Algorithmic Aspects of Graph Connectivity

Algorithmic Aspects of Graph Connectivity is the first book that thoroughly discusses graph connectivity, a central notion in graph and network theory, emphasizing its algorithmic aspects. This book contains various definitions of connectivity, including edge-connectivity, vertex-connectivity, and their ramifications, as well as related topics such as flows and cuts. With wide applications in the fields of communication, transportation, and production, graph connectivity has made tremendous algorithmic progress under the influence of theory of complexity and algorithms in modern computer science. New concepts and graph theory algorithms that provide quicker and more efficient computing, such as MA (maximum adjacency) ordering of vertices, are comprehensively discussed.

Covering both basic definitions and advanced topics, this book can be used as a textbook in graduate courses of mathematical sciences (such as discrete mathematics, combinatorics, and operations research) in addition to being an important reference book for all specialists working in discrete mathematics and its applications.

Hiroshi Nagamochi is a professor at the Graduate School of Informatics, Kyoto University. He is a member of the Operations Research Society of Japan and the Information Processing Society.

Toshihide Ibaraki is a professor with Kwansei Gakuin University and professor emeritus of Kyoto University. He is a Fellow of the ACM; Operations Research Society of Japan; the Institute of Electronic, Information and Communication Engineers; and the Information Processing Society.

ENCYCLOPEDIA OF MATHEMATICS AND ITS APPLICATIONS

The titles below, and earlier volumes in the series, are available from booksellers or from Cambridge University Press at www.cambridge.org.

ENCYCLOPEDIA OF MATHEMATICS AND ITS APPLICATIONS

Algorithmic Aspects of Graph Connectivity

HIROSHI NAGAMOCHI

Kyoto University

TOSHIHIDE IBARAKI

Kwansei Gakuin University

CAMBRIDGE
UNIVERSITY PRESS

CAMBRIDGE
UNIVERSITY PRESS

University Printing House, Cambridge CB2 8BS, United Kingdom

One Liberty Plaza, 20th Floor, New York, NY 10006, USA

477 Williamstown Road, Port Melbourne, VIC 3207, Australia

314-321, 3rd Floor, Plot 3, Splendor Forum, Jasola District Centre, New Delhi - 110025, India

79 Anson Road, #06-04/06, Singapore 079906

Cambridge University Press is part of the University of Cambridge.

It furthers the University's mission by disseminating knowledge in the pursuit of education, learning and research at the highest international levels of excellence.

www.cambridge.org
Information on this title: www.cambridge.org/9781108735490

© Hiroshi Nagamochi and Toshihide Ibaraki 2008

First published 2008
First paperback edition 2019

A catalogue record for this publication is available from the British Library

Library of Congress Cataloging in Publication data
Nagamochi, Hiroshi, 1960–
Algorithmic aspects of graph connectivity / Hiroshi Nagamochi and Toshihide Ibaraki.
p. cm.
Includes index.
ISBN 978-0-521-87864-7 (hardback)
1. Graph connectivity. 2. Graph algorithms. I. Ibaraki, Toshihide. II. Title.
QA166.243.N34 2008
511'.5–dc22 2008007560

ISBN 978-0-521-87864-7 Hardback
ISBN 978-1-108-73549-0 Paperback

Contents

Preface

Because the concept of a graph was introduced to represent how objects are connected, it is not surprising that connectivity has been a central notion in graph theory since its birth in the 18th century. Various definitions of connectivities have been proposed, for example, edge-connectivity, vertex-connectivity, and their ramifications. Closely related to connectivity are flows and cuts in graphs, where the cut may be regarded as a dual concept of connectivity and flows.

A recent general trend in the research of graph theory appears as a shift to its algorithmic aspects, and improving time and space complexities has been a strong incentive for devising new algorithms. This is also true for topics related to connectivities, flows, and cuts, and much important progress has been made. Such topics include computation, enumeration, and representation of all minimum cuts and small cuts; new algorithms to augment connectivity of a given graph; their generalization to more abstract mathematical systems; and so forth. In view of these, it would be a timely attempt to summarize those results and present them in a unified setting so that they can be systematically understood and can be applied to other related fields.

In these developments, we observe that a simple tool known as maximum adjacency (MA) ordering has been a profound influence on the computational complexity of algorithms for a number of problems. It is defined as follows.

MA ordering: Given a graph $G = (V, E)$, a total ordering $\sigma = (v_1, v_2, \ldots, v_n)$ of vertices is an MA ordering if $|E(V_{i-1}, v_i)| \geq |E(V_{i-1}, v_j)|$ holds for all i, j with $2 \leq i < j \leq n$, where $V_i = \{v_1, v_2, \ldots, v_i\}$ and $E(V', v)$ is the set of edges from vertices in V' to v.

To our knowledge, MA ordering was first introduced in a paper by R. E. Tarjan and M. Yannakakis [300], where it was called the Maximum Cardinality Search and used to test chordality of graphs, to test acyclicity of hypergraphs, and to solve other problems. We then rediscovered MA ordering [232], showing that it is effective for problems such as finding a forest decomposition and computing the minimum cuts of a graph. The extension in this direction has continued, and many problems are found to have faster algorithms.

The topics covered in this book are forest decomposition, minimum cuts, small cuts, cactus representation of cuts, connectivity augmentation, and source location problems. Mathematical tools used to solve these problems, such as maximum flows, extreme vertex sets, and edge splitting, are also discussed in detail. A generalization to a more abstract system than a graph is attempted on the basis of submodular and posimodular set functions.

The primary purpose of this book is to serve as a research monograph that covers the aforementioned algorithmic results attained in the area of graph connectivity, putting emphasis on results obtained from the introduction of MA ordering. However, this book is also appropriate as a textbook in graduate courses of mathematical sciences and operations research, because it starts with basic definitions of graph theory and contains most of the important results related to graph connectivities, flows, and cuts. Because the concept of connectivity is an important notion in many application areas, such as communication, transportation, production, scheduling, and power engineering, this book can be used as a reference for specialists working in such areas.

We would like to express our deep thanks to the many people who helped us to complete this project. First of all, we appreciate all the collaborations and comments given to us by Peter Eades, Andras Frank, Satoru Fujishige, Takuro Fukunaga, Magnús M. Halldórsson, Seokhee Hong, Toshimasa Ishii, Satoru Iwata, Tibor Jordán, Yoko Kamidoi, Kazuhisa Makino, Kiyohito Nagano, Mariko Sakashita, Kei Yamashita, and Liang Zhao, among others. We are particularly grateful to the late Professor Peter Hammer of Rutgers University for encouraging us to write this book. Finally we extend our thanks to our wives, Yuko and Mizuko, respectively, for their generous understanding.

Hiroshi Nagamochi
Toshihide Ibaraki
2007

Notation

$d(X; G)$	$d(X, V - X; G)$ for undirected graph G, where $d(\emptyset; G) = d(V; G) = 0$ is assumed	4
$d^+(X; G)$	$d(X, V - X; G)$ for directed graph G	4
$d^-(X; G)$	$d(V - X, X; G)$ for directed graph G	4
$\Gamma_G(v)$	set of neighbors of v in G	6
$\Gamma_G^+(X)$	set of out-neighbors of v in G	6
$\Gamma_G^-(X)$	set of in-neighbors of v in G	6
$G - F$	graph obtained from G by removing edges in F	7
G/F	graph obtained from G by contracting each edge in F into a single vertex and deleting any resulting loops	7
$G + E'$	graph obtained from G by adding the edges in E'	8
$G[X]$	subgraph induced from G by X	8
$G - X$	graph obtained from G by removing the vertices in X together with the edges incident with a vertex in X	8
G/X	graph obtained from G by contracting vertices in X into a single vertex and deleting any resulting loops	8
$G + b$	star augmentation of G defined by b	8
$\lambda(u, v; G)$	local edge-connectivity between u and v	9
$\lambda(S, v; G)$	size of a cut separating S and v	10
$\lambda(G)$	edge-connectivity of G	10
$\kappa(G)$	vertex-connectivity of G	10
$\kappa(u, v; G)$	local vertex-connectivity between u and v	10
$\kappa(S, v; G)$	minimum size of a vertex cut separating S and v	11
$\hat{\kappa}(S, v; G)$	maximum number of paths between S and v such that no two paths share any vertex other than v	11
e^r	reversal edge of e	22
$dist(u, v; G)$	distance from u to v in G	26
$\hat{G}$	digraph obtained by contracting all the strongly connected components in G	31
$\psi_G(v)$	$\sum\{c_G(e) \mid e = (v, u) \in E\} - \sum\{c_G(e) \mid e = (u, v) \in E\}$	33
$\lambda_\alpha(u, v; G)$	local α-connectivity	36
$\lambda_T(u, v; G)$	local T-connectivity	37
$\mu_\ell(u, v; G)$	local ℓ-mixed connectivity	37
$\lambda_s^+(G)$	$\min\{\lambda(s, v; G) \mid v \in V - s\}$	38
$\lambda_s^-(G)$	$\min\{\lambda(v, s; G) \mid v \in V - s\}$	38
$\overline{E}$	set of ordered pairs (u, v) such that $u, v \in V$, $u \neq v$ and $(u, v) \notin E$	39
$\overline{E}(X, Y)$	$\{(u, v) \in \overline{E} \mid u \in X, v \in Y\}$	39
$\kappa_s^+(G)$	$\min\{\kappa(s, v; G) \mid (s, v) \in \overline{E}(s, V - s)\}$	39
$\kappa_s^-(G)$	$\min\{\kappa(v, s; G) \mid (v, s) \in \overline{E}(V - s, s)\}$	39
G_S	digraph obtained by adding to G a new vertex s and directed edges (s, v) and (v, s) for every $v \in S$	40
$\kappa_{s,T}(G_S)$	$\min\{\kappa(s, v; G_S) \mid (s, v) \in \overline{E}(s, T; G_S)\}$	41

1

Introduction

In Chapter 1, we introduce basic definitions and notions. We also outline some of the known algorithms devised for solving problems related to flows, cuts, and connectivities. These algorithms will be used as a basis for the discussion in subsequent chapters. The standard definitions and other topics in graph theory can be found in the book by R. Diestel [52] or other textbooks on graph theory (e.g., [10, 33]). For basic data structures for graphs, standard graph algorithms, and their complexity, see the book by R. E. Tarjan [298], for example.

1.1 Preliminaries of Graph Theory

Let $\Re$ (resp. $\Re_+$ and $\Re_-$) denote the set of reals (resp. nonnegative reals and nonpositive reals) and $\mathbf{Z}$ (resp. $\mathbf{Z}_+$ and $\mathbf{Z}_-$) denote the set of integers (resp. nonnegative integers and nonpositive integers). For a real $a \in \Re$, $\lceil a \rceil$ (resp. $\lfloor a \rfloor$) denotes the smallest integer not smaller than a (resp. the largest integer not larger than a). For two reals $a, b \in \Re$ with $a \leq b$, we denote by $[a, b]$ and (a, b) the closed interval and open intervals; i.e., the sets of reals c with $a \leq c \leq b$ and $a < c < b$, respectively.

A singleton set $\{x\}$ may be simply written as x, and "$\subset$" implies proper inclusion, whereas "$\subseteq$" means "$\subset$ or $=$". The union of a set A and a singleton set $\{x\}$ may be denoted by $A + x$.

Let V be a finite set. The cardinality of (i.e., the number of elements in) V is denoted $|V|$. Let 2^V denote the *power set* of V, i.e., the family of all subsets of V (hence $|2^V| = 2^{|V|}$). The set of all pairs of elements in a set V is denoted $\binom{V}{2}$ (hence $|\binom{V}{2}| = \binom{|V|}{2}$). We say that a subset $X \subseteq V$ *divides* another subset $Y \subseteq V$ if $X \cap Y \neq \emptyset \neq Y - X$. For two subsets $A, B \subset V$, we say that a subset $X \subseteq V$ *separates* A and B if $A \subseteq X \subseteq V - B$ or $B \subseteq X \subseteq V - A$. For two subsets $X, Y \subseteq V$, we say that X and Y *intersect* each other if $X \cap Y \neq \emptyset$, $X - Y \neq \emptyset$, and $Y - X \neq \emptyset$ hold, and we say that X and Y *cross* each other if, in addition, $V - (X \cup Y) \neq \emptyset$ holds. For a weight function $a : V \to \Re$, we denote $\sum_{v \in X} a(v)$ by $a(X)$ for all $X \subseteq V$. A set of subsets of V, $\{V_1, V_2, \ldots, V_k\}$ with

$V_i \subseteq V (i = 1, 2, \ldots, k)$, is a *partition* of V if $\bigcup_{i=1}^{k} V_i = V$ and $V_i \cap V_j = \emptyset$ holds for all $i \neq j$.

An *undirected graph* (or a *graph*) G and a *directed graph* (or a *digraph*) G are defined by a pair composed of a vertex set V and an edge set $E \subseteq V \times V$, depending on whether edges are undirected and directed, respectively, and are denoted by $G = (V, E)$. The vertex set and edge set of a graph G may be denoted by $V(G)$ and $E(G)$, respectively. We use the notation $n = |V|$ and $m = |E|$ throughout this book.

An undirected edge e with end vertices u and v is denoted by $\{u, v\}$. We say that e is *incident* with u and v, u and v are the end vertices of e, and u (resp. v) is *adjacent* to v (resp. u). A directed edge e with tail u and head v is denoted by (u, v), and the *head* (resp. *tail*) of e is denoted by $h(e)$ (resp. $t(e)$). In this case, we say that $e = (u, v)$ is incident from u to v. An edge with the same end vertex (u, v) is called a *loop*.

A (di)graph G is called *trivial* if $|V(G)| = 1$. A graph (resp. digraph) G is called *complete* if there is an edge $\{u, v\}$ (i.e., a pair of edges (u, v) and (v, u)) for every two vertices $u, v \in V(G)$. A (di)graph G is called *bipartite* if $V(G)$ can be partitioned into two subsets, V_1 and V_2, so that every edge has one end vertex in V_1 and the other in V_2.

Undirected edges with the same pair of end vertices (or directed edges with the same tail and head) are called *multiple edges*. A graph (resp. digraph) is called a *multigraph* (a *multiple digraph*) if it is allowed to have multiple edges; otherwise it is called *simple*. We sometimes treat a multigraph G as a simple graph with integer-weighted edges, where the weight of each edge $e = \{u, v\}$ represents the number of multiple edges with the same end vertices u and v. In such an edge-weighted representation, the number m of edges means the number of pairs of adjacent vertices in G.

The *degree* of a vertex v in G is the number of edges incident with v. If G is a digraph, the *indegree* (resp. *outdegree*) denotes the number of edges incident to (resp. from) v. The minimum degree (resp. maximum degree) of the vertices in G is denoted by $\delta(G)$ (resp. $\Delta(G)$). An undirected graph (resp. digraph) G is called *Eulerian* if the degree of each vertex is even (resp. the indegree is equal to the outdegree at every vertex).

A graph $G' = (V', E')$ is called a *subgraph* of $G = (V, E)$ if $V' \subseteq V$ and $E' \subseteq E$, which we denote by $G' \subseteq G$. G' is a *spanning subgraph* if $V' = V$. A subgraph $G' = (V', E')$ of $G = (V, E)$ is *induced* by V' if E' is given by $E' = \{e \in E \mid \text{both end vertices of } e \text{ belong to } V'\}$, and G' may be denoted by $G[V']$. Given an edge set F (not necessarily a subset of $E(G)$), we denote by $V[F]$ the set of end vertices of edges in F.

A sequence of vertices and edges in G, $P = (v_1, e_1, v_2, e_2, \ldots, e_{k-1}, v_k)$, is called a *path* between v_1 and v_k (or from v_1 to v_k if G is a digraph) if $v_1, v_2, \ldots, v_k \in V$, $e_1, e_2, \ldots, e_{k-1} \in E$ and $e_i = \{v_i, v_{i+1}\}$ (or $e_i = (v_i, v_{i+1})$ if G is a digraph), $i = 1, 2, \ldots, k - 1$. Such a path P is also denoted as a sequence of vertices $P = (v_1, v_2, \ldots, v_k)$ or a sequence of edges $P = (e_1, e_2, \ldots, e_{k-1})$ if

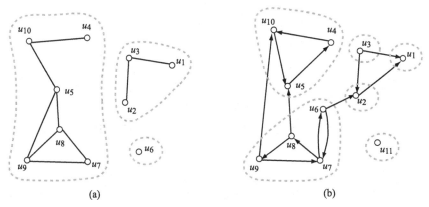

Figure 1.1. (a) A simple graph with three connected components; (b) a simple digraph with six strongly connected components, where each (strongly) connected component is enclosed by a gray dashed curve.

no confusion arises. For two vertices $u, v \in V$ in a graph (resp. digraph) G, a path between u and v (resp. a directed path from u to v) is called a (u, v)-*path*.

A graph (resp. digraph) G is called *connected* (resp. *strongly connected*) if G has a (u, v)-path for every pair of vertices u and v. A *connected component* (or a *component*) of a graph G is an inclusion-wise maximal vertex subset $X \subseteq V(G)$ such that every two vertices in X are connected by a path, where the induced subgraph $G[X]$ may also be called a (connected) component of G. A *strongly connected component* of a digraph G is an inclusion-wise maximal vertex subset $X \subseteq V(G)$ such that G has (u, v)- and (v, u)-paths for every two vertices u, $v \in X$, where the induced subgraph $G[X]$ may also be called a strongly connected component of G. Figure 1.1 illustrates examples of connected components of a graph and strongly connected components of a digraph.

An Eulerian connected graph has a sequence of edges by which we can visit all edges successively; we call such a sequence an *Eulerian trail*. Analogously an Eulerian strongly connected graph also admits an Eulerian trail, in which all directed edges are traversed along their directions. Figure 1.2(a) and (b) illustrate examples of Eulerian connected graph and strongly connected digraph, respectively.

1.1.1 Cut Functions of Weighted Graphs

When G is edge-weighted, the weight of an edge $e = \{u, v\}$ is denoted by $c_G(e)$ or $c_G(u, v)$, which are assumed to be nonnegative unless otherwise stated. Figure 1.3 shows a graph with integer edge weights, which can be viewed as a multigraph with multiplicity equal to the weight of each edge.

For two subsets $X, Y \subset V$ (not necessarily disjoint), $E(X, Y; G)$ denotes the set of edges e joining a vertex in X and a vertex in Y (i.e., $e = \{u, v\}$ satisfies $u \in X$ and $v \in Y$), and $d(X, Y; G)$ denotes $\sum_{e \in E(X,Y;G)} c_G(e)$. For a digraph $G = (V, E)$, we mean by $E(X, Y; G)$ the set of directed edges with a tail in X and

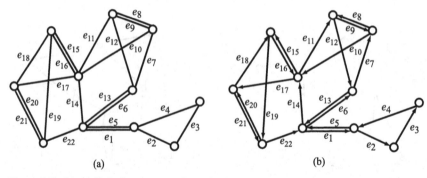

Figure 1.2. (a) An Eulerian connected graph; (b) an Eulerian strongly connected digraph, where the edges in the graph and digraph are indexed so that $(e_1, e_2, \ldots, e_{22})$ gives an Eulerian trail.

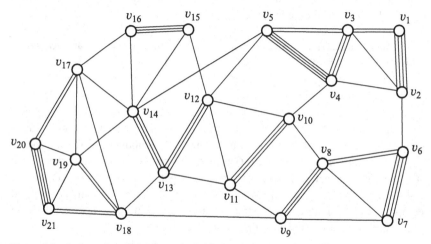

Figure 1.3. An integer-weighted graph G (the number of lines between two vertices represents the weight of the corresponding edge).

a head in Y. $E(X, Y; G)$ and $d(X, Y; G)$ may be written as $E(X; G)$ and $d(X; G)$, respectively, if $Y = V - X$, where $d(\emptyset; G) = d(V; G) = 0$ is assumed for convenience. In particular, the degree of v may be defined as $d(v; G)$. If G is clear from context, $E(X, Y; G)$ and $d(X, Y; G)$ may also be written as $E(X, Y)$ and $d(X, Y)$, respectively.

For a digraph $G = (V, E)$ and a subset $X \subseteq V$, we may write $d(X, V - X; G)$ and $d(V - X, X; G)$ as $d^+(X; G)$ and $d^-(X; G)$, respectively. The functions $d^+ : 2^V \rightarrow \Re_+$ with $d^+(X) = d^+(X; G)$, $X \in 2^V$, and $d^- : 2^V \rightarrow \Re_+$ with $d^-(X) = d^-(X; G)$, $X \in 2^V$, are called *cut functions* of a digraph G.

Lemma 1.1. *For two subsets X and Y of V in a digraph $G = (V, E)$, it holds that*

$$d^+(X; G) + d^+(Y; G) = d^+(X \cap Y; G) + d^+(X \cup Y; G)$$
$$+ d(X - Y, Y - X; G) + d(Y - X, X - Y; G) \quad (1.1)$$

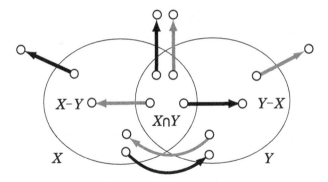

Figure 1.4. Illustration for $d^+(X; G)$ and $d^+(Y; G)$ of two subsets X and Y where black edges (resp. gray edges) represent $d^+(X; G)$ (resp. $d^+(Y; G)$).

and

$$d^-(X; G) + d^-(Y; G) = d^-(X \cap Y; G) + d^-(X \cup Y; G)$$
$$+ d(X - Y, Y - X; G) + d(Y - X, X - Y; G). \quad (1.2)$$

$\square$

Proof. For simplicity, we omit indicating G in $d(\cdot; G)$ and $d(\cdot, \cdot; G)$. We prove (1.1) ((1.2) can be treated symmetrically). The case where $X \subseteq Y$ or $Y \subseteq X$ is trivial since $\{X \cap Y, X \cup Y\} = \{X, Y\}$ and $\emptyset \in \{X - Y, Y - X\}$ hold. If $X \cap Y = \emptyset$, then we easily observe that $d^+(X) + d^+(Y) = d^+(X \cup Y) + d^+(X, Y) + d^+(Y, X)$ holds, implying (1.1). Consider the remaining case where X and Y intersect each other. In this case, we have

$$d^+(X \cap Y) = d(X \cap Y, X - Y) + d(X \cap Y, V - X)$$

and

$$d^+(X \cup Y) = d(Y, V - (X \cup Y)) + d(X - Y, V - (X \cup Y)).$$

See Fig. 1.4. On the other hand, we observe that the following equalities hold:

$$d^+(X) = d(X \cap Y, V - X) + d(X - Y, V - (X \cup Y)) + d(X - Y, Y - X),$$

$$d^+(Y) = d(X \cap Y, X - Y) + d(Y, V - (X \cup Y)) + d(Y - X, X - Y).$$

This proves the lemma. $\square$

Let G be an undirected graph. The function $d : 2^V \to \mathfrak{R}_+$ with $d(X) = d(X; G)$ for all $X \in 2^V$ is called a *cut function* of G. Let G' be the digraph obtained from G by replacing each edge $\{u, v\} \in E$ with two oppositely oriented directed edges (u, v) and (v, u). Then $d(X; G) = d^+(X; G') = d^-(X; G')$ holds for all $X \subseteq V$. Hence, by Lemma 1.1, function $d : 2^V \to \mathfrak{R}_+$ satisfies the following inequality:

$$d(X; G) + d(Y; G) = d(X \cap Y; G) + d(X \cup Y; G)$$
$$+ 2d(X - Y, Y - X; G). \quad (1.3)$$

By noting that $d(X; G) = d(V - X; G)$, we have $d(X; G) + d(Y; G) = d(V - X; G) + d(Y; G) = d((V - X) \cap Y; G) + d((V - X) \cup Y; G) + 2d((V - X) - Y, Y - (V - X); G) = d(X - Y; G) + d(Y - X; G) + 2d(X \cap Y, V - (X \cup Y); G)$. Thus,

$$d(X; G) + d(Y; G) = d(X - Y; G) + d(Y - X; G)$$
$$+ 2d(X \cap Y, V - (X \cup Y); G) \qquad (1.4)$$

for all $X, Y \subseteq V$.

1.1.2 Vertex Neighbors

For a vertex $v \in V$ in an undirected graph G, let $\Gamma_G(v)$ denote the set of *neighbors* of v (i.e., vertices adjacent to v). For a subset $X \subseteq V$, let $\Gamma_G(X) = \cup_{v \in X} \Gamma_G(v) - X$, where $\Gamma_G(\emptyset) = \Gamma_G(V) = \emptyset$ is assumed for convenience. For a subset X of V in a digraph G, a vertex $v \in V - X$ is called an *out-neighbor* (resp. *in-neighbor*) of X if there is an edge $(z, v) \in E$ (resp. $(v, z) \in E$) for some $z \in X$. The set of all out-neighbors (resp. in-neighbors) of X is denoted by $\Gamma_G^+(X)$ (resp. $\Gamma_G^-(X)$). We call a subset $X \subseteq V$ *dominating* in G if $V - X - \Gamma_G^-(X) = \emptyset$ and *nondominating* if $V - X - \Gamma_G^-(X) \neq \emptyset$.

Lemma 1.2. *For two subsets X and Y of V in a digraph $G = (V, E)$, it holds that*

$$|\Gamma_G^+(X)| + |\Gamma_G^+(Y)| = |\Gamma_G^+(X \cap Y)| + |\Gamma_G^+(X \cup Y)|$$
$$+ |(\Gamma_G^+(X - Y) - \Gamma_G^+(X \cap Y)) \cap (Y - X)|$$
$$+ |(\Gamma_G^+(Y - X) - \Gamma_G^+(X \cap Y)) \cap (X - Y)|$$
$$+ |(\Gamma_G^+(X - Y) \cap \Gamma_G^+(Y - X) - \Gamma_G^+(X \cap Y)) \cap (V - (X \cup Y))|$$
$$(1.5)$$

and

$$|\Gamma_G^-(X)| + |\Gamma_G^-(Y)| = |\Gamma_G^-(X \cap Y)| + |\Gamma_G^-(X \cup Y)|$$
$$+ |(\Gamma_G^-(X - Y) - \Gamma_G^-(X \cap Y)) \cap (Y - X)|$$
$$+ |(\Gamma_G^-(Y - X) - \Gamma_G^-(X \cap Y)) \cap (X - Y)|$$
$$+ |(\Gamma_G^-(X - Y) \cap \Gamma_G^-(Y - X)$$
$$- \Gamma_G^-(X \cap Y)) \cap (V - (X \cup Y))|. \qquad \square$$
$$(1.6)$$

Proof. We prove (1.5) ((1.6) can be treated symmetrically). From Fig. 1.5, we observe that

$$|\Gamma_G^+(X \cap Y)| = |\Gamma_G^+(X \cap Y) \cap (X - Y)| + |\Gamma_G^+(X \cap Y) \cap (V - X)|$$

and

$$|\Gamma_G^+(X \cup Y)| = |\Gamma_G^+(Y) \cap (V - (X \cup Y))|$$
$$+ |(\Gamma_G^+(X - Y) - \Gamma_G^+(Y)) \cap (V - (X \cup Y))|.$$

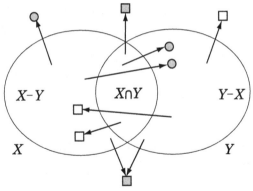

Figure 1.5. Illustration for $\Gamma_G^+(X)$ and $\Gamma_G^+(Y)$ of two intersecting subsets X and Y, where gray vertices represent $\Gamma_G^+(X)$ and square vertices represent $\Gamma_G^+(Y)$.

Furthermore, we observe that the following equalities also hold:

$$|\Gamma_G^+(X)| = |\Gamma_G^+(X \cap Y) \cap (V - X)| + |(\Gamma_G^+(X - Y) - \Gamma_G^+(Y)) \cap (V - (X \cup Y))|$$
$$+ |(\Gamma_G^+(X - Y) \cap \Gamma_G^+(Y - X) - \Gamma_G^+(X \cap Y)) \cap (V - (X \cup Y))|$$
$$+ |(\Gamma_G^+(X - Y) - \Gamma_G^+(X \cap Y)) \cap (Y - X)|,$$

$$|\Gamma_G^+(Y)| = |\Gamma_G^+(X \cap Y) \cap (X - Y)| + |\Gamma_G^+(Y) \cap (V - (X \cup Y))|$$
$$+ |(\Gamma_G^+(Y - X) - \Gamma_G^+(X \cap Y)) \cap (X - Y)|.$$

From these equalities, we obtain (1.5). $\qquad\square$

For an undirected graph $G = (V, E)$, let G' be the digraph obtained by replacing each edge $\{u, v\} \in E$ with two oppositely oriented directed edges, (u, v) and (v, u). Then $\Gamma_G(X) = \Gamma_{G'}^+(X) = \Gamma_{G'}^-(X)$ holds for all $X \subseteq V$. Hence, by Lemma 1.2, function $|\Gamma_G| : 2^V \to \mathbf{Z}_+$ satisfies the following inequality:

$$|\Gamma_G(X)| + |\Gamma_G(Y)| = |\Gamma_G(X \cap Y)| + |\Gamma_G(X \cup Y)|$$
$$+ |(\Gamma_G(X - Y) - \Gamma_G(X \cap Y)) \cap (Y - X)|$$
$$+ |(\Gamma_G(Y - X) - \Gamma_G(X \cap Y)) \cap (X - Y)| \qquad (1.7)$$
$$+ |(\Gamma_G(X - Y) \cap \Gamma_G(Y - X)$$
$$- \Gamma_G(X \cap Y)) \cap (V - (X \cup Y))|.$$

1.1.3 Graph Operations

For a subset $F \subseteq E$, $G - F$ denotes the graph obtained from G by removing the edges in F, and G/F denotes the graph obtained from G by contracting each edge $e \in F$ into a single vertex and deleting any resulting loops (and merging any resulting multiple edges into a single edge with the sum of their weights if G is an edge-weighted graph). See Fig. 1.6(b) and (c) for examples of $G - F$ and G/F. Note that G/F can be obtained in linear time by shrinking each connected component of (V, F) into a single vertex.

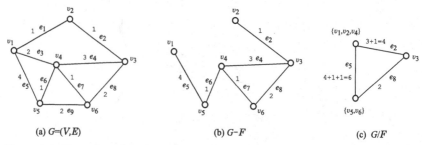

(a) G=(V,E)   (b) G−F   (c) G/F

Figure 1.6. Illustration of graphs (b) $G - F$ and (c) G/F for (a) graph $G = (V, E)$ and for $F = \{e_1, e_3, e_9\}$ (the number beside each edge e indicates the weight of e).

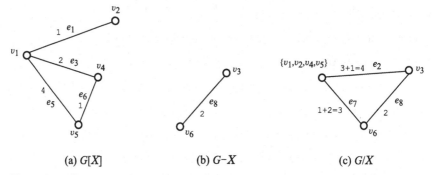

(a) G[X]   (b) G−X   (c) G/X

Figure 1.7. Illustration for graphs $G[X]$, $G - X$, and G/X of the graph $G = (V, E)$ in Fig. 1.6(a), where $X = \{v_1, v_2, v_4, v_5\}$.

For a set E' of new edges, we denote by $G + E'$ the graph obtained from G by adding the edges in E'.

Let X be a subset of V. We denote by $G[X]$ the subgraph induced from G by X, by $G - X$ the graph obtained from G by removing the vertices in X together with the edges incident with a vertex in X, and by G/X the graph obtained from G by contracting vertices in X into a single vertex and deleting any resulting loops (and merging any resulting multiple edges into a single edge with the sum of their weights if G is an edge-weighted graph). See Fig. 1.7(a), (b), and (c) as examples of $G[X]$, $G - X$, and G/X.

Given graph G, a *star augmentation* is a graph obtained by adding a new vertex s to G together with new weighted edges between s and some vertices in $V = V(G)$. A star augmentation H of G is defined by a vector $b \in \Re_+^V$ such that $b(v) = c_H(s, v)$ for each $v \in V$, where we let $b(v) = 0$ if edge $\{s, v\}$ is not introduced in the star augmentation. The star augmentation H defined by a vector $b \in \Re_+^V$ is denoted by $H = G + b$. See Fig. 1.8 for a star augmentation $H = G + b$ of graph $G = (V, E)$.

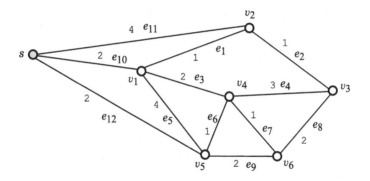

$H=G+b$

Figure 1.8. Illustration of the star augmentation $H = G + b$ of the graph $G = (V, E)$ defined in Fig. 1.6(a), where $b(v_1) = 2$, $b(v_2) = 4$, $b(v_5) = 2$, and $b(v_3) = b(v_4) = b(v_6) = 0$.

1.1.4 Edge-Connectivity

For an edge-weighted undirected graph (resp. digraph) G, a partition $\{X, V - X\}$ (resp. ordered partition $(X, V - X)$) of V, where X is a nonempty and proper subset X of V, is called a *cut* of G. A cut $\{X, V - X\}$ or $(X, V - X)$ is often denoted as X, for short, if no confusion arises. A subset $E' \subseteq E$ such that $E(X, V - X; G) \subseteq E'$ for some cut $\{X, V - X\}$ is called a *cut set* in G. An edge s is called a *cut edge* if $\{e\}$ is a cut set.

For a cut set E' such that $E' = E(X, V - X; G)$, we say that cut X is *generated* by E'. The *cut size* of a cut set E' (resp. cut X) is defined by $\sum_{e \in E'} c_G(e)$ (resp. $d(X; G)$). Let $S, T \subseteq V$. We say that a cut X *separates* S and T if $S \subseteq X \subseteq V - T$ or $T \subseteq X \subseteq V - S$, and that a cut X *separates* S *from* T if $S \subseteq X \subseteq V - T$. A cut separating S from T is called an (S, T)-*cut*. If S and T are singletons $\{s\}$ and $\{t\}$, respectively, we also refer to an (S, T)-cut as an (s, t)-*cut*. For two vertices, s and t, in an undirected graph/digraph G, an (s, t)-cut X (i.e., separating u and v) with the minimum cut size is called a *minimum* (s, t)-*cut*, and the cut size $d(X; G)$ is called *the local edge-connectivity* $\lambda(u, v; G)$ between u and v.

In an undirected graph/digraph G, we call a minimum (s, t)-cut X *minimal* (resp. *maximal*) if vertex set X is inclusion-wise minimal (resp. maximal) among all minimum (s, t)-cuts.

Lemma 1.3. *In an undirected graph/digraph G, a minimal (resp. maximal) minimum (s, t)-cut $X_{s,t}$ is unique; that is, $|X_{s,t}|$ is minimum (resp. maximum) among all minimum (s, t)-cuts.* $\square$

Proof. We deal with the case of minimal minimum (s, t)-cuts in a digraph; the case of maximal minimum (s, t)-cuts or undirected graphs can be treated analogously.

Assume that there are two minimal minimum (s, t)-cuts, X and X'. Then X and X' cross each other. By (1.1), we have

$$2\lambda(s, t; G) = d^+(X; G) + d^+(X'; G) \geq d^+(X \cap X'; G) + d^+(X \cup X'; G).$$

By the minimality of X and X', $d^+(X \cap X'; G) > \lambda(s, t; G)$. Hence, we have $d^+(X \cup X'; G) < \lambda(s, t; G)$, contradicting that $d^+(Y) \geq \lambda(s, t; G)$ holds for all (s, t)-cuts Y.   □

Given a subset $S \subseteq V$ and a vertex $v \in V - S$, we define the edge-connectivity $\lambda(S, v; G)$ by the minimum size of a cut X that separates S and v. Notice that $\lambda(S, v; G)$ is equal to $\lambda(s, v; G/S)$ of the graph G/S obtained by contracting S into a single vertex s.

The minimum cut size among all the cuts in G is called the *edge-connectivity* of G and is denoted by $\lambda(G)$. The edge connectivity of a graph consisting of a single vertex is set to be $+\infty$. Also by convention, $\lambda(v, v; G)$ is defined to be $+\infty$. These definitions tell that

$$\lambda(G) = \min_{u, v \in V} \lambda(u, v; G).$$

A cut X satisfying $d(X; G) = \lambda(G)$ is called a *minimum cut* in G. For a real $k \in \Re_+$, a graph G is *k-edge-connected* if $\lambda(G) \geq k$.

1.1.5 Vertex-Connectivity

For a connected undirected graph (resp. a strongly connected digraph) $G = (V, E)$, a subset $Z \subset V$ is called a *vertex cut* if $G - Z$ has at least two connected components (resp. at least two strongly connected components). The size of a vertex cut Z is defined by $|Z|$.

The minimum size of a vertex cut in G is called the (*global*) *vertex-connectivity* and is denoted by $\kappa(G)$. As a special case, we define the vertex-connectivity of a complete graph G by $\kappa(G) = n - 1$, where $n = |V(G)|$, since G has no vertex cut Z with $|Z| < n - 1$. A graph G is called *k-vertex-connected* if $n \geq k + 1$ and $\kappa(G) \geq k$ (i.e., there is no vertex cut S of size $k - 1$). By definition, $\kappa(G) \leq n - 1$ holds, where the equality holds only when G is a complete graph.

For two disjoint subsets $A, B \subseteq V$, we say that a subset $C \subset V - (A \cup B)$ *separates A from B* in G if $G - Z$ has no (u, v)-path for any pair $u \in A$ and $v \in B$. A vertex cut Z separating A from B is called an (A, B)-*vertex cut*. A vertex v is called a *cut vertex* if $\{v\}$ is a vertex cut.

Given two vertices, u and v, a set of (u, v)-paths is called *internally vertex-disjoint* if no two of them share any vertex other than u and v. *The local vertex-connectivity* between vertices u and v is defined to be the maximum number of internally vertex-disjoint (u, v)-paths and is denoted by $\kappa(u, v; G)$. As will be seen in Section 1.4, if $\{u, v\} \notin E$ in a graph (resp. $(u, v) \notin E$ in a digraph) G, then $\kappa(u, v; G)$ is equal to the minimum size $|Z|$ of a (u, v)-vertex cut Z. Observe that such a minimum (u, v)-vertex cut Z in an undirected graph (resp. a digraph) G is given by $Z = \Gamma_G(A) = \Gamma_G(B)$ (resp. $Z = \Gamma_G^+(A) = \Gamma_G^-(B)$) for some subsets $A, B \subseteq V - Z$ with $u \in A$ and $v \in B$. Thus, $\kappa(G) = \min\{\kappa(u, v; G) \mid u, v \in V\} = \min\{|\Gamma_G(X)| \mid X \subseteq V, \quad V - X - \Gamma_G(X) \neq \emptyset\}$ for an undirected graph G (resp. $\kappa(G) = \min\{\kappa(u, v; G) \mid u, v \in V\} = \min\{|\Gamma_G^+(X)| \mid X \subseteq V, V - X - \Gamma_G^+(X) \neq \emptyset\} = \min\{|\Gamma_G^-(X)| \mid X \subseteq V, V - X - \Gamma_G^-(X) \neq \emptyset\}$ for a digraph G).

Given a subset $S \subset V$ and a vertex $v \in V - S$, we define the vertex-connectivity between them in the following two ways. Let $\kappa(S, v; G)$ denote the minimum size of a vertex cut $C \subseteq V - S - v$ that separates S and v, and let $\hat{\kappa}(S, v; G)$ denote the maximum number of paths between S and v such that no two paths share any vertex other than v. Hence, $\hat{\kappa}(S, v; G) \geq k$ means that v remains connected to at least one vertex in S after deleting any $k - 1$ vertices in $V - v$, implying that $\hat{\kappa}(S, v; G) \leq |S|$.

1.1.6 Trees and Forests

For any graph G with $|V(G)| \geq 2$, it holds that

$$\kappa(G) \leq \lambda(G) \leq \delta(G) \leq 2|E(G)|/|V(G)| \tag{1.8}$$

since $\delta(G) \leq (1/|V(G)|) \sum_{v \in V(G)} d(v; G) = 2|E(G)|/|V(G)|$ holds, and $\{v, V(G) - v\}$ for a vertex v with $d(v; G) = \delta(G)$ is a cut with size $\delta(G)$, and $\kappa(G) = \min\{\kappa(u, v; G) \mid u, v \in V(G)\} \leq \min\{\lambda(u, v; G) \mid u, v \in V(G)\} = \lambda(G)$.

Let $G = (V, E)$ be an undirected graph. A connected graph is a *cycle* if the degree of every vertex is 2. A connected graph containing no cycle as its subgraph is called a *tree*. A tree with n vertices contains exactly $n - 1$ edges. A collection F of vertex-disjoint trees is called a *forest*. For a given graph G (possibly not connected), a spanning forest G' is *maximal* if the subgraph of G' induced by each connected component of G is connected. Thus, a spanning forest of a connected graph G is a spanning tree T such that $V(T) = V(G)$ and $E(T)$ contains $|V(G)| - 1$ edges from $E(G)$.

A tree with a designated vertex (called a *root*) is called a *rooted tree*. Let T be a rooted tree with root r. In T, the *depth* of a vertex v is defined to be the number of edges in the path of T that connects v and r. For two vertices u and v in T, u is called an *ancestor* of v (v is called a *descendant* of u) if u is in the path from v to r. In particular, if an ancestor u of v is adjacent to v, then u is called the *parent* of v and v is called a *child* of u.

For an edge-weighted graph G, a *minimum (weight) spanning tree* of G is a spanning tree T of G whose weight (i.e., the sum of the weights of all edges in $E(T)$) is minimum among all spanning trees of G. Similarly a *maximum (weight) spanning tree* of G is a spanning tree of G with the maximum weight.

Lemma 1.4. *For a connected graph $G = (V, E)$ with an edge weight $w : E \to \Re$, a spanning tree $T = (V, F)$ of G is minimum if and only if condition (i) or equivalently condition (ii) holds:*

(i) *For each edge $b \in E - F$, $w(b) \geq \max\{w(a) \mid a \in E(C_T(b)) - b\}$ holds, where $C_T(b)$ denotes the (unique) cycle in the graph $(V, F \cup \{b\})$.*
(ii) *For each edge $a \in F$, $w(a) \leq \min\{w(b) \mid b \in K_T(a) - a\}$ holds, where $K_T(a) = E(X, V - X; T)$ for the two components X and $V - X$ in the graph $(V, F - a)$.* $\square$

Proof. We first show that conditions (i) and (ii) are equivalent. Assume that condition (i) holds. For any edges $a \in F$ and $b \in K_T(a) - a$, the cycle C_b contains edges a and b, and $w(b) \geq w(a)$ holds by condition (i); that is, $\min\{w(b) \mid b \in K_T(a) - a\} \geq w(a)$, implying condition (ii). Now assume that condition (ii) holds. For any edges $b \in E - F$ and $a \in E(C_T(b)) - b$, the cut set $K_T(a)$ contains edges a and b, and $w(a) \leq w(b)$ holds by condition (ii); that is, $\max\{w(a) \mid b \in E(C_T(b)) - b\} \leq w(b)$, implying condition (i).

If a minimum spanning tree $T = (V, F)$ has edges $b \in E - F$ and $a \in E(C_T(b)) - b$ with $w(b) < w(a)$, then $T' = (V, (F - b) \cup \{a\})$ would be a spanning tree with a smaller weight than T, a contradiction. We show the converse. Let $T = (V, F)$ be a spanning tree satisfying condition (i). To lead to a contradiction, assume that T is not minimum, and let $T' = (V, F')$ be a minimum spanning tree, where we choose T' so that $|F \cap F'|$ is maximized among all minimum spanning trees without loss of generality. Since T' is minimum, conditions (i) and (ii) hold for T'. Choose an edge $b \in F' - F$ for which $(C_T(b) - b) \cap (K_{T'}(b) - b)$ contains an edge $a \in F - F'$. Since condition (i) holds for T (resp. condition (ii) holds for T'), we have $w(b) \geq w(a)$ (resp. $w(b) \leq w(a)$). Note that $(V, (F' - b) \cup \{a\})$ is a spanning tree with the same weight of T', which contradicts the choice of T'. This proves the lemma. $\square$

A maximum spanning tree is characterized by conditions (i) and (ii) with the modification of exchanging "max" and "min."

A spanning subgraph $T = (V, F)$ of a digraph $G = (V, E)$ is called a *forest* (resp. *tree*) if it is a forest (resp. tree) when we ignore the edge orientation. A tree $T = (V, F)$ (viewed as a digraph) of a digraph G is called an *s-out-arborescence* if it is an out-tree rooted at a vertex s; that is,

$$E(V - s, s; T) = \emptyset \text{ and } |E(V - v, v; T)| = 1 \quad (v \in V - s).$$

An *s*-in-arborescence is defined analogously.

1.1.7 Laminar Family

A family $\mathcal{X} \subseteq 2^V$ of subsets of V is called *laminar* if no two subsets in $\mathcal{X}$ intersect each other.

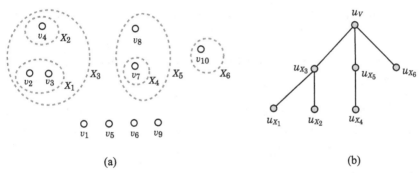

Figure 1.9. (a) A laminar family $\mathcal{X} = \{X_1 = \{v_2, v_3\}, X_2 = \{v_4\}, X_3 = \{v_2, v_3, v_4, v_5\}$, $X_4 = \{v_7\}, X_5 = \{v_7, v_8\}, X_6 = \{v_{10}\}\}$ of a finite set $V = \{v_1, v_2, \ldots, v_{10}\}$; (b) the corresponding tree representation $\mathcal{T} = (V, \mathcal{E})$.

A laminar family $\mathcal{X} \subseteq 2^V$ can be represented by a rooted tree $\mathcal{T} = (V, \mathcal{E})$ as follows, where we use term "nodes" for the vertices in the tree representation:

(i) Each node in V corresponds to the set V or a subset $X \in \mathcal{X}$, that is, $V = \mathcal{X} \cup \{V\}$, where the root corresponds to V. The node corresponding to a subset $X \subseteq V$ is denoted by u_X.

(ii) For two nodes u_X and u_Y, u_X is a child of u_Y in $\mathcal{T}$ if and only if $X \subset Y$ holds and $\mathcal{X}$ contains no set X' with $X \subset X' \subset Y$. The set of children of a node u is denoted by $Ch(u)$.

It is not difficult to see that $|\mathcal{X}| \leq 2|V| - 1$ holds. If each nonleaf in $\mathcal{T}$ has at least two children, then $|\mathcal{X}| \leq 2|L| - 1$ holds for the set L of leaves in $\mathcal{T}$.

For example, family $\mathcal{X} = \{X_1 = \{v_2, v_3\}, X_2 = \{v_4\}, X_3 = \{v_2, v_3, v_4, v_5\}$, $X_4 = \{v_7\}, X_5 = \{v_7, v_8\}, X_6 = \{v_{10}\}\}$ of a finite set $V = \{v_1, v_2, \ldots, v_{10}\}$ is laminar (see Fig. 1.9(a)), and its tree representation $\mathcal{T} = (V, \mathcal{E})$ is shown in Fig. 1.9(b).

1.2 Algorithms and Complexities

In this book, we present various algorithms for solving graph connectivity problems. In this section, we sketch fundamental notions for discussing algorithms and their efficiencies. See Aho, Hopcroft, and Ullman [1] and Cormen, Leiserson, and Rivest [48], for example, for more detailed arguments on algorithms.

Let $f : \mathbf{Z}_+ \to \Re_+$ and $g : \mathbf{Z}_+ \to \Re_+$ be functions. We mean by $f(n) = O(g(n))$ that there exist positive constants c and n_0 such that $f(n) \leq cg(n)$ holds for all $n \geq n_0$. On the other hand, we mean by $f(n) = \Omega(g(n))$ that there is a positive constant c such that $f(n) \geq cg(n)$ holds for infinitely many n. If $f(n) = O(g(n))$ and $f(n) = \Omega(g(n))$, then we denote this by $f(n) = \Theta(g(n))$.

To measure the running time and memory space required by an algorithm in the universal way, it is usually assumed that computation is executed on an abstract computer, called a *random-access machine*, where elementary operations, that is, arithmetical operations, comparisons, data movements, and control branching, can be carried out in constant time, and any integer can be stored in constant memory space. We say that an algorithm runs in $O(f(n))$ time and $O(g(n))$ space, where n stands for the size of an input, if it takes at most $cf(n)$ operations and $c'g(n)$ memory cells for some constants c and c'. An algorithm is called a *polynomial time* algorithm if it runs in $O(n^c)$ time for some constant c.

A problem is usually described as a mathematical statement that contains several parameters; a problem instance is obtained by assigning values to those parameters. Thus, a problem can be viewed as a collection of (usually infinitely many) such instances. A decision problem requires an answer of "yes" or "no." An optimization problem asks for a solution that minimizes (or maximizes) a given objective function among all feasible solutions.

The class $\mathcal{P}$, which stands for "polynomial," consists of all decision problems that admit polynomial time algorithms. The class $\mathcal{NP}$, which stands for "non-deterministic polynomial," consists of all decision problems with the following property: For an instance whose answer is yes, there is a proof (called a *certificate*) by which the correctness of the yes answer can be checked in polynomial time. Note that it is not required that such a certificate itself can be obtained in polynomial time.

A decision or optimization problem is called $\mathcal{NP}$-hard if a polynomial time algorithm for it would result in a polynomial time algorithm for every problem in $\mathcal{NP}$. A problem is called $\mathcal{NP}$-complete if it is an $\mathcal{NP}$-hard decision problem belonging to $\mathcal{NP}$. Clearly $\mathcal{P} \subseteq \mathcal{NP}$ holds. For a more detailed and formal introduction of the class $\mathcal{NP}$, see the book by Gary and Johnson [101].

Given a minimization problem P, a polynomial time algorithm is called an *approximation algorithm* with an *approximation ratio* α or an α-*approximation algorithm* if it delivers a feasible solution $APX(I)$ to a given instance I such that

$$\frac{cost(APX(I))}{cost(OPT(I))} \leq \alpha,$$

where $OPT(I)$ denotes an optimal solution to instance I and $cost(S)$ is the cost of a feasible solution S to I. Such a solution $APX(I)$ is called an α-*approximate solution*. See Ausiello et al. [7] for more on approximation algorithms.

1.2.1 Adjacency Lists

Any undirected simple graph G with n vertices can be represented as an $n \times n$ matrix $A = [a_{ij}]$, where $a_{ij} = 1$ if $\{v_i, v_j\} \in E(G)$ and $a_{ij} = 0$ otherwise. Since matrix A can be stored in a two-dimensional array, we can check whether or not $\{v_i, v_j\}$ belongs to $E(G)$ in $O(1)$ time. However, it takes $\Omega(n^2)$ space even for a sparse graph G. In this book, unless stated otherwise, we represent an undirected simple graph $G = (V, E)$ as *adjacency lists*, as shown in Fig. 1.10. For each vertex $v \in V$, we store the set of its neighbors, $\Gamma_G(v)$, in a linked list $Adj(v)$, which consists of linked cells, where each cell contains a vertex name and a

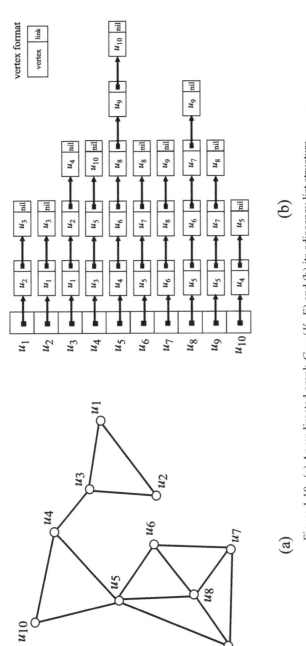

Figure 1.10. (a) An undirected graph $G = (V, E)$ and (b) its adjacency list structure.

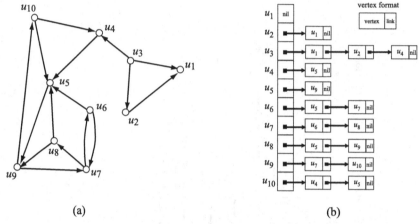

(a)   (b)

Figure 1.11. (a) A digraph $G = (V, E)$ and (b) its adjacency list structure.

pointer to the next cell. There is also a one-dimensional array that stores the vertex set $V(G)$, where each vertex v in the array is linked to the first cell of $Adj(v)$ by a pointer. The space for adjacency lists is $O(\sum_{v \in V(G)}(1 + d(v; G))) = O(n + m)$. With adjacency lists, we can find all edges incident with a given vertex v in $O(d(v; G))$ time by traversing all cells in $Adj(v)$.

To represent a multigraph G, we store an edge set $E(v; G)$ in a linked list $Adj(v)$, in which vertex u appears $|E(v, u; G)|$ times. In this case, the input size of a multigraph $G = (V, E)$ is measured by n and m, where $n = |V|$ and $m = |E|$. However, a multigraph $G = (V, E)$ can be represented as an edge-weighted graph, where each $\{u, v\}$ has multiplicity $c_G(\{u, v\})$ as its weight. This weight $c_G(\{u, v\})$ can be stored in a new field of the cell for each vertex v in $Adj(u)$. In this case, letting $\mu = |\{\{u, v\} \mid c_G(u, v) > 0\}|$, the input size of G becomes $O(n + \mu)$.

Analogously with the case of undirected graphs, a digraph G can be represented by adjacency lists such that, for each vertex $v \in V(G)$, all edges in $E(v; G)$ (those outgoing from v) are stored in a linked list $Adj(v)$ (see Fig. 1.11). With this data structure, G is stored in $O(n + m)$ space, and all edges outgoing from a given vertex v can be retrieved in $O(d(v; G))$ time by traversing all cells in $Adj(v)$.

1.2.2 Graph Search

A graph search is a procedure to scan all vertices and edges in a given graph, for example, in order to compute all connected components and to find a spanning forest. A similar procedure can be used for a digraph G to find strongly connected components and an s-out-arborescence (if $\lambda(s, v; G) \geq 1$ for all $v \in V(G)$).

During the execution of a graph search, each vertex v takes the three states "unseen," "visited," and "scanned," and each edge takes the states "unseen" and "scanned," where all vertices and edges are initially "unseen."

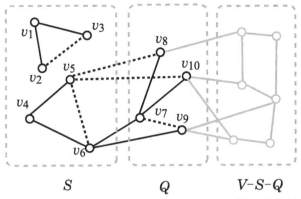

Figure 1.12. Illustration for sets S, Q, and $V - S - Q$ in an undirected graph $G = (V, E)$ observed at a certain instant during execution of GRAPHSEARCH, where edges in F (resp. edges not in F) are depicted by solid lines (resp. dotted lines), and unseen edges and vertices are depicted by gray lines and circles, respectively.

A graph search repeats the following procedure until all vertices are in the scanned state: First choose an unseen vertex as a *root*, making it visited, and then repeat the next iteration until no unseen edges are incident from any visited vertices. In each iteration, we choose an unseen edge $e = \{u, v\}$ (resp. directed edge $e = (u, v)$) incident from any visited vertex u, making e scanned, and we make vertex u scanned if no unseen edge is incident from it, and make vertex v visited if it is unseen. Hence, each application of the procedure finds a new root, which corresponds to each connected component (if G is an undirected graph).

The aforementioned search can find a subset $F \subseteq E(G)$ that induces a spanning forest in an undirected graph G or an s-out-arborescence F in a digraph G such that $\lambda(s, v; G) \geq 1$ for all $v \in V(G)$. We call the edges in such a set F *tree edges*. Such tree edges can be collected by storing those edges that are incident to unseen vertices when they are scanned.

The preceding graph search is formally described as follows, where Q, S, and R store all vertices that are visited but not yet scanned, all scanned vertices, and all roots, respectively, and B stores all scanned edges. Figure 1.12 illustrates the computation process of GRAPHSEARCH, where vertices v_i are visited in the order of the indices i, and v_1 and v_4 are stored as roots.

Procedure GRAPHSEARCH
Input: An undirected graph/digraph $G = (V, E)$ (possibly with a specified start
vertex $s \in V$).
Output: A vertex label ℓ of V ($\ell(v)$ denotes the order in which v has been visited)
and an edge set $F \subseteq E$ (F forms vertex disjoint forests).
1 $S := Q := R := B := \emptyset$; $i := 0$; /* S, Q, R, and B denote the sets of
"scanned" vertices, "visited" vertices, roots, and "scanned" edges,
respectively */

2   **while** $V - S \neq \emptyset$ **do**
        /* Choosing a visited or unseen vertex u^* */
3   **if** $Q \neq \emptyset$ **then** Choose a visited vertex $u^* \in Q$
        else
4   Choose an unseen vertex $u^* \in V - S$
        (choose s as u^*, if so specified, when $i = 0$);
5       $i := i + 1; \ell(u^*) := i; Q := Q \cup \{u^*\}$;
6       $R := R \cup \{u^*\}$
        end if;
        /* Choosing an unseen edge incident from u^* or making u^* "scanned" */
7   **if** $E(u^*; G) \subseteq B$ **then** $Q := Q - u^*; S := S \cup \{u^*\}$ /* u^* is scanned */
        else
8   Choose an unseen edge $e = \{u^*, v\} \in E(u^*; G) - B$
9       $(e = (u^*, v) \in E(u^*; G) - B$ if G is a digraph);
10      $B := B \cup \{e\}$; /* e is scanned */
11   **if** $v \in V - S - Q$ **then**
12      $i := i + 1; \ell(v) := i; Q := Q \cup \{v\}$;
13      $\rho(v) := e$ /* e is a tree edge entering into v */
        end /* **if** */
        end /* **if** */
        end; /* **while** */;
14 Output $\{\ell(u) \mid v \in V\}$ and $F := \{\rho(v) \mid v \in V - R\}$.

When a vertex $v \in V$ is visited, v is either stored in R as a root or reached via an edge $e = \{u^*, v\}$ (or $e = (u^*, v)$ for a digraph). In the latter case, such an edge e is stored in $\rho(v)$ as a tree edge. Therefore, $F = \{\rho(v) \mid v \in V - R\}$ gives a forest rooted at vertices in R.

Lemma 1.5. *For an undirected graph $G = (V, E)$,* GRAPHSEARCH *can be implemented to run in $O(m + n)$ time and space. Let $F \subseteq E$ and $R \subseteq V$ be obtained by* GRAPHSEARCH. *Then (V, F) is a spanning forest of G, and $|R|$ is the number of components of G. In particular, if G is connected then $T = (V, F)$ is a spanning tree of G.* $\square$

Proof. In line 8, we choose an edge $e = \{u^*, v\} \in E(u^*; G) - B$ in the order of the cells in its adjacency list $Adj(u^*)$ and maintain a pointer to indicate the cell that was scanned last. Then finding an edge $e = \{u^*, v\} \in E(u^*; G) - B$ in line 8 and testing whether or not $E(u^*; G) \subseteq B$ in line 7 can be executed in $O(1)$ time just by checking the cell next to the latest visited cell in $Adj(u^*)$. We can execute lines 3 and 4 in $O(1)$ time by choosing an arbitrary vertex u^* from $Q \neq \emptyset$ or from $V - S$. Note that a vertex u^* is chosen in line 8 at most $d(u^*; G) - 1$ times since $|E(u^*; G) - B|$ decreases by 1 after executing lines 7–13. Hence, line 4 (resp. line 5) is executed n (resp. $\sum_{u^* \in V} d(u^*; G) = O(m)$) times. Therefore, GRAPHSEARCH runs in $O(m + n)$ time and space.

If a vertex $v \in V - S$ is chosen in line 4, then no other vertex in $V - S$ is chosen until Q becomes empty; that is, all vertices reachable from v become scanned. Then a tree in (V, F) contains a vertex $r \in R$ and it is a spanning tree of the component containing r. Hence (V, F) is a maximal spanning forest. $\square$

Lemma 1.6. *For a digraph $G = (V, E)$, GRAPHSEARCH can be implemented to run in $O(m + n)$ time and space. Let $F \subseteq E$ and $R \subseteq V$ be obtained by GRAPHSEARCH. If a start vertex s is specified and s is reachable to any other vertices (i.e., $\lambda(s, v; G) \geq 1$, $v \in V$), then $T = (V, F)$ is an s-out-arborescence of G.* $\square$

Proof. As in the proof of Lemma 1.5, we easily see that GRAPHSEARCH runs in $O(m + n)$ time and space by using adjacency lists for digraphs.

If a start vertex s is specified, we first choose s as the first visited vertex. GRAPHSEARCH then visits all vertices and no longer executes line 4 (by the assumption that s is reachable to any other vertices). Then $R = \{s\}$ and F stores all edges that were used to find unseen vertices. Hence, F forms an s-out-arborescence of G. $\square$

If we introduce certain rules that describe how to choose a vertex u^* from Q in line 3, the resulting forest (V, F) has special structures.

Depth-First Search

The *depth-first search* is a graph search that chooses a new vertex u^* in line 3 from the most recently visited vertex; that is, the vertex u^* with the largest label ℓ is chosen from Q in line 3 of GRAPHSEARCH. Such a vertex $u^* \in Q$ can be found in $O(1)$ by maintaining a set Q of labeled vertices as a *stack*, which is a data structure that stores and returns data in a last-in/first-out manner. We call the spanning tree $T = (V, F)$ obtained in this manner a *depth-first search* (DFS) tree. Figure 1.13(a) shows a DFS tree $T = (V, F)$ of the connected graph $G = (V, E)$ defined in Fig. 1.10(a), where the number beside each vertex v denotes $\ell(v)$ and the edges in T are depicted by solid lines.

From the way vertices are visited in the depth-first search, we easily see that a DFS tree $T = (V, F)$ has the following property [297].

Lemma 1.7. *Let $T = (V, F)$ be a DFS tree of an undirected graph $G = (V, E)$. For each edge $e = \{u, v\} \notin F$, one end vertex u is a proper ancestor of the other end vertex v in T. Such a digraph G is termed a palm tree.* $\square$

Given a DFS tree $T = (V, F)$ and an edge $e = \{u, v\} \in E - F$, we can find a cycle C containing e in $|C|$ time by traversing the path from v to u along T, where we assume $\ell(u) < \ell(v)$ without loss of generality.

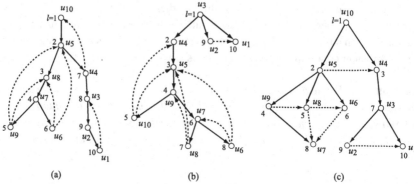

Figure 1.13. (a) A DFS tree $T = (V, F)$ of the graph $G = (V, E)$ defined in Fig. 1.10(a);
(b) a BFS tree $T = (V, F)$ of the digraph $G = (V, E)$ defined in Fig. 1.11(a); (c) a BFS
tree $T = (V, F)$ of the graph $G = (V, E)$ defined in Fig. 1.10(a), where edges in T (resp.
edges not in T) of (a)–(c) are depicted by solid lines (resp. dotted lines), and all undirected
edges are oriented in the direction of traversal in (a) and (c).

Breadth-First Search

Contrary to the depth-first search, the *breadth-first search* chooses a new vertex
u^* from the earliest visited vertex; that is, the vertex u^* with the smallest label ℓ
is chosen from Q in line 3 of GRAPHSEARCH. We can find such a vertex $u^* \in Q$
in $O(1)$ by maintaining the set Q of labeled vertices as a *queue*, which is a data
structure that stores and returns data in a first-in/first-out manner. We call the
spanning tree $T = (V, F)$ obtained in this manner a *breadth-first search* (BFS)
tree. Figure 1.13(b) shows a BFS tree $T = (V, F)$ of the digraph $G = (V, E)$
defined in Fig. 1.11(a), where the number beside each vertex v denotes $\ell(v)$ and
the edges in T are depicted by solid lines.

Consider a BFS tree T that is rooted at the vertex v with $\ell(v) = 1$. By the
construction of T, we see that the depth of each vertex u in T is equal to the
distance of u from the root in G. Thus, T gives the shortest paths from the root to
all other vertices. This is true for cases in which G is both undirected and directed.

1.3 Flows and Cuts

1.3.1 Maximum Flows in Digraphs

Let $G = (V, E)$ represent a digraph with a vertex set V and an edge set E,
where each edge $e \in E$ is weighted by $c_G(e) \in \Re_+$ (see Fig. 1.14). Let $s, t \in V$
be two designated vertices, which we call the source and sink of G, respectively.
A function $f : E \to \Re_+$ is called a *flow* (or an (s, t)-*flow*) of G if it satisfies the
following two types of constraints.

Flow conservation:

$$\sum_{e \in E(v, V-v)} f(e) - \sum_{e \in E(V-v, v)} f(e) \begin{cases} = 0 & \text{if } v \in V - \{s, t\}, \\ \geq 0 & \text{if } v = s, \\ \leq 0 & \text{if } v = t. \end{cases} \tag{1.9}$$

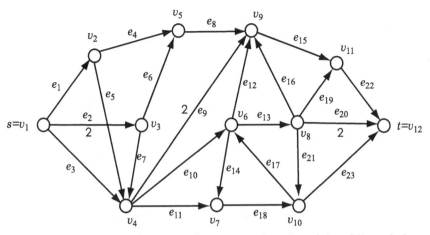

Figure 1.14. An edge-weighted digraph $G = (V, E)$, where the weights of directed edges e_2, e_9, and e_{20} are 2, and the weights of other edges are 1.

Capacity constraint:

$$0 \leq f(e) \leq c_G(e) \quad \text{for all } e \in E. \tag{1.10}$$

The *flow value* of f, $v(f)$, is defined by

$$v(f) = \sum_{e \in E(s, V-s)} f(e) - \sum_{e \in E(V-s, s)} f(e)$$

$$= \left(-\sum_{e \in E(t, V-t)} f(e) + \sum_{e \in E(V-t, t)} f(e) \right). \tag{1.11}$$

A flow f that maximizes $v(f)$ is called a *maximum flow* of G.

A simple directed path from s to t is called an (s, t)-*path*. Any (s, t)-flow f can be decomposed into a collection of weighted directed (s, t)-paths and weighted directed cycles as follows. By letting $f'(e) := f(e)$ ($e \in E$) initially, we take an (s, t)-path P in G that consists of some edges e with $f'(e) > 0$, and we reduce $f'(e)$ of the edges e on P by

$$f'(e) := \begin{cases} f'(e) - \alpha(P) & \text{for } e \in E(P), \\ f'(e) & \text{for } e \in E - E(P), \end{cases}$$

where $E(P)$ denotes the set of edges in P and

$$\alpha(P) = \min\{f(e) \mid e \in E(P)\} \, (> 0).$$

Observe that the resulting f' remains an (s, t)-flow. We continue this operation as long as such a path P exits (or equivalently $v(f') > 0$ holds). When f' has no such path (i.e., $v(f') = 0$), we can decompose the set of remaining edges e with $f'(e) > 0$ into a collection of weighted cycles by repeatedly finding cycles that consist of edges e with $f'(e) > 0$ and reducing f' of the edges in such cycles in a similar way.

Let f be an (s, t)-flow in G, and consider an (s, t)-cut X. By summing (1.9) over all vertices $v \in X$, we have

$$\sum_{e \in E(X, V-X)} f(e) - \sum_{e \in E(V-X, X)} f(e) = v(f). \tag{1.12}$$

Together with the capacity constraint, this implies

$$v(f) \le \sum_{e \in E(X, V-X)} f(e) \le \sum_{e \in E(X, V-X)} c_G(e) = d(X; G).$$

Therefore, the flow value of any (s, t)-flow cannot exceed the weight of any (s, t)-cut X. The next theorem, known as the *max-flow min-cut* theorem, is fundamental because it can provide many efficient algorithms for solving connectivity problems. The proof of this theorem will be given in the next subsection after introducing a maximum flow algorithm.

Theorem 1.8 ([63, 72]). *For an edge-weighted digraph G with a source s and a sink t, the following relation holds:*

$$\max\{v(f) \mid (s, t)\text{-flows } f\} = \min\{d(X; G) \mid (s, t)\text{-cuts } X\}. \qquad \square$$

Recall that the local edge-connectivity $\lambda(s, t; G)$ between two vertices s and t is defined to be $\min\{d(X; G) \mid (s, t)\text{-cuts } X\}$. Then Theorem 1.8 leads to the next corollary.

Corollary 1.9. *The local edge-connectivity $\lambda(s, t; G)$ is equal to the flow value of a maximum (s, t)-flow in an edge-weighted digraph G.* $\qquad \square$

1.3.2 Computing a Maximum (s, t)-Flow

In this subsection, we review some maximum flow algorithms. For simplicity (but without loss of generality), we assume the following:

- The given edge-weighted digraph $G = (V, E)$ is simple and symmetric, that is, for each directed edge $e = (u, v) \in E$, G has no other edge $e' = (u, v)$ with the same head and tail but has an edge (v, u) with the reverse direction (if necessary we add a new edge (v, u) with zero weight), where we denote by e^r the reversal edge (v, u) of $e = (u, v)$.
- We only consider a *skew-symmetric* (s, t)-flow f in G, that is, an (s, t)-flow f such that either $f(e) = 0$ or $f(e^r) = 0$ holds for every edge $e \in E$.

Let $f : E \to \Re_+$ be an (s, t)-flow in $G = (V, E)$. The *residual graph* $G^f = (V, E^f)$ of G with f is defined as follows. Let

$$c_{G^f}(e) = c_G(e) - f(e) + f(e^r) \qquad \text{for each } e \in E. \tag{1.13}$$

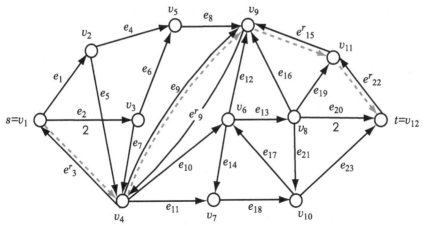

Figure 1.15. The residual graph G^f for the digraph G in Fig. 1.14 and an (s, t)-flow f such that $f(e_i) = 1$ for $i \in \{3, 9, 15, 22\}$ and $f(e_i) = 0$ otherwise, where these edges e_i with $f(e_i) > 0$ are depicted by dotted gray arrows.

The definition of $c_{G^f}(e)$ is interpreted as follows. Consider an edge e_1 with $f(e_1) > 0$ and $f(e_1^r) = 0$. Then $c_{G^f}(e_1) = c_G(e_1) - f(e_1)$ represents the remaining capacity of e (i.e., the maximum additional amount of flow that can be pushed along e) in G. On the other hand, the amount of the current flow $f(e_1)$ can also be interpreted as the amount of flow that can be pushed back in the reverse direction of e_1 (i.e., the amount of flow that can be sent along edge e_1^r). To represent this, we increase the weight of the reversal edge e_1^r by $f(e_1)$; that is, $c_{G^f}(e_1^r) = c_G(e_1^r) + f(e_1)$. Definition (1.13) is the result of these two considerations.

For example, Figure 1.15 illustrates the residual graph G^f for the digraph G in Fig. 1.14 and an (s, t)-flow f with $s = v_1$ and $t = v_{12}$ such that $f(e_i) = 1$ for $i \in \{3, 9, 15, 22\}$ and $f(e_i) = 0$ otherwise. This (s, t)-flow is shown by dotted gray arrows in Fig. 1.15.

A residual graph G^f has the following property. Let g be a skew-symmetric (s, t)-flow in G^f with flow value $v(g)$. Then we define the new skew-symmetric flow $f' : E \to \mathfrak{R}_+$ by $f' = f + g$, that is, a flow pair $(f(e), f(e^r))$ for each edge $e \in E$ with $f(e) \geq 0$ and $f(e^r) = 0$ is modified as follows:

$$(f'(e), f'(e^r)) = \begin{cases} (f(e) + g(e), 0) & \text{if } g(e) > 0, \\ (f(e) - g(e^r), 0) & \text{if } f(e) \geq g(e^r) > 0, \\ (0, g(e^r) - f(e)) & \text{if } f(e) < g(e^r) > 0, \\ (f(e), 0) & \text{otherwise.} \end{cases}$$

It is a simple matter to see that $f' = f + g$ is again a skew-symmetric (s, t)-flow of G, and its flow value satisfies

$$v(f') = v(f) + v(g).$$

In a residual graph G_f, the capacity of a directed path P is defined by

$$c_{G^f}(P) = \min\{c_{G^f}(e) \mid e \in E(P)\},$$

and an (s, t)-path P with $c_{G^f}(P) > 0$ is called an *augmenting path*. Given an augmenting path P of G^f, we define an (s, t)-flow $f_P : E \rightarrow \mathfrak{R}_+$ of G^f by

$$f_P(e) = \begin{cases} c_{G^f}(P) & \text{if } e \in E(P), \\ 0 & \text{otherwise.} \end{cases}$$

Then $f + f_P$ is an (s, t)-flow of G such that

$$v(f + f_P) = v(f) + c_{G^f}(P).$$

This means that, if we can find an augmenting path P in the current G^f, then an (s, t)-flow f' with a larger flow value can be constructed from f and P.

Maximality Test of a Flow

We can now explain how to test whether the current (s, t)-flow f is maximum or not. Assume that G^f has no augmenting path. Let X be the set of vertices that are reachable from s via edges in G^f. By the assumption and by the choice of X, $t \in V - X$ and $E(X, V - X; G^f) = \emptyset$ hold. Hence, by the definition of G^f we have

$$f(e) = \begin{cases} c_G(e) & \text{for } e \in E(X, V - X; G), \\ 0 & \text{for } e \in E(V - X, X; G). \end{cases} \tag{1.14}$$

From this,

$$\sum_{e \in E(X, V-X; G)} f(e) - \sum_{e \in E(V-X, X; G)} f(e) = \sum_{e \in E(X, V-X; G)} c_G(e),$$

and, hence, by (1.12) we have

$$v(f) = \sum_{e \in E(X, V-X; G)} c_G(e).$$

Thus, $v(f)$ is equal to the cut size of the (s, t)-cut X, implying, by the max-flow min-cut theorem (Theorem 1.8), that X is a minimum (s, t)-cut and the current f is a maximum (s, t)-flow of G.

For example, Fig. 1.16 shows the residual graph G^f for the digraph G defined in Fig. 1.14 and an (s, t)-flow f (depicted by broken gray arrows) with $s = v_1$ and $t = v_{12}$ such that $f(e_i) = 1$ for $i \in \{1, 2, 3, 5, 7, 9, 10, 11, 13, 15, 18, 20, 22, 23\}$ and $f(e_i) = 0$ otherwise. In this case, G^f has no augmenting path, and the X defined in the preceding manner is given by $X = \{v_1, v_2, v_3, v_4, v_5, v_9\}$, for which $d(X, V - X; G) = 3 = v(f)$ holds, implying that f is a maximum (s, t)-flow of G.

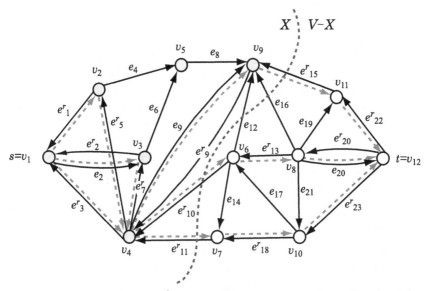

Figure 1.16. The residual graph G^f for the digraph G in Fig. 1.14 and (s, t)-flow f such that $f(e_i) = 1$ for $i \in \{1, 2, 3, 5, 7, 9, 10, 11, 13, 15, 18, 20, 22, 23\}$ and $f(e_i) = 0$ otherwise, where the edges e_i with $f(e_i) > 0$ are depicted by dotted gray arrows.

Maximum Flow Algorithms

From the argument so far, we obtain the following procedure for computing a maximum (s, t)-flow. Starting with the (s, t)-flow $f(e) = 0$ $(e \in E)$, we repeat the process of finding an augmenting path P and updating the current flow f by $f :=$ $f + f_P$ until there is no augmenting path. If all edge weights $c_G(e)$ in the original digraph G are integers, then the procedure constructs a maximum (s, t)-flow after a finite number of iterations (which is at most $\min\{d(s, V - s; G), d(V - t, t; G)\}$), during which the edge weights in residual graphs always remain integers. This proves the next theorem.

Theorem 1.10 ([72]). *If all edge weights in an edge-weighted digraph $G = (V, E)$ are integers, then there exists a maximum (s, t)-flow f such that $f(e)$ is an integer for every edge $e \in E$, and there is an algorithm to compute such f in finite computation time.*   □

However, the procedure in Theorem 1.10 is not efficient for digraphs with large edge weights and may not terminate in finite iterations if the digraph G has edges whose weights are irrational numbers [73]. Edmonds and Karp [61] first gave a maximum flow algorithm that runs in time polynomial in n and m. They chose the shortest augmenting path from s to t in each residual graph G^f, where the length of a path P is defined to be the number of edges in P.

Level Graphs

Dinits [53] proposed the use of level graphs to effectively find the shortest augmenting paths. The *level graph* L of a residual graph G^f is a subgraph of G^f that consists of the vertices and edges in all shortest paths from s to t. Let distance $dist(u, v; G^f)$ from u to v in G^f be defined as the length of the shortest (u, v)-path. Given $\ell = dist(s, t; G^f)$, let $level(v)$ denote the distance $dist(s, v; G^f)$, and let V_i ($i = 0, 1, \ldots, \ell$) denote the set of vertices v that satisfies $level(v) = i$ and $dist(v, t; G^f) = \ell - i$. Then L is given by the digraph $L = (\cup_{0 \le i \le \ell} V_i, \cup_{0 \le i \le \ell-1} E(V_i, V_{i+1}; G^f))$, where $V_0 = \{s\}$ and $V_\ell = \{t\}$. Observe that L contains all the shortest augmenting paths in G^f. For example, Figure 1.17(a) shows the level graph L for the digraph G in Fig. 1.14 and an (s, t)-flow $f = 0$ (i.e., $G^f = G$). Figure 1.17(b) is the level graph L corresponding to the residual graph G^f of Fig. 1.15.

Given a level graph L of G^f, an (s, t)-flow g is called a *blocking flow* if every (s, t)-path in L contains an edge e saturated by g (i.e., $g(e) = c_{G^f}(e)$). A blocking flow is a collection of the shortest augmenting paths in L. Then the (s, t)-flow $f + g$ augmented from f with g satisfies the following property.

Lemma 1.11. *For a blocking flow g in a residual graph G^f, the residual graph G^{f+g} of G with $f + g$ satisfies $dist(s, t; G^{f+g}) \ge dist(s, t; G^f) + 1$.*   □

Proof. Let $\ell = dist(s, t; G^f)$. Recall that the edge set of G^{f+g} is obtained from that of G^f by adding some edges e^r with $g(e) > 0$ and deleting those edges e with $(f + g)(e) = c_G(e)$. For any directed edge $e = (u, v)$ in a shortest path from s to t in G^f, the distance from s to t never decreases when we add its reverse edge $e^r = (v, u)$, since if G^f with added e^r has an (s, t)-path P with $e^r \in E(P)$ and $|E(P)| < \ell$, then it would hold that $\ell > dist(s, v; G^f) + 1 + dist(u, t; G^f) = dist(s, u; G^f) + dist(v, t; G^f) + 3$, contradicting the assumption that $\ell = dist(s, u; G^f) + 1 + dist(v, t; G^f)$. From this, we see that $dist(s, t; G^{f+g}) \ge dist(s, t; G^f)$. Also from the preceding observation, any (s, t)-path passing through e^r cannot be a path of length ℓ. This implies that, if G^{f+g} has an (s, t)-path of length ℓ, then it consists only of edges in G^f, contradicting that g is a blocking flow in G^f.   ⊔

Dinits' Algorithm

Now we are able to explain Dinits' algorithm. It repeats the phase that finds a blocking flow in G^f for the current (s, t)-flow and then updates f by $f + g$, until $dist(s, t; G^f) = +\infty$ holds (i.e., G^f has no (s, t)-path). For example, the algorithm finds a maximum (s, t)-flow for the digraph G in Fig. 1.14 as follows. It starts with an initial (s, t)-flow $f = 0$ in G. The first phase then constructs the level graph L for the digraph $G^f = G$ and finds a blocking flow g in L with $g(e_3) = g(e_9) = g(e_{15}) = g(e_{22}) = 1$, as shown in Fig. 1.17(a). After updating $f := f + g$, the residual graph G^f is obtained as in Fig. 1.15. The level graph L for the residual graph G^f is constructed in the second phase, and a blocking

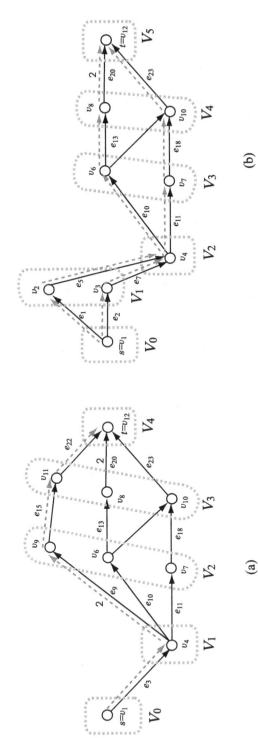

Figure 1.17. (a) The level graph L for the digraph G in Fig. 1.14 and (s, t)-flow $f = 0$ (i.e., $G^f = G$), and a blocking flow g in L with $g(e_3) = g(e_9) = g(e_{15}) = g(e_{22}) = 1$; (b) the level graph L for the residual graph G^f for the digraph G in Fig. 1.15 and a blocking flow g in L with $g(e_i) = 1$ for $i \in \{1, 2, 5, 7, 10, 11, 13, 18, 13, 18\}$; blocking flows are depicted by dotted gray arrows.

27

flow g in L is found with $g(e_i) = 1$ for $i \in \{1, 2, 5, 7, 10, 11, 13, 18, 13, 18\}$. The residual graph G^f is then reconstructed by updating $f := f + g$, as shown in Fig. 1.16. Since G^f has no augmenting path (i.e., $dist(s, t; G^f) = +\infty$), the algorithm halts in the third phase, concluding that the current f is a maximum (s, t)-flow of the digraph G in Fig. 1.14.

Since the length of any (s, t)-path is at most $n - 1$, the number of phases required is $O(n)$. A level graph can be constructed from G^f in $O(m + n)$ time by using the breadth-first search [298] (see Section 1.2.2). A blocking flow in a level graph L can be found in $O(n^2)$ time [184, 211, 299] or $O(m \log n)$ time [291]. Hence, Dinits' algorithm runs in $O(n^3)$ time or $O(mn \log n)$ time.

One of the fastest maximum flow algorithms currently in use is that of Goldberg and Tarjan [103]. Their algorithm runs in $O(mn \log(n^2/m))$ time. Faster randomized algorithms have been developed for computing a minimum (s, t)-cut in the case of undirected graphs [19, 105, 175, 178]. See [2, 3, 289] for more on network flow algorithms.

Because Dinits' algorithm correctly finds a maximum flow after a finite number of steps for any edge-weighted graph (possibly weighted by irrational numbers), the argument so far also establishes a proof for Theorem 1.8.

Dinits' Algorithm on Unweighted Digraphs

In the rest of this subsection, we consider an unweighted digraph which may have multiple edges (i.e., a multiple digraph such that each edge has unit capacity). Note that multiple edges are all counted in the total number $m = |E|$. We show that Dinits' algorithm runs faster on such digraphs.

In a residual graph for an unweighted digraph, a blocking flow can be found in $O(m)$ time because we can avoid traversing the same edge more than once. Therefore, a maximum (s, t)-flow in an unweighted digraph can be obtained in $O(mn)$ time.

Recall that, for a digraph $G = (V, E)$, $dist(s, t; G)$ denotes the distance from s to t. As observed in Corollary 1.9, $\lambda(s, t; G)$ also gives the maximum value of an (s, t)-flow in G.

Karzanov [183] and Even and Tarjan [66] have shown the following properties, based on which the time complexity of Dinits' algorithm will be further elaborated.

Lemma 1.12 ([66, 183]). *Let $G = (V, E)$ be an unweighted digraph, and $s, t \in V$ be given. Then*

    (i) $\lambda(s, t; G) \cdot dist(s, t; G) \leq m$.

    (ii) *If G has no multiple edges, then $\sqrt{\lambda(s, t; G)} \cdot dist(s, t; G) \leq n$.*

    (iii) *If G has no multiple edges and $|E(v, V - v; G)| \leq 1$ or $|E(V - v, v; G)| \leq 1$ holds for every $v \in V - \{s, t\}$, then $\lambda(s, t; G) \cdot (dist(s, t; G) - 1) \leq n - 2$.* $\qquad\square$

Proof. Let V_i be the set of vertices whose distance from s in G is i. Note that $E(V_0 \cup V_1 \cup \cdots \cup V_i, V - (V_0 \cup V_1 \cup \cdots \cup V_i); G) = E(V_i, V_{i+1}; G)$ holds for $i = 0, 1, \ldots, dist(s, t; G) - 1$ and that $E(V_i, V_{i+1}; G)$ and $E(V_j, V_{j+1}; G)$ are disjoint if $i \neq j$.

(i) Since $X = V_0 \cup V_1 \cup \cdots \cup V_i$ is an (s, t)-cut, $|E(X, V - X; G)| = |E(V_i, V_{i+1}; G)| \geq \lambda(s, t; G)$ by Theorem 1.8. Therefore, $m \geq \sum_{0 \leq i < dist(s,t;G)} |E(V_i, V_{i+1}; G)| \geq dist(s, t; G) \cdot \lambda(s, t; G)$.

(ii) Since there are no multiple edges, $|V_i| \cdot |V_{i+1}| \geq |E(V_i, V_{i+1}; G)| \geq \lambda(s, t; G)$ for each $i = 0, 1, \ldots, dist(s, t; G) - 1$. Hence, by $(|V_i| + |V_{i+1}|)/2 \geq \sqrt{|V_i| \cdot |V_{i+1}|}$, we have $(|V_i| + |V_{i+1}|)/2 \geq \sqrt{\lambda(s, t; G)}$ $(1 \leq i \leq dist(s, t; G) - 1)$. Therefore, $n \geq \sum_{0 \leq i \leq dist(s,t;G)-1} (|V_i| + |V_{i+1}|)/2 \geq dist(s, t; G) \cdot \sqrt{\lambda(s, t; G)}$.

(iii) In this case, each vertex $v \in V - \{s, t\}$ can be used by a path in an (s, t)-flow at most once. Therefore, $\lambda(s, t; G) \cdot (dist(s, t; G) - 1) \leq |V - \{s, t\}|$. $\square$

Based on Lemma 1.12, the following results can be proved.

Theorem 1.13 ([66, 183]). *Let $G = (V, E)$ be an unweighted digraph G. Then*

(i) *Dinits' algorithm runs in $O(m^{3/2})$ time.*

(ii) *If G has no multiple edges, then Dinits' algorithm runs in $O(n^{2/3}m)$ time.*

(iii) *If $|E(v, V - v; G)| \leq 1$ or $|E(V - v, v; G)| \leq 1$ holds for every vertex $v \in V - \{s, t\}$, then Dinits' algorithm runs in $O(n^{1/2}m)$ time.* $\square$

Proof. Since Dinits' algorithm runs in $O(Km)$ time for the total number of phases, K, it suffices to show that, under conditions (i)–(iii), K satisfies $K = O(m^{1/2})$, $O(n^{2/3})$, and $O(n^{1/2})$, respectively. Recall also that, in Dinits' algorithm, $dist(s, t; G^f)$ increases at least by 1 after each phase.

(i) Consider the phase when $\lambda(s, t; G^f)$ becomes less than $m^{1/2}$ for the first time. After this phase, there are at most $m^{1/2}$ phases. On the other hand, before the phase, $\lambda(s, t; G^f) \geq m^{1/2}$ always holds, and $dist(s, t; G^f) \leq m/\lambda(s, t; G^f) \leq m^{1/2}$ (by Lemma 1.12(i)) implies that there are at most $m^{1/2}$ phases until $\lambda(s, t; G^f) < m^{1/2}$ holds. Therefore, we have $K \leq 2m^{1/2}$.

(ii) Consider the phase when $\lambda(s, t; G^f)$ becomes less than $n^{2/3}$ for the first time. After this phase, there are at most $n^{2/3}$ phases. On the other hand, before the phase, $\lambda(s, t; G^f) \geq n^{2/3}$ holds, and $dist(s, t; G^f) \leq n/\sqrt{\lambda(s, t; G^f)} \leq n/n^{1/3} = n^{2/3}$ holds by Lemma 1.12(ii), which implies that there are at most $n^{2/3}$ phases until $\lambda(s, t; G^f) < n^{2/3}$ holds. Therefore, we have $K \leq 2n^{2/3}$.

(iii) Consider the phase when $\lambda(s, t; G^f)$ becomes less than $n^{1/2}$ for the first time. After this phase, there are at most $n^{1/2}$ phases. On the other hand, before the phase, $\lambda(s, t; G^f) \geq n^{1/2}$ holds, and $dist(s, t; G^f) \leq (n - 2)/$

$\lambda(s,t;G^f)+1 = O(n^{1/2})$ (by Lemma 1.12(iii)) implies that there are $O(n^{1/2})$ phases until $\lambda(s,t;G^f) < n^{1/2}$ holds. Therefore, we have $K \leq O(n^{1/2})$. ☐

Finally we show another property of Dinits' algorithm, which will be used in Chapter 2 to provide a faster implementation for unweighted simple undirected graphs.

Lemma 1.14 ([105]). *Let $G = (V, E)$ be an unweighted digraph G with no multiple edge. The number of edges e such that $f(e) = 1$ holds at least once during Dinits' algorithm is at most $4n^{3/2}$.* ☐

Proof. Dinits' algorithm can be viewed as a sequence of augmentations along the shortest path in the current residual graph. By Lemma 1.12(ii), the value of an (s,t)-flow g in a residual graph G^f is at most $\lambda(s,t;G^f) \leq (n/dist(s,t;G^f))^2$. Hence, when $d \leq dist(s,t;G^f) < 2d$ holds for some constant d, there are at most $(n/d)^2$ augmenting paths, each of which is of length at most $2d$, and at most $2n^2/d$ edges appear in these paths. Let d_0 be a constant. For all augmentations with $dist(s,t;G^f) \geq d_0$, the total number of edges appearing in these augmenting paths is bounded by $\sum_{i\geq 0} 2n^2/(2^i d_0) = 4n^2/d_0$, where the number of edges is counted on different intervals $d_0 \leq dist(s,t;G^f) \leq 2d_0, 2d_0 \leq dist(s,t;G^f) \leq 4d_0, \ldots$.

On the other hand, when $dist(s,t;G^f) < d_0$ holds, the length of an augmenting path is at most d_0, and there are at most n augmenting paths (since G has no multiple edges and satisfies $\lambda(s,t;G) \leq |E(s, V - s; G)| \leq n$).

Therefore, the total number of edges appearing in augmenting paths is $nd_0 + \sum_{i\geq 0} 2n^2/(2^i d_0) = nd_0 + 4n^2/d_0$. By choosing $d_0 = 2n^{1/2}$, this number becomes $nd_0 + 4n^2/d_0 = 4n^{3/2}$. ☐

Algorithm by Goldberg and Tarjan

A faster $O(mn \log(n^2/m))$ time maximum flow algorithm was obtained by Goldberg and Tarjan [103]. They construct a maximum (s, t)-flow by using *preflows* instead of flows. In a preflow $f : E \to \Re_+$ in a digraph $G = (V, E)$, the flow conservation (1.9) is relaxed to

$$\sum_{e\in E(v, V-v)} f(e) - \sum_{e\in E(V-v,v)} f(e) \geq 0 \text{ for all } v \in V - t.$$

The *excess* $e_f(v)$ of a vertex v in a preflow f is defined as

$$e_f(v) = \sum_{e\in E(v, V-v)} f(e) - \sum_{e\in E(V-v,v)} f(e).$$

For a given preflow, its residual graph G^f is defined as in the case of flows in Section 1.3.2. A *distance labeling* is a function $ds : V \to \mathbf{Z}_+$ such that $ds(u) \leq ds(v) + 1$ holds for every residual edge $(u, v) \in E(G^f)$ and $ds(s) - ds(t) \leq n$ also holds. An edge $(u, v) \in E(G^f)$ is called *admissible* if $ds(u) > ds(v)$. A vertex v is called *active* if $e_f(v) > 0$ and $ds(v) < ds(t) + n$. Given a preflow f and distance labeling ds, the operations *push* and *relabel* are defined to update f and ds, respectively, as follows. For an admissible edge (u, v) such that u is active, the push operation increases flow $f(u, v)$ as much as possible under the condition that the resulting f is a preflow, that is, by $\min\{c_{G^f}(u, v), e_f(u)\}$. On the other hand, for an active vertex v with no outgoing admissible edges, the relabel operation sets $ds(v)$ to be the highest value while maintaining the resulting labeling ds at a correct distance labeling, that is, one plus the smallest distance label of a vertex reachable from v via one residual edge. The idea of a push–relabel algorithm is to get rid of the positive excess of a vertex v by pushing it along edges (v, w) whose heads w are estimated by the distance labeling ds to be closer to the sink t. The goal is to transform a preflow into a maximum (s, t)-flow.

It is known [39] that there is an implementation of this push–relabel algorithm that finally obtains a maximum (s, t)-flow by performing $O(n^2 \sqrt{m})$ push operations in $O(n^2 \sqrt{m})$ time. Goldberg and Tarjan [103] gave an $O(mn \log(n^2/m))$ time implementation of a push–relabel algorithm by using a data structure of dynamic trees [291]. We refer to [2, 3] for more details of preflow algorithms.

1.3.3 Computing All (s, t)-Minimum Cuts

As we have already observed, a minimum (s, t)-cut X can be found from the residual graph G^f of a maximum (s, t)-flow f. In general, there is more than one minimum (s, t)-cut in G, and it is known [9, 273] that all minimum (s, t)-cuts can be enumerated from any maximum (s, t)-flow f. We now explain the basic ideas of such an algorithm.

Given an (s, t)-cut X in a digraph $G = (V, E)$, we say that two vertices $u, v \in V$ are separated by X if $|X \cap \{u, v\}| = 1$ holds. Let f be a maximum (s, t)-flow and G^f be its residual graph. An (s, t)-cut X in G is a minimum (s, t)-cut if and only if (1.14) holds. Therefore, for any directed cycle C in the residual graph G^f, the end vertices u and v of an edge (u, v) in C are not separated in G by any minimum (s, t)-cut. From this we see that all minimum (s, t)-cuts in G are preserved after contracting each strongly connected component of G^f into a single vertex.

Let $\hat{G}^f = (\hat{V}, \hat{E})$ denote the digraph obtained from G^f by contracting all the strongly connected components in G^f. Let $\hat{s}$ (resp. $\hat{t}$) denote the vertex in $\hat{G}^f$ that contains s (resp. t). Now $\hat{G}^f$ has no directed cycle and every vertex in $\hat{G}^f$ is contained in a $(\hat{t}, \hat{s})$-path. An ordered partition $(X, \overline{X} = V - X)$ of V is called a *dicut* if $E(X, \overline{X}; G) = \emptyset$. Then we easily observe the following.

Lemma 1.15 ([273]). *Let G, f, and $\hat{G}^f$ be as defined earlier. Given a subset $X \subset V$ such that $s \in X$ and $t \in V - X$, a cut $(X, V - X)$ is a minimum (s, t)-cut in G if and only if $(\hat{X}, \hat{V} - \hat{X})$ is a dicut in $\hat{G}^f$, where $\hat{X}$ is the set of vertices into which the vertices in X are contracted.* □

The digraph $\hat{G}^f$ is called a *directed acyclic graph* (DAG) representation of all minimum (s, t)-cuts in G. For example, strongly connected components

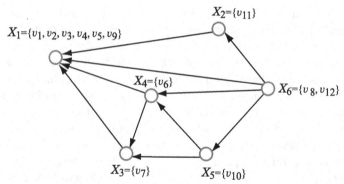

Figure 1.18. The DAG representation for all minimum (s, t)-cuts in the digraph G of Fig. 1.14 with $s = v_1$ and $t = v_{12}$.

of the residual graph G^f in Fig. 1.16 are given by vertex subsets $X_1 = \{v_1, v_2, v_3, v_4, v_5, v_9\}$, $X_2 = \{v_{11}\}$, $X_3 = \{v_7\}$, $X_4 = \{v_6\}$, $X_5 = \{v_{10}\}$, $X_6 = \{v_8, v_{12}\}$. By contracting each of these sets into a single vertex, we obtain the DAG representation shown in Fig. 1.18, where $s \in X_1$ and $t \in X_6$. In this DAG, we can find 10 dicuts: $(X, \overline{X})$ defined by $X = \cup_{i \in I} X_i$ for $I = \{1\}$, $\{1, 2\}$, $\{1, 3\}$, $\{1, 4\}$, $\{1, 2, 4\}$, $\{1, 2, 3\}$, $\{1, 3, 4\}$, $\{1, 3, 4, 5\}$, $\{1, 2, 3, 4\}$, $\{1, 2, 3, 4, 5\}$, respectively. Thus, the original digraph G in Fig. 1.14 has ten minimum (s, t)-cuts.

Given such a DAG representation of a digraph G with s and t, Ball and Provan [9] have given an algorithm for listing all minimum (s, t)-cuts in $O(n + m)$ time per cut. See also [276] for the paradigm for enumerating all (s, t)-cuts in a directed/undirected graph.

1.3.4 Reduction to Undirected Minimum (s, t)-Cuts

Given an edge-weighted graph G that has an undirected edge or a directed edge between every pair of vertices (possibly of weight zero), and given a source s and a sink t, Picard and Ratliff [274] have shown that the weights of edges can be changed while preserving the size of any minimum (s, t)-cut when we want to replace a directed edge with an undirected edge with the same set of end vertices. As a special case of their result, we show in the following that the problem of computing a minimum (s, t)-cut in a digraph with n vertices and m edges can be reduced in $O(n + m)$ time to the problem of computing a minimum (s, t)-cut in an undirected graph with n vertices and at most $m + n$ edges [223].

We describe a procedure to transform a given digraph $G = (V, E)$ with specified vertices s and t into an undirected graph $G_{s,t}$, where $G_{s,t}$ preserves all (s, t)-cuts X in G in the sense that

$$d(X; G) = \frac{1}{2}d(X; G_{s,t}) - \alpha$$

holds for some known constant $\alpha \geq 0$.

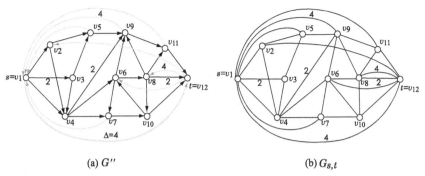

(a) G'' (b) $G_{s,t}$

Figure 1.19. (a) The Eulerian digraph G'' obtained from the digraph G in Fig. 1.14, where new edges are depicted by gray arrows and G satisfies $\Delta = 4$; (b) the undirected graph $G_{s,t}$ constructed from the G'' in (a).

Now define

$$\psi_G(v) \equiv \sum \{c_G(e) \mid e \in E(v, V - v; G)\}$$
$$- \sum \{c_G(e) \mid e \in E(V - v, v; G)\}, \quad v \in V.$$

First we convert the digraph G into an Eulerian digraph G'' by adding some edge weights, where a digraph G'' is called Eulerian if $\psi_{G''}(v) = 0$ for all $v \in V(G'')$ (i.e., for every vertex v, the sums of weights of incoming edges and that of outgoing edges are the same). For each vertex $v \in V - \{s, t\}$ with $\psi_G(v) > 0$, increase the weight of edge $e = (t, v)$ by $\psi_G(v)$, and, symmetrically for each vertex $v \in V - \{s, t\}$ with $\psi_G(v) < 0$, increase the weight of edge $e = (v, s)$ by $-\psi_G(v)$ (after creating edge (t, v) or (v, s) of zero weight if (t, v) or $(v, s) \notin E$). We then compute

$$\Delta = \psi_{G'}(t) \, (= -\psi_{G'}(s))$$

in the resulting digraph G', which satisfies $\psi_{G'}(v) = 0$ for all $v \in V - \{s, t\}$. Furthermore, if $\Delta > 0$, then increase the weight of edge $e = (s, t)$ by Δ (after creating edge (s, t) if $(s, t) \notin E$). If $\Delta < 0$, then increase the weight of edge $e = (t, s)$ by $-\Delta$ (after creating edge (t, s) if $(t, s) \notin E$). Let G'' denote the resulting digraph, which now satisfies $\psi_{G''}(s) = \psi_{G''}(t) = 0$ and, hence, is Eulerian. Let $G_{s,t}$ be the undirected graph obtained from G'' by neglecting its edge orientation. Figure 1.19(a) shows the Eulerian digraph G'' obtained from the digraph G in Fig. 1.14, and Fig. 1.19(b) shows $G_{s,t}$ obtained from this G''.

Theorem 1.16. *Given a digraph G with specified vertices s and t, let $G_{s,t}$ be the undirected graph obtained as before. Then for any (s, t)-cut X, it holds that*

$$d(X; G) = \frac{1}{2} d(X; G_{s,t}) - \max\{\Delta, 0\}. \qquad \square$$

Proof. Let X be an arbitrary (s, t)-cut. We easily see that $d(X; G') = d(X; G)$ holds because added edges are from t to v or from v to s. If $\Delta > 0$ (resp. $\Delta < 0$), then $d(X; G'') = d(X; G') + \Delta$ (resp. $d(X; G'') = d(X; G')$) holds. Since G'' is Eulerian, we have

$$d(X; G_{s,t}) = d(X; G'') + d(V - X; G'') = 2d(X; G'').$$

Therefore, $d(X; G) = d(X; G_{s,t})/2 - \max\{\Delta, 0\}$.   □

In particular, an (s, t)-cut X is minimum in G if and only if it also is in $G_{s,t}$. Clearly $G_{s,t}$ can be obtained from G in $O(n + m)$ time, and it has at most n more edges than the original digraph G.

1.4 Computing Connectivities

1.4.1 Menger's Theorem

Menger's theorem [217] states that the maximum number of edge-disjoint (resp. internally vertex-disjoint) (s, t)-paths is equal to the minimum size of an (s, t)-cut (resp. an (s, t)-vertex cut). This theorem characterizes the local edge-connectivity $\lambda(s, t; G)$ and the local vertex-connectivity $\kappa(s, t; G)$. In this subsection, we observe that this theorem follows from Theorems 1.8 and 1.10, and we then consider how to compute local connectivity and connectivity for both the edge and vertex versions.

Theorem 1.17. *Let $G = (V, E)$ be a digraph.*

   (i) *For two vertices $s, t \in V$, the maximum number of edge-disjoint (s, t)-paths in G is equal to the minimum size of an (s, t)-cut in G.*
   (ii) *For two vertices $s, t \in V$ with $(s, t) \notin E$, the maximum number of internally vertex-disjoint (s, t)-paths in G is equal to the minimum size of an (s, t)-vertex cut in G.*   □

Proof. (i) By letting $c_G(e) = 1$ for all edges e in the digraph $G = (V, E)$, we consider an integer-valued maximum (s, t)-flow f and a minimum (s, t)-cut X. By Theorems 1.8 and 1.10, $v(f) = d(X; G)$ holds, where $v(f)$ denotes the flow value of f. Now, as discussed in Section 1.2.1, we can decompose f into a set of weighted (s, t)-paths and weighted directed cycles such that the sum of weights of the paths is $v(f)$. Since f is integer-valued and $c_G(e) = 1$ for all edges e, the set of weighted paths consists of $v(f)$ edge-disjoint (s, t)-paths, as required.

(ii) Without loss of generality we assume that $G = (V, E)$ is simple since introducing multiple edges does not change the size of any vertex cut. We construct the following simple digraph $G^* = (V' \cup V'', E' \cup E'')$ from G (see Fig. 1.20), where

$$V' = \{v' \mid v \in V\}, \quad V'' = \{v'' \mid v \in V\},$$

$$E' = \{(u'', v') \mid (u, v) \in E\}, \quad E'' = \{(v', v'') \mid v \in V\}.$$

In other words, G^* is a bipartite digraph obtained from G by splitting each vertex v into two vertices v' and v'' and joining them via new directed edges.

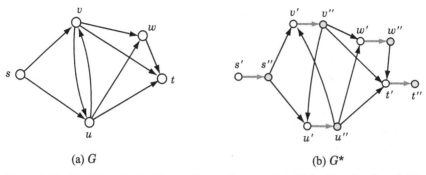

(a) G (b) G^*

Figure 1.20. (a) A digraph G with specified vertices s and t; (b) the bipartite digraph G^* obtained from G in (a) by splitting each vertex, where black (resp. gray) edges indicate edges in E' (resp. E'').

Regarding a directed path as a sequence of edges, any (s'', t')-path P^* in G^* is an alternating sequence of edges in E' and edges in E'', and the subsequence $P^* \cap E'$ defines an (s, t)-path P in G (after removing $'$ and $''$ from the vertex names). Conversely, from an (s, t)-path P, we can analogously construct an (s'', t')-path P^* in G^* such that $P^* \cap E' = P$. With this correspondence, we see that a set of internally vertex-disjoint (s, t)-paths in G corresponds to a set of the same number of edge-disjoint (s'', t')-paths in G^*, and vice versa. We define the weights of edges in G^* by $c_{G^*}(e) := 1$ $(e \in E'')$ and $c_{G^*}(e) := n$ $(e \in E')$, and we consider an integer-valued maximum (s'', t')-flow f in G^*. From this we obtain $v(f)$ internally vertex-disjoint (s, t)-paths in G. On the other hand, by Theorems 1.8 and 1.10, the size of a minimum (s'', t')-cut X^* in G^* is equal to $v(f)$. Since $|E(X^*; G^*)| = v(f) < n$ holds for this minimum cut X^*, it follows that $E(X^*; G^*) \subseteq E''$. Hence, the set of vertices corresponding to the edges in $E(X^*; G^*)$ (i.e., $v \in V$ corresponds to $(v', v'') \in E''$) is a minimum (s, t)-vertex cut in G. $\square$

Similar results for an undirected graph G can be obtained by applying Theorem 1.17 after replacing each edge in G with two oppositely oriented edges, which is stated in the following theorem.

Theorem 1.18. *Let $G = (V, E)$ be an undirected graph.*

  (i) *For two vertices $s, t \in V$, the maximum number of edge-disjoint (s, t)-paths in G is equal to the size of a minimum (s, t)-cut in G.*

  (ii) *For two nonadjacent vertices $s, t \in V$, the maximum number of internally vertex-disjoint (s, t)-paths in G is equal to the size of a minimum (s, t)-vertex cut in G.* $\square$

1.4.2 Unifying Local Connectivities: (k, α)-Connectivity

The local edge-connectivity and vertex-connectivity can be unified in the following manner. A *mixed cut* in a multigraph $G = (V, E)$ is defined as an ordered partition

(A, B, Z) of V^1 such that $A \neq \emptyset$ and $B \neq \emptyset$, where Z is allowed to be empty. We say that a mixed cut (A, B, Z) *separates* vertices u and v if one of u and v belongs to A and the other belongs to B; that is, u and v are disconnected in $G - Z - E(A, B; G)$.

Let $\alpha : V \to \mathbf{Z}_+$ be a vertex weight function. For a subset $X \subseteq V$, we denote $\alpha(X) = \sum_{v \in X} \alpha(v)$. Then the *size* of a mixed cut (A, B, Z) is defined to be $\alpha(Z) + d(A, B; G)$.

We define the local α-connectivity $\lambda_\alpha(u, v; G)$ between two vertices $u, v \in V$ to be the minimum size of a mixed cut (A, B, Z) separating u and v:

$$\lambda_\alpha(u, v; G) = \min\{\alpha(Z) + d(A, B; G) \mid (A, B, Z)$$
$$\text{is a mixed cut separating } u \text{ and } v\}.$$

We say that a family of paths connecting two vertices u and v is α-*independent* if the paths are edge-disjoint and each vertex $u' \in V - \{u, v\}$ is contained in at most $\alpha(u')$ paths of them. The two vertices u and v are called (k, α)-*connected* if $\lambda_\alpha(u, v; G) \geq k$. A graph is called (k, α)-connected if any two distinct vertices are (k, α)-connected.

Corollary 1.19. *Let G be an undirected multigraph and let s, t be two vertices. Then the maximum number of α-independent paths connecting s and t is equal to the minimum size of a mixed cut separating s and t in G.* □

Proof. Let $D = (V, E)$ be the digraph obtained from G by replacing each undirected edge $\{u, v\}$ with a pair of oppositely oriented edges (u, v) and (v, u). Let D^* be the digraph obtained from D by splitting each vertex $v \in V - \{s, t\}$ into two vertices v' and v'' and by joining them by $\alpha(v)$ copies of a new directed edge (v', v''). That is, $D^* = (V^*, E^*)$ is given by $V^* = V' \cup V'' \cup \{s'', t'\}$ and $E^* = E' \cup E_V$ such that

$$V' = \{v' \mid v \in V - \{s, t\}\}, \quad V'' = \{v'' \mid v \in V - \{s, t\}\},$$
$$E' = \{(u'', v') \mid (u, v) \in E\}, \quad E_V = \{\alpha(v) \text{ copies of } (v', v'') \mid v \in V - \{s, t\}\}.$$

This D^* is constructed so that a set of α-independent (s, t)-paths in G corresponds to a set of the same number of edge-disjoint (s, t)-paths in D^*, and vice versa. (This correspondence is analogous to that used in the proof of Theorem 1.17.) Similarly to Theorem 1.17(i), we can show that the maximum number of edge-disjoint (s, t)-paths in D^* (i.e., that of α-independent (s, t)-paths in G) is equal to the size of a minimum (s, t)-cut X^* in D^*. By letting $Z = \{v \in V - \{s, t\} \mid (v', v'') \in E(X^*; D^*)\}$ and $A = \{u \in V - Z \mid (u'', v') \in E(X^*; D^*)\}$, we see that $(A, B = V - Z - A, Z)$ is a mixed cut separating s and t, and it has the size $\alpha(Z) + d(A, B; G) = d(X^*; D^*)$. This proves the corollary. □

---

[1] (A, B, Z) is an ordered partition of V if A, B, Z are disjoint and satisfy $A \cup B \cup Z = V$.

Observe that $\lambda_\alpha(u, v; G)$ becomes the local edge-connectivity when $\alpha(x) > d(x; G)$ holds for all $x \in V$, whereas it implies the local vertex-connectivity when $\alpha(x) = 1$ for all $x \in V$. Moreover, this α-connectivity includes some of the previous generalizations [23, 89, 167] of edge and vertex connectivities.

For a specified subset $T \subseteq V$ of vertices, we say that a family of paths connecting two vertices u and v is T-*independent* if the paths are edge-disjoint and every element of T is contained in at most one path as an inner vertex. Frank et al. [89] defined local T-connectivity $\lambda_T(u, v; G)$ as the maximum number of T-independent paths connecting u and v. Observe that $\lambda_T(u, v; G) = \lambda_\alpha(u, v; G)$ holds if we set $\alpha(x) = 1, x \in T$ and $\alpha(x) > d(x; G), x \in V - T$.

On the other hand, Berg and Jordán [23] defined local ℓ-mixed connectivity between two vertices u and v by

$$\mu_\ell(u, v; G) = \min\{\ell|Z| + d(A, B; G) \,|$$
$$\text{mixed cuts } (A, B, Z) \text{ separating } u \text{ and } v\},$$

where $\ell \geq 1$ is a specified integer. They call a graph G ℓ-*mixed p-connected* if $|V| \geq (p/\ell) + 1$ and $\mu_\ell(u, v; G) \geq p$ for all pairs $u, v \in V$. This is an extension of (k, ℓ)-connectivity previously introduced by Kaneko and Ota [167] in the sense that (k, ℓ)-connectivity is equivalent to ℓ-mixed $k\ell$-connectivity (see also [62] for the (k, ℓ)-connectivity). Obviously we have $\mu_\ell(u, v; G) = \lambda_\alpha(u, v; G)$ if we use $\alpha(x) = \ell, x \in V$.

1.4.3 Computing Edge-Connectivity

Based on Menger's theorem, we can compute the edge (resp. vertex)-connectivity from the local edge (resp. vertex)-connectivity, where the latter can be computed by means of a maximum-flow algorithm in digraphs.

Theorem 1.20. *Let $G = (V, E)$ be an unweighted undirected/directed graph and let s and t be two vertices in V.*

(i) *$\lambda(s, t)$ edge-disjoint (s, t)-paths and a minimum (s, t)-cut in G can be found in $O(m^{3/2})$ time.*

(ii) *If G is simple, then $\lambda(s, t)$ edge-disjoint (s, t)-paths and a minimum (s, t)-cut in G can be found in $O(n^{2/3}m)$ time.*

(iii) *Let $k \geq 1$ be a given integer. Whether $\lambda(s, t) \geq k$ holds or not can be tested in $O(km)$ time. Furthermore, if $\lambda(s, t) < k$, then $\lambda(s, t)$ edge-disjoint (s, t)-paths and a minimum (s, t)-cut in G can be found in $O(km)$ time.* □

Proof. When a given graph is undirected, we redefine G to be the digraph obtained by replacing each edge with two oppositely oriented edges. Set the weight of each edge in G to be 1.

(i) and (ii): Immediate from Theorem 1.13(i) and (ii), respectively.

(iii) To compute $v(f)$, we repeat the iteration of finding an augmenting path at most k times. Since each iteration requires $O(m)$ time, the running time is then $O(km)$. If the algorithm terminates in less than k iterations, we have found a maximum (s, t)-flow f satisfying $v(f) = \lambda(s, t) < k$. On the other hand, if the algorithm is still running after $k - 1$ iterations, we conclude that $\lambda(s, t) \geq k$ holds. $\square$

Let $G = (V, E)$ be a weighted/unweighted digraph; we compute edge connectivity $\lambda(G)$. We choose an arbitrary vertex $s \in V$ as a designated vertex, and we define

$$\begin{aligned}
\lambda_s^+(G) &= \min\{\lambda(s, v; G) \mid v \in V - s\}, \\
\lambda_s^-(G) &= \min\{\lambda(v, s; G) \mid v \in V - s\}.
\end{aligned} \tag{1.15}$$

Given a minimum cut X of G, $\lambda(G) = \min\{\lambda(u, v) \mid u, v \in V(G)\}$ is equal to the $\lambda(u, v)$ of any $u \in X$ and $v \in V - X$. Considering two possible cases $s \in X$ and $s \in V - X$, it is immediately shown that it holds:

$$\lambda(G) = \min\{\lambda_s^+(G), \lambda_s^-(G)\}.$$

This method therefore computes maximum (s, v)-flows for all $v \in V - s$ and maximum (v, s)-flows for all $v \in V - s$, thus running a maximum flow algorithm $2(n - 1)$ times. It takes $O(m^{3/2}n)$ time for a multiple digraph G and $O(n^{5/3}m)$ time for a simple digraph G. If we only need to test whether or not G is k-edge-connected, then by Theorem 1.20(iii) we can test the k-edge-connectivity in $O(\min\{km, m^{3/2}\}n)$ time for a multiple digraph G and in $O(\min\{kmn, n^{5/3}m\})$ time for a simple digraph G.

Faster algorithms for unweighted digraphs have been proposed by Mansour and Schieber [212] and Gabow [96]. Mansour and Schieber gave an $O(\min\{nm, \lambda(G)^2n^2\})$ time algorithm for a simple graph $G = (V, E)$ by extending Matula's $O(nm)$ time algorithm for simple undirected graphs, which exploits a relation between minimum cuts and dominating sets. Gabow's algorithm is based on the idea of packing arborescences rooted at s, and it runs in $O(\lambda(G)m \log(n^2/m))$ time.

In Chapter 3, we show that $\lambda(G)$ of an undirected graph G can be computed in $O(mn + n^2 \log n)$ time by using a different mechanism.

1.4.4 Computing Vertex-Connectivity

We first note that the local vertex-connectivity can be computed in the following time complexity.

Theorem 1.21. Let $G = (V, E)$ be a simple unweighted undirected/directed graph, and let s and t be two vertices in V.

   (i) $\kappa(s, t)$ internally vertex-disjoint (s, t)-paths and a minimum (s, t)-vertex cut in G can be found in $O(n^{1/2}m)$ time.

   (ii) Let $k \geq 1$ be a given integer. Whether $\kappa(s, t) \geq k$ holds or not can be tested in $O(km)$ time. Furthermore, if $\kappa(s, t) < k$, then $\kappa(s, t)$ internally

> vertex-disjoint (s, t)-paths and a minimum (s, t)-vertex cut in G can be
> found in $O(km)$ time. □

Proof. When a given graph is undirected, we redefine G to be the digraph obtained by replacing each edge with two oppositely oriented edges.

(i) We apply a maximum flow algorithm to the simple digraph G^* constructed from G as in the proof for Theorem 1.17(ii). Since G^* satisfies $|E(v, V^* - v; G^*)| \leq 1$ or $|E(V^* - v, v; G^*)| \leq 1$ for every $v \in V$, the result is immediate from Theorem 1.13(iii).

(ii) An argument analogous to the proof of Theorem 1.20(iii) works for G^* of (i). □

Let $G = (V, E)$ be a simple undirected/directed graph. We consider how to compute vertex-connectivity $\kappa(G)$ via several lemmas. For an undirected (resp. directed) graph G, we denote by $\overline{E}$ the set of unordered pairs $\{u, v\}$ such that $u, v \in V$, $u \neq v$, and $\{u, v\} \notin E$ (resp. ordered pairs (u, v) such that $u, v \in V$, $u \neq v$ and $(u, v) \notin E$) and, for two subsets $X, Y \subseteq V$ (not necessarily disjoint), we define

$$\overline{E}(X, Y; G) = \{\{u, v\} \notin E \mid u \in X, v \in Y\}$$

(resp. $\overline{E}(X, Y; G) = \{(u, v) \notin E \mid u \in X, v \in Y\}$),

and

$$\kappa_{X,Y}(G) = \min\{\kappa(u, v; G) \mid \{u, v\} \in \overline{E}(X, Y; G)\}$$

(resp. $\kappa_{X,Y}(G) = \min\{\kappa(u, v; G) \mid (u, v) \in \overline{E}(X, Y; G)\}$),

where $\kappa_{X,Y}(G) = +\infty$ if $\overline{E}(X, Y; G) = \emptyset$, and we may write $\overline{E}(X, Y; G)$ and $\kappa_{X,Y}(G)$ as $\overline{E}(X, Y)$ and $\kappa_{X,Y}$, respectively, when G is clear from the context.

In what follows, we assume that G is not a complete undirected (resp. directed) graph and, hence, $\kappa(G) = \min\{\kappa(u, v; G) \mid \{u, v\} \in \overline{E}\}$ (resp. $\kappa(G) = \min\{\kappa(u, v; G) \mid (u, v) \in \overline{E}\}$). For a vertex s in a directed graph G, define

$$\kappa_s^+(G) = \min\{\kappa(s, v; G) \mid (s, v) \in \overline{E}(s, V - s)\},$$

$$\kappa_s^-(G) = \min\{\kappa(v, s; G) \mid (v, s) \in \overline{E}(V - s, s)\}.$$

Unlike $\lambda(G)$, $\kappa(G)$ may not be the minimum of $\kappa_s^+(G)$ and $\kappa_s^-(G)$ (since the (u, v) attaining the minimum in the preceding definition of $\kappa(G)$ may not contain s). By definition,

$$\kappa(G) = \min\{\kappa_{S,S}, \kappa_{S,T}, \kappa_{T,T}\}$$

holds for any partition $\{S, T = V - S\}$ of V in an undirected/directed graph $G = (V, E)$.

For an undirected (resp. directed) graph $G = (V, E)$, a subset $L \subseteq V$ is called k-*vertex-connected in a digraph* $G = (V, E)$ if $\kappa(u, v; G) \geq k$ holds for all $\{u, v\} \in$

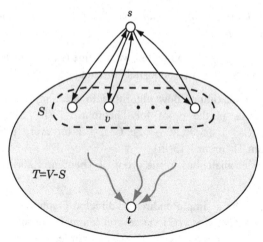

Figure 1.21. The augmented digraph G_S for a digraph G and a subset $S \subseteq V$.

$\overline{E}(L, L)$ (resp. $(u, v) \in \overline{E}(L, L)$) (note that L does not necessarily induce a k-vertex-connected subgraph from G). By definition, any subset $L \subseteq V$ is $\kappa_{L,L}$-vertex-connected, and, for any vertex cut C with $|C| < \kappa_{L,L}$, $S - C$ is contained in the same component (resp. strongly connected component) in $G - C$, since $\kappa(u, v; G - C) \geq \kappa_{L,L} - |C| \geq 1$ holds for all $\{u, v\} \in \overline{E}(L - C, L - C)$.

The next property gives a condition by which we can omit computing $\kappa_{T,T}$ to determine $\kappa(G)$.

Lemma 1.22 ([65]). *For a digraph $G = (V, E)$ which is not complete, let $\{S, T = V - S\}$ be a partition of V. Then*

    (i) *If $\kappa(u_1, u_2; G) < |S|$ for some pair $(u_1, u_2) \in \overline{E}(T, T)$, then there is a vertex $v \in S$ such that $(u_1, v) \in \overline{E}(T, S)$, $\kappa(u_1, v; G) \leq \kappa(u_1, u_2; G)$ or $(v, u_2) \in \overline{E}(S, T)$, $\kappa(v, u_2; G) \leq \kappa(u_1, u_2; G)$.*

    (ii) *If $\kappa(G) < |S|$, then $\kappa(G) = \min\{\kappa_{S,S}, \kappa_{S,T}, \kappa_{T,S}\}$.*   □

Proof. (i) Consider a minimum (u_1, u_2)-vertex cut C in G. That is, there is a partition $\{V_1, C, V_2\}$ of V such that $|C| = \kappa(u_1, u_2; G)$, $u_1 \in V_1$, $u_2 \in V_2$, and $E(V_1, V_2; G) = \emptyset$. Since $|C| < |S|$, $S - C \neq \emptyset$ contains a vertex v. Then if $v \in V_2$ (resp. $v \in V_1$), then C is a (u_1, v)-vertex cut (resp. (v, u_2)-vertex cut), indicating $(u_1, v) \in \overline{E}(T, S)$ and $\kappa(u_1, v; G) \leq |C|$ (resp. $(v, u_2) \in \overline{E}(S, T)$ and $\kappa(v, u_2; G) \leq |C|$).

(ii) By condition (i), $\kappa_{T,T} < |S|$ implies $\kappa_{T,T} \geq \min\{\kappa_{S,T}, \kappa_{T,S}\}$. From this and the assumption $\kappa(G) < |S|$, we get $\kappa(G) = \min\{\kappa_{S,S}, \kappa_{S,T}, \kappa_{T,S}, \kappa_{T,T}\} = \min\{\kappa_{S,S}, \kappa_{S,T}, \kappa_{T,S}\}$.   □

We easily see that Lemma 1.22(ii) also holds for the case of undirected graphs, in which $\kappa_{S,T} = \kappa_{T,S}$, holds by definition.

For a subset $S \subseteq V$ in an undirected (resp. directed) graph $G = (V, E)$, let G_S denote the graph obtained by adding to G a new vertex s and undirected edges

$\{s, v\}$ (resp. directed edges (s, v) and (v, s)) for every $v \in S$. This is illustrated in Fig. 1.21. The next property suggests how to compute $\kappa_{S,T}$ efficiently, where we denote

$$\kappa_{s,T}(G_S) = \min\{\kappa(s, v; G_S) \mid (s, v) \in \overline{E}(s, T; G_S)\},$$

$$\kappa_{T,s}(G_S) = \min\{\kappa(v, s; G_S) \mid (v, s) \in \overline{E}(T, s; G_S)\}.$$

Lemma 1.23 ([65, 120]). *For a noncomplete digraph $G = (V, E)$ and two disjoint subsets $S, T \subseteq V$, let G_S be the augmented graph as defined earlier.*

(i) *If* $\min\{\kappa_{S,T}, \kappa_{T,S}\} < \kappa_{S,S}$, *then* $\min\{\kappa_{S,T}, \kappa_{T,S}\} \geq \min\{\kappa_{s,T}(G_S), \kappa_{T,s}(G_S)\}$.

(ii) *If* $\min\{\kappa_{s,T}(G_S), \kappa_{T,s}(G_S)\} < |S|$, *then* $\min\{\kappa_{S,T}, \kappa_{T,S}\} \leq \min\{\kappa_{s,T}(G_S), \kappa_{T,s}(G_S)\}$.

(iii) *If* $\min\{\kappa_{S,T}, \kappa_{T,S}\} < \min\{|S|, \kappa_{S,S}\}$, *then* $\kappa_{S,T} = \min\{\kappa_{s,T}(G_S), \kappa_{T,s}(G_S)\}$. $\square$

Proof. Assume $\kappa_{S,T} \leq \kappa_{T,S}$ (since the case of $\kappa_{T,S} < \kappa_{S,T}$ can be treated analogously). (i) $\overline{E}(S, T) = \emptyset$ (i.e., $\kappa_{S,T} = +\infty$) implies the desired property. Consider the case of $\overline{E}(S, T) \neq \emptyset$, and $(u, v) \in \overline{E}(S, T)$ is a pair that has a (u, v)-vertex cut C with $|C| = \kappa_{S,T}$. Since $|C| = \kappa_{S,T} < \kappa_{S,S}$ and S is $\kappa_{S,S}$-vertex-connected in G, all vertices in $S - C \neq \emptyset$ belong to the same strongly connected component in $G - C$. Therefore, C is an (s, v)-vertex cut in G_S, implying that $\kappa_{S,T} \geq \kappa_{s,T}(G_S) \geq \min\{\kappa_{s,T}(G_S), \kappa_{T,s}(G_S)\}$.

(ii) Assume $\kappa_{s,T}(G_S) \leq \kappa_{T,s}(G_S)$ without loss of generality. Let C be an (s, u)-vertex cut with $|C| = \kappa_{s,T}(G_S)$ for some $u \in T$. Since $|S| > |C|$, $S - C$ contains a vertex v', for which $|C|$ is a (v', u)-vertex cut and $(v', u) \in \overline{E}(S, T)$, implying that $\min\{\kappa_{S,T}, \kappa_{T,S}\} \leq \min\{\kappa_{s,T}(G_S), \kappa_{T,s}(G_S)\}$.

(iii) By $\min\{\kappa_{S,T}, \kappa_{T,S}\} < \kappa_{S,S}$ and condition (i), we have $\kappa_{S,T} \geq \min\{\kappa_{s,T}(G_S), \kappa_{T,s}(G_S)\}$. Hence, by $\min\{\kappa_{S,T}, \kappa_{T,S}\} < |S|$, we have $\min\{\kappa_{s,T}(G_S), \kappa_{T,s}(G_S)\} \leq \min\{\kappa_{S,T}, \kappa_{T,S}\} < |S|$. From this and condition (ii), we have $\min\{\kappa_{S,T}, \kappa_{T,S}\} \leq \min\{\kappa_{s,T}(G_S), \kappa_{T,s}(G_S)\}$, i.e., $\min\{\kappa_{S,T}, \kappa_{T,S}\} = \min\{\kappa_{s,T}(G_S), \kappa_{T,s}(G_S)\}$. $\square$

Lemma 1.24. *For a noncomplete digraph $G = (V, E)$ and a nonempty proper subset S of V, let G_S be the augmented graph defined earlier. Then*

(i) *If* $\min\{\kappa_{S,S}, \kappa_s^+(G_S), \kappa_s^-(G_S)\} \geq |S|$, *then* $\kappa(G) \geq |S|$.

(ii) *If* $\min\{\kappa_{S,S}, \kappa_s^+(G_S), \kappa_s^-(G_S)\} < |S|$, *then* $\kappa(G) = \min\{\kappa_{S,S}, \kappa_s^+(G_S), \kappa_s^-(G_S)\}$. $\square$

Proof. Let $T = V - S$. Then $\kappa_{s,T}(G_S) = \kappa_s^+(G_S)$ and $\kappa_{T,s}(G_S) = \kappa_s^-(G_S)$ hold by the definition of G_S.

(i) To derive a contradiction, we assume $|S| > \kappa(G)$. By Lemma 1.22(ii), $\kappa(G) = \min\{\kappa_{S,S}, \kappa_{S,T}, \kappa_{T,S}\}$. If $\min\{\kappa_{S,T}, \kappa_{T,S}\} \geq \kappa_{S,S}$ $(= \kappa(G))$, then

$|S| \le \min\{\kappa_{S,S}, \kappa_s^+(G_S), \kappa_s^-(G_S)\} \le \kappa_{S,S} = \kappa(G) < |S|$, a contradiction. Then assume $\kappa_{S,S} > \min\{\kappa_{S,T}, \kappa_{T,S}\}$ $(= \kappa(G))$. By $\min\{\kappa_{S,T}, \kappa_{T,S}\} < \min\{|S|, \kappa_{S,S}\}$ and Lemma 1.23(i), we have $\min\{\kappa_{S,T}, \kappa_{T,S}\} \ge \min\{\kappa_s^+(G_S), \kappa_s^-(G_S)\}$. Hence, $|S| \le \min\{\kappa_{S,S}, \kappa_s^+(G_S), \kappa_s^-(G_S)\} \le \min\{\kappa_{S,S}, \kappa_{S,T}, \kappa_{T,S}\} = \min\{\kappa_{S,T}, \kappa_{T,S}\} = \kappa(G) < |S|$, a contradiction.

(ii) Observe that $\kappa(G) < |S|$ holds since by assumption $\kappa_{S,S} < |S|$ holds or $\min\{\kappa_{S,T}, \kappa_{T,S}\} < |S|$ follows from $\min\{\kappa_s^+(G_S), \kappa_s^-(G_S)\} < |S|$ by Lemma 1.23(ii).

First consider the case of $\kappa_{S,S} \le \min\{\kappa_s^+(G_S), \kappa_s^-(G_S)\}$. We claim that $\kappa_{S,S} \le \min\{\kappa_{S,T}, \kappa_{T,S}\}$ holds, from which $\min\{\kappa_{S,S}, \kappa_s^+(G_S), \kappa_s^-(G_S)\} = \kappa_{S,S} = \kappa(G)$ holds by Lemma 1.22(ii) and $|S| > \kappa(G)$. If $\kappa_{S,S} > \min\{\kappa_{S,T}, \kappa_{T,S}\}$, then $\min\{\kappa_{S,T}, \kappa_{T,S}\} \ge \min\{\kappa_s^+(G_S), \kappa_s^-(G_S)\}$ by Lemma 1.23(i). This, however, implies that $\min\{\kappa_{S,T}, \kappa_{T,S}\} \ge \kappa_{S,S}$, a contradiction. Therefore, $\kappa_{S,S} \le \min\{\kappa_{S,T}, \kappa_{T,S}\}$.

Next consider the case where $\kappa_{S,S} > \min\{\kappa_s^+(G_S), \kappa_s^-(G_S)\}$ holds. By assumption, $\min\{\kappa_s^+(G_S), \kappa_s^-(G_S)\} < |S|$ holds. Then by Lemma 1.23(ii) we have $\kappa_{S,T} \le \min\{\kappa_s^+(G_S), \kappa_s^-(G_S)\}$ $(< \min\{|S|, \kappa_{S,S}\})$. On the other hand, by $\min\{\kappa_{S,T}, \kappa_{T,S}\} < \min\{|S|, \kappa_{S,S}\}$ and Lemma 1.23(i), we have $\min\{\kappa_{S,T}, \kappa_{T,S}\} \ge \min\{\kappa_s^+(G_S), \kappa_s^-(G_S)\}$. Therefore, $\min\{\kappa_{S,T}, \kappa_{T,S}\} = \min\{\kappa_s^+(G_S), \kappa_s^-(G_S)\} < \kappa_{S,S}$, and, hence, $\min\{\kappa_{S,S}, \kappa_s^+(G_S), \kappa_s^-(G_S)\} = \min\{\kappa_{S,T}, \kappa_{T,S}\} = \kappa(G)$ follows from Lemma 1.22(ii) and $\min\{\kappa_{S,T}, \kappa_{T,S}\} < |S|$. $\square$

This lemma suggests the following algorithm for testing the k-vertex-connectivity of a given digraph.

Algorithm VERTEXCONN(G, k)
Input: A noncomplete digraph $G = (V, E)$ and an integer $k \in [1, n-2]$.
Output: A minimum vertex cut C of G if $\kappa(G) < k$; otherwise a message
  "$\kappa(G) \ge k$."
1 Choose arbitrarily a set S of k vertices from V;
2 Compute $\alpha_1 = \min\{k, \kappa_{S,S}\}$. If $\kappa_{S,S} < k$, then find a (u, v)-vertex cut C_1 with $(u, v) \in \overline{E}(S, S)$ that attains $|C_1| = \kappa_{S,S}$;
3 Construct the augmented graph G_S as defined earlier;
4 Compute $\alpha_2 = \min\{k, \kappa_s^+(G_S), \kappa_s^-(G_S)\}$. If $\alpha_2 < k$, then find a (u, v)-vertex cut C_2 with $(u, v) \in \overline{E}(S, T) \cup \overline{E}(S, T)$ that attains $|C_2| = \alpha_2$;
5 **if** $\min\{\alpha_1, \alpha_2\} = k$ **then**
6   Output "$\kappa(G) \ge k$"
7 **else**
8   Output $C = C_i$ with $|C_i| = \min\{\alpha_1, \alpha_2\}$.

Theorem 1.25. *Given a noncomplete digraph $G = (V, E)$ and an integer $k \in [1, n-2]$, VERTEXCONN correctly tests the k-vertex-connectivity of G and outputs a minimum vertex cut of G if $\kappa(G) < k$. VERTEXCONN runs in $O((k^2 n^{1/2} + kn)m)$ time.* $\square$

Proof. The validity of VERTEXCONN follows from Lemma 1.24. We consider its running time. Lines 2 and 4 of VERTEXCONN can be executed by testing the local k-vertex-connectivities at most $k(k-1)$ times and $2(n-k)$ times, respectively. The local k-vertex-connectivity for a pair of vertices can be tested in $O(\min\{k, n^{1/2}\}m)$ time by Theorem 1.21(i)–(ii). Therefore, the entire time complexity becomes

$$O((k^2 + n)\min\{k, n^{1/2}\}m) = O((\max\{k, n^{1/2}\})^2 \min\{k, n^{1/2}\}m)$$
$$= O(\max\{k, n^{1/2}\}kn^{1/2}m)$$
$$= O((k^2 n^{1/2} + kn)m). \qquad \square$$

If we set $k = \kappa(G) + 1$, VERTEXCONN(G, k) outputs a minimum vertex cut of G in $O((\kappa(G)^2 n^{1/2} + \kappa(G)n)m)$ time. However, $\kappa(G)$ is not known in advance. To overcome this dilemma, we use a *doubling technique* on parameter k. That is, we execute VERTEXCONN(G, k) for $k = 2, 2^2, 2^3, \ldots$ until a minimum vertex cut is found (i.e., $2^{i-1} \le \kappa(G) < 2^i$ holds for $k = 2^i$). The total time complexity is

$$O(\{(2)^2 + (2^2)^2 + \cdots + (2^i)^2\}n^{1/2}m + \{2 + 2^2 + \cdots + 2^i\}nm)$$
$$= O((2^i)^2 n^{1/2}m + 2^i nm)$$
$$= O(\kappa(G)^2 n^{1/2}m + \kappa(G)nm).$$

In this way, we can compute the exact value $\kappa(G)$ and a minimum vertex cut of G in the same time complexity as that of Theorem 1.25.

This idea can also be applied to any algorithm for testing the k-vertex-connectivity (resp. k-edge-connectivity) if it can deliver a minimum vertex cut (resp. a minimum cut) in case $\kappa(G) < k$ (resp. $\lambda(G) < k$) holds. For such an algorithm, a similar doubling technique enables us to compute $\kappa(G)$ (resp. $\lambda(G)$) in the same time bound in which k is replaced by $\kappa(G)$ (resp. $\lambda(G)$).

The time bound of VERTEXCONN(G, k) has been reduced by Henzinger et al. [121]. They have extended Hao and Orlin's algorithm [113] to compute $\lambda_s^+(G)$ so that $\kappa_s^+(G)$ can be computed in $O(nm)$ time. Hence, line 4 can be executed in $O(nm)$ time. Line 2 can be done in $O(knm)$ time by taking each vertex in S as s for $\kappa_s^+(G)$. By combining this with the results for the maximum flow algorithm, line 2 can be executed in $O(\min\{k^3 m, knm\})$ time. Therefore, VERTEXCONN(G, k) can be implemented to run in $O((n + \min\{k^3, kn\})m)$ time. Then by using a doubling technique on k, a minimum vertex cut can be found in $O((n + \min\{\kappa(G)^3, \kappa(G)n\})m)$ time.

Currently the fastest algorithm for computing the vertex-connectivity of a digraph is due to Gabow [98]. The algorithm makes use of expander graphs and runs in $O((n + \min\{k^{5/2}, kn^{3/4}\})m)$ time for checking the k-vertex-connectivity and in $O((n + \min\{\kappa(G)^{5/2}, \kappa(G)n^{3/4}\})m)$ time for finding a minimum vertex cut of G.

1.4.5 Reduction from Edge-Connectivity to Vertex-Connectivity

Given a multigraph $G = (V, E)$ (see Fig. 1.22(a)) and an integer $k \ge 1$, Galil and Italiano [100] construct a simple graph H_k such that H_k is k-vertex-connected if

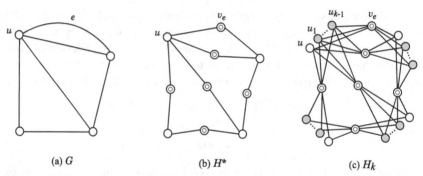

Figure 1.22. Illustration of graphs H^* and H_k: (a) graph G, (b) graph H^*, and (c) bipartite graph H_k.

and only if G is k-edge-connected. In this way, edge-connectivity is reduced to vertex-connectivity.

We first replace each edge $e = \{u, v\} \in E$ with two edges $\{u, v_e\}$ and $\{v_e, v\}$ introducing a new vertex v_e. Let $V_E = \{v_e \mid e \in E\}$, and denote by H^* the resulting graph on $V \cup V_E$ (see Fig. 1.22(b)). For each vertex $u \in V$, we denote by $N(u)$ the set of vertices $v_e \in V_E$ for all edges e incident with u, that is,

$$N(u) = \{v_e \in V_E \mid e \in E(u, V - u; G)\}.$$

Then each vertex $u \in V$ in H^* is adjacent to all vertices in $N(u)$.

We next create $k - 1$ copies $(u_1, u_2, \ldots, u_{k-1})$ of each vertex $u \in V$, and we let $V_u = \{u_1, u_2, \ldots, u_{k-1}\}$. We join each vertex in V_u and all vertices $N(u)$ by new edges, and we denote the resulting simple graph by $H_k = (W_k = V \cup V_E \cup (\cup_{u \in V} V_u), E_k)$ (see Fig. 1.22(c)), where

$$E_k = \{\{u, v_e\}, \{v_e, v\}, \{u_i, v_e\}, \{v_e, v_j\} \mid e = \{u, v\} \in E,$$
$$v_e \in V_E, \ u_i \in V_u, \ v_j \in V_v\}.$$

Observe that H_k can be constructed in $O(m + kn)$ time using an appropriate data structure. Clearly H_k is a bipartite graph between vertex sets V_E and $V \cup (\cup_{u \in V} V_u)$ and satisfies

$$|W_k| = |V| + |V_E| + |\cup_{u \in V} V_u| = |E| + k|V|, \quad |E_k| = 2k|E|.$$

For each $u \in V$, there are k paths of length 2 between any two $w, w' \in N(u)$ passing through only vertices in $\{u\} \cup V_u$. Hence,

$$\kappa(w, w'; H_k) \geq k. \tag{1.16}$$

Lemma 1.26. Let $G = (V, E)$, H^*, and H_k be as defined earlier.

(i) For any $F \subseteq E$ such that $G - F$ is not connected, $\{v_e \mid e \in F\}$ is a vertex cut in H_k.

(ii) For any vertex cut $Z \subseteq V_E$ in H_k, $G - \{e \in E \mid v_e \in Z\}$ is not connected.

(iii) *For any minimal vertex cut Z in H_k (i.e., a vertex cut such that any proper subset of Z is not a vertex cut), $|Z| \geq k$ holds if $Z - V_E \neq \emptyset$.*   □

Proof. (i) By construction, it is easy to see that, if $G - F$ is not connected, then $\{v_e \mid e \in F\}$ is a vertex cut in H^*. Also if $Z = \{v_e \mid e \in F\}$ is a vertex cut in H^*, then Z is a vertex cut in H_k.

(ii) Let $Z \subseteq V_E$ be a vertex cut in H_k, which is also a vertex cut in H^*. Since H^* is bipartite between vertex sets V_E and V, $Z \subseteq V_E$ separates some two vertices $u, v \in V$ in H^*. This means that edge set $\{e \in E \mid v_e \in Z\}$ separates these u and v in G.

(iii) Let Z be a minimal vertex cut in H_k such that $Z - V_E \neq \emptyset$. Consider $H_k - Z$, which has at least two connected components. By the minimality, $Z - u$ is not a vertex cut in H_k for any $u \in Z - V_E$. Hence, u has an edge incident with each of these components. This means that some two vertices $w, w' \in N(u)$ are separated by Z. Since $\kappa(w, w'; H_k) \geq k$ holds by (1.16), we then have $|Z| \geq k$.   □

Theorem 1.27. *For the graph H_k constructed from a multigraph G and an integer $k \geq 1$, it holds that*

$$\kappa(H_k) \begin{cases} \geq k & \text{if } \lambda(G) \geq k, \\ = \lambda(G) & \text{if } \lambda(G) \leq k - 1. \end{cases} \tag{1.17}$$
    □

Proof. By Lemma 1.26(i)–(iii), we see that there is a one-to-one correspondence between the edge cuts $F \subseteq E$ with $|F| \leq k - 1$ in G and the vertex cuts Z in H_k, where $|F| = |Z|$ holds. Hence, if $\lambda(G) \leq k - 1$, then we have

$$\kappa(H_k) = \lambda(G).$$

On the other hand, if $\lambda(G) \geq k$, then by Lemma 1.26(i)(iii), H_k has no vertex cut Z with $|Z| \leq k - 1$.   □

For a simple graph $G = (V, E)$, there is an $O(n + m)$ time algorithm [127] for testing the 3-vertex-connectivity and an $O(m + n\alpha(m, n))$ time algorithm [168] for testing the 4-vertex-connectivity of G, where $\alpha(m, n)$ is the inverse of the Ackermann function, which is very slowly growing [298]. By applying these algorithms to the graphs H_3 and H_4 constructed from a given multigraph G, we obtain the next result.

Corollary 1.28. *Let $G = (V, E)$ be a multigraph. The 3-edge-connectivity and 4-edge-connectivity of G can be tested in $O(n + m)$ time and $O(m + n\alpha(m, n))$ time, respectively.*   □

1.5 Representations of Cut Structures

In this section, we review some important tools and concepts related to cut structures of graphs such as the Gomory–Hu tree, maximal components, extreme vertex sets, and cactus representation.

1.5.1 Gomory–Hu Tree

For an edge-weighted undirected graph G, we have

$$\lambda(u, w; G) \geq \min\{\lambda(u, v; G), \lambda(v, w; G)\} \text{ for any three vertices } u, v, w \in V,$$
$$(1.18)$$

since any (u, w)-cut X is a (u, v)-cut or a (v, w)-cut, depending on whether v belongs to $V - X$ and X. From this, we can show that the set $\{\lambda(u, v; G) \mid u, v \in V\}$ of local edge-connectivities contains at most $n - 1$ different values. To see this, consider the complete graph K on V such that each edge $\{u, v\} \in E(K)$ is weighted by $c_K(u, v) = \lambda(u, v; G)$, and let T be a maximum spanning tree in K. It suffices to show that each nontree edge has the same weight as that of some tree edge. Take a nontree edge $\{u, v\}$ and consider the path $P_{u,v}$ connecting u and v in T. Let $\{u', v'\}$ be an edge in $P_{u,v}$ with the minimum weight. By the maximality of T, $\lambda(u, v; G) = c_K(u, v) \leq c_K(u', v') = \lambda(u', v'; G)$ holds (see the remark after Lemma 1.4). On the other hand, by repeated applications of property (1.18), we have $\lambda(u, v; G) = c_K(u, v) \geq c_K(u', v') = \lambda(u', v'; G)$. Hence, $\lambda(u, v; G) = \lambda(u', v'; G)$ holds, as required.

Definition 1.29. *For an edge-weighted graph $G = (V, E)$, an edge-weighted graph $H = (V, F)$ on the same vertex set V is called* flow equivalent *to G if $\lambda(u, v; H) = \lambda(u, v; G)$ holds for all $u, v \in V$, where H is not necessarily a subgraph of G. A tree T is* flow equivalent *to G if and only if*

> *for any two vertices $u, v \in V$, the minimum weight of the edges on the path between u and v in T is equal to $\lambda(u, v; G)$.* $\quad(1.19)$
> $\square$

The maximum spanning tree T on V constructed from the complete graph K in the preceding paragraph is flow equivalent to G, since, for any vertices $u, v \in V$, $\lambda(u, v; G) = \min\{c_K(e) \mid e \in P_{u,v}\}$ holds. It is known [72] that any graph G has a flow-equivalent tree T even if T is restricted to be a single path.

Definition 1.30. *A flow-equivalent tree T to G is called a* Gomory–Hu tree *of G if*

> *for each edge $e = \{u, v\} \in E(T)$, the cut $\{X, \overline{X} = V - X\}$ generated by e in T (i.e., $T - e$ has two components whose vertex sets are X and $\overline{X}$) has the same cut size as in G* $\quad(1.20)$

(i.e., $c_T(u, v) = d(X, \overline{X}; G)$ and $(X, \overline{X})$ is a minimum (u, v)-cut in G). $\quad\square$

Note that a flow-equivalent tree T to G is not always a Gomory–Hu tree of G. For example, if $G = (V, E)$ is a tree with unit edge weights, an arbitrary tree on V is flow equivalent to G but may not be a Gomory–Hu tree of G. Figure 1.23 shows a Gomory–Hu tree for the graph $G = (V, E)$ in Fig. 1.3.

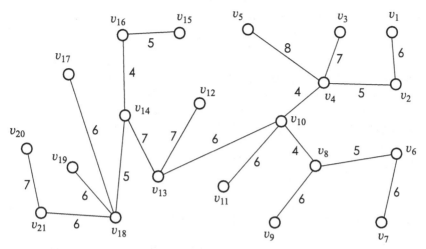

Figure 1.23. A Gomory–Hu tree $T = (V, F)$ for the graph $G = (V, E)$ in Fig. 1.3.

Theorem 1.31 ([107]). *For any edge-weighted undirected graph $G = (V, E)$, there exists a Gomory–Hu tree $T = (V, F)$.* $\square$

This theorem is based on the following observation.

Lemma 1.32 ([107]). *Let X be a minimum (s, t)-cut for some vertices $s, t \in V$ in a graph $G = (V, E)$. Then, for any pair of vertices $u, v \in V - X$, G has a minimum (u, v)-cut Y that does not cross X.* $\square$

Proof. Suppose that a minimum (u, v)-cut Y with $u, v \in V - X$ crosses X. By symmetry of X and $V - X$, assume $s \in X \cap Y$. Since $X \cap Y$ is an (s, t)-cut, we have $d(X \cap Y; G) \geq d(X; G)$. This and (1.3) imply $d(X \cup Y; G) \leq d(Y; G)$, indicating that $X \cup Y$ or $V - (X \cup Y)$ is a minimum (u, v)-cut. $\square$

By this lemma, the graph $G' = G/X$ obtained by contracting X into a vertex x satisfies

$$\lambda(u, v; G') = \lambda(u, v; G), \quad u, v \in V - X.$$

A *cut tree* T with respect to a partition $\mathcal{X} = \{X_1, X_2, \ldots, X_k\}$ of V is defined by vertex set $V(T) = \{x_1, x_2, \ldots, x_k\}$, where each vertex x_i corresponds to $X_i \in \mathcal{X}$, and edge set $E(T)$ such that

$$c_T(e) = d(X_e, \overline{X_e}; G), \quad e \in E(T),$$

where X_e and $\overline{X_e} = V - X_e$ denote the vertex subsets that correspond to the two components in $T - e$, respectively. A cut tree T is called a Gomory–Hu tree with respect to a partition $\mathcal{X}$ if it has the following property: For each edge $e \in E(T)$,

(i) $\lambda(u, v; G) \leq c_T(e)$ for all $u \in X_e$ and $v \in \overline{X_e}$.
(ii) Equality holds in condition (i) for some pair of $u \in X_e$ and $v \in \overline{X_e}$; that is, $\{X_e, \overline{X_e}\}$ is a minimum (u, v)-cut in G.

Lemma 1.33. *For a graph G, any Gomory–Hu tree T with respect to partition $\mathcal{X} = \{\{v\} \mid v \in V(G)\}$ satisfies (1.19) and (1.20).*   □

Proof. By definition of cut trees, T satisfies (1.20). To show (1.19), consider two vertices $u, v \in V(G)$ and let $e \in E(T)$ be an edge that has the minimum weight on the path between u and v in T. By property (i), we have $\lambda(u, v; G) \leq c_T(e)$. We show $\lambda(u, v; G) = c_T(e)$. If $\lambda(u, v; G) < c_T(e)$, then a minimum (u, v)-cut Y separates the endvertices of an edge e' in the path between u and v in T, where $\lambda(u, v; G) = d(Y; G) < c_T(e) \leq c_T(e')$. This, however, contradicts the implication of property (ii) that $\lambda(u', v'; G) = c_T(e')$ holds for some pair of $u' \in X_{e'}$ and $v' \in \overline{X_{e'}}$.   □

To prove Theorem 1.31, we consider a slightly more general property.

Lemma 1.34. *For a graph G and an integer $k \in [1, n]$, there exists a Gomory–Hu tree T_k with respect to a partition $\mathcal{X}$ of $V(G)$ satisfying $|\mathcal{X}| = k$.*   □

Proof. We prove this by induction on $k = |\mathcal{X}|$. For any graph G, a tree T_1 consisting of a single vertex is a Gomory–Hu tree T with respect to partition $\mathcal{X} = \{V(G)\}$. Now we assume that the lemma statement holds for all $k' \in [1, k]$. If $k = n$, then we are done. Consider the case of $k < n$. By the induction hypothesis, G has a Gomory–Hu tree T_k with respect to a partition $\mathcal{X}$ with $|\mathcal{X}| = k$. Since $k < n$, there is a subset $X \in \mathcal{X}$ such that $|X| \geq 2$. Choose two vertices $s, t \in X$ and consider a minimum (s, t)-cut S in G. Let $x \in V(T_k)$ be the vertex corresponding to X, and $e_1, e_2, \ldots, e_p \in E(T_k)$ be the edges incident to x. By property (ii), $\{X_{e_i}, \overline{X_{e_i}}\}$, for each edge e_i, is a minimum (u, v)-cut for some $u \in X_{e_i}$ and $v \in \overline{X_{e_i}}$, where we assume $X \cap X_{e_i} = \emptyset$ without loss of generality (see Fig. 1.24(a)). By Lemma 1.32, there is a minimum (s, t)-cut S that does not cross any of X_{e_i}, $i = 1, 2, \ldots, p$. Let $\{S, \overline{S} = V - S\}$ be such a minimum (s, t)-cut. (To find such a cut S, we contract each X_{e_i} into a single vertex x_i before computing a minimum (s, t)-cut S; see Fig. 1.24(b).) Based on S, we modify tree T_k into T_{k+1} by splitting vertex x into two vertices x' and x'' joined by a new edge $\{x', x''\}$ such that x' (resp. x'') corresponds to $X' = X \cap S$ (resp. $X'' = X \cap \overline{S}$). The weight of edge $\{x', x''\}$ is set to be $\lambda(s, t; G)$. Each edge e_i that was incident to x is now incident to x' if $X_{e_i} \subseteq S$ or x'' otherwise (see Fig. 1.24(c)). It is easy to see that the resulting tree T_{k+1} is a Gomory–Hu tree with respect to $\mathcal{X}' = (\mathcal{X} - X) \cup \{X', X''\}$. This proves the lemma.   □

The proof of Lemma 1.34 yields an algorithm for constructing a Gomory–Hu tree $T = T_n$, which runs in $O(n \cdot F(n, m))$ time, where $F(n, m)$ denotes the time bound for computing a minimum (s, t)-cut in a graph with n vertices and m weighted edges. This is currently the best time bound for computing a Gomory–Hu tree (or even for determining $\max_{u, v \in V(G)} \lambda(u, v; G)$). See [104] for an extensive experimental study on algorithms for computing Gomory–Hu trees.

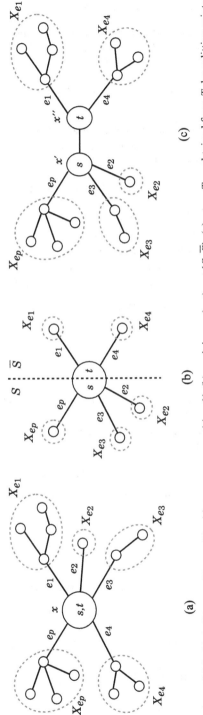

Figure 1.24. (a) A Gomory–Hu tree T_k with respect to a partition $\mathcal{X}$; (b) a minimum (s, t)-cut $\{S, \bar{S}\}$; (c) a tree T_{k+1} obtained from T_k by splitting x into x' and x''.

Pendent Pair

By definition, a leaf vertex v and its adjacent vertex u in a Gomory–Hu tree $T = (V, F)$ of a graph $G = (V, E)$ (e.g., $v = v_1$ and $u = v_2$ in Fig. 1.23) have a special property:

$$\lambda(v, u; G) = c_T(v, u) = d(v, V - v; T) = d(v; G).$$

We call an ordered pair (u, v) of vertices in G a *pendent pair* if $\lambda(v, u; G) = d(v; G)$. The preceding observation shows that any graph $G = (V, E)$ admits a pendent pair. This implies that, for the minimum degree $\delta(G) = \min_{v \in V} d(v; G)$ of G, the following inequality holds:

$$\min_{u,v \in V} \lambda(u, v; G) \le \delta(G) \le \max_{u,v \in V} \lambda(u, v; G).$$

One may be interested in a digraph version of a Gomory–Hu tree. A natural extension of the definition to digraphs is as follows. Let $G = (V, E)$ be an edge-weighted digraph. For an ordered pair (u, v), let $\lambda(u, v; G)$ denote the maximum flow value of a (u, v)-flow, or equivalently the minimum size of a (u, v)-cut X with $u \in X$ and $v \in V - X$. For an unordered pair $\{u, v\}$, define

$$\overline{\lambda}(u, v; G) = \min\{\lambda(u, v; G), \lambda(v, u; G)\}.$$

It can be shown that the property

$$\overline{\lambda}(u, w; G) \ge \min\{\overline{\lambda}(u, v; G), \overline{\lambda}(v, w; G)\} \text{ for any three vertices } u, v, w \in V$$

holds, and there is a flow-equivalent tree T that represents $\{\overline{\lambda}(u, v; G) \mid u, v \in V\}$. However, it is known [16, 284] that in general there is no Gomory–Hu tree T' of G in which each edge (u, v) in T' represents a minimum (u, v)- or (u, v)-cut in G with cut size $\overline{\lambda}(u, v; G)$. In fact, there is a digraph that has no pendent pair [284], whose definition is an ordered pair (u, v) such that

$$\overline{\lambda}(u, v; G) = \min\{d(v; G), d(V - v; G)\}.$$

See the digraph $G = (V, E)$ in Fig. 1.25, which consists of $2h \ge 2$ identical subgraphs $G_1, G_2, \ldots, G_{2h}$ sharing the same vertex s. It is not difficult to see that $\min_{v \in V}\{d(v; G), d(V - v; G)\} = 2h$, and $\overline{\lambda}(u, v; G) \le h + 1$ for any $u, v \in V$. Therefore, G has no pendent pair, and it cannot admit a Gomory–Hu tree either.

1.5.2 Components and Maximal Components

Let $G = (V, E)$ be an edge-weighted undirected graph.

Definition 1.35. *For a given $\ell \in \Re_+$, an ℓ-edge-connected component of G is defined to be a subset X of V such that*

(i) $\lambda(u, u'; G) \ge \ell$ *for any $u, u' \in X$ and*
(ii) $\lambda(u, v; G) < \ell$ *for any $u \in X$ and $v \in V - X$ (i.e., X is inclusion-wise maximal subject to condition* (i)).

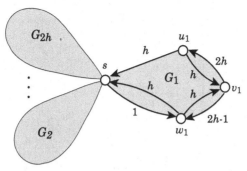

Figure 1.25. An edge-weighted digraph G that has no pendent pair (the number beside each edge e indicates the weight of e).

An ℓ-edge-connected component $X \subseteq V$ is called maximal *(with respect to ℓ) if $\ell = \min_{u,u' \in X} \lambda(u, u'; G)$.* □

Lemma 1.36. *For any $\ell \in \mathfrak{R}_+$, all ℓ-edge-connected components of a graph G give rise to a partition of $V(G)$.* □

Proof. Let two subsets X and Y of $V(G)$ satisfy property (i). By (1.18), if $X \cap Y \neq \emptyset$, then $X \cup Y$ also satisfies property (i). Hence, two subsets X and Y must be disjoint if they are inclusion-wise maximal subject to property (i). Note that, for any vertex $u \in V(G)$, subset $\{u\}$ satisfies property (i) by $\lambda(u, u; G) = +\infty$. Since every vertex belongs to some subset Z satisfying property (i), ℓ-edge-connected components give rise to a partition of $V(G)$. □

Note that the set of all maximal ℓ-edge-components may not be a partition of V, although such components are all disjoint.

Definition 1.37. *A maximal ℓ-edge-connected component for some ℓ is defined to be a* maximal component. *Let $\mathcal{Y}(G)$ denote the set of all maximal components.* □

Lemma 1.38. *$\mathcal{Y}(G)$ is a laminar family.* □

Proof. Consider two maximal components $X, Y \in \mathcal{Y}(G)$ with $X \cap Y \neq \emptyset$. Assume without loss of generality that X is an ℓ-edge-connected component and Y is an h-edge-connected component for some ℓ, h with $\ell \geq h$. Then $X \subseteq Y$ holds since any two vertices in an ℓ-edge-connected component are h-edge-connected. Hence, no two maximal components intersect each other, and $\mathcal{Y}(G)$ is a laminar family. □

We now show that the family $\mathcal{Y}(G)$ of maximal components can be constructed from a flow-equivalent tree $T = (V, F)$ of G. Let $\lambda_1 < \lambda_2 < \cdots < \lambda_p$ be the distinct values of the edge weights in T. For each λ_i, we construct the forest $T_i = T - \{e \in F \mid c_T(e) < \lambda_i\}$, which may have more than one connected

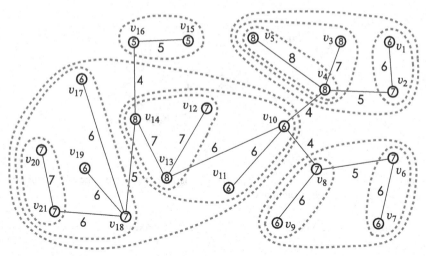

Figure 1.26. The set $\mathcal{Y}(G)$ of maximal components for the graph $G = (V, E)$ in Fig. 1.3, where the number inside the circle of vertex v_i indicates the cut size $d(v_i; G)$.

component. Then each connected component T' in T_i defines a λ_i-edge-connected component X of G such that $X = V(T')$. Such an X is a maximal λ_j-edge-connected component for the $\lambda_j = \min_{u,v \in X} \lambda(u, v; G) (\geq \lambda_i)$.

From this observation, we can construct the sets $\mathcal{Y}_i$ of maximal λ_i-edge-components for all i in the following manner. Let $F_i = \{e \in F \mid c_T(e) = \lambda_i\}$ for each $i \in \{1, 2, \ldots, p\}$. Initially we let $\mathcal{C}$ be the set of graphs for which each consists of a single vertex $v \in V$, and we repeat the next procedure in the order of $i = p, p - 1, \ldots, 1$: Join the connected components in $\mathcal{C}$ via edges in F_i, let $\mathcal{Y}_i := \{V(T') \mid$ newly created components T' in the ith iteration$\}$, and $\mathcal{C}$ be the set of all the resulting components. Sorting the weights of edges in T takes $O(n \log n)$ time, and the total time for joining components is $O(n \log n)$ (since each join can be executed in $O(\log n)$ time with an appropriate data structure for union-find operations [298]).

Conversely, it is not difficult to see that, once the family $\mathcal{Y}(G)$ of all maximal components is given, a flow-equivalent tree of G can be computed from $\mathcal{Y}(G)$. However, in general a Gomory–Hu tree cannot be constructed without knowing G.

Figure 1.26 shows the family $\mathcal{Y}(G)$ of all maximal components of the graph $G = (V, E)$ defined in Fig. 1.3, which are constructed from the Gomory–Hu tree in Fig. 1.23.

1.5.3 Extreme Vertex Sets

Let $G = (V, E)$ be an edge-weighted undirected graph.

Definition 1.39. *A nonempty proper subset X of V is called an* extreme vertex set *of G if $d(Y; G) > d(X; G)$ for all nonempty proper subsets Y of X.*   □

We denote by $\mathcal{X}(G)$ the family of all extreme vertex sets of G. Any singleton set $\{v\}$ with a vertex v is an extreme vertex set, which we call trivial. The concept of extreme vertex sets was first introduced by Watanabe and Nakamura [308] to solve the edge-connectivity augmentation problem.

Lemma 1.40. *For any graph* $G = (V, E)$, *the following properties hold.*

(i) *Any subset* $X \subset V$ *contains an extreme vertex set* $X'(\subseteq X)$ *such that* $d(X'; G) \leq d(X; G)$.

(ii) *There are at least two extreme vertex sets* X *and* Y *such that* $d(X; G) = d(Y; G) = \lambda(G)$ *and* $X \cap Y = \emptyset$. $\square$

Proof. (i) For a given $X \subset V$, let X' be an inclusion-wise minimal subset of X such that $d(X'; G) \leq d(X; G)$ (possibly $X' = X$). Then, for any proper subset Y of X', it holds that $d(Y; G) > d(X'; G)$, implying that X' is an extreme vertex set.

(ii) Let $\{Z, V - Z\}$ be a minimum cut in G. Then Z and $V - Z$ are disjoint subsets satisfying $d(Z; G) = d(V - Z; G) = \lambda(G)$. By condition (i), Z and $V - Z$ contain extreme vertex sets X and Y, respectively, such that $d(X; G) \leq \lambda(G)$ and $d(Y; G) \leq \lambda(G)$. Since $\lambda(G)$ is the size of a minimum cut, we have $d(X; G) = d(Y; G) = \lambda(G)$, as required. $\square$

Lemma 1.41. *No two extreme vertex sets in* $\mathcal{X}(G)$ *of a graph* G *intersect each other (hence,* $\mathcal{X}(G)$ *is laminar).* $\square$

Proof. Let X and Y be two subsets of V that intersect each other. Then $d(X; G) + d(Y; G) \geq d(X - Y; G) + d(Y - X; G)$ holds by (1.4). Thus, if X is an extreme vertex set, then $d(X; G) < d(X - Y; G)$ holds and thereby $d(Y; G) > d(Y - X; G)$ holds, implying that Y cannot be an extreme vertex set. $\square$

Figure 1.27 shows all the extreme vertex sets for the graph $G = (V, E)$ in Fig. 1.3.

Naor et al. observed the following characterization.

Lemma 1.42 ([259]). *Every extreme vertex set* $X \in \mathcal{X}(G)$ *is a maximal component for* $\ell = \min_{u,v \in X} \lambda(u, v; G)$. $\square$

Proof. Given an extreme vertex set X, fix two vertices $u_0 \in X$ and $v_0 \in V - X$ arbitrarily. It suffices to show that $\lambda(u_0, v_0; G) < \ell$. This is true if $d(X; G) < \ell$ (since cut X separates u_0 and v_0). Assume $d(X; G) \geq \ell$. Let $\{u, v\} = \operatorname{argmin}\{\lambda(u, v; G) \mid u, v \in X\}$, and let $\{U, V - U\}$ be a minimum (u, v)-cut.

Note that U and X intersect each other (otherwise $U \subset X$ would imply $\ell = d(U; G) > d(X; G)$ by the definition of extreme vertex sets, contradicting $d(X; G) \geq \ell$. Assume $v_0 \in U - X$ without loss of generality (if necessary, switch the roles of U and $V - U$). By (1.4), we have $d(X; G) + d(U; G) \geq d(X - U; G) + d(U - X; G)$, where $d(X - U; G) > d(X; G)$ since X is an

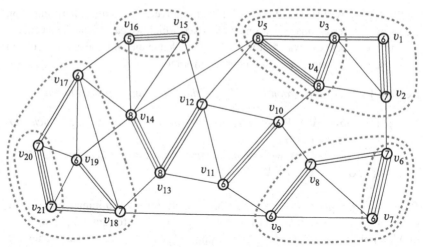

Figure 1.27. The set $\mathcal{X}(G)$ of extreme vertex sets for the graph $G = (V, E)$ in Fig. 1.3, where trivial extreme vertex sets are not indicated by broken curves but cut size is indicated inside the circle of each vertex.

extreme vertex set. Hence, we obtain $d(U - X; G) < d(U; G) = \ell$, which implies $\lambda(u_0, v_0; G) \leq d(U - X; G) < \ell$, as required.   □

Based on this lemma, we can easily obtain the family $\mathcal{X}(G)$ of all extreme vertex sets in G from the family of $\mathcal{Y}(G)$ of all maximal components in G. Note that a maximal component $Y \in \mathcal{Y}(G)$ is not an extreme vertex set only if there is a nonempty and proper subset $Y' \subset Y$ such that $d(Y'; G) \leq d(Y; G)$; that is, such an extreme vertex set Y' exists (recall that any subset contains at least one extreme vertex set). Such a set Y' is also a maximal component by Lemma 1.42. Therefore, a maximal component $Y \in \mathcal{Y}(G)$ is an extreme vertex set if and only if $d(Y'; G) > d(Y; G)$ for all maximal components Y' with $Y' \subset Y$. Let $\mathcal{T}$ be the rooted tree that represents the laminar family $\mathcal{Y}(G)$ of maximal components. We can discard nonextreme vertex sets from $\mathcal{Y}(G)$ by traversing $\mathcal{T}$ and checking the preceding condition of extreme vertex sets. Thus, we can identify $\mathcal{X}(G) \subseteq \mathcal{Y}(G)$ in $O(n)$ time if $\mathcal{T}$ and $\{d(Y; G) \mid Y \in \mathcal{Y}(G)\}$ are available.

Extreme vertex sets have the following useful property.

Lemma 1.43. *Given a graph $G = (V, E)$, a weight function $b : V \rightarrow \Re_+$, and a real $k \in \Re$, we have $d(Y; G) + \sum_{v \in Y} b(v) \geq k$ for all $Y \in 2^V - \{\emptyset, V\}$ if and only if $d(X; G) + \sum_{v \in X} b(v) \geq k$ holds for all extreme vertex sets $X \in \mathcal{X}(G)$.*   □

Proof. It suffices to show that, for each set $Y \in 2^V - \{\emptyset, V\}$, there is an extreme vertex set X such that $d(X; G) + \sum_{v \in X} b(v) \leq d(Y; G) + \sum_{v \in Y} b(v)$. If the set Y is not an extreme vertex set, then by Lemma 1.40(i) it contains an extreme vertex set $X \subseteq Y$ with $d(X; G) \leq d(Y; G)$. These X and Y satisfy $d(X; G) + \sum_{v \in X} b(v) \leq d(Y; G) + \sum_{v \in Y} b(v)$ by $\sum_{v \in Y - X} b(v) \geq 0$, as required.   □

1.5.4 Cactus Representation

Finally we consider a compact representation of all minimum cuts in an edge-weighted undirected graph $G = (V, E)$. We denote the set of all minimum cuts in G by $\mathcal{C}(G)$.

As no two vertices u and v with $\lambda(u, v; G) > \lambda(G)$ are separated by a minimum cut, we consider the family $\{V_1, \ldots, V_r\}$ of $\lambda(G)$-edge-connected components of G; that is, each V_i is an inclusion-wise maximal subset $X \subset V$ such that

$$\lambda(u, u'; G) > \lambda(G) \text{ for any distinct } u, u' \in X.$$

Let $\mathcal{A} = (U, E')$, where $U \cap V = \emptyset$ and $U = \{x_1, x_2, \ldots, x_r\}$, be the graph obtained from G by contracting each V_i into x_i and then deleting all resulting self-loops, if any. Then it is easy to see that all minimum cuts $\{X, V - X\}$ in G are preserved in $\mathcal{A}$, and every minimum cut in $\mathcal{A}$ corresponds to a minimum cut in G. For example, the graph G with $\lambda(G) = 4$ in Fig. 1.28(a) satisfies $\lambda(u, u'; G) > \lambda(G)$ only for $\{u, u'\} = \{u_5, u_6\}$, and the $\mathcal{A}$ is obtained from G by contracting these two vertices, as shown in Fig. 1.28(b).

A general representation for a subset of cuts in a graph G is given by introducing a cactus representation $(\mathcal{R}, \varphi)$ of G, where $\mathcal{R}$ is a graph and φ is a mapping from $V(G)$ to $V(\mathcal{R})$. Whenever we discuss a cactus representation in this book, we shall use *vertex* to denote an element in $V(G)$, and *node* to denote an element in $V(\mathcal{R})$. A set $V(\mathcal{R})$ may contain a node x such that there is no vertex $v \in V(G)$ with $\varphi(v) = x$, and such a node x is called an *empty node*. Let $\mathcal{C}(\mathcal{R})$ denote the set of all minimum cuts in $\mathcal{R}$.

Definition 1.44. *For a given set C' of cuts in a graph G, a pair $(\mathcal{R}, \varphi)$ of a graph $\mathcal{R}$ and a mapping φ is called a* representation *for C' if it satisfies the following conditions.*

(i) *For an arbitrary minimum cut $\{S, V(\mathcal{R}) - S\} \in \mathcal{C}(\mathcal{R})$, the cut $\{X, \overline{X}\}$ in G defined by $X = \{u \in V(G) \mid \varphi(u) \in S\}$ and $\overline{X} = \{u \in V \mid \varphi(u) \in V(\mathcal{R}) - S\}$ belongs to C'.*

(ii) *Conversely, for any cut $\{X, \overline{X}\} \in C'$, there exists a minimum cut $\{S, V(\mathcal{R}) - S\} \in \mathcal{C}(\mathcal{R})$ such that $X = \{u \in V \mid \varphi(u) \in S\}$ and $\overline{X} = \{u \in V \mid \varphi(u) \in V(\mathcal{R}) - S\}$.* □

Now we turn back to $\mathcal{A} = (U, E')$. By letting $\varphi : V \to U$ be the mapping such that $\varphi(u) = x_i$ for all $u \in V_i$, we see that $(\mathcal{A}, \varphi)$ is a representation for $\mathcal{C}(G)$. In general, $\mathcal{C}(G)$ admits a representation using a special class of graphs, as explained next, except for the case in which G is an unweighted multigraph with $\lambda(G) = 2$ [233] (see Section 2.3).

A connected graph is called a *cactus* if each edge belongs to exactly one cycle, where a pair of multiple edges with the same end vertices is treated as a cycle of length 2. A graph consisting of a single vertex is called a *trivial* cactus. Thus, every pair of cycles in a cactus, if any, has at most one vertex in common. Interestingly,

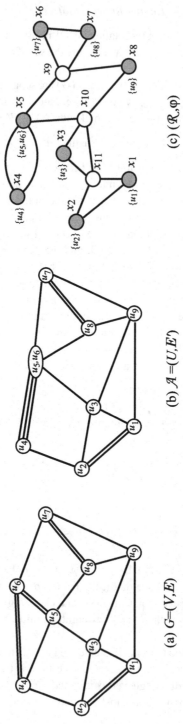

(a) $G=(V,E)$

(b) $\mathcal{A}=(U,E')$

(c) $(\mathcal{R},\varphi)$

Figure 1.28. Illustration of cactus representations: (a) an edge-weighted graph G with $\lambda(G) = 4$, (b) the contracted graph $A = (U, E')$, and (c) a cactus representation $(\mathcal{R}, \varphi)$ for $C(G)$, where $\varphi(u_1) = x_1$, $\varphi(u_2) = x_2$, $\varphi(u_3) = x_3$, $\varphi(u_4) = x_4$, $\varphi(u_5) = \varphi(u_6) = x_5$, $\varphi(u_7) = x_6$, $\varphi(u_8) = x_7$, and $\varphi(u_9) = x_8$, and x_9, x_{10}, and x_{11} are empty nodes, which are depicted as unshaded circles.

Dinits et al. [54] have proven that every graph G admits a representation $(\mathcal{R}, \varphi)$ for $\mathcal{C}(G)$ such that $\mathcal{R}$ is a cactus. How to construct such a cactus will be discussed in Section 5.3.

Theorem 1.45 ([54]). *For any edge-weighted graph G, there is a representation $(\mathcal{R}, \varphi)$ for $\mathcal{C}(G)$ such that $\mathcal{R}$ is an unweighted cactus.*   □

Note that any nontrivial cactus $\mathcal{R}$ satisfies $\lambda(\mathcal{R}) = 2$. Thus, $\{S, V(\mathcal{R}) - S\} \in \mathcal{C}(\mathcal{R})$ holds if and only if $E(S, V(\mathcal{R}) - S; \mathcal{R})$ is a set of two edges belonging to the same cycle in the cactus representation $\mathcal{R}$. Figure 1.28(c) shows a cactus representation $(\mathcal{R}, \varphi)$ for all minimum cuts in the graph G of Fig. 1.28(a), where, for example, a minimum cut $\{X = \{u_1, u_2, u_3\}, \overline{X}\}$ in G corresponds to the minimum cut $\{S = \{x_1, x_2, x_3, x_{11}\}, V(\mathcal{R}) - S\}$ in $\mathcal{R}$.

1.6 Connectivity by Trees

Although we devote ourselves mainly to the edge and vertex connectivities $\lambda(G)$ and $\kappa(G)$ in this book, we review in this subsection some other important measures of "connectedness of a graph."

1.6.1 Digraphs

A spanning subgraph $T = (V, F)$ of a digraph $G = (V, E)$ is called a *forest* (resp. *tree*) if it is a forest (resp. tree) when we neglect the edge orientation. A tree $T = (V, F)$ (viewed as a digraph) of G is called an *s-out-arborescence* if it is an out-tree rooted at a vertex s; that is,

$$E(V - s, s; T) = \emptyset \text{ and } |E(V - v, v; T)| = 1 \quad (v \in V - s).$$

An *s-in-arborescence* is defined symmetrically. We say that k forests $T_i = (V, F_i)$ of G, $i = 1, 2, \ldots, k$, are *edge-disjoint* if $F_i \cap F_{i'} = \emptyset$ for all $i \neq i'$ (see Fig. 1.29(a)). For a vertex s, a cut set $E(X, V - X)$ is called an *s-cut* if $s \in X$. Note that the minimum size of an s-cut is equal to $\lambda_s^+(G)$ (defined in (1.15)). Obviously, G can have k edge-disjoint s-out-arborescences only when the size of every s-cut in G is at least k. Edmonds has shown the following relation between s-cuts and s-out-arborescences.

Theorem 1.46 ([59]). *For a digraph $G = (V, E)$ with a designated vertex s, there exist k edge-disjoint s-out-arborescences if and only if*

$$d^-(X; G) \geq k \text{ for all nonempty } X \subseteq V - s, \tag{1.21}$$

where we denote $d^-(X; G) = d(V - X, X; G)$.   □

Proof. We follow a short proof due to Lovász [201]. Necessity: If G admits k edge-disjoint s-out-arborescences, then there are k edge-disjoint paths from s to each vertex v in any subset $X \subseteq V - s$, requiring $d^-(X; G) \geq k$.

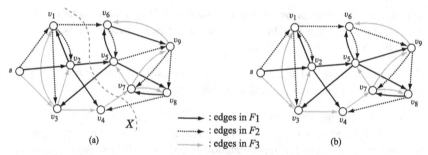

Figure 1.29. A digraph G consisting of three s-out-arborescences $T_1 = (V, F_1)$, $T_2 = (V, F_2)$, and $T_3 = (V, F_3)$, where T_1, T_2, T_3 are (a) edge-disjoint and (b) independent (see Section 2.1 for the definition of independent trees).

Sufficiency: Let $k \geq 1$. Assuming condition (1.21), we claim that there is an s-out-arborescence $T = (V, F)$ such that

$$d^-(X; G-F) \geq k - 1 \text{ for all } X \subseteq V - s. \tag{1.22}$$

Then by applying the same argument to the resulting graph repeatedly, we can obtain k edge-disjoint s-out-arborescences.

To prove the claim, we show that any s-out-arborescence $T = (W, F)$, $W \subset V$, satisfying (1.22), can be enlarged by adding an edge $e \in E - F$ while preserving (1.22). By the assumption of (1.21), $d^-(V - W; G) \geq k$ holds, implying that there is an edge $e = (u, v) \in E(W, V - W; G) = E(W, V - W; G - F)$ (see Fig. 1.30(a)). Assuming that $T' = (W \cup \{v\}, F \cup \{e\})$ violates (1.22) for all such edges $e \in E - F$ (otherwise we are done), we now derive a contradiction. That is, for such an edge e there is a subset $X \subseteq V - s$ such that $d^-(X; G - (F \cup \{e\})) < k - 1$. Since $d^-(X; G - F) \geq k - 1$ holds by assumption (1.21), we see that X satisfies $u \notin X$, $v \in X$ and $d^-(X; G - F) = k - 1$ holds (see Fig. 1.30(a)). Hence there exists a subset $Y \subseteq V - s$ with $Y - W \neq \emptyset$ and $d^-(Y; G - F) = k - 1$. We choose a minimal subset Y with such a property, where we assume $Y \cap W \neq \emptyset$ (otherwise $d^-(Y; G) = d^-(Y; G - F) = k - 1$ would hold). Then there is an edge $e' = (u', v') \in E(Y \cap W, Y - W; G - F)$ since $d^-(Y; G - F) = k - 1$ and $d^-(Y - W; G - F) = d^-(Y - W; G) \geq k$ hold (see Fig. 1.30(b)). To complete the proof, we show that there is no subset $X' \subset V - s$ with $u' \notin X'$, $v' \in X'$ and $d^-(X'; G - F) = k - 1$. If such a set X' exists, then we have by (1.2)

$$2(k - 1) = d^-(X'; G-F) + d^-(Y; G-F)$$
$$\geq d^-(X' \cap Y; G-F) + d^-(X' \cup Y; G-F),$$

from which we obtain $d^-(X' \cap Y; G - F) = k - 1$ by $d^-(X' \cup Y; G - F) \geq k - 1$, a contradiction to the minimality of Y. □

This theorem says that the minimum size of an s-cut is equal to the maximum number of edge-disjoint s-out-arborescences.

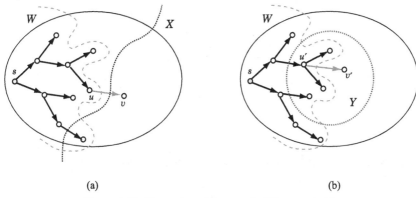

(a)   (b)

Figure 1.30. Illustration of the proof of Theorem 1.46.

Figure 1.29(a) illustrates a digraph G that has three edge-disjoint s-out-arborescences and a minimum s-cut $E(X, V - X; G)$ with $X = \{s, v_1, v_2, v_3, v_4\}$ whose size is $|E(X, V - X; G)| = 3$.

1.6.2 Undirected Graphs

We call an undirected graph k-*tree-connected* if it contains k edge-disjoint spanning trees. The class of k-tree-connected graphs $G = (V, E)$ is characterized by Tutte on the basis of partitions of V.

Theorem 1.47 ([304]). *An undirected multigraph $G = (V, E)$ is k-tree-connected if and only if*

$$\frac{1}{2}(d(V_1; G) + d(V_2; G) + \cdots + d(V_t; G)) \geq k(t - 1) \qquad (1.23)$$

holds for every partition $\{V_1, V_2, \ldots, V_t\}$ of V, where all V_i are nonempty. $\square$

The necessity of this theorem follows from an observation that, for k edge-disjoint spanning trees $T_1, \ldots, T_k$ in G and a partition $\{V_1, \ldots, V_t\}$ of V, it holds that $|E(V_i; G) \cap E(T_j)| \geq 1$, $1 \leq i \leq t$, $1 \leq j \leq k$. In particular, for the partition $\{\{v\} \mid v \in V\}$, the condition in (1.23) is written as $|E| \geq k(|V| - 1)$. The sufficiency, which requires some preparation, is omitted (see [52, 289] for proofs of the sufficiency). Figure 1.31 illustrates an example of a 2-tree-connected graph G.

Nash-Williams [263] proved the following result on covering by forests, which can be seen as a counterpart of Theorem 1.47.

Theorem 1.48 ([263]). *An undirected multigraph $G = (V, E)$ is the union of k-edge-disjoint forests if and only if*

$$d(X, X; G) \leq k|X| - k \qquad (1.24)$$

for every nonempty subset $X \subseteq V$, where $d(X, X; G)$ is the number of edges with both end vertices in X. $\square$

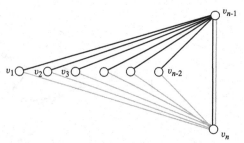

Figure 1.31. An example of a 2-tree-connected graph G, where black and gray lines represent two spanning trees in G, respectively, where $|E(G)| = 2(|V(G)| - 1)$ holds.

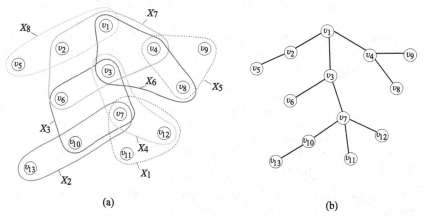

(a)   (b)

Figure 1.32. (a) A tree hypergraph $\mathcal{E} = \{X_1, X_2, \ldots, X_8\} \subseteq 2^V$, where $V = \{v_1, v_2, \ldots, v_{13}\}$; (b) a basic tree $T = (V, E)$ of the tree hypergraph in (a).

1.7 Tree Hypergraphs

Finally we introduce hypergraphs and discuss some properties of tree hypergraphs, an important class of hypergraphs, which will be the basis for the discussion in Sections 9.1.3 and 10.6.

A *hypergraph* G consists of a set V of vertices and a set $\mathcal{E}$ of *hyperedges*, where a hyperedge X is defined as a subset of V. Thus, a family $\mathcal{E} \subseteq 2^V$ defines a hypergraph $(V, \mathcal{E})$, which may be simply written as $\mathcal{E}$. For example, Figure 1.32(a) shows a hypergraph with a vertex set $V = \{v_1, v_2, \ldots, v_{13}\}$ and a hyperedge set $\mathcal{E} = \{X_1 = \{v_7, v_{11}, v_{12}\}, \ X_2 = \{x_7, v_{10}, v_{13}\}, \ X_3 = \{v_3, v_6, v_7, v_{10}\}, \ X_4 = \{v_3, v_7, v_{12}\}, \ X_5 = \{v_4, v_8, v_9\}, \ X_6 = \{v_1, v_3, v_4, v_8\}, \ X_7 = \{v_1, v_2, v_3, v_4, v_6\}, \ X_8 = \{v_1, v_2, v_5\}\} \subseteq 2^V$, where each hyperedge X_i is depicted by a closed curve.

For a hypergraph $\mathcal{E}$, a subset $R \subseteq V$ is called a *transversal* (or *hitting set*) of $\mathcal{E}$ if $R \cap X \neq \emptyset$ for all $X \in \mathcal{E}$. We denote by $\tau(\mathcal{E})$ the *transversal number* of $\mathcal{E}$, that is,

$$\tau(\mathcal{E}) = \min\{|R| \mid R \text{ is a transversal of } \mathcal{E}\}.$$

A subset $\mathcal{E}' \subseteq \mathcal{E}$ is called a *matching* of $\mathcal{E}$ if $X \cap X' = \emptyset$ holds for every pair of X, $X' \in \mathcal{E}'$ with $X \neq X'$; let $\nu(\mathcal{E})$ denote the *matching number* of $\mathcal{E}$, that is,

$$\nu(\mathcal{E}) = \max\{|\mathcal{E}'| \mid \mathcal{E}' \text{ is a matching of } \mathcal{E}\}.$$

From the definitions, it is clear that $\tau(\mathcal{E}) \geq \nu(\mathcal{E})$ holds for any hypergraph $\mathcal{E}$.

A hypergraph $\mathcal{E} \subseteq 2^V$ is called a *tree hypergraph* if there exists a tree $T = (V, E)$ on the same vertex set V such that each hyperedge $X \in \mathcal{E}$ induces a subtree of T, where an edge in E is not necessarily a hyperedge in $\mathcal{E}$. Such a tree T is called a *basic tree* for the hypergraph $\mathcal{E}$. Choose a root $r \in V$ in a basic tree T, and regard T as a tree rooted at r. Let $D(u)$ denote the set of all descendants of u in T (including u). For each hyperedge $X \in \mathcal{E}$, let $v_X \in X$ denote the (unique) vertex such that $X \subseteq D(v_X)$ (such a vertex exists since X induces a subtree from T). Number all hyperedges in $\mathcal{E}$ as $X_1, X_2, \ldots, X_{|\mathcal{E}|}$ such that

$$depth(v_{X_1}) \geq depth(v_{X_2}) \geq \cdots \geq depth(v_{X_{|\mathcal{E}|}}), \tag{1.25}$$

where $depth(v)$ denotes the depth of a vertex v in T.

For example, the hypergraph $\mathcal{E}$ in Figure 1.32(a) is a tree hypergraph, and a basic tree T is shown in Figure 1.32(b), where the hyperedges in $\mathcal{E}$ are numbered as $X_1, X_2, \ldots, X_8$ so that (1.25) holds when $v_1 \in V$ is chosen as the root of T. Note that $v_{X_1} = v_7$, $v_{X_2} = v_7$, $v_{X_3} = v_3$, $v_{X_4} = v_3$, $v_{X_5} = v_4$, $v_{X_6} = v_1$, $v_{X_7} = v_1$, and $v_{X_8} = v_1$ hold.

Lemma 1.49. *Let $\mathcal{E}$ be a tree hypergraph. For each hyperedge $X_i \in \mathcal{E}$ in a sequence of hyperedges $X_1, X_2, \ldots, X_{|\mathcal{E}|}$ of (1.25), any hyperedge X_j with $j \geq i$ and $X_j \cap X_i \neq \emptyset$ contains vertex v_{X_i}; that is, $\{v_{X_i}\}$ is a transversal of the hypergraph defined by $\{X_j \mid j \geq i, X_j \cap X_i \neq \emptyset\}$.* $\quad\square$

Proof. Assume that a hyperedge X_j satisfies $j \geq i$, $v_{X_i} \notin X_j$, and $(X_i \cap X_j) - v_{X_i} \neq \emptyset$. Since $j \geq i$ and $v_{X_i} \notin X_j$, we have $depth(v_{X_i}) > depth(v_{X_j})$. Furthermore, any vertex $u \in (X_i \cap X_j) - v_{X_i}$ satisfies $depth(u) > depth(v_{X_i})$ by the choice of $v_{X_i} \in X_i$. Hence, X_j contains v_{X_j} and u, but not v_{X_i} with $depth(u) > depth(v_{X_i}) > depth(v_{X_j})$. This, however, contradicts that X_j induces a subtree of T and satisfies $X_j \subseteq D(v_{X_j})$. Therefore, $v_{X_i} \in X_i \cap X_j$ holds if $X_i \cap X_j \neq \emptyset$. $\quad\square$

It is known that a tree hypergraph $\mathcal{E}$ satisfies the König property.

Theorem 1.50 (e.g., [29]). *Let $\mathcal{E} \subseteq 2^V$ be a tree hypergraph. Then $\tau(\mathcal{E}) = \nu(\mathcal{E})$ holds.* $\quad\square$

Proof. We proceed by induction on $|\mathcal{E}|$. If $\mathcal{E} = \emptyset$, then $\tau(\mathcal{E}) = \nu(\mathcal{E})$ holds for transversal $R = \emptyset$ and matching $\mathcal{M} = \emptyset$. Assume $\mathcal{E} \neq \emptyset$. Choose X_1 in the ordering of (1.25), and let $\mathcal{E}' = \mathcal{E} - \{X \in \mathcal{E} \mid X \cap X_1\}$. By induction hypothesis, $\mathcal{E}'$ has a transversal R' and a matching $\mathcal{M}'$ with $|R'| = |\mathcal{M}'|$. We see that $\mathcal{M} = \mathcal{M}' \cup \{X_1\}$ remains a matching since any hyperedge $X \in \mathcal{E}'$ is now disjoint with X_1. By Lemma 1.49, the vertex $v_{X_1} \in X$ is a transversal of $\{X \in \mathcal{E} \mid X \cap X_1\}$

and, hence, $R = R' \cup \{v_{X_1}\}$ is a transversal of $\mathcal{E}$. Therefore, $|R| = |\mathcal{M}|$ holds, proving $\tau(\mathcal{E}) = \nu(\mathcal{E})$. □

The inductive proof of Theorem 1.50 implies that a minimum transversal of a tree hypergraph $\mathcal{E} \subseteq 2^V$ can be computed from its basic tree T if a procedure for checking whether a given set $R \subseteq V$ is a transversal is available. This simple algorithm due to [14, 74] is described as follows.

Algorithm MINTRANSVERSAL

Input: A basic tree $T = (V, E)$ of a tree hypergraph $H = (V, \mathcal{E})$, where T is
    regarded as a tree rooted at a vertex $r \in V$.
Output: A minimum transversal R of H.
1 Initialize $R := \emptyset$ and $U := V$;
2 **while** $U \neq \emptyset$ **do**
3   Choose a leaf v of $T[U]$ and $U := U - \{v\}$;
4   **if** $R \cup U$ is not a transversal **then**
5     $R := R \cup \{v\}$ /* Any hyperedge $X \subseteq D(v) - R$ satisfies $v \in X$. */
6 **end**; /* **while** */;
7 Output R.

For example, MINTRANSVERSAL applied to the tree hypergraph $\mathcal{E}$ and its basic tree T in Fig. 1.32 chooses vertices from V as a leaf in line 3 on the order of $v_{13}, v_{12}, \ldots, v_1$, during which vertices v_7, v_4, and v_1 are added to R. The resulting minimum transversal is $R = \{v_7, v_4, v_1\}$. In this process, if we choose a hyperedge $X \subseteq D(v) - R$ in line 5 whenever $R \cup U$ is not a transversal in line 4, then we obtain a maximum matching $\mathcal{M} = \{X_1, X_5, X_8\}$, depicted as dotted curves in Fig. 1.32(a).

Note that, if $R \cup U$ in line 4 is not a transversal of $\mathcal{E}$, every hyperedge $X \in \mathcal{E}$ with $X \subseteq V - (R \cup U)$ contains the vertex v chosen in line 3. Let $C^*(\mathcal{E})$ denote the time complexity for deciding whether a given set $R' \cup U \subseteq V$ is a transversal of $\mathcal{E}$ under the condition that there is a vertex $v \in V - R$ such that every hyperedge $X \in \mathcal{E}$ with $X \subseteq V - R'$ (if any) contains the vertex v. Then we have the next lemma.

Lemma 1.51 ([74]). *Given a basic tree T of a tree hypergraph $H = (V, \mathcal{E})$,* MINTRANSVERSAL *computes a minimum transversal $R \subseteq V$ in $O(nC^*(\mathcal{E}))$ time.* □

1.7.1 Characterizations of Tree Hypergraphs

We now give two characterizations of tree hypergraphs. A hypergraph $\mathcal{E}$ is said to have the *Helly property* if any set of pairwise intersecting hyperedges has a nonempty intersection. The *line graph* $L(\mathcal{E})$ of a hypergraph $\mathcal{E}$ is a graph in which the nodes correspond to the hyperedges, two of them being adjacent if the corresponding hyperedges have a nonempty intersection. Figure 1.33 shows the line graph $L(\mathcal{E})$ of hypergraph $\mathcal{E}$ in Fig. 1.32(a).

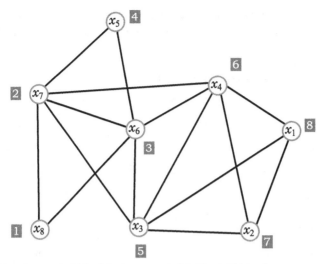

Figure 1.33. Line graph $L(\mathcal{E})$ of the hypergraph $\mathcal{E}$ in Fig. 1.32(a), where a vertex x_i in $L(\mathcal{E})$ corresponds to hyperedge $X_i \in \mathcal{E}$.

An undirected graph is called *chordal* if every cycle of length at least 4 has a chord. For a tree hypergraph, the following characterization has been discovered by several researchers (see [56, 216], for example).

Theorem 1.52. *A family $\mathcal{E} \subseteq 2^V$ is a tree hypergraph if and only if $\mathcal{E}$ has the Helly property and its line graph $L(\mathcal{E})$ is chordal.* $\square$

Proof. We first show the necessity. Let $T = (V, E)$ be a basic tree of a tree hypergraph $\mathcal{E}$. Since each hyperedge $X \in \mathcal{E}$ induces a subtree from T, any hyperedges $X_1, X_2, \ldots, X_k$ such that $X_i \cap X_j \neq \emptyset$, $1 \leq i < j \leq k$ contain a vertex in common, which shows the Helly propery. If $L(\mathcal{E})$ is not chordal, that is, $L(\mathcal{E})$ has a chordless cycle $(x_1, x_2, \ldots, x_k)$ of length $k \geq 4$, then $X_k \cap X_i = \emptyset$ for all $i = 2, 3, \ldots, k - 1$ and the union of hyperedges $X_i \in \mathcal{E}, i = 1, 2, \ldots, k - 1$ corresponding to x_i induces a subtree T' from T. However this contradicts that X_k induces a subtree T'' from T. Hence $L(\mathcal{E})$ is chordal. We show the sufficiency by induction on $|V| + |E|$. The case of $\min\{|V|, |E|\} = 1$ is clear. Assume $\min\{|V|, |E|\} \geq 2$. If E contains a hyperedge $\{v\}$ for some vertex $v \in V$, then by the induction hypothesis, $\mathcal{E} - X$ has a basic tree T, which is also a basic tree to $\mathcal{E}$ since $|X| = 1$. Now assume that every hyperedge $X \in \mathcal{E}$ contains at least two vertices. Since $L(\mathcal{E})$ is chordal, it contains a simplicial vertex, that is, a vertex whose neighbors form a complete subgraph (see Theorem 2.64 in Section 2.6). The simplicial vertex corresponds to a hyperedge $X \in \mathcal{E}$ such that every two hyperedges X' and X'' with $X' \cap X \neq \emptyset \neq X'' \cap X$ satisfy $X' \cap X'' \neq \emptyset$. By the Helly property, there is a vertex v contained in all hyperedges X' with $X \cap X' \neq \emptyset$. Let $u \in X - v$, and consider the new hypergraph $\mathcal{E}' = \{X - u \mid X \in \mathcal{E}\}$. Since any hyperedge $Y \in \mathcal{E}$ containing u intersects with X and, hence, contains v, the resulting $\mathcal{E}'$ also has the Helly property and its line graph is equal to $L(\mathcal{E})$. By the induction hypothesis, $\mathcal{E}'$ has a basic tree $T' = (V - u, E')$. Let T be the tree obtained from T' by adding a new vertex u together with a new edge $\{v, u\}$. By construction, T is a basic tree for $\mathcal{E}$. □

Another characterization is known as follows. For a given hypergraph $\mathcal{E} \subseteq 2^V$ with a positive weight function $w : \mathcal{E} \to \mathfrak{R}_+ - \{0\}$, we define the edge-weighted complete graph G_w on V by defining the weight $c(u, v)$ of edge $\{u, v\} \in E(G_w)$ by

$$c(u, v) = \sum_{X \in \mathcal{E}:\{u,v\}\subseteq X} w(X). \tag{1.26}$$

Theorem 1.53 ([14]). *Let $\mathcal{E} \subseteq 2^V$ be a hypergraph and $w : \mathcal{E} \to \mathfrak{R}_+ - \{0\}$ be any weight function. Then $\mathcal{E}$ is a tree hypergraph if and only if a maximum spanning tree in G_w is a basic tree for $\mathcal{E}$.* □

Proof. We only prove the only-if part. For any spanning tree T in G_w, its weight $c(T)$ is bounded by

$$(c(T) =) \sum_{\{u,v\}\in E(T)} c(u, v) \leq \sum_{X\in\mathcal{E}}(|X| - 1)w(X)$$

since each $X \in \mathcal{E}$ induces at most $|X| - 1$ edges of T. This inequality can be satisfied by equality since $\mathcal{E}$ has a basic tree T and such T satisfies the preceding inequality by equality. Then any maximum spanning tree T^* attains $c(T^*) = \sum_{X\in\mathcal{E}}(|X| - 1)w(X)$, and each $X \in \mathcal{E}$ must induce a connected subgraph from T^* since $w(X) > 0$. □

It follows that, for example, Kruskal's algorithm for minimum spanning trees can be applied to compute a basic tree for a tree hypergraph, and it runs in polynomial time in the number of hyperedges.

A hyperedge $X \in \mathcal{E} \subseteq 2^V$ is called a v-*avoiding* hyperedge if $v \notin X$, and is called a *maximal v-avoiding* hyperedge if, in addition, X is inclusion-wise maximal among all v-avoiding hyperedges in $\mathcal{E}$.

Lemma 1.54 ([14]). *Given a tree hypergraph $\mathcal{E}$, let*

$$\mathcal{E}^* = \{X \in \mathcal{E} \mid X \text{ is a maximal } v\text{-avoiding hyperedge for some } v \in V\}.$$

Then any basic tree T^* for $\mathcal{E}^*$ is a basic tree for $\mathcal{E}$. □

Proof. Assume that there is a hyperedge $X \in \mathcal{E} - \mathcal{E}^*$ that does not induce a subtree from T^*. That is, there are two vertices $u, u' \in X$ such that the unique path P connecting u and u' along T^* contains a vertex v not in X. Hence X is v-avoiding, and $\mathcal{E}^*$ contains a maximal v-avoiding hyperedge X^* with $X \subset X^*$. This, however, contradicts that T^* is a basic tree for $\mathcal{E}^*$ since P is not completely contained in X^*. □

2

Maximum Adjacency Ordering and Forest Decompositions

In this chapter, we discuss how to decompose a given multigraph G into a set of forests to obtain a spanning subgraph that preserves the edge/vertex-connectivity of G. We introduce a total ordering of the vertices in a multigraph G, called a maximum adjacency (MA) ordering, and then find such a forest decomposition. Based on this set of forests, we can convert G into a sparse graph in linear time while preserving the edge/vertex-connectivity. This sparsification technique can be used for many connectivity algorithms as a preprocessing that reduces the size of input graphs. We describe some of the applications of connectivity algorithms.

2.1 Spanning Subgraphs Preserving Connectivity

A *k-edge-connectivity certificate* (resp. *k-vertex-connectivity certificate*) of a multigraph G is a spanning subgraph H of G such that, for any two vertices u, v and any positive integer $k' \leq k$, there are k' edge-disjoint (resp. internally vertex-disjoint) paths between u and v in H if and only if there are k' edge-disjoint (resp. internally vertex-disjoint) paths between u and v in G. That is, a k-edge-connectivity (resp. k-vertex-connectivity) certificate is defined as a spanning subgraph that preserves the edge-connectivity (resp. vertex-connectivity) up to k. Therefore, when H is a k-edge-connectivity certificate (resp. k-vertex-connectivity certificate) of G, H is k-edge-connected (resp. k-vertex-connected) if and only if G is k-edge-connected (resp. k-vertex-connected). If a k-edge-connectivity certificate H of G is k-edge-connected, then $|E(H)| \geq \frac{kn}{2}$ holds since the degree of any vertex in H is at least k. Then we say that a k-edge-connectivity certificate H is *sparse* if $|E(H)| = O(kn)$. A sparse k-vertex-connectivity certificate is similarly defined. It is known that such a certificate exists [203].

Since we can reduce the edge size of a multigraph while preserving its k-edge-connectedness (resp. k-vertex-connectedness) by using an algorithm for a sparse k-edge-connectivity (resp. k-vertex-connectivity) certificate, this technique turns out to be useful for preprocessing some graph connectivity algorithms in order to obtain faster algorithms. However, in general, the problem of finding a

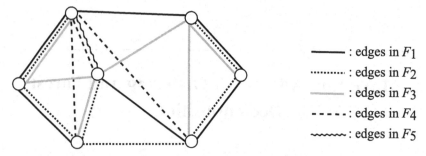

———— : edges in F_1

·········· : edges in F_2

———— : edges in F_3

- - - - : edges in F_4

∿∿∿ : edges in F_5

Figure 2.1. A forest decomposition $\mathcal{F} = (F_1, F_2, \ldots, F_5)$ of a multigraph G.

minimum spanning k-edge-connected (or k-vertex-connected) subgraph is known to be $\mathcal{NP}$-hard for any fixed $k \geq 2$ [64], and we have to give up the minimality in computing such certificates. As we shall see, constructing certificates is related to a decomposition of an edge set into forests or trees.

2.1.1 Constructing k-Edge-Connectivity Certificates

Let $G = (V, E)$ be an undirected multigraph, where we denote $m = |E|$ and $n = |V|$. A spanning subgraph (V, F) of G is called a *maximal spanning forest* if (V, F) is a forest (i.e., a graph with no cycle) and $(V, F \cup \{e\})$ is no longer forest for any edge $e \in E - F$. Such an F always satisfies $|F| \leq n - 1$.

Definition 2.1. *We partition the edge set E into $F_1, F_2, \ldots, F_m$ as follows. Let (V, F_1) be a maximal spanning forest of G. Similarly, for each $i = 2, 3, \ldots, m$, let (V, F_i) be a maximal spanning forest of the graph $G - (F_1 \cup F_2 \cup \cdots \cup F_{i-1})$. Then there is a $p \leq m$ such that $F_i \neq \emptyset \, (1 \leq i \leq p)$ and $F_i = \emptyset \, (p < i \leq m)$. We call such an ordered family $\mathcal{F} = (F_1, F_2, \ldots, F_m)$ (or $\mathcal{F} = (F_1, F_2, \ldots, F_p)$) of maximal spanning forests a* forest decomposition *of G.* □

For example, Fig. 2.1 illustrates a forest decomposition $\mathcal{F} = (F_1, F_2, \ldots, F_5)$ of a multigraph G.

Given a forest decomposition $\mathcal{F} = (F_1, F_2, \ldots, F_m)$ of G, we define spanning subgraphs $G_i = (V, E_i)$ by

$$E_i = F_1 \cup F_2 \cup \cdots \cup F_i, \quad i = 1, 2, \ldots, m,$$

where $|E_i| \leq i(n - 1)$ holds. Then the following property holds.

Lemma 2.2. *Let $\mathcal{F} = (F_1, F_2, \ldots, F_m)$ be a forest decomposition of a multigraph $G = (V, E)$, and define G_i as above for $i = 1, 2, \ldots, m$.*

(i) *For any edge $e = \{u, v\} \in F_k$, each forest (V, F_h) with $h < k$ contains a (u, v)-path.*

(ii) *For any edge $e = \{u, v\} \in F_k$, it holds $\lambda(u, v; G_h) \geq h \, (h = 1, 2, \ldots, k)$.* □

Proof. (i) By the maximality of forest (V, F_h), the subgraph $(V, F_h \cup \{e\})$ must have a cycle C containing e. Hence, forest (V, F_h) has the (u, v)-path $P = C - e$.

(ii) For each $h = 1, 2, \ldots, k - 1$, forest (V, F_h) contains a (u, v)-path by condition (i) and, hence, G_h has h edge-disjoint (u, v)-paths. Then G_k has k edge-disjoint (u, v)-paths, including a path $e = \{u, v\}$. Hence, $\lambda(u, v; G_h) \geq h$ holds for $h = 1, 2, \ldots, k$. □

We first observe that the spanning subgraph $G_k = (V, E_k)$ of G preserves any cut X with size up to k. Let $\mathcal{C}_k(G)$ be the set of cuts with size k, that is,

$$\mathcal{C}_k(G) = \{X \mid \emptyset \neq X \subset V, \ d(X; G) = k\}.$$

Lemma 2.3. *Let* $\mathcal{F} = (F_1, F_2, \ldots, F_m)$ *be a forest decomposition of a multigraph* $G = (V, E)$, *and let k be an integer with $1 \leq k \leq m$.*

(i) *For any nonempty and proper subset X of V,*

$$d(X; G_k) \begin{cases} \geq k & \text{if } d(X; G) \geq k \\ = d(X; G) & \text{if } d(X; G) \leq k - 1. \end{cases}$$

(ii) $\mathcal{C}_k(G_{k+1}) = \mathcal{C}_k(G)$. □

Proof. (i) It suffices to consider only the case of $d(X; G) \geq k$ (since the correctness for $k = d(X; G)$ will imply $d(X; G_h) = d(X; G)$ for all $h > d(X; G)$ by $d(X; G) = d(X; G_k) \leq d(X; G_h)$ and the definition of G_h). Assume $d(X; G_k) < d(X; G)$ (otherwise we are done by $d(X; G) \geq k$). Then there is an edge $e = \{u, v\} \in E(X, V - X; G) - E(X, V - X; G_k)$. By $e \notin F_1 \cup \cdots \cup F_k$, this means that e belongs to some forest F_i with $i > k$. By Lemma 2.2(ii), we have $\lambda(u, v; G_k) \geq k$. Since cut $\{X, V - X\}$ separates u and v in G_k, it must hold that $d(X; G_k) = |E(X, V - X; G_k)| \geq \lambda(u, v; G_k) \geq k$, as required.

(ii) For a cut $X \in \mathcal{C}_k(G)$, $d(X; G_{k+1}) = k$ holds by the second case of condition (i), implying that $\mathcal{C}_k(G_{k+1}) \supseteq \mathcal{C}_k(G)$. For a cut X with $d(X; G) \geq k + 1$, $d(X; G_{k+1}) \geq k + 1$ holds by condition (i). Hence, $d(X; G_{k+1}) = k < d(X; G)$ cannot occur for any cut X, indicating $\mathcal{C}_k(G_{k+1}) \subseteq \mathcal{C}_k(G)$. This proves condition (ii). □

We show that the spanning subgraph G_k of G is a k-edge-connectivity certificate of G.

Theorem 2.4 ([231]). *Let* $\mathcal{F} = (F_1, F_2, \ldots, F_m)$ *be a forest decomposition of a multigraph $G = (V, E)$, and k be an integer with $1 \leq k \leq m$. For every pair of vertices $u, v \in V$,*

$$\lambda(u, v; G_k) \begin{cases} \geq k & \text{if } \lambda(u, v; G) \geq k \\ = \lambda(u, v; G) & \text{if } \lambda(u, v; G) \leq k - 1. \end{cases}$$ □

Proof. It suffices to consider the case of $\lambda(u, v; G) \geq k$ (for the same reason as the proof of Lemma 2.3(i)). Since $\lambda(u, v; G) \geq k$ means that every cut X separating u

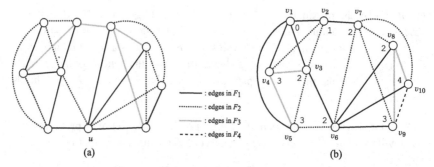

Figure 2.2. (a) A forest decomposition $\mathcal{F} = (F_1, F_2, F_3)$ of a simple graph G; (b) a forest decomposition $\mathcal{F}(G, \sigma) = (F_1, F_2, F_3, F_4)$ of the same simple graph G with an MA ordering $\sigma = (v_1, v_2, \ldots, v_{10})$.

and v satisfies $d(X; G) \geq k$, such X also satisfies $d(X; G_k) \geq k$ by Lemma 2.3(i). Thus, $\lambda(u, v; G_k) \geq k$. $\square$

This theorem says that a graph G is k-edge-connected if and only if G_k is k-edge-connected. Also by construction, $G_k = (V, E_k)$ satisfies

$$|E_k| \leq k(n - 1).$$

Recall that any graph with n vertices needs at least $\lceil kn/2 \rceil$ edges to be k-edge-connected. It is easy to see that G_k can be constructed in $O(km)$ time. Note that this complexity is faster than that of computing the edge-connectivity of G (see the discussion in Section 1.4).

Unfortunately, the spanning subgraph G_k of a k-vertex-connected graph G may not be k-vertex-connected in general. Figure 2.2(a) illustrates a forest decomposition $\mathcal{F} = (F_1, F_2, F_3)$ of a simple graph G, for which G_2 has a cut vertex $\{u\}$ even though G is 2-vertex-connected.

However, Nagamochi and Ibaraki [231] have proved that there is a forest decomposition $\mathcal{F}$ of a graph G such that the spanning subgraph G_k constructed from $\mathcal{F}$ is a k-vertex-connectivity certificate (see Fig. 2.2(b)), and that such an $\mathcal{F}$ can be found in linear time. We describe this result as Theorem 2.26 in the next subsection. Another characterization of a forest decomposition that gives rise to a vertex-connectivity certificate is given as follows.

Theorem 2.5 ([41, 43]). *For a simple undirected graph $G = (V, E)$, let $\mathcal{F}$ be a forest decomposition such that each maximal spanning forest (V, F_i) is chosen as a set of breadth-first search trees in the connected components of $G - (F_1 \cup F_2 \cup \cdots \cup F_{i-1})$. Then for every $u, v \in V$ in $G_k = (V, E_k = F_1 \cup F_2 \cup \cdots \cup F_k)$, we have*

$$\kappa(u, v; G_k) \begin{cases} \geq k & \text{if } \kappa(u, v; G) \geq k \\ = \kappa(u, v; G) & \text{if } \kappa(u, v; G) \leq k - 1. \end{cases}$$ $\square$

2.1.2 Edge-Connectivity of Digraphs

In general, a digraph has no sparse certificate that preserves the local edge/vertex-connectivity for every two vertices. To see this, consider an acyclic bipartite digraph $G = (V_1, V_2, E)$ such that $E \subseteq V_1 \times V_2$, where all edges are oriented from V_1 to V_2. In this G, deleting any edge $e = (u, v)$ results in a digraph $G - e$ such that $\lambda(u, v; G - e) = 0 < \lambda(u, v; G) = 1$, indicating that G has no sparse certificate.

For the global edge/vertex-connectivity, however, it is known [59, 209] that there is a sparse certificate; such an example will be discussed in this subsection. Unlike undirected graphs, it is still uncertain whether such a certificate can be constructed faster than testing of edge/vertex-connectivity.

Now we consider how to compute edge-connectivity of a digraph. Based on Edmonds' characterization of edge-disjoint arborescences (Theorem 1.46), Gabow [96] gave an efficient algorithm, as explained next.

Recall the following property of $\lambda_s^+(G)$. Let $\overline{G}$ denote the digraph obtained from a digraph G by reversing the directions of all edges. As discussed in (1.15) of Section 1.4, the edge-connectivity $\lambda(G)$ is given by taking the minimum of $\lambda_s^+(G)$ and $\lambda_s^+(\overline{G})$ $(= \lambda_s^-(G))$.

Theorem 1.46 due to Edmonds says that every k-edge-connected digraph $G = (V, E)$ has a set of k edge-disjoint s-out-arborescences $T_i = (V, F_i)$, $i = 1, 2, \ldots, k$. By applying Theorem 1.46 to the graph $\overline{G}$ with reversed orientation, G also has a set of k edge-disjoint s-in-arborescences $T_i' = (V, F_i')$, $i = 1, 2, \ldots, k$ for any vertex $s \in V$. Conversely, if G has such sets of s-out-arborescences and s-in-arborescences, then G is k-edge-connected, since $\lambda(u, s; G), \lambda(s, v; G) \geq k$ implies $\lambda(u, v; G) \geq k$ for any two vertices $u, v \in V$. Hence, the spanning subgraph $(V, F_1 \cup \cdots \cup F_k \cup F_1' \cup \cdots \cup F_k')$ preserves the k-edge-connectivity and has at most $2k(n - 1)$ edges. Instead of constructing these edge-disjoint s-out-arborescences, Gabow used the next characterization of such arborescences in order to test the k-edge-connectivity.

Theorem 2.6 ([57]). *For a digraph $G' = (V, E')$ with vertex $s \in V$, the following conditions* (i) *and* (ii) *are equivalent.*

(i) *E' can be partitioned into k edge-disjoint s-out-arborescences.*
(ii) *E' can be partitioned into k edge-disjoint trees, and $|E(V - v, v; G')| = k$ for all $v \in V - s$.* □

Interestingly, condition (ii) is just a necessary condition for E' to satisfy condition (i), but it is shown also to be sufficient. Therefore, one may expect a faster algorithm for finding a set of trees in condition (ii) than constructing s-out-arborescences in condition (i). Based on this, Gabow has actually designed an algorithm that finds edge-disjoint trees in conditions (ii) in $O(m \log(n^2/m))$ time per tree.

Theorem 2.7 ([96]). *For a simple digraph $G = (V, E)$, the k-edge-connectivity can be tested in $O(km \log(n^2/m))$ time, and the edge-connectivity $\lambda(G)$ can be computed in $O(\lambda(G)m \log(n^2/m))$ time.*   □

Given a digraph $G = (V, E)$ with $\lambda_s^+(G) \geq k$, there are k edge-disjoint (s, v)-paths for every vertex $v \in V$ by Menger's theorem. Such a digraph has k edge-disjoint s-out-arborescences by Theorem 1.46. By storing these s-out-arborescences, we can reconstruct k edge-disjoint (s, v)-paths for a vertex $v \in V$ in $O(\min\{kn, m\})$ time by traversing each of the s-out-arborescences.

2.1.3 Vertex-Connectivity of Digraphs

To consider vertex-connectivity of a digraph, we now construct a set of s-out-arborescences that preserves k internally vertex-disjoint (s, v)-paths for every $v \in V$. A set of k edge-disjoint s-out-arborescences $T_1, T_2, \ldots, T_k$ is called *independent* if k edge-disjoint (s, v)-paths consisting of the unique (s, v)-path on each T_i are internally vertex-disjoint for any $v \in V - s$. Figure 1.29(b) shows a digraph G that has three independent s-out-arborescences $T_i = (V, F_i), i = 1, 2, 3$. (Note that T_1 and T_2 in Fig. 1.29(a) are not independent since two paths from s to v_8 along T_1 and T_2 share v_5.)

A necessary condition for a digraph $G = (V, E)$ to admit k independent s-out-arborescences is given by

$$\kappa(s, v; G) \geq k \text{ for all } v \in V - s. \tag{2.1}$$

Moreover, G needs to contain a spanning subgraph $G_{s,k}$ satisfying (2.1) and having exactly $k(n - 1)$ edges. Cheriyan and Thurimella [41, 43] have proved that such a spanning subgraph $G_{s,k}$ always exists if (2.1) holds. However, it does not necessarily imply that such a spanning subgraph $G_{s,k}$ can be decomposed into k edge-disjoint s-out-arborescences. The statement was known as a conjecture.

Conjecture 2.8. *If a digraph $G = (V, E)$ satisfies (2.1), then it has k independent s-out-arborescences.*   □

If this conjecture is true, then we can use such a set of k independent s-out-arborescences as a sparse certificate that preserves property (2.1).

For $k = 2$, it is known [40, 312] that Conjecture 2.8 holds. However, for $k \geq 3$, Huck [135] has proved that Conjecture 2.8 does not holds for a general digraph. Hasunuma and Nagamochi [119] have proved that Conjecture 2.8 holds for all $k \geq 2$ if G is a line digraph, where a digraph G is called a *line digraph* if there is a digraph H such that $V(G) = E(H)$ and $(a, b) \in E(G)$ if and only if $a \in E(V(H) - v, v; H)$ and $b \in E(v, V(H) - v; H)$ hold for a vertex $v \in V(H)$.

2.1.4 Conjectures About Tree Decomposition

Now we consider the counterpart of the preceding argument of s-out-arborescences in undirected graphs. Let $T_i = (V, F_i), i = 1, 2, \ldots, k$, be spanning trees of a given undirected graph $G = (V, E)$, where two trees T_i and T_j are not necessarily edge disjoint. These trees are called s-*edge-independent* (resp. s-*vertex-independent*) if k (s, v)-paths each obtained by traversing a tree T_i are edge-disjoint (resp. internally vertex-disjoint) for all $v \in V - s$. Any graph G containing k s-edge-independent trees must satisfy

$$\lambda(s, v; G) \geq k \text{ for all } v \in V - s. \tag{2.2}$$

Thus, such a G must be k-edge-connected since $\lambda(s, u; G), \lambda(s, v; G) \geq k$ implies $\lambda(u, v; G) \geq k$ for any two vertices $u, v \in V$ by (1.18).

Conjecture 2.9. *If a graph $G = (V, E)$ satisfies (2.2), then it has k s-edge-independent trees.* □

It is known that Conjecture 2.9 is true for $k = 2$ [146] and $k = 3$ [190].

A necessary condition for a graph G to have k s-vertex-independent trees is

$$\kappa(s, v; G) \geq k \text{ for all } v \in V - s. \tag{2.3}$$

Note that (2.3) does not necessarily imply that G is k-vertex-connected (for example, any graph G'' obtained by joining two k (≥ 2)-vertex-connected graphs G and G' so that they share a vertex satisfies (2.3) with the shared vertex s, but is no longer k-vertex-connected). The next conjecture has been verified for a general graph with $k = 2$ [146] and $k = 3$ [38, 314], for a planar graph with $k = 4$ [134], for a product graph with any k [269], and for a chordal ring with any k [151].

Conjecture 2.10. *If a graph $G = (V, E)$ satisfies (2.3), then it has k s-vertex-independent trees.* □

It is also known that every 4-vertex-connected graph has four s-vertex-independent trees at any vertex s [51].

As an application of Theorem 1.27, Khuller and Schieber have shown that Conjecture 2.10 implies Conjecture 2.9.

Theorem 2.11 ([190]). *Let k be a positive integer. If Conjecture 2.10 with k holds for all graphs, then Conjecture 2.9 with k holds for all graphs.* □

Proof. Assume that Conjecture 2.10 holds for an integer $k \geq 1$. Let $G = (V, E)$ be a graph and $s \in V$ be a vertex that satisfies (2.2) (i.e., a k-edge-connected graph). We show that G admits k s-edge-independent trees. Let $H_k = (W_k = V \cup V_E \cup (\cup_{u \in V} V_u), F)$ be the k-vertex-connected graph defined from G and k in Lemma 1.26 and Theorem 1.27. Since H_k satisfies (2.3) for the vertex $s \in W_k$, H_k has k s-vertex-independent trees $T_i = (W, F_i), i = 1, 2, \ldots, k$, by the assumption. For each T_i, we define a spanning subgraph $T_i' = (V, \{p_i(u) \mid u \in V - s\})$ of G by defining edge $p_i(u) \in E$ for all vertices $u \in V - s$ in the following manner. For a vertex $u \in V - s$, we consider the vertex $u' \in \{u\} \cup V_u$ that is closest to s in T_i, and we choose edge $p_i(u) \in E$ as the edge e corresponding to the last vertex $v_e \in V_E$ before u' in the (s, u')-path in T_i. Then it is not difficult to see that $T_i' = (V, \{p_i(u) \mid u \in V - s\})$ for each $i = 1, 2, \ldots, k$ is a tree of G and that the s-vertex-independentness of $\{T_i \mid i = 1, 2, \ldots, k\}$ implies the s-edge-independentness of $\{T'_i \mid i = 1, 2, \ldots, k\}$. □

Finally we consider a set of trees in an undirected graph G. If there is a set of k edge-disjoint spanning trees $T_1, T_2, \ldots, T_k$ in G, we see that, for any two vertices u and v of G, the k paths from u to v in $T_1, T_2, \ldots, T_k$ are edge-disjoint. Thus, G is k-edge-connected. Nash-Williams [262] showed the following sufficient condition.

Theorem 2.12 ([262]). *Every 2k-edge-connected graph admits k edge-disjoint spanning trees.* □

This theorem follows from Theorem 1.47 since $(1/2)\sum_{1 \le i \le t} d(V_i; G) \ge 2kt/2 \ge k(t-1)$ holds for every partition $\{V_1, V_2, \ldots, V_t\}$ of V.

Let $T_1, T_2, \ldots, T_k$ be spanning trees in a graph G. If for any two vertices u and v of G, the paths from u to v in $T_1, T_2, \ldots, T_k$ are pairwise internally vertex disjoint, then we say that $T_1, T_2, \ldots, T_k$ are *completely independent* [117]. A characterization of completely independent spanning trees is given as follows.

Theorem 2.13 ([117]). *Let $T_1, T_2, \ldots, T_k$ be spanning trees in a graph G. Then, $T_1, T_2, \ldots, T_k$ are completely independent if and only if $T_1, T_2, \ldots, T_k$ are edge-disjoint and for each vertex v of G, there is at most one T_i such that the degree of v in T_i is greater than one.* □

Completely independent spanning trees are edge-disjoint spanning trees, although s-vertex-independent trees are not always edge-disjoint.

Analogously to Theorem 2.12, Hasunuma [117] poses the following statement as a conjecture.

Conjecture 2.14. *Every 2k-vertex-connected graph admits k completely independent spanning trees.* □

Currently the following results are known about completely independent spanning trees. For a digraph G, the undirected graph obtained from G by neglecting its edge orientation is called the *underlying graph* and is denoted by $U(G)$.

Theorem 2.15 ([117]). *Let $L(G)$ be a k-vertex-connected line digraph. Then the underlying graph $U(L(G))$ has k completely independent spanning trees.* □

Theorem 2.16 ([118]). *Every 4-vertex-connected maximal planar graph has two completely independent spanning trees. Such a pair of completely independent spanning trees can be found in linear time.* □

Theorem 2.17 ([118]). *Given a graph G, the problem of deciding whether there exist two completely independent spanning trees in G is $\mathcal{NP}$-complete.* □

2.2 MA Ordering

Computing a forest decomposition $\mathcal{F} = (F_1, F_2, \ldots, F_m)$ of a multigraph G according to Definition 2.1 may take $O(m^2)$ time if we repeat a graph search procedure $O(m)$ times. Nagamochi and Ibaraki [231] reduced this time bound to $O(m + n)$. The idea is to construct all $F_1, F_2, \ldots, F_m$ in a single scan of a graph search. During the graph search, we compute, for each edge e being scanned, the smallest j such that $F_j \cup \{e\}$ does not create a cycle, where sets $F_1, F_2, \ldots$ are those currently constructed and we grow such F_j by $F_j := F_j \cup \{e\}$. To avoid taking $O(|F_j|)$ time to check whether adding e to F_j creates a new cycle, we always choose an unscanned edge e that is adjacent to an edge $e' \in F_j$ with the largest j. An algorithm for scanning all edges with this rule is described as follows.

Algorithm FOREST
Input: A multigraph $G = (V, E)$ and a vertex $s \in V$.
Output: A forest decomposition $\mathcal{F} = (F_1, F_2, \ldots, F_m)$ of G and an ordering
    $\sigma = (v_1 = s, v_2, \ldots, v_n)$ of V.
1 $F_1 := F_2 := \cdots := F_m := \emptyset$;
2 $r(v) := 0$ for all $v \in V$; /*$r(v) = d(\{v_1, v_2, \ldots, v_i\}, v; G)$ holds for the
     current i */
3 **for** $i = 1$ to n **do**
4   Choose a vertex $u^* \in V - \{v_1, v_2, \ldots, v_{i-1}\}$ with the maximum $r(u^*)$;
     /* Choose s as u^* for $i = 1$ */
5     $v_i := u^*$;
6   **for** each edge $e = \{v_i, u\} \in E(v_i, V - \{v_1, v_2, \ldots, v_i\}; G)$ **do**
7       $r(u) := r(u) + 1$;
8       $F_{r(u)} := F_{r(u)} \cup \{e\}$
9   **end** /* for */
10 **end**; /* for */
11 Output $\mathcal{F} = (F_1, F_2, \ldots, F_m)$ and $\sigma := (v_1, v_2, \ldots, v_n)$.

An example of forest decomposition is shown in Fig. 2.2(b), in which the ordering $(v_1, v_2, \ldots, v_{10})$ tells how vertices are chosen in line 5 of FOREST. The numbers indicated beside vertices u show the $r(u)$ when u is selected as u^* in line 5.

After introducing some notions, we will prove in Lemma 2.25(iii) that $\mathcal{F} = (F_1, F_2, \ldots, F_m)$ obtained by FOREST is a forest decomposition satisfying Definition 2.1. In FOREST, after scanning vertex v_{i-1}, we see that, for each vertex $u \in V - \{v_1, v_2, \ldots, v_{i-1}\}, r(u)$ stands for $d(\{v_1, v_2, \ldots, v_{i-1}\}, u; G)$. Since v_i is chosen as a vertex u^* with the maximum $r(u^*) = d(\{v_1, v_2, \ldots, v_{i-1}\}, u^*; G)$, we observe that an ordering $\sigma := (v_1, v_2, \ldots, v_n)$ derived by FOREST satisfies

$$d(\{v_1, v_2, \ldots, v_{i-1}\}, v_i; G)$$
$$\geq d(\{v_1, v_2, \ldots, v_{i-1}\}, v_j; G) \quad \text{for all } i, j \text{ with } 2 \leq i < j \leq n.$$

A procedure for visiting vertices in the aforementioned ordering was first used by Tarjan and Yannakakis [300] to test chordality of a given simple graph and to test acyclicity of a given hypergraph. They call the procedure a maximum cardinality search. Unlike the algorithm FOREST, it does not partition an edge set E into subsets.

Definition 2.18. *For an undirected edge-weighted graph/multigraph* $G = (V, E)$, *a total ordering* $\sigma = (v_1, v_2, \ldots, v_n)$ $(|V| = n)$ *of vertices in* V *is called a* maximum adjacency (MA) ordering *if*

$$d(V_{i-1}, v_i; G) \geq d(V_{i-1}, v_j; G) \text{ for all } i, j \text{ with } 2 \leq i < j \leq n,$$

where

$$V_i = \{v_1, v_2, \ldots, v_i\} \ (1 \leq i \leq n). \qquad \square$$

As an example, we consider the integer-weighted graph $G = (V, E)$ in Fig. 1.3 interpreted as a multigraph. The numbering $v_1, v_2, \ldots, v_{21}$ is an MA ordering starting from v_1, since we can easily observe that $d(V_1, v_2; G) = 4 \geq d(V_1, v_j)$ $(3 \leq j \leq 21)$, $d(V_2, v_3; G) = 3 \geq d(V_2, v_j)$ $(4 \leq j \leq 21)$, $d(V_3, v_4; G) = 4 \geq d$ (V_3, v_j) $(5 \leq j \leq 21)$, $d(V_4, v_5; G) = 6 \geq d(V_4, v_j)$ $(6 \leq j \leq 21), \ldots, d(V_{19}, v_{20}; G) = 3 \geq d(V_{19}, v_{21})$. It is also easy to see that $\sigma = (v_1, v_2, \ldots, v_{10})$ in Fig. 2.2(b) is an MA ordering on the simple graph in Fig. 2.2(a).

The main aim of this chapter is to show that MA orderings can be used to construct a sparse k-edge/vertex-connectivity certificate. However, since MA orderings can also be used to identify a pendent pair (see Section 1.5.1), as will be discussed in Section 3.1, there are many articles that study properties of MA orderings [82, 89, 93, 232, 248, 250, 277, 283, 293]. An ordering in Definition 2.18 for unweighted graphs is called a legal ordering in [89]. An ordering in Definition 2.18 for edge-weighted graphs is called an MA ordering in [241] and called a max-back order in [283].

2.2.1 Computing MA Orderings in Undirected and Weighted Multigraphs

Lemma 2.19 ([231]). *Given a multigraph* $G = (V, E)$ *and a vertex* $s \in V$, *an MA ordering of* V *starting with* $v_1 = s$ *can be found in* $O(n + m)$ *time and space.* $\qquad \square$

Proof. Assuming that a given graph G is stored as a set of adjacency lists (as explained in Section 1.2.1), we show that an MA ordering $\sigma = (v_1, v_2, \ldots, v_n)$ can be obtained in $O(n + m)$ time and space. (See FOREST since the procedure is embedded in it.) Initialize $r(u) := d(v_1, u; G)$ for all neighbors u of $v_1 = s$ and $r(u) := 0$ for $u \in V - V_1 - \Gamma_G(v_1)$, where $V_1 = \{v_1\}$. Before choosing the ith vertex, it is not difficult to see that, for each $u \in V - V_{i-1}, r(u)$ stores $d(V_{i-1}, u; G)$. We maintain each nonempty set $S_r = \{v \in V - V_i \mid r(v) = r\}$ by a doubly linked list L_r, and the set $\{r \mid 0 \leq r \leq m, S_r \neq \emptyset\}$ by a doubly linked list L^*. The space complexity is $O(m + n)$. Then, for the current top r (i.e., largest r) in L^*, we can choose any vertex $v \in L_r$ as the ith vertex v_i . Note that $r(u)$ is updated to $r(u) := r(u) + d(v_i, u; G)$ for all $u \in \Gamma_G(v_i) - V_i$, upon completing the phase of v_i. This takes $O(d(v_i; G))$ time. For each $u \in \Gamma_G(v_i) - V_i$, the new $r(u)$ can be moved to the list L_r with $r = r(u)$ by traversing list L^* in $O(d(v_i, u; G))$ time since L_r and L^* are stored by doubly linked lists. Then the ith iteration takes $O(d(v_i; G))$ time, and the time complexity is also $O(n + m)$. □

An MA ordering in an edge-weighted graph $G = (V, E)$ can be found by choosing an arbitrary vertex s as v_1 and, after choosing the first $i - 1$ vertices $V_{i-1} = \{v_1, \ldots, v_{i-1}\}$, by choosing a vertex $u \in V - V_{i-1}$ that maximizes $d(V_{i-1}, u; G)$ as the ith vertex v_i. For an edge-weighted graph $G = (V, E)$, the algorithm can be described as follows.

Algorithm MAO
Input: An edge-weighted graph $G = (V, E)$ and a vertex $s \in V$.
Output: An MA ordering $\sigma = (v_1 = s, v_2, \ldots, v_n)$ of V.
1   $r(u) := 0$ for all $u \in V$;
2   **for** $i = 1$ to n **do**
3   Choose a vertex $u^* \in V - V_{i-1}$ with the maximum $r(u^*)$;
        /* Choose s as u^* for $i = 1$ */
4      $v_i := u^*$;
5      $r(u) := r(u) + d(v_i, u; G)$ for all vertices $u \in \Gamma_G(v_i) - V_i$;
6   **end**; /* for */
7   Output $\sigma := (v_1, v_2, \ldots, v_n)$.

Lemma 2.20 ([231]). *Given an edge-weighted graph $G = (V, E)$ and a vertex $s \in V$, an MA ordering of V starting with $v_1 = s$ can be found in $O(m + n \log n)$ time and $O(m + n)$ space.* □

Proof. We easily see that $r(u) = d(V_i, u; G)$ holds for all $u \in V - V_i$ before choosing v_{i+1} in MAO. Hence, the ordering σ output by MAO is an MA ordering.

We consider the complexity of MAO. As explained in Section 1.2.1, the graph $G = (V, E)$ is stored as a set of adjacency lists $Adj(u), u \in V$ in $O(m + n)$ space, by which we can find all vertices $u \in \Gamma_G(v_i) - V_i$ in line 5 in $O(|\Gamma_G(v_i)|)$ time. At each step i $(i = 1, \ldots, n)$, we maintain a data structure Q that contains all vertices $u \in V - V_i$ along with the key values $r(u), u \in V - V_i$. After choosing v_i in line 4, we update the key value $r(u)$ of each vertex $u \in \Gamma_G(v_i) - V_i$ by increasing by $d(v_i, u; G)$ in line 5. Thus, the number of updating keys is $|E|$. In line 3, we choose a vertex u^* with the maximum key $r(u^*)$ from Q, and then delete u^* from Q. The number of extracting a vertex with the maximum key from Q is $O(n)$.

By using data structure of Fibonacci heap [91] to maintain elements in Q, it is known that constructing Q with h elements, increasing a key value in Q k times, and extracting an element with the maximum key p times can be executed in $O(h + k + p \log h)$ time and $O(n)$ space. In MAO, $h = O(n)$, $k = O(m)$, and

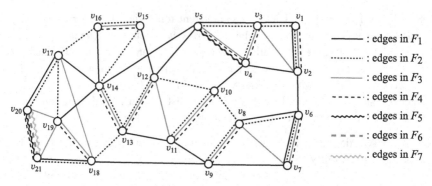

Figure 2.3. A forest decomposition $\mathcal{F}(G, \sigma) = (F_1, F_2, \ldots, F_7)$ of the multigraph G in Fig. 1.3 with an MA ordering $\sigma = (v_1, v_2, \ldots, v_{21})$.

$p = O(n)$ hold. Therefore, MAO can be implemented to run in $O(m + n \log n)$ time and $O(m + n)$ space.   □

2.2.2 Forest Decomposition by MA Ordering

Given an MA ordering $\sigma = (v_1, v_2, \ldots, v_n)$ of a multigraph $G = (V, E)$, let $\mathcal{F}(G, \sigma) = (F_1, F_2, \ldots, F_m)$ be the following partition of the edge set E. For each $i = 2, \ldots, n$, consider the set $E(V_{i-1}, v_i; G)$ of edges between V_{i-1} and v_i, and let $e_{k,i} \in E(V_{i-1}, v_i; G)$ be the edge that appears as the kth edge when the edges in $E(V_{i-1}, v_i; G)$ are arranged in the order $e_{1,i} = \{v_{j_1}, v_i\}, e_{2,i} = \{v_{j_2}, v_i\}, \ldots, e_{p,i} = \{v_{j_p}, v_i\}$, where $1 \leq j_1 \leq j_2 \leq \cdots \leq j_p$ holds. By letting

$$F_k = \{e_{k,2}, e_{k,3}, \ldots, e_{k,n}\}, \quad k = 1, 2, \ldots, m \qquad (2.4)$$

(some of $e_{k,i}$ may be void), we have a partition $\mathcal{F}(G, \sigma) = (F_1, \ldots, F_m)$ of E.

For the MA ordering $\sigma = (v_1, v_2, \ldots, v_{10})$ in Fig. 2.2(b) obtained for the simple graph in Fig. 2.2(a), the resulting forest decomposition $\mathcal{F}(G, \sigma) = (F_1, F_2, F_3, F_4)$ is also depicted in Fig. 2.2(b). Note that $F_k = \emptyset$ holds for $k > 4$ in this case. Figure 2.3 illustrates the forest decomposition $\mathcal{F}(G, \sigma)$ for the multigraph G (defined in Fig. 1.3) and MA ordering $\sigma = (v_1, v_2, \ldots, v_{21})$.

Lemma 2.21. *For each F_k, $k = 1, 2, \ldots, m$, defined earlier, $|E(V_{i-1}, v_i; G) \cap F_k| \leq 1$ $(2 \leq i \leq n)$ holds, F_k contains at most $n - 1$ edges, and (V, F_k) is a forest of G.*   □

Proof. Property $|E(V_{i-1}, v_i; G) \cap F_k| \leq 1$ $(2 \leq i \leq n)$ is clear from the definition. Note that, if (V, F_k) contains a cycle, then it would mean $|E(V_{i-1}, v_i; G) \cap F_k| \geq 2$ for some i. Hence, (V, F_k) is a forest and has at most $n - 1$ edges.   □

Lemma 2.22. *Let $\mathcal{F} = (F_1, \ldots, F_m)$ and $\sigma = (v_1, v_2, \ldots, v_n)$ be the outputs of algorithm* FOREST *applied to a multigraph $G = (V, E)$. Then $\mathcal{F} = \mathcal{F}(G, \sigma)$.*   □

Proof. Consider edge set $E(V_{i-1}, v_i; G)$ $(i > 1)$. When v_i is chosen as the ith vertex in σ by FOREST, every edge in $E(V_{i-1}, v_i; G)$ belongs to some set F_j. By lines 7 and 8 of FOREST, an edge $\{v_j, v_i\} \in E(V_{i-1}, v_i; G)$ is scanned before scanning any edge $\{v_h, v_i\} \in E(V_{i-1}, v_i; G)$ with $h > j$. Moreover, the jth scanned edge $e \in E(V_{i-1}, v_i; G)$ belongs to F_j. This is exactly equivalent to the manner of partitioning edge set E into $F_1, F_2, \ldots, F_m$ according to (2.4). □

From the preceding argument, we have the following lemma.

Lemma 2.23. *Given a multigraph G, an MA ordering σ of G and a forest decomposition $\mathcal{F}(G, \sigma) = (F_1, F_2, \ldots, F_m)$ can be obtained in $O(n + m)$ time and space.* □

By construction of $\mathcal{F}(G, \sigma)$, we easily have the following observation.

Lemma 2.24. *For an MA ordering $\sigma = (v_1, v_2, \ldots, v_n)$ of V in a multigraph $G = (V, E)$, let $\mathcal{F}(G, \sigma) = (F_1, \ldots, F_m)$ be the resulting forest decomposition. Then*

(i) *Exactly one edge $e_{k,n}$ from each F_k, $k = 1, \ldots, d(v_n; G)$ is incident to the last vertex v_n.*

(ii) *If $\{u, v\} \in F_i$ and $\{u, v\} \in F_j$ hold for two vertices u and v (i.e., $\{u, v\}$ is a multiple edge), where we assume $i < j$, then $\{u, v\} \in F_h$ for all h with $i \leq h \leq j$.* □

We here show a hierarchical property of $\mathcal{F}(G, \sigma)$ [266] and a consecutiveness of vertex indices in a forest (V, F_k) [67, 120].

Lemma 2.25. *Let $\sigma = (v_1, \ldots, v_n)$ be an MA ordering of a multigraph G, and let $\mathcal{F}(G, \sigma) = (F_1, F_2, \ldots, F_m)$ be the resulting forest decomposition.*

(i) *[266] For any integers i, j with $1 \leq i \leq j \leq m$, the ordering σ remains an MA ordering in the spanning subgraph $G_{i,j} = (V, F_i \cup F_{i+1} \cup \cdots \cup F_j)$.*

(ii) *For any connected component C in the spanning subgraph $\overline{G}_{k-1} = G - (F_1 \cup F_2 \cup \cdots \cup F_{k-1})$, all vertices in C appear in σ consecutively.*

(iii) *Each (V, F_k) is a maximal forest in the spanning subgraph $\overline{G}_{k-1} = G - (F_1 \cup F_2 \cup \cdots \cup F_{k-1})$. Hence, if two vertices u and v are connected in (V, F_k), then they are connected also in (V, F_j) for all $j < k$.*

(iv) *[67, 120] Let T be a tree in a forest $F_k \in \mathcal{F}(G, \sigma)$. Then T consists of consecutive vertices $v_i, v_{i+1}, \ldots, v_\ell$, and any subsequence $v_i, v_{i+1}, \ldots, v_h$ with $h \leq \ell$ induces a connected subgraph in T.* □

Proof. (i) It suffices to show that σ is an MA ordering in $G_{2,m}$ and $G_{1,m-1}$, since, by applying this repeatedly, we obtain the lemma. By construction of $\mathcal{F}(G, \sigma)$, we see that, for any $v_i \in V - v_1$, $|E(V_{i-1}, v_i; G_{1,m}) \cap F_k| = 1$ holds if and only if $d(V_{i-1}, v_i; G_{1,m}) \geq k$. For each $i = 2, \ldots, n$, we have

$$
\begin{aligned}
d(V_{i-1}, v_i; G_{2,m}) &= \max[0, \ d(V_{i-1}, v_i; G) - 1] \\
&= \max[0, \ \max\{d(V_{i-1}, u; G) \mid u \in V - V_{i-1}\} - 1] \\
&= \max\{\max[0, d(V_{i-1}, u; G) - 1] \mid u \in V - V_{i-1}\} \\
&= \max\{d(V_{i-1}, u; G_{2,m}) \mid u \in V - V_{i-1}\}.
\end{aligned}
$$

This implies that ordering σ is an MA ordering in $G_{2,m}$. Likewise, for each $i = 2, \ldots, n$, we have

$$
\begin{aligned}
d(V_{i-1}, v_i; G_{1,m-1}) &= \min[m - 1, \ d(V_{i-1}, v_i; G)] \\
&= \min[m - 1, \ \max\{d(V_{i-1}, u; G) \mid u \in V - V_{i-1}\}] \\
&= \max\{\min[m - 1, \ d(V_{i-1}, u; G)] \mid u \in V - V_{i-1}\} \\
&= \max\{d(V_{i-1}, u; G_{1,m-1}) \mid u \in V - V_{i-1}\},
\end{aligned}
$$

indicating that σ is an MA ordering in $G_{1,m-1}$.

(ii) By condition (i), σ is an MA ordering in $\overline{G}_{k-1}$. Hence, we easily see that all vertices in a connected component in $\overline{G}_{k-1}$ appear sequentially in σ.

(iii) As stated in Lemma 2.21, (V, F_k) is a forest. We then show the maximality of F_k in $\overline{G}_{k-1}$ by proving that it spans any connected component C in $\overline{G}_{k-1}$. By condition (ii), C consists of vertices with consecutive indices, say $v_i, v_{i+1}, \ldots, v_j$, in the MA ordering. Assume that F_k does not span C. Then there is an index h with $i < h \leq j$ such that $v_i, v_{i+1}, \ldots, v_{h-1}$ belong to the same connected component C' in (V, F_k), but v_h belongs to another connected component $C''(\neq C')$ in (V, F_k). Since F_k has no edge joining v_h and a vertex in V_{h-1}, it holds that $d(V_{h-1}, v_h; \overline{G}_{k-1}) = 0$. Since σ is an MA ordering in $\overline{G}_{k-1}$, $0 = d(V_{h-1}, v_h; \overline{G}_{k-1}) \geq d(V_{h-1}, u; \overline{G}_{k-1})$ for all $u \in V - V_{h-1}$. This implies that $E(V_{h-1}, V - V_{h-1}; \overline{G}_{k-1}) = \emptyset$, contradicting that v_{h-1} and v_h belong to the same connected component C in $\overline{G}_{k-1}$.

(iv) From conditions (ii) and (iii), all vertices in T appear in σ consecutively. Since σ is an MA ordering in forest F_k, we see that $(v_i, v_{i+1}, \ldots, v_\ell)$ is an MA ordering in T. Hence, we see that each vertex v_j ($i < j \leq \ell$) has at least one incident edge in T that joins v_j and a vertex $v_{j'}$ with $j' < j$. If v_j' is connected to v_i, then v_j is also connected to v_i via $v_{j'}$. Hence, any subsequence $v_i, v_{i+1}, \ldots, v_h$ ($h \leq \ell$) induces a connected graph from T.   □

By Lemmas 2.22 and 2.25(iii), a partition $\mathcal{F} = (F_1, \ldots, F_m)$ obtained from a multigraph $G = (V, E)$ by FOREST gives a forest decomposition that satisfies Definition 2.1.

We now show that a forest decomposition $\mathcal{F}(G, \sigma)$ of a multigraph G obtained from an MA ordering σ gives rise to a k-edge/vertex-connectivity certificate $G_k = (V, E_k = F_1 \cup F_2 \cup \cdots \cup F_k)$.

Theorem 2.26. *For a multigraph $G = (V, E)$ and an MA ordering σ of G, let $\mathcal{F}(G, \sigma) = (F_1, F_2, \ldots, F_m)$ be the resulting forest decomposition of G. Let*

$$G_k = (V, F_1 \cup F_2 \cup \cdots \cup F_k),$$

for $k = 1, 2, \ldots, m$. Then each G_k has at most $k(n - 1)$ edges and satisfies the following.

(i) [231] *For every vertex pair $u, v \in V$,*

$$\lambda(u, v; G_k) \begin{cases} \geq k & \text{if } \lambda(u, v; G) \geq k \\ = \lambda(u, v; G) & \text{if } \lambda(u, v; G) \leq k - 1. \end{cases}$$

(ii) [89] *Let G be simple. For every vertex pair $u, v \in V$,*

$$\kappa(u, v; G_k) \begin{cases} \geq k & \text{if } \kappa(u, v; G) \geq k \\ = \kappa(u, v; G) & \text{if } \kappa(u, v; G) \leq k - 1. \end{cases} \qquad \square$$

This theorem in particular shows that $G = (V, E)$ is k-edge-connected (resp. k-vertex-connected) if and only if $G_k = (V, E_k)$ is k-edge-connected (resp. k-vertex-connected).

We prove Theorem 2.26 in a more general setting of (k, α)-connectivity, which was introduced in Section 1.4 to unify edge-connectivity and vertex-connectivity, where α is a vertex weight function $\alpha : V \to \mathbf{Z}_+$. Theorem 2.26 is a special case of this more general result (Corollary 2.29). For the various notions of local connectivity as discussed in Section 1.4, sparse spanning subgraphs preserving such connectivities have been studied extensively [23, 43, 67, 89, 231].

2.2.3 (k, α)-Certificates and Their Properties

For (k, α)-connectivity, we define a certificate of a graph as follows. A spanning subgraph H of a graph G is called a (k, α)-*certificate* of G if

$$\lambda_\alpha(u, v; H) \geq \min\{\lambda_\alpha(u, v; G), k\} \text{ for every vertex pair } u, v \in V.$$

Clearly a (k, α)-certificate of G is (k, α)-connected if G is also (k, α)-connected. A (k, α)-certificate is called *sparse* if it has $O(kn)$ edges.

Let $\mathcal{C}_k(u, v; G)$ denote the set of all mixed cuts having size k and separating vertices u and v in G. For a (k, α)-certificate H of G, the size of a mixed cut in G may become smaller in H, but maintains its size as stated in the following lemma.

Lemma 2.27. *For a multigraph $G = (V, E)$, let H be a spanning subgraph of G. Let k be a positive integer, and α be a vertex weight function. Then the following three are equivalent.*

(i) *H is a (k, α)-certificate of G.*
(ii) *For any mixed cut (A, B, Z) in G such that $\alpha(Z) + d(A, B; G) > \alpha(Z) + d(A, B; H)$, it holds that $\alpha(Z) + d(A, B; H) \geq k$.*

(iii) *For every two distinct vertices* $u, v \in V$, *it holds that*

$$\mathcal{C}_j(u, v; G) = \mathcal{C}_j(u, v; H) \ (j < k), \quad \mathcal{C}_k(u, v; G) \subseteq \mathcal{C}_k(u, v; H),$$

$$\text{and} \bigcup_{i \geq k+1} \mathcal{C}_i(u, v; G) \subseteq \bigcup_{i \geq k} \mathcal{C}_i(u, v; H).$$

$\square$

Proof. (i)$\Rightarrow$(ii) Let (A, B, Z) be a mixed cut such that its size in H is smaller than that in G. Then there is an edge $e = \{u, v\} \in E(G) - E(H)$ joining a vertex $u \in A$ and a vertex $v \in B$. Hence, $\lambda_\alpha(u, v; H) < \lambda_\alpha(u, v; G)$. From condition (i), $\lambda_\alpha(u, v; H) \geq \min\{\lambda_\alpha(u, v; G), k\}$ and, hence, $\lambda_\alpha(u, v; H) \geq k$ must hold, implying $\alpha(Z) + d(A, B; H) \geq \lambda_\alpha(u, v; H) \geq k$.

(ii)$\Rightarrow$(iii) Let a mixed cut (A, B, Z) separate vertices u and v in G (then it separates u and v in any spanning subgraph of G). If the size of (A, B, Z) decreases in H, then it holds that $\alpha(Z) + d(A, B; G) > \alpha(Z) + d(A, B; H) \geq k$ by condition (ii), implying $\bigcup_{i \geq k+1} \mathcal{C}_i(u, v; G) \subseteq \bigcup_{i \geq k} \mathcal{C}_i(u, v; H)$. In particular, if $\alpha(Z) + d(A, B; G) = k$, then $\alpha(Z) + d(A, B; G) = \alpha(Z) + d(A, B; H) = k$, indicating $\mathcal{C}_k(u, v; G) \subseteq \mathcal{C}_k(u, v; H)$. For $j < k$, by assumption (ii), any mixed cut (A, B, Z) with size j in H (resp. (A, B, Z) with size j in G) has the same size in both G and H. This implies $\mathcal{C}_j(u, v; G) = \mathcal{C}_j(u, v; H)$.

(iii)$\Rightarrow$(i) For two distinct vertices $u, v \in V$, let $h = \lambda_\alpha(u, v; G)$ and let (A, B, Z) be a mixed cut with $\alpha(Z) + d(A, B; G) = h$. If $h \geq k$, then $\mathcal{C}_j(u, v; H) = \mathcal{C}_j(u, v; G) = \emptyset$ holds for all $j < k$ by assumption (iii), since (A, B, Z) is a minimum mixed cut in G, indicating $\lambda_\alpha(u, v; H) \geq k$. On the other hand, if $h < k$, then $(A, B, Z) \in \mathcal{C}_h(u, v; H)$ and $\mathcal{C}_j(u, v; H) = \mathcal{C}_j(u, v; G) = \emptyset$ $(j < h)$ by assumption (iii), implying $\lambda_\alpha(u, v; H) = h$. Therefore, $\lambda_\alpha(u, v; H) \geq \min\{\lambda_\alpha(u, v; G), k\}$. $\square$

2.2.4 Computing a Certificate in an α-Simple Graph

Given a vertex weight function $\alpha : V \to \mathbf{Z}_+$, a graph $G = (V, E)$ is called α-*simple* if for all pairs of vertices $u, v \in V$, $d(u, v; G)$ (i.e., the number of multiple edges joining u and v) is at most $\min\{\alpha(u), \alpha(v)\}$. Following the proof scheme for ℓ-mixed-connectivity certificates due to Berg and Jordán [23], we prove the next result.

Theorem 2.28 ([227]). *For an α-simple multigraph $G = (V, E)$, let $\mathcal{F}(G, \sigma) = (F_1, F_2, \ldots, F_m)$ be the forest decomposition obtained for an MA ordering σ of G. If two vertices u and v are connected in a forest (V, F_k), then $\lambda_\alpha(u, v; G_j) \geq j$ holds for $G_j = (V, F_1 \cup F_2 \cup \cdots \cup F_j)$, $j = 1, 2, \ldots, k$.* $\square$

Proof. We only have to show that $\lambda_\alpha(u, v; G_k) \geq k$, since $\lambda_\alpha(u, v; G_j) \geq j$ for $j < k$ will follow from the fact that u and v are connected in (V, F_j) by Lemma 2.25(i) and (iii).

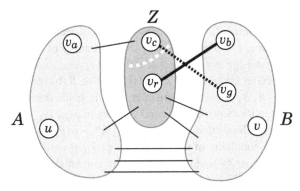

Figure 2.4. Illustration for a mixed cut (A, B, Z) in the proof of Theorem 2.28.

By induction on k, we prove that, for any mixed cut (A, B, Z) that separates these u and v in G_k, it holds that

$$\alpha(Z) + d(A, B; G_k) \geq k. \tag{2.5}$$

For $k = 1$, this trivially holds. Let $k \geq 2$, and assume that, for any $k' < k$, the inequality holds. Consider $G_{h,k} = (V, F_h \cup F_{h+1} \cup \cdots \cup F_k)$ with $2 \leq h \leq k$, which is clearly α-simple. By Lemma 2.25(i) and (iii), σ remains an MA ordering in $G_{h,k}$, and F_k is the $(k - h + 1)$-th forest in $G_{h,k}$. Hence, by $k - h + 1 < k$, our induction hypothesis tells that

$$\alpha(Z) + d(A, B; G_{h,k}) \geq k - h + 1 \tag{2.6}$$

holds for any mixed cut (A, B, Z) separating u and v, and for any integer h with $2 \leq h \leq k$.

Let (A, B, Z) be a mixed cut separating u and v in G_k. We first consider the case where $E(A, B; G_1) \neq \emptyset$. By (2.6), we have $\alpha(Z) + d(A, B; G_k) = \alpha(Z) + d(A, B; G_{2,k}) + d(A, B; G_1) \geq (k - 2 + 1) + 1 = k$, showing (2.5).

We then assume $E(A, B; G_1) = \emptyset$. Since u and v are connected in (V, F_k) by assumption, they belong to a tree T in $G_1 = (V, F_1)$ by Lemma 2.25(iii). By $E(A, B; G_1) = \emptyset$, we have $Z \cap V(T) \neq \emptyset$. Let $v_a \in A \cap V(T)$, $v_b \in B \cap V(T)$, and $v_c \in Z \cap V(T)$ be the vertices with the minimum index according to the MA ordering σ, respectively (see Fig. 2.4). Without loss of generality assume $a < b$. Then the vertex $v_{i^*} \in V(T)$ with the minimum index belongs to $A \cup Z$, and the set $\{v_{i^*}, v_{i^*+1}, \ldots, v_b\}$ of vertices in $V(T)$ with indices consecutively from i^* to b induces a connected graph in G_1 by Lemma 2.25(i), (iii), and (iv). This and $E(A, B; G_1) = \emptyset$ mean that $E(Z, B; G_1)$ contains an edge $\{v_r, v_b\}$ with $i^* \leq r < b$, and thereby it holds that $c \leq r < b$.

We here claim that, for $h^* = \alpha(v_c) + 1$,

$$d(v_c, B; G_{h^*,m}) = 0. \tag{2.7}$$

Assume that there is an edge $\{v_c, v_g\} \in E(v_c, B; G) \cap F_\ell$ for some $\ell \geq h^*$. By $\{v_c, v_g\} \in F_\ell$ and Lemma 2.25(iii), v_c and v_g are connected in G_1. Then $v_g \in B \cap V(T)$ and, hence, $c < b \leq g$ holds by the minimality of c and b in σ. Note then that there is an edge $e' = \{v', v_g\} \in E(\{v_{i^*}, v_{i^*+1}, \ldots, v_c\}, v_g; G_\ell) \cap F_1$ by construction of $\mathcal{F}(G, \sigma)$, where $v' \in Z$ holds since $v' \notin B$ (by the minimality of b) and $v' \notin A$ (by $E(A, B; G_1) = \emptyset$). Moreover, $v' = v_c$ holds since $v_c \in Z \cap V(T)$ has the minimum index. Since both F_1 and F_ℓ contain edge $\{v_c, v_g\}$ (i.e., $\{v_c, v_g\}$ is a multiple edge), it holds that $d(v_c, v_g) \geq \ell \geq h^* > \alpha(v_c)$ by Lemma 2.24(ii), contradicting the α-simplicity of G. This proves (2.7).

If $k \leq \alpha(v_c)$, then $\alpha(Z) + d(A, B; G_k) \geq k$ is immediate. Therefore, assume $k \geq h^* = \alpha(v_c) + 1 (\geq 2)$. Let $Z' = Z - v_c$ and $A' = A \cup \{v_c\}$. Then by (2.6) and (2.7)

$$
\begin{aligned}
\alpha(Z) + d(A, B; G_k) &\geq \alpha(Z) + d(A, B; G_{h^*,k}) \\
&= \alpha(v_c) + \alpha(Z') + d(A', B; G_{h^*,k}) \\
&\geq \alpha(v_c) + (k - h^* + 1) = k,
\end{aligned}
$$

indicating that (2.5) holds for the current k. This completes the induction on k.   □

Note that (k, α)-connectivity of a multigraph G remains well defined even if G is not α-simple, where we see that an edge between vertices u and v such that $d(u, v; G) > \min\{\alpha(u), \alpha(v)\}$ is redundant in considering (k, α)-connectivity of G. However, we need to assume that G is α-simple in order to show that $G_k = (V, F_1 \cup F_2 \cup \cdots \cup F_k)$ obtained from $\mathcal{F}(G, \sigma)$ is a (k, α)-certificate of G in the next corollary. For example, consider a 2-vertex-connected $G = (V, E)$ with $\alpha(v) = 1$, $v \in V$. Then a $(2, \alpha)$-certificate $G_2 = (V, F_1 \cup F_2)$ must be 2-vertex-connected. However, if we add a copy F_1' of F_1 to G, then the resulting graph G' is not α-simple, and we would have graph $(V, F_1 \cup F_1')$ as G_2', which is a tree of multiple edges and cannot be 2-vertex-connected.

Corollary 2.29 ([227]). *For an MA ordering σ of an α-simple multigraph $G = (V, E)$ with a vertex weight function α, let $\mathcal{F}(G, \sigma) = (F_1, F_2, \ldots, F_m)$ be the resulting forest decomposition. For each $k = 1, 2, \ldots, m$, $G_k = (V, F_1 \cup F_2 \cup \cdots \cup F_k)$ is a (k, α)-certificate of G with at most $k(n - 1)$ edges.*   □

Proof. Obviously $|E(G_k)| \leq k(n - 1)$. To prove that G_k is a (k, α)-certificate of G, it suffices to show that $H = G_k$ satisfies the condition of Lemma 2.27(ii). Consider a mixed cut (A, B, Z) with $\alpha(Z) + d(A, B; G) > \alpha(Z) + d(A, B; G_k)$. There is an edge $e = \{u, v\} \in E(A, B; G) \cap F_j$ for some $j \geq k + 1$; we choose such an edge e so that the index j is minimized. By the minimality of j, it holds that $\alpha(Z) + d(A, B; G_{j-1}) = \alpha(Z) + d(A, B; G_k)$. On the other hand, by Theorem 2.28, we have $\lambda_\alpha(u, v; G_{j-1}) \geq j - 1$. Therefore, $\alpha(Z) + d(A, B; G_k) = \alpha(Z) + d(A, B; G_{j-1}) \geq \lambda_\alpha(u, v; G_{j-1}) \geq j - 1 \geq k$.   □

Theorem 2.26(i) (resp. Theorem 2.26(ii)) follows from this corollary with $\alpha(v) > d(x; G)$, $v \in V(G)$ (resp. $\alpha(v) = 1$, $v \in V(G)$).

2.2.5 Sparsification

Corollary 2.29 together with Lemma 2.27 provides us a sparsification technique for many connectivity algorithms. Suppose that an algorithm for determining the k-edge/vertex-connectivity of a graph G (or between two vertices u, v in G) is available. Then by applying it to a (k, α)-certificate G_k instead of applying it to the original G, we can reduce the input size of the graph. Recall that G_k can be obtained in linear time (Lemma 2.19). A similar technique can also be used to design algorithms for enumerating all cuts of size exactly k (or less than $k + 1$). The following corollary lists some such results.

Corollary 2.30. *Let $G = (V, E)$ a multigraph.*

(i) *For two vertices $u, v \in V$, $\min\{k, \lambda(u, v; G)\}$ edge-disjoint (u, v)-paths can be found in $O(n + m + \min\{(kn)^{3/2}, m^{3/2}, k^2 n\})$ time (or in $O(m + \min\{kn^{5/3}, mn^{2/3}, k^2 n\})$ time if G is simple).*

(ii) *For two vertices $u, v \in V$, $\min\{k, \kappa(u, v; G)\}$ internally vertex-disjoint (u, v)-paths can be found in $O(n + m + \min\{kn^{3/2}, mn^{1/2}, k^2 n\})$ time.*

(iii) *For a simple graph G, the k-edge-connectivity can be tested in $O(m + k^2 n \log(n/k))$ time, and the edge-connectivity $\lambda = \lambda(G)$ together with a minimum cut can be computed in $O(m + \lambda^2 n \log(n/\lambda))$ time.*

(iv) *The k-vertex-connectivity of G can be tested in $O(n + m + \min\{k^{7/2}n, k^2 n^{7/4}\})$ time, and the vertex-connectivity $\kappa = \kappa(G)$ together with a minimum vertex cut can be computed in $O(m + \min\{\kappa^{7/2}n, \kappa^2 n^{7/4}\})$ time.* $\square$

Proof. (i) By using an MA ordering σ of G, we construct a certificate G_k from $\mathcal{F}(G, \sigma)$ in $O(n + m)$ time. By Theorem 2.26(i), G_k has $\min\{k, \lambda(u, v; G)\}$ edge-disjoint (u, v)-paths. By applying Theorem 1.20(i) and (iii) to G_k, such a set of (u, v)-paths can be found in $O(n + m + \min\{|E_k|^{3/2}, k|E_k|\}) = (n + m + \min\{(kn)^{3/2}, m^{3/2}, k^2 n\})$ time.

Similarly, conditions (ii)–(iv) follow from Theorem 1.21, Theorem 2.7, and Gabow's $O((n + \min\{k^{5/3}, kn^{3/4}\})m)$ time k-vertex-connectivity algorithm [98], respectively. $\square$

There are many other graph connectivity problems whose time bounds can be reduced by sparsification (see [96, 105, 121, 180, 179, 214, 232, 246, 247] for its applications).

2.2.6 Further Implications of Forest Decompositions

In the rest of this subsection, we derive some more useful properties which can be obtained from Theorem 2.28.

A subgraph H of a graph G is called (k, α)-*removable* in G if $G - E(H)$ remains to be a (k, α)-certificate of G. Mader [205] has proven that every k-vertex-connected graph G with the minimum degree $k + 2$ admits a cycle C whose removal still preserves the k-vertex-connectedness of G. Such a cycle is used as a key tool to prove some connectivity properties (see [24]). Berg and Jordán [23] first pointed out that the MA ordering can be used to obtain a (linear time) algorithm for the existence of such a removable cycle (in an ℓ-mixed p-connectivity version). A (k, α)-connectivity version of this result can be stated as follows.

Corollary 2.31 ([227]). *Let $G = (V, E)$ be an α-simple graph, and let k and h be positive integers such that $d(v; G) \geq k + h$ for all vertices $v \in V - s$, except for one vertex $s \in V$ for which $d(s; G) < k + h$ is allowed. Then G has a (k, α)-removable subgraph H which consists of h α-independent paths between some two adjacent vertices u and v.*   □

Proof. Consider $\mathcal{F}(G, \sigma) = (F_1, F_2, \ldots, F_m)$ for an MA ordering $\sigma = (v_1 = s, v_2, \ldots, v_n)$ of V in G starting with $v_1 = s$. Take G_k as a (k, α)-certificate of G, and consider the remaining subgraph $G_{k+1,m} = (V, F_{k+1} \cup F_{k+2} \cup \cdots \cup F_m)$, which is α-simple. By assumption on k and h, and $s \neq v_n$, $d(v_n; G) \geq k + h$ holds and there is an edge $e = \{v_j, v_n\} \in F_{k+h}$. By Lemma 2.25, σ is an MA ordering in $G_{k+1,m}$, and the e belongs to the hth forest in $\mathcal{F}(G_{k+1,m}, \sigma)$. Hence, by Theorem 2.28, $\lambda_\alpha(u, v; G_{k+1,m}) \geq h$, and $G_{k+1,m}$ contains a desired subgraph H.   □

From Corollary 2.31, we also have an extended result on removable cycles; that is, every α-simple graph G with $d(v; G) \geq k + 2, v \in V$ admits a (k, α)-removable cycle. By Corollary 2.31, Mader's result as noted earlier can be extended as follows: For a k-vertex-connected graph G with the minimum degree $k + h$, there are h internally vertex-disjoint paths between some two adjacent vertices whose removal leaves G k-vertex-connected.

Corollary 2.31 also tells that any edge-minimal (k, α)-connected spanning subgraph has a vertex u with degree k (otherwise we would have a removable edge). More generally we show that there is a pair of adjacent vertices u and v such that $\lambda_\alpha(u, v; G) = \min\{d(u; G), d(v; G)\}$.

Corollary 2.32 ([227]). *For an MA ordering $\sigma = (v_1, v_2, \ldots, v_n)$ of V in an α-simple graph $G = (V, E)$, let i^* be the largest index i with $\{v_i, v_n\} \in E$. Then for any integers j, h with $i^* \leq j < h \leq n$, it holds that $\lambda_\alpha(v_j, v_h; G) \geq d(v_n; G)$. In particular, $\lambda_\alpha(v_j, v_n; G) = d(v_n; G)$.*   □

Proof. Let $\ell = d(v_n; G)$. Since $\{v_{i^*}, v_n\} \in F_\ell$, all vertices $v_{i^*}, v_{i^*+1}, \ldots, v_{n-1}, v_n$ belong to the same component of (V, F_ℓ), as obvious from Lemma 2.25(iv). Hence, $\lambda_\alpha(v_j, v_h; G) \geq \ell$ holds by Theorem 2.28. Since $\lambda_\alpha(v_j, v_n; G) \leq \ell$ ($= d(v_n; G)$) is obvious, equality holds if $h = n$.   □

Mader [204, 207] has shown that every simple graph G has a pair of adjacent vertices u and v such that $\kappa(u, v; G) = \min\{d(u; G), d(v; G)\}$, and that every multigraph G has a pair of adjacent vertices u and v such that $\lambda(u, v; G) = \min\{d(u; G), d(v; G)\}$, where $\kappa(u, v; G)$ and $\lambda(u, v; G)$ denote the local vertex- and edge-connectivities, respectively. We see that the existence of such an edge e follows from Corollary 2.32 by setting $e = \{v_{i^*}, v_n\}$ and $\alpha(v) = 1$, $v \in V$ for the vertex-connectivity (resp. $\alpha(v) > d(v; G)$, $v \in V$ for the edge-connectivity). Thus, we have the following theorem.

Theorem 2.33 ([232]). *For a multigraph $G = (V, E)$, let v_{n-1} and v_n be the last two vertices in an MA ordering of G. Then*

(i) $\lambda(v_{n-1}, v_n; G) = d(v_n; G)$.
(ii) $\kappa(v_{n-1}, v_n; G) = d(v_n; G)$ *if G is simple.* □

This property that $\lambda(u, v; G)$ for some pair of vertices u and v can be determined by $d(v_n; G)$, where v_n can be computed by an MA ordering (i.e., in linear time), is used to design a simple and efficient algorithm for determining the edge connectivity of a multigraph G [232], as will be observed in Chapter 3.

2.2.7 k-Vertex-Connected Subset

We say that a subset $L \subseteq V$ of vertices is *k-vertex-connected* in a graph $G = (V, E)$ if $\kappa(u, v; G) \geq k$ for all $u, v \in L$ (note that L does not necessarily induces a k-vertex-connected subgraph). A pair of vertices u and v with $\kappa(u, v; G) = \min\{d(u; G), d(v; G)\} \geq k$ as discussed earlier can be considered as a k-vertex-connected set $L = \{u, v\}$. For $k \in \{2, 3, 4\}$, Mader [205] has proved that any graph G with degree at least k contains a k-vertex-connected subset L with $|L| \geq k$. By using MA ordering, Henzinger [120] has proven that any simple graph G with degree at least δ contains a k-vertex-connected subset L with $|L| \geq \delta + 2 - k$ for any $k \leq \delta$.

Lemma 2.34. *For a simple graph $G = (V, E)$, let $\sigma = (v_1, v_2, \ldots, v_n)$ be an MA ordering of V and let k be an integer with $0 \leq k \leq d(v_n; G)$. Then the set of last $d(v_n; G) + 2 - k$ vertices in σ is k-vertex-connected in G.* □

Henziger [120] and Nagamochi [222] used this property to design an efficient algorithm for approximating the vertex connectivity in a graph.

For the existence of a set of vertices that are (k, α)-connected, a common generalization of Corollary 2.32 and Lemma 2.34 can be stated in the following form.

Corollary 2.35 ([227]). *Let $G = (V, E)$ be an α-simple graph and let δ be a positive integer such that $d(v; G) \geq \delta$ holds for all vertices $v \in V - s$ (possibly $d(s; G) < \delta$ for $s \in V$). Then, for each positive integer $k \leq \delta$, G has a subset $X_k \subseteq V$ such that $\lambda_\alpha(u, v; G) \geq k$ for all pairs $u, v \in X_k$ and $|X_k| \geq (\delta - k + 1)/\overline{\alpha} + 1$, where $\overline{\alpha} = \alpha(X_k)/|X_k|$.* □

Proof. Let $\sigma = (v_1 = s, v_2, \ldots, v_n)$ be an MA ordering of V in G. By Lemma 2.24(i), forest $F_k \in \mathcal{F}(G, \sigma)$ has an edge $e = \{v_p, v_n\}$ incident to v_n. Let $X_k = \{v_p, v_{p+1}, \ldots, v_n\}$. Then $d(X_k - v_n, v_n; G) \geq d(v_n; G) - k + 1$. Analogously to the proof of Corollary 2.32, we see that $\lambda_\alpha(u, v; G) \geq k$ for all pairs $u, v \in X_k$. By the α-simplicity of G,

$$\sum_{u \in X_k - v_n} \min\{\alpha(u), \alpha(v_n)\} \geq d(X_k - v_n, v_n; G).$$

Hence, we have

$$
\begin{aligned}
(|X_k| - 1)\overline{\alpha} &\geq (|X_k| - 1)\min\{\alpha(v_n), \overline{\alpha}\} = \min\{\alpha(X_k) - \overline{\alpha}, (|X_k| - 1)\alpha(v_n)\} \\
&\geq \min\{\alpha(X_k) - \alpha(v_n), (|X_k| - 1)\alpha(v_n)\} \\
&\geq \sum_{u \in X_k - v_n} \min\{\alpha(u), \alpha(v_n)\} \\
&\geq d(X_k - v_n, v_n; G) \geq d(v_n; G) - k + 1 \geq \delta - k + 1,
\end{aligned}
$$

as required. □

Lemma 2.34 follows from Corollary 2.35 by setting $\alpha(v) = 1$, $v \in V$.

2.3 3-Edge-Connected Components

As a first application of the forest decomposition, in this section we devise a linear time algorithm for computing all 3-edge-connected components of a multigraph $G = (V, E)$. The forest decomposition used here can be any including the one obtained by an MA ordering.

A cut $E' = E(X, V - X) \subseteq E$ (defined in Section 1.1) is called a k-cut if $|E'| = k$. Let us define

$$
\begin{aligned}
E^1(G) &= \{\{u, v\} \in E \mid \lambda(u, v; G) = 1\}, \\
E^2(G) &= \{\{u, v\} \in E \mid \lambda(u, v; G) = 2\}, \\
E^3(G) &= \{\{u, v\} \in E \mid \lambda(u, v; G) \geq 3\}.
\end{aligned}
$$

Any edge $\{u, v\} \in E^1(G)$ is a 1-cut, and any edge $e \in E^2(G)$ is contained in a 2-cut. An inclusion-wise maximal subset $X \subseteq V$ such that $\lambda(u, v; G) \geq k$ for all $u, v \in X$ is called a k-edge-connected component (k-component, for short) of G, as defined in Section 1.5.2. A 1-component is simply a (connected) component.

By Lemma 1.36, the set of all k-components

$$M_k(G) = \{X_1, X_2, \ldots, X_p\}$$

of G is a partition of V. Clearly, $M_k(G) = \{V\}$ if and only if $\lambda(G) \geq k$. The purpose of this section is to compute $M_3(G)$ in linear time.

2.3.1 Properties of 2-Cuts in Maximal Spanning Forests F_1 and F_2

Let G be a graph that may not be connected. Clearly, $M_3(G)$ is the union of $M_3(G')$ for all connected components G' of G. Therefore, we assume in the rest of this section, unless otherwise stated, that G is connected. Now we show some properties of spanning forests and 2-cuts in a connected graph G.

Lemma 2.36. *Let F_1 be the edge set of a spanning tree of a connected graph $G = (V, E)$ (hence, F_1 is maximal), let F_2 be the edge set of an arbitrary maximal forest of $G - F_1$, and let $F_3 = E - F_1 - F_2$. Such F_1 and F_2 can be found in $O(n + m)$ time (e.g., by applying the depth-first search twice) and satisfy the following properties.*

(i) *$|F_i| \leq |V| - 1$ for $i = 1, 2$.*

(ii) *For each edge $e = \{u, v\} \in F_3$, there are three paths $P_i \subseteq F_i$, $i = 1, 2, 3$ connecting u and v (i.e., $\lambda(u, v; G) \geq 3$).*

(iii) *$E^2(G) \subseteq F_1 \cup F_2$.*

(iv) *All edges in the graph $G/(F_2 - E^2(G))$ belong to $F_1 \cup F_2$, where G/F denotes the graph obtained by contracting each edge $e \in F$ into a single vertex (see Section 1.1).* □

Proof. (i) Obvious.

(ii) Immediate from the maximality of forests F_1 and F_2.

(iii) Immediate from condition (ii).

(iv) It suffices to show that all edges in F_3 will be deleted in $G/(F_2 - E^2(G))$. Consider an edge $e = \{u, v\} \in F_3$. Then there is a path P in F_2 connecting u and v. Any edge $e' = \{u', v'\}$ in the path P satisfies $\lambda(u', v'; G) \geq 3$ (i.e., $e' \in E^3(G)$), since u' and v' are connected by a path $(P \cup \{e\}) - \{e'\}$ which is edge-disjoint to the path $P_1 \subseteq F_1$ of condition (ii), connecting u' and v'. Then $e' \in F_2 - E^2(G)$. Therefore, all such e' and, hence, e will be deleted as self-loops in $G/(F_2 - E^2(G))$. □

Lemma 2.37. *Let G be a connected graph.*

(i) *For an edge $e = \{u, v\} \in E^2(G)$, there is a path P connecting u and v without using e. This P contains all edges e' such that $\{e, e'\}$ is a 2-cut of G.*

(ii) *If $\{e_0, e_1\}$ and $\{e_0, e_2\}$ are 2-cuts of G, then $\{e_1, e_2\}$ is also a 2-cut.* □

Proof. (i) Such a P exists by Menger's theorem. If there is a 2-cut $\{e, e'\}$ such that $e' \notin P$, then u and v are connected by P in $G - \{e, e'\}$. This is a contradiction since 2-cut $\{e, e'\}$ must disconnect u and v by definition.

(ii) $G - \{e_0\}$ is connected by definition of a 2-cut. Then it is easy to see that e_1 and e_2 are two 1-cuts in $G - e_0$ and, hence, $G - \{e_0, e_1, e_2\}$ has exactly three components, G_1, G_2, and G_3. Thus, $G - \{e_1, e_2\}$ is not connected since edge e_0 can connect only two of G_1, G_2, and G_3. Therefore, $\{e_1, e_2\}$ is a 2-cut. □

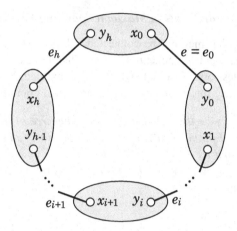

Figure 2.5. Edge set $S_e = \{e_0, e_1, \ldots, e_h\}$.

For an edge $e = \{x_0, y_0\} \in E^2(G)$ of a connected graph G, let S_e denote the edge set such that $e \in S_e$ and $e' \in S_e$ if and only if $\{e, e'\}$ is a 2-cut of G. By Lemma 2.37(i), $S_e - \{e\}$ is contained in any path P that connects x_0 and y_0 without using e. Lemma 2.37(ii) then tells us that any pair of edges in S_e is a 2-cut. Denote all the edges in S_e by

$$e = e_0 = \{x_0, y_0\}, \ e_1 = \{x_1, y_1\}, \ e_2 = \{x_2, y_2\}, \ldots, e_h = \{x_h, y_h\}, \qquad (2.8)$$

where edges are arranged in the order appearing in P from y_0 to x_0, as shown in Fig. 2.5.

We show that G is decomposed into $h + 1$ components in $G - S_e$. Clearly, vertices y_i and x_{i+1} (y_h and x_0) are connected by a subpath (possibly a null path) in $P - S_e$, and the number of components in $G - S_e$ is at most $h + 1$ (because any connected component contains at least one of these end vertices). If some x_i and x_j satisfying $0 \le i < j \le h$ are in the same connected component, it is easily seen that $G - \{e_i, e_j\}$ is connected, contradicting the preceding property that $\{e_i, e_j\}$ is a 2-cut. Moreover, $\lambda(y_i, x_{i+1 \ (\mathrm{mod}\ h+1)}; G - S_e) \ge 2$ since otherwise S_e would contain another 2-cut separating y_i and $x_{i+1 \ (\mathrm{mod}\ h+1)}$, contradicting the definition of S_e. Consequently, we have the following lemma.

Lemma 2.38. *For each edge $e \in E^2(G)$ in a connected graph G, define the edge set $S_e = \{e = \{x_0, y_0\}, \{x_1, y_1\}, \ldots, \{x_h, y_h\}\}$ as before. Then $G - S_e$ has exactly $h + 1$ components G_i, $i = 0, 1, \ldots, h$, where each G_i contains y_i and $x_{i+1 \ (\mathrm{mod}\ h+1)}$ (which are possibly identical) and $\lambda(y_i, x_{i+1 \ (\mathrm{mod}\ h+1)}; G) \ge 3$ holds.*   □

The order of edges (2.8) is independent of the choice of P, because if another path P' visits these end vertices in a different order, then $G - S_e$ has at least one component X containing $\{x_i, x_j\}$ with $i \ne j$ (or $\{x_i, y_j\}$ with $i + 1 \ne j$), contradicting Lemma 2.38.

2.3.2 Computing $E^2(G)$ from F_1 and F_2

Before presenting an algorithm for computing all 3-components of a graph G, we show that the set $E^2(G) \cap F_2$ and sets S_e for all $e \in E^2(G) \cap F_2$ can be found in linear time. Let $P_{uv} \subseteq F_1$ denote the unique path in F_1 connecting vertices u and v in G.

Lemma 2.39. *Let G be a 2-edge-connected graph. Then, an edge $e = \{u, v\} \in F_2$ belongs to $E^2(G)$ if and only if there is an edge $e' \in P_{uv}(\subseteq F_1)$ such that no other edge $e'' = \{u'', v''\} \in F_2 \cup F_3 - e$ satisfies $e' \in P_{u''v''}$. If $e \in E^2(G) \cap F_2$, then S_e is obtained by collecting all $e' \in F_1$ with such property.* □

Proof. Since the end vertices u and v of e are connected by path P_{uv}, a 2-cut E' with $e \in E'$ (if any) contains an edge $e' \in P_{uv} \subseteq F_1$. The only-if part is trivial, since if each $e' = \{u', v'\} \in P_{uv}(\subseteq F_1)$ is in path $P_{u''v''}$ for some $e'' = \{u'', v''\} \in F_2 \cup F_3$, then u' and v' remain connected in $G - \{e, e'\}$. We show the if part. Assume that, for some edge $e' \in P_{uv}$, there is no edge $e'' = \{u'', v''\} \in F_2 \cup F_3$ such that $e' \in P_{u''v''}$. Since G is 2-edge-connected, (V, F_1) is a spanning tree of G, and $(V, F_1 - e')$ consists of two connected components X and $V - X$. Since $e' \in P_{uv}$, it holds that $e \in E(X, V - X; G)$. If there is an edge $\hat{e} = \{\hat{u}, \hat{v}\} \in E(X, V - X; G) - \{e, e'\}$, then the end vertices of $\hat{e}$ are connected by path $P_{\hat{u},\hat{v}}(\subseteq F_1)$, which must contain e', contradicting the assumption. Moreover, $S_e - e$ consists of all such edges $e' \in F_1$. □

We first describe a naïve algorithm to find $E^2(G) \cap F_2$ and S_e for all $e \in E^2(G) \cap F_2$ by checking the condition of Lemma 2.39. Its time complexity will be improved later in this section. Let (V, F_1) be a spanning tree obtained by applying the depth-first search from a vertex, say z, and let the label $\ell[v]$ of vertex $v \in V$ be defined by the order visited by the depth-first search (see Section 1.2.2). The root vertex z has $\ell[z] = 1$. We orient each edge $e = \{u, v\} \in E$ from u to v so that e is visited when u is being visited by the depth-first search. Thus, $e \in F_1$ is directed from the end vertex with smaller label to the other end vertex with larger label while $e \in E - F_1$ is directed from the end vertex with larger label to the other end vertex with smaller label. We regard G and tree (V, F_1) as a digraph and an out-tree with root z, respectively. Let e_v denote the directed edge in F_1 with head v (which is unique unless $v = z$, in which case $e_z = \emptyset$). As observed in Section 1.2.2, each edge $e \notin F_1$ has its $h(e)$ in the path of F_1 from z to $t(e)$ (such a digraph G is termed a palm tree by Tarjan [297]). Therefore, such a path $P_{h(e)t(e)} \subseteq F_1$ for each $e \in E$ can be found in $O(|P_{h(e)t(e)}| + 1)$ time by traversing F_1 from $t(e)$ toward z.

The following algorithm to compute edges in $E^2(G) \cap F_2$ and their S_e consists of two major steps. In the first step, for each edge $e \in E_1$, we compute

$$count(e) = \begin{cases} +\infty & \text{if } e \in P_{h(e')t(e')} \text{ for some } e' \in F_3, \\ |\{e' \in F_2 \mid e \in P_{h(e')t(e')}\}| & \text{otherwise.} \end{cases}$$

$$(2.9)$$

If $count(e) = 1$, we also compute the edge $partner(e) := e' \in F_2$ with $e \in S_{e'}$. In the second step, we compute S_e for all $e \in F_2$, and then $E^2(G) \cap F_2$. To facilitate computing $\{count(e) \mid e \in F_1|\}$, we use the following weights for edges $e' \in F_2 \cup F_3$:

$$weight(e') = \begin{cases} 1 & \text{if } e' \in F_2, \\ +\infty & \text{if } e' \in F_3. \end{cases} \tag{2.10}$$

Algorithm TRACE

Input: A 2-edge-connected graph $G = (V, E)$ and a partition F_1, F_2, F_3 of E as defined in Lemma 2.36, where each vertex $v \in V$ has label $\ell[v]$ of the depth-first search, each edge $e \in E$ has its head $h(e)$ and tail $t(e)$, and e_v denotes the edge $e \in F_1$ with $h(e) = v$.

Output: $E^2(G) \cap F_2$ and $\{S_e \mid e \in E^2(G) \cap F_2\}$.

/* Step 1 */
$count(e) := 0$ and $partner(e) := \emptyset$ for all $e \in F_1$;
$weight(e') := 1$ for all $e' \in F_2$;
$weight(e') := +\infty$ for all $e' \in F_3$;
$Q := F_2 \cup F_3$;
while $Q \neq \emptyset$ **do**
   Choose an edge e' from Q and let $Q := Q - \{e'\}$; $v := t(e')$;
   while $\ell[v] > \ell[h(e')]$ **do** /* Tracing path $P_{h(e')t(e')}$ */
      $count(e_v) := count(e_v) + weight(e')$; $partner(e_v) := e'$; $v := t(e_v)$
   end /* inner while */
end; /* outer while */
/* Step 2 */
$S_{e'} := \{e'\}$ for $e' \in F_2$;
/* $S_{e'}$ will represent an ordered set of the edges arranged as in (2.8) */
for each $e \in F_1$ (picking up $e \in F_1$ in the order visited by the depth-first search) **do**
   if $count(e) = 1$ **then** $S_{e'} := S_{e'} \cup \{e\}$ for $e' = partner(e)$
   end; /* for */
$E^2(G) \cap F_2 := \{e' \in F_2 \mid S_{e'} \neq \{e'\}\}$
end.

The correctness of the TRACE algorithm follows from Lemma 2.39. The time complexity of Step 1 is $O(|F_2 \cup F_3||F_1|)$ as a path in F_1 is traced for each $e' \in Q$ in Step 1, while the time complexity of Step 2 is obviously $O(n + m)$.

Example 2.40. Figure 2.6 shows a graph G^1 to which TRACE is applied, where $z = v_1$ is the root and v_i ($i = 1, 2, \ldots, 13$) represents the ith vertex visited by the depth-first search to find F_1 (i.e., $\ell[v_i] = i$). By applying TRACE, we obtain $E^2(G^1) \cap F_2 = \{e_1 = \{v_{13}, z\}, e_2 = \{v_{11}, v_8\}\}$, $S_{e_1} = \{e_1, e_3 = \{z, v_8\}, e_4 = \{v_9, v_{12}\}\}$ and $S_{e_2} = \{e_2, e_5 = \{v_9, v_{10}\}\}$. $\qquad\qquad\square$

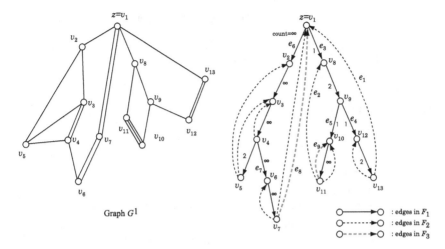

Figure 2.6. Graph G^1 and its orientation (the numbers beside edges e in F_1 denote $count(e)$ upon completion of TRACE).

To make the computation time linear, we modify Step 1 of TRACE so that, once $count(e) \geq 2$ holds for an edge $e \in F_1$, e will never be traversed later. During the execution of TRACE, denote by F_1^* the set of edges $e \in F_1$ with $count(e) \geq 2$, and prepare a pointer $p : V \to V$ such that $p(v)$ is the highest ancestor of v such that $P_{vp(v)} \subseteq F_1^*$ (i.e., $count(e_{p(v)}) < 2$ or $p(v) = z$). In particular, $p(v) = v$ holds if $count(e_v) < 2$. While tracing up the path $P_{h(e')t(e')}$ for a given edge $e' \in Q$, this pointer p enables us to skip all subpaths contained in F_1^*. However, p must be updated carefully. In general, whenever a new edge $e \in F_1$ is labeled $count(e) \geq 2$, $p(v)$ of all v with $p(v) = h(e)$ must be updated as $p(v) := p(t(e))$ (i.e., the subpath in F_1^* ending at $h(e)$ is merged with the subpath starting from $t(e)$), and the overall time required for this can be $O(nm)$. However, we show below that, if edges $e' \in Q$ in Step 1 are selected in the nondecreasing order of $\ell[h(e')]$, then no two maximal subpaths $\subseteq F_1^*$ are merged (i.e., the update chain mentioned earlier does not occur). Such an order of selecting $e' \in Q$ is realized by visiting all the vertices v in V in the depth-first search manner, each time picking up all the edges that are remaining in Q and are incident to v.

Lemma 2.41. *Assume that edges e' in Q are selected in Step 1 of the* TRACE *algorithm in the nondecreasing order of $\ell[h(e')]$. Then, when a new edge $e \in F_1$ is labeled $count(e) \geq 2$, there is no vertex $v \in V$ except for $h(e)$ such that $p(v) = h(e)$.* $\square$

Proof. Assume that there is a vertex $v \neq h(e)$ with $p(v) = h(e)$, when $e \in F_1$ is labeled $count(e) \geq 2$ by tracing path $P_{h(e')t(e')} \subseteq F_1$ for the current $e' \in Q$. Since $p(v) = h(e)$ means $P_{vh(e)} \subseteq F_1^*$, there was an edge $e'' \in Q$ with $h(e'') = h(e)$ which was scanned before e'. However, since e is in path $P_{h(e')t(e')}$, we have $\ell[h(e')] < \ell[h(e'')]$, a contradiction. $\square$

Now we are ready to describe a linear time implementation of Step 1 of TRACE.

/* Step 1 */
$count(e) := 0$ and $partner(e) := \emptyset$ for all $e \in F_1$;
$weight(e') := 1$ for all $e' \in F_2$;
$weight(e') := +\infty$ for all $e' \in F_3$;
$p(v) := v$ for all $v \in V$;
$Q := F_2 \cup F_3$;
while $Q \neq \emptyset$ **do**
    Choose an edge $e' \in Q$ with the smallest $\ell[h(e')]$, and let $Q := Q - \{e'\}$;
    $v := p(t(e'))$;
    while $\ell[v] > \ell[h(e')]$ **do**
        $count(e_v) := count(e_v) + weight(e')$; $partner(e_v) := e'$;
        if $count(e_v) \geq 2$ **then** $p(v) := p(t(e_v))$;
        /* After this, edges from $t(e_v)$ to $p(v)$ will be skipped */
        $v := p(t(e_v))$
    end /* inner while */
end. /* outer while */

Lemma 2.42. *The modified Step* 1 *of the* TRACE *algorithm runs in* $O(n + m)$ *time.* ◻

Proof. It is clear by Lemma 2.41 that the pointer p computed in the preceding algorithm is correct; that is, $P_{vp(v)}$ for each $v \in V$ denotes the subpath of $P_{vz} \subseteq F_1$ such that $P_{vp(v)} \subseteq F_1^*$ and either $count(e_{p(v)}) < 2$ or $p(v) = z$. This means that each edge $e \in F_1$ is traversed at most three times when $count(e)$ is updated to 0, 1, and 2 (or $+\infty$) during the whole computation of Step 1. Therefore, the total time of the inner while-loop is $O(|E| + |F_1|) = O(n + m)$. Choosing all edges e' from Q in the nondecreasing order of $\ell[t(e')]$ is also done in $O(n + m)$ time by following the depth-first search used to compute F_1. The rest of the computation is minor. ◻

Note that the sets S_e for $e \subset F_2 \cap E^2(G)$ computed by TRACE can detect some 2-cuts in G, that is, those $\{e', e''\}$ such that $e', e'' \in S_e$ for some $e \in F_2 \cap E^2(G)$. However, there are other types of 2-cuts $\{e_1, e_2\}$ such that $e_1, e_2 \in F_1 \cap E^2(G)$, but neither $\{e_1, e\}$ nor $\{e_2, e\}$ is the 2-cut for any $e \in F_2$. These are not found by the algorithm TRACE. For example, the 2-cut $\{e_6 = \{z, v_2\}, e_7 = \{v_4, v_6\}\}$ in G^1 of Fig. 2.6 is not found by TRACE. To detect such 2-cuts, we will transform G into a smaller graph and apply TRACE recursively, as will be described next.

2.3.3 Graph Transformations Preserving 3-Edge Connectivity

We introduce transformations of a 2-edge-connected graph $G = (V, E)$, which preserve all 3-components of G. If G has a vertex v with degree 2, then we construct the graph

$$G_v = (V, E \cup \{e'\} - E(v, V - v; G)) \text{ for a vertex } v \text{ with degree 2,}$$

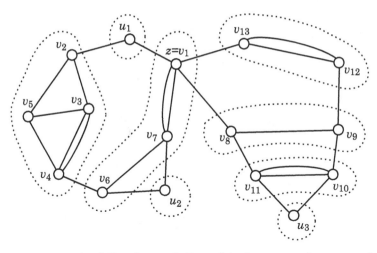

Figure 2.7. Graph G^2 (dotted curves indicate all 3-edge-connected components).

where e' is the new edge connecting the two vertices adjacent to v (note that v is not deleted but isolated). It is easy to see $M_3(G_v) = M_3(G)$. Let $G{\downarrow} \deg 2$ denote the graph obtained by repeating this operation for all vertices v with degree 2. Then

$$M_3(G{\downarrow} \deg 2) = M_3(G).$$

Also $E^1(G{\downarrow} \deg 2) = \emptyset$ holds (as $E^1(G) = \emptyset$ holds since G is 2-edge-connected) and each nontrivial component H' of $G{\downarrow} \deg 2$ satisfies $\delta(H') \geq 3$, where δ denotes the minimum degree. For example, $G^2{\downarrow} \deg 2$ for G^2 in Fig. 2.7, which has vertices u_1, u_2, u_3 with degree 2, becomes G^1 of Fig. 2.6, where three isolated vertices u_1, u_2, u_3 are not shown.

We now consider another transformation. Let $G = (V, E)$ be a 2-edge-connected graph. Take an edge $e \in E^2(G)$ together with the edge set $S_e = \{e = \{x_0, y_0\}, \{x_1, y_1\}, \ldots, \{x_h, y_h\}\}$ of (2.8) and consider the graph

$$G{\downarrow}e = (V, (E - S_e) \cup D_e) \tag{2.11}$$

by defining a set of new edges

$$D_e = \{\{y_0, x_1\}, \{y_1, x_2\}, \ldots, \{y_{h-1}, x_h\}, \{y_h, x_0\}\} \tag{2.12}$$

from which any $\{y_i, x_{i+1 \ (\text{mod } h+1)}\}$ with $y_i = x_{i+1}$ is deleted as a self-loop. Figure 2.8 illustrates $G{\downarrow}e$, corresponding to Fig. 2.5.

Note that $G{\downarrow}e$ is unique. By Lemma 2.38, any two sets $\{y_i, x_{i+1}\}$ and $\{y_j, x_{j+1}\}$ with $i \neq j$ belong to different components in $G{\downarrow}e$. Thus, $G{\downarrow}e$ has $h + 1$ components, whose vertex sets are the same as those in G_i of Lemma 2.38. We show

$$\lambda(y_i, x_{i+1}; G{\downarrow}e) \geq 3 \text{ for each } \{y_i, x_{i+1}\} \in D_e. \tag{2.13}$$

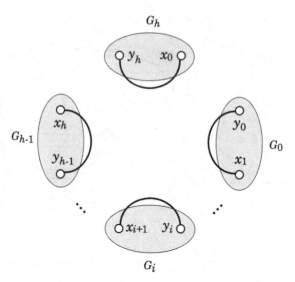

Figure 2.8. Transformed graph $G{\downarrow}e$.

Assume $y_i \neq x_{i+1}$, since otherwise $\lambda(y_i, x_{i+1}; G{\downarrow}e) = \infty$. First $\lambda(y_i, x_{i+1}; G{\downarrow} e) \geq 2$ holds since these end vertices are now connected by edge $\{y_i, x_{i+1}\}$ and a subpath of $P - S_e$, where P is any path in G connecting the end vertices of e without using e. On the other hand, if $\lambda(y_i, x_{i+1}; G{\downarrow}e) = 2$, then there is a 2-cut $\{(y_i, x_{i+1}), e'\}$ with $e' \in P - S_e$. In this case, it is easy to see that x_{i+1} and y_{i+1} are disconnected in $G - \{e', e_{i+1} = (x_{i+1}, y_{i+1})\}$, i.e., $\{e', e_{i+1}\}$ is a 2-cut in G. Since $\{e, e_{i+1}\}$ is a 2-cut in G by definition, $\{e', e\}$ is also a 2-cut in G by Lemma 2.37(ii). However, this implies $e' \in S_e$, a contradiction.

Lemma 2.43. *Let G be a 2-edge-connected graph, and define $G{\downarrow}e$ for an $e \in E^2(G)$ as before.*

  (i) *$M_3(G) = M_3(G{\downarrow}e)$.*
 (ii) *Any 2-cut F in G with $F \cap S_e = \emptyset$ is a 2-cut in $G{\downarrow}e$.*
(iii) *Any 1-cut F (resp. 2-cut F) in $G{\downarrow}e$ is a 1-cut (resp. 2-cut) in G and satisfies $F \cap S_e = \emptyset$.*
 (iv) *$E^1(G{\downarrow}e) = \emptyset$, that is, each component of $G{\downarrow}e$ is 2-edge-connected.*   □

Proof. Let D_e be the set of the new edges in (2.12) added to $G{\downarrow}e$ in (2.11).

  (i) It suffices to show that, for $u \neq v$, $\lambda(u, v; G) \geq 3$ if and only if $\lambda(u, v; G{\downarrow}e) \geq 3$. It is easy to see that any $u, v \in V$ with $\lambda(u, v; G) \geq 3$ belong to the same component of $G - S_e$ (i.e., a G_i of Lemma 2.38). Any path in G, connecting u and v without using $\{e_i = \{x_i, y_i\}, e_{i+1} = \{x_{i+1}, y_{i+1}\}\}$ is in $G{\downarrow}e$, whereas any path P that connects u and v via edges e_i and e_{i+1} becomes the path P' in $G{\downarrow}e$ obtained from P by replacing the subpath of P outside G_i with edge $\{y_i, x_{i+1}\} \in D_e$. Thus, $\lambda(u, v; G) \geq 3$ means $\lambda(u, v; G{\downarrow}e) \geq 3$. The converse can be similarly shown.

(ii) For such F, let $X \subseteq V$ satisfy $E(X, V - X; G) = F$. If $E(X, V - X; G \downarrow e) - F$ has an edge $\{u, v\}$, then $\{u, v\} \in D_e$ and $\lambda(u, v; G) \geq 3$ from (2.13) and condition (i). This contradicts $|E(X, V - X; G)| \leq 2$.

(iii) For such F, let $G_F = (V_F, E_F)$ be the component of $G \downarrow e$ containing the edges in F, whose vertex set is equal to one of G_i in Lemma 2.38; that is, V_F contains y_i and x_{i+1}. Let $G' = (X', E')$ be one of the components in $G_F - F$. Therefore, $E(X', V - X'; G \downarrow e) = F$ and $F \cap D_e = \emptyset$ by (2.13). Hence, $\{y_i, x_{i+1}\}$ is contained in X' or $V_F - X'$ (i.e., $E(X', V - X'; G) = E(X'; G \downarrow e) = F$).

(iv) Obvious from condition (iii) and $E^1(G) = \emptyset$.   □

Call two edges $e, e' \in E^2(G)$ *independent* if $\{e, e'\}$ is not a 2-cut. The following lemma gives some properties of an independent pair.

Lemma 2.44. *Let G be a 2-edge-connected graph.*

(i) *Any pair of $e, e' \in E^2(G) \cap F_2$ is independent.*

(ii) *If a pair of $e, e' \in E^2(G)$ is independent, then $S_e \cap S_{e'} = \emptyset$ and $e' \in E^2(G \downarrow e)$. Furthermore, the order (2.8) of edges in $S_{e'}$ in G remains unchanged in $G \downarrow e$.*   □

Proof. (i) Obvious since $G - \{e, e'\}$ is connected by the edge set F_1.

(ii) If $S_e \cap S_{e'}$ has an edge e'', then $\{e, e''\}$ and $\{e', e''\}$ are 2-cuts in G and so is $\{e, e'\}$ by Lemma 2.37(ii), contradicting the independence of e and e'. Then $e' \in E^2(G \downarrow e)$ by Lemma 2.43(ii). Therefore, $S_{e'}$ is in one component of $G \downarrow e$ (i.e., of $G - S_e$). From the maximality of S_e, it is easy to see that no edge in $S_{e'}$ is a 1-cut in $G - S_e$. Thus, $e' \in E^2(G - S_e)$, and $S_{e'}$ is included in a cycle C' containing e' in $G - S_e$. Since such C' is also a cycle in $G \downarrow e$, we see that the ordering of edges (2.8) in $S_{e'}$ is the same in G and $G \downarrow e$.   □

Now we consider the edge contraction G/E' for an edge set $E' \subseteq E$. Let $[X]_G$ for a subset X of vertices in G/E' stand for the set of all vertices in V that are contracted to some vertices in X. Similarly, $\{[X_1]_G, [X_2]_G, \ldots, [X_p]_G\}$ for $M_3(G/E') = \{X_1, X_2, \ldots, X_p\}$ is denoted by $[M_3(G/E')]_G$. For example, the 3-components of G^1/E' for the graph G^1 in Fig. 2.6 with $E' = \{e_8 = \{v_1, v_7\}, e_9 = \{v_{10}, v_{11}\}\}$ are given by $M_3(G^1/E') = \{X_1 = \{v_1', v_6\}, X_2 = \{v_2, v_3, v_4, v_5\}, X_3 = \{v_8, v_9\}, X_4 = \{v_{10}'\}, X_5 = \{v_{12}, v_{13}\}\}$, where v_1' and v_{10}' denote the vertices contracted from edges e_8 and e_9, respectively. See Fig. 2.9, which shows G^1/E' and $M_3(G^1/E')$. For this example, we have $[M_3(G^1/E')]_{G^1} = \{[X_1]_{G^1} = \{v_1, v_6, v_7\}, [X_2]_{G^1} = X_2, [X_3]_{G^1} = X_3, [X_4]_{G^1} = \{v_{10}, v_{11}\}, [X_5]_{G^1} = X_5\}$.

Lemma 2.45. *Let a multigraph G be 2-edge-connected and let an edge set $E'' \subseteq E^3(G)$ be given. Then the following properties hold.*

(i) $M_3(G) = [M_3(G/E'')]_G$.

(ii) $E^1(G/E'') = \emptyset$, *i.e.,* G/E'' *is 2-edge-connected.*   □

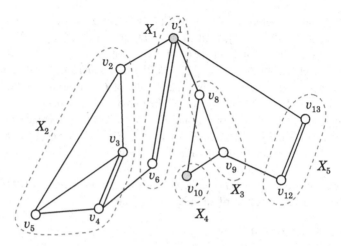

Figure 2.9. Graph G^1/E' obtained from graph G^1 in Fig. 2.6 and $E' = \{e_8 = \{v_1, v_7\}, e_9 = \{v_{10}, v_{11}\}\}$, where dotted curves indicates all 3-components in $M_3(G^1/E')$.

Proof. (i) It is sufficient to consider the case of $E'' = \{e\}$ with $e = \{u, v\} \in E^3(G)$. Let w denote the vertex contracted from u and v, and $G/\{e\} = (V', E')$, where $V' = (V \cup \{w\}) - \{u, v\}$. We have the following properties (a) and (b).

(a) $\lambda(x, y; G) \geq 3$ for vertices x and y such that $\{x, y\} \neq \{u, v\}$ means $\lambda(x, y; G/\{e\}) \geq 3$, because any cut in $G/\{e\}$ is a cut in G.
(b) $\lambda(x, y; G/\{e\}) \geq 3$ for vertices $x \neq y$ means $\lambda(x, y; G) = \lambda(x, y; G/\{e\}) \geq 3$, because any cut $E(X, V - X; G)$ in G satisfying $x \in X, y \in V - X$, and $|E(X, V - X; G)| < 3$ has the property that $u, v \in X$ or $u, v \in V - X$ by the assumption $e = \{u, v\} \in E^3(G)$ and, hence, is a cut in $G/\{e\}$.

Let $M_3(G/\{e\}) = \{X_1, X_2, \ldots, X_p\}$, where X_1 is assumed to contain w. For any vertex $z \in X_i$ ($i = 2, 3, \ldots, p$), we have

$$\{y \in V' \mid \lambda(z, y; G/\{e\}) \geq 3\} = \{y \in V \mid \lambda(z, y; G) \geq 3\}$$

from properties (a) and (b). Similarly, we have

$$\{y \in V' \mid \lambda(w, y; G/\{e\}) \geq 3\} = (\{y \in V \mid \lambda(u, y; G) \geq 3\} \cup \{w\}) - \{u, v\}$$

for vertex $w \in X_1$ from properties (a) and (b) (since $e = \{u, v\} \in E^3(G)$ implies that $\lambda(u, y; G) \geq 3$ if and only if $\lambda(v, y; G) \geq 3$). This shows

$$M_3(G) = \{[X_1]_G, [X_2]_G, \ldots, [X_p]_G\}.$$

(ii) Obvious from the property that any 1-cut in $G/\{e\}$ is a 1-cut in G, since G is assumed to be 2-edge-connected.   □

Now we combine the preceding transformations $G \downarrow \deg 2$, $G \downarrow e$, and G/E''. For each S_e, $e \in E^2(G) \cap F_2$, found by the TRACE algorithm, we apply transformation $G := G \downarrow e$ successively (this is possible via Lemma 2.44). The resulting graph G' satisfies $M_3(G') = M_3(G)$ by Lemma 2.43(i). Let

$$D = \cup\{D_e \mid e \in E^2(G) \cap F_2\}$$

be the set of all the added edges in the process of obtaining G'. Clearly, $\lambda(u, v; G') \geq 3$ for any edge $e = \{u, v\} \in F_2 - E^2(G)$ by definition and for any edge $e = \{u, v\} \in D$ by (2.13).

Next consider the transformation

$$G'' = G'/(D \cup (F_2 - E^2(G))). \tag{2.14}$$

By Lemma 2.45(i), $M_3(G) = M_3(G') = [M_3(G'')]_G$ holds. Also every component of G'' is 2-edge-connected by Lemmas 2.43(iv) and 2.45(ii). Furthermore, all edges in $F_3 \cup (F_2 - E^2(G)) \cup D$ are deleted in $G/(D \cup (F_2 - E^2(G)))$ by Lemma 2.36(iv); that is,

$$\text{all edges remaining in } G'' \text{ belong to } F_1. \tag{2.15}$$

2.3.4 Algorithm to Compute all 3-Components of G

The following algorithm finds the set of all 3-components $M_3(G)$ of a 2-edge-connected multigraph G. It applies the aforementioned recursive procedure to compute G'' of (2.14) from G. REDUCE is a key procedure that returns $M_3(G)$ from a given 2-edge-connected G by such a recursive algorithm.

Algorithm 3COMPONENTS
Input: A 2-edge-connected connected multigraph G.
Output: $M_3(G)$.
$\quad G := G \downarrow \deg 2;$
$\quad$ Let $G_i, i = 1, 2, \ldots, q$, be the connected components of G;
$\quad M := \emptyset;$
$\quad$ **for** $i := 1, 2, \ldots, q$ **do**
$\quad\quad$ **if** $G_i = (V_i, E_i)$ is trivial **then** $M := M \cup \{V_i\}$
$\quad\quad\quad$ **else** REDUCE $(G_i, M_i);\quad M := M \cup M_i$
$\quad\quad$ **end** /* if */
$\quad$ **end**; /* for */
$\quad M_3(G) := M.$

Procedure REDUCE(G, M)
Input: A nontrivial 2-edge-connected multigraph $G = (V, E)$ with $\delta(G) \geq 3$.
Output: $M = M_3(G)$.
$\quad$ Compute a spanning tree (V, F_1) by the depth-first search and a partition
$\quad\quad F_1, F_2,$ and F_3 of E as stated in Lemma 2.36;
$\quad$ Find $E^2(G) \cap F_2$ and S_e for all $e \in E^2(G) \cap F_2$ by Algorithm TRACE;
$\quad G' := G; D := \emptyset;$
$\quad$ **for** each $e \in E^2(G) \cap F_2$ **do**
$\quad\quad G' := G' \downarrow e;\quad D := D \cup D_e$
$\quad$ **end**; /* for */

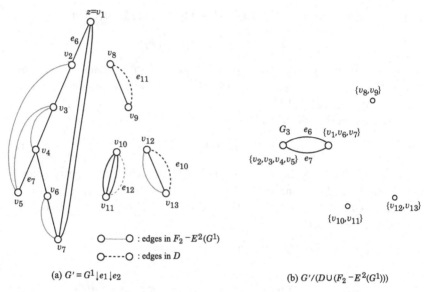

Figure 2.10. Computation of all 3-edge-connected components of G^1 in Fig. 2.6.

$G'' := G'/(D \cup (F_2 - E^2(G)))$;
$G'' := G'' \downarrow \deg 2$;
Let G_i, $i = 1, 2, \ldots, q$, be the connected components of G'';
$M := \emptyset$;
for $i := 1, 2, \ldots, q$ **do**
  if G_i is trivial **then** $M_i := M \cup G_i$
  else REDUCE(G_i, M_i); $M := M \cup [M_i]_{G''}$
  end /* if */
end; /* for */
Return M.

Example 2.46. We apply the 3COMPONENTS algorithm to G^2 in Fig. 2.7. After obtaining $G^2 \downarrow \deg 2$, which is G^1 of Fig. 2.6 and three isolated vertices $\{u_1\}$, $\{u_2\}$, $\{u_3\}$ (trivial 3-components), it executes REDUCE(G^1, M). It then calls the TRACE algorithm and obtains $E^2(G^1) \cap F_2 = \{e_1, e_2\}$, $S_{e_1} = \{e_1, e_3, e_4\}$, and $S_{e_2} = \{e_2, e_3\}$ as discussed in Example 2.40. Based on these, G^1 is partitioned into four components, which are shown in Fig. 2.10(a), after executing operation $G^1 \downarrow e$ for $e_1, e_2 \in E^2(G^1) \cap F_2$, where $D = D_{e_1} \cup D_{e_2}$, $D_{e_1} = \{e_{10} = \{v_{12}, v_{13}\}, e_{11} = \{v_8, v_9\}\}$ and $D_{e_2} = \{e_{12} = \{v_{10}, v_{11}\}\}$. We then contract edges in $D \cup (F_2 - E^2(G^1))$, and we obtain three trivial graphs and G^3 with edges $\{e_6, e_7\}$ as shown in Fig. 2.10(b). After performing REDUCE(G^3, M) recursively, REDUCE(G^1, M) returns

$$M = M_3(G^1) = \{\{v_1, v_6, v_7\}, \{v_2, v_3, v_4, v_5\}, \{v_8, v_9\}, \{v_{10}, v_{11}\}, \{v_{12}, v_{13}\}\}.$$

Finally, $M_3(G^2) = M_3(G^1) \cup \{\{u_1\}, \{u_2\}, \{u_3\}\}$ is output by 3COMPONENTS. □

Theorem 2.47. *For a 2-edge-connected graph* $G = (V, E)$, *algorithm* 3COMPONENTS *correctly computes* $M_3(G)$, *in* $O(n + m)$ *time.* □

Proof. The correctness follows from the discussion so far. We now analyze its time complexity. Clearly, one execution of REDUCE(G, M) is done in $O(n + m)$ time by Lemmas 2.42–2.45, if the time for recursive calls of REDUCE is ignored. Now consider a 2-edge-connected graph $G = (V, E)$ with $\delta(G) \geq 3$ to which REDUCE(G, M) is applied. Since $\delta(G) \geq 3$,

$$|E| \geq |V|\delta(G)/2 \geq 1.5|V|. \tag{2.16}$$

Let $G'' = (V'', E'')$ be the graph obtained after edge contraction $G'/(D \cup (F_2 - E^2(G)))$. By (2.15),

$$|E''| \leq |F_1| \leq |V| - 1.$$

Combining this and (2.16), we have

$$|E''| < |V| \leq (2/3)|E|,$$

where E'' may also be considered the set of edges in all components G_i, $i = 1, 2, \ldots, q$, of $G'' := G'' \downarrow \deg 2$. From this, the total time required to perform 3COMPONENTS (i.e., recursive calls of REDUCE) to compute $M_3(G)$ is proportional to

$$|E| + (2/3)|E| + (2/3)^2|E| + \cdots = O(|E|). \qquad \Box$$

Corollary 2.48. *Deciding whether or not a connected graph* $G = (V, E)$ *is 3-edge-connected is done in* $O(n + m)$ *time.* □

Proof. Obvious from Theorem 2.47 since G is 3-edge-connected if and only if $M_3(G) = \{V\}$. □

2.3.5 Computing All 2-Cuts

All 2-cuts in a 2-edge-connected graph $G = (V, E)$ can be listed as follows. First compute $M_3(G)$ by the preceding algorithm and let $G' = (V', E')$ be the graph obtained from G by contracting each 3-component of G into a vertex (Fig. 2.11 shows such graph G' corresponding to G^2 of Fig. 2.7). Note that $E^1(G') = \emptyset$ by the assumption that G is 2-edge-connected. Furthermore, $E^2(G') \neq \emptyset$ if and only if $\lambda(G) = 2$. If $\lambda(G) = 2$, it holds that $E^2(G') = E^2(G)$ and $E^3(G') = \emptyset$. Therefore, the set of all 2-cuts in G is the same as that of G'. By Lemma 2.38, we see that, for each edge $e \in E^2(G)$, two vertices y_i and $x_{i+1 \pmod{h+1}}$ in (2.8) for $i = 0, 1, \ldots, h$ will be contracted into the single vertex in G', implying that the edges in S_e form a cycle in G'. Hence, G' is a cactus (defined in Section 1.5.4). Cactus G' in Fig. 2.11 consists of five cycles $C_1, C_2, \ldots, C_5$, where, for example, C_1 is the cycle consisting of edges in S_e for edge $e = \{v_4, v_6\}$ in graph G^2 of Fig. 2.7.

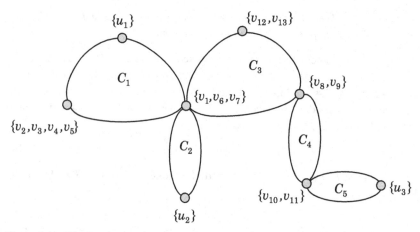

Figure 2.11. The graph obtained from multigraph G^1 in Fig. 2.6 by contracting each 3-edge-connected component into a single vertex.

Therefore, to obtain all 2-cuts of G', we find all cycles $C_1, C_2, \ldots, C_q$ in G', which constitute $E^2(G')$, by applying the depth-first search to G' (see Section 1.2.2), and the set of all 2-cuts is given by

$$\bigcup_{i=1,2,\ldots,q} \{\{e, e'\} \mid e \text{ and } e' \text{ are in one } C_i\}.$$

In other words, G' is a cactus representation $(\mathcal{R}, \varphi)$, as discussed in Section 1.5.4, for all minimum cuts in a 2-edge-connected graph, where $\mathcal{R} = G'$ and φ is the mapping from a vertex v to the node in G' into which v is contracted. In this case, no empty node is introduced to $\mathcal{R} = G'$. Any minimum cut $\{X, V - X\}$ in G corresponds to a minimum cut $\{S, V(\mathcal{R}) - S\}$ in $\mathcal{R}$ such that $S = \cup_{v \in X} \varphi(v)$. For example, minimum cut $\{X = \{u_1, v_2, v_3, v_4, v_5\}, V - X\}$ in graph G^2 of Fig. 2.7 is represented by minimum cut $\{S = \{\{u_1\}, \{v_2, v_3, v_4, v_5\}\}, V(\mathcal{R}) - S\}$ in the cactus $\mathcal{R} = G'$ of Fig. 2.11.

2.4 2-Approximation Algorithms for Connectivity

2.4.1 $(2 + \varepsilon)$-Approximation to Edge-Connectivity

Based on a forest decomposition, Matula [214] has given a linear time algorithm for finding a cut in a multigraph whose size is at most $(2 + \varepsilon)$ as large as the minimum, where $\varepsilon > 0$ can be arbitrarily specified. That is, it is a $(2 + \varepsilon)$-approximation algorithm (see Section 1.2) for the edge-connectivity of a given graph G. Here we describe a version refined by Karger and Motwani [180].

Algorithm EC-APPROX

Input: A connected multigraph $G = (V, E)$ $(n \geq 2)$ and a constant $\varepsilon > 0$.
Output: A subset $X \subset V$ such that $d(X, V - X; G) \leq (2 + \varepsilon)\lambda(G)$.

$G' := G; \bar{\lambda} := +\infty;$
while $|V(G')| > 1$ **do**
  if $\delta(G') < \bar{\lambda}$ **then**
    $\bar{\lambda} := \delta(G');$ /*(G') denotes the minimum degree of G' */
    Let $x^* \in V(G')$ be a vertex with $d(x^*; G') = \delta(G')$
  end; /* if */
  Find a forest decomposition $\mathcal{F} = (F'_1, F'_2, \ldots, F'_{|E'|})$ of $G' = (V', E')$;
  $k := \left\lceil \dfrac{\bar{\lambda}}{2 + \varepsilon} \right\rceil;$
  $G' := G'/F'_k$
end; /* while */
Output the set X of all vertices in V that have been contracted into the current x^*.

Theorem 2.49 ([214]). *For a connected multigraph G, EC-Approx correctly finds a cut X in G such that*

$$d(X, V - X; G) \le (2 + \varepsilon)\lambda(G) \tag{2.17}$$

after $O(\log m)$ iterations of the while-loop. EC-Approx can be implemented to run in $O(n + m)$ time. □

Proof. We first show that EC-Approx halts after $O(\log m)$ iterations. For this, we prove that, after each iteration of the while-loop, the number of edges in $G'/F'_k = (V'', E'')$ decreases by a constant factor $2/(2 + \varepsilon)$ compared to that of $G' = (V', E')$. Recall that by (1.8) it holds that

$$|E'| \ge \delta(G')|V'|/2. \tag{2.18}$$

By Lemma 2.2(i), we see that contracting the edges in F'_k in G' also removes all edges in F'_j with $j > k$ as self-loops in the resulting graph G'/F'_k. Hence,

$$|E''| \le |F'_1 \cup F'_2 \cup \cdots \cup F'_{k-1}| \le (k - 1)(|V'| - 1). \tag{2.19}$$

From (2.18), (2.19), $k := \lceil \bar{\lambda}/(2 + \varepsilon) \rceil$, and $\bar{\lambda} \le \delta(G')$ as defined in EC-Approx, we get

$$|E''| \le \left(\left\lceil \frac{\bar{\lambda}}{2 + \varepsilon} \right\rceil - 1 \right)(|V'| - 1) < \frac{\delta(G')|V'|}{2 + \varepsilon} \le \frac{2|E'|}{2 + \varepsilon},$$

which proves the claim by $2/(2 + \varepsilon) < 1$. Since the graph remains connected after any edge contraction, it will be contracted into a single vertex after $O(\log m)$ iterations, and the procedure halts.

We next show that the output X satisfies (2.17). By construction, X has been contracted to the last x^* and $\bar{\lambda} = \delta(G') = d(x^*; G')$, i.e., $\bar{\lambda} = d(X; G)$. Then it suffices to show that $\lambda(G) \ge \bar{\lambda}/(2 + \varepsilon)$. Assume otherwise, that is, G has a cut Y with $d(Y; G) < \bar{\lambda}/(2 + \varepsilon)$. In each iteration of the while-loop, $k \ge \lceil \bar{\lambda}/(2 + \varepsilon) \rceil$ holds. Hence, by Lemma 2.2(ii) we see that, for any edge $\{u, v\}$ contracted during the while-loop, $\lambda(u, v; G) \ge k \ge \lceil \bar{\lambda}/(2 + \varepsilon) \rceil$ holds. This implies that any edge in $E(Y, V - Y; G)$ will never be contracted since $d(Y; G) < \bar{\lambda}/(2 + \varepsilon)$, contradicting that $|V(G')| = 1$ holds upon completion. Therefore, (2.17) holds for the output X.

We finally show that EC-APPROX runs in linear time. A forest decomposition of E' can be found in $O(|V'| + |E'|)$ time by computing an MA ordering in the graph G' (see Lemma 2.23). Thus, each iteration of the while-loop can be executed in $O(|E'|)$ time. Hence, the entire running time is at most

$$m + \left(\frac{2}{2 + \varepsilon}\right)m + \left(\frac{2}{2 + \varepsilon}\right)^2 m + \cdots = O(m). \qquad \square$$

This theorem tells that, for a sufficiently small ε, we obtain a near 2-approximation solution to the minimum cut in linear time.

2.4.2 2-Approximation to Vertex-Connectivity

Faster algorithms for approximating the vertex connectivity have been proposed based on the observation that $\kappa(G) \leq \delta(G)$ holds for any graph G. Let $\kappa = \kappa(G)$ and $\delta = \delta(G)$ in this section. Henzinger [120] has given a 2-approximation algorithm for computing κ, based on the forest decomposition $\mathcal{F}(G, \sigma)$ by an MA ordering σ. Her algorithm returns the vertex connectivity κ in $O(n^2 \min\{\kappa, \sqrt{n}\})$ time and $O(n^2)$ space if $\kappa \leq \lfloor \delta/2 \rfloor$; it returns a message "$\kappa > \lfloor \delta/2 \rfloor$" otherwise.

For a fixed $\alpha < 1$, Gabow [98] has given an $O(m + \kappa^2 n^{3/2} + \kappa n^2)$ time algorithm that delivers a minimum vertex cut C of G if $\kappa \leq \alpha\delta$; it returns a message "$\kappa > \alpha\delta$" otherwise.

In this section, we present an improved version of Henzinger's algorithm. This algorithm delivers in $O(n^2(1 + \min\{\kappa^2, \kappa\sqrt{n}\}/\delta))$ time and $O(n + m)$ space a minimum vertex cut C of G if $\kappa \leq \lfloor \delta/2 \rfloor$; it returns a message "$\kappa > \lfloor \delta/2 \rfloor$" otherwise. In the latter case, a vertex cut $C = \Gamma_G(v)$ for a vertex $v \in V$ with minimum degree δ has the cut size $\delta < 2\kappa$. Since $\kappa \leq \delta$ holds by definition, such an algorithm can be regarded as a 2-approximation algorithm to the problem of finding a minimum vertex cut in graph.

For two subsets $X, Y \subseteq V$ (not necessarily disjoint) in $G = (V, E)$, we define a set of vertex pairs

$$\overline{E}(X, Y; G) = \{\{u, v\} \notin E \mid u \in X, v \in Y\}$$

and

$$\kappa_{X,Y}(G) = \min\{\kappa(u, v; G) \mid \{u, v\} \in \overline{E}(X, Y; G)\},$$

where $\kappa_{X,Y}(G) = +\infty$ if $\overline{E}(X, Y; G) = \emptyset$, and we may write $\overline{E}(X, Y; G)$ and $\kappa_{X,Y}(G)$ as $\overline{E}(X, Y)$ and $\kappa_{X,Y}$, respectively, when G is clear from the context.

Given a partition $\{S, T = V - S\}$ of V,

$$\kappa(G) = \min\{\kappa_{S,S}, \kappa_{S,T}, \kappa_{T,T}\}$$

holds by definition.

For a subset $X \subseteq V$ and a new vertex $a \notin V$, we denote by $G + a \times X$ the graph obtained by adding vertex a and an edge $\{a, u\}$ for every vertex $u \in X$. For a subset $X \subseteq V$, we denote by $G + X \times X$ the graph obtained by adding edges $\{u, v\}$ for all nonadjacent pairs of vertices $u, v \in X$.

Lemma 2.50 ([120]). *For a graph $H = (V_H, E_H)$, let K be a subset of V_H such that K induces a complete subgraph from H. For a subset $Z \subseteq V_H$, let $H' = H + (K \cup Z) \times (K \cup Z)$. Then for any vertex $s \in K$*

$$\kappa_{s, V_H - K}(H) = \min\{\kappa_{s, Z}(H), \ \kappa_{s, V_H - K - Z}(H')\}. \qquad \square$$

Proof. We easily see by definition that $\kappa_{s, V_H - K}(H) = \min\{\kappa_{s, Z}(H), \kappa_{s, V_H - K - Z}(H)\} \leq \min\{\kappa_{s, Z}(H), \kappa_{s, V_H - K - Z}(H')\}$. We show the converse. Consider an (s, u)-vertex cut C in H for a vertex $u \in V_H - K$, which gives rise to a partition $\{V_s, C, V_u\}$ of V_H such that $E(V_s, V_u; G) = \emptyset$, $s \in V_s$, and $u \in V_u$. Since K induces a complete subgraph from H, $K \subseteq V_s \cup C$. If $Z \cap V_u \neq \emptyset$, then C is an (s, v)-vertex cut for any vertex $v \in Z \cap V_u$ in H. Hence $\kappa_{s, V_H - K}(H) \geq \kappa_{s, Z}(H)$. Assume that $Z \cap V_u = \emptyset$. Then C does not separate any two vertices in Z, and remains a vertex cut in $H' = H + (K \cup Z) \times (K \cup Z)$. Then C is an (s, v')-vertex cut in H' for a vertex $v' \in V_u \subseteq V_H - K - Z$. Hence, $\kappa_{s, V_H - K}(H) \geq \kappa_{s, V_H - K - Z}(H')$. Putting these together, we have $\kappa_{s, V_H - K}(H) \geq \min\{\kappa_{s, Z}(H), \ \kappa_{s, V_H - K - Z}(H')\}$, as required. $\square$

Definition 2.51. *For a graph $G = (V, E)$, a set $S \subseteq V$ with $|S| = q$ is a (p, q)-core if it is a p-vertex-connected set. We then call an ordered family $(S_1, S_2, \ldots, S_{\lceil n/q \rceil})$ of subsets of V a (p, q)-core collection of G if it satisfies the following conditions, where we denote $S_{i,j} = S_i \cup S_{i+1} \cup \cdots \cup S_j$ ($i \leq j$) (see Fig. 2.12 after Claim 2.53).*

(i) S_1 *is a (p, q)-core in G.*
(ii) *For $i = 2, 3, \ldots, \lceil n/q \rceil - 1$, S_i is a (p, q)-core in the graph $G + S_{1, i-1} \times S_{1, i-1}$.*
(iii) $S_{1, \lceil n/q \rceil} = V$ *holds, and $S_{\lceil n/q \rceil}$ is a (p, q)-core in the graph $G + (V - S_{\lceil n/q \rceil}) \times (V - S_{\lceil n/q \rceil})$.* $\square$

Lemma 2.52 ([120]). *Given a graph $G = (V, E)$ with a minimum degree δ, positive integers p and q with $q \geq 2$ and $p + q \leq \delta + 2$, a (p, q)-core collection of G can be found in $O((m + n)n/q)$ time and $O(n + m)$ space.* $\square$

Proof. To obtain S_1, we compute an MA ordering σ_1 of G. Let S_1 be the set of last q vertices in σ_1. By Lemma 2.34, the set of last $\delta + 2 - p$ ($\geq q$) vertices in σ_1 is p-vertex-connected in G. Then S_1 is a (p, q)-core in G, satisfying Definition 2.51(i).

Observe that, if a subset $X \subseteq V$ induces a complete subgraph from G, then any ordering of X can be used as the first $|X|$ vertices in an MA ordering of G. Suppose that h disjoint (p, q)-cores $S_1, S_2, \ldots, S_h$ ($h < \lceil n/q \rceil$) satisfying Definition 2.51(ii) have been obtained. Then S_{h+1} is computed as follows: First compute an MA ordering σ_{h+1} in $G + S_{1,h} \times S_{1,h}$ starting with an arbitrary ordering of the vertices in $S_1 \cup S_2 \cup \cdots \cup S_h$ and let S_{h+1} be the set of last q vertices in σ_{h+1}. As in condition (i), S_{h+1} is a (p, q)-core in $G + S_{1,h} \times S_{1,h}$.

For $i = \lceil n/q \rceil$, let $S_{\lceil n/q \rceil}$ be an arbitrary superset of $V - S_{1, \lceil n/q \rceil - 1}$ such that $|S_{\lceil n/q \rceil}| = q$ holds. Then $G + (V - S_{\lceil n/q \rceil}) \times (V - S_{\lceil n/q \rceil})$ admits an MA ordering in which the set of the last q vertices is equal to $S_{\lceil n/q \rceil}$, and $S_{\lceil n/q \rceil}$ is p-vertex-connected by Lemma 2.34. This shows that $S_{\lceil n/q \rceil}$ satisfies Definition 2.51(iii). Therefore, we can find a desired partition by computing $\lceil n/q \rceil$ MA orderings. Although each $G + S_{1,i} \times S_{1,i}$ may have many more edges than G has in its definition, we can conduct the algorithm for finding an MA ordering σ_i in $G + S_{1,i} \times S_{1,i}$ without explicitly referring to the added edges. Therefore, the time and space bounds are $O((n + m)n/q)$ and $O(n + m)$, respectively, by Lemma 2.19. $\square$

Let G be a given graph with a minimum degree $\delta \geq 1$, and let

$$p = \lfloor \delta/2 \rfloor + 1 \text{ and } q = \lceil \delta/2 \rceil + 1. \tag{2.20}$$

We compute an MA ordering σ of G, by which we first sparsify G into

$$G_p = (V, F_1 \cup F_2 \cup \cdots \cup F_p)$$

by using the forest decomposition $\mathcal{F}(G, \sigma) = (F_1, F_2, \ldots, F_m)$ (see Theorem 2.26 in Section 2.2). We then find a (p, q)-core collection $(S_1, S_2, \ldots, S_{\lceil n/q \rceil})$ of G_p. A 2-approximation algorithm for the vertex-connectivity $\kappa(G)$ will be designed so that it outputs either a vertex cut C of G with $|C| \leq \lfloor \delta/2 \rfloor$ or a message "$\kappa(G) > \lfloor \delta/2 \rfloor$".

Now we consider the case of

$$\kappa(G) \leq \lfloor \delta/2 \rfloor \ (< p). \tag{2.21}$$

By Theorem 2.26,

$$\kappa(G_p) = \kappa(G)$$

holds in this case, and the set of vertex cuts with cardinality $\kappa(G)$ remains unchanged in G_p.

Let $(S_1, S_2, \ldots, S_{\lceil n/q \rceil})$ be a (p, q)-core collection of G_p. For S_1 and $T_1 = V - S_1$, we have $\kappa(G_p) = \min\{\kappa_{S_1,S_1}(G_p), \kappa_{S_1,T_1}(G_p)\}$ by $|S_1| = q \geq p > \kappa(G_p)$ and Lemma 1.22(ii) (where Lemma 1.22(ii) for digraphs remains valid for undirected graphs). Since S_1 is p-vertex-connected and $\kappa_{S_1,S_1}(G_p) \geq p > \kappa(G_p)$, we have

$$\kappa(G_p) = \kappa_{S_1,T_1}(G_p) < |S_1|.$$

Now introducing a new vertex s, we define

$$\tilde{H} = G_p + s \times S_1 \text{ and } H_2 = G_p + s \times S_1 + S_1 \times S_1.$$

Claim 2.53. $\kappa_{S_1,T_1}(G_p) = \kappa_{s,T_1}(\tilde{H}) = \kappa_{s,V-S_1}(H_2).$ $\square$

Proof. Since $\kappa_{S_1,T_1}(G_p) < \min\{|S_1|, \kappa_{S_1,S_1}(G_p)\}$ by assumption (2.21), we have $\kappa_{S_1,T_1}(G_p) = \kappa_{s,T_1}(\tilde{H})$ by Lemma 1.23(iii) (where Lemma 1.23(iii) for digraphs

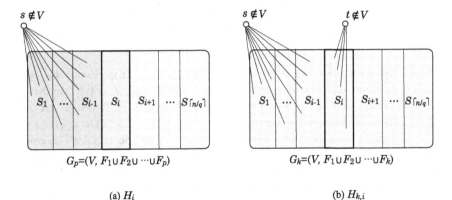

$$G_p=(V, F_1 \cup F_2 \cup \cdots \cup F_p)$$

(a) H_i

$$G_k=(V, F_1 \cup F_2 \cup \cdots \cup F_k)$$

(b) $H_{k,i}$

Figure 2.12. (a) Graph $H_i = G_p + s \times S_{1,i-1} + S_{1,i-1} \times S_{1,i-1}$; (b) graph $H_{k,i} = G_k + s \times S_{1,i-1} + t \times S_i$.

remains valid for undirected graphs). By definition, $\kappa_{s,T_1}(\tilde{H}) = \min\{\kappa(u, v) \mid \{u, v\} \in \overline{E}(s, T_1; \tilde{H})\} = \min\{\kappa(u, v) \mid \{u, v\} \in \overline{E}(s, T_1; H_2)\} = \kappa_{s,T_1}(H_2) = \kappa_{s,V-S_1}(H_2)$. $\square$

The remaining task is to compute $\kappa_{s,V-S_1}(H_2)$ $(= \kappa(G))$. For $i = 2, 3, \ldots, \lceil n/q \rceil$, define

$$H_i = G_p + s \times S_{1,i-1} + S_{1,i-1} \times S_{1,i-1}$$

(see Fig. 2.12(a)). By applying Lemma 2.50 to the graph H_2 with $K = \{s\} \cup S_1$ and $Z = S_2$, we have

$$(\kappa(G) =) \kappa_{s,V-S_1}(H_2) = \min\{\kappa_{s,S_2}(H_2), \kappa_{s,V-S_1-S_2}(H_3)\}.$$

Repeating this for $i = 2, 3, \ldots, \lceil n/q \rceil$, we have

$$\kappa_{s,V-S_1}(H_2) = \min\{\kappa_{s,S_2}(H_2), \kappa_{s,V-S_1-S_2}(H_3)\}$$
$$= \min\{\kappa_{s,S_2}(H_2), \kappa_{s,S_3}(H_3), \kappa_{s,V-S_1-S_2-S_3}(H_4)\}$$
$$= \cdots$$
$$= \min\{\kappa_{s,S_2}(H_2), \kappa_{s,S_3}(H_3), \ldots, \kappa_{s,V-S_{1,\lceil n/q \rceil-1}}(H_{\lceil n/q \rceil})\}$$
$$= \min\{\kappa_{s,S_2}(H_2), \kappa_{s,S_3}(H_3), \ldots, \kappa_{s,S_{1,\lceil n/q \rceil}}(H_{\lceil n/q \rceil})\}.$$

Hence,

$$(\kappa(G) =) \kappa_{S_1,T_1}(G_p) = \min\{\kappa_{s,S_i}(H_i) \mid i = 2, 3, \ldots, \lceil n/q \rceil\}. \quad (2.22)$$

We now test whether or not $\kappa_{s,S_i}(H_i) \geq k$ holds for a given integer $k \geq 1$ by using the next observation. Introducing another new vertex t, we define graphs

$$H_{k,i} = G_k + t \times S_{1,i-1} + s \times S_i \text{ for } i = 2, 3, \ldots, \lceil n/q \rceil$$

(see Fig. 2.12(b)).

Claim 2.54. *If $\kappa_{S_i,t}(H_i) \leq k < p$ for some integer $k \geq 1$, then any minimum (s,t)-vertex cut C in $H_{k+1,i}$ is a vertex cut in G_p, and $\kappa(s,t; H_{k+1,i}) = \kappa_{S_i,t}(H_i)$ holds.*   □

Proof. By assumption, $\kappa_{S_i,t}(H_i) < p \leq \min\{|S_i|, \kappa_{S_i,S_i}(H_i)\}$. Hence by applying Lemma 1.23(iii) to graph H_i with $S = S_i$ and $T = \{s\}$, we have $\kappa_{s,S_i}(H_i) = \kappa(s,t; H_i + t \times S_i)$. Let C be a minimum (s,t)-vertex cut in $H_{k+1,i}$. By assumption, $|C| = \kappa(s,t; H_{k+1,i}) \leq \kappa(s,t; H_i + t \times S_i) = \kappa_{s,S_i}(H_i) \leq k < p \leq |S_i|$. Then C is a vertex cut in G_{k+1}, and in G_p by Theorem 2.26. By construction of $H_{k+1,i}$, no two vertices in $S_{1,i-1}$ are separated by C in $H_{k+1,i}$. Then C is also a vertex cut in $H_t + t \times S_i$, proving $\kappa(s,t; H_i + t \times S_i) \leq \kappa(s,t; H_{k+1,i})$. Since $\kappa(s,t; H_i + t \times S_i) \geq \kappa(s,t; H_{k+1,i})$ is obvious by definition, we have the equality.   □

Lemma 2.55. *Assume $\kappa(G) < p$. Then $\kappa(G) = \min_{2 \leq i \leq \lceil n/q \rceil} \kappa(s,t; H_{k+1,i}) < p$ holds for some positive integer $k < p$.*   □

Proof. By (2.22) and assumption, $\kappa(G) = \kappa_{s,S_i}(H_i) < p$ holds for some i. For this i and a positive integer k with $\kappa_{s,S_i}(H_i) \leq k < p$, we have $\kappa(s,t; H_{k+1,i}) = \kappa_{s,S_i}(H_i) = \kappa(G) < p$ by Claim 2.54.   □

For each $i = 2, 3, \ldots, \lceil n/q \rceil$, we test whether or not $\kappa(s,t; H_{k+1,i}) \geq k$ holds by doubling k to determine whether there is an integer $k = 2^j < p$ such that $\min_{2 \leq i \leq \lceil n/q \rceil} \kappa(s,t; H_{k+1,i}) < p$ or not (if not, $\kappa(G) \geq p$ by Lemma 2.55). An algorithm based on this is described as follows.

Algorithm APPROXVCON
Input: A noncomplete connected graph $G = (V, E)$ with a minimum degree δ.
Output: A minimum vertex cut C of G if $\kappa = \kappa(G) \leq \lfloor \delta/2 \rfloor$ or a message "$\kappa > \lfloor \delta/2 \rfloor$" otherwise.
1   $p := \lfloor \delta/2 \rfloor + 1$; $q := \lceil \delta/2 \rceil + 1$;
2   Compute an MA ordering σ of G and its forest decomposition $\mathcal{F}(G, \sigma) = (F_1, F_2, \ldots, F_m)$;
    /* We denote $G_k = (V, F_1 \cup \cdots \cup F_k)$ */
3   Find a (p, q)-core collection $(S_1, S_2, \ldots, S_{\lceil n/q \rceil})$ of graph G_p;
    /* For each $i = 2, \ldots, \lceil n/q \rceil$ and new vertices t and s, we denote $H_{k,i} = G_k + s \times S_{1,i-1} + t \times S_i$, where $S_{1,i-1} = S_1 \cup S_2 \cup \cdots \cup S_{i-1}$ */
4   $k := 1$;
5   **while** $\min_{2 \leq i \leq \lceil n/q \rceil} \kappa(s,t; H_{k+1,i}) \geq k$ and $k < p$ **do**
6      $k := \min\{2k, p\}$;
7   Test whether $\min_{2 \leq i \leq \lceil n/q \rceil} \kappa(s,t; H_{k+1,i}) \geq k$
    end; /* while */
    /* Either (a) $\min_{2 \leq i \leq \lceil n/q \rceil} \kappa(s,t; H_{k+1,i}) < k \leq p$ or
       (b) $\min_{2 \leq i \leq \lceil n/q \rceil} \kappa(s,t; H_{k+1,i}) \geq k = p$ */
8   **if** (a) holds **then**
9   Let $i^* := \arg\min\{\kappa(s,t; H_{k+1,i}) \mid 2 \leq i \leq \lceil n/q \rceil\}$;

10   Output a minimum (s, t)-vertex cut C in $H_{i^*, k+1}$ as a minimum vertex
      cut of G
11 **else** /* (b) holds */
12   Output "$\kappa > \lfloor \delta/2 \rfloor$."

Theorem 2.56. *Given a noncomplete connected graph G with a minimum degree δ, APPROXVCON correctly delivers a minimum vertex cut C of G if $\kappa = \kappa(G) \leq \lfloor \delta/2 \rfloor$ or returns a message "$\kappa > \lfloor \delta/2 \rfloor$" otherwise, in $O(n^2(1 + \min\{\kappa^2, \kappa\sqrt{n}\}/\delta))$ time and $O(n + m)$ space.* □

Proof. The correctness of the algorithm follows from the preceding argument. We consider its time complexity. An MA ordering σ of G and the forest decomposition $\mathcal{F}(G, \sigma)$ can be found in $O(n + m)$ time by Lemma 2.23. A (p, q)-core collection in G_p can be obtained in $O((n + \delta n)n/\delta) = O(n^2)$ time by Lemma 2.52. Since graph $H_{k+1,i}$ has $O(kn)$ edges, we can test whether or not $\kappa(s, t; H_{k+1,i}) \geq k$ (and obtain $\kappa(s, t; H_{k+1,i})$ if $\kappa(s, t; H_{k+1,i}) \leq k$) in $O(\min\{k, \sqrt{n}\}kn)$ time and $O(n + m)$ space by using Corollary 2.30(ii). Hence, the space complexity is $O(n + m)$. The j-iteration of the while-loop can be executed in $O((n/\delta)\min\{2^j, \sqrt{n}\}2^j n)$ time since $k = O(2^j n)$ and $|E(H_{k+1,i})| = O(2^j n)$ hold for all $i = 2, \ldots, \lceil n/q \rceil$. By $\kappa \leq \delta$, we have $p = O(\kappa)$ when the while-loop ends up with $k = p$. Therefore, the entire run time is given by $O(m + n^2 + (n/\delta) \sum_{0 \leq j \leq \log_2 \min\{2\kappa, p\}} \min\{2^j, \sqrt{n}\}2^j n) = O(m + n^2 + \min\{\kappa, \sqrt{n}\}\kappa n^2/\delta)$.

Note that we do not have to maintain all graphs $H_{k+1,1}, H_{k+1,2}, \ldots, H_{k+1,\lceil n/q \rceil}$ separately during the while-loop, since each of these graphs can be constructed from G_p in $O(kn)$ time. □

2.5 Fast Maximum-Flow Algorithms

In this section, we describe two maximum-flow algorithms as applications of MA orderings. The first algorithm is due to Goldberg and Rao [105]. They proved that, for undirected multigraphs, the time bound of Dinits' algorithm (Section 1.3.2) can be improved to $O(\min\{m, n^{3/2}\}m^{1/2})$ just by plugging a sparsification procedure by MA ordering to reduce the time to compute a blocking flow in L. The second algorithm is designed by Fujishige [95], who extended the definition of MA ordering to digraphs so that an (s, t)-flow having a large flow value in the residual digraph can be found by such an MA ordering. His algorithm augments flows along such (s, t)-flows instead of blocking (s, t)-flows in level graphs of Dinits' algorithm. It runs in $O(n(m + n \log n) \log nU)$ time for an integer-weighted digraph, where U denotes the maximum edge weight. Basic definitions about maximum flows, such as residual graphs and level graphs, can be found in Section 1.3.2.

2.5.1 Goldberg and Rao's Algorithm

Let us consider an unweighted undirected graph with no multiple edge. By Theorem 1.13(i) and (ii), Dinits' algorithm runs in $O(\min\{m^{1/2}, n^{2/3}\}m)$ time for such a graph. Goldberg and Rao [105] have shown that this can be improved to $O(\min\{m, n^{3/2}\}m^{1/2})$ by sparsifying the residual graphs by MA orderings during the algorithm.

We denote by $G_0 = (V, E)$ the given graph with no multiple edge. As observed in Lemma 1.14, the number of edges e assigned $f(e) = 1$ during Dinits' algorithm is $4n^{3/2}$. Hence, if G_0 has $m \gg 4n^{3/2}$ edges, then most edges will not be used in the construction of a maximum flow. We try to discard some such edges by a sparsification technique to reduce the time for scanning edges. For this, we use Lemma 1.12(i) to estimate the value of a maximum flow in a residual digraph, and we sparsify the current graph obtained during the algorithm while maintaining the maximum flow value of the residual digraph.

The value $v(f)$ of a maximum (s, t)-flow f in an undirected graph or digraph H is denoted by $val(s, t; H)$, that is, $val(s, t; H)$ is the maximum number of edge-disjoint (s, t)-paths (resp. directed (s, t)-paths) in an undirected graph H (resp. in a digraph H). For an undirected graph $G = (V, E)$, let $\widetilde{G} = (V, E')$ denote the digraph obtained by replacing each edge e with two oppositely oriented edges e' and e''. We define an (s, t)-flow f in an undirected graph G to be an (s, t)-flow $f : E' \to \{0, 1\}$ in $\widetilde{G}$. For an (s, t)-flow f in an undirected graph G, we let G^f denote the residual digraph defined by $\widetilde{G}$ and f, and we let $E^{f1}(G)$ (resp. $E^{f0}(G)$) denote the set of edges e in G such that $f(e') = 1$ or $f(e'') = 1$ (resp. $f(e') = f(e'') = 0$) holds for the corresponding directed edges e' and e'' in $\widetilde{G}$. Furthermore, for a forest decomposition $(F_1, F_2, \ldots, F_m)$ of $E^{f0}(G)$ in the graph $(V, E^{f0}(G))$ and an integer $k \geq 1$, we define the spanning subgraph of G,

$$G_{f,k} = (V, E^{f1}(G) \cup F_1 \cup F_2 \cup \cdots \cup F_k),$$

where $G_{f,k}$ has at most $|E^{f1}(G)| + k(n-1) = O(n^{3/2} + kn)$ edges if f is a flow constructed during Dinits' algorithm. Since $G_{f,j}$ is a subgraph of G, $val(s, t; G_{f,j}) \leq val(s, t; G)$ is obvious.

Lemma 2.57 ([105]). *Given an (s, t)-flow f in an undirected graph G and any integer $k > 0$, it holds $val(s, t; G_{f,k}) \geq \min\{v(f) + k, val(s, t; G)\}$.*   □

Proof. Notice that $val(s, t; G_{f,k}) \geq v(f)$ holds since $E^{f1}(G) \subseteq E(G_{f,k})$, showing that the stated inequality holds for $k = 0$. Assume conversely that the stated inequality does not hold in general; that is, there is an integer $j \geq 0$ such that $val(s, t; G_{f,j}) \geq \min\{v(f) + j, val(s, t; G)\}$ but $val(s, t; G_{f,j+1}) < \min\{v(f) + j + 1, val(s, t; G)\}$. This implies that $val(s, t; G_{f,j}) = val(s, t; G_{f,j+1}) = v(f) + j < val(s, t; G)$. By Menger's theorem (Theorem 1.18(i)), $G_{f,j}$ has an (s, t)-cut $(S, \overline{S})$ with the cut size $v(f) + j$. Since $val(s, t; G_{f,j}) < val(s, t; G)$, we see that $E(S, \overline{S}; G) - E(S, \overline{S}; G_{f,j})$ contains an edge $e = \{u, v\} \in E^{f0}(G)$, indicating that u and v are connected in graph $(V, E^{f0}(G) - \cup_{i=1,\ldots,j} F_i)$. Hence, u and v must be connected in the $(j + 1)$-st maximal spanning forest F_{j+1}, and this means that $val(s, t; G_{f,j}) < val(s, t; G_{f,j+1})$, contradicting $val(s, t; G_{f,j}) = val(s, t; G_{f,j+1}) = v(f) + j$.   □

Lemma 2.58 ([105]). *For an (s, t)-flow f in an undirected graph G and any integer $k \geq \lceil (n/dist(s, t; G^f))^2 \rceil$, it holds that*

$$val(s, t; G_{f,k}) = val(s, t; G),$$

where $dist(s, t; G^f)$ denotes the length (i.e., the number of edges) of a shortest (s, t)-path P in digraph G^f.   □

Proof. Note that $val(s, t; G) = val(s, t; \tilde{G}) = v(f) + val(s, t; G^f)$ by the definition of residual graph G^f. By Lemma 1.12(ii), it holds that $n \geq \sqrt{val(s, t; G^f)}$ $\cdot dist(s, t; G^f)$. Hence, $k \geq \lceil (n/dist(s, t; G^f))^2 \rceil \geq val(s, t; G^f) = val(s, t; G) - v(f)$ holds. From this and Lemma 2.57, we have $val(s, t; G_{f,k}) \geq \min\{v(f) + k, val(s, t; G)\} = val(s, t; G)$, indicating $val(s, t; G_{f,k}) = val(s, t; G)$ since $val(s, t; G_{f,k}) \leq val(s, t; G)$ is obviously true.   □

Based on this lemma, we can modify Dinits' algorithm so that, after each phase, the current graph G is sparsified into $G_{f,k}$ with $k = \lceil (n/dist(s, t; G^f))^2 \rceil$ without losing the correctness of the algorithm. By Lemma 2.23 such a subgraph $G_{f,k}$ can be constructed in linear time. The entire algorithm is described as follows.

Algorithm MAXFLOW1
Input: An undirected graph $G_0 = (V, E)$ with no multiple edges, and a pair
    (s, t) of a source and a sink.
Output: A maximum (s, t)-flow $f : E \rightarrow \{0, 1\}$ in G_0.
    $G := G_0$; $f(e) := 0$ for all $e \in E$;
    while $val(s, t; G^f) > 0$ **do**
    $k := \lceil (n/dist(s, t; G^f))^2 \rceil$;
    $G := G_{f,k}$; /* sparsification preserving $val(s, t; G) = val(s, t; G_0)$ by
        Lemma 2.58 */
    Find a blocking flow g (see Dinits' algorithm in Section 1.3.2)
        in the level digraph of the residual digraph G^f;
    $f := f + g$
    end; /* while */
    Output f.

We now evaluate the running time of MAXFLOW1.

Lemma 2.59. *After each phase of MAXFLOW1, G has at most $4n^{3/2} + n((n/dist(s, t; G^f))^2 + 1)$ edges.*   □

Proof. By Lemma 1.14, the number of edges e with $f(e) = 1$ in G is at most $4n^{3/2}$. Since the set $E^{f0}(G)$ of edges e with $f(e) = 0$ is sparsified into a set $F_1 \cup \cdots \cup F_k$ with $k = \lceil (n/dist(s, t; G^f))^2 \rceil$, $G = G_{f,k}$ has at most $4n^{3/2} + k(n - 1) \leq 4n^{3/2} + n((n/dist(s, t; G^f))^2 + 1)$ edges.   □

Theorem 2.60. MAXFLOW1 *runs in $O(\min\{m, n^{3/2}\}m^{1/2})$ time.*   □

Proof. If $m \leq n^{3/2}$, then by Lemma 1.13(i) Dinits' algorithm finds a maximum flow in $O(m^{3/2}) = O(n^{3/2}m^{1/2})$ time. Therefore, we assume $m > n^{3/2}$. Let *dist* denote $dist(s, t; G^f)$ and let $\overline{m}$ denote the number of edges in the current graph G in MAXFLOW1.

(i) While $dist < n^{3/2}/m^{1/2}$ holds, there are at most $n^{3/2}/m^{1/2}$ such phases. Then the time bound for these phases is $O((n^{3/2}/m^{1/2})m) = O(n^{3/2}m^{1/2})$.

(ii) While $n^{3/2}/m^{1/2} \leq dist < n^{3/4}$ holds, in the phase for $dist = i$, we see by Lemma 2.59 that the number $\overline{m}$ of edges in the residual graph is bounded by

$$\overline{m} \leq 4n^{3/2} + n(n/i)^2 + n \leq 5n(n/i)^2.$$

Let $\rho = \lceil n^{3/2}/m^{1/2} \rceil$. Then the total time during these phases is at most

$$\sum_{i=\rho}^{\infty} 5n(n/i)^2 = 5n^3 \sum_{i=\rho}^{\infty} \frac{1}{i^2} \leq \frac{5n^3}{\rho^2} \sum_{i=\rho}^{\infty} \frac{1}{\lfloor i/\rho \rfloor^2} \leq \frac{5n^3}{\rho} \sum_{i=1}^{\infty} \frac{1}{i^2} \leq \frac{5n^3}{\rho} \cdot \frac{\pi^2}{6}.$$

Therefore, we obtain a time bound of $O(n^3/\rho) = O(n^{3/2}m^{1/2})$.

(iii) When $n^{3/4} \leq dist$ holds, the number $\overline{m}$ of edges in the residual graph is at most $4n^{3/2} + n(n/dist)^2 + n = O(n^{3/2})$ by Lemma 2.59. By Lemma 1.12(i), we obtain $val(s, t; G^f) \leq \overline{m}/dist = O(n^{3/2}/n^{3/4}) = O(n^{3/4})$. Hence, there are $O(n^{3/4})$ such phases, and the total run time in this case is $O(n^{3/4} \cdot n^{3/2}) = O(n^{3/2}m^{1/2})$ (since $m > n^{3/2}$ by assumption).   □

2.5.2 Fujishige's Algorithm

In this subsection, we consider a digraph $G = (V, E)$ with edges weighted by nonnegative integers. Fujishige [95] has shown that, for such a digraph, a fast maximum-flow algorithm can be designed by making use of MA ordering generalized for digraphs.

In a digraph G, an MA ordering is defined by an ordering $\sigma = (v_1, v_2, \ldots, v_n)$ of V such that the following inequalities hold, where $V_{i-1} = \{v_1, v_2, \ldots, v_{i-1}\}$.

$$d(V_{i-1}, v_i; G) \geq d(V_{i-1}, v_j; G) \text{ for all } i, j \text{ with } 2 \leq i \leq j \leq n.$$

Such an MA ordering can be found in $O(m + n \log n)$ time, as in the case of weighted undirected graphs, which will be discussed in Section 3.1.

Given a digraph G with a source s and a sink t, we find an MA ordering $\sigma = (v_1 = s, v_2, \ldots, v_k = t, \ldots, v_n)$ starting from $v_1 = s$. We denote $d(v_i) = d(V_{i-1}, v_i; G), i = 2, 3, \ldots, n$.

Lemma 2.61 ([95]). *Given an MA ordering $\sigma = (v_1 = s, v_2, \ldots, v_k = t, \ldots, v_n)$ in a digraph G, an (s, t)-flow f with $v(f) \geq \min_{2 \leq i \leq k} d(v_i)$ can be found in $O(n + m)$ time.*   □

Proof. Let $\delta = \min_{2 \leq i \leq k} d(v_i)$. The following procedure finds a desired flow f. We start from $b_k := \delta$ and $b_i := 0$ for $i = 1, 2, \ldots, k-1$, and $f(u, v) := 0$ for all directed edges $(u, v) \in E$. In the order of $j = k, k-1, \ldots, 2$, we push back a flow with amount b_j along edges in $E(V_{j-1}, v_j; G)$, where we set $f(e) \geq 0$ arbitrarily under the constraints $f(e) \leq c_G(e)$ $(e \in E(V_{j-1}, v_j; G))$ and $\sum_{e \in E(V_{j-1}, v_j; G)} f(e) = b_j$. Then we update b_j and b_i $(1 \leq i < j)$ by $b_j := 0$ and $b_i := b_i + f(v_i, v_j)$ for all $(v_i, v_j) \in E(V_{j-1}, v_j; G)$. After each iteration, $\sum_{1 \leq i \leq k} b_i = \delta$ always holds (since $\sum_{e \in E(V_{j-1}, v_j; G)} f(e) = b_j$) and, hence, $b_i \leq \delta$ $(1 \leq i \leq k)$ holds. This means that, in each iteration for j, $b_j \leq \delta \leq d(v_j)$ holds and we can update $f(e)$ $(e \in E(V_{j-1}, v_j; G))$ according to the preceding procedure. Thus, this procedure eventually constructs an (s, t)-flow f with flow value δ. $\qquad\square$

Lemma 2.62 ([95]). *Let f be an (s, t)-flow f in a digraph G, obtained by the procedure of Lemma 2.61, based on an MA ordering σ starting from s. Then $v(f) \geq \max\{c_G(P), val(s, t; G)/n\}$ holds for any augmenting path P from s to t in G, where $c_G(P)$ denotes the minimum capacity of the edges in P.* $\qquad\square$

Proof. Let $\sigma = (v_1 = s, v_2, \ldots, v_k = t, \ldots, v_n)$ be the MA ordering. Then $v(f) = \delta = \min_{2 \leq i \leq k} d(v_i)$ holds by Lemma 2.61, where we assume that v_j attains $\delta = d(v_j)$. Let f' be an arbitrary (s, t)-flow in G. Then consider a vertex u that maximizes $\sum_{e \in E(V_{j-1}, u; G)} f'(e)$ over all $u \in V - V_{j-1}$. By the choice of v_j in σ, we have

$$\delta = d(v_j) \geq d(V_{j-1}, u; G) \geq \sum_{e \in E(V_{j-1}, u; G)} f'(e).$$

Now assume that f' is the (s, t)-flow along an augmenting path P. Then we have $\sum_{e \in E(V_{j-1}, u; G)} f'(e) \geq v(f') = c_G(P)$, proving $\delta \geq c_G(P)$. Next assume that f' is a maximum (s, t)-flow in G. Then at least one of the vertices $u \in V - V_{j-1}$ satisfies $\sum_{e \in E(V_{j-1}, u; G)} f'(e) \geq v(f')/n$ since otherwise $v(f') \leq \sum_{e \in E(V_{j-1}, V-V_{j-1}; G)} f'(e) < |V - V_{j-1}| v(f')/n < v(f')$, a contradiction. Therefore, $\delta \geq val(s, t; G)/n$ also holds. $\qquad\square$

Based on this lemma, we obtain the following algorithm for finding a maximum (s, t)-flow.

Algorithm MAXFLOW2
Input: A digraph $G = (V, E)$ with edges weighted by nonnegative integers and
    with a pair (s, t) of a source and a sink.
Output: A maximum (s, t)-flow $f : E \to \mathbf{Z}_+$.
  $f(e) := 0$ for all $e \in E$;
  while $val(s, t; G^f) > 0$ **do**
    Find an MA ordering σ starting from s in the residual digraph G^f
      for the current f;
    Construct an (s, t)-flow g in G^f by following Lemma 2.61;
    $f := f + g$
  end; /* while */
  Output f.

Each iteration of the while-loop can be executed in $O(m + n \log n)$ time. Let $f^{(i)}$ denote the (s, t)-flow f obtained after the ith iteration. For a maximum (s, t)-flow f^* in G, we see by Lemma 2.62 that

$$v(f^*) - v(f^{(i+1)}) \leq \left(1 - \frac{1}{n}\right)(v(f^*) - v(f^{(i)})).$$

Then we see that, after each $O(n)$ iterations, the difference $v(f^*) - v(f)$ (i.e., the maximum flow value in the residual graph G^f) is reduced by at least half. For this, we show that there are constants c and c' such that $(1 - 1/n)^{cn} \leq 1/2$ holds for all $n \geq c'$. Since $\alpha(n) = (1 + 1/n)^n$ is an increasing function such that $\alpha(n) \leq e$ (< 2.8) for all $n \geq 1$, where e is the base of the natural logarithm. Hence, $(1 - 1/(n + 1))^{cn} = 1/\alpha(n)^c \leq 1/2$ $(n > c')$ for some constants c and c'. By denoting the maximum weight of an edge by U, there is an obvious bound $v(f^*) \leq n^2 U$. Therefore, after $i = O(\log nU)$ iterations, the difference $v(f^*) - v(f^{(i)})$ becomes less than 1; that is, $v(f^*) - v(f^{(i)}) = 0$ by the integrality of weights, and the algorithm finds a maximum (s, t)-flow $f^* = f^{(i)}$.

Theorem 2.63 ([95]). MAXFLOW2 *correctly finds a maximum (s, t)-flow in* $O(n(m + n \log n) \log nU)$ *time.*   □

2.6 Testing Chordality

For a cycle C in a graph G, an edge $e = \{u, v\} \in E(G)$ is called a *chord* if $\{u, v\} \in V(C)$ but $e \notin E(C)$. A graph G is called *chordal* if every chordless cycle in G is of length 3. We present in this subsection a characterization of a chordal graph, which is based on MA ordering.

A *simplicial vertex* is a vertex v whose neighbor set $\Gamma_G(v)$ induces a clique (i.e., a complete subgraph) of G. An ordering $(u_1, u_2, \ldots, u_n)$ of vertices of a graph G is called a *perfect elimination ordering* if

$$u_i \text{ is a simplicial vertex of graph } G[\{u_i, u_{i+1}, \ldots, u_n\}], i = 1, 2, \ldots, n - 1.$$

$$(2.23)$$

Theorem 2.64. *Let $G = (V, E)$ be a simple graph with $|V| \geq 2$, and $\sigma = (v_1, v_2, \ldots, v_n)$ be an MA ordering of G.*

  (i) *If G is chordal, then v_n is a simplicial vertex of G.*
  (ii) *G is chordal if and only if the reverse ordering $(v_n, v_{n-1}, \ldots, v_1)$ of σ is a perfect elimination ordering of G.*   □

Proof. (i) The case of $d(v_n; G) \leq 1$ is clear. Assume that $d(v_n; G) \geq 2$ and let $\Gamma_G(v_n) = \{v_{i_1}, v_{i_2}, \ldots, v_{i_d}\}$, where $i_1 < i_2 < \cdots < i_d$ $(d = d(v_n; G))$. It suffices to derive a contradiction, assuming that there are indices h and ℓ with $1 \leq h < \ell \leq d$ such that v_{i_h} and v_{i_ℓ} are not adjacent. Let $G' = G - \{v_i \mid i_\ell < j < n\}$ (note that G' remains chordal). By Corollary 2.32 with $\alpha(u) = 1, v \in V(G'), j = i_l$ and $h = n$, we have $\kappa(v_n, v_{i_\ell}; G') = \ell$. This means that there are ℓ internally vertex-disjoint

(v_n, v_{i_ℓ})-paths P_k, $k = 1, 2, \ldots, \ell$, each starting with edge $\{v_n, v_{i_k}\}$. Two paths P_h and P_ℓ form a cycle C, which satisfies $E(C) \cap E(v_n; G') = \{\{v_n, v_{i_h}\}, \{v_n, v_{i_\ell}\}\}$. Note that $|E(C)| \geq 4$ since $\{v_{i_h}, v_{i_\ell}\} \notin E(G')$ (even if $\ell = d$). Since G' is chordal, C has a chord e, by which we have a shorter cycle C' than C such that $E(C') \cap E(v_n; G') = E(C) \cap E(v_n; G')$. Choose C' as the shortest one among such cycles C'. Since $\{v_{i_h}, v_{i_\ell}\} \notin E(G')$ and $E(C') \cap E(v_n; G') = \{\{v_n, v_{i_h}\}, \{v_n, v_{i_\ell}\}\}$ hold, we see that such C' still satisfies $|C'| \geq 4$, a contradiction to that C' is chordless. Therefore, $\Gamma_G(v_n)$ induces a clique in G.

(ii) Let $\hat{G}_i = G[\{v_i, v_{i-1}, \ldots, v_1\}]$, $i = 1, 2, \ldots, n$. Necessity: It is clear that any induced subgraph of a chordal graph is chordal. Then $\hat{G}_i$ is chordal for each $i = 1, 2, \ldots, n$, and by condition (i), v_i is a simplicial vertex in the graph $\hat{G}_i$. This means that $(v_n, v_{n-1}, \ldots, v_1)$ is a perfect elimination ordering of G.

Sufficiency: Let $(v_n, v_{n-1}, \ldots, v_1)$ be a perfect elimination ordering of G. We prove by induction on the number of vertices that G is chordal. It is clear that $\hat{G}_1$ is chordal. Assuming that $\hat{G}_i$ is chordal, we show that $\hat{G}_{i+1}$ remains chordal. If $\hat{G}_{i+1}$ has a chordless cycle C of length 4, then C must pass through v_{i+1}. However, C cannot be chordless since all neighbors of v_{i+1} form a clique in $\hat{G}_{i+1}$. Therefore, by induction, we see that G is chordal.   □

Since an MA ordering in a graph can be obtained in linear time by Lemma 2.19, Theorem 2.64 provides a linear time algorithm for testing whether a given graph is chordal or not. The testing algorithm is given by Tarjan and Yannakakis [300].

For example, the graph in Fig. 1.33 is a chordal graph. The shaded numbers beside vertices denote an MA ordering of the graph. The reverse of the MA ordering is easily shown to be a perfect elimination ordering, showing by Theorem 2.64(ii) that the input graph is chordal.

3

Minimum Cuts

In this chapter we show, as applications of maximum adjacency (MA) ordering, that a minimum cut in an edge-weighted graph can be found efficiently and that a maximum flow between certain vertices, called a pendent pair, can be computed efficiently.

There are various applications of minimum cut algorithms such as cutting plane algorithms [8, 47, 199], the traveling salesman problem (TSP) [164, 219, 311], the vehicle routing problem [15, 280], network reliability theory [176, 292, 281], large-scale circuit placement [31, 46, 114, 210], information retrieval [28], image segmentation [102], automatic graph drawing [218], compilers for parallel languages [34], and computational biology [115, 116, 124, 313].

A standard algorithm to compute a minimum cut in an edge-weighted graph $G = (V, E)$ was to solve $n - 1$ (s, t)-maximum flow problems by changing the source sink pair (s, t) over all $t \in V - s$, where s was fixed to an arbitrary vertex in V. Using an $O(nm \log(n^2/m))$ time maximum flow algorithm [103] yields an $O(n^2 m \log(n^2/m))$ time algorithm for computing a minimum cut in G.

In Section 3.1, we show that the last two vertices in an MA ordering is a pendent pair; that is, the local edge-connectivity between them is equal to the degree of the last vertex. Using this property, in Section 3.2 we give a novel algorithm for computing a minimum cut in a graph, which runs in $O(mn + n^2 \log n)$ time. Section 3.3 deals with an application of the minimum-cut algorithm. In Section 3.4, we derive a hierarchical structure of MA orderings, and in Section 3.5 we see that a maximum flow between a pendent pair can be constructed in linear time. In Section 3.6, we extend the definition of pendent pairs to a set function. Finally Section 3.7 surveys practical performance of several efficient minimum-cut algorithms.

3.1 Pendent Pairs in MA Orderings

For any specified pair of vertices $u, v \in V$ in an edge-weighted graph $G = (V, E)$, we can compute the local edge-connectivity $\lambda(u, v; G)$ by applying a maximum-flow algorithm. As noted in Corollary 1.9, this takes $O(mn \log(n^2/m))$ time by using one of the fastest maximum-flow algorithms [103]. However, in this section, we show that $\lambda(u, v; G)$ for some pair of vertices $u, v \in V$ (which are specified by the algorithm) can be computed by a significantly simpler method. As observed in Section 1.5.1, every edge-weighted graph G admits a *pendent pair* (u, v), that is, an ordered pair of vertices u and v such that $\lambda(u, v; G) = d(v; G)$. Our first observation is that, without constructing a Gomory–Hu tree from Section 1.5, a pendent pair of a graph can be identified from an MA ordering.

As defined in Section 2.2, an MA ordering in an edge-weighted graph $G = (V, E)$ is an ordering $\sigma = (v_1, v_2, \ldots, v_n)$ of vertices in V such that

$$d(V_{i-1}, v_i; G) \geq d(V_{i-1}, v_j; G) \text{ for all } i, j \text{ with } 2 \leq i \leq j \leq n, \tag{3.1}$$

where $V_j = \{v_1, v_2, \ldots, v_j\}$ ($1 \leq j \leq n$). Such an ordering can be found by choosing an arbitrary vertex as v_1 and choosing a vertex $u \in V - V_{i-1}$ that has the maximum sum of weights of edges between V_{i-1} and u as the ith vertex v_i, after choosing the first $i-1$ vertices $v_1, \ldots, v_{i-1}$. For example, the numbering $(v_1, v_2, \ldots, v_{21})$ of the vertices in the graph $G = (V, E)$ in Fig. 1.3 is an MA ordering of G starting from v_1.

The following property of an MA ordering is the starting point of the rest of development.

Theorem 3.1 ([82, 93, 231, 232, 293]). *For an edge-weighted graph $G = (V, E)$, let $\sigma = (v_1, v_2, \ldots, v_n)$ be an MA ordering of V. Then the pair of the last two vertices v_{n-1} and v_n is a pendent pair; that is,*

$$\lambda(v_{n-1}, v_n; G) = d(v_n; G). \tag{3.2}$$

$\square$

Since (3.2) holds for a multigraph G by Theorem 2.33(i), it remains valid for a graph with edges weighted by integers (or by rational numbers). For general real weights, it was first proved by Nagamochi and Ibaraki [232] in the form that $\lambda(v_h, v_n; G) = d(v_n; G)$ holds for the largest index h, such that $c_G(v_h, v_n) > 0$, under the assumption for simplicity that every edge has a positive weight. However, the result can be easily extended to nonnegative weights because allowing edges with zero weights in algorithm CAPFOREST of [232] does not affect the correctness of the proof. Then, introducing the edge $\{v_{n-1}, v_n\}$ with zero weight, the preceding result implies (3.2). The proof [232] is rather technical since the result is first verified in the case of rational-valued weights and then extended to the case of real-valued weights.

As will be discussed in subsequent chapters, MA orderings can be applied to design numerous important graph-connectivity algorithms. Many researchers have studied properties of MA ordering and discovered simple proofs of Theorem 3.1 [82, 93, 232, 248, 250, 283, 293].

To complete Theorem 3.1, here we describe a simple proof for the case of real weights, which is due to Frank [82]. (In Section 3.4 we will give an alternative proof, which also tells how to construct a maximum flow between the last two vertices v_{n-1} and v_n in an MA ordering.)

Proof of Theorem 3.1. By definition, $\lambda(v_{n-1}, v_n; G) \le d(v_n; G)$ is obvious. We show the converse, $\lambda(v_{n-1}, v_n; G) \ge d(v_n; G)$, by an induction on the numbers of vertices. The theorem is true for $|V| = 2$. Assume $n = |V|$ for a given graph $G = (V, E)$ and as sume that the theorem holds for all graphs with $n'(< n)$ vertices. Consider an MA ordering $\sigma = (v_1, v_2, \ldots, v_{n-2}, v_{n-1}, v_n)$ in G. Without loss of generality we assume that the last two vertices v_{n-1} and v_n are not adjacent (since an edge $e = \{v_{n-1}, v_n\}$ contributes to both $\lambda(v_{n-1}, v_n; G)$ and $d(v_n; G)$ by $c_G(e)$). Then we will show that $d(\{v_1, \ldots, v_{n-2}\}, v_{n-1}; G) = d(v_{n-1}; G)$ and $d(\{v_1, \ldots, v_{n-2}\}, v_n; G) = d(v_n; G)$ hold. Notice that the ordering $\sigma' = (v_1, v_2, \ldots, v_{n-2}, v_{n-1})$ is an MA ordering in the graph $G - v_n$ and, hence, by induction hypothesis we have

$$\lambda(v_{n-2}, v_{n-1}; G - v_n) = d(v_{n-1}; G - v_n) \, (= d(v_{n-1}; G)).$$

Similarly, we have

$$\lambda(v_{n-2}, v_n; G - v_{n-1}) = d(v_n; G - v_{n-1}) \, (= d(v_n; G))$$

since $\sigma'' = (v_1, v_2, \ldots, v_{n-2}, v_n)$ is an MA ordering in $G - v_{n-1}$. Therefore, we obtain

$$\begin{aligned}\lambda(v_{n-1}, v_n; G) &\ge \min\{\lambda(v_{n-2}, v_{n-1}; G), \lambda(v_{n-2}, v_n; G)\} \quad \text{(by (1.18))} \\ &\ge \min\{\lambda(v_{n-2}, v_{n-1}; G - v_n), \lambda(v_{n-2}, v_n; G - v_{n-1})\} \\ &= \min\{d(v_{n-1}; G), d(v_n; G)\} = d(v_n; G).\end{aligned}$$

This proves Theorem 3.1. $\square$

Figure 3.1 illustrates an MA ordering $\sigma = (s, u_3, u_4, u_2, u_5, u_1, u_6)$ and a pendent pair (u_1, u_6), implying that $\lambda(u_1, u_6; G) = d(u_6; G) = 80$.

By Lemma 2.20, we can find a pendent pair (u, v) in $O(m + n \log n)$ time and $O(m + n)$ space by computing an MA ordering σ and by setting (u, v) to be its last two vertices (v_{n-1}, v_n). Also by this lemma, we can find an MA ordering σ with a prescribed starting vertex s. Therefore, we can avoid a specified vertex being used in the last two vertices in σ (if $n > 2$). This property is crucial in designing efficient algorithms for computing the extreme vertex sets in Chapter 6 and edge splittings in Chapter 7.

Lemma 3.2 ([232]). *For an edge-weighted graph $G = (V, E)$ and a vertex $s \in V$, a pendent pair (u, v), where $u \ne s \ne v$ if $n > 2$, can be found in $O(m + n \log n)$ time and $O(m + n)$ space.* $\square$

Queyranne [277] and Rizzi [283] generalized Theorem 3.1 for the cut function $d : 2^V \to R^+$ to a more general setting of set functions. We describe the results by Rizzi and Queyranne in Sections 3.6 and 10.2, respectively.

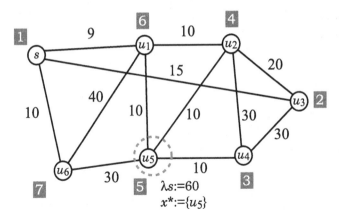

Figure 3.1. An MA ordering in an edge-weighted graph G, where the numbers next to the edges indicate their weights and the shaded numbers beside vertices denote an MA ordering.

3.2 A Minimum-Cut Algorithm

As observed in the previous section, we can compute the local edge-connectivity $\lambda(u, v; G)$ for a pendent pair u and v in $O(m + n \log n)$ time. This implies that, if an edge-weighted graph G has a cut $\{X, V - X\}$ with cut size smaller than $\lambda(u, v; G)$, then it does not separate u and v and, hence, is preserved in the graph $G/\{u, v\}$ obtained by contracting u and v into a single vertex. That is, the following relation holds:

$$\lambda(G) = \min\{\lambda(G/\{u, v\}), \lambda(u, v; G)\}. \tag{3.3}$$

Thus, the problem of finding a minimum cut in G is reduced to finding a minimum cut in $G/\{u, v\}$ with one less vertex. Based on this, Nagamochi and Ibaraki [232] have devised an $O(nm + n^2 \log n)$ time algorithm for computing the edge-connectivity $\lambda(G)$ and a minimum cut in G by computing MA orderings $n - 2$ times.

For a graph G with a designated vertex s, a cut $\{X, V - X\}$ is called s-proper if neither $X = \{s\}$ nor $V - X = \{s\}$ holds. The s-proper edge-connectivity is defined to be the minimum cut size of s-proper cuts and is denoted by $\lambda_s(G)$, where $\lambda_s(G)$ is defined to be $+\infty$ if $|V| \le 2$. In other words,

$$\lambda_s(G) = \min\{\lambda(u, v; G) \mid u, v \in V - s\}.$$

Hence, we see

$$\lambda(G) = \min\{\lambda_s(G), d(s; G)\}.$$

Based on observation (3.3), a minimum s-proper cut in a graph can be obtained by choosing the same vertex s as the first vertex v_1 in the MA orderings in the preceding algorithm. In the following, we describe such an algorithm.

Algorithm CONTRACT

Input: An edge-weighted graph $G = (V, E)$ with $|V| \geq 3$ and a vertex $s \in V$.

Output: A minimum s-proper cut $\{X, V - X\}$ of G.

1   $H := G; \lambda_s := +\infty;$
2   **while** $|V(H)| \geq 3$ **do**
3   Find a pendent pair (u, v) with $u, v \in V(H) - s$ in H;
4   **if** $d(v; H) < \lambda_s$ **then**
5           $\lambda_s := d(v; H);$ $x^* := v \in V(H)$
        end; /* if */
6       $H := H/\{u, v\}$
    end; /* while */
7   Let X be the set of all vertices in V that have been contracted into the
        current x^*;
8   Output $\{X, V - X\}$.

We also give a slightly different version of this algorithm so that the minimum degree $\min_{v \in V(H)} d(v; H)$ of the current graph H is available before contracting the next pendent pair. The modified version will be a basis of the algorithms in the subsequent chapters.

Algorithm MINCUT

Input: An edge-weighted graph $G = (V, E)$ with $|V| \geq 3$ and a vertex $s \in V$.

Output: A minimum s-proper cut $\{X, V - X\}$ of G.

1   $x^* := \operatorname{argmin}_{v \in V - s} d(v; G); \lambda_s := \min_{v \in V - s} d(v; G);$
2   $H := G;$
3   **while** $|V(H)| \geq 4$ **do**
4   Find a pendent pair (u, v) with $u, v \in V(H) - s$ in H;
        /* $\lambda(u, v; H) = d(v; H) \geq \lambda_s$ */
5   Contract u and v, call the resulting vertex as w, and let $H := H/\{u, v\}$;
6   **if** $d(w; H) < \lambda_s$ **then** $\lambda_s := d(w; H);$ $x^* := w$ **end** /* if */
    end; /* while */
7   Let $X \subseteq V - s$ be the set of all vertices that have been contracted into x^*;
8   Output $\{X, V - X\}$.

Theorem 3.3. *For an edge-weighted graph $G = (V, E)$ with a designated vertex $s \in V$, MINCUT correctly computes the s-proper edge-connectivity $\lambda_s(G)$ and a minimum s-proper cut in $O(n(m + n \log n))$ time.* $\square$

Proof. By construction, a cut $\{X, V - X\}$ computed by the algorithm is s-proper and $d(X; G) = \lambda_s$ holds. We show that there is no s-proper cut $\{Y, V - Y\}$ with $d(Y; G) < \lambda_s$. Assume conversely that such a cut $\{Y, V - Y\}$ exists. Before the while-loop, it holds that $d(v; G) \geq \lambda_s$ for all $v \in V - s$. Since we update λ_s as $d(w; H)$ whenever it is less than the current λ_s, a pendent pair (u, v) in H obtained in line 4 always satisfies $\lambda(u, v; H) \geq \lambda_s$ after the update. Since such a pair of vertices is contracted into a single vertex in each iteration of the while-loop, we

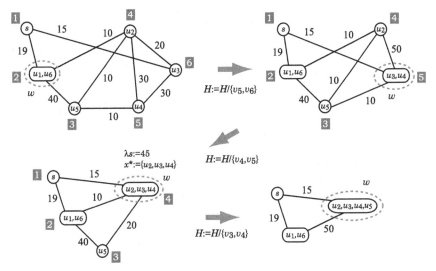

Figure 3.2. Illustration of MINCUT computation for the graph G in Fig. 3.1, where in each graph the numbers beside edges indicate their weights and the shaded numbers beside vertices denote an MA ordering of the graph.

see that no two vertices $u' \in Y$ and $v' \in V - Y$ with $d(Y, V - Y; G) < \lambda_s$ have been contracted before completion of the while-loop. Hence, $\{Y, V - Y\}$ must be $\{s, V - s\}$, which contradicts that $\{Y, V - Y\}$ is an *s*-proper cut.

The time complexity follows from Lemma 3.2. $\square$

Figures 3.1 and 3.2 illustrate a process of MINCUT applied to the graph G in Fig. 3.1, where the first graph in Fig. 3.2 is obtained from Fig. 3.1 by $H := H/\{v_1, v_6\}$. In the third graph of Fig. 3.2, λ_s is updated to 45. Therefore, we conclude that $\lambda_s(G) = 45$, and $\{\{u_2, u_3, u_4\}, \{s, u_1, u_5, u_6\}\}$ is output as a minimum *s*-proper cut. Note that $\lambda(G) \neq \lambda_s(G)$ holds in this example since $d(s; G) = 34 < \lambda_s(G) = 45$.

Computing the *s*-proper edge-connectivity will be a basis for solving other connectivity problems. MINCUT will be used, for example, for edge splitting and the edge-connectivity augmentation problems in Chapters 7 and 8, respectively.

From the preceding result and relation $\lambda(G) = \min\{\lambda_s(G), d(s; G)\}$, we obtain a minimum cut by choosing a smaller one between $(\{s\}, V - s)$ and the cut $(X, V - X)$ output by MINCUT. This is an $O(n(m + n \log n))$ time minimum-cut algorithm, which is currently one of the best among the existing deterministic algorithms.

Corollary 3.4. *For an edge-weighted graph* $G = (V, E)$, *a minimum cut can be computed in* $O(n(m + n \log n))$ *time and* $O(n + m)$ *space.* $\square$

3.3 *s*-Proper *k*-Edge-Connected Spanning Subgraphs

In this section, we extend the algorithm MINCUT in the previous section to solve some problems related to *s*-proper edge-connectivity.

3.3.1 h-Minimal Subset of $E(s; G)$

Let $G = (V, E)$ be a multigraph. For edge sets E' and E'' such that $E' \subseteq E$ and $E'' \cap E = \emptyset$, the graphs $(V, E - E')$ and $(V, E \cup E'')$ are denoted by $G - E'$ and $G + E''$, respectively. Let $s \in V$ be a designated vertex in G. For a positive integer $h \leq \lambda_s(G)$, we say that a subset $F \subseteq E(s; G)$ is *h-minimal* (with respect to s) if

$$\lambda_s(G - (E(s; G) - F)) \geq h > \lambda_s(G - (E(s; G) - F')) \text{ for any } F' \subset F.$$

We now show that an h-minimal subset $F \subseteq E(s; G)$ can be obtained by modifying MINCUT in Section 3.2.

First delete all edges incident with s to obtain a graph

$$G_s = G - E(s; G),$$

then check degree $d(v; G_s)$ for all vertices $v \in V - s$ in G_s. If there is a vertex $v \in V - s$ with $d(v; G_s) < h$ then $E(s, v; G)$ must contain at least $h - d(v; G_s)$ edges (since G originally satisfies $\lambda_s(G) \geq h$). We put back arbitrary $h - d(v; G_s)$ edges in $E(s, v; G)$ to G_s for all vertices $v \in V - s$ with $d(v; G) < h$, and we denote by F (tentatively) the set of all edges added to G_s.

We now compute $\lambda_s(G_s + F)$ by algorithm MINCUT. If $\lambda_s(G_s + F) \geq h$, then F is an h-minimal set. On the other hand, if $\lambda_s(G_s + F) < h$, then after line 5 of MINCUT we check whether $d(X; G_s + F) < h$ holds for the set X of vertices contracted to w so far. This implies that there are least $h - d(X; G_s + F)$ edges in $E(s, X; G) - F$ by $\lambda_s(G) \geq h$. We add to F arbitrary $h - d(X; G_s + F)$ edges in $E(s, X; G) - F$ and then continue this modified iteration of MINCUT until $|V(H)| = 3$ holds. We call a subset $Y \subset V - s$ *h-critical* in a graph G' if $d(Y; G') = h$. By collecting inclusion-wise maximal subsets X detected in the while-loop, we can obtain a family of disjoint h-critical subsets $X_1, X_2, \ldots, X_p$ such that

$$\sum_{1 \leq i \leq p} d(s, X_i; G_s + F) = d(s; G_s + F) \tag{3.4}$$

holds in the final graph $G_s + F$. The entire algorithm is described as follows.

Algorithm h-MINIMALEDGESET
Input: A multigraph $G = (V, E)$ with a designated vertex s and a positive integer $h \in [1, \lambda_s(G)]$.
Output: An h-minimal subset $F \subseteq E(s; G)$, and a family $\mathcal{X} = \{X_1, X_2, \ldots, X_p\}$ of disjoint h-critical subsets satisfying (3.4).
1   $G_s := G - E(s; G)$; $F := \emptyset$; $\mathcal{X} := \emptyset$;
2   **for** each $v \in V - s$ with $d(v; G_s) < h$ **do**
3   Add to F arbitrary $h - d(v; G_s)$ edges in $E(s, v; G)$;
4   Add $\{v\}$ to $\mathcal{X}$
    end; /* for */
5   $H := G_s + F$; /* $d(v; H) \geq h$ for all $v \in V - s$ */

6 **while** $|V(H)| \geq 4$ **do**
7   Find a pendent pair (u, v) with $u, v \in V(H) - s$ in H (by computing an
      MA ordering from the initial vertex s);
      /* $\lambda(u, v; H) = d(v; H) \geq h$ */
8   Contract u and v, call the resulting vertex x^*, and let $H := H/\{u, v\}$;
      /* $d(x^*; H) = d(X; G_s + F)$ */
      if $d(x^*; H) < h$ **then**
9   Let $X \subseteq V - s$ be the set of all vertices that have been contracted
        into x^*;
10   Add to F arbitrary $h - d(X; G_s + F)$ edges in $E(s, X; G) - F$;
11   Add X to $\mathcal{X}$, discarding any subsets $X' \in \mathcal{X}$ with $X' \subset X$;
12   Let H denote the graph obtained from H by adding $h - d(x^*; H)$ edges
        between s and x^*
      end /* if */
    end. /* while */

The correctness and time complexity of algorithm h-MINIMALEDGESET are summarized in the next theorem.

Theorem 3.5. *For a multigraph* $G = (V, E)$, $s \in V$ *and a positive integer* $h \in$ $[1, \lambda_s(G)]$, h-MINIMALEDGESET *correctly computes an* h-*minimal subset* $F \subseteq$ $E(s; G)$ *and a family* $\mathcal{X}$ *of* h-*critical subsets satisfying* (3.4). *Furthermore,* h-MINIMALEDGESET *runs in* $O(n(m + n \log n))$ *time* (*if* G *is given as an edge-weighted graph*) *or in* $O(m + hn^2)$ *time* (*if* E *is given as a set of unweighted edges*), *where* $m = |E|$. $\square$

Proof. It is obvious that, by construction, the obtained $\mathcal{X}$ is a family of disjoint h-critical subsets satisfying (3.4). We show that the output F is h-minimal. Before entering the while-loop, it holds that $d(v; H) \geq h$ for all $v \in V - s$. Since we increase the degree $d(x^*; H)$ to h in line 12 whenever it is less than h, it inductively holds that $d(v; H) \geq h$ for all $v \in V(H) - s$ before each iteration of the while-loop. Therefore, any pendent pair (u, v) in H found in line 7 satisfies $\lambda(u, v; H) \geq \min\{d(u; H), d(v; H)\} \geq h$. Hence, h-MINIMALEDGESET never contracts two vertices $u' \in Y$ and $v' \in V - Y$ such that $d(Y, V - Y; G_s + F) < h$ for the current F. This implies that $\lambda_s(G_s + F) \geq h$ holds for the final graph $G_s + F$. Since $\mathcal{X}$ satisfies (3.4), any edge $e = \{s, v\} \in F$ has an h-critical subset $X_i \in \mathcal{X}$ with $v \in X_i$, for which $d(X_i; G_s + (F - e)) = h - 1 < h$ holds. This implies that F is minimal to the property $\lambda_s(G_s + F) \geq h$. The time complexity for an edge-weighted graph follows from Lemma 3.2 since the computation in the while-loop (i.e., finding a pendent pair by an MA ordering) is repeated at most n times. For the case where E is given as an edge set, we can sparsify the given multigraph G into a spanning subgraph with $O(hn)$ edges in $O(n + m)$ time (see Theorem 2.26) before applying h-MINIMALEDGESET to G. This reduces the time bound $O(n(n + m))$ to $O(m + n + n(hn)) = O(m + hn^2)$. $\square$

3.3.2 Minimal h-Edge-Connected Spanning Subgraph

An edge e in an h-edge-connected graph G is called h-*irremovable* if $G - e$ is no longer h-edge-connected. A graph is called a *minimal h-edge-connected* graph if every edge is h-irremovable. We consider the problem of finding a minimal h-edge-connected spanning subgraph G' of a given h-edge-connected multigraph. If we inspect the removability of each edge $e = \{u, v\}$ by computing a maximum flow from u to v in $G - e$, then it would require $O(m)$ maximum flow computations. By using Theorem 3.5, however, we can find a desired spanning subgraph in the following time complexity.

Corollary 3.6. *Given an h-edge-connected multigraph $G = (V, E)$, a minimal h-edge-connected spanning subgraph $G' = (V, E')$ can be obtained in $O(n^2(m + n \log n))$ time (if G is given as an edge-weighted graph) or in $O(m + hn^3)$ time (if E is given as a set of unweighted edges).* $\qquad\square$

Proof. A desired edge set $E' \subseteq E$ can be obtained as follows. Let $V = \{v_1, v_2, \ldots, v_n\}$ and let $G^0 = G$. For $i = 1, 2, \ldots, n$, we compute an h-minimal subset $F_i \subseteq E(v_i; G^{i-1})$ by applying h-MINIMALEDGESET. Letting

$$\hat{F}_i := \begin{cases} F_i & \text{if } |F_i| \geq h, \\ \text{a subset } F \text{ with } F_i \subset F \subseteq E(v_i; G^{i-1}) \text{ and } |F| = h & \text{otherwise,} \end{cases}$$

we remove the edges in $E(v_i; G^{i-1}) - \hat{F}_i$ from G^{i-1}, denoting the resulting graph by G^i. Let $G' = (V, E')$ denote the final graph G^n. By the choice of F_i, each graph G^i is v_i-proper h-edge-connected. Since F_i with $|F_i| < h$ is replaced with a superset $\hat{F}_i$ of F, we always have $d(v_i; G^i) \geq h$. Therefore, G^i is h-edge-connected for $i = 0, 1, 2, \ldots, n$. To show the minimality of G^n, note that all edges incident to v_i (i.e., $\hat{F}_i$) are h-irremovable in G^i and any edge h-irremovable in G^i remains h-irremovable in G^j with $j > i$, since G^j is a subgraph of G^i. Hence, such edges will never be deleted by the application of h-MINIMALEDGESET. Therefore, every edge in G^n is h-irremovable. Finally the time bound follows from Theorem 3.5. $\qquad\square$

3.3.3 Minimum Star Augmentation

As another application of the h-MINIMALEDGESET algorithm, we consider how to increase the edge-connectivity of a given multigraph G by adding a new vertex s and new edges between s and G. Given a multigraph $G = (V, E)$ and an integer $k \geq 1$, the problem asks to find a star augmentation $G + b$ of G (see Section 1.1) that minimizes

$$b(V) = \sum_{v \in V} c_{G+b}(s, v)$$

subject to the condition

$$d(X; G + b) \, (= d(X; G) + b(X)) \geq k \text{ for all } X \subset V \tag{3.5}$$

or, equivalently, $\lambda_s(G + b) \geq k$.

To solve this problem, we first consider the star augmentation $G' = G + b'$ such that $b'(v) = k$ for all $v \in V$. Note that $\lambda_s(G') \geq k$ holds. Then by applying the h-MINIMALEDGESET algorithm to G' and $h := k$, we compute a k-minimal subset $F \subseteq E(s; G')$ and a family $\mathcal{X} = \{X_1, X_2, \ldots, X_p\}$ of k-critical subsets satisfying (3.4). The star augmentation $G + b$ defined by $b(v) = |F \cap E(s, v; G')|$, $v \in V$, satisfies

$$
\begin{aligned}
d(X_i; G + b) &= k, \ X_i \in \mathcal{X} \\
\textstyle\sum_{1 \leq i \leq p} d(s, X_i; G + b) &= d(s; G + b) = b(V).
\end{aligned}
\tag{3.6}
$$

On the other hand, for each cut $\{X_i, V - X_i\}$, we have to add at least $d(s, X_i; G + b) = k - d(X_i; G)$ edges between X_i and $V - X_i$ to increase the cut size to k. By noting that subsets in $\mathcal{X}$ are pairwise disjoint, this tells that we need at least $\sum_{1 \leq i \leq p} d(s, X_i; G + b)$ $(= b(V))$ new edges to obtain a star augmentation of G satisfying (3.5). Therefore, the aforementioned star augmentation $G + b$ is optimal, and we have the next result.

Theorem 3.7. *For a multigraph $G = (V, E)$ and a positive integer k, a minimum star augmentation $G + b$ can be obtained in $O(n(m + n \log n))$ time.* $\square$

3.4 A Hierarchical Structure of MA Orderings

In this section we describe a hierarchical structure of MA orderings, which will be used in designing a maximum-flow algorithm in the next section and other algorithms in Chapters 6 and 8.

Let $G = (V, E)$ be an edge-weighted graph, let $\sigma = (v_1, v_2, \ldots, v_n)$ be an MA ordering on G, and let $\delta \geq 0$ be a real. We consider constructing spanning subgraphs of G such that σ remains an MA ordering to each of them. For this, we define that a spanning subgraph G' of G is obtained from an MA ordering $\sigma = (v_1, v_2, \ldots, v_n)$ on G by a δ-reduction if G' satisfies

$$c_{G'}(e) \leq c_G(e) \text{ for all } e \in E,$$
$$d(V_{i-1}, v_i; G') = \min\{d(V_{i-1}, v_i; G), \delta\} \text{ for all } i = 2, 3, \ldots, n$$

where $V_{i-1} = \{v_1, v_2, \ldots, v_{i-1}\}$.

Lemma 3.8 ([6]). *Let G' be a graph obtained from an MA ordering $\sigma = (v_1, v_2, \ldots, v_n)$ of an edge-weighted graph G by a δ-reduction. Then σ is also an MA ordering to G'.* $\square$

Proof. It suffices to show that

$$d(V_{i-1}, v_i; G') \geq d(V_{i-1}, v_j; G') \text{ for all } i \text{ and } j \text{ with } 2 \leq i < j \leq n.$$

If $d(V_{i-1}, v_i; G') = \delta$, then we have

$$d(V_{i-1}, v_i; G') \geq d(V_{i-1}, v_j; G'),$$

since $\delta \geq d(V_{j-1}, v_j; G') \geq d(V_{i-1}, v_j; G')$ by the δ-reduction and $V_{j-1} \supseteq V_{i-1}$. Therefore, assume $\delta > d(V_{i-1}, v_i; G') = d(V_{i-1}, v_i; G)$. Then by the definitions of G' and an MA ordering, we have

$$d(V_{i-1}, v_i; G) \geq d(V_{i-1}, v_j; G) \geq d(V_{i-1}, v_j; G').$$

Then

$$d(V_{i-1}, v_i; G') \geq d(V_{i-1}, v_j; G')$$

follows, as required.   □

We now show how to decompose G into two spanning subgraphs such that σ is still an MA ordering to them and their union becomes the original G. Given an MA ordering $\sigma = (v_1, v_2, \ldots, v_n)$ in G, we write $u \leq u'$ if $u = v_i$ and $u' = v_{i'}$ satisfy $i \leq i'$, and we arrange the edges in $E(V_{i-1}, v_i; G)$ ($i = 2, 3, \ldots, n$) in the order of

$$e_{i,1} = \{u_{i,1}, v_i\}, \; e_{i,2} = \{u_{i,2}, v_i\}, \ldots, e_{i,r_i} = \{u_{i,r_i}, v_i\}, \tag{3.7}$$

where $r_i = |E(V_{i-1}, v_i; G)|$, so that $u_{i,1} \leq u_{i,2} \leq \cdots \leq u_{i,r_i}$ holds. Given a real $\delta \geq 0$, we define two subgraphs $G_\delta = (V, E)$ and $\overline{G}_\delta = (V, E)$ by the edge weights c_{G_δ} and $c_{\overline{G}_\delta}$:

$$c_{G_\delta}(u_{i,j}, v_i) = \begin{cases} c_G(u_{i,j}, v_i), & \text{if } j \leq p_i - 1 \\ \delta - \displaystyle\sum_{1 \leq j \leq p_i - 1} c_G(u_{i,j}, v_i), & \text{if } j = p_i \\ 0, & \text{if } j > p_i \end{cases}$$

$$c_{\overline{G}_\delta}(e) = c_G(e) - c_{G_\delta}(e) \text{ for all edges } e \in E,$$

where p_i denotes the smallest index such that

$$\sum_{1 \leq j \leq p_i} c_G(u_{i,j}, v_i) \geq \delta$$

(we interpret $p_i = r_i + 1$ if $\sum_{1 \leq j \leq r_i} c_G(u_{i,j}, v_i) < \delta$). We call the resulting graphs G_δ and $\overline{G}_\delta$ the δ-*skeleton* and δ-*skin* of G (with respect to ordering σ), respectively. Figure 3.3(b) shows the 3-skeleton G_3 and the 3-skin $\overline{G}_3$ of the graph G with an MA ordering in Fig. 3.3(a).

Note that, by definition, for each $i = 2, 3, \ldots, n$ and $u \in V - V_{i-1}$,

$$d(V_{i-1}, u; G_\delta) = d(V_{i-1}, u; G) \text{ and } d(V_{i-1}, u; \overline{G}_\delta) = 0$$

hold if $d(V_{i-1}, u; G) \leq \delta$, while

$$d(V_{i-1}, u; G_\delta) = \delta \text{ and } d(V_{i-1}, u; \overline{G}_\delta) = d(V_{i-1}, u; G) - \delta$$

hold if $d(V_{i-1}, u; G) > \delta$.

The following is an edge-weighted version of Lemma 2.25.

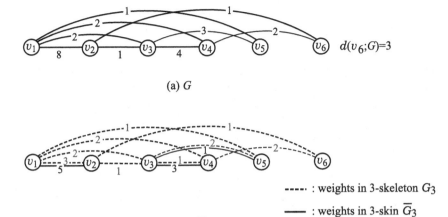

(a) G

----- : weights in 3-skeleton G_3

——— : weights in 3-skin $\overline{G}_3$

(b) G_3 and $\overline{G}_3$

Figure 3.3. (a) An edge-weighted graph G with an MA ordering $\sigma = (v_1, v_2, v_3, v_4, v_5, v_6)$, where the numbers beside edges indicate the weights of the edges; (b) the 3-skeleton G_3 and the 3-skin $\overline{G}_3$, where weights in G_3 and $\overline{G}_3$ are depicted by broken edges and solid edges, respectively.

Lemma 3.9. *For an MA ordering* $\sigma = (v_1, v_2, \ldots, v_n)$ *of an edge-weighted graph* G *and a real* $\delta \geq 0$, *let* G_δ *and* $\overline{G}_\delta$ *be the* δ-*skeleton and* δ-*skin of* G, *respectively. Then the ordering* σ *remains an MA ordering in both* G_δ *and* $\overline{G}_\delta$. $\qquad\square$

Proof. By the definition of G_δ and $\overline{G}_\delta$, we see that, for each $i = 2, 3, \ldots, n$ and $u \in V - V_{i-1}$, it holds that

$$d(V_{i-1}, u; G_\delta) = \min[\delta, d(V_{i-1}, u; G)],$$
$$d(V_{i-1}, u; \overline{G}_\delta) = \max[0, d(V_{i-1}, u; G) - \delta].$$

The first relation says that G_δ is obtained from G by a δ-reduction, and σ is an MA ordering in G_δ by Lemma 3.8. For the δ-skin $\overline{G}_\delta$, we have for each $i = 2, \ldots, n$ that

$$\begin{aligned}
d(V_{i-1}, v_i; \overline{G}_\delta) &= \max[0, d(V_{i-1}, v_i; G) - \delta] \\
&= \max[0, \max\{d(V_{i-1}, u; G) - \delta \mid u \in V - V_{i-1}\}] \\
&= \max\{\max[0, d(V_{i-1}, u; G) - \delta] \mid u \in V - V_{i-1}\} \\
&= \max\{d(V_{i-1}, u; \overline{G}_\delta) \mid u \in V - V_{i-1}\},
\end{aligned}$$

implying that ordering σ is also an MA ordering in $\overline{G}_\delta$. $\qquad\square$

Note that the δ-skin $\overline{G}_\delta$ may not be obtained from G by the δ-reduction. For example, the 3-skin $\overline{G}_3$ in Fig. 3.3 is not a graph obtained from G by any δ-reduction.

Based on this lemma, we can give an alternative proof for Theorem 3.1 after proving the following observation. The next lemma is an edge-weighted version of Lemma 2.25(ii).

Lemma 3.10. *Let* $\sigma = (v_1, v_2, \ldots, v_n)$ $(n \geq 2)$ *be an MA ordering in an edge-weighted graph* $G = (V, E)$. *Then each connected component of* G *(a maximal subset of vertices connected each other via edges with positive weights) consists of vertices* $v_j, v_{j+1}, \ldots, v_h$ *having consecutive indices from some* j *to* h. *In particular,* v_{n-1} *and* v_n *belong to the same connected component if* $d(v_n; G) > 0$. □

Proof. Assume that there is a connected component Z consisting of vertices whose indices are not consecutive. Let Z contain the smallest index among such components. Then there are three vertices $v_i, v_j \in Z$ and $v_{i+1} \notin Z$ for some $1 \leq i < i + 1 < j \leq n$. Let Z' be the connected component containing v_{i+1}. By the choice of Z, Z' contains no vertex v_k with index $k \leq i$; hence, $d(V_i, v_{i+1}; G) = 0$. On the other hand, $d(V_i, v_j; G) > 0$ holds since v_i and v_j are in the same connected component. Thus, $d(V_i, v_{i+1}; G) < d(V_i, v_j; G)$ contradicts the definition of MA orderings. This proves the first statement in the lemma, from which the second statement immediately follows. □

We now prove Theorem 3.1 by constructing a maximum flow between the last two vertices, v_{n-1} and v_n, in an MA ordering in G.

Proof of Theorem 3.1. We assume without loss of generality that $d(v_n; G) > 0$ holds in a given MA ordering $\sigma = (v_1, v_2, \ldots, v_n)$, since $d(v_n; G) = 0$ trivially implies (3.2). Let $E^+(G)$ denote the set of edges with positive weights. For each $i = 2, 3, \ldots, n$ with $E(V_{i-1}, v_i; G) \cap E^+(G) \neq \emptyset$, let $\tilde{e}(v_i)$ denote the edge $\{u_{i'}, v_i\}$ with the smallest index i' among the edges in $E(V_{i-1}, v_i; G) \cap E^+(G)$. Let $F = \{\tilde{e}(v_i) \mid i = 2, \ldots, n, \ E(V_{i-1}, v_i; G) \cap E^+(G) \neq \emptyset\}$. By construction, we see that the graph (V, F) is a forest. For $\delta = \min\{c_G(e) \mid e \in F\}$ (> 0), the δ-skeleton G_δ satisfies

$$E(G_\delta) = F \text{ and } c_{G_\delta}(e) \leq c_G(e) \text{ for all } e \in E(G_\delta).$$

By Lemma 3.9, σ is also an MA ordering in G_δ. From the assumption $d(v_n; G) > 0$, $d(v_n; G_\delta) > 0$ holds. Then by Lemma 3.10, v_{n-1} and v_n are connected by a path P in G_δ. We push a flow from v_{n-1} to v_n along P by an amount δ, and we reduce the weights of edges $e \in E(P)$ by δ in G. Note that the resulting graph G' contains the δ-skin $\overline{G}_\delta$ of G; that is,

$$E(\overline{G}_\delta) \subseteq E(G') \text{ and } c_{\overline{G}_\delta}(e) \leq c_{G'}(e) \text{ for all } e \in E(\overline{G}_\delta).$$

Note that $d(v_n; \overline{G}_\delta) = d(v_n; G) - \delta$ holds and one of the edges in G now has weight zero in $\overline{G}_\delta$. Since σ remains an MA ordering in $\overline{G}_\delta$ by Lemma 3.9, we can repeat the preceding procedure to $\overline{G}_\delta$ until we have a (v_{n-1}, v_n)-flow with

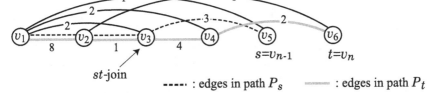

Figure 3.4. Example of paths P_t and P_s and their st-join, where P_t and P_s are depicted by gray solid lines and black broken lines, respectively.

flow value $d(v_n; G)$ after at most m iterations. When this procedure halts, (3.2) is proved. □

It was shown [250] that this algorithm for finding a maximum (v_{n-1}, v_n)-flow can be implemented to run in $O(m \log n)$ time by using the data structure of a dynamic tree [291]. In the next subsection, however, we show that a maximum (v_{n-1}, v_n)-flow for the last two vertices, v_{n-1} and v_n, in an MA ordering can be found in linear time without using a sophisticated data structure.

3.5 Maximum Flows Between a Pendent Pair

We describe a linear time algorithm that constructs a maximum (s, t)-flow between a pendent pair (s, t) in a given MA ordering. This algorithm was proposed by Arikati and Mehlhorn [6].

Fix an MA ordering $\sigma = (v_1, v_2, \ldots, v_n)$ of a graph $G = (V, E)$ and let (s, t) be the pendent pair (v_{n-1}, v_n). For a vertex $v = v_i \in V$, let $h(v)$ denote the vertex $h(v) = v_j$ with the largest j such that $j < i$ and $c_G(v_j, v_i) > 0$. For $t = v_n$, let

$$P_t = (u_0 = t, u_1 = h(u_0), u_2 = h(u_1), \ldots, u_r = h(u_{r-1}))$$

be the maximal path obtained by repeatedly visiting the vertices $u_{i+1} = h(u_i)$ from $u_0 = t$. Analogously define P_s from $s = v_{n-1}$. The vertex v_i with the largest i that belongs to both P_t and P_s is called the st-join. For example, Fig. 3.4 illustrates an MA ordering $\sigma = (v_1, v_2, \ldots, v_6)$ in the graph G of Fig. 3.3, and paths $P_t = (t = v_6, v_4, v_3, v_2, v_1)$, $P_s = (s = v_5, v_3, v_2, v_1)$, and the st-join v_3.

Lemma 3.11 ([6]). *For the pendent pair* $(s, t) = (v_{n-1}, v_n)$ *of an MA ordering* $\sigma = (v_1, v_2, \ldots, v_n)$ *in an edge-weighted graph* $G = (V, E)$, *which is not necessarily connected, let paths* P_s *and* P_t *be defined as before.*

(i) *For each i such that no v_j with $i \leq j$ belongs to both P_t and P_s, it holds that $d(V_{i-1}, v_i; G) \geq d(v_n; G)$.*

(ii) *If $d(v_n; G) > 0$, then the st-join v_ℓ exists and $d(V_{i-1}, v_i; G) \geq d(v_n; G)$ holds for all $i = \ell + 1, \ell + 2, \ldots, n$.* □

Proof. (i) We show by induction on i. The stated property holds for $i = n$. Assume that a vertex v_i with $i < n$ satisfies condition (i); we assume that v_i is not in P_t (the other case can be treated analogously). Let v_ℓ be the vertex in P_t with the minimum $\ell > i$. Then $d(V_{i-1}, v_\ell; G) = d(V_{\ell-1}, v_\ell; G)$ since $d(\{v_i, v_{i+1}, \ldots, v_{\ell-1}\}, v_\ell; G) = 0$ by the definition of P_t. By induction hypothesis, $d(V_{\ell-1}, v_\ell; G) \geq d(v_n; G)$. By the definition of MA orderings, $d(V_{i-1}, v_i; G) \geq d(V_{i-1}, v_\ell; G)$. Therefore, $d(V_{i-1}, v_i; G) \geq d(v_n; G)$, as required.

(ii) By condition (ii), we only need to show that the st-join exists. Assume that one of P_t and P_s does not reach v_1; say, P_t ends up with v_i $(i > 1)$. This means $d(V_{i-1}, v_i; G) = 0$, contradicting the property $d(V_{i-1}, v_i; G) \geq d(v_n; G) > 0$ of condition (i). Therefore, both P_t and P_s reach v_1 and the st-join exists.   □

Based on paths P_t and P_s and their st-join v_k, we can send a flow from s to t by the following procedure.

1. For the st-join v_k, consider the path P from s to t obtained by following P_s from s to v_k and then by following P_t from v_k to t. Let ε be the smallest weight of the edges in P.

2. We send the ε amount of flow from s to t along P. Thus, we reduce the weights of all edges in P by ε; that is, for each vertex v_i in P except for v_k, we reduce the weight of edge $\{v_j, v_i\}$ in P with $j < i$ by ε (where such an edge $\{v_j, v_i\}$ has the largest j in $E(V_{i-1}, v_i; G)$ by the choice of P_t and P_s).

3. For each vertex $v_\ell \in (V - V(P) - v_1) \cup \{v_k\}$, we reduce the weights of edges in $E(V_{\ell-1}, v_\ell; G)$ arbitrarily so that the sum of these weights becomes $\min\{d(v_n; G) - \varepsilon, d(V_{\ell-1}, v_\ell; G)\}$. (In other words, the resulting graph G' is obtained by a $(d(v_n; G) - \varepsilon)$-reduction from G.)

By Lemma 3.8, the same ordering σ is an MA ordering in G'. Also observe that it holds that $d(v_n; G') = d(v_n; G) - \varepsilon$. If $d(v_n; G') = 0$ then we are done since the obtained flow is a maximum (s, t)-flow. Otherwise if $d(v_n; G') > 0$ then G' has an st-join by Lemma 3.11 and we can again apply the aforementioned procedure to G'. Hence, by repeating the procedure for $G := G'$ until the new G' satisfies $d(v_n; G') = 0$, we can construct a collection of weighted paths that together gives a maximum flow of value $d(v_n; G)$ from s to t. This proves the correctness of the preceding algorithm.

We now show that the algorithm can be implemented to run in linear time. For this, we observe in the following that, in each iteration, the weight reduction in step 3 may not be explicitly executed. First note that we can first choose the edge $(v_j, v_\ell) \in E(V_{\ell-1}, v_\ell; G)$ with the smallest j in step 3. Then we see that such weight reductions for vertices $v_\ell \in (V - V(P) - v_1) \cup \{v_k\}$ in step 3 may be skipped before starting the next iteration of the procedure. This is because sending a flow in step 2 reduces the weight of the edge $\{v_j, v_i\} \in E(V_{i-1}, v_i; G)$ with the largest j, and such a flow from s to t can be found in steps 1 and 2 even if the weight reductions in step 3 are skipped in the previous iterations of the procedure. From this observation, we conclude that we do not have to take a path from s to

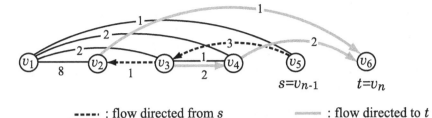

----- : flow directed from s ——— : flow directed to t

Figure 3.5. A maximum (v_{n-1}, v_n)-flow obtained by PENDENTFLOW in the graph G of Fig. 3.3(a).

t one by one; we visit vertices from v_n to v_1, pushing flows from s to t via all possible paths. More precisely, the algorithm is described as follows, where flow value $f(v_j, v_i)$ with $j < i$ takes a positive real (resp. negative real) if a flow of amount $|f(v_j, v_i)|$ moves from v_j to v_i (resp. v_i to v_j).

Algorithm PENDENTFLOW
Input: An MA ordering $\sigma = (v_1, v_2, \ldots, v_n)$ of a graph $G = (V, E)$.
Output: A maximum (v_{n-1}, v_n)-flow $f : E \to \mathfrak{R}$.
1   $f(e) := 0$ for all $e \in E$;
2   $b(v) := 0$ for all $v \in V - \{v_{n-1}, v_n\}$; $b(v_{n-1}) := d(v_n; G)$;
     $b(v_n) := -d(v_n; G)$;
     /* $b(v) > 0$ (resp. $b(v) < 0$) means that a flow of amount $|b(v)|$
       is pushed from v_{n-1} to v (resp., from v to v_n) */
3   **for** $i = n, n-1, \ldots, 2$ **do**
4   **if** $b(v_i) \neq 0$ **then**
5   **for** each edge $\{v_j, v_i\} \in E(V_{i-1}, v_i; G)$ in the decreasing order of
      $j \, (< i)$ **do**
6      $f(v_j, v_i) := \min\{c_G(v_j, v_i), |b(v_i)| - \sum_{j < \ell < i} |f(v_\ell, v_i)|\}$;
      /* pushing flow on edge $\{v_j, v_i\}$ */
7   **if** $b(v_i) < 0$ **then** $f(v_j, v_i) := -f(v_j, v_i)$; **end** /* if */
8      $b(v_j) := b(v_j) + f(v_j, v_i)$;
9   **end** /* for */
10   **end** /* if */
11 **end.** /* for */

As an example, Fig. 3.5 shows a maximum (v_{n-1}, v_n)-flow obtained by PEN-DENTFLOW in the graph G of Fig. 3.3(a).

In PENDENTFLOW, we push the flow of amount $b(v_i)$ from v_i (or to v_i) by the inner for-loop of lines 5–9. Although we do not explicitly maintain paths P_t and P_s, the algorithm correctly finds the directions of flows at each vertex v_k by comparing the minimum of the amount of flow from s to v_k (i.e., $\sum\{-f(v_k, v_i) \mid f(v_k, v_i) < 0, \, i > k\}$) and the amount of flow to t from v_k (i.e., $\sum\{f(v_k, v_i) \mid f(v_k, v_i) > 0, \, i > k\}$). We see that, after the iteration for v_{k-1} in the outer for-loop of lines 3–11, $b(v_k)$ becomes equal to $\sum\{f(v_k, v_i) \mid f(v_k, v_i) > 0, i > k\} - \sum\{-f(v_k, v_i) \mid f(v_k, v_i) < 0, \ i > k\}$.

We can sort via bucket sort all edges $\{v_j, v_i\}$ in each set $E(V_{i-1}, v_i; G)$ according to j in linear time. Also it is easy to see that each edge is scanned $O(1)$ times during the entire algorithm. Hence, PENDENTFLOW can be implemented to run in linear time. This establishes the next theorem.

Theorem 3.12. *For the pendent pair* $(s, t) = (v_{n-1}, v_n)$ *of an MA ordering* $\sigma = (v_1, v_2, \ldots, v_n)$ *in an edge-weighted graph* $G = (V, E)$, *a maximum* (v_{n-1}, v_n)-*flow can be computed in* $O(n + m)$ *time.* $\square$

3.6 A Generalization of Pendent Pairs

In this section, we show that Theorem 3.1 holds under a more general setting, as studied by Rizzi [283].

For a finite set V, let d be a function $g : 2^V \times 2^V \to \Re$ such that

$$g(X, Y) = g(Y, X) \text{ for all subsets } X, Y \subseteq V.$$

A function d is called *monotone* if it holds that $g(X', Y) \le g(X, Y)$ for any subsets $X', X, Y \subseteq V$ with $X' \subseteq X$ and $X \cap Y = \emptyset$, and the function is called *consistent* if it holds that

$$g(A, X \cup B) \ge g(B, X \cup A)$$

for any disjoint sets $X, A, B \subseteq V$ with $g(A, X) \ge g(B, X)$.

A subset S of V is called *nontrivial* if $\emptyset \ne S \ne V$. An ordered pair (s, t) is called a *pendent pair* if $g(V - T, T) \ge g(V - t, t)$ holds for any disjoint sets $T \subseteq V$ with $s \in V - T$ and $t \in T$. Then an MA ordering of V on a monotone and consistent function g is defined as an order $\sigma = (v_1, v_2, v_3, \ldots, v_n)$ such that

$$g(V_{i-1}, v_i) \ge g(V_{i-1}, v_j) \text{ for } i, j \text{ with } 2 \le i \le j \le n,$$

where V_{i-1} denotes the set $\{v_1, v_2, \ldots, v_{i-1}\}$.

For two elements $a, b \in V$, the set obtained from V by identifying $\{a, b\}$ as a single element $v[a, b]$ is denoted by $V_{a,b}$. Hence, $V_{a,b} = (V - \{a, b\}) \cup \{v[a, b]\}$. A function $g : 2^V \times 2^V \to \Re$ can be naturally modified to a function $g : 2^{V_{a,b}} \times 2^{V_{a,b}} \to \Re$ by interpreting $g(X_1, X_2)$ for sets $X_1, X_2 \subseteq V_{a,b}$ as $g(X_1', X_2')$, where $X_i' = (X_i - v[a, b]) \cup \{a, b\}$ if $v[a, b] \in X_i$ and $X_i' = X_i$ otherwise. When $a = v_i$ and $b = v_j$, we may write $v[a, b]$ as $v_{[i,j]}$ for simplicity.

Lemma 3.13 ([283]). *Let* $\sigma = (v_1, v_2, v_3, \ldots, v_n)$ $(n \ge 3)$ *be an MA ordering of a finite set* V *on a monotone and consistent function* $g : 2^V \times 2^V \to \Re$. *Then*

(i) $\sigma_{1,2} = (v_{[1,2]}, v_3, v_4, \ldots, v_n)$ *is an MA ordering of* V_{v_1, v_2} *on g.*

(ii) $\sigma_{2,3} = (v_1, v_{[2,3]}, v_4, \ldots, v_n)$ *is an MA ordering of* V_{v_2, v_3} *on g.*

(iii) $\sigma_{1,3} = (v_2, v_{[1,3]}, v_4, \ldots, v_n)$ *is an MA ordering of* V_{v_1, v_3} *on g.* $\square$

Proof. (i) Immediate from the definition. (ii) It suffices to show that $g(v_1, v_{[2,3]}) \geq g(v_1, v_k)$ holds for any $k = 4, 5, \ldots, n$. This is true since $g(v_1, v_2) \geq g(v_1, v_k)$ in σ and $g(v_1, \{v_2, v_3\})$ $(= g(v_1, v_{[2,3]})) \geq g(v_1, v_2)$ by the monotonicity of g.

(iii) It suffices to show that $g(v_2, v_{[1,3]}) \geq g(v_2, v_k)$ holds for any $k = 4, 5, \ldots, n$. Since σ is an MA ordering of V, it holds that $g(v_1, v_2) \geq g(v_1, v_3)$, which implies $g(\{v_1, v_3\}, v_2)$ $(= g(v_2, v_{[1,3]})) \geq g(\{v_1, v_2\}, v_3)$ by the consistency of g. Since σ is an MA ordering of V and g is monotone, we have $g(\{v_1, v_2\}, v_3) \geq g(\{v_1, v_2\}, v_k) \geq g(v_2, v_k)$. Therefore, $g(v_2, v_{[1,3]}) \geq g(v_2, v_k)$, as required. $\qquad\square$

Theorem 3.14 ([283]). *For an MA ordering* $\sigma = (v_1, v_2, v_3, \ldots, v_n)$ *of a finite set V on a monotone and consistent function* $g : 2^V \times 2^V \to \Re$, (v_{n-1}, v_n) *is a pendent pair.* $\qquad\square$

Proof. We prove by induction on n. For $n = 3$, the theorem is true since $g(v_1, v_2) \geq g(v_1, v_3)$ implies $g(\{v_1, v_3\}, v_2) \geq g(\{v_1, v_2\}, v_3)$ by the consistency of g. Let $n > 3$ and assume that the theorem holds for all $n' < n$. For an MA ordering $\sigma = (v_1, v_2, v_3, \ldots, v_n)$ and a subset T of V with $v_n \in T$ and $v_{n-1} \in V - T$, we show that

$$g(V - T, T) \geq g(V - v_n, v_n).$$

For the first three elements, v_1, v_2, and v_3, there is a pair v_i and v_j ($1 \leq i < j \leq 3$) not separated by T. Hence $g(V_{v_i,v_j} - T, T) = g(V - T, T)$ and, $g(V_{v_i,v_j} - v_n, v_n) = g(V - v_n, v_n)$. For such i and j, we contract v_i and v_j into $v_{[i,j]}$, and we consider the MA orderings $\sigma_{i,j}$ discussed in Lemma 3.13. Then $g(V_{v_i,v_j} - T, T) \geq g(V_{v_i,v_j} - v_n, v_n)$ holds in V_{v_i,v_j} by the induction hypothesis. This also implies $g(V - T, T) \geq g(V - v_n, v_n)$. $\qquad\square$

For example, $g(X, Y) = d(X, Y; G)$ for subsets $X, Y \subseteq V(G)$ in an edge-weighted undirected graph G is a monotone and consistent function. Thus, Theorem 3.1 is a special case of this theorem.

Another extension of a pendent pair to symmetric submodular set functions due to Queyranne [277] will be discussed in Chapter 10. Theorem 3.14 is slightly more general than the result by Queyranne since there is a monotone and consistent function g that cannot be represented as a symmetric submodular set function. As such an example, function g with $g(S, T) = \max\{c_G(u, v) \mid e = \{u, v\} \in E(S, T; G)\}$, $S, T \subseteq V$, for an edge-weighted graph $G = (V, E)$ is monotone and consistent, but function f with $f(S) = g(S, V - S)$, $S \in 2^V$ is not a submodular set function.

3.7 Practically Efficient Minimum-Cut Algorithms

As observed in this chapter, a minimum cut can be computed in the time bound of $O(mn + n^2 \log n)$, which is smaller by a factor of $O(n)$ than the naïve $O(n^2 m \log(n^2/m))$ algorithm consisting of $n - 1$ maximum flow computations. However, since computing a minimum cut has numerous applications, study of the practical efficiency of minimum-cut algorithms is an important issue, and there are reports on experimental study of various minimum-cut algorithms by Chekuri et al. [35] and Jünger et al. [165]. Based on these reports, this section provides several practically efficient minimum-cut algorithms.

We call a set F of edges in a graph G *contractible* if $\lambda(G/F) = \lambda(G)$ holds, where G/F denotes the graph obtained from G by contracting each edge $e \in F$ into a single vertex (see Section 1.1).

3.7.1 Padberg and Rinaldi's Algorithm

Padberg and Rinaldi [271] observed some sufficient conditions for a graph to have a contractible edge.

Lemma 3.15 ([271]). *Let $G = (V, E)$ be an edge-weighted graph and let $\overline{\lambda}$ be a real such that $\overline{\lambda} \geq \lambda(G)$. Then an edge $e = \{u, v\}$ is contractible if one of the following conditions holds:*

$$c_G(u, v) \geq \overline{\lambda}, \tag{3.8}$$

$$2c_G(u, v) \geq \min\{d(u; G), d(v; G)\}, \tag{3.9}$$

$$\begin{aligned} 2c_G(u, v) \geq \max\{d(u; G) - c_G(u, w), d(v; G) - c_G(v, w)\} \\ \textit{for some } w \in V - \{u, v\}, \end{aligned} \tag{3.10}$$

$$\begin{aligned} c_G(u, v) + \sum_{w \in S} \min\{c_G(u, w), c_G(v, w)\} \geq \overline{\lambda} \\ \textit{for some subset } S \subseteq V - \{u, v\}. \end{aligned} \tag{3.11}$$

$\square$

By maintaining $d(u; G)$ and $c_G(u, v)$ as explicit data for all $v \in V$ and $e = \{u, v\} \in E$, conditions (3.8) and (3.9) can be examined for an edge $\{u, v\}$ in $O(1)$ time. Conditions (3.10) and (3.11) can be checked in $O(n)$ time.

Padberg and Rinaldi [271] proposed the following minimum-cut algorithm based on Lemma 3.15. Whenever some edge meets one of conditions (3.8)–(3.11), the edge can be contracted to a single vertex x, and the cut size $d(x; G')$ of the new vertex in the resulting graph G' possibly updates the incumbent cut size by $\overline{\lambda} := \min\{d(x; G'), \overline{\lambda}\}$. If none of the conditions holds for any in a certain edge set, then a maximum-flow algorithm is invoked for some pair of vertices s and t to contract s and t after computing the minimum (s, t)-cut size $\lambda(s, t; G)$ and updating $\overline{\lambda} := \min\{\lambda(s, t; G), \overline{\lambda}\}$. This is the general scheme of minimum-cut algorithms by Padberg and Rinaldi. However, in implementing this scheme, there is some freedom to decide how many and which edges are tested before invoking an (s, t)-maximum-flow computation and to choose which vertices as (s, t)-pair for the (s, t)-maximum flow computation. Several strategies for this scheme have been proposed [35, 165, 271], and it is reported that, in many instances, the number of invoked (s, t)-maximum-flow computations is extremely small compared with the worst-case bound n.

3.7.2 A Practical Version of MINCUT

In Section 3.2, we observed that a minimum cut can be found by algorithm MINCUT. The algorithm needs to compute MA orderings $O(n)$ times and thereby its running time is $O(n(m + n \log n))$ (see Theorem 3.3). In practice, we may find more than one edge to be contracted from a given MA ordering. Let $\sigma = (v_1, v_2, \ldots, v_n)$ be an MA ordering of an edge-weighted simple graph $G = (V, E)$, and $\overline{\lambda}$ is an upper bound on $\lambda(G)$. Then we choose an edge set $E_{\sigma,\overline{\lambda}}$ as follows. Let

$$V(\overline{\lambda}) = \{v \in V - v_1 \mid d(V_{i-1}, v_i; G) \geq \overline{\lambda}\}.$$

For each vertex $v_i \in V(\overline{\lambda})$, let $p(i) < i$ be the index such that

$$d(V_{p(i)}, v_i; G) \geq \overline{\lambda} > d(V_{p(i)-1}, v_i; G),$$

and define

$$E_{\sigma,\overline{\lambda}} = \{\{v_{p(i)}v_i\} \in E \mid v_i \in V(\overline{\lambda})\}.$$

For example, graph G with an MA ordering in Fig. 3.3(a) has $V(\overline{\lambda}) = \{v_2, v_4, v_5\}$ and $E_{\sigma,\overline{\lambda}} = \{\{v_1, v_2\}, \{v_3, v_4\}, \{v_3, v_5\}\}$ for $\overline{\lambda} = 4$.

Lemma 3.16. *For each edge $\{u, v\} \in E_{\sigma,\overline{\lambda}}$, we have $\lambda(u, v; G) \geq \overline{\lambda}$. Moreover, $E_{\sigma,\overline{\lambda}}$ forms a forest in which each tree consists of consecutive vertices in σ.* □

Proof. Let $\{v_j, v_i\} \in E_{\sigma,\overline{\lambda}}$, where $j < i$. Then we easily see that $(v_1, v_2, \ldots, v_j, v_i)$ is an MA ordering in the graph $G' = G[\{v_1, v_2, \ldots, v_j, v_i\}]$, and $\lambda(v_j, v_i; G) \geq d(v_i; G') \geq \overline{\lambda}$, by Theorem 3.1. We see that $E_{\sigma,\overline{\lambda}}$ is acyclic, since otherwise there must be a vertex $v_i \in V - v_1$ that is adjacent to at least two vertices $v_j, v_{j'}$, with $j, j' < i$ in forest $(V, E_{\sigma,\overline{\lambda}})$. For a positive $\varepsilon < \min\{c_G(e) \mid e \in E\}$, $E_{\sigma,\overline{\lambda}}$ is the edge set of the ε-skin $\overline{(G_{\overline{\lambda}})}_\varepsilon$ of the $\overline{\lambda}$-skeleton of G, and each tree in $E_{\sigma,\overline{\lambda}}$ consists of consecutive vertices in σ, since σ is still an MA ordering in $\overline{(G_{\overline{\lambda}})}_\varepsilon$ by Lemma 3.9. □

By this lemma, edge set $E_{\sigma,\overline{\lambda}}$ is contractible. In fact, $G/E_{\sigma,\overline{\lambda}}$ can be obtained by contracting the set of consecutive vertices in each tree in $E_{\sigma,\overline{\lambda}}$ into a single vertex. For graph G in Fig. 3.3(a) and $\overline{\lambda} = 4$ the components in $(V, E_{\sigma,\overline{\lambda}})$ is $\{X_1 = \{v_1, v_2\}, X_2 = \{v_3, v_4, v_5\}, X_3 = \{v_6\}\}$, and $G/E_{\sigma,\overline{\lambda}}$ is obtained by contracting each X_i into a vertex x_i. Based on Lemma 3.16, Nagamochi et al. [248] proposed the following minimum-cut algorithm, whose description is slightly different from that in the literature [248].

Algorithm MINCUT2
Input: An edge-weighted graph $G = (V, E)$ with $|V| \geq 3$.
Output: A minimum cut $\{X, V - X\}$ of G.
1   $x^* := \operatorname{argmin}_{v \in V} d(v; G)$; $\overline{\lambda} := \min_{v \in V} d(v; G)$;
2   $H := G$;
3   **while** $|V(H)| \geq 3$ **do**
4   Compute an MA ordering σ and edge set $E_{\sigma,\overline{\lambda}}$ in H;

5   Contract each component X_i of $(V, E_{\sigma,\bar{\lambda}})$ into a single vertex x_i;
6   **if** $\min_{x \in V(H)} d(x; H) < \bar{\lambda}$ **then**
7        $\bar{\lambda} := \min_{x \in V(H)} d(x; H);\ \ x^* := \operatorname{argmin}_{x \in V(H)} d(x; H)$
    end /* if */
    end; /* while */
8   Let $X \subseteq V$ be the set of all vertices that have been contracted into x^*;
9   Output $\{X, V - X\}$.

3.7.3 Hao and Orlin's Algorithm

Let $G = (V, E)$ be a digraph with edges weighted by nonnegative reals. We can determine $\lambda_s^+(G)$ by computing local edge-connectivities as follows (see Section 1.1 for definition of $\lambda_s^+(G)$).

Algorithm DirectMinCut
Input: An edge-weighted digraph $G = (V, E)$ with a vertex s.
Output: A cut $X \subset V$ such that $s \in X$ and $d(X; G) = \lambda_s^+(G)$.
1   $S = \{s\};\ X := \emptyset;\ \bar{\lambda} := +\infty$;
2   **while** $V - S \neq \emptyset$ **do**
3   Choose a vertex $t \in V - S$;
4   Compute a minimum (S, t)-cut Z in G, that is,
              a set Z with $S \subseteq Z \subseteq V - t$ and $d(Z; G) = \lambda(S, t; G)$;
5   **if** $\lambda(S, t; G) < \bar{\lambda}$ **then** $\bar{\lambda} := \lambda(S, t; G);\ X := Z;\ S := S \cup \{t\}$ **end**; /* if */
    end; /* while */
6   Output X.

Note that $\lambda(S, t; G) = \lambda(s', t; G/S)$ holds for the digraph G/S obtained from G by contracting S into a single vertex s'. We claim that a cut X output by the algorithm satisfies $d(X; G) = \lambda_s^+(G)$. Let $v_1 (= s), v_2, \ldots, v_n$ ($|V| = n$) be an ordering of the vertices in G, where vertices $v_2, \ldots, v_n$ are chosen as t in line 3 of DirectMinCut. Consider a cut $X^* \subset V$ such that $s \in X^*$ and $d(X^*; G) = \lambda_s^+(G)$ and let i be the index such that $\{v_1, v_2, \ldots, v_i\} \cap X^* = \{v_1, v_2, \ldots, v_{i-1}\}$. When a minimum (S, t)-cut Z is computed in line 4 for $t = v_i$, $S = \{v_1, v_2, \ldots, v_{i-1}\}$ holds and $d(Z; G) = \lambda(S, t; G) = d(X^*; G)$ must hold, indicating that this Z is a solution. A naïve implementation of DirectMinCut needs $O(n)$ maximum-flow computations, indicating an $O(n^2 m \log(n^2/m))$ time bound if Goldberg and Tarjan's $O(nm \log(n^2/m))$ time maximum-flow algorithm [103] is used.

By using Goldberg and Tarjan's push-relabel maximum-flow algorithm [103] for computing a minimum (S, t)-cut in line 4, Hao and Orlin [113] reduced the time to $O(nm \log(n^2/m))$. They exploited information such as distance labeling obtained from the previous iterations in the while-loop and cleverly chose sink t in line 3 such that the entire time complexity to compute a minimum cut is that of a single run of the push-relabel maximum-flow algorithm (see [113] for the details of the algorithm). This currently yields the fastest $O(mn \log(n^2/m))$ time algorithm for computing $\lambda_s^+(G)$ in an edge-weighted digraph G. Needless to say, a minimum cut in an edge-weighted undirected graph G can be found in the same time complexity by applying Hao and Orlin's algorithm to the digraph G' obtained by replacing each undirected edge with two oppositely oriented edges with the same edge weight. Fleischer [71] proved that a cactus representation of all minimum cuts can be contructed in $O(mn \log(n^2/m))$ time by Hao and Orlin's algorithm (see Chapter 5).

3.7.4 Randomized Algorithms

We mention that there are randomized algorithms that compute minimum cuts with high probability without using maximum-flow computation. Karger and Stein [181, 182] proposed the following algorithm.

Procedure RANDOMMINCUT$(G, \bar{\lambda})$
Input: An edge-weighted undirected graph G and an upper bound $\bar{\lambda}$ on $\lambda(G)$.
Output: A cut $W \subset V(G)$.
  if $|V(G)| = 2$ and $c_G(u, v) < \bar{\lambda}$ for $\{e = \{u, v\}\} = E(G)$ **then**
  $\bar{\lambda} := c_G(u, v)$;
  Let W be of all vertices contracted into u so far
  else
    repeat twice
    $threshold := \lceil |V(G)|/\sqrt{2} \rceil$;
    while $|V(G)| > threshold$ **do**
      Choose an edge $\{u, v\}$ with probability proportional to $c_G(u, v)$;
      $G := G/\{u, v\}$, contracting u and v into a single vertex s;
      if $d(s; G) < \bar{\lambda}$ **then**
      $\bar{\lambda} := d(s; G)$;
      Let W be the set of all vertices contracted into s so far
      end /* if */
    end /* while */
    RANDOMMINCUT$(G, \bar{\lambda})$;
    end /* repeat */
  end. /* if */

Karger and Stein [181, 182] showed that the algorithm can be implemented to run in $O(n^2 \log n)$ time and found a particular minimum cut with probability $\Omega(1/\log n)$. They proposed to execute $O(\log^2 n)$ independent runs of this algorithm to obtain an $O(n^2 \log n)$ time algorithm that finds all minimum cuts with high probability. Karger [177] further proved that a minimum cut can be found in near linear time with high probability.

3.7.5 Experimental Results

Jünger et al. [165] claimed that they conducted computational experiments to test the practical efficiency of the minimum-cut algorithms originally proposed in their papers. According to their report, MinCut2 and Hao and Orlin's algorithm are the fastest among the four aforemetioned algorithms. Chekuri et al. [35] proposed new and improved implementations for these four algorithms. Among their efficient codes, one based on Hao and Orlin's algorithm is the fastest. Both reports [35, 165] emphasize the great effect of the use of heuristics due to Padberg and Rinaldi [271] before resorting to any minimum-cut algorithm. After preprocessing a given graph by applying (3.8) and (3.9) as much as possible, the instance becomes considerably small, leading to a significant reduction in the running time.

4

Cut Enumeration

The number of cuts with small weights in a graph G is an important topic in the reliability analysis of probabilistic graphs whose edges are subject to failure [45], in the minimum k-way cut problem (i.e., the problem of computing a minimum edge subset whose removal creates at least k connected components [239, 251]), and other problems. In this chapter, we consider counting the number of small cuts, as well as deriving the upper and lower bounds.

In Section 4.1, we give an algorithm for enumerating all cuts in order of non-decreasing weights. The first r smallest cuts can be enumerated by $O(rn)$ maximum flow computations.

In Section 4.2, we show that, for an arbitrary $k > 1$, all $O(n^{2k})$ cuts with weights at most $k\lambda(G)$ can be enumerated in $O(n^{2k+2})$ time without relying on the maximum-flow algorithm. This enumeration algorithm makes use of an edge-splitting operation (see Chapter 7 for more details) to reduce the number of vertices by one while preserving the edge-connectivity.

In Section 4.3, we review some basic properties of a set of minimum cuts, and we give an algorithm for counting the number of minimum cuts, by which we can also prove that an upper bound on the number of minimum cuts is $\binom{n}{2} = \frac{n}{2}(n - 1)$ [27, 54]. This algorithm will become the design basis for an efficient algorithm for constructing a cactus representation in Chapter 5.

In Section 4.4, we prove that the number of cuts with weights less than $\frac{4}{3}\lambda(G)$ is at most $\binom{n}{2}$. With this bound, the time complexity of the aforementioned algorithm for enumerating all the cuts with weights less than $\frac{4}{3}\lambda(G)$ becomes $O(n^4)$.

4.1 Enumerating All Cuts

In this section, we present an algorithm that finds all cuts in an edge-weighted graph G on the order of nondecreasing weights [111, 112, 307]. The algorithm finds the next minimum cut by solving at most $2n - 3$ maximum-flow problems.

Theorem 4.1 ([111, 112, 307]). *Given an edge-weighted graph $G = (V, E)$, all cuts in G can be enumerated in order of nondecreasing weights with $O(nF(n, m))$*

time delay between two consecutive outputs, where $n = |V|$ and $m = |E|$, and $F(n, m)$ is the time required to find a minimum cut (i.e., maximum flow) in G between a given source and sink. The space required to output the first r minimum cuts is $O(rn)$.   □

Proof. Let $V = \{v_1, \ldots, v_n\}$, and let $\mathcal{C}_G$ denote the set of all cuts $\{X, V - X\}$ ($X \in 2^V - \{\emptyset, V\}$). To enumerate cuts in order of nondecreasing weights, we partition $\mathcal{C}_G$ into subsets systematically. We introduce a subset $\mathcal{C}(v)$ of $\mathcal{C}_G$ defined by a p-dimensional $\{0, 1\}$-vector v for some $p \in [1, n]$, where the ith entry of vector v is denoted by $v(i)$. We assume that $v(1) = 1$ for all the vectors v in the subsequent discussion. Then $\mathcal{C}(v)$ represents the set of all cuts separating the following two subsets:

$$S_v = \{v_i \mid i \in \{1, \ldots, p\}, \ v(i) = 1\},$$
$$T_v = \{v_i \mid i \in \{1, \ldots, p\}, \ v(i) = 0\}.$$

That is,

$$\mathcal{C}(v) = \{\{X, V - X\} \mid S_v \subseteq X \subseteq V - T_v\}.$$

In particular, $\mathcal{C}(v)$ with the one-dimensional vector v represents all cuts $\{X, V - X\}$ with $v_1 \in X$ (i.e., $\mathcal{C}(v) = \mathcal{C}_G$), whereas $\mathcal{C}(v)$ with an n-dimensional vector v consists of a single cut $\{S_v, T_v = V - S_v\}$.

Given v, we can find a minimum cut $\{X, V - X\} \in \mathcal{C}(v)$ as follows. If $T_v \neq \emptyset$ (i.e., v contains at least one zero-value entry), then a minimum cut $\{X, V - X\} \in \mathcal{C}(v)$ can be obtained in $F(n, m)$ time by computing a minimum (s, t)-cut in the graph $(G/S_v)/T_v$ obtained by contracting S_v and T_v into vertices s and t, respectively. On the other hand, if $T_v = \emptyset$ (i.e., $v(i) = 1$ for all $i \in \{1, \ldots, p\}$), then such a minimum cut $\{X, V - X\}$ can be found by running the minimum cut algorithm $(n - p)$ times to separate S and T for all $T = \{v_i\}$ with $v_i \in V - S_v$.

For a p-dimensional $\{0, 1\}$-vector v, we denote by $\mu(v)$ the n-dimensional $\{0, 1\}$-vector that represents a cut $\{X, V - X\} \in \mathcal{C}(v)$ with the minimum weight and by $d(v)$ its weight. Let $\mu = \mu(v)$ for simplicity and let $\{X^*, V - X^*\}$ be the minimum cut represented by μ.

We then remove $\{X^*, V - X^*\}$ from $\mathcal{C}(v)$ and replace the vector v by $(n - p)$ vectors $\overline{\mu}^{p+1}, \overline{\mu}^{p+2}, \ldots, \overline{\mu}^n$ such that

$$\mathcal{C}(v) - \{\{X^*, V - X^*\}\} = \mathcal{C}(\overline{\mu}^{p+1}) \cup \mathcal{C}(\overline{\mu}^{p+2}) \cup \cdots \cup \mathcal{C}(\overline{\mu}^n),$$

where $\overline{\mu}^q$ is the q-dimensional vector defined by

$$\overline{\mu}^q(i) = \begin{cases} \mu(i) & \text{if } 1 \leq i \leq q - 1, \\ 1 - \mu(i) & \text{if } i = q. \end{cases}$$

With these notations, the following algorithm enumerates all cuts in order of nondecreasing weights. We start from the one-dimensional vector v with $v(1) = 1$, and we compute $\mu(v)$ and its weight $d(v)$ and let $Q := \{v\}$. Then we enumerate cuts one after another in nondecreasing order by repeatedly executing the following procedure, NEXTMIN.

Procedure NEXTMIN

Choose a vector $v \in Q$ with the minimum weight $d(v)$;
return $\mu(v)$;
$Q := Q - \{v\}$;
$\mu := \mu(v)$;
for each $q = p + 1, p + 2, \ldots, n$ **do** /* Let p be the dimension of v */
  $\tau := \overline{\mu}^q$;
  Compute $\mu(\tau)$ and $d(\tau)$;
  $Q := Q \cup \{\tau\}$
end. /* for */

From the preceding argument, we see that Q always has the property $\bigcup_{v \in Q} C(v) = C - $ (the set of cuts already output). Therefore, it is not difficult to see that the procedure NEXTMIN correctly finds the next smallest cut. In each execution of NEXTMIN, it computes at most $n - 1$ $\mu(\tau)$, each of which can be obtained by computing a minimum (s, t)-cut once, except for the case where all entries of τ are 1 (in this case $\mu(\tau)$ is computed by computing minimum (s, t)-cuts at most $n - 1$ times). Thus, the procedure calls the minimum-cut algorithm at most $(n - 2) + (n - 1) = 2n - 3$ times. By maintaining set $\text{argmin}\{d(v) \mid v \in Q\}$ by using a heap data structure, a vector $v \in Q$ with the minimum $d(v)$ can be obtained in $O(\log |Q|) = O(\log(2^n)) = O(n)$ time. Thus, the time delay to find the next smallest cut is $O((2n - 3)(F(n, m) + n)) = O(nF(n, m))$.

Finally, we consider the space complexity of the preceding algorithm. After outputting a cut $\mu = \mu(v)$, we generate $n - p$ vectors $\tau = \overline{\mu}^q$, where these vectors can be implicitly represented by $O(n)$ space. Thus, we need $O(n)$ space per cut, and the space required for enumerating the first minimum r cuts is $O(rn)$. □

If graph G is planar, we can enumerate cuts more efficiently by making use of the fact that a cut in the original G corresponds to a cycle in its dual graph $G^* = (V^*, E)$. Let $S(n, m)$ denote the time to compute a shortest (s, t)-path in an edge-weighted graph G with n vertices and m edges. The next lemma is necessary for this purpose.

Lemma 4.2. *For an edge-weighted graph $G = (V, E)$, cycles in G can be enumerated in order of nondecreasing lengths with $O(S(n, m))$ time delay between two consecutive outputs, where the first cycle can be found in $O(mS(n, m))$ time. The space required for enumerating the first r shortest cycles is $O(rm + nm + m^2)$.* □

Proof. It is known [187] that (s, t)-paths can be enumerated in order of nondecreasing lengths with $O(S(n, m))$ time delay between two consecutive outputs and that the space required to output the first r shortest (s, t)-paths is $O(r + n + m)$. Based on this, we enumerate cycles in G in order of nondecreasing lengths as follows. Let $E = \{e_1 = (s_1, t_1), e_2 = (s_2, t_2), \ldots, e_m = (s_m, t_m)\}$. Then the set $\mathcal{S}$ of all cycles in G can be partitioned into m sets $\mathcal{S}_i, i = 1, \ldots, m$, of cycles, where $\mathcal{S}_i$ is the set of cycles $C \subseteq E$ such that $e_i \in C \subseteq E - \{e_1, \ldots, e_{i-1}\}$. Then a cycle $C \in \mathcal{S}_i$ is obtained by combining an (s_i, t_i)-path $P \subseteq E - \{e_1, \ldots, e_{i-1}\}$ and the edge $e_i = \{s_i, t_i\}$. The shortest cycle in G can be obtained as the cycle with the minimum length among $P_i^* \cup \{e_i\}, i = 1, \ldots, m$, where P_i^* is the shortest (s_i, t_i)-path in the graph $(V, E - \{e_1, \ldots, e_{i-1}\})$. If $P_j^* \cup \{e_j\}$ is chosen as the cycle of minimum length, then we compute the next shortest (s_j, t_j)-path P in the graph $(V, E - \{e_1, \ldots, e_{j-1}\})$, and we replace P_j^* with this P. Then the second shortest cycle in G can be chosen as the cycle with minimum length among all $P_i^* \cup \{e_i\}$, $i = 1, \ldots, m$. Thus, by updating P_j^* by the next shortest (s_j, t_j)-path P after $P_j^* \cup \{e_j\}$ is chosen, we can repeatedly enumerate cycles in order of nondecreasing weights, with $O(S(n, m))$ time delay. The required space for outputting the first r shortest cycles is $O(m(r + n + m))$, since each $\mathcal{S}_i$ requires $O(r + n + m)$ space. □

Corollary 4.3. *For an edge-weighted planar graph $G = (V, E)$, cuts in G can be enumerated in order of nondecreasing weights with $O(n)$ time delay between two consecutive outputs, where the first cut can be found in $O(n^2)$ time. The space required for enumerating the first r minimum cuts is $O(rn + n^2)$.* □

Proof. As noted before, cuts in a planar graph $G = (V, E)$ can be enumerated by enumerating cycles in the dual graph $G^* = (V^*, E)$. By Lemma 4.2, cycles in G^* can be enumerated in order of nondecreasing lengths with $O(S(|V^*|, |E|))$ time delay. For a planar graph G^*, it is known that $|V^*| = O(|V| + |E|)$ and $S(|V^*|, |E|) = O(|V^*| + |E|) = O(|V|)$ [122] hold. The space complexity also follows from Lemma 4.2. □

4.2 Enumerating Small Cuts

In this section, we show that all cuts of weight less than $k\lambda(G)$ (where $\lambda(G)$ is the weight of a minimum cut) for a given real $k \geq 1$ can be enumerated in $O(n^{2k+2})$ time without using the maximum-flow algorithm. For this, we use the technique of *edge splitting*, for which we present fast algorithms in Chapter 7. In this section, we first introduce basic terminologies and some results on edge splitting, which are necessary for designing our enumeration algorithm in Section 4.2.2.

4.2.1 Weighted Edge Splitting

The purpose of edge splitting is to reduce the size of a graph while preserving the edge-connectivity. Let $G = (V, E)$ be an edge-weighted graph with a designated vertex $s \in V$ and let $u, v \in \Gamma(s; G)$ be vertices adjacent to s (possibly $u = v$), where

$$\delta_{max} = \min\{c_G(s, u), c_G(s, v)\}.$$

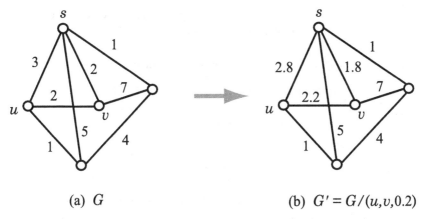

(a) G (b) $G' = G/(u,v,0.2)$

Figure 4.1. Edge splitting: (a) A graph G and (b) $G' = G/(u, v, \delta = 0.2)$.

Given a nonnegative real $\delta \leq \delta_{max}$, we say that a graph G' is obtained from G by *splitting* edges $\{s, u\}$ and $\{s, v\}$ by *weight* δ (or by an edge splitting with edges $\{s, u\}$ and $\{s, v\}$ and weight δ) if $G' = (V, E)$ is a graph such that

$$c_{G'}(e) = \begin{cases} c_G(e) - \delta & \text{if } e \in \{\{s, u\}, \{s, v\}\} \\ c_G(e) + \delta & \text{if } e = \{u, v\} \\ c_G(e) & \text{if } e \in E - \{\{s, u\}, \{s, v\}, \{u, v\}\}, \end{cases}$$

where we create a new edge $\{u, v\}$ in G' if $\{u, v\} \notin E$. In the case of $u = v$, we interpret the preceding description as

$$c_{G'}(e) = \begin{cases} c_G(e) - 2\delta & \text{if } e = \{s, u\} \\ c_G(e) & \text{if } e \in E - \{s, u\}. \end{cases}$$

We denote the resulting graph G' by $G/(u, v, \delta)$. Figure 4.1(b) shows the graph G' obtained from a graph in Fig. 4.1(a) by splitting edges $\{s, u\}$ and $\{s, v\}$ by weight $\delta = 0.2$.

Clearly, for any cut X, it holds that

$$d_{G/(u,v,\delta)}(X) = \begin{cases} d(X; G) - 2\delta & \text{if cut } X \text{ separates } s \text{ and } \{u, v\} \\ d(X; G) & \text{otherwise.} \end{cases} \tag{4.1}$$

Hence, for the s-proper edge-connectivity (defined in Section 3.2), we have $\lambda_s(G/(u, v, \delta)) \leq \lambda_s(G)$ for any $\delta \leq \delta_{max}$. Let $\delta_s(u, v; G)$ denote the maximum δ with $\delta \leq \delta_{max}$ and $\lambda_s(G/(u, v, \delta)) = \lambda_s(G)$. Then any minimum s-proper cut in G remains a minimum s-proper cut in the graph $G/(u, v, \varepsilon)$ for any $\varepsilon \in [0, \delta_s(u, v; G)]$. An edge splitting (u, v, δ) is called *feasible* in G if $\delta \leq \delta_s(u, v; G)$. We say that a graph G'' with $d(s; G'') = 0$ is obtained from G by *isolating* s if G'' is constructed by a finite sequence of feasible edge splittings (u_i, v_i, δ_i), $i = 1, 2, \ldots, p$ (i.e., $\delta_i \leq \delta_s(u_i, v_i; G'_i)$ for $G'_i = G'_{i-1}/(u_{i-1}, v_{i-1}, \delta_{i-1})$, where $G'_0 = G$ and $G'' = G'_{p+1}$). As we shall see in Chapter 7 given any designated vertex s, there always exists such a sequence of feasible edge splittings [202]. (To be more precise, in Chapter 7 we handle a more restricted case where a given graph is integer-weighted and an edge splitting needs to be carried out with an integer weight δ.)

The next property follows from the preceding definitions.

Lemma 4.4. *For an edge-weighted graph $G = (V, E)$ with a designated vertex $s \in V$, let G' be the graph obtained from G by isolating s and let $G_s = (V - s, E')$ be the graph obtained from G' by eliminating s. Then*

> (i) *For every nonempty $X \subset V - s$, $d(X; G_s) = d(X; G') \le d(X; G)$,*
> (ii) *$\lambda(G_s) = \lambda_s(G') = \lambda_s(G) \ge \lambda(G)$.*   □

Proof. By definition of G', we have $d(X; G_s) = d(X; G')$ for all nonempty $X \subset V - s$, in particular, $\lambda(G_s) = \lambda_s(G')$. Since G' is obtained by a sequence of edge splittings at s, $d(X; G') \le d(X; G)$ holds for all nonempty $X \subset V - s$. By definitions, $\lambda_s(G) \ge \lambda(G)$ also holds. Finally, since all edge splittings in the sequence are feasible, we have $\lambda_s(G') = \lambda_s(G)$. From these inequalities and equalities, conditions (i) and (ii) follow.   □

As a corollary of Theorem 7.10 in Chapter 7, we have the following result for the time and space complexity for isolating a vertex s.

Corollary 4.5. *Given an edge-weighted graph G and a designated vertex s, we can find in $O(mn + n^2 \log n)$ time a sequence of $O(|\Gamma(s; G)|)$ edge splittings that isolates s.*   □

4.2.2   Enumerating All Small Cuts

A cut $\{X, V - X\}$ in an edge-weighted graph G is called an α-*cut* if it has weight α. For a given $\alpha > 0$, let $\mathcal{C}(\alpha; G)$ denote the set of all β-cuts in G satisfying $\beta < \alpha$. We do not distinguish subset X from its complement, $V - X$. To avoid the duplication of X and $V - X$, therefore, we choose an arbitrary vertex $r \in V$ as a *reference vertex*, and we denote by $\mathcal{C}_r(\alpha; G)$ the set of all β-cuts X with $r \notin X$. Note that $|\mathcal{C}(\alpha; G)| = |\mathcal{C}_r(\alpha; G)|$ by definition; in what follows, we compute $\mathcal{C}_r(\alpha; G)$ to avoid confusion.

We first give an outline of the algorithm for enumerating all cuts $\mathcal{C}_r(\alpha; G)$. Given an ordered set of vertices $V = \{v_1, v_2, \ldots, v_n\}$, define a sequence of graphs G_i, $i = n, n - 1, \ldots, 2$, as follows. Let $G_n = G$ and let G_{i-1}, $i = n, \ldots, 3$, be the graph obtained from G_i by isolating vertex v_i, where $V_i = \{v_1, v_2, \ldots, v_i\}$ denotes the vertices in G_i. The following relation exists between G_i and G_{i-1}. Any cut X with $\{v_i\} \ne X \ne V_i - v_i$ in G_i is also a cut in G_{i-1}, and $d(X; G_i) \ge d(X; G_{i-1})$ holds by Lemma 4.4(i). Also, note that two cuts X and X' in G_i such that $v_i \notin X$ and $X' = X \cup \{v_i\}$ become the same cut in G_{i-1} (see Fig. 4.2).

Choose v_1 as the reference vertex r. From the preceding observation, we see that any cut $X \in \mathcal{C}_r(\alpha; G_i)$ appears in exactly one of the three sets: $\mathcal{C}_r(\alpha; G_{i-1})$,

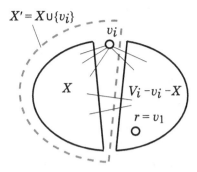

Figure 4.2. Illustration of two cuts, X and $X' = X \cup \{v_i\}$.

$\{X \cup \{v_i\} \mid X \in C_r(\alpha; G_{i-1})\}$, or $\{\{v_i\}\}$. In other words, the set

$$C^*_{v_i} = C_r(\alpha; G_{i-1}) \cup \{X \cup \{v_i\} \mid X \in C_r(\alpha; G_{i-1})\} \cup \{\{v_i\}\} \qquad (4.2)$$

includes $C_r(\alpha; G_i)$ (the inclusion is possibly proper); hence, it holds that

$$C_r(\alpha; G_i) = \{X \in C^*_{v_i} \mid d(X; G_i) < \alpha\}. \qquad (4.3)$$

Suppose that we have stored weights of the cuts in $C_r(\alpha; G_{i-1})$, $\{d(X; G_{i-1}) \mid X \in C_r(\alpha; G_{i-1})\}$, and the set Q_{v_i} of triplets (u, v, δ) that are used to isolate v_i in G_i. For each cut $Y \in C^*_{v_i}$, its weight $d(Y; G_i)$ can be easily computed from $C_r(\alpha; G_{i-1})$ and Q_{v_i} as follows. If $Y = \{v_i\}$, then clearly

$$d(Y; G_i) = 2 \sum_{(u,v,\delta) \in Q_{v_i}} \delta.$$

If $Y \in C_r(\alpha; G_{i-1})$, then we have

$$d(Y; G_i) = d(Y; G_{i-1}) + 2 \sum \{\delta \mid (u, v, \delta) \in Q_{v_i} \text{ such that } \{u, v\} \subseteq Y\},$$

since $d(Y; G_{i-1})$ decreases by 2δ at each edge splitting $(u, v, \delta) \in Q_{v_i}$ if Y separates $\{v_i\}$ and $\{u, v\}$ (see (4.1)). Analogously, if $Y = Y' \cup \{v_i\}$ for a $Y' \in C_r(\alpha; G_{i-1})$, then

$$d(Y; G_i) = d(Y'; G_{i-1}) + 2 \sum \{\delta \mid (u, v, \delta) \in Q_{v_i} \text{ such that } \{u, v\} \cap Y' = \emptyset\}.$$

To compute $d(Y; G_i)$ efficiently, we use a data structure that enables us to check if $w \in Y$ in $O(1)$ time, for example, by preparing a membership mapping $f_Y : V \mapsto \{0, 1\}$ with $f_Y(v) = 1$ ($v \in Y$) and $f_Y(v) = 0$ ($v \in V - Y$). By using an algorithm in Corollary 4.5, s can be isolated by creating $O(|\Gamma(s; G)|)$ split edges; hence, it holds that

$$|Q_{v_i}| = O(|\Gamma(v_i; G_i)|).$$

Then each $d(Y; G_i)$ can be computed in $|Q_{v_i}| = O(|\Gamma(v_i; G_i)|)$ time by using $\{d(X; G_{i-1}) \mid X \in C_r(\alpha; G_{i-1})\}$, Q_{v_i}, and a membership mapping f_Y.

Consequently, all cuts in $\mathcal{C}(k\lambda(G); G)$ can be enumerated in the following manner.

Algorithm ENUMERATE
Input: An edge-weighted graph $G = (V, E)$ with $V = \{v_1, \ldots, v_n\}$ and a real
    number $k > 1$.
Output: $\mathcal{C}(k\lambda(G); G)$.

 1 **begin**
 2   Compute $\lambda(G)$; $\alpha := k\lambda(G)$; $G_n := G$;
 3   **for** $i = n, n - 1, \ldots, 2$ **do**
 4   **begin**
 5   Isolate v_i in G_i by using Corollary 4.5;
 6   Let Q_{v_i} be the set of triplets (u, v, δ) used to isolate s;
 7   Denote the resulting graph by G_{i-1}
 8   **end**;
 9   Choose the reference vertex r as v_1;
10    $\mathcal{C}_r(\alpha; G_1) := \emptyset$;
11   **for** $j = 2, 3, \ldots, n$ **do**
12   **begin**
13          $d(\{v_j\}; G_{j-1}) := 2\sum\{\delta \mid (u, v, \delta) \in Q_{v_j}\}$;
14   **for** each $X \in \mathcal{C}_r(\alpha; G_{j-1})$
15          $d(X; G_j) := d(X; G_{j-1}) + 2\sum\{\delta \mid (u, v, \delta) \in Q_{v_j}$
                      such that $\{u, v\} \subseteq X\}$;
16          $d(X \cup \{v_j\}; G_j) := d(X; G_{j-1}) + 2\sum\{\delta \mid (u, v, \delta) \in Q_{v_j}$
                      such that $\{u, v\} \cap X = \emptyset\}$
          /* Whether $v \in X$ or not is tested by using membership function f_X */
17   **end**;
18       $\mathcal{C}_{v_j}^* := \mathcal{C}_r(\alpha; G_{j-1}) \cup \{X \cup \{v_j\} \mid X \in \mathcal{C}_r(\alpha; G_{j-1})\} \cup \{\{v_j\}\}$;
19       $\mathcal{C}_r(\alpha; G_j) := \{X \in \mathcal{C}_{v_j}^* \mid d(X; G_j) < \alpha\}$
       /* For each $X \in \mathcal{C}_r(\alpha; G_j)$, update its membership function f_X */
20   **end**;
21   Output $\mathcal{C}(k\lambda(G); G) := \mathcal{C}_r(\alpha; G_n)$
22 **end**.

Theorem 4.6. *For an edge-weighted graph $G = (V, E)$ and a real number $k > 1$,* ENUMERATE *computes the set $\mathcal{C}(k\lambda(G); G)$ correctly and runs in $O(n^{2k+2})$ time.* $\square$

Proof. The correctness of ENUMERATE follows from the discussion so far, in particular from (4.2) and (4.3). In line 2, $\lambda(G)$ can be computed in $O(nm + n^2 \log n)$ time via Corollary 3.4. Let m_i denote the number of edges with positive weights in G_i, $i = 2, \ldots, n$. By Corollary 4.5, all values for G_i in the loop of lines 3–8 can be constructed in $O(\sum_{i=2}^{n}(i \cdot m_i + i^2 \log i)) = O(n^4)$ time. Now we consider the time required in the loop of lines 11–20. By Lemma 4.4(ii),

$$\lambda(G) = \lambda(G_n) \le \lambda(G_{n-1}) \le \cdots \le \lambda(G_2)$$

holds for the graphs G_i.

Since the number of cuts with weights less than $k\lambda(G)$ in a graph G with i vertices is known to be $O(i^{2k})$ [174], we have $|\mathcal{C}_r(\alpha; G_i)| = |\mathcal{C}_r(k\lambda(G); G_i)| \le |\mathcal{C}_r(k\lambda(G_i); G_i)| = O(i^{2k})$, $i = 2, 3, \ldots, n$.

As discussed before the description of ENUMERATE, each $d(X; G_i)$ for a cut $X \in \mathcal{C}_{v_i}^*$ can be updated from $d(X; G_{i-1})$ in $O(|Q_{v_i}|)$ ($\le v$) time. Updating the i membership mapping f_X for each cut X requires $O(|X|) = O(|V|)$ time. Then computing $\mathcal{C}_r(\alpha; G_i)$ for all i in lines 11–20 requires

$$\sum_{i=2}^{n} (|\mathcal{C}_r(k\lambda(G_i)); G_i)||Q_{v_i}|) = O\left(\sum_{i=2}^{n} (i^{2k}|Q_{v_i}|)\right)$$

$$= O\left(\sum_{i=2}^{n} (i^{2k+1})\right) = O(n^{2k+2})$$

time. Therefore, the entire running time of ENUMERATE is $O(n^4 + n^{2k+2}) = O(n^{2k+2})$. $\square$

4.3 Enumerating Minimum Cuts

We denote by $\mathcal{C}(G)$ the set of all minimum cuts in an edge-weighted graph G. In this section, after observing basic properties of minimum cuts, we show how to enumerate all cuts in $\mathcal{C}(G)$ and also prove an upper bound on $|\mathcal{C}(G)|$.

Lemma 4.7. *For an edge-weighted graph G with $\lambda(G) > 0$ (i.e., G is connected), let $\{X, \overline{X}\} \in \mathcal{C}(G)$. The graphs $G[X]$ and $G[\overline{X}]$ induced from G by X and $\overline{X}$ are both connected.* $\square$

Proof. If the lemma were not true, there would be a cut $\{Y, \overline{Y}\}$ such that either $Y \subset X$ or $Y \subset \overline{X}$ with $d(Y, \overline{Y}; G) < \lambda(G)$, a contradiction. $\square$

The following elegant lemma lays the groundwork for the subsequent discussion in this section and in Chapter 5.

Lemma 4.8 ([27, 54]). *In an edge-weighted graph $G = (V, E)$, for any two cuts $\{X, \overline{X}\}, \{Y, \overline{Y}\} \in \mathcal{C}(G)$ that cross each other, let $V_1 = X \cap Y$, $V_2 = \overline{X} \cap Y$, $V_3 = \overline{X} \cap \overline{Y}$, and $V_4 = X \cap \overline{Y}$ (see Fig. 4.3). Then*

(i) $d(V_1, V_2) = d(V_2, V_3) = d(V_3, V_4) = d(V_4, V_1) = \lambda(G)/2$, *and*
(ii) $d(V_1, V_3) = d(V_2, V_4) = 0$. $\square$

Proof. By (1.4), it holds that

$$2\lambda(G) = d(X) + d(Y) = d(V_4) + d(V_2) + 2d(V_1, V_3).$$

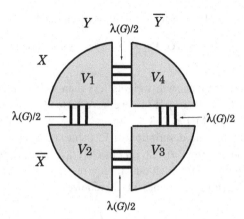

Figure 4.3. Illustration for edges between V_i and V_j in two crossing minimum cuts $\{X, \overline{X}\}, \{Y, \overline{Y}\}$.

By $d(V_4), d(V_2) \geq \lambda(G)$ and $d(V_1, V_3) \geq 0$, we see that $d(V_4) = d(V_2) = \lambda(G)$ and $d(V_1, V_3) = 0$ must hold. Similarly $d(V_1) = d(V_3) = \lambda(G)$ and $d(V_2, V_4) = 0$ hold from $2\lambda(G) = d(\overline{X}) + d(Y) = d(V_3) + d(V_1) + 2d(V_2, V_4)$. Hence, condition (ii) holds and the sum of any two in $\{d(V_1, V_2), d(V_2, V_3), d(V_3, V_4), d(V_4, V_1)\}$ is equal to $\lambda(G)$, indicating condition (i).   □

An ordered set $(V_1, V_2, \ldots, V_r)$, $r \geq 2$, is called an *ordered partition* (or *o-partition* for short) of a vertex set V if $\{V_1, \ldots, V_r\}$ is a partition of V. Given an o-partition $(V_1, \ldots, V_r)$ and two indices h and k ($1 \leq h \leq k \leq r$), we define

$$V_{(h,k)} = V_h \cup V_{h+1} \cup \cdots \cup V_k.$$

We say that an edge $e = \{s, t\}$ in G is *critical* if $\lambda(s, t; G) = \lambda(G)$ and $c_G(e) > 0$. Thus, removal of a critical edge e decreases the edge-connectivity. It is known that the set of minimum cuts in $\mathcal{C}(G)$ separating the end vertices of a critical edge $\{s, t\}$ has the following simple structure.

Lemma 4.9 ([185]). *For each critical edge $e = \{s, t\}$ in an edge-weighted graph $G = (V, E)$, no two cuts in $\mathcal{C}(G)$ separating s and t cross each other. Thus, there is an o-partition $\pi_{(s,t)} = (V_1, \ldots, V_r)$ of V such that $s \in V_1$ and $t \in V_r$ hold, and the set of $r - 1$ cuts of the form*

$$\left\{ V_{(1,i)}, V_{(i+1,r)} \right\}, \quad 1 \leq i < r,$$

is equal to the set of all cuts in $\mathcal{C}(G)$ that separate s and t.   □

Proof. We first show that no two minimum cuts $\{X, \overline{X}\}$ and $\{Y, \overline{Y}\}$ in $\mathcal{C}(G)$ that separate s and t cross each other, where $\overline{X} = V - X$ and $\overline{Y} = V - Y$. Assume $s \in X \cap Y$ without loss of generality. If these cuts cross each other, edge $e = \{s, t\}$ is contained in $E(X \cap Y, \overline{X} \cap \overline{Y}; G)$ and, hence, $d(X \cap Y, \overline{X} \cap \overline{Y}; G) \geq c_G(e) > 0$.

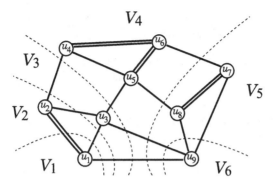

Figure 4.4. Illustration of the (s, t)-MC partition $\pi_{(s,t)}$ with $(s, t) = (u_1, u_9)$ of the graph G in Fig. 1.28.

However, by Lemma 4.8(ii), $d(X \cap Y, \overline{X} \cap \overline{Y}; G) = 0$ must hold, a contradiction. Therefore, $\{X, \overline{X}\}$ and $\{Y, \overline{Y}\}$ do not cross each other.

This implies that all minimum cuts $\{X_i, \overline{X}_i\}$ $(i = 1, \ldots, q)$ in $\mathcal{C}(G)$ that separate s and t, where we assume $s \in X_i$ without loss of generality, can be arranged so that

$$\{s\} \subseteq X_1 \subset X_2 \subset \cdots \subset X_q \subseteq V - \{t\}$$

holds. Thus, $(X_1, X_2 - X_1, \ldots, X_q - X_{q-1}, \overline{X}_q)$ is the desired o-partition that represents all minimum cuts $\{X_i, \overline{X}_i\}$ $(i = 1, \ldots, q)$. $\qquad \square$

For a subset $\mathcal{C}' \subseteq \mathcal{C}(G)$ of minimum cuts in G, an o-partition $\pi = (V_1, V_2, \ldots, V_r)$ of V is called a *minimum-cut o-partition* (or *MC partition*, for short) over $\mathcal{C}'$, if

$$\left\{ \left\{ V_{(1,k)}, V_{(k+1,r)} \right\} \mid 1 \leq k \leq r - 1 \right\} \subseteq \mathcal{C}'.$$

The o-partition $\pi_{(s,t)}$ in Lemma 4.9 is called the (s, t) *minimum-cut o-partition* $((s, t)$-*MC partition*, for short). For example, the (s, t)-MC partition $\pi_{(s,t)}$ with $(s, t) = (u_1, u_9)$ of the graph G in Fig. 1.28(a) is given by $(V_1 = \{u_1\}, V_2 = \{u_2\}, V_3 = \{u_3\}, V_4 = \{u_4, u_5, u_6\}, V_5 = \{u_7, u_8\}, V_6 = \{u_9\})$ and is shown Fig. 4.4.

Lemma 4.10 ([185, 258]). *Let $\{s, t\}$ be a critical edge in an edge-weighted graph G. Then given an arbitrary maximum flow between s and t, the (s, t)-MC partition can be obtained in $O(m + n)$ time and $O(m + n)$ space.* $\qquad \square$

Proof. (Sketch) As described in Section 1.3.3, Picard and Queyranne [273] have introduced a directed acyclic graph (DAG) that represents all (s, t)-cuts with weight $\lambda(s, t; G)$. Based on this DAG representation, Ball and Provan [9] have given an algorithm for listing all minimum (s, t)-cuts in $O(n + m)$ time per cut. However, the algorithm can be implemented to run in $O(n + m)$ time for all such cuts based on the nested structure in Lemma 4.9, as Karzanov and Timofeev [185] and Naor and Vazirani [258] have shown.   □

From this observation, we can compute the set $\mathcal{C}(G)$ of all minimum cuts in a given edge-weighted graph G by the following algorithm.

Algorithm EDGECONTRACT
Input: An edge-weighted graph $G = (V, E)$.
Output: $\mathcal{C}(G)$.
 1 $\mathcal{C} := \emptyset$; $G^{(1)} := G$; $\lambda := \lambda(G)$;
 2 **for** $i = 1, 2, \ldots, n - 1$ **do**
 3   Choose a critical edge $\{s_i, t_i\}$ in $G^{(i)}$;
 4   Compute an (s_i, t_i)-MC partition $\pi_{(s_i, t_i)}$ over $\mathcal{C}(G^{(i)})$
      (where we set $\pi_{(s_i, t_i)} = (V(G^{(i)}))$ if $\lambda(s_i, t_i; G^{(i)}) > \lambda$);
 5   Let C_i be the set of cuts with size λ that separate s_i and t_i, which can be
      computed from $\pi_{(s_i, t_i)}$ by Lemma 4.9;
 6    $\mathcal{C} := \mathcal{C} \cup C_i$;
 7   Let $G^{(i+1)}$ be the graph obtained from $G^{(i)}$ by contracting s and t into a
      single vertex
 8 **end**; /* for */
    /* The final graph $G^{(n)}$ consists of a single vertex */
 9 Output $\mathcal{C}(G) := \mathcal{C}$.

Clearly, the (s_i, t_i)-MC partitions $\pi_{(s_i, t_i)}$, $i = 1, \ldots, n - 1$, for the sequence of graphs $G^{(1)}, \ldots, G^{(n-1)}$ contain all minimum cuts in the original graph G. The following theorem is a direct consequence of the algorithm.

Theorem 4.11. *For an edge-weighted graph G,* EDGECONTRACT *can be implemented to run in $O(nF(n, m))$ time, where $F(n, m)$ is the time required to find a minimum cut (i.e., maximum flow) in G between a given source and sink.*   □

From the preceding result, we can show that the number of minimum cuts in G is at most $\binom{n}{2}$. In each graph $G^{(i)}$, the number of cuts with size λ that are destroyed by contracting edge $\{s_i, t_i\}$ is at most $|V(G^{(i)})| - 1 = (n - i + 1) - 1$ by Lemma 4.9. Therefore, we have

$$|\mathcal{C}(G)| \leq (|V| - 1) + (|V| - 2) + \cdots + 1 = \binom{n}{2}.$$

Theorem 4.12 ([27, 54]). *For any edge-weighted graph G, it holds that $|\mathcal{C}(G)| \leq \binom{n}{2}$.*   □

We note that this bound is actually attained by a ring graph consisting of $n \geq 2$ vertices, in which $\lambda(G) = 2$ holds.

Now we consider the case in which there is no pair of crossing minimum cuts in $\mathcal{C}(G)$. Then we can show that

$$|\mathcal{C}(G)| \leq 2|V| - 3$$

holds by the following induction. If $|X| = 1$ or $|V - X| = 1$ for all $\{X, V - X\} \in$ $\mathcal{C}(G)$, then it holds that $|\mathcal{C}(G)| \leq |V|$. Otherwise take a minimum cut $\{X, V - X\} \in \mathcal{C}(G)$, contract X (resp. $V - X$) into a single vertex, and denote $G_1 = G/X$ and $G_2 = G/(V - X)$. By the induction hypothesis,

$$|\mathcal{C}(G)| = |\mathcal{C}(G_1)| + |\mathcal{C}(G_2)| - 1$$
$$\leq (2(|X| + 1) - 3) + (2(|V - X| + 1) - 3) - 1 = 2|V| - 3.$$

In the next section, we prove that $\binom{n}{2}$ is also a tight upper bound on the number of cuts of weight less than $\frac{4}{3}\lambda(G)$.

4.4 Upper Bounds on the Number of Small Cuts

We prove in this section that $|\mathcal{C}(k\lambda(G); G)|$ for $k \leq \frac{4}{3}$ is at most $\binom{n}{2}$. This bound $\binom{n}{2}$ is the same as the upper bound in Theorem 4.12 for all the minimum cuts. The time complexity of ENUMERATE in Section 4.2.2 can also be improved to $O(n^4)$ for such k.

Theorem 4.13. *For an edge-weighted graph G, it holds that $|\mathcal{C}(\frac{4}{3}\lambda(G); G)| \leq \binom{n}{2}$.* □

Note that, for a cycle G such that each edge is weighted 1, there are $\binom{n}{2}$ minimum cuts and all other cuts X satisfy $d(X) \geq 4 > \frac{4}{3}\lambda(G)$. Therefore, this bound is tight. We then see that the coefficient $k = \frac{4}{3}$ of $\alpha = \frac{4}{3}\lambda(G)$ is the largest possible value for $\binom{n}{2}$ to be an upper bound. For this, consider a complete graph K_4 with four vertices, where each edge is weighted 1. Clearly, $\lambda(K_4) = 3$, and K_4 has four cuts of weight 3 and three cuts of weight 4, indicating $|\mathcal{C}((\frac{4}{3} + \varepsilon)\lambda(K_n); K_n)| \geq 7 > \binom{4}{2}(= 6)$ for any $\varepsilon > 0$.

The proof of Theorem 4.13 will be given after mentioning the next corollary.

Corollary 4.14. *For an edge-weighted graph $G = (V, E)$ and $1 < k \leq \frac{4}{3}$, $\mathcal{C}(k\lambda(G); G)$ can be computed in $O(n^4)$ time.* □

Proof. A closer look at the proof of Theorem 4.6 tells that the running time of ENUMERATE is $O(n^4 + \sum_{i=2}^{n}(|\mathcal{C}_r(k\lambda(G_i)); G_i)||Q_{v_i}|))$. Therefore, by Theorem 4.13, ENUMERATE runs in $O(n^4 + \sum_{i=2}^{n}(\binom{i}{2}n)) = O(n^4)$ time for $1 < k \leq \frac{4}{3}$. □

Now we prove Theorem 4.13 via several lemmas. For an edge-weighted graph $G = (V, E)$ with a designated vertex $s \in V$ and a real $\alpha > 0$, if two cuts X and $X' = X \cup \{s\}$ both belong to $\mathcal{C}(\alpha; G)$, then we call $\{X, X'\}$ a pair of *twin cuts* with respect to (s, α). Let $r \in V - s$ be a reference vertex, and we define the set of partners of such twin cuts by

$$\mathcal{T}_r(s, \alpha; G) \equiv \{X | X \subseteq V - \{s, r\}, \text{ and } X, X \cup \{s\} \in \mathcal{C}_r(\alpha; G)\}.$$

From (4.2) and (4.3), we have $\mathcal{C}_r(\alpha; G) \subseteq \mathcal{C}_r(\alpha; G_s) \cup \{X \cup \{s\} \mid X \in \mathcal{C}_r(\alpha; G_s), d(X \cup \{s\}; G_s) \leq d(X \cup \{s\}; G) < \alpha\} \cup \{\{s\}\}$ and, hence

$$|\mathcal{C}_r(\alpha; G)| \leq |\mathcal{C}_r(\alpha; G_s)| + |\mathcal{T}_r(s, \alpha; G)| + 1, \tag{4.4}$$

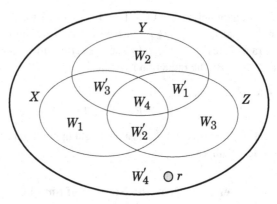

Figure 4.5. Illustration of three cuts, X, Y, and Z.

where G_s denotes the graph obtained from G by eliminating s after isolating s in G (see Lemma 4.4).

Based on this inequality, we prove Theorem 4.13 by induction on $n = |V|$. The theorem clearly holds for $n = 2$. Assume here that Theorem 4.13 holds for any graph with less than n vertices. If we can show

$$|\mathcal{T}_r\left(s, \tfrac{4}{3}\lambda(G); G\right)| \le n - 2, \tag{4.5}$$

then we have from (4.4) that

$$
\begin{aligned}
|\mathcal{C}_r\left(\tfrac{4}{3}\lambda(G); G\right)| &\le |\mathcal{C}_r\left(\tfrac{4}{3}\lambda(G); G_s\right)| + |\mathcal{T}_r\left(s, \tfrac{4}{3}\lambda(G); G\right)| + 1 \\
&\le |\mathcal{C}_r\left(\tfrac{4}{3}\lambda(G_s); G_s\right)| + |\mathcal{T}_r\left(s, \tfrac{4}{3}\lambda(G); G\right)| + 1 \\
&\quad \text{(from } \lambda(G_s) \ge \lambda(G) \text{ (Lemma 4.4(ii)))} \\
&\le \binom{n-1}{2} + (n - 2) + 1 \quad \text{(induction hypothesis and (4.5))} \\
&= \binom{n}{2}. \tag{4.6}
\end{aligned}
$$

Therefore, property (4.5) proves Theorem 4.13. The proof of (4.5) will be given below via Lemmas 4.15–4.19.

Lemma 4.15. *For an edge-weighted graph $G = (V, E)$ with a reference vertex $r \in V$, let X, Y, and Z be three distinct cuts in $\mathcal{C}_r(\tfrac{4}{3}\lambda(G); G)$ and define a partition $\{W_i, W_i' \mid i = 1, 2, 3, 4\}$ of V as follows (see Fig. 4.5):*

$$
\begin{aligned}
W_1 &= X \cap \overline{Y} \cap \overline{Z}, & W_2 &= \overline{X} \cap Y \cap \overline{Z}, & W_3 &= \overline{X} \cap \overline{Y} \cap Z, & W_4 &= X \cap Y \cap Z, \\
W_1' &= \overline{X} \cap Y \cap Z, & W_2' &= X \cap \overline{Y} \cap Z, & W_3' &= X \cap Y \cap \overline{Z} & W_4' &= \overline{X} \cap \overline{Y} \cap \overline{Z}.
\end{aligned}
\tag{4.7}
$$

Then at least one of W_1, W_2, W_3, and W_4 is empty, and at least one of W_1', W_2', and W_3' is also empty. □

Proof. If none of W_1, W_2, W_3, and W_4 is empty, then we would have

$$3 \times \tfrac{4}{3}\lambda(G) > d(X) + d(Y) + d(Z)$$
$$\geq 2 \sum_{1 \leq i < j \leq 4} d(W_i, W_j) + \sum_{1 \leq i, k \leq 4} d(W_i, W_k')$$
$$\geq d(W_1) + d(W_2) + d(W_3) + d(W_4) \geq 4\lambda(G),$$

which is a contradiction. Analogously, since $r \in W_4' \neq \emptyset$, one of W_1', W_2', and W_3' must be empty. $\qquad\square$

Lemma 4.16. *For an edge-weighted graph $G = (V, E)$, let $s \in V$ and $r \in V - s$ and let X, Y, and Z be three cuts in $\mathcal{T}_r(s, \tfrac{4}{3}\lambda(G); G)$. Define W_i and W_i' ($i = 1, 2, 3, 4$) as in (4.7). Then at least two of W_1, W_2, W_3, and W_4 are empty, and at least two of W_1', W_2' and W_3' are also empty.* $\qquad\square$

Proof. Since $X, Y, Z \subseteq V - \{s, r\}$, we see $s \in W_4'$. Since no cut in $\mathcal{T}_r(s, \tfrac{4}{3}\lambda(G); G)$ contains r, it holds that $r \in W_4' - s \neq \emptyset$. By Lemma 4.15, one of $W_i (i = 1, 2, 3, 4)$, say W_1, is empty (other cases can be treated analogously). Then assume $X' = X \cup \{s\} \in \mathcal{C}(\tfrac{4}{3}\lambda(G); G)$, where X and X' are a pair of twin cuts. Again, by applying Lemma 4.15 to three cuts X', Y, and Z, we see that one of $W_1 \cup \{s\}$, W_2, W_3, and W_4 must be empty. Since $W_1 \cup \{s\} \neq \emptyset$, one of W_2, W_3, and W_4 is also empty. A similar argument also proves the result for subsets W_i' ($i = 1, 2, 3$). $\qquad\square$

Lemma 4.17. *If there are two cuts in $\mathcal{T}_r(s, \tfrac{4}{3}\lambda(G); G)$ that cross each other in G, then $n \geq 4$ and $|\mathcal{T}_r(s, \tfrac{4}{3}\lambda(G); G)| = 2 \ (\leq n - 2)$.* $\qquad\square$

Proof. Suppose that two cuts X and Y in $\mathcal{T}_r(s, \tfrac{4}{3}\lambda(G); G)$ cross each other in G. Clearly $n \geq 4$. In this case, if $\mathcal{T}_r(s, \tfrac{4}{3}\lambda(G); G)$ contains other cut (say Z), then Lemma 4.16 applies to W_i and W_i' ($i = 1, 2, 3, 4$). However, this is impossible since two crossing cuts X and Y have already produced four nonempty subsets among W_i and W_i'. Hence, the third cut Z cannot exist. Thus, $|\mathcal{T}_r(s, \tfrac{4}{3}\lambda(G); G)| = 2$ follows. $\qquad\square$

Lemma 4.18. *Let $G = (V, E)$ be as defined earlier. Then any cut $X \in \mathcal{T}_r(s, \tfrac{4}{3}\lambda(G); G)$ satisfies $d(s, X) > \tfrac{1}{3}d(s)$.* $\qquad\square$

Proof. For a cut $X \in \mathcal{T}_r(s, \tfrac{4}{3}\lambda(G); G)$, define $X' = X \cup \{s\}$ and $\tilde{X} = V - s - X$. Then we have

$$\tfrac{4}{3}\lambda(G) > d(X') = d(X) - d(s, X) + d(s, \tilde{X}) \geq \lambda(G) - d(s, X) + d(s, \tilde{X}),$$

from which follows

$$d(s, X) - d(s, \tilde{X}) > -\frac{1}{3}\lambda(G).$$

This and $d(s, X) + d(s, \tilde{X}) = d(s) \geq \lambda(G)$ then imply that $d(s, X) > \tfrac{1}{3}d(s)$. $\qquad\square$

Lemma 4.19. *If no two cuts in $T_r(s, \frac{4}{3}\lambda(G); G)$ cross each other in G, then* $|T_r(s, \frac{4}{3}\lambda(G); G)| \le n - 2$. □

Proof. We call a cut X in $T_r(s, \frac{4}{3}\lambda(G); G)$ *minimal* if there is no X' such that $X \supset X' \in T_r(s, \frac{4}{3}\lambda(G); G)$. All minimal cuts are disjoint. Hence, there are at most two minimal cuts, because otherwise, for three minimal cuts, X, Y, and Z, $d(s, X) + d(s, Y) + d(s, Z) > d(s)$ would follow from Lemma 4.18, which is a contradiction. Assume that there are two minimal cuts, X_A and X_B (the case where $T_r(s, \frac{4}{3}\lambda(G); G)$ contains exactly one minimal cut can be treated analogously). By definition, $X_A \cap X_B = \emptyset$ and $X_A \cup X_B \subseteq V - \{s, r\}$. Since no two cuts in $T_r(s, \frac{4}{3}\lambda(G); G)$ cross each other, all cuts in $T_r(s, \frac{4}{3}\lambda(G); G)$ can be numbered as $X_1, X_2, \ldots, X_p$ so that

$$X_A = X_1 \subset X_2 \subset \cdots \subset X_k, \quad X_{k+1} \supset X_k \supset \cdots \supset X_p = X_B,$$

where $X_k \cap X_{k+1} = \emptyset$ and $\{s, r\} \subseteq V - (X_k \cup X_{k+1})$ hold. From this, we see that $p \le |X_k| + |X_{k+1}| \le n - 2$. □

Lemmas 4.17 and 4.19 prove property (4.5), which completes the proof of Theorem 4.13.

Henzinger and Williamson [123] extended the preceding argument to prove an $O(n^2)$ upper bound on the number of cuts with weight less than $\frac{3}{2}\lambda(G)$. Based on a probabilistic analysis, Karger [174] derived, for arbitrary $k \ge 1$, an upper bound $O(n^{2k})$ on the number of cuts of weight no more than $k\lambda(G)$.

In concluding this section, we cite other results on the number of minimum cuts. For any unweighted multigraph G with an odd $\lambda(G)$, Bixby [27] proved $|\mathcal{C}(G)| \le \lfloor \frac{3n}{2} \rfloor - 2$. Lehel, Maffray, and Preissmann [198] showed that any *simple* unweighted graph G satisfies $|\mathcal{C}(G)| \le \frac{2n^2}{(k+1)^2} + \frac{(k-1)n}{k+1}$ (if $k = \lambda(G)$ is an even integer ≥ 4) and $|\mathcal{C}(G)| \le (1 + \frac{4}{k+5})n$ (if $k = \lambda(G)$ is an odd integer ≥ 5). For an edge-weighted graph G, Chandran and Ram [32] derived upper bounds on $|\mathcal{C}(G)|$ in terms of other graph parameters such as radius, diameter, maximum degree, minimum degree, cordality, and girth.

5

Cactus Representations

In this chapter, we investigate structures and algorithms of cactus representations, which were introduced in Section 1.5.4 to represent all minimum cuts in an edge-weighted graph G. Throughout this chapter, we assume that $\lambda(G) > 0$ for a given graph G, which implies that G is connected. Let $\mathcal{C}(G)$ denote the set of all minimum cuts in G. In Section 5.1, we define a canonical form of cactus representations. In Section 5.2, we show that a subset of $\mathcal{C}(G)$ that consists of minimum cuts separating two given vertices, s and t, can be represented by a simple cactus structure. In Section 5.3, we design an $O(mn + n^2 \log n)$ time algorithm for constructing a cactus representation $\mathcal{R}$ of $\mathcal{C}(G)$.

5.1 Canonical Forms of Cactus Representations

In this section, we discuss cactus representations for a subset of minimum cuts, and we prove the existence of two canonical forms, which we call the cycle-type and junction-type normal cactus representations. Such a canonical representation is useful in designing an efficient algorithm that constructs a cactus representation for all the minimum cuts of a given graph [244]. It also helps to efficiently test whether two given graphs have the same "structure" with respect to their minimum cuts, which is based on a planar isomorphism algorithm due to Hopcroft and Tarjan [126].

A cactus representation for a given subset $\mathcal{C} \subseteq \mathcal{C}(G)$, if one exists, may not be unique unless we impose further structural restrictions.

We say that two distinct cuts of G, $\{X, \overline{X}\}$ and $\{Y, \overline{Y}\}$, where $\overline{X} = V - X$ and $\overline{Y} = V - Y$, are *complementary* if they do not cross each other (i.e., if either X or $\overline{X}$ properly contains Y).

We call an ordered set $(V_1, V_2 \ldots, V_r)$, $r \geq 2$, an *ordered partition* of V if $\{V_1, \ldots, V_r\}$ is a partition of V, that is, $\cup_{i=1}^{r} V_i = V$ and $V_i \cap V_j = \emptyset$, $i \neq j$. Given an ordered partition $(V_1, \ldots, V_r)$ and two indices h and k ($1 \leq h \leq k \leq r$), we define

$$V_{(h,k)} = V_h \cup V_{h+1} \cup \cdots \cup V_k.$$

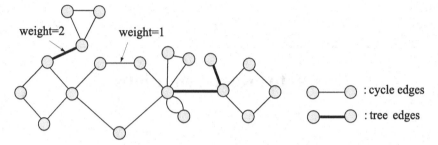

Figure 5.1. An example of a cactus.

For a subset $C' \subseteq C(G)$, an ordered partition $\pi_1 = (V_1, V_2, \ldots, V_r)$ of V is called a *minimum-cut ordered partition* (or *MC partition*, for short) over C' if $\{V_{(1,k)}, \overline{V_{(1,k)}}\}$, $1 \le k \le r - 1$, are minimum cuts in C', that is,

$$\mathcal{C}_1 = \left\{ \{V_{(1,k)}, \overline{V_{(1,k)}}\} \mid 1 \le k \le r - 1 \right\} \subseteq C'.$$

An ordered partition $\pi_2 = (V_1', V_2', \ldots, V_{r'}')$ of V is called a *circular* MC partition (or *CMC partition*, for short) over C', if

$$\mathcal{C}_2 = \left\{ \left\{ V_{(h,k)}', \overline{V_{(h,k)}'} \right\} \mid 1 \le h \le k \le r' - 1 \right\} \subseteq C'. \tag{5.1}$$

In these cases, we say that π_1 (resp. π_2) *represents* $\mathcal{C}_1$ (resp. $\mathcal{C}_2$) and that a cut in the previous $\mathcal{C}_1$ (resp. $\mathcal{C}_2$) *belongs* to the MC partition π_1 (resp. CMC partition π_2).

A CMC partition $(V_1, V_2, \ldots, V_r)$ over C' is said to be *maximal* if for any $X \subset V_i$ with $1 \le i \le r$, $(V_1, \ldots, V_{i-1}, X, V_i - X, V_{i+1}, \ldots, V_r)$, is no longer a CMC partition over C'.

Clearly, any CMC partition over C' is an MC partition over C', but not vice versa. With these notions, Lemma 4.8 can be restated as follows.

Lemma 5.1. *Let $\{X, \overline{X}\}$ and $\{Y, \overline{Y}\}$ be two minimum cuts of a graph $G = (V, E)$. If these cuts cross each other, then (V_1, V_2, V_3, V_4) is a CMC partition over $C(G)$, where $V_1 = X \cap Y$, $V_2 = \overline{X} \cap Y$, $V_3 = \overline{X} \cap \overline{Y}$, and $V_4 = X \cap \overline{Y}$.*   □

A cycle on n vertices is called an *n-cycle*. A graph is called a *cactus* if any two cycles have at most one vertex in common, if any. In particular, a graph that consists of a single vertex is called a *trivial* cactus. An edge in a cactus is called a *cycle edge* if it is in a cycle; otherwise it is called a *tree edge* (see Fig. 5.1). Among examples of cacti are a chain, a tree, a cycle, and a star (in which all vertices except one have degree 1). A cactus R is called *uniform* if each cycle edge e (if any) satisfies $c_R(e) = 1$ and each tree edge e (if any) satisfies $c_R(e) = 2$. It is easy to see that if R is a connected, nontrivial, and uniform cactus, then $\lambda(R) = 2$ holds and each minimum cut consists of either two cycle edges in the same cycle or a single tree edge (see Fig. 5.1).

5.1.1 Relation Between Cycles in $\mathcal{R}$ and Minimum Cuts in G

Given a graph $G = (V, E)$, we map it to another graph $\mathcal{R} = (W, F)$ (which is a cactus in our discussion) by $\varphi : V \rightarrow W$. Throughout the remainder of the chapter, we shall use *vertex* to denote an element in V, and *node* to denote an element in W. We normally use u and v with or without subscript/superscript to denote vertices, and x, y, and z with or without subscript/superscript to denote nodes. Define

$$\varphi(X) = \{\varphi(v) \in W \mid v \in X\} \quad \text{for } X \subseteq V, \text{ and}$$
$$\varphi^{-1}(S) = \{v \in V \mid \varphi(v) \in S\} \quad \text{for } S \subseteq W.$$

For a subset $\mathcal{C} \subseteq \mathcal{C}(G)$ of minimum cuts, $(\mathcal{R}, \varphi)$ is a *representation* for $\mathcal{C}$ if it satisfies conditions (i) and (ii) in Definition 1.44 in Section 1.5.4. As before, $\mathcal{C}(G)$ and $\mathcal{C}(\mathcal{R})$ denote the set of all minimum cuts of G and $\mathcal{R}$, respectively, and, for $X \subseteq V$ and $S \subseteq W$, we use notations $\bar{X} = V - X$ and $\tilde{S} = W - S$, respectively. For a subset $\mathcal{C}' \subseteq \mathcal{C}(\mathcal{R})$, let

$$\varphi^{-1}(\mathcal{C}') = \{\{\varphi^{-1}(S), \varphi^{-1}(\tilde{S})\} \mid \{S, \tilde{S}\} \in \mathcal{C}'\}.$$

Then the condition that $(\mathcal{R}, \varphi)$ is a cactus representation for $\mathcal{C}$ (i.e., satisfying conditions (i) and (ii) in Definition 1.44) can be stated as follows:

$$\varphi^{-1}(\mathcal{C}(\mathcal{R})) = \mathcal{C}.$$

Suppose that $(\mathcal{R}, \varphi)$ is a representation for $\mathcal{C} \subseteq \mathcal{C}(G)$. We say that a cut $\{X, \bar{X}\} \in \mathcal{C}$ and a cut $\{S, \tilde{S}\} \in \mathcal{C}(\mathcal{R})$ *correspond* to each other if $\varphi(X) \subseteq S$ and $\varphi(\bar{X}) \subseteq \tilde{S}$. For the special case of $\mathcal{C} = \emptyset$, we consider that $(\mathcal{R}, \varphi)$ with a trivial cactus $\mathcal{R} = (x, \emptyset)$ with $\varphi(V) = x$ is a cactus representation for it. A node $x \in W$ with $\varphi^{-1}(x) = \emptyset$ is called an *empty node*. Note that, if $\mathcal{R}$ has an empty node, a minimum cut in $\mathcal{C}$ may correspond to more than one minimum cut in $\mathcal{C}(\mathcal{R})$, whereas any minimum cut in $\mathcal{C}(\mathcal{R})$ always corresponds to exactly one minimum cut in $\mathcal{C}$. This implies that if S contains only empty nodes then $\{S, \tilde{S}\} \notin \mathcal{C}(\mathcal{R})$.

As observed in Theorem 1.45, there is a uniform cactus representation $(\mathcal{R}, \varphi)$ for $\mathcal{C}(G)$. For example, the graph G^* in Fig. 5.2 satisfies $\lambda(G^*) = \lambda(v_1, v_{19}; G^*) = 4$ and $\lambda(v_9, v_{12}; G^*) = 5$ (i.e., no cut separating v_9 and v_{12} is minimum). Figure 5.3 shows a uniform cactus representation for $\mathcal{C}(G^*)$ for the graph G^* in Fig. 5.2.

Normal Cactus Representation

Note that not all subsets $\mathcal{C} \subseteq \mathcal{C}(G)$ have cactus representations. We observe that if $\mathcal{C} \subseteq \mathcal{C}(G)$ has a cactus representation $(\mathcal{R}, \varphi)$ then it has a cactus representation $(\mathcal{R}', \varphi')$ such that $\mathcal{R}'$ has no tree edges. Such $\mathcal{R}'$ is obtained from $\mathcal{R}$ by replacing each tree edge $\{u, v\}$ in $\mathcal{R}$ with two edges, converting $\{u, v\}$ into a 2-cycle on u and v while keeping the same φ (i.e., $\varphi' = \varphi$). Therefore, in the rest of this chapter we consider only uniform cacti without tree edges. In this case, every edge

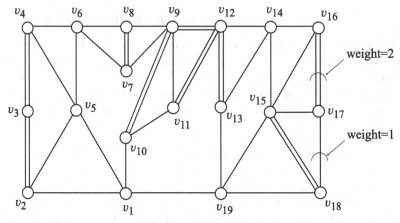

Figure 5.2. A graph G^* with $\lambda(G^*) = 4$.

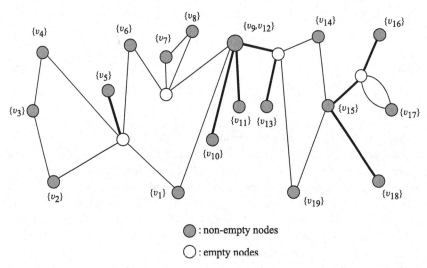

: non-empty nodes

: empty nodes

Figure 5.3. A cactus representation for $\mathcal{C}(G^*)$ (bold edges are tree edges, and $\{\cdot\}$ beside a node x shows $\varphi^{-1}(x)$).

belongs to a cycle and has the same cost. This will simplify discussion on cactus representations.

We call a node v in a cactus a *k-junction node* if v belongs to exactly k cycles.

Definition 5.2. *A cactus representation* $(\mathcal{R}, \varphi)$ *is said to be* normal *if it has no tree edge and no empty 2-junction node belonging to a 2-cycle.*   □

We will see in Section 5.1.2 that, if there is a cactus representation for $\mathcal{C} \subseteq \mathcal{C}(G)$, then there is a normal cactus representation for $\mathcal{C}$. Figure 5.4 shows a normal cactus representation for all minimum cuts $\mathcal{C}(G^*)$ in graph G^* of Fig. 5.2.

Table 5.1. Relationship Among Subgraphs of $\mathcal{R}$, Minimum Cuts in G, and CMC partitions of V

Subgraph of $\mathcal{R}$	Minimum cuts of G	CMC partition of V
2-cycle	one cut	MC partition of size 2
3-cycle, or empty 3-junction node	3 cuts, each pair of which is complementary	CMC partition of size 3
r-cycle ($r \geq 4$)	$\binom{r}{2}$ cuts, each pair of which is crossing or complementary	CMC partition of size r

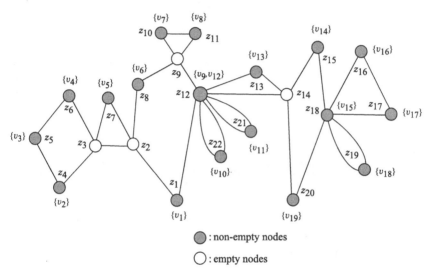

Figure 5.4. A normal cactus representation for $\mathcal{C}(G^*)$ ($\{\cdot\}$ beside a node x shows $\varphi^{-1}(x)$).

Cycles in $\mathcal{R}$ and Minimum Cuts in G

The major goal of this section is to investigate the relationship between a subgraph of $\mathcal{R}$ and minimum cuts in G. In particular, we want to know the structural properties of minimum cuts in G that correspond to distinct cycles in $\mathcal{R}$, and vice versa. The main results are summarized in Table 5.1.

Before giving rigorous proofs of the relationships in Table 5.1, we first informally explain the implication of cycles of different lengths in $\mathcal{R}$. Given a graph $G = (V, E)$, let $(\mathcal{R}, \varphi)$ be a normal cactus representation for $\mathcal{C}(G)$. In the following, we associate each node $x \in W$ with the set $\varphi^{-1}(x) \subset V$ (see Fig. 5.4, for example).

It is clear that a 2-cycle through nodes x and y in $\mathcal{R}$ represents the cut $\{X, \overline{X}\}$ in G, where $X = \varphi^{-1}(W_1)$ and $\overline{X} = \varphi^{-1}(\tilde{W}_1)$ are defined by the two components W_1 and $\tilde{W}_1$ in $\mathcal{R}$ resulting from the removal of the two edges $\{x, y\}$. This is stated in the first and second columns in the first row of Table 5.1. In this case, we obtain the

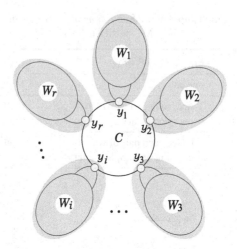

Figure 5.5. A cycle C in a normal cactus representation.

MC partition (V_1, V_2) of V of size $r = 2$, where $V_1 = X$ and $V_2 = \overline{X}$ (i.e., $\{V_1, V_2\}$ is a minimum cut). This explains the third entry in the first row of Table 5.1.

For a cycle C in a cactus $\mathcal{R} = (W, F)$, we define $W(C)$ and $F(C)$ to be the sets of nodes and edges in C, respectively. Let (W_i, F_i), $i = 1, 2, \ldots, r$, denote the components of $\mathcal{R} - F(C)$, where each (W_i, F_i) appears in C in the order $i = 1, 2, \ldots, r$ (see Fig. 5.5). We assume $r \geq 2$. Since any two cycles have at most one node in common, each component (W_i, F_i) $(i = 1, \ldots, r)$ contains exactly one node (call it y_i) in $W(C)$. In this case, the ordered partition $\pi_C = (V_1, V_2, \ldots, V_r)$ defined by $V_i = \varphi^{-1}(W_i)$, $i = 1, 2, \ldots, r$, is a CMC partition of V over C. Here we define the following terminology.

Definition 5.3. *We say that a cycle C in $\mathcal{R}$ yields the CMC partition π_C and that a cut in G belongs to π_C if it is one of the cuts in the C_2 of* (5.1). □

This is what is implied by an r-cycle C in $\mathcal{R}$ (see the last column of Table 5.1).

The second row of Table 5.1 for $r = 3$ can be best explained with the help of Fig. 5.6. Figure 5.6(a) shows a 3-cycle in $\mathcal{R}$, while Figure 5.6(b) shows an empty 3-junction node. Each of these two cases gives rise to three cuts belonging to the CMC partition $(V_1, V_2, V_3) = (\varphi^{-1}(W_1), \varphi^{-1}(W_2), \varphi^{-1}(W_3))$. It is clear that any two of them are complementary. We also say that an empty 3-junction node *yields* a CMC partition of size 3.

Before explaining the last entry (the middle column of the third row) of Table 5.I by using Theorem 5.12, we obtain more preparation in Section 5.1.2.

5.1.2 Normal Cactus Representation with Additional Restrictions

We shall now move on to more rigorous discussion that includes the proof of one-to-one correspondence between cycles (in column 1) and CMC partitions (in

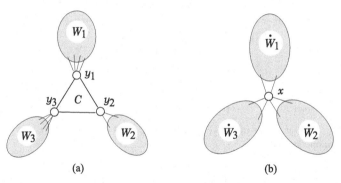

Figure 5.6. Two possible structures for a CMC partition of size 3.

column 3) of Table 5.1. Our immediate goal is to show that if a cactus representation exists at all for $C \subseteq C(G)$ then a normal cactus representation with some restrictions always exists (Lemma 5.6).

Lemma 5.4. *Let* $(\mathcal{R}, \varphi)$ *be a* (*not necessarily normal*) *cactus representation for* $C \subseteq C(G)$. *Then the following properties hold:*

(i) $\mathcal{R}$ *has no empty node of degree 1 and no empty node of degree 2 in a cycle.*
(ii) *For any two nonempty nodes* v_1, v_2 *in* $\mathcal{R}$, *there is a cut* $\{X, \overline{X}\} \in C$ *with* $\varphi^{-1}(v_1) \subseteq X$ *and* $\varphi^{-1}(v_2) \subseteq \overline{X}$. □

Proof. (i) Assume that $\mathcal{R}$ had an empty node x of degree 1 or an empty node x of degree 2 in a cycle. Then the cut $\{x, W - x\} \in C(\mathcal{R})$ would not correspond to any cut in $C(G)$, contradicting the definition of $\mathcal{R}$.

(ii) Consider a path P between v_1 and v_2 in $\mathcal{R}$. If P contains a cycle edge e, let $F' = \{e, e'\}$, where e' is an edge in the same cycle but not on P. Otherwise, let $F' = \{e\}$, where e is a tree edge in P. Obviously, $\mathcal{R} - F'$ has two connected components, S and S', containing v_1 and v_2, respectively, implying that the cut $\{S, S'\} \in C(\mathcal{R})$ corresponds to the cut $\{X, \overline{X}\}$, satisfying condition (ii). □

Next we introduce three operations for transforming cactus representations.

2-Cycle contraction: Contract a 2-cycle C containing an empty 2-junction node x into the other node x' in C, eliminating the resulting self-loop (see Fig. 5.7(a)).
3-Cycle insertion: Replace an empty 3-junction node x with the three new empty nodes y_1, y_2, and y_3, which form a new 3-cycle (see Fig. 5.7(b)).
3-Cycle elimination: Replace a 3-cycle $\{y_1, y_2, y_3\}$ with the three 2-cycles $\{x, y_1\}, \{x, y_2\}$, and $\{x, y_3\}$ after introducing a new node x (see Fig. 5.7(c)).

Note that none of the three operations changes $\varphi^{-1}(C(\mathcal{R}))$. For example, a 2-cycle contraction eliminates a minimum cut $(S, \tilde{S})$ of $\mathcal{R}$ that separates x and x' such that $x \in S$ and $x' \in \tilde{S}$, but $\{S' = S - x, \tilde{S}' = \tilde{S}\}$ is a minimum cut in

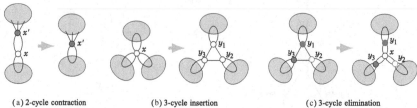

(a) 2-cycle contraction　　　　　　(b) 3-cycle insertion　　　　　　(c) 3-cycle elimination

Figure 5.7. Illustration for (a) 2-cycle contraction, (b) 3-cycle insertion, and (c) 3-cycle elimination operations.

the contracted cactus satisfying $\varphi^{-1}(S') = \varphi^{-1}(S)$ and $\varphi^{-1}(\tilde{S}') = \varphi^{-1}(\tilde{S}')$ (hence, $\varphi^{-1}(\mathcal{C}(\mathcal{R}))$ remains unchanged).

Lemma 5.5. *For a graph $G = (V, E)$ and a subset $C \subseteq \mathcal{C}(G)$, if there is a cactus representation for C, then there is a normal cactus representation for C.*　□

Proof. It is easy to see that a cactus representation can be transformed into a normal cactus representation by replacing each tree edge with a 2-cycle and applying 2-cycle contractions as many times as possible.　□

We can further assume that the normal cactus representation $\mathcal{R}$ satisfies some additional restrictions.

Lemma 5.6. *Given a graph $G = (V, E)$, both of the following conditions hold for any $C \subseteq \mathcal{C}(G)$:*

  (i) *If C has a cactus representation, then C has a normal cactus representation $\mathcal{R}$ without any empty 3-junction node.*
 (ii) *If C has a cactus representation, then C has a normal cactus representation $\mathcal{R}$ without any 3-cycle.*　□

(However, C may not have a representation $\mathcal{R}$ satisfying (i) and (ii) simultaneously.)

Proof. (i) Let $\mathcal{R}$ be a cactus representation for C, where we assume that tree edges, if any, have been replaced with 2-cycles. We apply the following procedures:

  (a) Apply the 3-cycle insertion (Fig 5.7(b)) to all empty 3-junction nodes, if any.
  (b) Normalize the resulting cactus by repeatedly applying 2-cycle contractions.

After procedure (a) is completed, all empty 3-junction nodes are eliminated, and procedure (b) re-creates no empty 3-junction node. This proves condition (i).

(ii) Apply the transformations (c) and (b), where (c) is defined as follows:

  (c) Apply the 3-cycle elimination (Fig. 5.7(c)) to all 3-cycles, if any.

Normalization (b) will not reintroduce any 3-cycle.　□

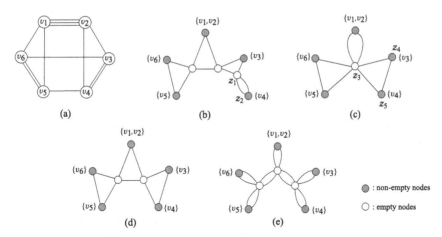

Figure 5.8. Four examples of cactus representations.

5.1.3 Cycle-Type and Junction-Type Cactus Representations

We now investigate the more detailed structure of normal cactus representations.

Definition 5.7. *We call a normal cactus representation without empty 3-junction nodes a* cycle-type *normal cactus representation. Similarly, we call a normal cactus representation without 3-cycles a* junction-type *normal cactus representation.* □

Lemma 5.6 tells that there are both normal cactus representations cycle-type and junction type. Figure 5.8(b), (c), (d), and (e) shows four cactus representations for the same graph in Fig. 5.8(a). The cactus representation in Fig. 5.8(b) is not normal since it has an empty 2-junction node, z_1, belonging to 2-cycle $\{z_1, z_2\}$. The cactus representation in Fig. 5.8(c) is normal but is neither of cycle-type nor of junction-type since it has an empty 3-junction node, z_3, and a 3-cycle, $\{z_3, z_4, z_5\}$, whereas the ones in Fig. 5.8(d) and (e) are of cycle type and junction type, respectively. (Note that two empty 2-junction nodes belong to a 3-cycle and do not prevent it from being normal.)

Since cycle-type normal cactus representations often enable us to prove lemmas and theorems more easily, this is the type of representation we mainly consider in the rest of this section. However, we need to introduce a few more terms.

Given a cactus $\mathcal{R} = (W, F)$ and a node $x \in W$, suppose that $\mathcal{R} - x$ has k components $\mathcal{R}_i = (W_i, F_i)$, $i = 1, 2, \ldots, k$, where we see that W_i contains at least one node of degree 2, which is a nonempty node (Lemma 5.4(i)). For each i, we call the graph induced by $W_i \cup \{x\}$ in $\mathcal{R}$ a *blockcactus* at x. For example, an empty 3-junction node x in $\mathcal{R}$ of Fig. 5.6(b) has three blockcacti. From a cactus $\mathcal{R} = (W, F)$, we define the *cycle distance* in $\mathcal{R}$, $\delta : W \times W \to \mathbf{Z}_+$, as follows:

$$\delta(x, y) = \text{the number of cycles } C \text{ such that } F(C) \cap F(P) \neq \emptyset$$
$$\text{for a path } P \text{ from } x \text{ to } y.$$

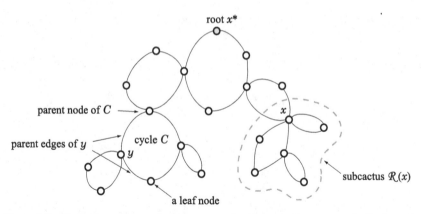

Figure 5.9. Illustration of root node x^*, parent node of a cycle C, parent cycle C of a node y, parent edges of a node y, and subcactus $\mathcal{R}(x)$ at a node x.

Note that $\delta(x, y)$ does not depend on the choice of path P since $\mathcal{R}$ is a cactus. By definition, $\delta(x, x) = 0$ for all $x \in W$. For example, $\delta(x, y) = 4$ for the nodes x and y in the cactus of Fig. 5.9.

In the following it is often convenient to fix a node $x^* \in W$ as the *root* node of $\mathcal{R}$. Observe that, for any cycle C in $\mathcal{R}$, one node in C is at a cycle distance, say j, from x^*, and all the other nodes in C are at a cycle distance $j + 1$ from x^*. We call the former node the *parent node* of cycle C. For cycle C in the cactus in Fig. 5.9, the parent node of C has cycle distance 2 and other nodes in C have cycle distance 3. For a node y in C, which is not its parent node, C is called the *parent cycle* of y, and the two edges of C incident to y are called the *parent edges* of y. See Fig. 5.9 for these definitions.

For any node x in $\mathcal{R}$ with $\delta(x^*, x) \geq 1$, the two parent edges of x give a minimum cut; that is, their removal disconnects $\mathcal{R}$ into exactly two components. We call one of them containing x the *subcactus* of $\mathcal{R}$ at x, and we denote it by $\mathcal{R}(x) = (W(x), F(x))$, where $W(x)$ (resp. $F(x)$) is its node (resp. edge) set. Figure 5.9 illustrates an example of the subcactus $\mathcal{R}(x)$. For convenience, we define the subcactus at the root x^* to be $\mathcal{R}$ itself. From the property $\varphi^{-1}(\mathcal{C}(\mathcal{R})) = \mathcal{C}$ of the representation $(\mathcal{R}, \varphi)$, we see that the subcactus $\mathcal{R}(x)$ at any node x contains at least one nonempty node. A node x with $W(x) = \{x\}$ is called a *leaf* node. Clearly all nodes of degree 2 on a cycle C, except the parent node, are leaf nodes. A leaf node is neither the root node nor an empty node (see Lemma 5.4(i)).

We now prove a series of lemmas to investigate properties of normal cactus representations. To start with, the next lemma shows when a minimum cut of G corresponds to more than one minimum cut in a normal cactus representation.

Lemma 5.8. *For a graph $G = (V, E)$ and a normal cactus representation $(\mathcal{R}, \varphi)$ for $\mathcal{C} \subseteq \mathcal{C}(G)$, let $\{S, \tilde{S}\} \in \mathcal{C}(\mathcal{R})$. Then $E(S, \tilde{S}; \mathcal{R})$ consists of two edges incident to an empty 2-junction node $x \in S$ if and only if there is another cut*

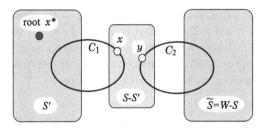

Figure 5.10. Two cycles C_1, C_2 in the proof of Lemma 5.8

$\{S', \tilde{S}'\} \in C(\mathcal{R})$ such that $\varphi^{-1}(S) = \varphi^{-1}(S')$. Moreover, such S' is unique and given by $S - \{x\}$. $\qquad \square$

Proof. From the structure of cacti, the only-if part is trivial. To show the if part, let $\mathcal{R} = (W, F)$ and let $\{S, \tilde{S}\}$, $\{S', \tilde{S}'\} \in C(\mathcal{R})$ be two distinct minimum cuts satisfying $\varphi^{-1}(S) = \varphi^{-1}(S')$. Then $(S - S') \cup (S' - S)$ consists only of empty nodes. Note that if the two cuts S and S' intersect each other in $\mathcal{R}$, then they cross each other, since $W - (S \cup S')$ must contain a nonempty node. However, if these two cuts cross each other, then, by Lemma 4.8(iii), $\{(S - S'), W - (S - S')\}$ would be a minimum cut in $\mathcal{R}$ with $\varphi^{-1}(S - S') = \emptyset$, but it would not correspond to any cut in G, a contradiction to the definition of a cactus representation. Therefore, S and S' cannot intersect each other, and we can assume without loss of generality that $S' \subset S$.

We claim that $E(S', \tilde{S}; \mathcal{R}) = \emptyset$, where $\tilde{S} = W - S$. To prove this claim, let $d(S', \tilde{S}; \mathcal{R}) = \alpha$, $d(S', S - S'; \mathcal{R}) = \beta$, and $d(S - S', \tilde{S}; \mathcal{R}) = \gamma$. The situation is illustrated in Fig. 5.10. Since $\{S, \tilde{S}\}$, $\{S', \tilde{S}'\} \in C(\mathcal{R})$ and $\{S - S', W - (S - S')\} \notin C(\mathcal{R})$, we have $\alpha + \beta = \alpha + \gamma = 2$ and $\beta + \gamma > 1$, where α can take only one of the three possible values: 0, 1, or 2. It is easy to see that the only possible solution is given by $\alpha = 0$ and $\beta = \gamma = 2$. In other words, we have $E(S', \tilde{S}; \mathcal{R}) = \emptyset$ and $d(S', S - S'; \mathcal{R}) = d(S - S', \tilde{S}; \mathcal{R}) = 2$.

Now, let C_1 (resp. C_2) be the cycle containing the edges in $E(S', S - S'; \mathcal{R})$ (resp. $E(S - S', \tilde{S}; \mathcal{R})$). To facilitate the rest of the proof, we fix an arbitrary nonempty node $x^* \in S'$ as the root and consider cycle distances from x^*. We see that cycle C_1 can contain at most one node (say x) in $S - S'$ because if C_1 contained two nodes $x_1, x_2 \in S - S'$ then the subcactus either at x_1 or at x_2 would consist only of nodes in $S - S'$ (i.e., empty nodes), a contradiction to Lemma 5.4(i). Similarly, C_2 also contains at most one node (say y) in $S - S'$ (see Fig. 5.10). We now show $C_1 \neq C_2$. If $C_1 = C_2$, then cycle $C_1 = C_2$ would contain exactly one node $x = y$ in $S - S'$, and the subcactus at $x = y$ would contain only empty nodes in $S - S'$, again a contradiction to Lemma 5.4(i).

In addition to the parent cycle C of x, there is at most one cycle C_x that passes through x, because if there were two such cycles then one of them would contain an empty node $z \in S - S'$ such that the subcactus $\mathcal{R}(z)$ at z consists of empty nodes in $S - S'$, a contradiction. It then follows that x is an empty 2-junction node, and C_x is not a 2-cycle since the representation is normal.

To complete the proof, we want to show that $C_x = C_2$. Since $\mathcal{R}$ is normal, if $C_x \neq C_2$ then C_x is not a 2-cycle; that is, it would contain at least two nodes, z_1, z_2, other than x, where we assume $z_1 \neq y$ without loss of generality. If so, the subcactus $\mathcal{R}(z_1)$ at z_1 would again consist only of empty nodes in $S - S'$, a contradiction. Therefore, we have $C_x = C_2$ and, hence, $S - S' = \{x\}$, proving the lemma.   □

Lemma 5.9. *Given a normal cactus representation $(\mathcal{R} = (W, F), \varphi)$ for $\mathcal{C} \subseteq \mathcal{C}(G)$, let us fix an arbitrary node $x^* \in W$ as the root node. Then, for any two distinct $x, x' \in W$, their subcacti $R(x) = (W(x), F(x))$ and $R(x') = (W(x'), F(x'))$ satisfy $\varphi^{-1}(W(x)) \neq \varphi^{-1}(W(x'))$.*   □

Proof. Assume that there are distinct nodes x and x' with $\varphi^{-1}(W(x)) = \varphi^{-1}(W(x'))$. As we remarked after defining a subcactus before Lemma 5.8, each of $W(x)$ and $W(x')$ contains a nonempty node.

Since $W(x) \neq W(x')$, there is, without loss of generality, an empty 2-junction node z such that $W(x) \cup \{z\} = W(x')$ by Lemma 5.8. However, this means that $x' = z$ is the parent of x, and we have a 2-cycle passing through z and x, contradicting the assumption that the cactus (W, F) is normal.   □

A CMC partition $(V_1, V_2, \ldots, V_r), r \geq 2$, over $\mathcal{C} \subseteq \mathcal{C}(G)$ is *maximal* if, for any $i, 1 \leq i \leq r$, and $X \subset V_i, (V_1, \ldots, V_{i-1}, X, V_i - X, V_{i+1}, \ldots, V_r)$, is no longer a CMC partition over $\mathcal{C}$. We are now in a position to prove two important lemmas in this section.

Lemma 5.10. *Given a graph $G = (V, E)$, let $(\mathcal{R}, \varphi)$ be a cycle-type normal cactus representation for $\mathcal{C} \subseteq \mathcal{C}(G)$. Let $\pi = (V_1, V_2, \ldots, V_r)$ be a maximal CMC partition over $\mathcal{C}$ with $r \geq 2$. Then $\mathcal{R}$ has a cycle C of length r which yields π.* □

Proof. From the definition of π, for each $i \in \{1, 2, \ldots, r\}$, there is a minimum cut $\{W_i, \tilde{W}_i\} \in \mathcal{C}(\mathcal{R})$ such that $\varphi^{-1}(W_i) = V_i$ and $\varphi^{-1}(\tilde{W}_i) = \bar{V}_i$. We assume without loss of generality that such W_i is inclusion-wise maximal in the sense that any $W' \supset W_i$ with $\varphi^{-1}(W') = V_i$ implies $\{W', \tilde{W}'\} \notin \mathcal{C}(\mathcal{R})$. By Lemma 4.7, for each $i = 1, 2, \ldots, r$, the graphs induced from $\mathcal{R}$ by W_i and $\tilde{W}_i$ are both connected.

We first show $W_i \cap W_j = \emptyset$ for distinct $i, j \in \{1, 2, \ldots, r\}$. Since $\varphi^{-1}(W_i) \cap \varphi^{-1}(W_j) = V_i \cap V_j = \emptyset$, neither $W_i \subseteq W_j$ nor $W_i \supseteq W_j$ holds (otherwise we would have $\varphi^{-1}(W_i) \cap \varphi^{-1}(W_j) = V_i$). Moreover, if $W_i \cap W_j \neq \emptyset$, then the cuts $\{W_i, \tilde{W}_i\}, \{W_j, \tilde{W}_j\} \in \mathcal{C}(\mathcal{R})$ cross each other and, by Lemma 4.8(i), $\mathcal{C}(\mathcal{R})$ would contain cut $\{W_i \cap W_j, W - W_i \cap W_j\}$ with $\varphi^{-1}(W_i \cap W_j) = \emptyset$, a contradiction to the definition of a cactus representation. Therefore, $W_i \cap W_j = \emptyset$ for distinct $i, j \in \{1, 2, \ldots, r\}$.

Let $W^{\#} = W - \cup_{i=1}^{r} W_i$. Next we prove the lemma for the case $W^{\#} = \emptyset$ (Case 1), and we show that $W^{\#} \neq \emptyset$ (Case 2) is impossible. In the rest of the proof, W_{r+1} and V_{r+1} mean W_1 and V_1, respectively.

Case 1: $W^{\#} = \emptyset$. Note first that, for any $i \in \{1, 2, \ldots, r\}$, $E(W_i, \tilde{W}_i; \mathcal{R})$ consists of two edges in the same cycle, since $\mathcal{R}$ has no tree edge. If $r = 2$, then let C

be the cycle that contains the two edges in $E(W_1, W_2; \mathcal{R})$, where $W_2 = \tilde{W}_1$ and $W_1 = \tilde{W}_2$. For $r \geq 3$, before choosing a cycle C, we claim that $E(W_i, W_{i+1}; \mathcal{R})$ contains exactly one edge for each $i \in \{1, 2, \ldots, r\}$. If $E(W_i, W_j; \mathcal{R})$ contains two edges for some $i < j$, then $d(W_i, \tilde{W}_i; \mathcal{R}) = d(W_j, \tilde{W}_j; \mathcal{R}) = 2$ would imply $d(W_i \cup W_j, W - (W_i \cup W_j); \mathcal{R}) = \emptyset$ (where $W - (W_i \cup W_j) \neq \emptyset$ by $r \geq 3$), a contradiction. By noting that $d(W_i, \tilde{W}_i; \mathcal{R}) = 2$ for all i and, by the assumption $W = \cup_{i=1}^{r} W_i$, the only possibility is that $E(W_i, W_j; \mathcal{R})$ consists of at most one edge, and all such edges are in a single cycle C. If W_k and W_{k+1} are not adjacent in C for some k, then for the cut $\{S, \tilde{S}\} \in \mathcal{C}(\mathcal{R})$ corresponding to $\{V_k \cup V_{k+1}, \overline{V_k \cup V_{k+1}}\} \in \mathcal{C}(G)$, $d(S, \tilde{S}; \mathcal{R}) \geq 4$ would hold (since each W_i induces a connected subgraph in $\mathcal{R}$), which is a contradiction. Hence, for each $i = 1, 2, \ldots, r$, $E(W_i, W_{i+1}; \mathcal{R})$ contains exactly one edge, and $W_1, W_2, \ldots, W_r$ appear in C in this order. This proves the claim, and we choose the cycle C in this argument.

Now we assume $r \geq 2$, and we show that the chosen cycle C satisfies the lemma. If the length of C is more than r and, hence, some W_k has two or more nodes, then $(V_1, \ldots, V_{k-1}, X, X - V_k, V_{k+1}, \ldots, V_r)$, where $X(\neq \emptyset) \subset V_k$, would be a CMC partition of length $r + 1$, contradicting the maximality of π. Therefore, C has length r and it yields π by $W^\# = \emptyset$, implying that C satisfies the lemma.

Case 2: $W^\# \neq \emptyset$. Clearly, $W^\#$ contains only empty nodes. Let $z \in W^\#$ and let $\{\dot{\mathcal{R}}_j \mid j = 1, 2, \ldots, h\}$ be the set of blockcacti of $\mathcal{R}$ at z, where $\dot{\mathcal{R}}_j = (\dot{W}_j, \dot{F}_j)$. Note that $h \geq 2$ holds, since z is an empty node. Also, $h \neq 3$ holds since $\mathcal{R}$ is of cycle type. Since each W_i ($i = 1, 2, \ldots, r$) is connected and $z \notin W_i$, it is totally contained in some $\dot{W}_j$. Conversely, each $\dot{W}_j$ ($j = 1, 2, \ldots, h$) contains some W_i, since otherwise the blockcactus $\dot{\mathcal{R}}_j$ would consist only of empty nodes, a contradiction. Therefore, there is a k such that W_k and W_{k+1} are contained in distinct sets $\dot{W}_i$ and $\dot{W}_j$, respectively. We assume $W_k \subseteq \dot{W}_1$ and $W_{k+1} \subseteq \dot{W}_2$ without loss of generality.

We first consider the case where $h \geq 4$ (see Fig. 5.11(a)). In this case, if there is a cut $\{S, \tilde{S}\} \in \mathcal{C}(\mathcal{R})$ that corresponds to $\{V_k \cup V_{k+1}, \overline{V_k \cup V_{k+1}}\} \in \mathcal{C}(G)$, then at least one of the graphs induced by S and $\tilde{S}$ is not connected, which is a contradiction to Lemma 4.7.

Finally, we consider the case $h = 2$. Then z is an empty 2-junction node (see Fig. 5.11(b)). We show that $\dot{W}_1$ and $\dot{W}_2$ each contain at least two sets out of $\{W_1, \ldots, W_r\}$. To see this, note that if $\dot{W}_j \cap (W_1 \cup \cdots \cup W_r) = W_i$ holds for some i and j then $\varphi^{-1}(\dot{W}_j) = V_i$ and $\{\dot{W}_j, W - \dot{W}_j\} \in \mathcal{C}(\mathcal{R})$ hold, contradicting the maximality of W_i, since $W_i \cup \{z\} \subseteq \dot{W}_j$. Therefore, for some i, j, $W_i \cup W_k \subseteq \dot{W}_1$ and $W_j \cup W_{k+1} \subseteq \dot{W}_2$. From this configuration, a contradiction can be derived as in the case of $h \geq 4$. $\qquad\square$

We also note that the cycle C in Lemma 5.10 for a given maximal CMC partition π is unique by Lemma 5.9. The next lemma shows that the converse of Lemma 5.10 is also true.

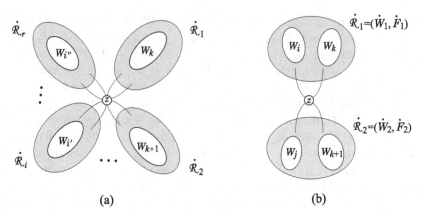

Figure 5.11. Illustration for the cases (a) $h \geq 4$ and (b) $h = 2$ in Case 2 of the proof of Lemma 5.10.

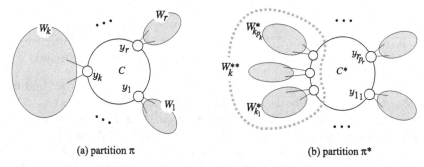

Figure 5.12. Two cycles, (a) C and (b) C^*, in the proof of Lemma 5.11.

Lemma 5.11. *Given a graph $G = (V, E)$, let $(\mathcal{R}, \varphi)$ be a cycle-type normal cactus representation for $\mathcal{C} \subseteq \mathcal{C}(G)$. For any cycle C of length $r \geq 2$ in $\mathcal{R}$, the ordered partition $\pi_C = (V_1, V_2, \ldots, V_r)$ that C yields is a maximal CMC partition over $\mathcal{C}$.* $\square$

Proof. As observed in the paragraph before Definition 5.3, each component (W_i, F_i), $i = 1, \ldots, r$, in $\mathcal{R} - F(C)$ contains exactly one node (call it y_i) in $W(C)$ (see Fig. 5.12(a)), and the ordered partition $\pi_C = (V_1, V_2, \ldots, V_r)$ that C yields is a CMC partition over $\mathcal{C}$. Hence, we only have to show the maximality of π_C.

Assume that π_C is not maximal. Then there is a maximal CMC partition π^* over $\mathcal{C}$ such that

$$\pi^* = (X_{1_1}, X_{1_2}, \ldots, X_{1_{p_1}}, X_{2_1}, \ldots, X_{2_{p_2}}, \ldots, X_{r_1}, \ldots, X_{r_{p_r}}),$$

where $V_i = X_{i_1} \cup \cdots \cup X_{i_{p_i}}$, $i = 1, \ldots, r$, and $p_k \geq 2$ for some k.

By Lemma 5.10, $\mathcal{R}$ has a cycle C^* of length $r^* = p_1 + p_2 + \cdots + p_r$ $(>r)$ that yields π^*. This means that $\mathcal{R} - F(C^*)$ has r^* components, (W_j^*, F_j^*),

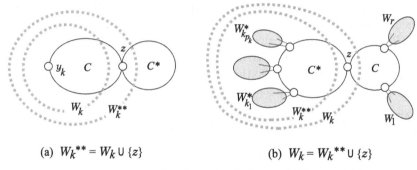

(a) $W_k^{**} = W_k \cup \{z\}$ (b) $W_k = W_k^{**} \cup \{z\}$

Figure 5.13. Empty 2-junction node z in the proof of Lemma 5.11.

$j = 1_1, \ldots, 1_{p_1}, \ldots, r_1, \ldots, r_{p_r}$, such that $\varphi^{-1}(W_j^*) = X_j$ for all j. Let $W_k^{**} = W_{k_1}^* \cup \cdots \cup W_{k_{p_k}}^*$, where $p_k \geq 2$ (see Fig. 5.12(b)). Obviously, $\varphi^{-1}(W_k^{**}) = V_k = \varphi^{-1}(W_k)$. From $r < r^*$, we have $C \neq C^*$, and this implies that $E(W_k^{**}, \tilde{W}_k^{**}) \neq E(W_k, \tilde{W}_k)$, since distinct cycles C and C^* can share at most one node in a cactus. Therefore, by Lemma 5.8, there is an empty 2-junction node z such that $W_k^{**} \cup \{z\} = W_k$ or $W_k^{**} = W_k \cup \{z\}$ (see Fig. 5.13). If $W_k^{**} = W_k \cup \{z\}$ (Fig. 5.13(a)), then no set $W_{k_i}^*$ contains a node in C and, hence, C can have at most two nodes, z and y_k, implying that C is a 2-cycle, a contradiction to the fact that a normal cactus representation has no empty 2-junction node belonging to a 2-cycle. So, assume $W_k^{**} \cup \{z\} = W_k$ (Fig. 5.13(b)). In this case, however, we claim that there is no minimum cut in $\mathcal{R}$ corresponding to a minimum cut $\{(V_1 \cup \cdots \cup V_{k-1} \cup X_{k_1}), (X_{k_2} \cup \cdots \cup X_{k_{p_k}} \cup V_{k+1} \cup \cdots \cup V_r)\}$ in G, which is obtained from π^*. To prove this claim, let $(S, \tilde{S})$ be a cut in $\mathcal{R}$ such that $\varphi^{-1}(S) = V_1 \cup \cdots \cup V_{k-1} \cup X_{k_1}$. One of S and $\tilde{S}$ does not include z and induces a disconnected subgraph in $\mathcal{R}$. Hence, by Lemma 4.7, $(S, \tilde{S})$ is not a minimum cut in $\mathcal{R}$, proving the claim. $\square$

The preceding result, which establishes a one-to-one correspondence between the maximal CMC partitions and the cycles in a cycle-type normal cactus representation, is summarized as follows.

Theorem 5.12. *Given $G = (V, E)$ and $\mathcal{C} \subseteq \mathcal{C}(G)$, let $(\mathcal{R}, \varphi)$ be a cycle-type normal cactus representation for $\mathcal{C}$. Then an ordered partition $\pi = (V_1, V_2, \ldots, V_r)$ of V is a maximal CMC partition over $\mathcal{C}$ if and only if $\mathcal{R}$ has an r-cycle that yields π.* $\square$

For example, the 5-cycle $C_0 = \{z_1, z_2, z_9, z_{10}, z_{13}\}$ in Fig. 5.4 yields a CMC partition,

$$\pi_{C_0} = \{\{v_1\}, \{v_2, \ldots, v_5\}, \{v_6\}, \{v_7, v_8\}, \{v_9, \ldots, v_{19}\}\},$$

over $\mathcal{C}(G^*)$ in the graph G^* of Fig. 5.2. Since the representation in Fig. 5.4 is the cycle-type normal cactus representation for $\mathcal{C}(G^*)$, π_{C_0} is a maximal CMC partition over $\mathcal{C}(G^*)$ by Theorem 5.12.

Conversely, Theorem 5.12 implies that a maximal CMC partition over $C(G)$ uniquely determines a cycle in the cycle-type normal cactus representation for $C(G)$.

Let $\Pi^3(C)$ denote the set of all maximal CMC partitions of size 3 over a subset $C \subseteq C(G)$. In this case, the following lemma shows that, for each $\pi \in \Pi^3(C)$, any given normal cactus representation for C has a unique subgraph that yields π.

Lemma 5.13. *Given a graph $G = (V, E)$, let $(\mathcal{R}, \varphi)$ be a normal cactus representation for a subset $C \subseteq C(G)$. Let $\pi \in \Pi^3(C)$. Then either*

(a) $\mathcal{R}$ *has a cycle C of length 3 which yields π, or*
(b) $\mathcal{R}$ *has a 3-junction node y which yields π,*

but not both.   □

Proof. We show that conditions (a) and (b) cannot occur at the same time. Assume that $\mathcal{R}$ has both a cycle C satisfying condition (a) and an empty 3-junction node satisfying condition (b). Apply the 3-cycle insertion to the empty 3-junction node, followed by normalization, generating a 3-cycle C^*. Note that this transformation does not destroy C. Thus, both C and C^* yield π, a contradiction to Lemma 5.9.   □

5.1.4 Canonical Cactus Representations

Our goal in this subsection is to prove the following theorem, which states that the normal cactus representation for C introduced in the previous subsection, is unique within isomorphism.

Theorem 5.14. *Let $(\mathcal{R}_i = (W_i, F_i), \varphi_i)$, $i = 1, 2$, be two normal cactus representations for $C \subseteq C(G)$ such that, for each $\pi \in \Pi^3(C)$, a 3-cycle in $\mathcal{R}_1$ yields π if and only if a 3-cycle in $\mathcal{R}_2$ yields π. Then there is a bijection $\alpha : W_1 \to W_2$ such that $\varphi_1^{-1}(x) = \varphi_2^{-1}(\alpha(x))$ holds for any $x \in W_1$, and $\{x, x'\} \in F_1$ holds if and only if $\{\alpha(x), \alpha(x')\} \in F_2$ holds.*   □

We first prove this theorem via the following three lemmas for the special case, in which both $(\mathcal{R}_1, \varphi_1)$ and $(\mathcal{R}_2, \varphi_2)$ are cycle-type normal cactus representations. Choose a nonempty node $x^* \in W_1$ and a node $y^* \in W_2$ with $\varphi_1^{-1}(x^*) \cap \varphi_2^{-1}(y^*) \neq \emptyset$ as the root nodes of $\mathcal{R}_1$ and $\mathcal{R}_2$, respectively. As before, we denote the subcactus at $x \in W_i$ by $(W_i(x), F_i(x))$.

Lemma 5.15. *Let $(\mathcal{R}_i = (W_i, F_i), \varphi_i)$, $i = 1, 2$, be two cycle-type normal cactus representations for $C \subseteq C(G)$. Then for an r-cycle C in $\mathcal{R}_1$, where nodes $x_1, x_2, \ldots, x_r$ appear in this order, there is a unique r-cycle C' in $\mathcal{R}_2$, where nodes $y_1, y_2, \ldots, y_r$ appear in this order, such that $\varphi_1^{-1}(W_1(x_i)) = \varphi_2^{-1}(W_2(y_i))$ for $i = 2, 3 \ldots, r$ and $\varphi_1^{-1}(W_1 - \cup_{i=2}^r W_1(x_i)) = \varphi_2^{-1}(W_2 - \cup_{i=2}^r W_2(y_i))$ hold, where x_1 (resp. y_1) is the parent node of C (resp. C'). The converse relation (i.e., from $\mathcal{R}_2$ to $\mathcal{R}_1$) is also true, that is, the correspondence between cycles is one-to-one.*   □

Proof. Consider the maximal CMC partition $\pi = (V_1, V_2, \ldots, V_r)$ that C yields and apply Lemmas 5.10 and 5.11.   □

Lemma 5.16. *Let* $(\mathcal{R}_i = (W_i, F_i), \varphi_i)$, $i = 1, 2$, *be two cycle-type normal cactus representations for* $C \subseteq \mathcal{C}(G)$. *Then* $|W_1| = |W_2|$ *holds, and there is a bijection* $\alpha : W_1 \rightarrow W_2$ *such that* $\varphi_1^{-1}(W_1(x)) = \varphi_2^{-1}(W_2(\alpha(x)))$ *holds for all* $x \in W_1$.   □

Proof. The lemma clearly holds for the root pair, x^* and y^*. Take any node $x \neq x^*$ in $\mathcal{R}_1$. Let $\mathcal{R}_1(x) = (W_1(x), F_1(x))$ be the subcactus at x, and let C_x be the parent cycle of x in $\mathcal{R}_1$. By Lemma 5.15, $\mathcal{R}_2$ has a cycle C'_x containing a node y such that $\varphi_1^{-1}(W_1(x)) = \varphi_2^{-1}(W_2(y))$. By Lemma 5.9, no other node in $\mathcal{R}_1$ has this property, and vice versa. Then the correspondence $\alpha : W_1 \rightarrow W_2$ defined by $y = \alpha(x)$ is a bijection. This proves the lemma.   □

Lemma 5.17. *Let* $(\mathcal{R}_i = (W_i, F_i), \varphi_i)$, $i = 1, 2$, *be two cycle-type normal cactus representations for* $C \subseteq \mathcal{C}(G)$. *Then there is a bijection* $\alpha : W_1 \rightarrow W_2$ *such that* $\varphi_1^{-1}(x) = \varphi_2^{-1}(\alpha(x))$ *for all* $x \in W_1$, *and* $\{x, x'\} \in F_1$ *holds if and only if* $\{\alpha(x), \alpha(x')\} \in F_2$ *holds*.   □

Proof. Let $\alpha : W_1 \rightarrow W_2$ denote the bijection obtained in Lemma 5.16. We first show that if $\{x, x'\} \in F_1$ holds then $\{\alpha(x), \alpha(x')\} \in F_2$ holds (the converse can be treated analogously since α is a bijection). Let $\{x, x'\}$ be an edge in F_1 and let C be an r-cycle in $(\mathcal{R}_1, \varphi_1)$ such that $\{x, x'\} \in F(C)$. Assume that neither x not x' are the parent node of C (the case where one of x and x' is the parent node of C can be treated in a similar manner). By Lemma 5.15, $(\mathcal{R}_2, \varphi_2)$ has an r-cycle C' such that $\varphi_1^{-1}(W_1(x)) = \varphi_2^{-1}(W_2(y))$ and $\varphi_1^{-1}(W_1(x')) = \varphi_2^{-1}(W_2(y'))$ hold for an edge $\{y, y'\} \in F(C')$. Since α is a bijection in Lemma 5.16, we have $\varphi_1^{-1}(W_1(x)) = \varphi_2^{-1}(W_2(\alpha(x)))$ and $\varphi_1^{-1}(W_1(x')) = \varphi_2^{-1}(W_2(\alpha(x')))$. Hence, it holds that $\varphi_2^{-1}(W_2(y)) = \varphi_2^{-1}(W_2(\alpha(x)))$ and $\varphi_2^{-1}(W_2(y')) = \varphi_2^{-1}(W_2(\alpha(x')))$, which imply, by Lemma 5.9, $y = \alpha(x)$ and $y' = \alpha(x')$, respectively. Therefore, $\{\alpha(x), \alpha(x')\} \in F_2$.

To complete the proof, we next show that $\varphi_1^{-1}(x) = \varphi_2^{-1}(\alpha(x))$ holds for $x \in W_1$. Take any node $x \in W_1$. Clearly, for each node $x' \in W_1(x) - x$, we have $\varphi_1^{-1}(W_1(x')) \subseteq \varphi_1^{-1}(W_1(x))$. Therefore, $\emptyset \neq \varphi_2^{-1}(W_2(\alpha(x'))) \subseteq \varphi_2^{-1}(W_2(\alpha(x)))$ by Lemma 5.16, which implies that $\alpha(x') \in W_2(\alpha(x))$. Conversely, for any $y' \in W_2(\alpha(x))$, $\alpha^{-1}(y') \in W_1(x)$ holds. Thus, α gives a bijection between $W_1(x) - x$ and $W_2(\alpha(x)) - \alpha(x)$. From this we obtain

$$\varphi_1^{-1}(x) = \varphi_1^{-1}(W_1(x)) - \bigcup_{x' \in W_1(x) - x} \varphi_1^{-1}(W_1(x'))$$

$$= \varphi_2^{-1}(W_2(\alpha(x))) - \bigcup_{y' \in W_2(\alpha(x)) - \alpha(x)} \varphi_2^{-1}(W_2(y'))$$

$$= \varphi_2^{-1}(\alpha(x)).$$

This completes the proof.   □

Now we prove Theorem 5.14 by extending the result in this lemma.

Proof of Theorem 5.14. The assumption on $\pi \in \Pi^3(\mathcal{C})$ says that π is represented in the same manner in both $\mathcal{R}_1$ and $\mathcal{R}_2$, namely, either by a 3-cycle or an empty 3-junction node (see Lemma 5.13). Then let Π' be the set of all $\pi \in \Pi^3(\mathcal{C})$, which are represented by empty 3-junction nodes in both $\mathcal{R}_1$ and $\mathcal{R}_2$. Pick an element $\pi \in \Pi'$ and let x and y be the empty 3-junction nodes in $\mathcal{R}_1$ and $\mathcal{R}_2$, respectively, that yield π. Now apply the 3-cycle insertion to x and y in $\mathcal{R}_1$ and $\mathcal{R}_2$, respectively, and let $\mathcal{R}_1'$ and $\mathcal{R}_2'$ be the resulting cacti, respectively. It is clear that there is a bijection α between the node sets of $\mathcal{R}_1$ and $\mathcal{R}_2$ as described in Theorem 5.14 if and only if there is a bijection α' between the node sets of $\mathcal{R}_1'$ and $\mathcal{R}_2'$. By repeating this until no element is left in Π', we obtain cycle-type normal cactus representations $\mathcal{R}_1^*$ and $\mathcal{R}_2^*$ such that the bijection α between the node sets of $\mathcal{R}_1$ and $\mathcal{R}_2$ exists if and only if there is a bijection α^* between the node sets of $\mathcal{R}_1^*$ and $\mathcal{R}_2^*$. However, by Lemma 5.17, there is such a bijection α^*, showing that there is a bijection α between the node sets of $\mathcal{R}_1$ and $\mathcal{R}_2$ as stated in Theorem 5.14. $\square$

Before concluding this section, we present some complexity results.

Lemma 5.18. *Let $(\mathcal{R}, \varphi)$ be a normal cactus representation for $\mathcal{C} \subseteq \mathcal{C}(G)$, where $G = (V, E)$. Then the number of empty nodes in $\mathcal{R}$ is at most that of nonempty nodes, which is at most $|V|$.* $\square$

Proof. Let $W^+(\mathcal{R})$ (resp. $W^{\emptyset}(\mathcal{R})$) be the set of nonempty nodes (resp. empty nodes) in $\mathcal{R}$. We show that $|W^+(\mathcal{R})| \geq |W^{\emptyset}(\mathcal{R})|$ by induction on $|W^{\emptyset}(\mathcal{R})|$. Fix an arbitrary nonempty node $x^* \in W^+(\mathcal{R})$ as the root. Assume $|W^{\emptyset}(\mathcal{R})| \neq \emptyset$ (otherwise the lemma is trivially true) and choose an empty node $z \in W^{\emptyset}(\mathcal{R})$ that has the largest cycle distance from x^* (defined before Lemma 5.8). This means that the subcactus $\mathcal{R}(z) = (W(z), F(z))$ contains no empty node other than z. On the other hand, by Lemma 5.4(i), we have $W(z) \neq \{z\}$. Let C_z be the parent cycle of z.

Case 1: C_z is not a 2-cycle. In this case, $W(z)$ contains at least two nonempty nodes. Otherwise, only one cycle $C \neq C_z$ would pass z, and this C would be a 2-cycle, contradicting that $\mathcal{R}$ is normal.

Case 2: C_z is a 2-cycle. In this case, since z is not an empty 2-junction node, there are at least two other cycles that pass through z. This implies that $W(z)$ contains at least two nonempty nodes.

Let $\mathcal{R}'$ be the cactus obtained from $\mathcal{R}$ by coalescing the subcactus $\mathcal{R}(z)$ into a single nonempty node. Clearly, $\mathcal{R}'$ is normal. In the preceding two cases, we have

$$|W^{\emptyset}(\mathcal{R}')| = |W^{\emptyset}(\mathcal{R})| - 1, \quad |W^+(\mathcal{R}')| \leq |W^+(\mathcal{R})| - 1.$$

Therefore, by induction, we have proved that $|W^+(\mathcal{R})| \geq |W^{\emptyset}(\mathcal{R})|$ holds for any normal cactus $\mathcal{R}$.

Finally, a normal cactus representation $(\mathcal{R}, \varphi)$ has at most $|\{\varphi(v) \mid v \in V\}|$ $(\leq |V|)$ nonempty nodes. Hence, the number of empty nodes is at most $|V|$. $\square$

Theorem 5.19. *Given a cactus representation* $(\mathcal{R}', \varphi')$ *for* $\mathcal{C} \subseteq \mathcal{C}(G)$, *a cycle-type or junction-type normal cactus representation* $(\mathcal{R}, \varphi)$ *for* $\mathcal{C}$ *can be constructed in linear time and linear space.* □

Proof. Let $\mathcal{R}' = (W', F')$. To obtain a cycle-type normal cactus representation, we perform transformations (a) and (b) required in the proof of Lemma 5.6(i). Transformation (a) replaces all empty 3-junction nodes with 3-cycles, taking $O(1)$ time for each 3-junction node, and then transformation (b) contracts all empty 2-junction nodes, taking $O(1)$ time for each 2-junction node. Since the number of empty nodes is $O(|W'|)$ and no new empty 2- or 3-junction node is created during the transformations, a cycle-type normal cactus representation can be obtained in $O(|W'| + |F'|)$ time and $O(|W'| + |F'|)$ space, where $|F'| = O(|W'|)$ holds for any cactus $\mathcal{R}' = (W', F')$. Also φ can be constructed in $O(|V| + |W'|)$ time and $O(|V| + |W'|)$ space. Similarly a junction-type normal cactus representation can be obtained in linear time and space by performing transformations (c) and (b) as required in the proof of Lemma 5.6(ii). □

5.2 (s, t)-Cactus Representations

Call an edge $e = \{s, t\}$ in a graph $G = (V, E)$ *critical* (as defined in Section 4.3) if $\lambda(s, t; G) = \lambda(G)$ and $c_G(e) > 0$. In this section, we consider the subset $\mathcal{C} \subseteq \mathcal{C}(G)$, which consists of all minimum cuts that separate the end vertices of a given critical edge $\{s, t\}$, and we show that there is a cactus representation for $\mathcal{C}$. Such a representation can be constructed in linear time from a given maximum (s, t)-flow and plays a crucial role in Section 5.3 to design an algorithm for constructing a cactus representation for the set of all minimum cuts $\mathcal{C}(G)$.

5.2.1 Union of Cactus Representations

We first introduce an operation that combines two representations for different sets of minimum cuts of G into a single representation.

We say that a representation $(\mathcal{R}, \varphi)$ *induces* a partition $\{V_1, V_2, \ldots, V_r\}$ of V if $\mathcal{R}$ has exactly r nonempty nodes, $x_1, x_2, \ldots, x_r$, such that $\varphi^{-1}(x_i) = V_i$. Two partitions $\{V_1, \ldots, V_r\}$ and $\{V'_1, \ldots, V'_{r'}\}$ (or two ordered partitions $(V_1, \ldots, V_r)$ and $(V'_1, \ldots, V'_{r'})$) of V, where $r, r' \geq 2$, are said to be *complementary* (with respect to V_i and V'_j) if there are two subsets V_i, V'_j such that

$$V_i \cup V'_j = V$$

(see Fig. 5.14). Thus, two cuts $\{V_1, V - V_1\}$ and $\{V'_1, V - V'_1\}$ (considered partitions) either cross each other or are complementary.

Consider two cacti $\mathcal{R} = (W, F)$ and $\mathcal{R}' = (W', F')$, where $W \cap W' = \emptyset$, such that $(\mathcal{R}, \varphi)$ and $(\mathcal{R}', \varphi')$ are representations for $\mathcal{C} \subseteq \mathcal{C}(G)$ and $\mathcal{C}' \subseteq \mathcal{C}(G)$, respectively. These two representations are said to be *complementary* if the two partitions of V, $\{V_1, V_2, \ldots, V_r\}$ and $\{V'_1, V'_2, \ldots, V'_{r'}\}$ induced by $(\mathcal{R}, \varphi)$ and $(\mathcal{R}', \varphi')$,

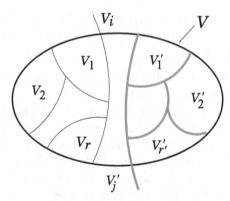

Figure 5.14. Illustration of two complementary partitions $\{V_1, V_2, \ldots, V_r\}$ and $\{V_1', V_2', \ldots, V_{r'}'\}$ such that $V_i \cup V_j' = V$.

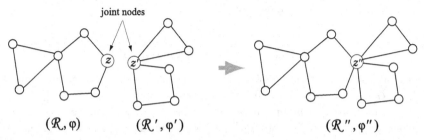

Figure 5.15. Illustration for the union of two representations, $(\mathcal{R}, \varphi)$, and $(\mathcal{R}', \varphi')$, into a new representation $(\mathcal{R}'', \varphi'')$.

respectively, are complementary. (This implies $r, r' \geq 2$.) If $(\mathcal{R}, \varphi)$ and $(\mathcal{R}', \varphi')$ are complementary, then there are two nodes, $z \in W$ and $z' \in W'$, such that

$$\varphi^{-1}(z) \cup \varphi'^{-1}(z') = V.$$

We call these z and z' *joint nodes*. The *union* of two complementary representations $(\mathcal{R}, \varphi)$ and $(\mathcal{R}', \varphi')$, denoted by

$$(\mathcal{R}'', \varphi'') = (\mathcal{R}, \varphi) \oplus (\mathcal{R}', \varphi'),$$

is then defined as the cactus obtained from $\mathcal{R}$ and $\mathcal{R}'$ by identifying the two joint nodes z and z' as a new node, say z'', and by defining a mapping $\varphi'' : V \to W \cup W' \cup \{z''\} - \{z, z'\}$ as follows (see Fig. 5.15):

$$\varphi''^{-1}(z'') = \varphi^{-1}(z) \cap \varphi'^{-1}(z'),$$
$$\varphi''^{-1}(x) = \varphi^{-1}(x) \text{ for } x \in W - z,$$
$$\varphi''^{-1}(x') = \varphi'^{-1}(x') \text{ for } x' \in W' - z'.$$

Note that the new node z'' is an empty node if and only if the joint nodes z and z' satisfy $\varphi^{-1}(z) \cap \varphi'^{-1}(z') = \emptyset$, that is, $\varphi^{-1}(W-z) = \varphi'^{-1}(z')$ or, equivalently,

$\varphi'^{-1}(W' - z') = \varphi^{-1}(z)$. The significance of the union operation is given by the following lemma.

Lemma 5.20. *Suppose that a representation* $\mathcal{R} = (W, F)$ *for* $\mathcal{C} \subseteq \mathcal{C}(G)$ *and a representation* $\mathcal{R}' = (W', F')$ *for* $\mathcal{C}' \subseteq \mathcal{C}(G)$ *are complementary. Then* $(\mathcal{R}'', \varphi'') = (\mathcal{R}, \varphi) \oplus (\mathcal{R}', \varphi')$ *is a representation for* $\mathcal{C} \cup \mathcal{C}'$. $\qquad\square$

Proof. Note that $\mathcal{R}'' = (W'', F'')$ has a node set $W'' = W \cup W' \cup \{z''\} - \{z, z'\}$. Let $\{X, \overline{X}\} \in \mathcal{C} \cup \mathcal{C}'$. Consider the case $\{X, \overline{X}\} \in \mathcal{C}$ (the other possibility, i.e., $\{X, \overline{X}\} \in \mathcal{C}'$, can be treated analogously) and let $\{S, W - S\}$ be the corresponding cut in $\mathcal{C}(\mathcal{R})$, where we assume $X = \varphi^{-1}(S)$ and $z \in W - S$ without loss of generality. By definition, we have $\{S, W'' - S\} \in \mathcal{C}(\mathcal{R}'')$, $\varphi''^{-1}(S) = X$, and $\varphi''^{-1}(W'' - S) = \overline{X}$. Conversely, we let $\{T, W'' - T\}$ be an arbitrary cut in $\mathcal{C}(\mathcal{R}'')$, where we assume $z'' \in W'' - T$ without loss of generality. Then either $T \subseteq W - z$ or $T \subseteq W' - z'$ holds, because otherwise (i.e., $T \cap W \neq \emptyset \neq T \cap W'$) the cut node z'', which separates $T \cap W$ and $T \cap W'$, is not contained in T, implying that $\{T \cap W, W - T\}$ or $\{T \cap W', W' - T\}$ would be a cut smaller than a minimum cut in $\mathcal{R}''$, a contradiction. Therefore, $\{T, W'' - T\}$ corresponds to a cut in $\mathcal{C} \cup \mathcal{C}'$. $\qquad\square$

5.2.2 Minimum Cuts Represented by (s, t)-MC Partitions

We first introduce two basic types of cactus representations, which represent the set of all minimum cuts belonging to an MC partition and a CMC partition, respectively. We call a cactus a *chain* if it consists only of 2-cycles and each node is either a 1- or a 2-junction node. A representation $(\mathcal{R}, \varphi)$ in which $\mathcal{R}$ is a chain is called a *chain representation*.

Let $\pi_1 = (V_1, V_2, \ldots, V_r)$ be an MC partition and let

$$\mathcal{C}_1 = \left\{ \{V_{(1,k)}, \overline{V_{(1,k)}}\} \mid 1 \leq k \leq r - 1 \right\}.$$

Clearly, $\mathcal{C}_1$ has a chain representation $(\ddot{\mathcal{R}}_{\pi_1}, \psi_{\pi_1})$, which is defined by

$$\ddot{\mathcal{R}}_{\pi_1} = (\{x_i \mid 1 \leq i \leq r\}, \{e_1, e_1', e_2, e_2', \ldots, e_{r-1}, e_{r-1}'\}),$$
$$\psi_{\pi_1}^{-1}(x_i) = V_i \quad (1 \leq i \leq r),$$

where $e_i = \{x_i, x_{i+1}\}$, $e_i' = \{x_i, x_{i+1}\}$, $1 \leq i \leq r - 1$.

Let $\pi_2 = (V_1', V_2', \ldots, V_{r'}')$ be a CMC partition and let

$$\mathcal{C}_2 = \left\{ \{V_{(h,k)}', \overline{V_{(h,k)}'}\} \mid 1 \leq h \leq k \leq r' - 1 \right\}.$$

Similarly, $\mathcal{C}_2$ has a *cycle representation* $(\mathring{\mathcal{R}}_{\pi_2}, \phi_{\pi_2})$, which is defined by

$$\mathring{\mathcal{R}}_{\pi_2} = (\{x_i \mid 1 \leq i \leq r'\}, \{e_1, e_2, \ldots, e_{r'}, \}),$$
$$\phi_{\pi_2}^{-1}(x_i) = V_i' \quad (1 \leq i \leq r'),$$

where $e_i = \{x_i, x_{i+1}\}$, $1 \leq i \leq r' - 1$, and $e_{r'} = \{x_{r'}, x_1\}$.

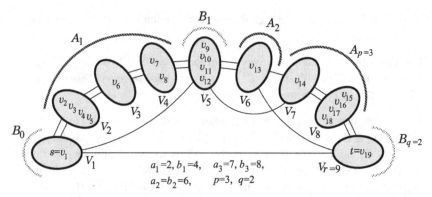

Figure 5.16. The (v_1, v_{19})-MC partition $\pi_{(v_1,v_{19})}$ over $\mathcal{C}(G^*)$ and its segments $\{A_i\}$ and $\{B_i\}$.

As observed in Lemmas 4.9 and 4.10, the (s, t)-*MC partition* $\pi_{(s,t)}$ over $\mathcal{C}(G)$ for a given critical edge $\{s, t\}$ is unique and can be constructed in linear time from a maximum (s, t)-flow in G. For example, the (v_1, v_{19})-MC partition $\pi_{(v_1,v_{19})}$ of the graph G^* in Fig. 5.2 is

$$\pi_{(v_1,v_{19})} = (\{v_1\}, \{v_2, v_3, v_4, v_5\}, \{v_6\}, \{v_7, v_8\}, \{v_9, v_{10}, v_{11}, v_{12}\},$$
$$\{v_{13}\}, \{v_{14}\}, \{v_{15}, v_{16}, v_{17}, v_{18}\}, \{v_{19}\}),$$

which is shown in Fig. 5.16.

Minimum Cuts Not Separating a Critical Edge

We now consider other minimum cuts that *do not separate* s and t for any critical edge $\{s, t\}$, that is, those not belonging to any (s, t)-MC partition.

Let π be a partition $\{V_1, V_2, \ldots, V_r\}$ (or an ordered partition $(V_1, V_2, \ldots, V_r)$) of V and let $\{X, \overline{X}\}$ be a cut in G. We say that

- cut $\{X, \overline{X}\}$ *crosses* π if $\{X, \overline{X}\}$ crosses some cut of the form $\{V_i, V - V_i\}$,
- cut $\{X, \overline{X}\}$ is *compatible* with π if

$$X = \bigcup_{i \in I} V_i \text{ for some } I \subset \{1, 2, \ldots, r\}, \text{ and}$$

- cut $\{X, \overline{X}\}$ is *indivisible* with π if

$$X \subset V_i \text{ for some } i \in \{1, 2, \ldots, r\}.$$

Notice that any cut that does not cross π is either compatible or indivisible with π. We denote by $\mathcal{C}_{comp}(\pi)$ (resp. $\mathcal{C}_{indv}(\pi)$) the set of all minimum cuts in $\mathcal{C}(G)$ that are compatible with π (resp. indivisible with π).

We prove next via three lemmas that, from the (s, t)-MC partition $\pi_{(s,t)}$ for a critical edge $\{s, t\}$, not only the minimum cuts that separate s and t but also many other minimum cuts which do not separate s and t can be obtained.

Lemma 5.21. *Let $\{s,t\}$ be a critical edge in a graph G and let $\pi_{(s,t)}$ be the (s,t)-MC partition $\pi_{(s,t)}$ over $C(G)$. Then a minimum cut $\{X,\overline{X}\} \in C(G)$ is either compatible or indivisible with $\pi_{(s,t)}$, that is, $C(G) = C_{comp}(\pi_{(s,t)}) \cup C_{indv}(\pi_{(s,t)})$.* $\square$

Proof. By the definition of compatibility and indivisibility, it suffices to show that no minimum cut $\{X,\overline{X}\} \in C(G)$ crosses $\pi_{(s,t)}$. Assume that a cut $\{X,\overline{X}\} \in C(G)$ crosses $\pi_{(s,t)}$. By Lemma 4.9, no minimum cut separating s and t crosses $\pi_{(s,t)}$; hence, we can assume $X \cap \{s,t\} = \emptyset$. Then there are two subsets V_k and V_ℓ in $\pi_{(s,t)}$ such that $X \cap V_k \neq \emptyset \neq \overline{X} \cap V_k$ and $X \cap V_\ell \neq \emptyset$ (possibly $X \supset V_\ell$). Without loss of generality, we assume $k < \ell$ (the case $k > \ell$ can be treated by the reversal of $\pi_{(s,t)}$). This means that the minimum cut $\{V_{(1,k)}, V_{(k+1,r)}\}$ crosses $\{X,\overline{X}\}$ and, by (1.4), we have

$$d(V_{(1,k)}; G) + d(X; G) \geq d(V_{(1,k)} - X; G) + d(X - V_{(1,k)}; G),$$

which, by $\lambda(G) = d(V_{(1,k)}; G) = d(X; G)$, implies $d(V_{(1,k)} - X; G) = d(X - V_{(1,k)}; G) = \lambda(G)$. Therefore, $\{V_{(1,k)} - X, \overline{V_{(1,k)}} - X\}$ is a minimum cut that separates s and t but does not belong to $\pi_{(s,t)}$. This contradicts Lemma 4.9. $\square$

Lemma 5.22. *For a critical edge $\{s,t\}$ in a graph $G = (V,E)$, let $\pi_{(s,t)} = (V_1, \ldots, V_r)$ be the (s,t)-MC partition over $C(G)$ and let $\{X,\overline{X}\} \in C_{comp}(\pi_{(s,t)})$. Then we have the following:*

(i) *If $\{X,\overline{X}\}$ does not separate s and t then $X = V_{(k,\ell)}$ or $\overline{X} = V_{(k,\ell)}$ for some k, ℓ ($1 < k \leq \ell < r$).*

(ii) *If $X = V_{(k,\ell)}$ or $\overline{X} = V_{(k,\ell)}$ for some k, ℓ ($1 < k \leq \ell < r$) then $\{V_{(i,j)}, \overline{V_{(i,j)}}\} \in C(G)$ for all i and j ($k \leq i \leq j \leq \ell$).* $\square$

Proof. (i) Assume that $\{X,\overline{X}\}$ does not separate s and t (i.e., $\{s,t\} \subseteq \overline{X}$, without loss of generality). Then $V_1 \cup V_r \subseteq \overline{X}$ holds since $\{X,\overline{X}\}$ is compatible with $\pi_{(s,t)}$. Let k and ℓ be the smallest and largest indices such that $V_k \subseteq X$ and $V_\ell \subseteq X$. It suffices to show that there is no $V_h \subseteq \overline{X}, k < h < \ell$. Assume indirectly that such a V_h exists. Then cut $\{X,\overline{X}\}$ crosses another minimum cut $\{V_{(1,k)}, V_{(k+1,r)}\} \in C(G)$. Hence, by Lemma 4.8, $\{V_{(1,k)} \cup X, \overline{V_{(1,k)}} \cup X\}$ is also a minimum cut in G. Note that this cut separates s and t but does not have the form of $V_{(1,j)}$ ($1 \leq j < r$). This contradicts Lemma 4.9, as required.

(ii) We first show that any cut $\{V_{(k,j)}, \overline{V_{(k,j)}}\}$ with $k \leq j \leq \ell$ is a minimum cut in G. Since this is obvious if $j = \ell$, we assume $k \leq j < \ell$. Then cut $\{X,\overline{X}\}$ crosses another minimum cut $\{V_{(1,j)}, \overline{V_{(1,j)}}\}$. Hence, by Lemma 4.8 and $V_{(1,j)} \cap X = V_{(k,j)}$, $\{V_{(k,j)}, \overline{V_{(k,j)}}\}$ is also a minimum cut in G. Similarly, any cut $\{V_{(i,\ell)}, \overline{V_{(i,\ell)}}\}$ with $k \leq i \leq \ell$ is a minimum cut in G. Therefore, we are done for $i = k$ or $j = \ell$. Now, we let $k < i \leq j < \ell$. Then two minimum cuts $\{V_{(k,j)}, \overline{V_{(k,j)}}\}$ and $\{V_{(i,\ell)}, \overline{V_{(i,\ell)}}\}$ cross each other. Hence, by Lemma 4.8 and $V_{(k,j)} \cap V_{(i,\ell)} = V_{(i,j)}, \{V_{(i,j)}, \overline{V_{(i,j)}}\}$ is also a minimum cut in G, proving condition (ii). $\square$

Using Lemma 5.22, one could enumerate all minimum cuts in $C_{comp}(\pi_{(s,t)})$ by checking whether $d(V_{(i,j)}, \overline{V_{(i,j)}}; G) = \lambda(G)$ holds for all possible pairs (i,j).

However, there are $O(r^2) = O(|V|^2)$ such pairs. To find them more efficiently, we first show that the set $\mathcal{C}_{comp}(\pi_{(s,t)})$ can be represented by a collection of MC or CMC partitions or both over $\mathcal{C}(G)$, based on which $\mathcal{C}_{comp}(\pi_{(s,t)})$ can be computed from $\pi_{(s,t)}$ in linear time.

Let $\pi_{(s,t)} = (V_1, V_2, \ldots, V_r)$ be the (s, t)-MC partition over $\mathcal{C}(G)$ for a critical edge $e = \{s, t\}$ in a graph G. To apply Lemma 5.22, we first partition $\{V_1, V_2, \ldots, V_r\}$ into

$$A = \{V_i \mid d(V_i, \overline{V_i}; G) = \lambda(G), \ 1 < i < r\}, \text{ and}$$
$$B = \{V_1, V_r\} \cup \{V_i \mid d(V_i, \overline{V_i}; G) > \lambda(G), \ 1 < i < r\}.$$

If we remove all $V_i \in A$ from $\pi = (V_1, V_2, \ldots, V_r)$, then we are left with a sequence of *segments*, each consisting of one or more $\{V_i\}$ with contiguous indices. Suppose that there are $q+1$ such segments $B_0, B_1, \ldots, B_q$, with $V_1 \in B_0$ and $V_r \in B_q$. Clearly, $\{B_j \mid j = 0, 1, \ldots, q\}$ is a partition of B.

We also partition A into p segments, $A_1, A_2 \ldots, A_p$, where each segment A_k is given as

$$V_\ell \in A \text{ and } d(V_{(a_k,\ell)}, \overline{V_{(a_k,\ell)}}; G) = \lambda(G) \text{ hold for } \ell = a_k, a_k + 1, \ldots, b_k. \quad (5.2)$$

Furthermore, we assume that each A_k is maximal with the aforementioned properties.

More specifically, indices $a_1, b_1, a_2, b_2, \ldots, a_p, b_p$ are defined as follows: Let $b_0 = 0$ for convenience and set $k := 0$. We repeatedly set $k := k + 1$ and choose the smallest index a_k and the largest index b_k with $b_{k-1} < a_k \le b_k < r$ that satisfy (5.2), until such a pair of indices no longer exists. Since no $V_i \in B$ is included in any A_k, we see that, for each B_j, $j = 0, 1, \ldots, q$, there is an index k such that

$$B_j = \{V_{b_k+1}, V_{b_k+2}, \ldots, V_{a_{k+1}-1}\}.$$

Hence, $p \ge q$. A procedure for determining all A_k, $k = 1, 2, \ldots, p$ using (5.2) is given as follows.

Procedure SEGMENT
$a := \ell := 2; \ \ k := \Delta := 0;$
while $a < r$ **do**
    while $d(V_{(a,\ell)}, \overline{V_{(a,\ell)}}; G) = \lambda(G)$ **do** $\Delta := 1; i := i+1$ **end**; /* while */
    if $\Delta = 1$ **then** $\Delta := 0; \ k := k + 1; \ \ A_k := V_{(a,i-1)}; \ell := \ell - 1$ **end**; /* if */
    $a := \ell + 1; \ell := \ell + 1$
end. /* while */

For example, Figure 5.16 shows the preceding partitions $\{A_1, A_2, A_3\}$ and $\{B_0, B_1, B_2\}$ for the (v_1, v_{19})-MC partition $\pi_{(v_1,v_{19})} = (V_1, V_2, \ldots, V_9)$ over $\mathcal{C}(G^*)$ for the critical edge $\{v_1, v_{19}\}$ in G^* of Fig. 5.2, where we obtain $p = 3, q = 2$ and $r = 9$.

Characterization of $\mathcal{C}_{comp}(\pi_{(s,t)})$

Based on these preparations, we can now characterize $\mathcal{C}_{comp}(\pi_{(s,t)})$.

Lemma 5.23. *Let $\{A_k \mid k = 1, 2, \ldots, p\}$ and $\{B_j \mid j = 0, 1, \ldots, q\}$ be as defined earlier for the (s, t)-MC partition for a critical edge $\{s, t\} \in E$ in $G = (V, E)$. Then the following conditions (i), (ii), and (iii) hold.*

(i) *The ordered partition $\pi_{B_0} = (V_1, \ldots, V_{a_1-1}, V_{(a_1,r)})$ of V associated with $B_0 = \{V_1, V_2, \ldots, V_{a_1-1}\}$, the ordered partition $\pi_{B_q} = (V_{(1,b_p)}, V_{b_p+1}, \ldots, V_r)$ of V associated with $B_q = \{V_{(1,b_p)}, V_{b_p+1}\}$, and the ordered partition of V associated with $B_j = \{V_{b_k+1}, V_{b_k+2}, \ldots, V_{a_{k+1}-1}\}$,*

$$\pi_{B_j} = (V_{(1,b_k)}, V_{b_k+1}, V_{b_k+2}, \ldots, V_{a_{k+1}-1}, V_{(a_{k+1},r)}), \quad 1 \le j \le q$$

are all MC partitions over $\mathcal{C}(G)$.

(ii) *For each k $(1 \le k \le p)$, the ordered partition of V associated with $A_k = \{V_{a_k}, V_{a_k+1}, \ldots, V_{b_k}\}$,*

$$\pi_{A_k} = (V_{(1,a_k-1)}, V_{a_k}, V_{a_k+1}, \ldots, V_{b_k}, V_{(b_k+1,r)})$$

is a maximal CMC partition over $\mathcal{C}(G)$.

(iii) *Let $\mathcal{M}$ be the set of minimum cuts that belong to some MC partitions in conditions (i) and (ii). Then $\mathcal{M} = \mathcal{C}_{comp}(\pi_{(s,t)})$.*   □

Proof. (i) Immediate from Lemma 4.9.

(ii) We first show that the ordered partition π_{A_k} is a CMC partition in G. By construction, $\{V_{(a_k,b_k)}, \overline{V_{(a_k,b_k)}}\} \in \mathcal{C}(G)$. Hence, by Lemma 5.22(ii) we see that, for each $A_k = \{V_{a_k}, V_{a_k+1}, \ldots, V_{b_k}\}$, any cut $\{V_{(h,\ell)}, \overline{V_{(h,\ell)}}\}$ with $a_k \le h \le \ell \le b_k$ is a minimum cut. Note that all the other cuts belonging to π_{A_k} are minimum cuts that separate s and t by Lemma 5.22. Hence, π_{A_k} is a CMC partition in G.

We next prove that π_{A_k} is a maximal CMC partition over $\mathcal{C}(G)$. Assume that a CMC partition π_{A_k} is not maximal. Since no minimum cut crosses π_{A_i} by Lemma 5.21, no ordered partition of V of the form $(V_{(1,a_k-1)}, V_{a_k}, \ldots, V_{j-1}, V_j - X, X, V_{j+1}, \ldots, V_{b_k}, V_{(b_k+1,r)})$ $(a_k \le j \le b_k)$ is a CMC partition over $\mathcal{C}(G)$. Assume that $\mathcal{C}(G)$ has a CMC partition of V of the form

$$\pi' = (X, Y, V_{a_k}, \ldots, V_{b_k}, V_{(b_k+1,r)}) \text{ for some } X \subset V_{(1,a_k-1)} \text{ and } Y = V_{(1,a_k-1)} - X$$

(the case where $X, Y \subset V_{(b_k+1,r)}$ can be treated analogously). Since two minimum cuts, $\{Y \cup V_{a_k}, \overline{Y \cup V_{a_k}}\}$ and $\{V_{(a_k,b_k)}, \overline{V_{(a_k,b_k)}}\}$, cross each other, we see by Lemma 4.8 that $\{Y \cup V_{(a_k,b_k)}, \overline{Y \cup V_{(a_k,b_k)}}\}$ is a minimum cut that belongs to π'. Since $t \notin Y \cup V_{(a_k,b_k)}$, we see by Lemma 5.22(i) that $Y \cup V_{(a_k,b_k)}$ has the form of $V_{(h,b_k)}$ for some $h \in \{2, a_k - 1\}$ (where $h \ne 1$ holds by $Y \ne V_{(1,a_k-1)}$). By Lemma 5.22(ii), it holds that $\{V_{(i,j)}, \overline{V_{(i,j)}}\} \in \mathcal{C}(G)$ for all i and j with $h \le i \le j \le b_k$. This, however, contradicts that segment A_k is maximal subject to (5.2).

(iii) Clearly, $\mathcal{M} \subseteq \mathcal{C}_{comp}(\pi_{(s,t)})$. To show $\mathcal{M} \supseteq \mathcal{C}_{comp}(\pi_{(s,t)})$, we assume that there was a minimum cut $\{X, \overline{X}\} \in \mathcal{C}_{comp}(\pi_{(s,t)})$ not considered in condition (i) or (ii). As all minimum cuts in $\mathcal{C}_{comp}(\pi_{(s,t)})$ that separate s and t are included in condition (i) or (ii) (since $\{V_{(1,h)}, \overline{V_{(1,h)}}\}$ for any $1 \le h \le r$ is represented by a partition in condition (i) or (ii)), $\{X, \overline{X}\}$ does not separate s and t and, hence, has the form $X = V_{(h,\ell)}$ $(1 < h \leq \ell < r)$ by Lemma 5.22(i). Then, by Lemma 5.22(ii), each $V_{(j,j)} = V_j$ with $h \leq j \leq \ell$ is a minimum cut in $\mathcal{C}(G)$, that is, $\{V_h, V_{h+1}, \ldots, V_\ell\} \subseteq A$. Let k be the index such that $V_h \in A_k$. Hence, $a_k \leq h$. If $\ell \leq b_k$ (i.e., $\{V_h, V_{h+1}, \ldots, V_\ell\} \subseteq A_k$) then $\{X, \overline{X}\}$ would belong to π_{A_k}. Hence, $b_k < \ell$ holds. Then by Lemma 5.22(ii) we have $\{V_{(h,b_k+1)}, \overline{V_{(h,b_k+1)}}\} \in \mathcal{C}(G)$. We here claim that $\{V_{(a_k,b_k+1)}, \overline{V_{(a_k,b_k+1)}}\} \in \mathcal{C}(G)$. This is trivial if $a_k = h$. If $a_k < h$ then two minimum cuts $\{V_{(h,b_k+1)}, \overline{V_{(h,b_k+1)}}\}$ and $\{V_{(a_k,b_k)}, \overline{V_{(a_k,b_k)}}\}$ cross each other and, by Lemma 4.8, we see that $\{V_{(a_k,b_k+1)}, \overline{V_{(a_k,b_k+1)}}\}$ is also a minimum cut in $\mathcal{C}(G)$. This claim, however, contradicts the maximality of A_k. □

Note that a cut in $\mathcal{C}(G)$ may belong to more than one MC partition in $\{\pi_{B_j} \mid j = 1, \ldots, q\} \cup \{\pi_{A_k} \mid k = 1, \ldots, p\}$ of the preceding lemma. For example, cut $\{V_{(1,b_k)}, V_{(b_k+1,r)}\}$ belongs to π_{A_k} and also to π_{B_j} for some B_j.

5.2.3 (s, t)-Cactus Representations

Given the (s, t)-MC partition $\pi_{(s,t)} = (V_1, \ldots, V_r)$ over $\mathcal{C}(G)$ for a critical edge $\{s, t\}$ of a graph $G = (V, E)$, we are now ready to prove that there *exists* a cactus representation for $\mathcal{C}_{comp}(\pi_{(s,t)})$. For each MC partition π_{B_j}, $j = 0, 1, \ldots, q$, of Lemma 5.23, we let $(\ddot{\mathcal{R}}_{\pi_{B_j}}, \psi_{\pi_{B_j}})$ be the chain representation for the minimum cuts belonging to π_{B_j}, and for each CMC partition π_{A_i}, $i = 1, 2, \ldots, p$, we let $(\mathring{\mathcal{R}}_{\pi_{A_i}}, \phi_{\pi_{A_i}})$ be the cycle representation for the minimum cuts belonging to π_{A_i}.

For our running example of Fig. 5.16, $\ddot{\mathcal{R}}_{\pi_{B_0}}$ has two nodes and represents the MC partition $\pi_{B_0} = (V_1, V_{(2,9)})$. Similarly, $\mathring{\mathcal{R}}_{\pi_{A_1}}$ has five nodes and represents the CMC partition $\pi_{A_1} = (V_1, V_2, V_3, V_4, V_{(5,9)})$. Since $V_1 \cup V_{(2,9)} = V$, these two MC partitions are complementary and, therefore, their union $\mathcal{R}' = (\ddot{\mathcal{R}}_{\pi_{B_0}}, \psi_{\pi_{B_0}}) \oplus (\mathring{\mathcal{R}}_{\pi_{A_1}}, \phi_{\pi_{A_1}})$ can be formed, with the nodes corresponding to $V_{(2,9)}$ of π_{B_0} and V_1 of π_{A_1} as the joint nodes. By Lemma 5.20, the resulting cactus $\mathcal{R}'$ represents all minimum cuts that are represented by $(\ddot{\mathcal{R}}_{\pi_{B_0}}, \psi_{\pi_{B_0}})$ or $(\mathring{\mathcal{R}}_{\pi_{A_1}}, \phi_{\pi_{A_1}})$.

Continuing as before, we can construct a single cactus $(\mathcal{R}_{(s,t)}, \varphi_{(s,t)})$ that represents $\mathcal{C}_{comp}(\pi_{(s,t)})$ by the following procedure.

Procedure CHAIN
Input: A chain representation $(\ddot{\mathcal{R}}_{\pi_{B_j}}, \psi_{\pi_{B_j}})$ for each MC partition π_{B_j},
    $j = 0, 1, \ldots, q$, and a cycle representation $(\mathring{\mathcal{R}}_{\pi_{A_i}}, \phi_{\pi_{A_i}})$, for each CMC
    partition π_{A_i}, $i = 1, 2, \ldots, p$, in Lemma 5.23.
Output: A cactus representation for $\mathcal{C}_{comp}(\pi_{(s,t)})$.
    $(\mathcal{R}, \varphi) := (\ddot{\mathcal{R}}_{\pi_{B_0}}, \psi_{\pi_{B_0}})$;
    for $k = 1, 2, \ldots, p$ **do**
        $(\mathcal{R}, \varphi) := (\mathcal{R}, \varphi) \oplus (\mathring{\mathcal{R}}_{\pi_{A_k}}, \phi_{\pi_{A_k}})$;
        if $b_k + 1 \neq a_{k+1}$ **then** $(\mathcal{R}, \varphi) := (\mathcal{R}, \varphi) \oplus (\ddot{\mathcal{R}}_{\pi_{B_j}}, \psi_{\pi_{B_j}})$,
            where B_j is determined by $V_{b_k+1} \in B_j$
    end; /* for */
    $(\mathcal{R}_{(s,t)}, \varphi_{(s,t)}) := (\mathcal{R}, \varphi)$.

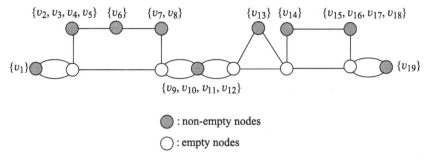

Figure 5.17. The (v_1, v_{19})-cactus representation for $\mathcal{C}_{comp}(\pi_{(v_1, v_{19})})$ by Theorem 5.24.

Note that the condition $b_k + 1 \neq a_{k+1}$ in the CHAIN procedure means that there is an intervening B-segment B_j between A_k and A_{k+1}. Since the two operands in union $(\mathcal{R}, \varphi) \oplus (\mathring{\mathcal{R}}_{\pi_{A_k}}, \phi_{\pi_{A_k}})$ (or $(\mathcal{R}, \varphi) \oplus (\ddot{\mathcal{R}}_{\pi_{B_j}}, \psi_{\pi_{B_j}})$) are complementary, Lemma 5.20 is always applicable. Therefore, the obtained $(\mathcal{R}_{(s,t)}, \varphi_{(s,t)})$ is a cactus representation for $\mathcal{C}_{comp}(\pi_{(s,t)})$.

Note also in the CHAIN procedure that, every time a union is formed, the two joint nodes becomes an empty node. This implies that the mapping $\varphi_{(s,t)}$ can be easily obtained just by combining $\{\psi_{\pi_{B_j}}\}$ and $\{\phi_{\pi_{A_k}}\}$ and discarding the mapping from joint nodes. (See the paragraph just before Lemma 5.20.) Therefore, $\mathcal{R}_{(s,t)}$ contains exactly r nonempty nodes and $p + q$ empty nodes.

For the example of Fig. 5.16, we obtain the (v_1, v_{19})-cactus representation of Fig. 5.17 by the CHAIN procedure. It is confirmed from Fig. 5.17 that the procedure introduces $p + q$ empty nodes and inserts cycles (for $\{A_k\}$) and chains (for $\{B_j\}$) in the order of their appearance in the (s, t)-MC partition $\pi_{(v_1, v_{19})}$.

From the preceding discussion we have the following theorem.

Theorem 5.24. *Let $\{s, t\}$ be a critical edge in a graph $G = (V, E)$. Then there is a cactus representation for the set of all minimum cuts that are compatible with the (s, t)-MC partition $\pi_{(s,t)}$ over $\mathcal{C}(G)$.* $\square$

We call the resulting cactus representation $(\mathcal{R}_{(s,t)}, \varphi_{(s,t)})$ for $\mathcal{C}_{comp}(\pi_{(s,t)})$ the (s, t)-*cactus representation*. Note that this (s, t)-cactus representation may not be a cycle-type normal cactus representation. For example, the (v_1, v_{19})-cactus representation of Fig. 5.17 is not normal. However, this can be transformed into a cycle-type normal cactus representation by applying Theorem 5.19. The result is shown in Fig. 5.18.

Theorem 5.25. *The cycle-type normal (s, t)-cactus representation $\mathcal{R}_{(s,t)}$ for a critical edge $\{s, t\}$ in a graph $G = (V, E)$ can be constructed from the (s, t)-MC partition $\pi_{(s,t)}$ in $O(|E| + |V|)$ time and $O(|E| + |V|)$ space.* $\square$

Proof. Let $\pi_{(s,t)} = (V_1, V_2, \ldots, V_r)$. To analyze the complexity of the SEGMENT procedure, imagine that $V_1, V_2, \ldots, V_r$ are arranged from left to right. During the execution SEGMENT, the set $V_{(a, \ell)}$ moves from left to right, and the edge set $E(V_{(a, \ell)}, \overline{V_{(a, \ell)}})$ may expand or shrink. As a and i change during execution, each

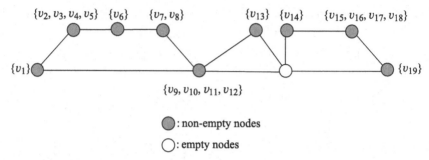

Figure 5.18. The cycle-type normal (v_1, v_{19})-cactus representation for $C_{comp}(\pi_{(v_1,v_{19})})$.

edge enters the set $E(V_{(a,\ell)}, \overline{V_{(a,\ell)}})$ and leaves it at most twice. Therefore, the time complexity of the SEGMENT procedure is $O(|E|+|V|)$. From the computed segments $\{B_j\}$ and $\{A_k\}$, we prepare chain representations $(\ddot{\mathcal{R}}_{\pi_{B_j}}, \psi_{\pi_{B_j}})$ and cycle representations $(\mathring{\mathcal{R}}_{\pi_{A_k}}, \phi_{\pi_{A_k}})$ in $O(|V|)$ time and $O(|V|)$ space. We can then construct the cactus $\mathcal{R}_{(s,t)}$ via the CHAIN procedure in $O(|V|)$ time and $O(|V|)$ space, since $\mathcal{R}_{(s,t)}$ has at most $O(|V|)$ nodes and edges. Computing the mapping $\varphi_{(s,t)}$ for $\mathcal{R}_{(s,t)}$ can be done in $O(|V|)$ time and $O(|V|)$ space as commented in the paragraph preceding Theorem 5.24. By Theorem 5.19, we then transform $\mathcal{R}_{(s,t)}$ into the cycle-type normal cactus representation in $O(|V|)$ time and $O(|V|)$ space.   □

Based on these results, an algorithm for constructing an entire cactus representation for $\mathcal{C}(G)$ will be given in the next subsection.

5.3 Constructing Cactus Representations

A cycle-type normal cactus representation is called a *CNC representation*. We observed in Section 4.3 that the set of all minimum cuts $\mathcal{C}(G)$ in a given graph G can be computed as follows. After initializing $G^{(1)} := G$, $\lambda := \lambda(G)$, and $i := 1$, we repeat the cycle of choosing a critical edge $\{s_i, t_i\}$ in $G^{(i)}$, computing an (s_i, t_i)-MC partition $\pi_{(s_i,t_i)}$ over $\mathcal{C}(G^{(i)})$, and updating $G^{(i+1)} := G^{(i)}/\{s, t\}$ and $i := i + 1$. Based on these data, Karzanov and Timofeev [185] proposed the following algorithm to construct a cactus representation for $\mathcal{C}(G)$. For the last graph $G^{(n-1)}$ with a single vertex, we can easily find a cactus representation $(\mathcal{R}^{(n-1)}, \varphi^{(n-1)})$ for $\mathcal{C}(G^{(n-1)})$. Now suppose by induction that a cactus representation $(\mathcal{R}^{(i+1)}, \varphi^{(i+1)})$ for $\mathcal{C}(G^{(i+1)})$ is at hand. Then a cactus representation $(\mathcal{R}^{(i)}, \varphi^{(i)})$ for $\mathcal{C}(G^{(i)})$ can be obtained by combining $(\mathcal{R}^{(i+1)}, \varphi^{(i+1)})$ and the (s_i, t_i)-MC partition $\pi_{(s_i,t_i)}$. By repeating this process from $G^{(n-1)}$ to $G^{(1)}$, we can construct a cactus representation $(\mathcal{R}^{(1)}, \varphi^{(1)})$ for $\mathcal{C}(G^{(1)})$ in polynomial time.

However, to combine $(\mathcal{R}^{(i+1)}, \varphi^{(i+1)})$ and $\pi_{(s_i,t_i)}$ into a cactus representation, we need to find out the correspondence between the nodes in $(\mathcal{R}^{(i+1)}, \varphi^{(i+1)})$ and the sets in the partition $\pi_{(s_i,t_i)}$. This task is considerably complicated. Nagamochi and Kameda [243] and Nagamochi et al. [253] simplified this process so that the entire algorithm runs in $O(nm + n^2 \log n + n^*m \log n)$ time, where n^* denotes the number of nodes in the CNC representation, for which $n^* \le 2n$ follows from Lemma 5.18. However, in this algorithm, the minimum cuts in $\mathcal{C}_{comp}(\pi_{(s_i,t_i)})$, which do not separate s_i and t_i, are again represented in $(\mathcal{R}^{(i+1)}, \varphi^{(i+1)})$. Thus, the same minimum cut repeatedly appears in graphs $G^{(i)}$, $G^{(i+1)}$, ..., $G^{(j)}$ for some j $(> i)$, thereby increasing the resulting running time. In the subsequent algorithm in this section, we introduce a different decomposition of a given graph to reduce the number of such duplications.

5.3.1 Divide-and-Conquer Procedure for Cactus Representations

As a notational convenience to describe an algorithm for constructing an entire cactus representation for $\mathcal{C}(G)$, we define the (u, v)-cactus representation for a noncritical edge $\{u, v\}$ to be $(\mathcal{R}, \varphi)$ such that $\mathcal{R}$ consists only of a single node x (i.e., $\mathcal{R} = (\{x\}, \emptyset)$ and $\varphi(V) = x$).

Let $\{s, t\}$ be a critical edge in a graph G and let $\pi_{(s,t)} = (V_1, \ldots, V_r)$ be the (s, t)-MC partition. The set $\mathcal{C}_{comp}(\pi_{(s,t)})$, that is, minimum cuts compatible with $\pi_{(s,t)}$, is represented by an (s, t)-cactus representation, which we denote by $(\mathcal{R}_{(s,t)}, \varphi_{(s,t)})$. There may remain other minimum cuts in $\mathcal{C}(G) - \mathcal{C}_{comp}(\pi_{(s,t)}) = \mathcal{C}_{indv}(\pi_{(s,t)})$, that is, those indivisible with $\pi_{(s,t)}$. According to Lemma 5.21, each minimum cut $\{X, \overline{X}\} \in \mathcal{C}_{indv}(\pi_{(s,t)})$ has a subset V_i in $\pi_{(s,t)}$ such that

$$X \subset V_i \ (\text{or } \overline{X} \subset V_i)$$

(that is, X or $\overline{X}$ is a subset of V_i, and some two vertices $u, v \in V_i$ are separated by $\{X, \overline{X}\}$).

For each V_i in $\pi_{(s,t)} = (V_1, \ldots, V_r)$, consider the graph

$$G_i = G/(V(G) - V_i) \tag{5.3}$$

constructed from G by contracting $V(G) - V_i$ into a single vertex $x_{\overline{V_i}}$. Obviously, $\lambda(G_i) \ge \lambda(G)$ holds. The graph G_i is called *critical* if $\lambda(G_i) = \lambda(G)$ holds. Assume that G_i is critical and consider a minimum cut $\{Y, V(G_i) - Y\} \in \mathcal{C}(G_i)$. By Lemma 5.21, we see that either

(i) $\{Y, V(G_i) - Y\}$ separates some two vertices u and v in V_i and satisfies $Y \subset V_i$ (or $V(G_i) - Y \subset V_i$) or

(ii) $\{Y, V(G_i) - Y\} = \{V_i, x_{\overline{V_i}}\}$.

Note that the cut $\{V_i, x_{\overline{V_i}}\}$ in condition (ii) is already represented in $(\mathcal{R}_{(s,t)}, \varphi_{(s,t)})$ as $\{V_i, V(G) - V_i\}$. The ordered collection $(G_1, G_2, \ldots, G_r)$ of graphs obtained by (5.3) is called an (s, t)-*decomposition* of G.

Figure 5.19 shows the (s, t)-decomposition $G_i = G/(V(G) - V_i)$, $i = 1, 2, \ldots, 9$, for the (s, t)-MC partition $\pi_{(s,t)} = (V_1, V_2, \ldots, V_9)$ in Fig. 5.16 obtained from the graph G^* in Fig. 5.2 with $s = v_1$ and $t = v_{19}$.

Suppose that, for every critical graph G_i in the collection, we prepare a cactus representation $(\mathcal{R}_{G_i}, \varphi_{G_i})$ for $\mathcal{C}(G_i)$ or for $\mathcal{C}(G_i) - \{V_i, x_{\overline{V_i}}\}$. For a noncritical

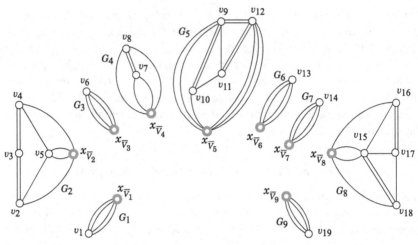

Figure 5.19. The (s, t)-decomposition $G_i = G/(V(G) - V_i), i = 1, 2, \ldots, 9$, for the (s, t)-MC partition $\pi_{(s,t)} = (V_1, V_2, \ldots, V_9)$ in Fig. 5.16 obtained from graph G^* in Fig. 5.2 with $s = v_1$ and $t = v_{19}$.

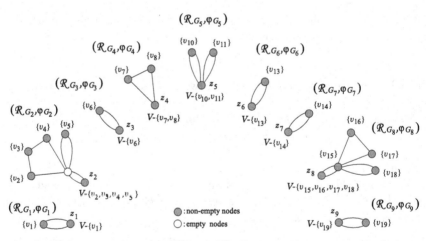

Figure 5.20. Cactus representations $(\mathcal{R}_{G_i}, \varphi_{G_i})$ for $\mathcal{C}(G_i), i = 1, 2, \ldots, r = 9$, for the (s, t)-MC partition $\pi_{(s,t)} = (V_1, V_2, \ldots, V_9)$ in Fig. 5.16 obtained from the graph G^* in Fig. 5.2 with $s = v_1$ and $t = v_{19}$.

graph G_i, we prepare the trivial cactus representation $(\mathcal{R}_{G_i}, \varphi_{G_i})$ consisting of a single node x; that is, $\mathcal{R}_{G_i} = (\{x\}, \emptyset)$ and $\varphi_{G_i}(V(G_i)) = x$. Figure 5.20 shows cactus representations $(\mathcal{R}_{G_i}, \varphi_{G_i})$ for the (s, t)-decomposition $G_i = G/(V(G) - V_i)$, $i = 1, 2, \ldots, 9$, in Fig 5.19 obtained from the (s, t)-MC partition $\pi_{(s,t)} = (V_1, V_2, \ldots, V_9)$, in Fig. 5.16. In this example, all $G_i, i = 1, 2, \ldots, 9$, are critical, where G_i with $i \neq 5$ still has minimum cut $\{V_i, x_{\overline{V_i}}\}$ and G_5 does not have such a minimum cut but has some other cut with size $\lambda(G)$.

Each minimum cut $\{X, \overline{X}\} \in C_{indv}(\pi_{(s,t)})$ is represented by $(\mathcal{R}_{G_i}, \varphi_{G_i})$ of the graph G_i with $X \subset V_i$ (or $\overline{X} \subset V_i$). Therefore, to obtain a cactus representation for $C(G) = C_{comp}(G) \cup C_{indv}(G)$, we must combine cactus representations $(\mathcal{R}_{G_i}, \varphi_{G_i})$, $i = 1, 2, \ldots, r$, and $(\mathcal{R}_{(s,t)}, \varphi_{(s,t)})$. For this purpose, we use the union operation $\oplus$ introduced in Section 5.2.1. For each $i = 1, \ldots r$, the vertex $x_{\overline{V_i}}$ in G_i is mapped into a node z_i in $\mathcal{R}_{G_i}$ (hence, $x_{\overline{V_i}} \in \varphi_{G_i}^{-1}(z_i)$), and we let x_{V_i} be the node in $(\mathcal{R}_{(s,t)}, \varphi_{(s,t)})$ such that $\varphi_{(s,t)}^{-1}(x_{V_i}) = V_i$. By interpreting $\varphi_{G_i}(v) = z_i$ for all $v \in V(G) - V_i$, this implies that

$$\varphi_{(s,t)}^{-1}(x_{V_i}) \cup \varphi_{G_i}^{-1}(z_i) = V(G)$$

holds. Thus, two partitions of $V(G)$, $\pi_{(s,t)}$ and $\{\varphi_{G_i}^{-1}(x) \mid x$ nonempty nodes in $\mathcal{R}_{G_i}\}$, are complementary. Then, as shown in Lemma 5.20, it is possible to combine an (s, t)-cactus representation $(\mathcal{R}_{(s,t)}, \varphi_{(s,t)})$ and a cactus representation $(\mathcal{R}_{G_i}, \varphi_{G_i})$ by performing the union operation $(\mathcal{R}_{(s,t)}, \varphi_{(s,t)}) \oplus (\mathcal{R}_{G_i}, \varphi_{G_i})$. By repeating this process, the (s, t)-cactus representation $(\mathcal{R}_{(s,t)}, \varphi_{(s,t)})$ and all cactus representations $(\mathcal{R}_{G_i}, \varphi_{G_i})$, $i = 1, 2, \ldots, r$, can be combined into a single cactus representation $(\mathcal{R}, \varphi)$ for $C(G)$ as follows:

Let $(\mathcal{R}, \varphi) := (\mathcal{R}_{(s,t)}, \varphi_{(s,t)})$ initially;
for $i = 1, \ldots, r$ **do**
  $(\mathcal{R}, \varphi) := (\mathcal{R}, \varphi) \oplus (\mathcal{R}_{G_i}, \varphi_{G_i})$

By Lemma 5.20, the resulting $(\mathcal{R}, \varphi)$ represents all minimum cuts in those represented by $(\mathcal{R}_{G_i}, \varphi_{G_i})$, $i = 1, 2, \ldots, r$, and $(\mathcal{R}_{(s,t)}, \varphi_{(s,t)})$, that is, all minimum cuts in $C(G)$.

Now we summarize the previous procedure for constructing a CNC representation for $C(G)$ of a given graph G^* as the following recursive algorithm, which is applied to G^* after initializing $\lambda := \lambda(G^*)$ and $G := G^*$.

Procedure CACTUSNAIVE(G)

1. Choose an edge $\{s, t\}$ in G if any (return a trivial cactus $(\mathcal{R}, \varphi)$ otherwise, i.e., if G is a single vertex).
2. If $\lambda(s, t; G) > \lambda$, then contract s and t into a single vertex and apply the CACTUSNAIVE(G') procedure to the resulting graph G'.
3. Otherwise (i.e., if $\lambda(s, t; G) = \lambda$), compute the (s, t)-MC partition $\pi_{(s,t)} = (V_1, V_2, \ldots, V_r)$ and the corresponding (s, t)-cactus representation $(\mathcal{R}_{(s,t)}, \varphi_{(s,t)})$.
4. Find the (s, t)-decomposition $(G_1, \ldots, G_r)$ of G (see (5.3) for the definition).
5. Apply the CACTUSNAIVE(G_i) procedure to each G_i to obtain the CNC representation $(\mathcal{R}_{G_i}, \varphi_{G_i})$ for $C(G_i)$, where the CACTUSNAIVE(G_i) procedure returns a trivial cactus if G_i is not critical.
6. Combine all $\{(\mathcal{R}_{G_i}, \varphi_{G_i}), i = 1, \ldots, r\}$ and $(\mathcal{R}_{(s,t)}, \varphi_{(s,t)})$ into a cactus representation $(\mathcal{R}, \varphi)$ for $C(G)$ by using the union operation $\oplus$.
7. Simplify $(\mathcal{R}, \varphi)$ into the CNC representation and return the resulting $(\mathcal{R}, \varphi)$.

5.3.2 Modification into an Algorithm

If CACTUSNAIVE(G') for a graph G' is invoked in the aforementioned procedure during the execution of CACTUSNAIVE(G''), then we call graph G' a *child* of G'', and G'' the *parent* of G'. The parent–child relation between graphs G' and G'' induces a tree $\mathcal{T}$ rooted at the input graph G^* that represents the recursive computation of CACTUSNAIVE.

However, the algorithm is tricky because if $d(V_i, V(G) - V_i; G) = \lambda$ for some i then cut $\{V_i, \overline{v_i}\}$ remains a minimum cut in its child, G_i, even though it has already been detected in its parent, G. This may result in infinitely many recursive calls. Not to invoke such an unnecessary call, we maintain the set of old minimum cuts; we call a minimum cut *new* at G' if it has not been detected in the ancestor of G', and *old* otherwise. Note that a minimum cut is old in G' if and only if it is of the form $\{v, V(G') - v\}$ and v is a contracted vertex $x_{\overline{V_i}}$ in the ancestor of G'. Therefore, we can maintain the set of old minimum cuts in a graph G' just by marking such vertices "old."

Now we consider when an (s, t)-cactus representation $(\mathcal{R}_{(s,t)}, \varphi_{(s,t)})$ for a graph G' contains a new minimum cut (whereby, the call to G' is necessary). Thus, with the set V^{old} of vertices marked "old," we can test whether the (s, t)-cactus representation $(\mathcal{R}_{(s,t)}, \varphi_{(s,t)})$ contains a new minimum cut in $O(|V(\mathcal{R}_{(s,t)})|)$ time.

If the (s, t)-cactus representation contains no new minimum cut, then $V_1 = \{s\}$ or $V_r = \{t\}$ holds in the (s, t)-MC partition $(V_1, \ldots, V_r)$ of $V(G')$ (otherwise, a minimum cut $\{V_1, V(G') - V_1\}$ or $\{V_r, V(G') - V_r\}$ does not separate a single vertex from the rest). In this case, we contract s and t into a single vertex, resulting in a graph with one less vertex, and then we update the set of old minimum cuts by $V^{old} := V^{old} - \{s, t\}$ (recall that by Theorem 5.24 all minimum cuts separating s and t are represented by $(\mathcal{R}_{(s,t)}, \varphi_{(s,t)})$). With this modification, a new minimum cut is detected or the number of vertices decreases after each recursive call.

5.3.3 Entire CONSTRUCT Algorithm

With the preceding modification, the previous divide-and-conquer procedure is now described as follows, where we want to construct a cactus representation for $\mathcal{C}(G^*)$ of a given graph G^*.

Procedure CACTUS(G, V^{old}, λ)
Input: A graph G, a subset $V^{old} \subset V(G)$, and a real number $\lambda > 0$.
Output: A cactus representation $(\mathcal{R}, \varphi)$ for a set $\mathcal{C}'$ of minimum cuts (whose
    weights are equal to λ) such that $\mathcal{C}(G) - \{\{\overline{v}, V(G) - \{\overline{v}\}\} \mid \overline{v} \in V^{old}\} \subseteq \mathcal{C}'$
    $\subseteq \mathcal{C}(G)$.
1 **if** $|V(G)| = 1$ **then return** the trivial cactus $(\mathcal{R}, \varphi)$
2 **else**
3   Choose an edge $e = \{s, t\} \in E(G)$ with $c_G(e) > 0$;
4   **if** $\lambda(s, t; G) > \lambda$ or the (s, t)-cactus representation $(\mathcal{R}_{(s,t)}, \varphi_{(s,t)})$ represents
        no minimum cut other than those $\{\overline{v}, V(G) - \{\overline{v}\}\}$, $\overline{v} \in V^{old}$

5   **then**
6       $G := G/\{s, t\};$
7       $V^{old} := V^{old} - \{s, t\};$
8       $(\mathcal{R}, \varphi) :=$CACTUS$(G, V^{old}, \lambda)$
9   **return** $(\mathcal{R}, \varphi)$
10 **else**
11   **for** each V_i in the (s, t)-MC partition $\pi_{(s,t)} = (V_1, V_2, \ldots, V_r)$ **do**
12          $G_i := G/(V(G) - V_i)$, denoting by $x_{\overline{V_i}}$ the vertex obtained by contracting $V(G) - V_i$;
13   **if** $d(V_i; G) = \lambda$ **then** $V_i^{old} := (V^{old} \cap V_i) \cup \{x_{\overline{V_i}}\}$ **end**; /* if */
14          $(\mathcal{R}_{G_i}, \varphi_{G_i}) :=$CACTUS$(G_i, V_i^{old}, \lambda)$
15   **end**; /* for */
16      $(\mathcal{R}, \varphi) := (\mathcal{R}_{(s,t)}, \varphi_{(s,t)}) \oplus (\mathcal{R}_{G_1}, \varphi_{G_1}) \oplus \cdots \oplus (\mathcal{R}_{G_r}, \varphi_{G_r});$
17   Convert $(\mathcal{R}, \varphi)$ into the CNC representation and denote it as $(\mathcal{R}, \varphi)$;
18   **return** $(\mathcal{R}, \varphi)$
19 **end** /* if */
20 **end**. /* if */

Algorithm CONSTRUCT
Input: An edge-weighted graph G^*.
Output: The CNC representation $(\mathcal{R}, \varphi)$ for $\mathcal{C}(G^*)$.
    Compute $\lambda := \lambda(G^*)$;
    $V^{old} := \emptyset$;
    $(\mathcal{R}, \varphi) :=$CACTUS$(G^*, V^{old}, \lambda)$.

We show the computation process of the CONSTRUCT algorithm applied to graph G^* with $\lambda(G^*) = 4$ in Fig. 5.2. After setting $\lambda := 4$ and $V^{old} := \emptyset$, the CACTUS $(G^*, \emptyset, 4)$ procedure is invoked. In the execution of CACTUS$(G, \emptyset, 4)$, where $G = G^*$, edge $\{v_1, v_{19}\}$ with $\lambda(v_1, v_{19}; G) = 4$ is chosen as $\{s, t\}$ in line 4, where the (s, t)-MC partition $\pi_{(s,t)} = (V_1, V_2, \ldots, V_9)$, is shown in Fig. 5.16. Then the (s, t)-decomposition $G_i = G/(V(G) - V_i)$, $i = 1, 2, \ldots, 9$, shown in Fig. 5.19 is computed in lines 11 and 12. In line 13, $V_i^{old} := \{x_{\overline{V_i}}\}$ is performed for each $i \in \{1, 2, \ldots, 9\} - \{5\}$. After executing CACTUS$(G_i, V_i^{old}, 4)$ for all $i = 1, 2, \ldots, 9$, the outputs $(\mathcal{R}_{G_i}, \varphi_{G_i}) :=$CACTUS$(G_i, V_i^{old}, 4)$ are combined with the (s, t)-cactus representation $(\mathcal{R}_{(s,t)}, \varphi_{(s,t)})$ shown in Fig. 5.17 in line 16.

We next describe the computation process of CACTUS$(G_i, V_i^{old}, 4)$ for each of $i = 1, 2, \ldots, 9$. In the execution of CACTUS$(G = G_1, V^{old} = \{x_{\overline{V_1}}\}, 4)$, edge $\{s = v_1, t = x_{\overline{V_1}}\}$ with $\lambda(s, t; G)$ is chosen in line 4. Since the (s, t)-cactus representation $(\mathcal{R}_{(s,t)}, \varphi_{(s,t)})$ represents no minimum cut other than $\{x_{\overline{V_1}}, V(G_1) - \{x_{\overline{V_1}}\}\}$, $x_{\overline{V_1}} \in V^{old}$, it performs $G := G/\{s, t\}$ and $V^{old} := V^{old} - \{s, t\}$ in lines 6 and 7, where the resulting graph G consists of a single vertex and $V^{old} = \emptyset$ holds. In line 9, CACTUS(G, V^{old}, λ) is invoked, but it returns a trivial cactus (since $|V(G)| = 1$ holds in line 1 in its execution). Hence, $(\mathcal{R}, \varphi) :=$CACTUS$(G, V^{old}, \lambda)$ is a trivial cactus, which CACTUS$(G = G_1, V^{old} = \{x_{V_1}\}, 4)$ returns in line 9 as its output.

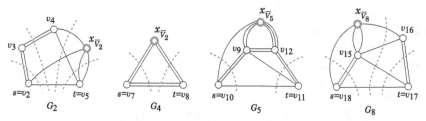

Figure 5.21. The (s, t)-MC partitions for graphs G_2, G_4, G_5, and G_8.

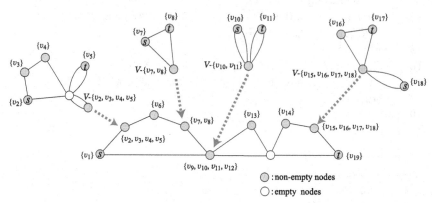

Figure 5.22. Nontrivial (s, t)-cactus representations generated during the execution of CACTUS($G^*, \emptyset, 4$).

We see that CACTUS($G = G_i$, $V^{old} = \{x_{V_i}\}$, 4) for $i \in \{3, 6, 7, 9\}$ also returns trivial cacti.

Finally we consider CACTUS($G = G_i$, V^{old}, 4) for $i \in \{2, 4, 5, 8\}$. For graph G_2 (resp. G_4, G_5, and G_8), edge $\{s = v_2, t = v_5\}$ (resp. $\{s = v_7, t = v_8\}$, $\{s = v_{10}, t = v_{11}\}$, and $\{s = v_{18}, t = v_{17}\}$) with $\lambda(s, t; G) = 4$ is chosen in line 4. The (s, t)-MC partitions for graphs G_2, G_4, G_5, and G_8 are shown in Fig. 5.21. For each graph of G_2, G_4, G_5, and G_8, its (s, t)-cactus representation is shown in Fig. 5.22. CACTUS($G = G_i$, V^{old}, 4) for each $i \in \{2, 4, 5, 8\}$ invokes the CACTUS procedure for each graph in its (s, t)-decomposition. However, any of the calls to CACTUS returns a trivial cactus; hence, CACTUS($G = G_i$, V^{old}, 4) for $i \in \{2, 4, 5, 8\}$ returns the (s, t)-cactus representation of G_i. Therefore, combining the four cactus representations in Fig. 5.22 yields a cactus representations in Fig. 5.4 for $\mathcal{C}(G^*)$, where graph G^* was given in Fig. 5.2. Note that trivial cacti generated during the execution of CACTUS($G^*, \emptyset, 4$) are not shown in Fig. 5.22 and Fig. 5.4.

5.3.4 Complexity Analysis of CONSTRUCT

We analyze the time and space complexities of the CONSTRUCT algorithm. Computing $\lambda = \lambda(G^*)$ can be executed in $O(mn + n \log n)$ time and $O(m)$ space via Corollary 3.4. For a fast implementation of CACTUS, we use maximum adjacency

(MA) orderings to compute the (s, t)-cactus representations. In line 3 of CACTUS, we compute an MA ordering $\sigma = (u_1, u_2, \ldots, u_{n'})$ for the current graph G, and we choose the edge $e = \{s, t\}$ as the edge between the vertex u_p with the largest index in σ such that $\{u_p, u_{n'}\} \in E(G)$ and the last vertex $u_{n'}$. Since $\sigma' = (u_1, u_2, \ldots, u_{p-1}, u_p, u_{n'})$ is an MA ordering in $G - \{u_{p+1}, \ldots, u_{n'-1}\}$, $\lambda(s, t; G) = d(t; G)$ holds by Theorem 3.1, and a maximum (s, t)-flow f can be found in linear time by Theorem 3.12. Hence, by Lemma 4.10 and Theorem 5.25, the (s, t)-MC partition and the cycle-type normal (s, t)-cactus representation can be constructed in linear time. Therefore, we have the next property.

Lemma 5.26. *Lines 3 and 4 of* CACTUS *can be executed in* $O(|E(G)| + |V(G)| \log |V(G)|)$ *time.* $\qquad \square$

We then consider the time and space for executing CACTUS recursively. Let n_{calls} be the number of times that CACTUS is invoked during the entire execution of CONSTRUCT. Notice that contracting V_i in line 11 creates a new vertex, $x_{\overline{V_i}}$, during the computation of CACTUS(G, V^{old}, λ). Let V_{new} be the set of all these vertices, $x_{\overline{V_i}}$, newly created by CACTUS during the entire execution of CONSTRUCT.

Lemma 5.27. $n_{calls} \leq 9n - 7$ *and* $|V_{new}| \leq 5n - 5$. $\qquad \square$

Proof. Let n_{new} be the number of times that the (s, t)-cactus representation for a chosen edge $\{s, t\}$ contains a new minimum cut. Any two new minimum cuts found in different (s, t)-cactus representations never cross each other. This is because, in constructing a descendent G' from a graph G'', all vertices $V''(G'') - V(G')$ (if any) are contracted into a single vertex, and G' cannot have a cut that crosses a cut in G'', where each minimum cut $\{X, V - X\}$ is considered one of the sets X and $V - X$ that does not contain a reference vertex r. Thus, considering that the number of noncrossing cuts in G^* is at most $2|V(G^*)| - 2$, we have

$$n_{new} \leq 2n - 2.$$

Let n_{edge} be the number of times that an edge is chosen as $\{s, t\}$ in line 3 and let n_{cntr} be the number of times that the chosen edge $\{s, t\}$ is contracted in line 6. From these definitions, we have

$$n_{edge} = n_{cntr} + n_{new}.$$

Let n_{trvi} be the number of times that CACTUS returns the trivial cactus in line 1. Note that n_{trvi} is the number of leaves in the tree $\mathcal{T}$ representing the recursive call to CACTUS in CONSTRUCT (see the explanation in the beginning of Sec. 5.3.2). To count the number of leaves in $\mathcal{T}$, let $\sum |\pi_{(s,t)}|$ denote the size of (s, t)-MC partitions $\pi_{(s,t)}$ such that their cactus representations contain new minimum cuts. Since such an (s, t)-MC partition $\pi_{(s,t)}$ increases the number of leaves in $\mathcal{T}$ by $|\pi_{(s,t)}| - 1$, we have

$$n_{trvi} = 1 + \left(\sum |\pi_{(s,t)}| - n_{new} \right). \tag{5.4}$$

The number of new vertices of the form $x_{\overline{V_i}}$ increases by $|\pi_{(s,t)}|$ whenever an (s,t)-cactus representation that contains a new minimum cut is constructed. Thus, $|V_{new}| = \sum |\pi_{(s,t)}|$ holds. Contracting an edge $\{s, t\}$ reduces the number of vertices by 1. Hence, we have

$$n_{trvi} = n + \sum |\pi_{(s,t)}| - n_{cntr},$$

and, hence, by (5.4) we have

$$n_{cntr} = n + n_{new} - 1 \le 3n - 3,$$
$$n_{edge} = n_{new} + n_{cntr} = n - 1 + 2n_{new} \le 5n - 5.$$

By charging $r = |\pi_{(s,t)}|$ credits to each child G_i of G (i.e., the number of new vertices created to produce G_i), we see that the total number of newly created vertices is equal to the number of all (s, t)-cactus representations (including those that do not produce new minimum cuts), which is bounded from above as follows:

$$\sum |\pi_{(s,t)}| \le n_{cntr} + n_{new}.$$

Thus, we obtain

$$|V_{new}| = \sum |\pi_{(s,t)}| \le n_{cntr} + n_{new} \le 5n - 5.$$

This, together with (5.4), then implies that

$$n_{trvi} = 1 + \sum |\pi_{(s,t)}| - n_{new} \le 1 + n_{cntr} \le 3n - 2.$$

In T, the parent G in line 6 of CACTUS has exactly one child, whereas the parent G in lines 11–16 of CACTUS has at least two children. Line 6 is executed n_{cntr} times and the number of leaves is equal to n_{trvi} ($\le 3n - 2$). Therefore, we obtain the following bound:

$$n_{calls} \le n_{cntr} + 2n_{trvi} \le 9n - 7. \qquad \square$$

In the following, we denote by T_i the total time of executing line i of CACTUS during the computation of CONSTRUCT, and we derive their upper bounds. For this, we also show how to maintain the following data in $O(m)$ space during the execution of CONSTRUCT:

D1. Graphs G used as inputs of calls to CACTUS,
D2. The (s, t)-MC partitions used to produce children G_i during the execution of CACTUS,
D3. The sets of old vertices V^{old} in the inputs of CACTUS, and
D4. Cactus representations in the outputs of CACTUS.

Suppose that CACTUS(G, V^{old}, λ) has just been invoked; let

$$G^{(0)} = G^*, G^{(1)}, \ldots, G^{(k)} = G$$

be the graphs stored in the current stack for recursive calls (i.e., those on the path from the root G^* to G in T), where $G^{(j)}$ is the parent of $G^{(j+1)}$ and k is the depth

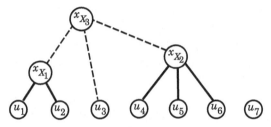

Figure 5.23. Forest $\mathcal{F}$ that keeps track of the contraction process, where the current graph has been obtained from the original graph G having vertices $\{u_1, u_2, \ldots, u_7\}$ by contracting $X_1 = \{u_1, u_2\}$ into x_{X_1}, $X_2 = \{u_4, u_5, u_6\}$ into x_{X_2}, and $X_3 = \{x_{X_1}, u_3, x_{X_2}\}$ into x_{X_3}.

of the current call. By Lemma 5.27, $k \leq n_{calls} \leq 9n - 7$ holds. Let $V^{old(j)}$ and $(\mathcal{R}^{(j)}, \varphi^{(j)})$ be the set of old vertices and the cactus representation in the call of CACTUS$(G^{(j)}, V^{old(j)}, \lambda)$, respectively.

We first consider D1. Since the depth of recursions is $O(n)$ and each call CACTUS(G, V^{old}, λ) needs $O(m)$ space for maintaining the current graph G, a naïve implementation of CONSTRUCT would require $O(mn)$ space. To reduce this to $O(m)$, we avoid creating a copy of $G^{(k)}$ before invoking CACTUS$(G^{(k)}, V^{old(k)}, \lambda)$ in line 14 of CACTUS. Instead, we construct $G^{(k)}$ in $O(m)$ time by retrieving from the original input graph G^* (which is always maintained). For this, we keep the record of the sequence of contractions from $G^{(0)} = G^*$ down to the current graph $G^{(k)}$ in $\mathcal{T}$. We use a forest $\mathcal{F}$ to keep such a record. Initially $\mathcal{F}$ is the set of n isolated vertices in $V(G^*)$. When a subset $X \subseteq V(G^*)$ is contracted into a single vertex x_X, we create a new vertex x_X together with the new edges $\{x_X, u\}$, $u \in X$, and we let x_X be the parent of each $u \in X$ (see Fig. 5.23). Each time a set $X' \subseteq V(G')$ is contracted, we update the set $\mathcal{F}$ by creating the new vertex $x_{X'}$ with the edges joining $x_{X'}$ and all vertices in X'. When we need to recover graph $G^{(k-1)}$ after executing CACTUS$(G^{(k)}, V^{old(k)}, \lambda)$ for its child $G^{(k)}$, we simply remove from $\mathcal{F}$ the vertex x_X that has been created to obtain $G^{(k)}$ by contracting set $X \subseteq V(G)$. (For example, in Fig. 5.23, the vertex x_{X_3} created at the time of constructing G will be removed when the parent of G is constructed.) Note that the number of vertices in $\mathcal{F}$ is at most $n + |V_{new}| = O(n)$ by Lemma 5.27. In this way, we can maintain the forest $\mathcal{F}$ in $O(n)$ time per update, and we can construct a child G_i or recover its parent in $O(m)$ time. Hence, by Lemma 5.26, $T_3 + T_4$ is $O(n_{calls}(m + n \log n)) = O(mn + n^2 \log n)$ time.

We next consider D2. Let $\pi_{(s,t)}^{(j)}$, $j = 0, 1, \ldots, k$, denote the (s, t)-MC partition of graph $G^{(j)}$. If we keep the full (s, t)-MC partition $\pi_{(s,t)}^{(j)}$ in each call of CACTUS$(G^{(j)}, V^{old(j)}, \lambda)$, the required space for recursive calls would be $O(\sum_{0 \leq j \leq k} |\pi_{(s,t)}^{(j)}|) = O(n^2)$ space. To reduce this, we discard the ith subset $V_i^{(k)} \in \pi_{(s,t)}^{(k)}$ and store only $\pi_{(s,t)}^{(k)} - V_i^{(k)}$ before calling CACTUS$(G^{(k+1)} = G^{(k)}/(V(G^{(k)} - V_i^{(k)}), V^{old(k+1)}, \lambda)$, but we regain $\pi_{(s,t)}^{(k)}$ from $\pi_{(s,t)}^{(k)} - V_i^{(k)}$ and $V_i^{(k)}$ (where CACTUS$(G^{(k+1)}, V^{old(k+1)}, \lambda)$ will return $V_i^{(k)}$ upon completion). Thus, no two copies of a vertex in the input graph G^* are stored over all graphs stored in the stack, and, hence, $O(n)$ space suffices to maintain all the (s, t)-MC partitions $\pi_{(s,t)}^{(j)}$, $j = 0, 1, \ldots, k$, during CONSTRUCT.

We now consider D3. Suppose that, in CACTUS($G^{(k)}, V^{old(k)}, \lambda$), a child $G^{(k+1)} = G^{(k)}/(V(G^{(k)}) - V_i^{(k)})$ is constructed and $V_i^{old(k+1)} = (V^{old(k-1)} \cap V_i^{(k)}) \cup \{x_{\overline{V_i}}^{(k)}\})$ is computed. If we store the entire $V^{old(j)}$ in every call of CACTUS($G^{(j)}, V^{old(j)}, \lambda$), then it will require $O(\sum_{0 \le j \le k} |V^{old(j)}|) = O(n^2)$ space. Similarly to D2, this can be reduced to $O(n)$ space. For this, we remove $V^{old(k)} \cap V_i^{(k)}$ from $V^{old(k)}$ and store only $V^{old(k)} - V_i^{(k)}$ and $x_{\overline{V_i}}^{(k)}$ before calling CACTUS($G^{(k+1)}, V_i^{old(k+1)}, \lambda$), but we regain $V^{old(k)}$ from $V_i^{old(k+1)}$ and $x_{\overline{V_i}}^{(k)}$ after finishing CACTUS($G^{(k+1)}, V_i^{old(k+1)}, \lambda$). Hence, no vertex in V_{new} is maintained in more than one graph except for those $x_{\overline{V_i}}$ kept to regain $V^{old} \cap V_i$. Since $|V_{new}| \le 5n - 5$ and the depth k is at most $n_{calls} \le 9n - 7$ by Lemma 5.27, we need an $O(n_{calls} + |V_{new}|) = O(n)$ space for maintaining old cuts during CONSTRUCT.

With the preceding data structure for D1–D3, we see that each of lines 6, 7, 12, and 13 of CACTUS can be executed in $O(mn + n)$ time. Since there are $O(n_{calls})$ such executions, the total time of $T_6 + T_7 + T_{12} + T_{13}$ is $O(n_{calls}(m + n)) = O(mn)$.

We finally consider D4. Note that each $\mathcal{R}^{(j)}$ ($j = 0, 1, \ldots, k - 1$) has a special node $x^{(j)}$ that corresponds to the subset V_i used for $G^{(j+1)} = G^{(j)}/(V(G^{(j)}) - V_i)$. No vertex $v \in V(G^*)$ is mapped to two nodes $x \in V(\mathcal{R}^{(j)})$ and $y \in V(\mathcal{R}^{(j')})$ ($j < j'$) unless x and y are special. Thus, $\cup_{0 \le j \le k} V(\mathcal{R}^{(j)})$ contains at most n non-special nonempty nodes and at most k ($\le 9n - 7$) special nonempty nodes. Recall that the (s, t)-cactus representation $(\mathcal{R}_{(s,t)}, \varphi_{(s,t)})$ and the cactus representations returned by CACTUS(G_i, V_i^{old}, λ) are all CNC representations, and their sizes are bounded from above by twice the number of nonempty nodes by Lemma 5.18. Therefore, $\sum_{0 \le j \le k} |V(\mathcal{R}^{(j)})|$ is $O(n)$. As to the space for storing mappings φ, we discard $\varphi_{(s,t)}^{-1}(z_i)$ in line 14 before invoking CACTUS(G_i, V_i^{old}, λ), where z_i denotes the node such that $z_i = \varphi_{(s,t)}(V_i)$ (where $\varphi_{(s,t)}^{-1}(z_i)$ can be regained easily while executing line 16). Hence, no vertex may be mapped to any two cactus representations $(\mathcal{R}_{(s,t)}, \varphi_{(s,t)})$ and $(\mathcal{R}_i, \varphi_i)$ in line 15, and the space for maintaining mapping φ is also $O(n)$. Then combining cactus representations in line 16 can be done in $O(n)$ time. Converting the resulting representation into the CNC representation in line 17 takes $O(n)$ time by Theorem 5.19. Hence, $T_{16} + T_{17}$ is $O(n_{calls}n) = O(n^2)$ time.

Summarizing the discussion so far, the next theorem is established.

Theorem 5.28 ([257]). *A cactus representation for all minimum cuts in an edge-weighted graph G can be constructed in $O(mn + n^2 \log n)$ time and $O(n + m)$ space.* □

6

Extreme Vertex Sets

The concept of extreme vertex sets, defined in Section 1.5.3, was first introduced by Watanabe and Nakamura [308] to solve the edge-connectivity augmentation problem. The fastest deterministic algorithm currently known for computing all extreme vertex sets was given by Naor, Gusfield, and Martel [259]. Their algorithm first computes the Gomory–Hu cut tree of the graph and then finds all maximal k-edge-connected components for some k, from which all extreme vertex sets are identified by Lemma 1.42, taking $O(n(mn \log(n^2/m)))$ running time. Benczúr and Karger [20] have given a Monte Carlo–type randomized algorithm, which runs in $O(n^2 \log^5 n)$ time but is rather involved. Notice that computing all extreme vertex sets is not easier than finding a minimum cut since at least one of the extreme vertex sets is a minimum cut.

In this chapter, we give a simple and efficient algorithm for computing all extreme vertex sets in a given graph, and we show some applications of extreme vertex sets. The algorithm will be used to solve the edge-connectivity augmentation problem in Section 8.3. In Section 6.1, we design a deterministic $O(nm + n^2 \log n)$ time algorithm for computing the family $\mathcal{X}(G)$ of extreme vertex sets in a given edge-weighted graph G, which is a laminar family, as observed in Lemma 1.41. As a new application of extreme vertex sets, in Section 6.2 we consider a dynamic graph G in which the weight of edges incident to a designated vertex may increase or decrease with time and we give a dynamic minimum cut algorithm that reports a minimum cut of the current G whenever the weight of an edge is updated. In Section 6.3, we consider the problem of finding an optimal contraction ordering of vertices in a graph G by which its edge-connectivity increases as quickly as possible. Such an ordering of vertices will be used in Section 9.1 to solve the source location problem with edge-connectivity requirement.

Finally, in Section 6.4, we give an efficient algorithm for the problem of choosing k disjoint subsets in a graph to minimize the sum of their cut sizes.

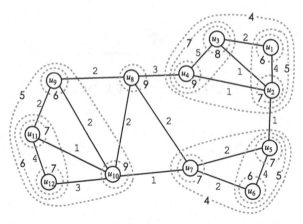

Figure 6.1. A graph G_1 and all extreme vertex sets in G_1, where the numbers beside edges indicate their weights and each extreme vertex set X is depicted by a dotted closed curve with a number that indicates the cut size $d(X; G_1)$.

6.1 Computing Extreme Vertex Sets in Graphs

A nonempty proper subset X of V is called an *extreme vertex set* of G if

$$d(Y; G) > d(X; G)$$

holds for all nonempty proper subsets Y of X. Any singleton set $\{v\}$ with a vertex v is an extreme vertex set, which is called *trivial*. Let $\mathcal{X}(G)$ denote the family of all extreme vertex sets in a graph G, which is laminar (see Section 1.1.7 and Lemma 1.41). Let $\mathcal{T}$ denote the tree representation defined for the laminar family $\mathcal{X}(G) \cup \{V\}$ (see Section 1.1). Figure 6.1 illustrates the family $\mathcal{X}(G_1)$ of extreme vertex sets in a graph G_1 and Fig. 6.2 shows its tree representation $\mathcal{T}$, where V is its root.

A pair of vertices $u, v \in V$ is called a *flat pair* if no nontrivial extreme vertex set $X \in \mathcal{X}(G)$ separates u and v (i.e., any extreme vertex set $X \in \mathcal{X}(G)$ with $|\{u, v\} \cap X| = 1$ is either $\{u\}$ or $\{v\}$). A flat pair $\{u, v\}$ corresponds to a pair of leaves that have the same parent in the tree representation $\mathcal{T}$ of $\mathcal{X}(G)$. For example, $\{u_1, u_2\}$, $\{u_3, u_4\}$, $\{u_5, u_6\}$, $\{u_9, u_{10}\}$, and $\{u_{11}, u_{12}\}$ are all the flat pairs of graph G_1 in Fig. 6.1.

Consider an ordering of vertices $\pi = (v_1, v_2, \ldots, v_n)$ which is obtained by repeating a procedure of choosing a vertex with the minimum degree and removing it from the graph. That is, π satisfies

$$d(v_i; G - V_{i-1}) \le d(v_j; G - V_{i-1}) \text{ for all } i, j \text{ with } 1 \le i \le j \le n, \quad (6.1)$$

where $V_0 = \emptyset$ and $V_j = \{v_1, v_2, \ldots, v_j\}$ $(1 \le j \le n)$. An ordering π in (6.1) is called a *minimum-degree (MD) ordering* [229]. This ordering is also known as δ-slicings [203] or smallest-last ordering [215] if G is an unweighted simple graph and was introduced to study the structure of induced subgraphs.

As in Lemma 3.2, we see the following.

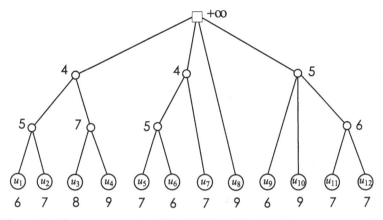

Figure 6.2. The tree presentation $\mathcal{T}$ for $\mathcal{X}(G_1) \cup \{V\}$, where its root represents V.

Lemma 6.1 ([229]). *For an edge-weighted graph with n vertices and m edges, an MD ordering π can be found in $O(m + n \log n)$ time and $O(m + n)$ space.* □

We prove that a flat pair can be found via an MD ordering.

Theorem 6.2 ([229]). *For an edge-weighted graph $G = (V, E)$, let $\pi = (v_1, v_2, \ldots, v_n)$ be an MD ordering. Then the pair of the last two vertices, v_{n-1} and v_n, is a flat pair.* □

For example, the vertices of graph G_1 in Fig. 6.1 are indexed by an MD ordering, and the last two vertices, u_{11} and u_{12}, give a flat pair. We prove Theorem 6.2 via several lemmas based on maximum adjacency (MA) orderings. For a graph $G = (V, E)$ and a weight function $b : V \to \Re_+$, a star augmentation $G + b$ with a designated vertex s (see Section 1.1.3 for the definition of star augmentation) is called a *k-regular star augmentation* if $d(v; G + b) = \max\{k, d(v; G)\}$ (i.e., $b(v) = \max\{0, k - d(v; G)\}$) for all $v \in V$. The k-regular star augmentation was introduced [20, 78] as a building block of algorithms for solving the edge-connectivity augmentation.

Lemma 6.3. *Let $X \in \mathcal{X}(G)$ be a nontrivial extreme vertex set of a graph G and let k be a real with $d(X; G) < k \leq \min_{u \in X} d(u; G)$. Then X does not separate two vertices v and w if $\lambda(v, w; G + b) \geq k$ holds in the k-regular star augmentation $G + b$.* □

Proof. By $k \leq \min_{u \in X} d(u; G)$, it holds that $d(u; G + b) = d(u; G)$ (i.e., $b(u) = 0$) for all $u \in X$. Then $d(X; G + b) = d(X; G)$. Hence, $|X \cap \{v, w\}| = 1$ would imply $\lambda(v, w; G + b) \leq d(X; G + b) = d(X; G) < k$, a contradiction to the assumption $\lambda(v, w; G + b) \geq k$. □

Lemma 6.4 ([238]). *For a graph $G = (V, E)$ and a real $K \geq 0$, let $G + b$ be the K-regular star augmentation and let $\sigma = (v_0 = s, v_1, v_2, \ldots, v_{n-1}, v_n)$ be*

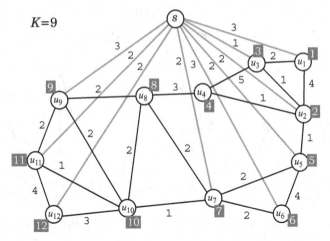

Figure 6.3. The K-regular star augmentation $G + b$ and its MA ordering σ for graph G_1 of Fig. 6.1, where the numbers beside edges indicate their weights and the numbers beside vertices indicate an MA ordering σ (equivalently an MD ordering π of G_1).

an MA ordering starting with s in $G + b$. Then, for any k with $0 \le k \le K$, $\lambda(v_{n-1}, v_n; G + b') \ge k$ holds in the k-regular star augmentation $G + b'$. $\qquad\square$

Proof. Let k be a real with $0 \le k \le K$ and let $G + b'$ be the k-regular star augmentation of G. Let $\delta = K - k$ and let B be the δ-skin of the K-regular star augmentation $G + b$. (The δ-skin was defined in Section 3.4.) By construction of $G + b'$ and B, we see that $c_{G+b'}(v, w) \ge c_B(v, w)$ for all $v, w \in V \cup \{s\}$. In particular, $\lambda(v_{n-1}, v_n; G + b') \ge \lambda(v_{n-1}, v_n; B)$. By applying Lemma 3.9 to $\delta = K - k$, we have $\lambda(v_{n-1}, v_n; B) = d(v_n; G + b) - \delta \ge K - \delta = k$. Therefore, $\lambda(v_{n-1}, v_n; G + b') \ge k$ holds, as required. $\qquad\square$

Lemma 6.5 ([220, 221]). *For a graph $G = (V, E)$ and a real $K \ge \max_{u \in V} d(u; G)$, let $G + b$ be the K-regular star augmentation and let $\sigma = (v_0 = s, v_1, v_2, \dots, v_{n-1}, v_n)$ be an MA ordering σ starting with s in $G + b$. Then no nontrivial extreme vertex set X in G separates v_n and v_{n-1}.* $\qquad\square$

Proof. For each nontrivial extreme vertex set X in G, there is a real k_X with $d(X; G) < k_X \le \min_{u \in X} d(u; G)$. By $K \ge \max_{u \in V} d(u; G)$, we have $k_X \le K$. Therefore, by Lemma 6.4, $\lambda(v_{n-1}, v_n; G + b') \ge k_X$ holds in the k_X-regular star augmentation $G + b'$ of G. Then, by Lemma 6.3, X does not separate v_n and v_{n-1}. $\qquad\square$

    Figure 6.3 shows the K-star augmentation $G + b$ with $K = 9$ and its MA ordering σ for graph G_1 of Fig. 6.1. We are ready to prove Theorem 6.2. In fact, since $d(v; G + b) = K$ holds for all $v \in V$ in the K-regular star augmentation $G + b$ with $K \ge \max_{u \in V} d(u; G)$, we see that $d(V_{i-1} \cup \{s\}, v_i; G + b) = d(v_i; G + b) - d(v_i, V - V_i; G + b) = K - d(v_i; G - V_i)$ holds for any ordering

$(s, v_1, v_2, \ldots, v_{n-1}, v_n)$, where $V_i = \{v_1, v_2, \ldots, v_i\}$. By (3.1) and (6.1), this implies that an ordering $(s, v_1, v_2, \ldots, v_{n-1}, v_n)$ is an MA ordering in $G + b$ if and only if $(v_1, v_2, \ldots, v_{n-1}, v_n)$ is an MD ordering in G. Therefore, Theorem 6.2 follows from Lemma 6.5.

For the last two vertices v and w in an MD ordering of a given graph G, Theorem 6.2 tells that v and w can be contracted into a single vertex, say z, without losing any nontrivial extreme vertex set in G. Based on this property, the following algorithm for computing all extreme vertex sets repeats such a contraction operation of v and w until only two vertices remain. Notice that in this process the set of all vertices contracted into a vertex z may form an extreme vertex set in the original graph G and will be retained as a candidate of an extreme vertex set before executing the contraction procedure in the resulting graph. When we reach a graph with only two vertices, the set of all extreme vertex sets of G can be retrieved from the set of candidates after discarding all nonextreme vertex sets. The entire algorithm can be described as follows.

Algorithm EXTREME
Input: A graph $G = (V, E)$.
Output: The family $\mathcal{X}(G)$ of all extreme vertex sets of G.
1    $\mathcal{X} := \{\{u\} \mid u \in V\}$; $G' := G$;
2   **while** $|V(G')| \geq 3$ **do**
3   Find an MD ordering π in G';
4   Contract the last two vertices $v, w \in V(G')$ in π into a single vertex z
          and let G' denote the resulting graph;
5   Let X_z denote the set of vertices in V that have been contracted into z
          so far, and set $\mathcal{X} := \mathcal{X} \cup \{X_z\}$;
6   **end**; /* while */
7    $\mathcal{X} := \mathcal{X} - \{X \in \mathcal{X} \mid d(Y; G) \leq d(X; G) \text{ for some } Y \in \mathcal{X} \text{ with } Y \subset X\}$;
8   Output $\mathcal{X}(G) := \mathcal{X}$.

Figure 6.3 shows an MD ordering π of line 4 obtained in the first iteration of the while-loop of EXTREME applied to graph G_1 of Fig. 6.1. Figure 6.4 illustrates all graphs G' and MD orderings π in the subsequent iterations of the while-loop, where the family

$$\mathcal{X} = \{\{u_i\} \mid i = 1, 2, \ldots, 12\} \cup \{\{u_{11}, u_{12}\}, \{u_{10}, u_{11}, u_{12}\},$$
$$\{u_9, u_{10}, u_{11}, u_{12}\}, \{u_1, u_2\}, \{u_3, u_4\}, \{u_1, u_2, u_3, u_4\},$$
$$\{u_8, u_9, u_{10}, u_{11}, u_{12}\}, \{u_5, u_6\}, \{u_5, u_6, u_7\},$$
$$\{u_5, u_6, u_7, u_8, u_9, u_{10}, u_{11}, u_{12}\}\}$$

is computed after the while-loop. Then $\mathcal{X}(G)$ is obtained by discarding sets $\{u_{10}, u_{11}, u_{12}\}$ and $\{u_5, u_6, u_7, u_8, u_9, u_{10}, u_{11}, u_{12}\}$ from $\mathcal{X}$.

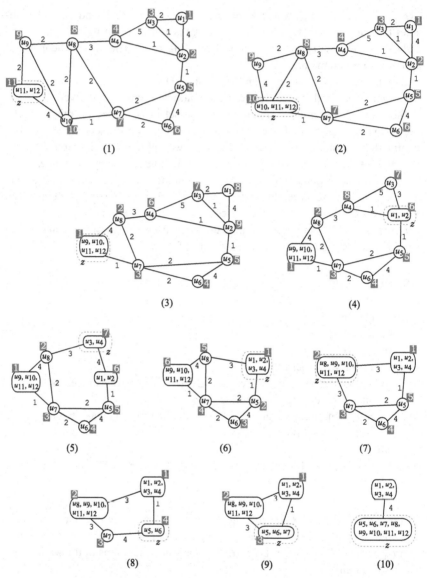

Figure 6.4. Illustration of EXTREME for computing all extreme vertex sets in G_1 of Fig. 6.1, where the numbers beside edges indicate their weights and the numbers beside vertices indicate the MD orderings of the corresponding graphs.

Theorem 6.6 ([220, 221]). *The* EXTREME *algorithm correctly finds the family of all extreme vertex sets of an edge-weighted graph in* $O(mn + n^2 \log n)$ *time and* $O(m + n)$ *space.* □

Proof. Since $\mathcal{X}$ in line 7 is a laminar family that has a tree representation with at most n leaves, $|\mathcal{X}|$ (which is the number of nodes in the tree representation) is at most $2n - 1$. The time bound is then immediate from the complexity of computing MD orderings (see Lemma 6.1).

We then show the correctness of EXTREME. As observed in Theorem 6.2, no nontrivial extreme vertex set in the current graph G' separates the last two vertices $\{v, w\}$ in the MD ordering computed during the while-loop. Since $\mathcal{X}$ stores all X_z, where z are vertices newly created by the contraction procedure, the set $\mathcal{X}$ after the while-loop contains all extreme vertex sets of G. Obviously no set discarded in line 7 is an extreme vertex set. For correctness, therefore, it suffices to show that every set remaining in the final $\mathcal{X}$ is in fact an extreme vertex set of G. Assume that such an $X \in \mathcal{X}$ is not an extreme vertex set for which there is an extreme vertex set X' such that $X' \subset X$ and $d(X'; G) \leq d(X; G)$. However, since $\mathcal{X}$ contains all extreme vertex sets, X' is in the final $\mathcal{X}$, and X must have been discarded in line 7, a contradiction. Thus, the final $\mathcal{X}$ is equal to $\mathcal{X}(G)$. $\square$

In the next subsection, we consider an algorithm for computing the edge-connectivity of a graph that has a designated vertex s such that the weights of edges incident to s may change with time. For this, we prepare the following corollaries. The first corollary considers a relation between $\mathcal{X}(G)$ and $\mathcal{X}(G[Z])$, where $G[Z]$ denotes the subgraph of G induced by $Z \subseteq V$.

Corollary 6.7. *For a graph $G = (V, E)$ and a subset $Z \subseteq V$, it holds that $\mathcal{X}(G) \cap (2^Z - \{Z\}) \subseteq \mathcal{X}(G[Z])$, and $\mathcal{X}(G) \cap (2^Z - \{Z\})$ can be computed in $O(m + n + m'n' + n'^2 \log n)$ time and $O(m + n)$ space, where $n' = |Z|$ and m' is the number of weighted edges in $G[Z]$.* $\square$

Proof. For a subset $X \subset Z$, it holds that $d(X; G[Z]) = d(X; G) - d(X, V - Z; G)$. Any $X \in \mathcal{X}(G) \cap (2^Z - \{Z\})$ satisfies $d(X; G) < d(Y; G)$ and $d(X, V - Z; G) \geq d(Y, V - Z; G)$ for all $Y \subset X$ and, thereby, $d(X; G[Z]) < d(Y; G[Z])$ for all $Y \subset X$. This implies that X remains an extreme vertex set in $G[Z]$, proving $\mathcal{X}(G) \cap (2^Z - \{Z\}) \subseteq \mathcal{X}(G[Z])$. To obtain $\mathcal{X}(G) \cap (2^Z - \{Z\})$, first construct $G[Z]$ and compute the family $\mathcal{X}(G[Z])$ of all extreme vertex sets in $G[Z]$ by applying EXTREME; then discard all sets X such that $d(X; G) \geq d(Y; G)$ for some $Y \in \mathcal{X}(G[Z])$ with $Y \subset X$ to obtain $\mathcal{X}(G) \cap (2^Z - \{Z\})$. The time and space complexities follow from Theorem 6.6. $\square$

In general, $\mathcal{X}(G) \cap (2^Z - \{Z\}) \subset \mathcal{X}(G[Z])$ is possible. For example, for the subgraph $G_1[A]$ induced from graph G_1 in Fig. 6.1 by set $A = \{u_4, u_8, u_9\}$, we have $\{u_4, u_8\} \in \mathcal{X}(G_1[A]) - \mathcal{X}(G_1) \cap (2^A - \{A\})$.

From Corollary 6.7, we have the following property of the edge-connectivity of a star augmentation $G + b$, where $b(X)$ denotes $\sum_{v \in X} b(v)$ for any $X \subseteq V$.

Corollary 6.8. *For a graph $G = (V, E)$ and a weight function $b : V \to \Re_+$, the star augmentation $G + b$ satisfies*

$$\lambda(G + b) = \min\{b(V), \ \min\{d(X; G) + b(X) \mid X \in \mathcal{X}(G)\}\}.$$ $\square$

Proof. A minimum cut in $G + b$ is either $\{s, V - s\}$ or a member of $\mathcal{X}(G + b) \cap (2^V - V)$. By Corollary 6.7, we have $\mathcal{X}(G + b) \cap (2^V - V) \subseteq \mathcal{X}((G + b)[V]) = \mathcal{X}(G)$. Therefore, $\lambda(G + b) = \min\{d(s; G + b), \min\{d(X; G + b) \mid X \in \mathcal{X}(G + b) \cap (2^V - V)\}\} \geq \min\{d(s; G + b), \min\{d(X; G + b) \mid X \in \mathcal{X}(G)\}\} = \min\{b(V), \min\{d(X; G) + b(X) \mid X \in \mathcal{X}(G)\}\}$. On the other hand, by the definition of $\lambda(G + b)$, we have $\lambda(G + b) \leq \min\{b(V), \min\{d(X; G) + b(X) \mid X \in \mathcal{X}(G)\}\}$, and thereby $\lambda(G + b) = \min\{b(V), \min\{d(X; G) + b(X) \mid X \in \mathcal{X}(G)\}\}$.   □

This corollary says that we can obtain $\lambda(G + b')$ for a different b' only by updating $b'(X) = \sum_{v \in X} b'(v)$ for all $X \in \mathcal{X}(G) \cup \{V\}$, without recomputing $\mathcal{X}(G)$.

6.2 Algorithm for Dynamic Edges Incident to a Specified Vertex

In this section, we consider a dynamic graph G in which the weight of each edge may increase or decrease with time (unless no negative weight appears). A dynamic minimum-cut algorithm reports the edge-connectivity of the current G after some edge weights have been updated. The current fastest dynamic algorithm is due to Thorup [302] and deals with an unweighted multigraph G such that $\lambda(G) = O(\log^k n)$ and can maintain the edge-connectivity in $\tilde{O}(\sqrt{n})$ time per edge insertion or deletion (i.e., increase or decrease by weight 1).

In the sequel, we consider a restricted dynamic graph model in which edge weight may change only for the edges that are incident to a designated vertex v_0. As shown by the next result, this makes the dynamic problem much easier.

Theorem 6.9 ([228]). *Let $G = (V, E)$ be an edge-weighted graph with a designated vertex $v_0 \in V$ such that weights of the edges incident to v_0 may change. Then, with an $O(mn + n^2 \log n)$ time preprocessing, the edge-connectivity $\lambda(G)$ can be reported in $O(\log n)$ time per update. The corresponding minimum cut can be found in $O(\log n)$ time from the set of cuts registered by preprocessing.*   □

Remark. The result in the theorem is optimal in the following sense.

(i) The preprocessing time $O(mn + n^2 \log n)$ matches the current best time bound for computing the edge-connectivity deterministically [232]. Note that we need to obtain the edge-connectivity of the initial input graph.

(ii) The time $O(\log n)$ after each update matches the time for updating a priority queue. This is the best possible outcome since our problem includes the problem of sorting n nonnegative elements $a_1, a_2, \ldots, a_n$ by comparisons. The initial graph $G = (V, E)$ has $V = \{v_0, v_1, \ldots, v_n\}$ and $E = \{\{v_0, v_i\} \mid i = 1, 2, \ldots, n\}$, where edges $\{v_0, v_i\}$, $i = 1, 2, \ldots, n$, have weights a_i. Then we repeat (n times) the operation of reporting the current minimum cut $\{v_h\}$ and increasing weight of edge $\{v_0, v_h\}$ to $+\infty$. Observe that the resulting order of reported cuts $\{v_h\}$ is a sorted order of all a_i.

Now we prove Theorem 6.9. Let G be a graph with a designated vertex v_0, where weights of edges in $G - v_0$ remain unchanged. We first compute the family

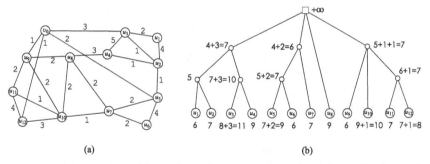

(a)   (b)

Figure 6.5. (a) A graph G with a designated vertex v_0, where $G - v_0$ is equal to the graph G_1 in Fig. 6.1; (b) the tree representation T for $\mathcal{X} = \mathcal{X}(G - v_0) \cup \{V\}$ of the current graph G.

$\mathcal{X}(G - v_0)$ of extreme vertex sets in $G - v_0$ as preprocessing. This takes $O(mn + n^2 \log n)$ time by Theorem 6.6. Then let $b : V(G - v_0) \to \mathfrak{R}_+$ be a vertex weight that represents the current weights of edges incident to v_0; that is, $b(v) = c_G(v_0, v)$ for $v \in V(G - v_0)$. By applying Corollary 6.8 to graph $G - v_0$, we have

$$\lambda(G) = \min\{d(v_0; G), \min\{d(X; G - v_0) + b(X) \mid X \in \mathcal{X}(G - v_0)\}\}. \qquad (6.2)$$

When the weight of an edge $\{v_0, v\}$ changes, the new $\lambda(G)$ can be obtained by recomputing $\min\{d(X; G - v_0) + b(X) \mid X \in \mathcal{X}(G - v_0)\}$ for the new b. For this, we only need to update the second terms of $d(X; G - v_0) + b(X)$ for all $X \in \mathcal{X}(G - v_0)$. (Note that we do not have to recompute family $\mathcal{X}(G - v_0)$ itself).

To facilitate the process, we maintain the laminar family $\mathcal{X} = \mathcal{X}(G - v_0) \cup \{V\}$ by its tree representation T (see Section 6.1). For each node $u = u_X$ in T (i.e., u corresponds to a cut $X \in \mathcal{X}$), we assign $cost(u)$, which is initialized by

$$cost(u) := d(X; G - v_0) + b(X) \text{ for } u = u_X, X \in \mathcal{X}(G - v_0), \qquad (6.3)$$

where $cost(r) = +\infty$ for the root r. For example, for the graph G in Fig. 6.5(a), the graph $G - v_0$ is already shown as Fig. 6.1 and its tree representation is shown in Fig. 6.2. The tree representation T initialized by the current edges $\{v_0, u_3\}$, $\{v_0, u_5\}$, $\{v_0, u_9\}$, and $\{v_0, u_{12}\}$ incident to v_0 is shown in Fig. 6.5(b). The number beside each node $u = u_X$ denotes $d(X; G - v_0) + b(X)$.

Relation (6.2) tells that the edge-connectivity of the current graph G after weight changes is the minimum of $d(v_0; G)$ and $cost(u)$ for all nodes u in T. An increase (resp. decrease) of the weight of an edge $\{v_0, v\}$ by $\Delta \geq 0$ changes $cost(u)$ of all $u = u_X$ with $v \in X$ to $cost(u) + \Delta$ (resp. $cost(u) - \Delta$). All nodes u whose $cost(u)$ needs to be changed per update lie on the path from the leaf $u_{\{v\}}$ to the root in T, where node $u_{\{v\}}$ corresponds to set $\{v\}$ in T. This idea can also be applied to obtain the tree representation for $\mathcal{X}(G - v_0) \cup \{V\}$ with initial b from that of $b = 0$, since it can be obtained by updating by $b(v)$ the $cost$ of all nodes u that are in the path from leaf $u_{\{v\}}$ corresponding to each edge $\{v_0, v\}$ to the root. $\square$

To consider a data structure for the preceding computation, let T be a rooted tree that has $cost(u)$ for each node u and define the following operations on T:

addcost(v, Δ): Add a real Δ to the costs of all nodes in the path from node v to the root.

findmin: Return the minimum $cost(u)$ over all nodes u in T and the node attaining the minimum.

A data structure supporting operation addcost is known; it can be executed in amortized $O(\log n)$ time per update [291] and in $O(\log n)$ time per update [22], where n is the number of nodes in T. Recently, it has been shown that findmin can also be executed in $O(\log n)$ time per update [4, 278]. Thus, we have the following result.

Lemma 6.10 ([4, 278]). *Let T be a rooted tree with n nodes. With $O(n \log n)$ preprocessing time, any operation of* addcost *or* findmin *to T can be executed in $O(\log n)$ time.*   □

This lemma implies Theorem 6.9. We first construct a tree representation $\mathcal{T}$ for $\mathcal{X} = \mathcal{X}(G - v_0) \cup \{V\}$ in $O(mn + n^2 \log n)$ time as a preprocess, where each node u has initial $cost(u)$ in (6.3). Whenever the weight of an edge $\{v_0, v\}$ incident to v_0 changes by a real number Δ, the costs of nodes in $\mathcal{T}$ can be updated in $O(\log n)$ time by using addcost($u_{\{v\}}, \Delta$), and the minimum $cost(u)$ in $\mathcal{T}$ together with the node $u = u_X$ attaining the minimum (and the corresponding extreme vertex set $X \in \mathcal{X}(G - v_0)$) can be reported in $O(\log n)$ time by using findmin. The value $d(v_0; G)$ can be updated in $O(1)$ time after each weight change. Therefore, we can compute $\lambda(G)$ of (6.2) as well as the minimum cut $\{X, V - X\}$ in $O(\log n)$ time per weight change. This proves Theorem 6.9.

6.3 Optimal Contraction Ordering

In this section, we consider the problem of finding an optimal order of contracting vertices by which the edge-connectivity of the graph increases as quickly as possible. The result will be used to solve the source location problem in Chapter 9. More precisely, we show the following result, where G/X denotes the graph G with all vertices in X being contracted into a single vertex.

Theorem 6.11 ([225]). *For a graph $G = (V, E)$ with $n \geq 2$ vertices and two disjoint subsets $A, B \subseteq V$, there exists an ordering $v_1, v_2, \ldots, v_p$ of the vertices in B ($p = |B|$) such that, for each $i = 1, 2, \ldots, p$, it holds that*

$$\lambda(G/(A \cup \{v_1, v_2, \ldots, v_i\})) \geq \lambda(G/(A \cup Y)) \text{ for all } Y \subseteq B \text{ with } |Y| = i.$$

Given a family of extreme vertex sets of G, it takes $O(n \log n)$ time to find such an ordering and to compute the edge-connectivities $\lambda(G/(A \cup \{v_1, v_2, \ldots, v_i\}))$ for all $i \in \{1, 2, \ldots, p\}$.   □

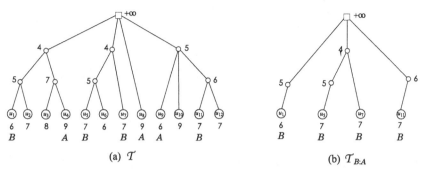

Figure 6.6. (a) Tree representation T for the family $\mathcal{X}(G_1)$ of extreme vertex sets in the graph G_1 in Fig. 6.1; (b) tree representation $T_{B:A}$ for $\mathcal{X}_{B:A} \cup \{V\}$ with $A = \{u_4, u_8, u_9\}$ and $B = \{u_1, u_5, u_7, u_{11}\}$.

We show the existence of such an ordering of B via a few observations, starting with the following.

Lemma 6.12. *Given a nonempty subset $Y \subset V$ in a graph G, let $G + b$ be the star augmentation such that $b(v) = +\infty$ for all $v \in Y$ and $b(v) = 0$ for all $v \in V - Y$. Then*

$$\lambda(G/Y) = \lambda(G + b).$$

Furthermore, given the family $\mathcal{X}(G)$ of extreme vertex sets of G, it holds that

$$\lambda(G/Y) = \min\{d(X; G) \mid X \in \mathcal{X}(G),\ X \cap Y = \emptyset\}. \qquad \square$$

Proof. For a minimum cut $\{Z, V(G/Y) - Z\}$ of the graph G/Y (where $Z \cap Y = \emptyset$ can be assumed without loss of generality), we have $\lambda(G/Y) = d(Z; G/Y) = d(Z; G + b) \geq \lambda(G + b)$. For a minimum cut $\{W, V(G + b) - W\}$ of the graph $G + b$ (where $W \cap (Y \cup \{s\}) = \emptyset$ can be assumed without loss of generality by assumption $d(s; G + b) = +\infty$), $\lambda(G + b) = d(W; G + b) = d(W; G/Y) \geq \lambda(G/Y)$. Hence, $\lambda(G/Y) = \lambda(G + b)$ holds. For the second half, recalling Corollary 6.8 and the definition of b, we have $\lambda(G + b) = \min\{d(X; G) + b(X) \mid X \in \mathcal{X}(G)\} = \min\{d(X; G) \mid X \in \mathcal{X}(G),\ X \cap Y = \emptyset\}. \qquad \square$

For disjoint subsets $A, B \subseteq V$, we define

$$\mathcal{X}_{B:A} = \{X \in \mathcal{X}(G) \mid X \subseteq V - A,\ X \cap B \neq \emptyset\},$$

and we let $T_{B:A}$ be the tree representation for $\mathcal{X}_{B:A} \cup \{V\}$. For each node u in $T_{B:A}$, let $cost(u)$ denote the cut size $d(X; G)$ of the corresponding subset X such that $u = u_X$, where $cost(u) = +\infty$ for the root $u = u_V$. For example, Fig. 6.6(a) (copied from Fig. 6.2) shows the tree representation T of extreme vertex sets in the graph G_1 in Fig. 6.1, and Figure 6.6(b) shows $T_{B:A}$ with $A = \{u_4, u_8, u_9\}$ and $B = \{u_1, u_5, u_7, u_{11}\}$.

Let Y be a nonempty subset of B. We say that Y *covers* a node u in $T_{B:A}$ if u is contained in the path from the root to a leaf node $u_{\{v\}}$ with some $v \in Y$. A node in

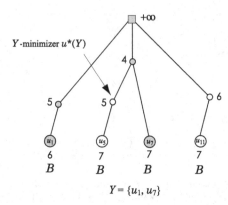

$$Y = \{u_1, u_7\}$$

Figure 6.7. Illustration of a Y-minimizer $u^*(Y)$ for $Y = \{u_1, u_7\}$ in $T_{B:A}$ of Fig. 6.6(b); the nodes covered by Y are shaded and the number beside each node indicates $cost$ of the node.

$T_{B:A}$ not covered by Y is called a *Y-minimizer* if it has the minimum $cost$ among all nodes not covered by Y. Note that there exists a Y-minimizer whose parent is covered by Y, since the cost of a node ($\neq$ root) is not larger than that of its child. For notational convenience, we denote by $u^*(Y)$ one of the Y-minimizers (although there may be more than one Y-minimizer), and we define the cost of a Y-minimizer to be $cost(u^*(Y))$. Figure 6.7 shows a Y-minimizer $u^*(Y)$ for $Y = \{u_1, u_7\}$ in $T_{B:A}$ of Fig. 6.6(b).

By Lemma 6.12, we have

$$\lambda(G/(A \cup Y)) = \min[\min\{d(X; G) \mid X \cap (A \cup B) = \emptyset, \ X \in \mathcal{X}(G)\},$$
$$\min\{d(X; G) \mid X \cap (A \cup Y) = \emptyset, \ X \cap B \neq \emptyset, \ X \in \mathcal{X}(G)\}]$$
$$= \min\{\lambda(G/(A \cup B)), \ cost(u^*(Y))\},$$

where $\lambda(G/(A \cup B)) = \min\{d(X; G) \mid X \cap (A \cup B) = \emptyset, \ X \in \mathcal{X}(G)\}$ is independent of the choice of Y. From this observation, the remaining task in the proof of Theorem 6.11 is to find an ordering $v_1, \ldots, v_p$ of B such that

$$cost(u^*(Y_i)) = \max\{cost(u^*(Y)) \mid Y \subseteq B, |Y| = i\}$$
$$\text{for each } Y_i = \{v_1, v_2, \ldots, v_i\}, 1 \le i \le p. \tag{6.4}$$

Such an ordering can be obtained by the following algorithm.

Algorithm TRAVERSE

Input: The tree representation $T_{B:A}$ of $\mathcal{X}_{B:A} \cup \{V\}$ with node costs $cost(u_X)$, $X \in \mathcal{X}_{B:A} \cup \{V\}$.

Output: An ordering $v_1, \ldots, v_p$ of B satisfying (6.4).

Initialize by setting $i := 1$ and $T_1 := T_{B:A}$;

for each $i = 1, 2, \ldots, p$ **do** /* determine the ith vertex $v_i \in B$ as follows */

   Traverse the rooted tree T_i from the root to a leaf node by choosing a child $u' \in Ch(u)$ with the minimum $cost(u')$ whenever we step downward from a node u;

Let leaf node $u_{\{v_i\}}$ in T_i be reached by this traversal;
Let T_{i+1} be the rooted tree obtained from T_i by contracting all the traversed
    nodes into a single node (as a new root)
end. /* for */

For example, we consider the graph G_1 in Fig. 6.1 with $A = \{u_4, u_8, u_9\}$ and
$B = \{u_1, u_5, u_7, u_{11}\}$, where $\lambda(G_1/(A \cup B)) = d(u_6; G_1) = 6$ holds. TRAVERSE is
then applied to $T_{B:A}$ in Fig. 6.6(b) and we compute a sequence of trees $T_1 (= T_{B:A})$,
T_2, T_3, and T_4 as shown in Fig. 6.8. Then TRAVERSE finds an ordering $(v_1 = u_5, v_2 =
u_1, v_3 = u_{11}, v_4 = u_7)$, for which subsets $Y_i = \{v_1, \ldots, v_i\}$, $i = 1, 2, \ldots, p = 4$,
satisfy $cost(u^*(Y_1)) = 5, cost(u^*(Y_2)) = 6, cost(u^*(Y_3)) = 7$, and $cost(u^*(Y_4)) =
+\infty$, and $\lambda(G_1/(A \cup Y_1)) = \min\{6, 5\} = 5$, $\lambda(G_1/(A \cup Y_2)) = \min\{6, 6\} = 6$,
$\lambda(G_1/(A \cup Y_3)) = \min\{6, 7\} = 6$, and $\lambda(G_1/(A \cup Y_4)) = \min\{6, +\infty\} = 6$.

Finally we prove the correctness of the resulting sets $Y_i = \{v_1, v_2, \ldots, v_i\}$
$(1 \le i \le p)$ by introducing a min-max formula. A subset AT of the nodes in $T_{B:A}$
is called an *antichain* if any path from the root to a leaf node contains exactly
one node from AT (see Fig. 6.9). Hence, any two nodes in an antichain AT are
incomparable; that is, neither of them is an ancestor of the other.

Let AT be an antichain in $T_{B:A}$ with $|AT| > i$, let Y be a subset of B with
$|Y| = i$, and let C be the set of nodes in AT covered by Y. Then $|C| \le i$ holds,
and

$$cost(u^*(Y)) \le \min\{cost(u) \mid u \in AT - C\} \le cost(u')$$

holds for the $(i + 1)$-st smallest nodes u' in AT. Therefore, we have the following
inequality:

$$\max_{Y \subseteq B, \, |Y|=i} cost(u^*(Y)) \le \min_{\text{antichains } AT} [\text{the } (i + 1)\text{-st smallest } cost \text{ in } AT].$$

For example, $AT = \{u_a, u_b, u_{v_2}, u_c, u_d, u_e\}$ in Fig. 6.9 is an antichain in which
the fourth smallest cost is 7, implying that, for any subset $Y \subseteq B$ with $|Y| = 3$,
$cost(u^*(Y))$ is at most 7. To prove that $cost(u^*(Y_i))$ is maximized over all subsets
$Y \subseteq B$ with $|Y| = i$, it then suffices to show that, for Y_i, there is an antichain AT_i
such that the preceding inequality holds by equality.

Claim 6.13. *For each Y_i, $i = 1, 2, \ldots, p$, obtained by* TRAVERSE, *there is an
antichain AT_i such that*

$$cost(u^*(Y_i)) = [\text{the } (i + 1)\text{-st smallest } cost \text{ in } AT_i]. \tag{6.5}$$
□

Proof. By induction on i, we prove that there is a pair of a Y_i-minimizer $u^*(Y_i)$
and an antichain AT_i such that, for the set C_i of the nodes in AT_i covered by Y_i,

$$u^*(Y_i) \in AT_i \text{ and } |C_i| = i, \tag{6.6}$$

$$cost(u') \le cost(u^*(Y_i)) \text{ holds for all nodes } u' \in C_i, \tag{6.7}$$

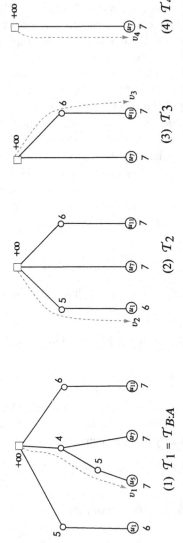

Figure 6.8. Illustration of TRAVERSE, computing tree representations $\mathcal{T}_1 = \mathcal{T}_{B:A}$ (see Fig. 6.6(b)), $\mathcal{T}_2$, $\mathcal{T}_3$, and $\mathcal{T}_4$ with $A = \{u_4, u_8, u_9\}$ and $B = \{u_1, u_5, u_7, u_{11}\}$, where TRAVERSE outputs an ordering $(v_1 = u_5, v_2 = u_1, v_3 = u_{11}, v_4 = u_7)$ of B.

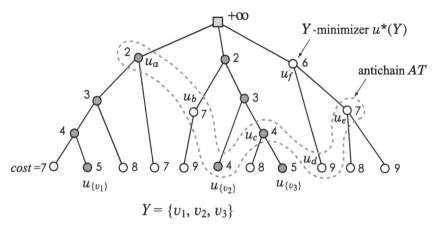

$$Y = \{v_1, v_2, v_3\}$$

Figure 6.9. Illustration of an antichain AT and a Y-minimizer $u^*(Y)$ for $Y = \{v_1, v_2, v_3\}$ in a rooted tree; the nodes covered by Y are depicted by shaded circles and the number beside each node indicates its *cost*.

where $cost(u^*(Y_i)) \le cost(u)$ holds for all nodes $u \in AT_i - C_i$ since $u^*(Y_i)$ is a Y_i-minimizer. Therefore, properties (6.6) and (6.7) imply (6.5).

For each Y_i, we construct a desired antichain AT_i as follows. Let C_i be a set of distinct i nodes $u_1', u_2', \ldots, u_i'$ such that each u_k' ($1 \le k \le i$) is covered by $\{v_k\}$ ($v_k \in Y_i$) but not covered by $Y_i - \{v_k\}$ (such i nodes can be chosen as will be explained later). Based on such C_i, let $U(C_i)$ denote the set of uncovered nodes u'' whose parent is a proper ancestor of some node in C_i. Observe that $AT_i = C_i \cup U(C_i)$ is an antichain with $|C_i| = i$. In Fig. 6.9, supposing that $Y_i = \{v_1, v_2, v_3\}$ has been constructed during TRAVERSE, we have a set $C_i = \{u_a, u_{\{v_2\}}, u_c\}$; then $U(C_i) = \{u_b, u_f\}$ and antichain $AT_i = C_i \cup U(C_i)$, where u_f is a Y_i-minimizer.

Now we show that a set C_i can be chosen for each Y_i such that the resulting antichain $AT_i = C_i \cup U(C_i)$ satisfies properties (6.6) and (6.7).

First consider the case of $i = 1$. Let $Y_1 = \{v_1\}$ be chosen by TRAVERSE and let $u^*(Y_1)$ be a Y_1-minimizer whose parent is covered by Y_1. Then there is a sibling u_a of $u^*(Y_1)$ that is covered by Y_1 (see Fig. 6.10(a)). We define $u_1' = u_a$ and $C_1 = \{u_1'\}$, which satisfies (6.6). The resulting antichain $AT_1 = C_1 \cup U(C_1)$ satisfies (6.7), since $cost(u_a) \le cost(u^*(Y_1))$ holds by the choice of u_a in T_1.

Let $j \ge 1$. Assuming that there is a set $C_j = \{u_1', u_2', \ldots, u_j'\}$ of j covered nodes such that $AT_j = C_j \cup U(C_j)$ is an antichain satisfying (6.6) and (6.7), we will construct a desired set C_{j+1} from the C_j.

Case 1: The $u_{\{v_{j+1}\}}$ chosen by TRAVERSE covers no node in $U(C_j)$; that is, all nodes in $U(C_j)$ remain uncovered by Y_{j+1}. In this case, a Y_j-minimizer $u^*(Y_j) \in U(C_j)$ is not covered by Y_{j+1} and is also a Y_{j+1}-minimizer $u^*(Y_{j+1})$.

Let u_a be the highest ancestor of $u_{\{v_{j+1}\}}$ in $T_{B:A}$ that is not covered by Y_j (see Fig. 6.10(b)). By the assumption of this case, u_a is a descendant of some node

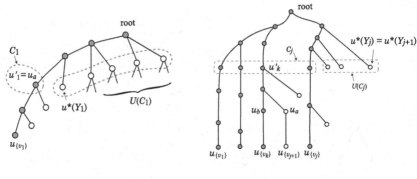

(a) antichain $AT_1 = C_1 \cup U(C_1)$ (b) antichain $AT_j = C_j \cup U(C_j)$

Figure 6.10. (a) Antichain $AT_1 = C_1 \cup U(C_1)$ for $i = 1$; (b) nodes u_a and u_b in the antichain $AT_j = C_j \cup U(C_j)$ in Case 1.

$u'_k \in C_j$; hence, there exists exactly one sibling u_b of u_a that has been covered by Y_j. We define $C_{j+1} = (C_j - u'_k) \cup \{u_a, u_b\}$, and we denote $C_{j+1} = \{u'_1, \ldots, u'_{j+1}\}$ by letting $u'_{j+1} := u_a$ and redefining $u'_k := u_b$. Let $AT_{j+1} = C_{j+1} \cup U(C_{j+1})$. Then (6.6) holds for Y_{j+1}, C_{j+1}, and AT_{j+1}.

For $u' \in C_{j+1} - \{u_a, u_b\} = C_j - \{u'_k\}$, we have $cost(u') \le cost(u^*(Y_j))$ by induction hypothesis. For $u' = u'_{j+1}(= u_a)$, we have $cost(u_a) \le cost(u^*(Y_j)) = cost(u^*(Y_{j+1}))$ since, in the $(j + 1)$-th iteration of TRAVERSE, both u_a and $u^*(Y_j)$ were children of the root of T_j and $u_a = u'_{j+1}$ was chosen as a child with the smallest cost. For $u' = u'_k(= u_b)$, we have $cost(u_b) \le cost(u_a) (\le cost(u^*(Y_j)))$ since u_a and u_b were siblings during construction of T_k and u_b was chosen before u_a. Therefore, (6.7) holds for Y_{j+1} and AT_{j+1}.

Case 2: The $u_{\{v_{j+1}\}}$ covers a node $u_a \in U(C_j)$. Since all nodes in $U(C_j)$ appear as children of the root of T_j, u_a is a Y_j-minimizer. This implies $cost(u_a) \le cost(u^*(Y_{j+1}))$. There are two subcases.

(a) A Y_{j+1}-minimizer $u^*(Y_{j+1})$ belongs to $U(C_j) - \{u_a\}$ (see Fig. 6.11(a)). Let $u'_{j+1} := u_a$ and $C_{j+1} = C_j \cup \{u'_{j+1}\}$. Then we have $U(C_{j+1}) = U(C_j) - \{u_a\}$, and (6.6) holds. By induction hypothesis, $cost(u') \le cost(u^*(Y_j)) = cost(u_a)$ holds for all $u' \in C_j$. Hence, $cost(u') \le cost(u_a) \le cost(u^*(Y_{j+1}))$ holds for all $u' \in C_{j+1} = C_j \cup \{u_a\}$, implying that $AT_{j+1} = C_{j+1} \cup U(C_{j+1})$ satisfies (6.7).

(b) No Y_{j+1}-minimizer belongs to $U(C_j) - \{u_a\}$. Let $u^*(Y_{j+1})$ be a Y_{j+1}-minimizer whose parent is covered by Y_{j+1}. Let u_b be the sibling of $u^*(Y_{j+1})$ that is covered by Y_{j+1} (see Fig. 6.11(b)). Let $u'_{j+1} := u_a$. There is a node $u'_k \in C_j \cup \{u'_{j+1}\}$ that is a proper ancestor of $u^*(Y_{j+1})$, where possibly $u'_k = u_a$. Redefine u'_k by $u'_k := u_b$ and let $C_{j+1} = \{u'_1, \ldots, u'_{j+1}\}$. Then $|C_{j+1}| = j + 1$, and $u^*(Y_{j+1}) \in U(C_{j+1})$ (since $u_b \in C_{j+1}$). Then (6.6) holds. By induction hypothesis, $cost(u') \le cost(u^*(Y_j)) \le cost(u^*(Y_{j+1}))$ holds for all $u' \in C_j$. For $u' = u_b$, we have $cost(u_b) \le cost(u^*(Y_{j+1}))$ since u_b and $u^*(Y_{j+1})$ were siblings during the construction of T_k. Therefore, for each $u' \in C_j \cup \{u_a, u_b\} \supseteq C_{j+1}$,

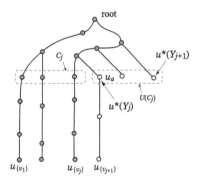

(a) antichain $AT_j = C_j \cup U(C_j)$ in Case-2(a)

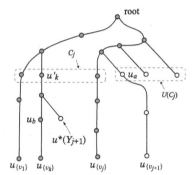

(b) antichain $AT_j = C_j \cup U(C_j)$ in Case-2(b)

Figure 6.11. (a) Node $u_a \in U(C_j)$ in an antichain $AT_j = C_j \cup U(C_j)$ in Case 2, subcase (a); (b) node u_b for an antichain $AT_j = C_j \cup U(C_j)$ in Case 2, subcase (b).

$cost(u') \leq cost(u^*(Y_{j+1}))$ holds, implying that $AT_{j+1} = C_{j+1} \cup U(C_{j+1})$ satisfies (6.7).

This completes the induction proof of Claim 6.13. □

We finally consider the running time of TRAVERSE. It suffices to show that, for each u in T_i, a child in $Ch(u)$ with the minimum $cost$ can be found in $O(\log n)$ time. For this, we maintain $Ch(u)$ by a priority queue such as a Fibonacci heap. By contracting a path in T_i to obtain T_{i+1}, we need to merge the priority queues of the nodes in the path. The total number of times that two child sets are merged during TRAVERSE is $O(n)$. Since Fibonacci heaps for two sets can be merged in $O(\log n)$ amortized time [91], the entire time for computing an ordering is $O(n \log n)$. This proves Theorem 6.11.

6.4 Minimum k-Subpartition Problem

This section gives another application of extreme vertex sets. Given an edge-weighted graph $G = (V, E)$, a subset $S \subseteq V$, an integer $k \geq 1$, and a real $b \geq 0$, the minimum subpartition problem asks to find a family of k nonempty disjoint subsets $X_1, X_2, \ldots, X_k \subseteq S$ with $d(X_i) \leq b$, $1 \leq i \leq k$, which minimizes $\sum_{1 \leq i \leq k} d(X_i)$, where $d(X)$ denotes the total weight of edges between X and $V - X$. In this section, we show that the minimum subpartition problem can be solved in $O(mn + n^2 \log n)$ time by using extreme vertex sets. The result is then applied to the minimum k-way cut problem and the graph strength problem, for which we obtain $O(mn + n^2 \log n)$ time 2-approximation algorithms.

6.4.1 Properties of Minimum (k, b)-Subpartitions

Let $G = (V, E)$ be a simple undirected graph with a vertex set V and an edge set E such that each edge e is weighted by a nonnegative real $w(e)$. For a subset $F \subseteq E$, we denote $\sum_{e \in F} w(e)$ by $w(F)$. A *k-partition* S of a subset $S \subseteq V$ is a family of k disjoint nonempty subsets of S such that $\cup_{X \in S} X = S$ holds. A *k-subpartition* S of a subset $S \subseteq V$ consists of k disjoint nonempty subsets of S and is called *proper* if $\cup_{X \in S} X$ is a proper subset of S.

Given a real $b \geq 0$, a k-subpartition (resp. k-partition) S of a subset $S \subseteq V$ is called a (k, b)-subpartition (resp. (k, b)-partition) if $d(X) \leq b$ for all $X \in S$. A *minimum* (k, b)-*subpartition* S minimizes $cost(S) := \sum_{X \in S} d(X)$. In this section, we consider the problem of computing a minimum (k, b)-subpartition and prove the next result.

Theorem 6.14. *Given an edge-weighted graph $G = (V, E)$, a subset $S \subseteq V$, and a real $b \geq 0$, a minimum (proper) (k, b)-subpartition of S (if any) for all $k \in [1, |S|]$ can be obtained in $O(mn + n^2 \log n)$ time, where $n = |V|$ and $m = |E|$.* □

Let $\mathcal{X} \subseteq 2^S$ be a laminar family of subsets of a subset $S \subseteq V$. As discussed in Sections 1.1.7 and 6.1, a laminar family can be represented by a rooted tree T, and $|\mathcal{X}| \leq 2|S| - 1$ holds. Based on such representation, we then show that $2|S| - 1 - |\mathcal{X}|$ new subsets of S can be added to $\mathcal{X}$ so that the resulting family $\mathcal{X} \cup \mathcal{X}'$ remains laminar, where $\mathcal{X}'$ denotes the set of added subsets. We first add all trivial sets $\{v\} \notin \mathcal{X}$, and then we consider the tree representation T' of the resulting laminar family $\mathcal{X} \cup \{\{v\} \notin \mathcal{X}\}$. We transform T' into a binary rooted tree T by inserting $2|S| - 1 - |\mathcal{X} \cup \{\{v\} \notin \mathcal{X}\}|$ new nodes, where each new node constitutes a new subset in $\mathcal{X}'$. We call such a binary tree T *consistent with S and $\mathcal{X}$*. As an example, consider a graph G_1 and its family $\mathcal{X}(G_1)$ of extreme vertex sets as shown in Fig. 6.1. Its tree presentation is given in Fig. 6.2. From this, we have the following binary tree consistent with $S = V$ (see Fig. 6.12):

$$\mathcal{X} = \{X_i \mid i = 1, 2, \ldots, 23\},$$
$$X_i = \{u_i\}, i = 1, 2, \ldots, 12,$$
$$X_{13} = \{u_1, u_2\}, X_{14} = \{u_3, u_4\}, X_{15} = \{u_5, u_6\}, X_{16} = \{u_9, u_{10}\},$$
$$X_{17} = \{u_{11}, u_{12}\}, X_{18} = X_{15} \cup \{u_7\}, X_{19} = X_{13} \cup X_{14}, X_{20} = X_{18} \cup \{u_8\},$$
$$X_{21} = X_{16} \cup X_{17}, X_{22} = X_{20} \cup X_{21}, X_{23} = X_{19} \cup X_{22} = V,$$

where extreme vertex sets of G_1 (indicated by circles in Fig.6.12) are given by

$$\mathcal{X}(G_1) = \{X_i \mid i \in \{1, 2, \ldots, 12\} \cup \{13, 14, 15, 17, 19, 21\}\},$$

and additional sets to form a binary tree are given by

$$\mathcal{X}' = \{X_i \mid i \in \{16, 20, 22, 23\}\}.$$

For a subset $S \subseteq V$ and a real $b \geq 0$, we denote by $\mathcal{X}_S(G)$ (resp. $\mathcal{X}_{S,b}(G)$) the family of all extreme vertex sets $X \in \mathcal{X}(G)$ with $X \subseteq S$ (resp. $X \subseteq S$ and $d(X) \leq b$).

Lemma 6.15. *Given an edge-weighted graph G, a subset $S \subseteq V$, an integer $k \geq 1$, and a real $b \geq 0$, if there is a minimum (proper) (k, b)-subpartition S of S, then there is such a subpartition that consists only of extreme vertex subsets in $\mathcal{X}_{S,b}(G)$.* □

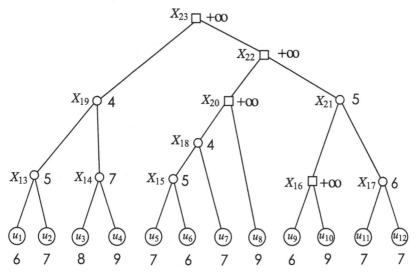

Figure 6.12. A binary tree representation $\mathcal{T} = (\mathcal{X}(G_1) \cup \mathcal{X}', \mathcal{E})$ consistent with $\mathcal{X}(G_1)$.

Proof. Let $\mathcal{S} = \{X_1, \ldots, X_k\}$ be a minimum (k, b)-subpartition of S; the case where $\mathcal{S}$ is proper can be treated analogously. We assume without loss of generality that $\mathcal{S}$ minimizes $\sum_{1 \le i \le k} |X_i|$ among all minimum (k, b)-subpartitions of S. Since $d(X_i) \le b$ by definition, it suffices to show that each X_i is an extreme vertex set. If X_i contains a subset Y with $d(Y) \le d(X_i)$, then $(\mathcal{S} - \{X_i\}) \cup \{Y\}$ remains a minimum (k, b)-subpartition of S, which, however, contradicts the minimality of $\sum_{1 \le i \le k} |X_i|$. Therefore, each X_i is an extreme vertex set, and $\mathcal{S}$ consists of subsets in $\mathcal{X}_{S,b}(G)$. □

We remark that considering a subpartition in the lemma is crucial since a graph G may not have a k-partition of V that consists of extreme vertex subsets. Moreover, even if G has a k-partition of V that consists of extreme vertex subsets, a minimum k-partition may not be such a family of k extreme vertex subsets. For example, consider graph G_0 in Fig. 6.13. Observe that G has two nontrivial extreme vertex sets $\{v_1, v_2\}$ and $\{v_3, v_4, v_5\}$ and five trivial extreme vertex sets $\{v_i\}$, $1 \le i \le 5$. For $k = 3$, $\mathcal{S} = \{\{v_1\}, \{v_2\}, \{v_3, v_4, v_5\}\}$ with $cost(\mathcal{S}) = 14$ is a 3-partition of V that consists of extreme vertex subsets. However, a minimum 3-partition of G is given by $\mathcal{S}^* = \{\{v_1, v_2, v_3\}, \{v_4\}, \{v_5\}\}$ with $cost(\mathcal{S}^*) = 12$. Note that G_0 has a minimum 3-subpartition $\mathcal{S}' = \{\{v_1, v_2\}, \{v_4\}, \{v_5\}\}$ with $cost(\mathcal{S}') = 10$ consisting of extreme vertex sets.

6.4.2 Algorithm for Minimum (k, b)-Subpartitions

This section gives an algorithm for computing a minimum (k, b)-subpartition, which will be modified in the next section to find a minimum proper (k, b)-subpartition.

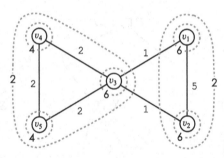

Figure 6.13. A graph G_0 and all extreme vertex sets in G_0, where the numbers beside edges indicate their weights and each extreme vertex set X is depicted by a dotted closed curve with a number that indicates the cut size $d(X; G_0)$.

We first compute the family $\mathcal{X}(G)$ of all extreme vertex sets in G via the EXTREME algorithm of Section 6.1. This can be done in $O(mn + n^2 \log n)$ time by Theorem 6.6. We then obtain $\mathcal{X}_S(G)$ from $\mathcal{X}(G)$, and we construct a binary tree $\mathcal{T} = (V = \mathcal{X}_S(G) \cup \mathcal{X}', \mathcal{E})$ consistent with S and $\mathcal{X}_S(G)$. (Actually the EXTREME algorithm, without executing line 7, outputs such a binary tree in the same time complexity.)

Let $opt(X, k)$ denote the minimum cost of a (k, b)-subpartition of a subset X, where we define $opt(X, 0) = 0$ and $opt(X, k) = +\infty$ for all k such that G has no (k, b)-subpartition of X. We now compute all $opt(X, k)$, $k \in [1, |X|]$, $X \in V$ by dynamic programming as follows.

The set of leaves in $\mathcal{T}$ consists of trivial sets $\{u\}$, $u \in S$. For each leaf $X = \{u\} \in \mathcal{X}_S(G)$, we have

$$opt(X, 1) = \begin{cases} d(\{u\}) & \text{if } d(\{u\}) \le b, \\ +\infty & \text{if } d(\{u\}) > b. \end{cases} \tag{6.8}$$

Consider a nonleaf $X \in V$ and let Y_1 and Y_2 be the two children of X in $\mathcal{T}$, where it holds that

$$\mathcal{X}_{X,b}(G) - \{X\} = \mathcal{X}_{Y_1,b}(G) \cup \mathcal{X}_{Y_2,b}(G) \text{ and } \mathcal{X}_{Y_1,b}(G) \cap \mathcal{X}_{Y_2,b}(G) = \emptyset. \tag{6.9}$$

By Lemma 6.15, there is a minimum (k, b)-subpartition of X (if any) which consists of subsets in $\mathcal{X}_{X,b}(G)$. Hence, by (6.9) we see that, for each $k \in [2, |X|]$, there is an integer $i \in [0, k]$ such that $opt(X, k) = opt(Y_1, i) + opt(Y_2, k - i)$. Thus, it holds that

$$opt(X, k) = \min_{0 \le i \le k} \{opt(Y_1, i) + opt(Y_2, k - i)\}. \tag{6.10}$$

For $k = 1$, we have

$$opt(X, 1) = \begin{cases} d(X) & \text{if } X \in \mathcal{X}_{S,b}(G), \\ \min\{opt(Y_1, 1), opt(Y_2, 1)\} & \text{if } X \notin \mathcal{X}_{S,b}(G), \end{cases} \tag{6.11}$$

since $d(Y) > d(X)$ holds for all proper subsets Y of $X \in \mathcal{X}(G)$.

Algorithm SUBPARTITION(S, b)
Input: A binary tree $\mathcal{T} = (\mathcal{V} = \mathcal{X}_S(G) \cup \mathcal{X}', \mathcal{E})$ consistent with S and $\mathcal{X}_S(G)$,
  and a real $b \geq 0$.
Output: $\{opt(X, k) \mid 1 \leq k \leq |X|\}$ for all nodes $X \in \mathcal{V}$.
  For each leaf $X = \{u\} \in \mathcal{X}_S(G)$, compute $opt(X, 1)$ according to (6.8);
  while there is an unprocessed node in $\mathcal{T}$ **do**
    Choose a lowest unprocessed node X, and compute $opt(X, 1)$ and
      $\{opt(X, k) \mid 2 \leq k \leq |X|\}$ according to (6.11) and (6.10), respectively
  end. /* while */

Then the dynamic programming recursion of SUBPARTITION(S, b) for the preceding example (see Fig. 6.12) proceeds as follows, where we set $S = V$ and
$b = +\infty$ and each cell in the table indicates $opt(X_i, k)$, $i = 1, 2, \ldots, 23$ and
$k = 1, 2, \ldots, 12$, and each empty cell implies that the corresponding $opt(X_i, k)$
is $+\infty$.

$k =$	1	2	3	4	5	6	7	8	9	10	11	12
X_1	6											
X_2	7											
X_3	8											
X_4	9											
X_5	7											
X_6	6											
X_7	7											
X_8	9											
X_9	6											
X_{10}	9											
X_{11}	7											
X_{12}	7											
X_{13}	5	13										
X_{14}	7	17										
X_{15}	5	13										
X_{16}	6	15										
X_{17}	6	14										
X_{18}	4	12	20									
X_{19}	4	12	20	30								
X_{20}	4	12	20	29								
X_{21}	5	12	20	29								
X_{22}	4	9	16	24	33	40	49	59				
X_{23}	4	8	13	20	28	36	44	52	60	69	79	89

For example, for $k = 5$, a minimum 5-subpartition of V has total weight
$opt(X_{23}, 5) = 28$, and the corresponding subpartition is $\{X_9, X_{11}, X_{12}, X_{18}, X_{19}\}$.
Such a subpartition can be retrieved from the process of computing $opt(X, k)$
as follows. Whenever we compute $opt(X, k)$ according to (6.10), we store

$i_{(X,k)} = i \in [0, k]$ that attains the minimum. After computing $opt(X, k)$ (<0), we can construct a minimum k-subpartition $\mathcal{S}_k$ of X by checking the index $i = i_{(X,k)}$; $\mathcal{S}_k$ consists of a minimum i-subpartition $\mathcal{S}_i$ of Y_1 and a minimum $(k - i)$-subpartition $\mathcal{S}_{k-i}$ of Y_2, where Y_1 and Y_2 are the children of X. These subpartitions $\mathcal{S}_i$ and $\mathcal{S}_{k-i}$ can also be identified recursively.

The time complexity of the SUBPARTITION algorithm is analyzed as follows. Note that the combination $opt(Y_1, i_1) + opt(Y_2, i_2)$ with fixed i_1 and i_2 appears exactly once in (6.10) with $0 \leq k \leq |X|$. This implies that $\{opt(X, k) \mid 1 \leq k \leq |X|\}$ can be computed in $O(|Y_1||Y_2|)$ time if $\{opt(Y_j, k) \mid 1 \leq k \leq |Y_j|\}$, $j = 1, 2$ is already available.

Lemma 6.16 ([245]). *Given a binary tree $\mathcal{T} = (\mathcal{V}, \mathcal{E})$ consistent with S and $\mathcal{X}_S(G)$ and a real $b \geq 0$, we can compute $\{opt(X, k) \mid 1 \leq k \leq |X|\}$ for all nodes $X \in \mathcal{V}$ in $O(|S|^2)$ time.* □

Proof. Let $t(n)$ denote the time required to compute $\{opt(X, k) \mid 1 \leq k \leq |X|\}$ for a subset X with $|X| = n$. Choose a constant c such that $t(1) \leq c$ and $\{opt(X, k) \mid 1 \leq k \leq |X|\}$ can be computed in at most $2c|Y_1||Y_2|$ time from $\{opt(Y_j, k) \mid 1 \leq k \leq |Y_j|\}$, $j = 1, 2$, where Y_1 and Y_2 are the children of X in $\mathcal{T}$. We show that $t(n) \leq cn^2$ holds. For $n = 1$, this is trivial. Assuming that $t(\hat{n}) \leq c\hat{n}^2$ holds and $\hat{n} \in [1, n - 1]$, we prove $t(n) \leq cn^2$. Consider a nonleaf $X \in \mathcal{V}$ and its two children Y_1 and Y_2 of X in $\mathcal{T}$. Let $n = |X|$, $n_1 = |Y_1|$, and $n_2 = |Y_2|$, where $n = n_1 + n_2$. Then by induction hypothesis, we have

$$t(n) \leq t(n_1) + t(n_2) + 2cn_1n_2 \leq cn_1^2 + cn_2^2 + 2cn_1n_2 = cn^2.$$

This proves the lemma.   □

If $opt(S, k) = +\infty$ holds for some $k \in [1, |S|]$, then S has no (k, b)-subpartition. Otherwise, as explained earlier, a minimum (k, b)-subpartition of S can be obtained by retrieving the integers i that attain the minimum in the recursive formula, which takes $O(|S|)$ time. This establishes the result on minimum (k, b)-subpartitions in Theorem 6.14.

6.4.3 Algorithm for Proper Minimum (k, b)-Subpartitions

Let $\alpha(X, k)$ denote the minimum cost of a family $\mathcal{S}$ of k disjoint extreme vertex sets in $\mathcal{X}_{X,b}(G)$ such that $\cup_{Z \in \mathcal{S}} Z = X$ (i.e., $\mathcal{S}$ is a (k, b)-partition of X by extreme vertex sets), where $\alpha(X, 0) = 0$ and $\alpha(X, k) = +\infty$ for all k such that G has no such family $\mathcal{S}$. Let $\beta(X, k)$ denote the minimum cost of a family $\mathcal{S}$ of k disjoint extreme vertex sets in $\mathcal{X}_{X,b}(G)$ such that $\cup_{Z \in \mathcal{S}} Z \subset X$ (i.e., $\mathcal{S}$ is a proper (k, b)-subpartition of X by extreme vertex sets), where $\beta(X, 0) = 0$ and $\beta(X, k) = +\infty$ for all k such that G has no such family $\mathcal{S}$. By Lemma 6.15, $\beta(X, k)$ gives the cost of a minimum *proper* (k, b)-subpartition of X. By definition, we observe that $opt(X, k) = \min\{\alpha(X, k), \beta(X, k)\}$ holds.

Now we show that $\alpha(X, k)$ and $\beta(X, k)$ together can be computed for all $k \in [1, |X|]$ and $X \in V$ in a similar manner to SUBPARTITION. Because $\beta(X, k)$ gives the minimum cost of proper (k, b)-subpartition of X, this is considered as a proof of Theorem 6.14 for the proper subpartition version.

Let T be a binary tree consistent with S and $\mathcal{X}_S(G)$. For a nonleaf $X \in \mathcal{X}_{S,b}(G)$, let Y_1 and Y_2 be the children of X in T. Note that, for $k \geq 2$, a (k, b)-partition of X that consists of extreme vertex sets in $\mathcal{X}_{S,b}(G)$ is achieved by an (i, b)-partition of Y_1 and a $(k - i, b)$-partition of Y_2, both of which consist of extreme vertex sets in $\mathcal{X}_{S,b}(G)$. Also observe that a proper (k, b)-subpartition of $X \in \mathcal{X}_{S,b}(G)$ is achieved by an (i, b)-subpartition of Y_1 and a $(k - i, b)$-subpartition of Y_2, one of which is proper. From these observations, we obtain the following algorithm, which computes all $\alpha(X, k)$ and $\beta(X, k)$.

Algorithm PROPERSUBPARTITION(S, b)
Input: A binary tree $T = (V = \mathcal{X}_S(G) \cup \mathcal{X}', \mathcal{E})$ consistent with S and $\mathcal{X}_S(G)$, and a real $b \geq 0$.
Output: $\{\alpha(X, k), \beta(X, k) \mid 1 \leq k \leq |X|\}$ for all nodes $X \in V$.
For each leaf $X = \{u\} \in \mathcal{X}_S(G)$, compute
$$\alpha(X, 1) := \begin{cases} d(\{u\}) & \text{if } d(\{u\}) \leq b, \\ +\infty & \text{if } d(\{u\}) > b; \end{cases}$$
$\beta(X, 1) := +\infty$;
while there is unprocessed node in T **do**
Choose a lowest unprocessed node X;
$$\alpha(X, 1) := \begin{cases} d(X) & \text{if } X \in \mathcal{X}_{S,b}(G), \\ +\infty & \text{otherwise}, \end{cases}$$
$\beta(X, 1) := \min\{\alpha(Y_1, 1), \beta(Y_1, 1), \alpha(Y_2, 1), \beta(Y_2, 1)\}$;
For each $k = 2, 3, \ldots, |X|$, compute
$\alpha(X, k) := \min_{1 \leq i \leq k-1}\{\alpha(Y_1, i) + \alpha(Y_2, k - i)\}$;
$\beta(X, k) := \min_{0 \leq i \leq k}\{\alpha(Y_1, i) + \beta(Y_2, k - i), \beta(Y_1, i) + \alpha(Y_2, k - i),$
$\qquad\qquad\qquad \beta(Y_1, i) + \beta(Y_2, k - i)\}$
end. /* while */

Analogously with the analysis of SUBPARTITION, we see that the PROPER-SUBPARTITION algorithm runs in $O(|S|^2)$ time. Also, for each $k \in [1, |S|]$ with $\beta(S, k) < +\infty$, a minimum proper (k, b)-subpartition of S can be obtained in $O(|S|)$ time. This establishes the result for the minimum proper (k, b)-subpartitions in Theorem 6.14.

6.4.4 Minimum k-Way Cut

We apply the fact that the minimum subpartition problem can be solved efficiently to obtain an approximation algorithm for computing a minimum k-way cut in a given graph, where $k \geq 2$ is assumed. For an edge-weighted graph $G = (V, E)$, a subset F of edges is called a *k-way cut* if removal of F from G results in at least

k connected components. We denote by $\mu(G, k)$ the cost of a minimum k-way cut of G.

We easily see that there is a minimum k-way cut F which is given by $\cup_{1 \leq i < j \leq k} E(V_i, V_j)$ for some k-partition $\{V_1, V_2, \ldots, V_k\}$ of V. Thus, the minimum k-way cut problem asks to find a k-partition $\mathcal{Z} = \{V_1, V_2, \ldots, V_k\}$ of V that minimizes $cost(\mathcal{Z}) = \sum_{V_i \in \mathcal{Z}} d(V_i)$. Goldschmidt and Hochbaum [106] proved that the problem is NP-hard if k is an input parameter, and they presented an $O(n^{k^2/2 - 3k/2 + 4} F(n, m))$ time algorithm, where $F(n, m)$ denotes a time bound of a maximum-flow algorithm in an edge-weighted graph with n vertices and m edges. Recently the time bound was improved to $O(n^{4k/(1 - 1.71/\sqrt{k}) - 31})$ by Kamidoi et al. [166]. Karger and Stein [182] proposed a Monte Carlo algorithm with time bound of $O(n^{2(k-1)} \log^3 n)$.

Several 2-approximation algorithms for the minimum k-way cut problem have been proposed. Saran and Vazirani [287] first proposed a $2(1 - 1/k)$-approximation algorithm that successively finds minimum cuts until the graph is partitioned into k components and runs in $O(mn^2 \log(n^2/m))$ time. Kapoor [173] gave an $O(k(nm + n^2 \log n))$ time $2(1 - 1/k)$-approximation algorithm. Zhao et al. [315] presented an $O(kmn^3 \log(n^2/m))$ time approximation algorithm that has a performance ratio of $2 - 3/k$ for an odd value of k and $2 - (3k - 4)/(k^2 - k)$ for an even value of k. Naor and Rabani [260] had a 2-approximation algorithm based on an LP relaxation of the minimum k-way cut. Ravi and Sinha [282] gave a 2-approximation algorithm based on an algorithm for computing the strength of graphs.

Based on Theorem 6.14, here we give two new and faster $2(1 - 1/k)$-approximation algorithms for the minimum k-way cut problem. Let $\mathcal{S}_k^* = \{V_i^* \mid i = 1, 2, \ldots, k\}$ denote a minimum k-partition of V, where $d(V_k^*) = \max_{1 \leq i \leq k} d(V_i^*)$ is assumed without loss of generality. Let $cost(\mathcal{S}_k^*) = \sum_{1 \leq i \leq k} d(V_i^*)$. Note that $cost(\mathcal{S}_k^*) = 2\mu(G, k)$ and $d(V_k^*) \geq 2\mu(G, k)/k$ hold.

The first algorithm, called APPROX1, computes a minimum k-subpartition $\mathcal{S}_k$ of V. Let $cost(\mathcal{S}_k) = \sum_{Y \subset \mathcal{S}_k} d(Y)$. If $\mathcal{S}_k$ is a k-partition, then we output edge set $F = \cup_{Y, Y' \in \mathcal{S}_k} E(Y, Y')$ as a minimum k-way cut. Otherwise (i.e., if it is a proper k-subpartition of V), we choose a subset $X \in \mathcal{S}_k$ with a maximum $d(X)$, and we let $F_1 = \cup_{Y, Y' \in \mathcal{S}_k - \{X\}} E(Y, Y')$ and $F_2 = E(S', V - S')$ for $S' = \cup_{Y \in \mathcal{S}_k - \{X\}} Y$. Then we output edge set $F = F_1 \cup F_2$ as a k-way cut.

Lemma 6.17 ([245]). *Let $\mathcal{S}_k$ be a minimum k-subpartition of V and let F be an edge set output by* APPROX1. *Then*

$$\mu(G, k) \geq \frac{1}{2} cost(\mathcal{S}_k) \tag{6.12}$$

and

$$w(F) \leq 2\left(1 - \frac{1}{k}\right)\left[\frac{1}{2} cost(\mathcal{S}_k)\right] \leq 2\left(1 - \frac{1}{k}\right) \mu(G, k). \tag{6.13}$$

$\square$

Proof. Since any k-partition of V is a k-subpartition of V, we have

$$cost(\mathcal{S}_k) \leq cost(\mathcal{S}_k^*) = 2\mu(G, k),$$

proving (6.12). If $\mathcal{S}_k$ is a k-partition of V, then $F = \cup_{Y,Y' \in \mathcal{S}_k} E(Y, Y')$ satisfies $w(F) = cost(\mathcal{S}_k)/2 \leq \mu(G, k)$ and is a minimum k-way cut, where (6.13) holds since $w(F) = cost(\mathcal{S}_k)/2 \leq \mu(G, k) \leq 2(1 - 1/k)\mu(G, k)$ for $k \geq 2$. Otherwise, $F = F_1 \cup F_2$ satisfies

$$w(F) \leq cost(\mathcal{S}_k) - d(X) - w(F_1) \leq \left(1 - \frac{1}{k}\right) cost(\mathcal{S}_k) \leq 2\left(1 - \frac{1}{k}\right)\mu(G, k),$$

proving (6.13). □

The second algorithm, called APPROX2, computes a minimum proper $(k-1)$-subpartition $\mathcal{S}_{k-1}$ of V and lets $F_1 = \cup_{Y,Y' \in \mathcal{S}_{k-1}} E(Y, Y')$ and $F_2 = E(S', V - S')$ for $S' = \cup_{Y \in \mathcal{S}_{k-1}} Y$. Then it outputs edge set $F = F_1 \cup F_2$ as a k-way cut.

Lemma 6.18 ([245]). *Let $\mathcal{S}_{k-1}$ be a minimum proper $(k-1)$-subpartition S of V, and F be an edge set output by* APPROX2. *Then*

$$\mu(G, k) \geq \frac{k}{2(k-1)} cost(\mathcal{S}_{k-1}), \tag{6.14}$$

and

$$w(F) \leq 2\left(1 - \frac{1}{k}\right)\left[\frac{k}{2(k-1)} cost(\mathcal{S}_{k-1})\right] \leq 2\left(1 - \frac{1}{k}\right)\mu(G, k). \tag{6.15}$$
□

Proof. Let $\mathcal{S}_k^*$ be defined as before. Since $\{V_i^* \mid 1 \leq i \leq k-1\}$ in $\mathcal{S}_k^*$ is a proper $(k-1)$-subpartition of V, we have

$$cost(\mathcal{S}_{k-1}) \leq 2\mu(G, k) - d(V_k^*) \leq \frac{2(k-1)}{k}\mu(G, k),$$

proving (6.14). From this, we have

$$w(F) \leq cost(\mathcal{S}_{k-1}) = 2\left(1 - \frac{1}{k}\right)\left[\frac{k}{2(k-1)} cost(\mathcal{S}_{k-1})\right] \leq 2\left(1 - \frac{1}{k}\right)\mu(G, k),$$

proving (6.13). □

Unlike the $2(1 - 1/k)$-algorithms in the literature [173, 287, 315], excluding the 2-approximation algorithms [260, 282], we can also obtain lower bounds (6.12) and (6.14) on $\mu(G, k)$. Hence, if the ratio of the cost $w(F)$ of an approximate solution F to these lower bounds is smaller than the worst-case ratio $2(1 - 1/k)$, then we can derive a better ratio.

Since minimum k-subpartitions and minimum proper k-subpartitions for all $k \in [2, n]$ can be obtained in $O(mn + n^2 \log n)$ time by Theorem 6.14 with $b = +\infty$, we have the following result.

Theorem 6.19 ([245]). *Given an edge-weighted graph $G = (V, E)$, $2(1 - 1/k)$-approximate solutions to the minimum k-way cut problem for all $k \in [2, n]$ can be obtained in $O(mn + n^2 \log n)$ time.*   □

6.4.5 Graph Strength

Based on the preceding result, we now give an approximation algorithm for computing the strength of a graph. Given an edge-weighted graph $G = (V, E)$, the *strength* $\sigma(G)$ of G was introduced by Gusfield [109] and Cunningham [49] as a measure of network invulnerability, which is defined as

$$\sigma(G) = \min\left\{ \frac{w(F)}{c(G-F) - 1} \mid F \subseteq E,\ c(G-F) \geq 2 \right\},$$

where $c(G - F)$ denotes the number of connected components in the graph $G - F$ obtained from G by deleting the edges in F. In other words, $\sigma(G) = \min_{2 \leq k \leq n} \mu(G, k)/(k-1) = \mu(G, k^*)/(k^* - 1)$ for some k^*. The strength $\sigma(G)$ can be found in $O(mn^2(m + n \log n))$ time [49].

We can compute 2-approximate solutions F'_k for the minimum k-way cut problem for all $k \in [2, n]$ in $O(mn + n^2 \log n)$ time by Theorem 6.19. We choose a solution F'_k that minimizes $w(F'_k)/(k-1)$ among $F'_2, F'_3, \ldots, F'_n$. Then we see by Theorem 6.19 that

$$w(F'_k)/(k-1) \leq w(F'_{k^*})/(k^* - 1) \leq 2w(F_{k^*})/(k^* - 1) = 2\sigma(G),$$

where k^* was defined earlier. Hence, we have the next result.

Theorem 6.20 ([245]). *Given an edge-weighted graph $G = (V, E)$, a partition $\mathcal{S}$ of V such that $\sigma(G) \leq cost(\mathcal{S})/(|\mathcal{S}| - 1) \leq 2\sigma(G)$ can be determined in $O(mn + n^2 \log n)$ time.*   □

7

Edge Splitting

In this chapter we discuss edge splitting, which is a proof technique that detaches a pair of adjacent edges at a vertex while preserving the vertex/edge-connectivity, and it is used to solve many graph connectivity problems, such as the graph orientation problem and the connectivity augmentation problem.

After giving a brief preparation in Section 7.1, we show in Sections 7.2 and 7.3 $O(nm + n^2 \log n)$ time edge-splitting algorithms for weighted graphs and unweighted multigraphs, respectively. In Section 7.4, we describe the results of edge-splitting problems for local edge connectivity and for edge connectivity in digraphs. In Section 7.4.3, we give results for edge splitting with various additional constraints. In Section 7.5, we briefly review the recent results on detachments, an extended operation of edge splitting. In Section 7.6, we mention some applications of edge splitting.

7.1 Preliminaries

7.1.1 Splitting in Multigraphs

Let H be a multigraph and let $s \in V(H)$ be a *designated vertex* in H. Given vertices $u, v \in \Gamma_H(s)$ adjacent to s (possibly $u = v$) and a nonnegative integer $\delta \in [0, \min\{c_H(s, u), c_H(s, v)\}]$, let us consider the graph H' constructed from H by deleting δ edges from $E(s, u; H)$ and $E(s, v; H)$, respectively, and adding new δ edges to $E(u, v; H)$:

$$c_{H'}(e) = \begin{cases} c_H(e) - \delta & \text{if } e \in \{\{s, u\}, \{s, v\}\} \\ c_H(e) + \delta & \text{if } e = \{u, v\} \\ c_H(e) & \text{if } e \in E(H) - \{\{s, u\}, \{s, v\}, \{u, v\}\}, \end{cases} \tag{7.1}$$

where we create a new edge $\{u, v\}$ in H' if $\{u, v\} \notin E(H)$. In the case of $u = v$, we interpret the preceding description as

$$c_{H'}(e) = \begin{cases} c_H(e) - 2\delta & \text{if } e = \{s, u\} \\ c_H(e) & \text{if } e \in E(H) - \{s, u\}, \end{cases} \tag{7.2}$$

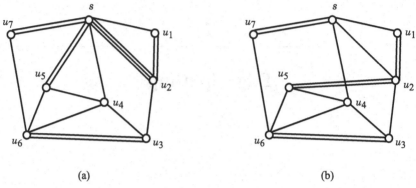

Figure 7.1. (a) A multigraph H with a designated vertex s; (b) the graph H' obtained from H by splitting $\delta = 2$ pairs of edges $\{s, u_2\}$ and $\{s, u_5\}$.

where $\delta \in [0, \frac{1}{2}c_H(s, u)]$. We say that H' is obtained from H by *splitting* δ pairs of edges $\{s, u\}$ and $\{s, v\}$. Clearly, the resulting graph H' satisfies, for any cut X with $X \subseteq V(H) - s$,

$$d(X; H') = \begin{cases} d(X; H) - 2\delta & \text{if } u, v \in X \\ d(X; H) & \text{otherwise.} \end{cases} \quad (7.3)$$

For example, Fig. 7.1(a) and 7.1 (b) illustrate a multigraph H with a designated vertex s and the graph H' obtained from H by splitting $\delta = 2$ pairs of edges $\{s, u_2\}$ and $\{s, u_5\}$.

For an integer $k \in [2, \lambda_s(H)]$, we say that splitting a pair of edges $\{s, u\}$ and $\{s, v\}$ is *k-feasible* if $\lambda_s(H') \geq k$ holds in the graph H' resulting from the splitting (see Section 3.2 for the definition of s-proper edge-connectivity $\lambda_s(H)$). A set of splitting operations at s is called *complete* if the resulting graph H' does not have any edge incident to s. In order to have a complete splitting at s, $d(s; H)$ must be an even integer. For this reason, throughout this chapter we assume that the designated vertex s of a given multigraph H has an even $d(s; H)$. Lovász [202] showed the following important property.

Theorem 7.1 ([78, 202]). *Let H be a multigraph with a designated vertex $s \in V(H)$ with even $d(s; H)$ and let k be an integer with $2 \leq k \leq \lambda_s(H)$. Then for each $u \in \Gamma_H(s)$ there is a vertex $v \in \Gamma_H(s)$ such that splitting one pair of edges $\{s, u\}$ and $\{s, v\}$ is k-feasible.* □

(The theorem statement is not valid for $k = 1$; consider a star H with a center s.) By repeatedly applying this property we see that, for such s and k, there always exists a complete k-feasible splitting. It is also easily observed that the order of splitting operations in such a sequence does not affect its feasibility. Since a complete k-feasible splitting reduces the number of vertices in a graph while preserving its s-proper edge-connectivity, it is widely used as a powerful tool in inductive proofs of various edge-connectivity problems (e.g., see [13, 17, 78, 97, 153, 249, 234, 235]).

Since the s-proper edge-connectivity can be computed by $O(n)$ maximum-flow computations (e.g., constructing a Gomory–Hu cut tree in Section 1.5.1) and there are at most $\binom{n}{2} = O(n^2)$ pairs of neighbors of s, a complete feasible splitting can be found by $O(n^3)$ maximum-flow computations. By using an $O(mn \log(n^2/m))$ time maximum-flow algorithm [103], this naïve implementation for finding a complete feasible splitting would take $O(mn^4 \log(n^2/m))$ time, where m is the number of weighted edges when H is stored as an edge-weighted simple graph. Frank [78] first showed that a complete k-feasible splitting can be obtained by considering only $O(n)$ pairs of splitting at s; hence, $O(mn^3 \log(n^2/m))$ time is required for computing a complete k-feasible splitting. Afterward, the time complexity was improved to $O(mn^2 \log(n^2/m))$ by Gabow [97] and Nagamochi and Ibaraki [249] and to $O(n(m + n \log n) \log n)$ by Nagamochi and Ibaraki [235].

In this chapter, we shall give an $O(nm + n \log n)$ time algorithm for finding a complete edge splitting in a multigraph H.

7.1.2 Splitting in Weighted Graphs

As already observed in Section 4.2.1, the edge splitting in weighted graphs is defined as follows. Let H be an edge-weighted graph with a designated vertex $s \in V(H)$ and let $u, v \in \Gamma(s; H)$ be vertices adjacent to s (possibly $u = v$). Given a nonnegative real $\delta \leq \min\{c_H(s, u), c_H(s, v)\}$ ($\delta \leq \frac{1}{2}c_H(s, u)$ if $u = v$), we say that a graph H' is obtained from H by *splitting* edges $\{s, u\}$ and $\{s, v\}$ by *weight* δ (or by an edge splitting with edges $\{s, u\}$ and $\{s, v\}$ and weight δ) if H' satisfies (7.1) and (7.2) for the real δ. For a real $k \in \Re_+$, an edge splitting (u, v, δ) is called k-*feasible* in H if $\lambda_s(H') \geq k$ holds for the resulting graph H'.

In Sections 7.2 and 7.3, we show $O(nm + n \log n)$ time algorithms for finding a complete edge splitting in an edge-weighted graph and a multigraph, respectively. These algorithms are based on the structure of extreme vertex sets. The idea was originally used by Benczúr and Karger [20] to design an $O(n^2 \log^5 n)$ time Monte Carlo–type randomized algorithm to solve the edge-connectivity augmentation problem.

Before describing the algorithms, we introduce some terminology. Let H be an edge-weighted graph. Note that a multigraph H can also be stored as an integer-weighted simple graph. For a designated vertex $s \in V(H)$, let k satisfy $0 \leq k \leq \lambda_s(H)$. Throughout this chapter, we denote by $G = (V, E)$ the graph $H - s$, and by $b(v)$ the edge weight $c_H(s, v)$ for each $v \in V(H) - s$. That is,

$$G = (V, E) = H - s,$$
$$b(v) = c_H(s, v), \quad v \in V(H) - s.$$

In other words, $H = (V + s, E \cup E(s; H))$ is the star augmentation $G + b$ (defined in Section 1.1). By $k \leq \lambda_s(H)$, we see that

$$d(X; G + b) (= d(X; G) + b(X)) \geq k \text{ for all } X \in 2^V - \{\emptyset, V\}. \tag{7.4}$$

For the family $\mathcal{X}(G)$ of extreme vertex sets of G, define

$$\mathcal{X}_k(G) = \{X \in \mathcal{X}(G) \mid d(X; G) < k\}.$$

Then by Lemma 1.43, condition (7.4) is equivalent to

$$d(X; G + b) \geq k \text{ for all } X \in \mathcal{X}_k(G). \tag{7.5}$$

For a subset $X \subseteq V$ and a set E' of edges, we denote $d(X; (V, E'))$ by $d(X; E')$ for convenience. A set of split edges obtained by a complete k-feasible splitting can be interpreted as a set F of new weighted edges such that the augmented graph $G + F$ satisfies

$$\lambda(G + F) \geq k \text{ and } d(v; F) \leq b(v) \text{ for all } v \in V. \tag{7.6}$$

On the other hand, if such a set F of weighted edges satisfying (7.6) is given, a complete k-feasible splitting of H is obtained by splitting edges $\{u, s\}, \{s, v\}$ with weight $c_F(e)$ for each edge $e = \{u, v\} \in F$ (where $c_F(e)$ denotes the weight of each edge $e \in F$) and by splitting edges $\{s, v\}$ with the remaining weights $b(v) - d(v; F)$. Then the resulting graph is k-edge-connected by $\lambda(G + F) \geq k$.

7.2 Edge Splitting in Weighted Graphs

In this subsection, we describe an algorithm for finding a complete k-feasible splitting in a given graph H whose edges are weighted by nonnegative reals. For this purpose it suffices to find a set F of new edges that satisfies (7.6) for $G = H - s$ and k.

7.2.1 Path Augmentation

We construct an edge set F in (7.6) by repeatedly choosing a new edge set E' with the following three properties and by setting F to be the union of those edge sets E':

$$d(v; E') \leq b(v) \text{ for all } v \in V, \tag{7.7}$$

$$\begin{array}{l} \text{no edge in } E' \text{ has both end vertices} \\ \text{in an extreme vertex set } X \in \mathcal{X}(G), \end{array} \tag{7.8}$$

$$\mathcal{X}(G + E') \subseteq \mathcal{X}(G). \tag{7.9}$$

After showing the next property, we will discuss how to obtain such an E'.

Claim 7.2. *For any new edge set E' satisfying conditions (7.7)–(7.9), the augmented graph $G' = G + E'$ and the reduced weight $b'(v) = b(v) - d(v; E')$ remain to satisfy $b'(v) \geq 0$ and $d(v; G' + b') = d(v; G + b)$ for every $v \in V$, and condition (7.4).* □

Proof. For each $v \in V$, $b'(v) = b(v) - d(v; E') \geq 0$ holds by (7.7), and it holds that

$$d(v; G' + b') = d(v; G') + b'(v) = d(v; G) + d(v; E') + b(v) - d(v; E')$$
$$= d(v; G) + b(v) = d(v; G + b),$$

as required. To show that G' and b' satisfy condition (7.4), we first see by (7.8) that

$$d(X; E') = \sum_{v \in X} d(v; E') \text{ for all } X \in \mathcal{X}(G).$$

Then by (7.9) it holds that $\mathcal{X}(G + E') \subseteq \mathcal{X}(G)$, in particular $\mathcal{X}_k(G + E') \subseteq \mathcal{X}_k(G)$. Therefore, for each $X \in \mathcal{X}_k(G + E')$,

$$d(X; G + E') + b'(X) = d(X; G) + d(X; E') + b'(X)$$
$$= d(X; G) + \sum_{v \in X}(d(v; E') + b'(v))$$
$$= d(X; G) + b(X) \geq k,$$

where the last inequality follows from (7.5) for G and b. Hence, (7.5) holds for G' and b'. By Lemma 1.43, this is equivalent to condition (7.4). □

Based on this claim, we see that a set F satisfying (7.6) can be constructed as follows. Let $E_1', E_2', \ldots, E_r'$ be the sets such that E_j' for each $j = 1, 2, \ldots, r$ is an edge set satisfying conditions (7.7)–(7.9) in $G + \cup_{1 \leq i \leq j-1} E_i'$ with vertex weights $b''(v) = b(v) - d(v; \cup_{1 \leq i \leq j-1} E_i')$, $v \in V$. By Claim 7.2, condition (7.4) holds for $G' = G + \cup_{1 \leq i \leq r} E_i'$ and $b'(v) = b(v) - d(v; \cup_{1 \leq i \leq r} E_i')$, $v \in V$. Hence, by choosing such sets until $\lambda(G + \cup_{1 \leq i \leq q} E_i') \geq k$ holds, we have $F = \cup_{1 \leq i \leq q} E_i'$ satisfying (7.6); the existence of such a finite sequence $E_1', \ldots, E_q'$ is shown in the end of this subsection. In what follows, we show that such a set F can be obtained by a sequence of $O(n)$ such sets.

Constructing an E' Satisfying Conditions (7.7)–(7.9)

To find a new edge set E' satisfying conditions (7.7)–(7.9) in $G = H - s$, we consider all inclusion-wise maximal extreme vertex sets in $\mathcal{X}_k(G)$, which we denote by

$$\widehat{\mathcal{X}}(G) = \{X_1, X_2, \ldots, X_p\}, \tag{7.10}$$

where we assume without loss of generality that $d(X_1; G)$ and $d(X_p; G)$ satisfy

$$d(X_p; G) = d(X_1; G) \leq \min\{d(X_i; G) \mid i = 1, 2, \ldots, p\}.$$

By Lemma 1.40(ii), such a numbering is possible and

$$d(X_p; G) = d(X_1; G) = \lambda(G)$$

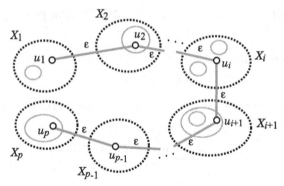

Figure 7.2. Illustration of maximal extreme vertex sets X and a choice of an edge set E' of (gray lines).

holds. Choose a vertex $u_i \in X_i$ with $b(u_i) > 0$ arbitrarily for each $i = 1, 2, \ldots, p$; define a set E' of new edges of a weight ε by

$$E' = \{e_i = \{u_i, u_{i+1}\} \mid u_i \in X_i,\ u_{i+1} \in X_{i+1},\ 1 \le i \le p - 1\} \qquad (7.11)$$

(see Fig. 7.2); and denote $V(E') = \{u_1, u_2, \ldots, u_p\}$. Define the weight ε of every edge in E' by

$$\varepsilon = \min\{\varepsilon', \varepsilon''\}, \qquad (7.12)$$

where

$$\varepsilon' = \min\{\min\{b(u_1), b(u_p)\},\ \min\{b(u_i)/2 \mid i = 2, \ldots, p - 1\}\},$$
$$\varepsilon'' = \min\{d(Y; G) - \lambda(G) \mid Y \in \mathcal{X}(G),\ Y \cap V(E') = \emptyset\}.$$

Then $d(X_1; E') = d(X_p; E') = \varepsilon$ and $d(X_i; E') = 2\varepsilon$ hold for all $i = 2$, $3, \ldots, p - 1$. Since the set E' forms a path of length p, we call the graph $G + E'$ a *path augmentation* of G.

Given a family $\mathcal{X}(G)$ of extreme vertex sets, the family $\widehat{\mathcal{X}}(G)$ and an edge set E' can be found in $O(n)$ time. More important, by condition (7.9) we can obtain the family $\mathcal{X}(G + E')$ from $\mathcal{X}(G)$ in $O(|E'| \log n) = O(n \log n)$ time by computing $d(X; G + E')$ for all $X \in \mathcal{X}(G)$ with an appropriate data structure such as dynamic trees.

Now we show that the aforementioned E' satisfies properties (7.7)–(7.9). It is easy to see that (7.7) holds by the choice of ε ($\le \varepsilon'$), and (7.8) holds since each extreme vertex set $Y \in \mathcal{X}(G)$ is contained in some $X_i \in \widehat{\mathcal{X}}(G)$ or disjoint with any $X_i \in \widehat{\mathcal{X}}(G)$. To prove property (7.9), we assume indirectly that there exists an extreme vertex set

$$U \in \mathcal{X}(G + E') - \mathcal{X}(G). \qquad (7.13)$$

We consider properties of such a set U in the following claims, and we derive a contradiction.

Claim 7.3. *Such a set U in (7.13) satisfies $d(U; E') \in \{0, \varepsilon\}$ and there is an edge $e \in E'$ that joins two vertices in U. In particular, U is not contained in any set $X_i \in \widehat{\mathcal{X}}(G)$.* $\square$

Proof. By Lemma 1.40(i), U contains an extreme vertex set $X \in \mathcal{X}(G)$ with $d(X; G) \leq d(U; G)$. Since $U \notin \mathcal{X}(G)$, X is a proper subset of U. On the other hand, $U \in \mathcal{X}(G + E')$ means $d(X; G + E') > d(U; G + E')$. By noting that $d(X; G + E') = d(X; G) + d(X; E')$ and $d(U; G + E') = d(U; G) + d(U; E')$, from $d(U; G) - d(X; G) \geq 0$ and $d(X; G + E') - d(U; G + E') > 0$ it holds that

$$d(X; E') - d(U; E') > 0.$$

By construction of E', this means $d(X; E') - \varepsilon \geq d(U; E')$. Also, by construction of E', $d(X; E') \leq 2\varepsilon$ holds, indicating $d(U; E') \in \{0, \varepsilon\}$. Since $d(X; E') = d(X, U - X; E') + d(X, V - U; E')$ and $d(U; E') \geq d(X, V - U; E')$, from $d(X; E') - d(U; E') > 0$ it holds that

$$0 < d(X; E') - d(U; E') = d(X, U - X; E') + d(X, V - U; E') - d(U; E')$$
$$\leq d(X, U - X; E'),$$

indicating that an edge $e \in E'$ joins two vertices in U. Hence, U is not contained in any $X_i \in \widehat{\mathcal{X}}(G)$ since no edge $e \in E'$ has its end vertices in a single set $X_i \in \widehat{\mathcal{X}}(G)$). $\square$

Claim 7.4. *If the U in (7.13) intersects a set $X \in \mathcal{X}(G)$, then $d(U \cap X, U - X; E') \geq \varepsilon$.* $\square$

Proof. By the definition of extreme vertex sets, $d(X - U; G) > d(X; G)$ and $d(U - X; G + E') > d(U; G + E')$ (i.e., $d(U - X; G) > d(U; G) + d(U; E') - d(U - X; E')$). By (1.4), $d(X; G) + d(U; G) \geq d(X - U; G) + d(U - X; G)$ and, hence, we have $d(U - X; E') > d(U; E')$. This implies that $d(U \cap X, U - X; E') > 0$ and, hence, $d(U \cap X, U - X; E') \geq \varepsilon$, as required. $\square$

Claim 7.5. *For each $X_i \in \widehat{\mathcal{X}}(G)$ with $i \in \{1, p\}$, either $X_i \subset U$ or $X_i \cap U = \emptyset$ holds.* $\square$

Proof. Let $X = X_i$ ($i \in \{1, p\}$). Since $U \notin \mathcal{X}(G)$ and $X \in \mathcal{X}(G)$, we have $U \neq X$. By Claim 7.3, U is not contained in X. Hence, it suffices to derive a contradiction from the assumption that U intersects X. By Claim 7.4, $d(U \cap X, U - X; E') \geq \varepsilon$. Since $d(X; E') \leq \varepsilon$ by construction of E' and $d(U \cap X, U - X; E') \leq d(X; E')$, we have $d(X; E') = d(U \cap X, U - X; E') = \varepsilon$. Hence, $u_i \in U \cap X$. Since U is an extreme vertex set in $G + E'$, we have $d(U - X; G + E') > d(U; G + E')$. From this and $d(X; G + E') + d(U; G + E') \geq d(X - U; G + E') + d(U - X; G + E')$ (by (1.4)), we obtain $d(X - U; G + E') < d(X; G + E')$, where $d(X - U; G + E') = d(X - U; G)$ holds by $u_i \in U \cap X$. Since $d(X; G + E') = d(X; G) + \varepsilon$ holds by the choice of E', it holds that $d(X - U; G) < d(X; G) + \varepsilon$. Then by Lemma 1.40(i) there is an extreme vertex set $Y \in \mathcal{X}(G)$ such that

$Y \subseteq X - U$ (hence, Y does not contain u_i) and $d(Y; G) \leq d(X - U; G) < d(X; G) + \varepsilon$. This, however, implies that $d(Y; G) - d(X; G) < \varepsilon$ for an extreme vertex set $Y \in \mathcal{X}(G)$ with $Y \cap V(E') = \emptyset$, contradicting the choice of ε. □

Claim 7.6. *If at least one of X_1 and X_p is contained in U, then there is an extreme vertex set $Y \in \mathcal{X}(G)$ with $d(Y; G) - \lambda(G) < \varepsilon$ and $Y \cap V(E') = \emptyset$.* □

Proof. Assume $X_i \subseteq U$ for some $i \in \{1, p\}$. Then we have $d(X_i; G + E') = \lambda(G) + \varepsilon$. Hence, U can be an extreme vertex set in $G + E'$ only when $d(U; G + E') < d(X_i; G + E') = \lambda(G) + \varepsilon$. By noting that $d(U; G + E') = d(U; G) + d(U; E') \geq \lambda(G) + d(U; E')$ and $d(U; E') \in \{0, \varepsilon\}$ by Claim 7.3, we have $d(U; E') = 0$ and $d(U; G) = d(U; G + E') < d(X_i; G + E') = \lambda(G) + \varepsilon$. By Lemma 1.40(i), $V - U$ contains an extreme vertex set $Y \in \mathcal{X}(G)$ such that $Y \subseteq V - U$ and $d(Y; G) \leq d(V - U; G) = d(U; G) < \lambda(G) + \varepsilon = d(X_i; G) + \varepsilon$, as required. Since E' forms a path, $u_i \in X_i \subseteq U$ and $d(U; E') = 0$ imply that $V(E') \subseteq U$, indicating that $Y \cap V(E') = \emptyset$. □

Claim 7.7. *If none of X_1 and X_p is contained in U, then $d(U; E') \geq 2\varepsilon$.* □

Proof. By assumption and Claim 7.5, it holds that $X_1 \cup X_p \subseteq V - U$. Since there is an edge in E' that joins two vertices in U by Claim 7.3, we see that the path consisting of edges in E' starts from $u_1 \in X_1$ and ends up with $u_p \in X_p$, crossing the border of U at least twice. This implies that $d(U; E') \geq 2\varepsilon$. □

Now we come to the final stage of proving property (7.9). Claim 7.6 contradicts the choice of ε while Claim 7.7 is a contradiction to Claim 7.3. Therefore, there is no U satisfying (7.13), proving that any path augmentation $G + E'$ as defined by (7.11) satisfies condition (7.9).

Lemma 7.8. *The edge set E' defined by (7.11) from $\widehat{\mathcal{X}}(G)$ of (7.10) satisfies properties (7.7), (7.8), and (7.9).* □

By the choice of ε and properties (7.7)–(7.9), we also have the following property.

Lemma 7.9. *After the aforementioned path augmentation $G + E'$, it holds that $\lambda(G + E') = \lambda(G) + \varepsilon = d(X_1; G + E') = d(X_p; G + E')$.* □

Proof. For $X_1 \in \widehat{\mathcal{X}}(G)$, $d(X_1; G + E') = d(X_1; G) + \varepsilon = \lambda(G) + \varepsilon$ holds, implying $\lambda(G + E') \leq \lambda(G) + \varepsilon$. We show its converse. By Lemma 1.43 with $b = 0$, it suffices to prove that $d(Y; G + E') \geq \lambda(G) + \varepsilon$ holds for every $Y \in \mathcal{X}(G + E')$. Let $Y \in \mathcal{X}(G + E')$. If $Y \cap V(E') \neq \emptyset$, then $d(Y; G + E') \geq d(Y; G) + \varepsilon \geq \lambda(G) + \varepsilon$. Assume that $Y \cap V(E') = \emptyset$. In this case, by the choice of ε, we have $d(Y; G) - d(X_1; G) \geq \varepsilon$, which implies that $d(Y; G + E') \geq d(Y; G) \geq d(X_1; G) + \varepsilon = \lambda(G) + \varepsilon$, as required. □

Augmenting G with Edge Set F to Achieve $\lambda(G + F) \geq k$

To augment a graph $G = H - s$ to a graph $G' = G + F$ such that $\lambda(G') \geq k$ holds, we repeat the following procedure until $\mathcal{X}_k(G') = \emptyset$ holds in the resulting graph G':

Find a path augmentation $G + E'$ in G and update $G := G + E'$ and $b(v) := b(v) - d(v; E')$ for all $v \in V$.

We now prove that such a graph G' is obtained after $O(n)$ iterations, and then we give an efficient implementation of this algorithm. Given a graph G and its weight function $b : V \to \Re_+$, let

$$V_b = \{v \in V \mid b(v) > 0\}(= \Gamma_H(s)),$$

$$n_b = |V_b|(= |\Gamma_H(s)|), \text{ and } n_k = |\mathcal{X}_k(G)|.$$

By (7.4), each extreme vertex set $X \in \mathcal{X}_k(G)$ contains a vertex in V_b. Hence,

$$n_k \leq 2n_b - 2 \tag{7.14}$$

since $\mathcal{X}_k(G)$ is a laminar family. Let $E'_1, E'_2, \ldots, E'_q$ be all sets of edges constructed by (7.11) in this order during the iterations of the algorithm. Then we let

$$F = \cup_{1 \leq j \leq q} E'_j.$$

We let ε_j be the weight of each edge in E'_j, and we let $G^{(j)}$ denote the graph $G + E'_1 + E'_2 + \cdots + E'_j$ after the jth iteration. If $\varepsilon = \varepsilon_j$ achieves $\varepsilon = b(u_i)$ for $i \in \{1, p\} \subseteq V(E'_j)$ or $\varepsilon = b(u_i)/2$ for $i \in V(E'_j) - \{1, p\}$, then $b(u_i)$ becomes 0 in $G^{(j)}$ after adding E'_j to $G^{(j-1)}$. On the other hand, if $\varepsilon_j = d(Y; G^{(j-1)}) - \lambda(G^{(j-1)})$ holds for some $Y \in \mathcal{X}(G^{(j-1)})$ with $Y \cap V(E'_j) = \emptyset$ in the current graph $G^{(j-1)}$, then $d(Y; G^{(j)}) = \lambda(G^{(j-1)}) + \varepsilon_j$ by Lemma 7.9, which implies that Y becomes a new member of $\widehat{\mathcal{X}}(G^{(j+1)})$. Therefore, the number of iterations, q, is at most $n_b + n_k = O(n_b)$. Since each iteration can be executed to run in $O(n \log n)$ time, the algorithm can be implemented to run in $O(n_b(n \log n))$ time.

Finally we show that the number of pairs of vertices that are joined by new edges in F can be bounded from above by $O(|\Gamma_H(s)|)$. As already observed in the definition of $\widehat{\mathcal{X}}(G)$, there are at least two sets $X^*, X^{**} \in \mathcal{X}(G)$ with $d(X^*; G) = d(X^{**}; G) = \lambda(G)$. After each iteration, we try to construct the next edge set E'_{h+1} using as many edges in the previous edge set E'_h as possible. Such sets X^* and X^{**} can always be used as the first and last sets in $\widehat{\mathcal{X}}(G^{(j)})$ for all j, since $d(X^*; G)$ and $d(X^{**}; G)$ remain $\lambda(G^{(j)})$ by Lemma 7.9. Hence, we can reuse each edge $\{u, v\} \in E'_h$ as an edge in E'_{h+1} if the sets $X_i, X_j \in \widehat{\mathcal{X}}(G^{(h-1)})$ containing u and v, respectively, remain members of $\widehat{\mathcal{X}}(G^{(h)})$, and the current weights $b'(u) = b(u) - d(u; \cup_{1 \leq j \leq h} E'_j)$ and $b'(v) = b(v) - d(v; \cup_{1 \leq j \leq h} E'_j)$ are both positive. Let E^*_h be the set of such edges $\{u, v\} \in E'_h$ and let $X^*_1, X^*_2, \ldots, X^*_r$ be the sets in $\widehat{\mathcal{X}}(G^{(h)}) \cap \widehat{\mathcal{X}}(G^{(h-1)})$ (hence, each edge $\{u, v\} \in E^*_h$ joins some two sets X^*_i and $X^*_{i'}$, and each X^*_j receives at most two edges from E^*_h). Let

$X_1^h, X_2^h, \ldots, X_{r'}^h$ be the sets in $\widehat{\mathcal{X}}(G^{(h)}) - \widehat{\mathcal{X}}(G^{(h-1)})$. By the definition of E_h^*, we see that an edge set E_{h+1}' defined in (7.11) can be constructed so that $E_{h+1}' \supseteq E_h^*$ holds. We choose edges $\{u, v\} \in E_{h+1}' - E_h^*$ so that two sets X_j^* and $X_{j'}^*$ joined by an edge in $E_h' - E_h^*$ will be joined again. Then each edge $e = \{u, v\} \in E_{h+1}' - E_h^*$ satisfies one of the following three conditions:

(a) e is incident to some set X_i^h, or
(b) e joins X_j^* and $X_{j'}^*$ that were not joined by any edge in E_h', or
(c) e joins X_j^* and $X_{j'}^*$ that were joined by an edge in E_h'.

The number of edges e in E_{h+1}' of type (a) is at most $2r'$. The number of edges e in E_{h+1}' of type (b) is at most the number of sets that disappear (i.e., $|\widehat{\mathcal{X}}(G^{(h-1)}) - \widehat{\mathcal{X}}(G^{(h)})|$) since X_j^* or $X_{j'}^*$ has an old set $X \in \widehat{\mathcal{X}}(G^{(h-1)}) - \widehat{\mathcal{X}}(G^{(h)})$ that was joined with the set X_j^* or $X_{j'}^*$ but is now not a member of $\widehat{\mathcal{X}}(G^{(h)})$. Finally, the number of edges in E_{h+1}' of type (c) is at most the number of vertices v such that $b(v) - d(v; \cup_{1 \leq j \leq q} E_h') = 0 < b(v) - d(v; \cup_{1 \leq j \leq q} E_{h-1}')$. With this observation, the number of pairs of vertices joined by the edges in $F = \cup_{1 \leq j \leq q} E_j'$ is at most

$$2n_k + n_k + n_b \leq 7n_b - 6 = O(|\Gamma_H(s)|).$$

From the preceding argument, we have established the following result.

Theorem 7.10 ([226]). *Given an edge-weighted graph H with a designated vertex s and a real $0 \leq k \leq \lambda_s(H)$, there is a complete k-splitting at s such that the number of pairs of vertices joined by the split edges is at most $O(|\Gamma_H(s)|)$. Moreover, such a splitting can be found in $O(n^2 \log n)$ time and $O(n + m)$ space if the set of all extreme vertex sets of G, $\mathcal{X}(G)$, is available.* □

7.3 Edge Splitting in Multigraphs

In this section, we give an $O(mn + n^2 \log n)$ time algorithm for finding a complete k-feasible splitting at a designated vertex s in a multigraph H with n vertices and m edges, where H is assumed to be stored as a simple graph such that each edge is weighted by a nonnegative integer. Let

$$G = (V, E) = H - s,$$

$$b(v) = c_H(s, v), \quad v \in V(H) - s.$$

We design a splitting algorithm by repeatedly computing an edge set E' satisfying conditions (7.7)–(7.9). However, we cannot apply the algorithm in the previous section directly to the case of multigraphs, since the ε of (7.12) may not be an integer. To overcome this, we find a set F' of split edges from a subset of $E(s; H)$ such that $\lambda(G + F') \geq k - 1$, in the first phase; then, in the second phase, we find a set F'' of split edges from the remaining edges incident to s such that $\lambda(G + F' + F'') \geq k$. These two phases are presented in the following subsections, respectively.

7.3.1 Chain Augmentation

Our goal in the first phase is to find a set F' of split edges such that the graph $G + F'$ augmented from G by F' satisfies the following:

$$\lambda(G + F') \geq k - 1 \text{ (i.e., } d(X; G + F') \geq k - 1 \text{ for all } X \in 2^V - \{\emptyset, V\}),$$

$$d(v; F') \leq b(v) \text{ for all } v \in V.$$

Thus, to obtain a minimum edge set F such that $\lambda(G + F) \geq k$, we first increase any cut size $d(X; G) < k$ to at least $k - 1$, not to k. This is because increasing the edge-connectivity optimally by 1 needs a more careful consideration in the structure of minimum cuts. Such an edge set F' can be constructed by repeatedly choosing a new edge set E' with properties (7.7)–(7.9) and by setting F' to be the union of all edge sets E'. By Claim 7.2, $b'(v) = c_H(s, v) - d(v; F')(\geq 0)$ holds for all $v \in V$, and (7.4) holds for $G' = G + F'$ and b'.

Constructing an E' Satisfying Conditions (7.7)–(7.9)

To find a new edge set E' satisfying conditions (7.7)–(7.9), we consider all extreme vertex sets X with $d(X; G) < k - 1$ (i.e., those in $\mathcal{X}_{k-1}(G)$), where $b(X) \geq 2$ since $d(X; G) + b(X) \geq k$ holds by (7.5). Now we denote all inclusion-wise maximal extreme vertex sets in $\mathcal{X}_{k-1}(G)$ by

$$\widehat{\mathcal{X}}(G) = \{X_1, X_2, \ldots, X_{p-1}, X_p\}, \tag{7.15}$$

where we assume without loss of generality by Lemma 1.40(ii) that $d(X_1; G)$ and $d(X_p; G)$ satisfy

$$d(X_p; G) = d(X_1; G) \leq \min\{d(X_i; G) \mid i = 1, 2, \ldots, p\}.$$

Choose a vertex $u_1 \in X_1$, a vertex $\overline{u}_p \in X_p$, and vertices $u_i, \overline{u}_i \in X_i$ (possibly $u_i = \overline{u}_i$), $i = 2, 3, \ldots, p - 1$, such that

$$\min\{b(u_i), b(\overline{u}_i)\} = 1 \text{ if } u_i \neq \overline{u}_i, \quad b(u_i) = b(\overline{u}_i) \geq 2 \text{ if } u_i = \overline{u}_i. \tag{7.16}$$

(Such a choice of vertices $u_i, \overline{u}_i$ from each $X_i \in \widehat{\mathcal{X}}(G)$ is possible since $b(X_i) \geq 2$ now holds.) Define a set E' of new edges of weight ε by

$$E' = \{e_i = \{u_i, \overline{u}_{i+1}\} \mid u_i \in X_i, \overline{u}_{i+1} \in X_{i+1}, 1 \leq i \leq p - 1\} \tag{7.17}$$

and let $V(E')$ be the set of end vertices of the edges in E' (see Fig. 7.3). The weight ε of each edge in E' is defined by

$$\varepsilon = \min\{\varepsilon', \varepsilon''\}, \tag{7.18}$$

where

$$\varepsilon' = \min\{\min\{b(u_i), b(\overline{u}_i) \mid u_i \neq \overline{u}_i, 1 \leq i \leq p\},$$
$$\min\{\lfloor b(u_i)/2 \rfloor \mid u_i = \overline{u}_i, 1 < i < p\}\}, \tag{7.19}$$
$$\varepsilon'' = \min\{d(Y; G) - \lambda(G) \mid Y \in \mathcal{X}(G), Y \cap V(E') = \emptyset\}. \tag{7.20}$$

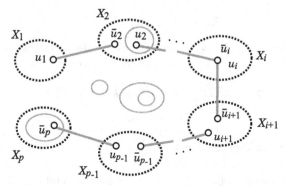

Figure 7.3. Illustration of maximal extreme vertex sets $X \in \widehat{\mathcal{X}}(G)$ and a choice of an edge set E' (gray lines).

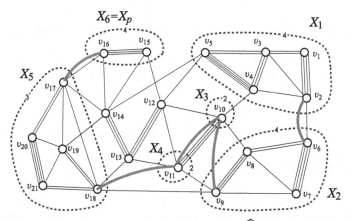

Figure 7.4. Maximal extreme vertex sets $X_1, X_2, \ldots, X_p \in \widehat{\mathcal{X}}(G)$ in Fig. 1.27, and a chain augmentation $G + E'$, where the edges in E' are depicted by thick gray lines.

In this case, note that ε is a positive integer, since any set $Y \in \mathcal{X}(G)$ with $d(Y; G) = \lambda(G)$ must belong to $\widehat{\mathcal{X}}(G)$ by definition of $\widehat{\mathcal{X}}(G)$. Then $d(X_1; E') = d(X_p; E') = \varepsilon$ and $d(X_i; E') = 2\varepsilon$ hold for all $i = 2, 3, \ldots, p - 1$. The set E' forms a path of length p when we contract each X_i to a single vertex. We call the graph $G + E'$ a *chain augmentation*. Given a family $\mathcal{X}(G)$ of extreme vertex sets, the family $\widehat{\mathcal{X}}(G)$ and the preceding edge set E' can be found in $O(n \log n)$ time, and $\mathcal{X}(G + E')$ can be obtained from $\mathcal{X}(G)$ in $O(|E'| \log n) = O(n \log n)$ time via (7.9), as in the real-weighted case of the previous subsection.

For the example in Fig. 1.27, Fig. 7.4 shows the maximal extreme vertex sets $X_1, X_2 \ldots, X_p \in \widehat{\mathcal{X}}(G)$ and a chain augmentation $G + E'$.

Now we show that the E' satisfies properties (7.7)–(7.9). We easily see that the E' satisfies conditions (7.7) and (7.8). To prove (7.9), assuming indirectly that there exists an extreme vertex set

$$U \in \mathcal{X}(G + E') - \mathcal{X}(G), \tag{7.21}$$

we derive a contradiction after proving some properties of U. The next claim can be obtained analogously to Claim 7.3.

Claim 7.11. *Such a set U satisfies $d(U; E') \in \{0, \varepsilon\}$ and there is an edge $e \in E'$ that joins two vertices in U. In particular, U is not contained in any set $X_i \in \widehat{\mathcal{X}}(G)$.* $\square$

Claim 7.12. *If the U in (7.21) intersects a set $X \in \mathcal{X}(G)$, then $d(U \cap X, U - X; E') \geq \max\{\varepsilon, 2\}$.* $\square$

Proof. We have $d(U \cap X, U - X; E') \geq \varepsilon$, as in Claim 7.4. We show that $d(U \cap X, U - X; E') \geq 2$. By the definition of extreme vertex sets, $d(X - U; G) \geq d(X; G) + 1$ and $d(U - X; G + E') \geq d(U; G + E') + 1$ (i.e., $d(U - X; G) \geq d(U; G) + 1 + d(U; E') - d(U - X; E')$). By (1.4), $d(X; G) + d(U; G) \geq d(X - U; G) + d(U - X; G)$; hence, we have $d(U - X; E') \geq d(U; E') + 2$. This implies that $d(U \cap X, U - X; E') \geq 2$. $\square$

Claim 7.13. *For each $X_i \in \widehat{\mathcal{X}}(G)$ $(2 \leq i \leq p - 1)$, either $\{u_i, \overline{u}_i\} \subseteq U$ or $\{u_i, \overline{u}_i\} \cap U = \emptyset$ holds.* $\square$

Proof. Assume indirectly that $|\{u_i, \overline{u}_i\} \cap U| = 1$, from which we have $d(U \cap X_i, U - X_i; E') \leq \varepsilon$. By (7.16), $|\{u_i, \overline{u}_i\} \cap U| = 1$ means $u_i \neq \overline{u}_i$ and, hence, $\varepsilon = \varepsilon' = 1$. By Claim 7.11, U is not a proper subset of X_i. Then U intersects X_i and, by Claim 7.12 $d(U \cap X_i, U - X_i; E') \geq 2$ holds, a contradiction to $d(U \cap X_i, U - X_i; E') \leq \varepsilon = 1$. $\square$

The next three claims hold analogously to Claims 7.4, 7.6, and 7.7.

Claim 7.14. *If U intersects an extreme vertex set $X \in \mathcal{X}(G)$, then $d(X; E') \geq d(U \cap X, U - X; E') \geq 2$. In particular, U intersects none of X_1 and X_p.* $\square$

Claim 7.15. *If at least one of X_1 and X_p is contained in U, then there is an extreme set $Y \in \mathcal{X}(G)$ with $d(Y; G) - \lambda(G) < \varepsilon$ and $Y \cap V(E') = \emptyset$.* $\square$

Claim 7.16. *If none of X_1 and X_p is contained in U, then $d(U; E') \geq 2\varepsilon$.* $\square$

Claims 7.15 and 7.16 contradict the choice of ε and Claim 7.11, respectively. This proves that any chain augmentation $G + E'$ defined by (7.17) also satisfies condition (7.9).

The next property holds analogously to Lemma 7.9.

Lemma 7.17. *The aforementioned chain augmentation $G + E'$ satisfies $\lambda(G + E') = \lambda(G) + \varepsilon = d(X_1; G + E') = d(X_p; G + E')$.* $\square$

Augmenting G with F' to Achieve $\lambda(G + F') \geq k - 1$

Based on this result, we can augment a given graph G to a $(k - 1)$-edge-connected graph $G' = G + F'$ by repeating the following procedure from $F' := \emptyset$ until $\mathcal{X}_{k-1}(G') = \emptyset$ holds:

> Find a chain augmentation $G + E'$ in G and update $G := G + E'$, $F' := F' \cup E'$, and $b(v) := b(v) - d(v; E')$ for all $v \in V$.

When $\mathcal{X}_{k-1}(G') = \emptyset$ holds, $G' = G + F'$ is $(k - 1)$-edge-connected; that is, $d(X; G + F') \geq k - 1$ holds for all nonempty subsets $X \subset V$. By Claim 7.2, such an F' satisfies $b'(v) := c_H(s, v) - d(v; F') \geq 0$, $v \in V$ and $d(X; G + F' + b') \geq k$ for all $X \in 2^V - \{\emptyset, V\}$.

The run time of this algorithm is analyzed analogously to the real-weighted case. For the initial G and weight function b, let

$$V_b = \{v \in V \mid b(v) > 0\} \, (= |\Gamma_H(s)|),$$
$$n_b = |V_b|, \text{ and } n_k = |\mathcal{X}_k(G)|,$$

where $n_k \leq 2n_b - 2$ holds since any extreme vertex set $X \in \mathcal{X}_k(G)$ contains a vertex in V_b. Let $E_1', E_2', \ldots, E_q'$ be all sets of edges constructed by (7.17) in this order during the algorithm. Then $F' = \cup_{1 \leq j \leq q} E_j'$. Let ε_j be the weight of each edge in E_j' and let $G^{(j)}$ denote the graph $G + E_1' + E_2' + \cdots + E_j'$ after the jth iteration. If $\varepsilon = \varepsilon_j$ of (7.18) is attained by ε' of (7.19), then $b(u)$ for some vertex u becomes 0 or 1 in $G^{(j)}$ after adding E_j' to $G^{(j-1)}$. On the other hand, if $\varepsilon_j = d(Y; G^{(j-1)}) - \lambda(G^{(j-1)})$ holds for some $Y \in \mathcal{X}(G^{(j-1)})$ with $Y \cap V(E_j') = \emptyset$, then $d(Y; G^{(j)}) = \lambda(G^{(j-1)}) + \varepsilon_j$ by Lemma 7.17, and Y becomes a new member of $\widehat{\mathcal{X}}(G^{(j)})$. Therefore, the number of iterations, q, is at most $2n_b + n_k = O(n_b)$. Since each iteration can be executed in $O(n \log n)$ time, the algorithm can be implemented to run in $O(n_b(n \log n))$ time.

Also analogous to the real-weighted case, we can show that the number of pairs of vertices that are joined by new edges in F' can be bounded by $O(|\Gamma_H(s)|)$. There are at least two sets $X^*, X^{**} \in \mathcal{X}(G)$ with $d(X^*; G) = d(X^{**}; G) = \lambda(G)$. By Lemma 7.17, X^* and X^{**} can always be used as the first and last sets in $\widehat{\mathcal{X}}(G^{(j)})$ for all j. Hence, we can reuse an edge $\{u, v\} \in E_h'$ as an edge in E_{h+1}' if the sets $X_i, X_j \in \widehat{\mathcal{X}}(G^{(h-1)})$ containing u and v, respectively, remain members of $\widehat{\mathcal{X}}(G^{(h)})$ and the current vertex weights $b'(u) = b(u) - d(u; \cup_{1 \leq j \leq h} E_j')$ and $b'(v) = b(v) - d(v; \cup_{1 \leq j \leq h} E_j')$ are both at least 2 (so as to meet condition (7.16)). Let E_h^* be the set of such edges $\{u, v\}$ and let $X_1^*, X_2^*, \ldots, X_r^*$ be the sets in $\widehat{\mathcal{X}}(G^{(h)}) \cap \widehat{\mathcal{X}}(G^{(h-1)})$. Let $X_1^h, X_2^h, \ldots, X_{r'}^h$ be the sets in $\widehat{\mathcal{X}}(G^{(h)}) - \widehat{\mathcal{X}}(G^{(h-1)})$. By the definition of E_h^*, we see that an edge set E_{h+1}' defined in (7.17) can be constructed so that $E_{h+1}' \supseteq E_h^*$ holds. We choose edges $\{u, v\} \in E_{h+1}' - E_h^*$ so that two sets, X_j^* and $X_{j'}^*$, joined by an edge in $E_h' - E_h^*$ will be joined again.

Then each edge $e = \{u, v\} \in E'_{h+1} - E^*_h$ satisfies one of the following three conditions:

(a) e is incident to some new set X^h_i,
(b) e joins X^*_j and $X^*_{j'}$ that were not joined by any edge in E'_h, or
(c) e joins X^*_j and $X^*_{j'}$ that were joined by an edge in E'_h.

The number of edges e in E'_{h+1} of condition (a) is at most $2r'$. The number of edges in E'_{h+1} of condition (b) is at most the number of sets that disappear, that is, $|\widehat{\mathcal{X}}(G^{(h-1)}) - \widehat{\mathcal{X}}(G^{(h)})|$. Finally, the number of edges in E'_{h+1}, condition (c) is at most the number of vertices v such that $b(v)$ becomes 0 or 1 in $G^{(h)}$. Therefore, the number of pairs of vertices joined by the edges in F' is at most

$$2n_k + n_k + n_b + (n_b - n') \leq 8n_b - n' - 6, \tag{7.22}$$

where n' denotes the number of vertices u with $b'(u) = b(v) - d(v; F') \geq 1$ after the final iteration in the first phase.

Lemma 7.18. *Given a multigraph H stored as an integer-weighted graph, a designated vertex s with even $d(s; H)$, and an integer $0 \leq k \leq \lambda_s(H)$, the first phase finds a set F' of new edges such that*

$$b'(v) = c_H(s, v) - d(v; F') \geq 0 \text{ for all } v \in V,$$

$$\lambda(G + F') \geq k - 1,$$

$$d(X; G + F' + b') \geq k \text{ for all } X \in 2^V - \{\emptyset, V\},$$

$$b'(V) \text{ is even,}$$

and the number of pairs of vertices joined by the edges in F' is at most $8n_b - n' - 6$. It runs in $O(n_b(n \log n))$ time if the set of all extreme vertex sets of G, $\mathcal{X}(G)$, is available. □

7.3.2 Augmentation on the Resulting Cactus

Let F' be the set of edges obtained after the first phase, let b' be the vertex weight in the resulting graph $G + F'$, and let n' denote the number of vertices $v \in V$ with $b'(v) \geq 1$. The remaining task for the second phase is to increase the edge connectivity of the current graph $G + F'$ by 1 by adding a set F'' of new edges such that

$$\lambda(G + F' + F'') \geq k,$$

$$d(v; F'') \leq b'(v) \text{ for all } v \in V.$$

An algorithm for obtaining such F'' will be given in Section 8.1 by using the structure of cactus representations; here we give its outline. A nonempty subset $Z \subset V$ is called a *minimal minimum cut* if $\{Z, V - Z\}$ is a minimum cuts but

$\{Z', V - Z'\}$ is not a minimum cut for any proper subset $Z' \subset Z$. It is easy to see that all minimal minimum cuts are disjoint. Let $\mathcal{M}(G + F')$ be the set of all minimal minimum cuts in $G + F'$. For each $Z \in \mathcal{M}(G + F')$, we can choose a vertex $v_Z \in Z$ with $b'(v_Z) \geq 1$ since $d(Z; G + F') = k - 1$ and $d(Z; G + F' + b') \geq k$ imply $b'(Z) \geq 1$. Based on this observation, Lemma 8.3 in Section 8.1 will tell that we can find a set F'' of $\lceil |\mathcal{M}(G + F')|/2 \rceil$ new edges such that $\lambda(G + F' + F'') \geq \lambda(G + F') + 1 = k$ and $d(v; F'') \leq b'(v)$, $v \in V$. Therefore, we obtain a set $F = F' \cup F''$ of new edges such that $\lambda(G + F) \geq k$ and the total weights of edges in F is at most $b(V)/2$.

Note that the second phase introduces at most $\lceil n'/2 \rceil$ new edges. Hence, F consists of at most $|F'| + |F''| \leq 8n_b - n' - 6 + \lceil n'/2 \rceil \leq 8n_b - 6$ weighted edges. To find an edge set F'' by Lemma 8.3, we need to compute a cactus representation for all minimum cuts in $G + F'$. Thus, by Theorem 5.28, the entire run time for the two phases is $O(n(m + n_b) + n^2 \log n)$, including the time for computing the family $\mathcal{X}(G)$ of all extreme vertex sets in G, which is $O(nm + n^2 \log n)$ by Theorem 6.6.

By summarizing the arguments for the first and second phases, we establish the next result.

Theorem 7.19. *Given a multigraph H with n vertices and m edges stored as an integer-weighted graph, a designated vertex s with even $d(s; H)$, and an integer $0 \leq k \leq \lambda_s(H)$, there is a complete k-feasible splitting at s such that the number of pairs of vertices joined by the split edges is $O(|\Gamma_H(s)|)$. Moreover, such a splitting can be found in $O(mn + n^2 \log n)$ time and $O(n + m)$ space.* $\square$

7.4 Other Splittings

The concept of edge splitting is not restricted to the edge-connectivity of undirected graphs. This section reviews some attempts of generalizations for the cases of local edge-connectivity and digraphs, and for the case where some constraints are imposed on the method of pairing. Proofs will be all omitted throughout this section for the sake of simplicity.

7.4.1 Edge Splitting for Local Edge-Connectivity

Theorem 7.1 shows the existence of an edge splitting that preserves global edge-connectivity. An edge splitting that preserves local edge-connectivity is defined as follows. For a function

$$r : \binom{V - s}{2} \rightarrow \mathbf{Z}_+,$$

where $\binom{V-s}{2}$ denotes the set of all pairs of vertices u and v in $V - s$, an edge splitting at s is called r-*feasible* if the graph G' resulting from the edge splitting satisfies $\lambda(u, v; G) \geq r(u, v)$ for all vertices $u, v \in V - s$. Mader [206] proved the existence of such an edge splitting.

Theorem 7.20 ([206]). *Let $G = (V, E)$ be a graph with $d(s; G) \notin \{1, 3\}$ and let $r(u, v) = \lambda(u, v; G)$, $u, v \in V - s$. Then*

(a) *If s is not a cut vertex, then there is an r-feasible splitting pair of edges $\{s, w\}$ and $\{s, w'\}$.*

(b) *If s is a cut vertex but there is no cut edge incident to s, then any pair of edges $\{s, w\}$ and $\{s, w'\}$ such that w and w' belong to distinct components in $G - s$ is r-feasible.* $\square$

Frank [79] gave a shorter proof for this theorem, and Gabow [97] showed that a complete r-feasible splitting in the sense of this theorem can be found in $O(n^2 m \log(n^2/m))$ time.

7.4.2 Edge Splitting in Digraphs

In a digraph $G = (V, E)$ with a designated vertex $s \in V$, a splitting operation replaces two edges (w, s) and (s, w'), one directed to s and the other from s, with a single edge (w, w') directed from w to w'. Mader [209] proved that there always exists an edge splitting that preserves the global edge-connectivity of a given digraph G.

Theorem 7.21 ([209]). *Let $G = (V, E)$ be a digraph with a designated vertex $s \in V$ satisfying $d(s, V - s; G) = d(V - s, s; G)$ and let $k \geq 0$ be an integer such that $\lambda(u, v; G) \geq k$ for all $u, v \in V - s$. Then for any edge $(w, s) \in E(V - s, s; G)$ there is an edge $(s, w') \in E(s, V - s; G)$ such that the graph G' obtained by splitting (w, s) and (s, w') satisfies $\lambda(u, v; G') \geq k$ for all $u, v \in V - s$.* $\square$

For a digraph G with a designated vertex s in Fig. 7.5(a), $\lambda(u, v; G) \geq 2$ for all $u, v \in V - s$. For edge (u_1, s), (s, u_3) is one of the edges such that $\lambda(u, v; G') \geq 2$ still holds for all $u, v \in V - s$ in the graph G' after splitting (u_1, s) and (s, u_3). Similarly splitting (u_2, s) and (s, u_4) preserves the local edge-connectivity. Figure 7.5(b) shows the digraph G'' obtained from G by splitting pairs of edges $\{(u_1, s), (s, u_3)\}$ and $\{(u_2, s), (s, u_4)\}$ and it satisfies $\lambda(G'') = 2$.

Frank [77] and Jackson [153] proved that, for an Eulerian digraph, there is an edge splitting that preserves local edge-connectivities.

Theorem 7.22 ([77, 153]). *Let $G = (V, E)$ be an Eulerian digraph with a designated vertex $s \in V$. Then for any edge $(w, s) \in E(V - s, s; G)$ there is an edge $(s, w') \in E(s, V - s; G)$ such that the graph G' obtained by splitting (w, s) and (s, w') satisfies $\lambda(u, v; G') \geq \lambda(u, v; G)$ for all $u, v \in V - s$.* $\square$

Figure 7.5(c) shows an example of a non-Eulerian digraph G with a designated vertex s such that no edge splitting meets the condition $\lambda(u, v; G') \geq \lambda(u, v; G)$ for all $u, v \in V - s$; $\lambda(u_2, u_4; G') < 2 = \lambda(u_2, u_4; G)$ holds (resp. $\lambda(u_3, u_4; G'') < 2 = \lambda(u_3, u_4; G)$) for the digraph G' (resp. G'') obtained by splitting edges (u_2, s) and (s, u_1) (resp. (u_3, s) and (s, u_1)).

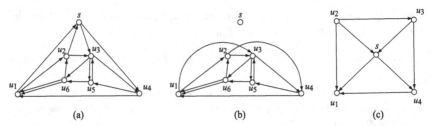

Figure 7.5. (a) A digraph G with $\lambda(G) = 2$. (b) A digraph G'' obtained from G by splitting pairs of edges $\{(u_1, s), (s, u_3)\}$ and $\{(u_2, s), (s, u_4)\}$, where $\lambda(G'') = 2$ holds. (c) A digraph G with a designated vertex s which has no edge splitting that preserves the local edge-connectivity.

7.4.3 Splitting with Constraints

This subsection shows some results for edge splitting with additional constraints in the combination of pairs of edges.

Partition Constraint

Jackson [153] observed that an Eulerian multigraph satisfies the next property.

Theorem 7.23 ([153]). *Given an Eulerian multigraph with a designated $s \in V$, and an even integer k such that $2 \le k \le \lambda_s(G)$, each edge $\{s, u\} \in E(s; G)$ has at least $d(s; G)/2$ edges $(s, v) \in E$ (possibly $u = v$) such that splitting $\{s, u\}$ and $\{s, v\}$ is k-feasible.* □

We conclude from this theorem that, given a partition $\{F_1, F_2, \ldots, F_r\}$ of $E(s; G)$ such that

$$|F_i| \le d(s; G)/2 \quad \text{for } 1 \le i \le r,$$

there is a complete feasible splitting in which no pair of edges $\{s, u\}$ and $\{s, v\}$ both belonging to the same subset F_i is selected. An extension of this result is also known.

Theorem 7.24 ([252]). *Given a multigraph $G = (V, E)$ with a designated $s \in V$ of even degree, an even integer k with $k \le \lambda_s(G)$, and a partition $\{F_1, F_2, \ldots, F_r\}$ of $E(s; G)$ such that $|F_i| \le d(s; G)/2$ $(1 \le i \le r)$, there is a complete k-feasible splitting in which no pair of edges $\{s, u\}$ and $\{s, v\}$ both belonging to the same subset F_i is selected. Such a complete splitting can be found in $O(n(n + |E(s; G)|) \log |\Gamma_G(s)|)$ time.* □

This implies the next result, based on which Bang-Jensen et al. [13] solved the edge-connectivity augmentation problems with partition constraint for an even target k.

Corollary 7.25 ([13]). *Given a multigraph $G = (V, E)$ with a designated $s \in V$ of even degree, an even integer k with $k \le \lambda_s(G)$, and a partition $\{P_1, P_2, \ldots, P_r\}$*

of $V - s$ such that $d(s, P_i; G) \leq d(s; G)/2$ $(1 \leq i \leq r)$, there is a complete k-feasible splitting in which no pair of edges $\{s, u\}$ and $\{s, v\}$ whose u and v belong to the same subset P_i is selected. □

Clearly, this is a special case of Theorem 7.24.

Noncrossing Splitting

Let $G = (V, E)$ be a multigraph with a designated vertex s and let $\pi = (w_0, w_1, \ldots, w_{p-1})$ be a cyclic order for the vertex set $\Gamma_G(s) = \{w_0, w_1, \ldots, w_{p-1}\}$, $(p = |\Gamma_G(s)|)$ of neighbors of s. Two edges $\{w_h, w_i\}$ and $\{w_j, w_\ell\}$ are called *crossing* (with respect to π) if $h + a = j + b = i + c = \ell \pmod{p}$ holds for some $1 \leq c < b < a \leq p - 1$; they are called *noncrossing* otherwise. A sequence of splittings at s is called *noncrossing* if any two split edges are noncrossing.

Theorem 7.26 ([230]). *Given a multigraph $G = (V, E)$ with a designated vertex $s \in V$ of even degree, a positive even integer $k \leq \lambda_s(G)$, and a cyclic order π of neighbors of s, there always exists a complete and noncrossing k-feasible splitting. Such a complete splitting can be found in $O(|\Gamma_G(s)|n(m + n \log n))$ time (if the weight function c_G is given as input) or in $O(|E| + |\Gamma_G(s)|kn^2)$ time (if the set E is given as input).* □

Planarity-Preserving Splitting

Let $G = (V, E)$ be a planar multigraph with a vertex $s \in V$ of even degree. A complete splitting at s is called *planarity-preserving* if the resulting graph remains planar. Based on the result of noncrossing splitting, we prove that if k is an even integer with $k \leq \lambda_s(G)$ then there always exists a complete k-feasible and planarity-preserving splitting. For $k = 3$, we also prove by a separate argument that there exists a complete k-feasible and planarity-preserving splitting if the resulting graph is allowed to be re-embedded in the plane. In both cases, such a complete splitting can be obtained in polynomial time, but the latter case requires slightly less running time.

Let us examine some examples of complete splittings in planar graphs.

(i) Figure 7.6(a) shows a graph $G_1 = (V, E)$ with $c_{G_1}(s, w_i) = 1$ and $c_{G_1}(w_i, w_{i+1 \pmod 4}) = a, 0 \leq i \leq 3$ for a given integer $a \geq 1$. Clearly, $\lambda_s(G_1) = k$ with $k = 2a + 1$. For a cyclic order $\pi = (w_0, w_1, w_2, w_3)$, G_1 has unique complete k-feasible splitting (i.e., a splitting pair of $\{s, w_0\}$, $\{s, w_2\}$ and a pair of $\{s, w_1\}$, $\{s, w_3\}$), that is crossing with respect to π. This implies that, for every odd $k \geq 3$, there is a graph G with a designated vertex s and a cyclic order of $\Gamma_G(s)$ that has no complete and noncrossing k-feasible splitting. Note that, if we remove the noncrossing constraint, G_1 has a complete and planarity-preserving

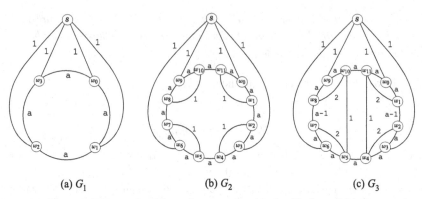

(a) G_1 (b) G_2 (c) G_3

Figure 7.6. Example of three planar graphs: (a) G_1, (b) G_2, and (c) G_3.

k-feasible splitting (by placing one of the split edges in the interior of cycle $C_1 = \{w_0, w_1, w_2, w_3\}$).

(ii) Figure 7.6(b) shows a planar graph $G_2 = (V, E)$ with $c_{G_2}(w_i, w_{i+1(\text{mod } 12)}) = a$ for $0 \leq i \leq 11$ and $c_{G_2}(e) = 1$ otherwise, where a is an integer satisfying $a \geq 1$. G_2 satisfies $\lambda_s(G_2) = k$ with $k = 2a + 1$ and has unique complete k-splitting at s (i.e., a pair of $\{s, w_0\}, \{s, w_6\}$ and a pair of $\{s, w_3\}, \{s, w_9\}$), which is not planarity-preserving unless the embedding of subgraph $G_2[V - s]$ is changed; if $G_2[V - s]$ is re-embedded in the plane so that block components $\{w_2, w_3, w_4\}$ and $\{w_8, w_9, w_{10}\}$ of $G_2[V - s]$ are flipped (i.e., two vertices w_3 and w_9 share the same inner face), then the complete k-splitting becomes planarity-preserving. From this we see that, for every odd $k \geq 3$, there is a planar graph G with a designated vertex s which has no complete and planarity-preserving k-feasible splitting (unless the embedding of G is re-embedded).

(iii) Let $a \geq 2$ be an integer and consider the graph $G_3 = (V, E)$ in Fig. 7.6(c), where $c_{G_3}(w_i, w_{i+1}) = a - 1$ for $i \in \{1, 7\}$, $c_{G_3}(w_i, w_{i+1 \text{ (mod } 12)}) = a$ for $i \subset \{0, 1, \dots, 11\} - \{1, 7\}$, $c_{G_3}(w_i, w_{i+2 \text{ (mod } 12)}) = 2$ for $i \in \{2, 5, 8, 11\}$, and $c_{G_3}(e) = 1$ otherwise. Clearly, $\lambda_s(G_3) = k$ with $k = 2a + 1$ (≥ 5). It is easily observed that the unique complete k-feasible splitting (i.e., a pair of $\{s, w_0\}, \{s, w_6\}$ and a pair of $\{s, w_3\}, \{s, w_9\}$) is not planarity-preserving for any choice of re-embedding G_3 in the plane. This implies that, for every odd $k \geq 5$, there exists a graph that has no complete and planarity-preserving k-feasible splitting even if re-embedding after splitting is allowed.

In what follows, we assume that a given graph G is *planar*, and we consider whether there is a complete and planarity-preserving k-feasible splitting for a designated vertex s of even degree and an integer $k \leq \lambda_s(G)$. We prove that such a splitting always exists if k is even or $k = 3$. Note that we have already observed in (iii) that such a splitting may not exist if k is odd and $k \geq 5$.

We first consider the case of an even value of k. We initially fix an embedding ψ of G in the plane, and we let π_ψ be the order of neighbors of s that appear around s in the embedding ψ of G. Clearly, a complete splitting at s is planarity-preserving if it is noncrossing with respect to π_ψ. Therefore, in the case of even integers k, the next theorem is immediate from Theorem 7.26 and the fact that m is $O(n)$ ([267]) in a planar graph G.

Theorem 7.27. *Given a planar multigraph $G = (V, E)$ with a designated vertex $s \in V$ of even degree, and given a positive even integer $k \leq \lambda_s(G)$, there exists a complete and planarity-preserving k-feasible splitting (which also preserves the embedding of $G - s$ in the plane). Such a splitting can be found in $O(|\Gamma_G(s)|n^2 \log n)$ time (if the weight function c_G is given as input) or in $O(|E| + |\Gamma_G(s)|kn^2)$ time (if the set E is given as input).* $\quad\square$

As already observed in the preceding (ii), in general this theorem may not be valid for odd integers k.

We next consider the case of $k = 3$. For $k = 3 \leq \lambda_s(G)$, we prove that there is a complete and planarity-preserving k-feasible splitting. However, in this case we may need to re-embed the subgraph $G - s$ in the plane to obtain such a splitting.

Theorem 7.28 ([230]). *Given a planar multigraph $G = (V, E)$ with a designated vertex $s \in V$ of even degree, and given $\lambda_s(G) \geq 3$, there exists a complete and planarity-preserving 3-feasible splitting, and such a splitting can be found in $O(n^2)$ time (if the weight function c_G is given as input) or in $O(|E| + n^2)$ time (if the set E is given as input).* $\quad\square$

Jordán [161, 162] defined a nice notion of nonadmissible graphs to handle edge splitting problems with constraints. For a given graph $G = (V \cup \{s\}, E)$ with a designated vertex s, the nonadmissible graph $B = (\Gamma_G(s), E_B)$ on the vertex set $\Gamma_G(s)$ of neighbors of s is such that B has an edge $\{u, v\} \in E_B$ if and only if splitting a pair of edges $\{s, u\}, \{s, v\}$ at s is not k-feasible. He then gave a characterization of the nonadmissible graphs and showed that, using this result, several edge-splitting theorems such as Theorem 7.24 and Corollary 7.25 are derived effectively.

7.5 Detachments

In this section we describe a graph transformation called *detachment*, which is regarded as an extension of edge splitting or as a reverse operation of the contraction of a vertex set.

7.5.1 Detachments at a Designated Vertex s

Fleiner [69] first studied the problem of detaching a single vertex s. For a designated vertex s in a graph $G = (V, E)$ with no loops, a degree specification $f(s)$ is a sequence $(d_1, d_2, \ldots, d_p)$ of positive integers such that $\sum_{1 \le i \le p} d_i = d(s; G)$. An $f(s)$-*detachment* of G is a graph G' with $V(G') = (V - s) \cup \{s_1, s_2, \ldots, s_p\}$ and $E(G') = E'$ obtained by splitting s into p vertices $s_1, s_2, \ldots, s_p$, called the pieces of s in G', such that each edge $e \in E(s; G)$ is incident to one of the pieces and $d(s_i; G') = d_i$ holds for each $i = 1, 2, \ldots, p$ (other edges in E do not change). Fleiner [69] proved the following result.

Theorem 7.29 ([69]). *Let $G = (V, E)$ be a graph with a designated vertex $s \in V$ such that $\lambda(u, v; G) \ge k$ holds for each pair $u, v \in V - s$, where k is an integer $k \ge 2$. Then, given a degree specification $f(s) = (d_1, d_2, \ldots, d_p)$, where $d_i \ge 2$, $i = 1, 2, \ldots, p$, there is an $f(s)$-detachment G' of G such that $\lambda(u, v; G') \ge k$ for each pair $u, v \in V - s$ if and only if $\lambda(u, v; G - s) \ge k - \sum_{1 \le i \le p} \lfloor d_i/2 \rfloor$ for each pair $u, v \in V - s$.* □

Jordán and Szigeti [163] proved a more general result, which is also an extension of Theorem 7.20.

Theorem 7.30 ([163]). *Let $G = (V, E)$ be a graph with a designated vertex $s \in V$ such that no cut edge is incident to s and $\lambda(u, v; G) \ge r(u, v)$ for each pair $u, v \in V - s$, where r is a function $r : \binom{V-s}{2} \to \mathbf{Z}_+$. Then, given a degree specification $f(s) = (d_1, d_2, \ldots, d_p)$, where $d_i \ge 2$, $i = 1, 2, \ldots, p$, there is an $f(s)$-detachment G' of G such that $\lambda(u, v; G') \ge r(u, v)$ for each pair $u, v \in V - s$ if and only if $\lambda(u, v; G - s) \ge r(u, v) - \sum_{1 \le i \le p} \lfloor d_i/2 \rfloor$ for each pair $u, v \in V - s$.* □

7.5.2 Global Detachments

We consider an undirected multigraph $G = (V, E)$ which may have loops, where $E(X, X; G)$ for a subset $X \subseteq V$ denotes the set of edges between vertices in X (including loops incident to a vertex in X), $d(X, X; G)$ denotes $|E(X, X; G)|$, and the *degree* of a vertex v in G is defined to be $deg(v; G) = d(v; G) + 2d(v, v; G)$. Given a function $p : V \to \mathbf{Z}_+$, a graph G' with $E(G') = E$ is called a *p-detachment* of G if G' is obtained by splitting each vertex $v \in V$ into $p(v)$ vertices (i.e., $V(G')$ consists of $n = |V|$ disjoint subsets V_v, $v \in V$ such that contracting each subset V_v into a single vertex v results in the original G). Given a function $p : V \to \mathbf{Z}_+$, a *p-degree specification* is a set f of vectors $f(v) = (f_1^v, f_2^v, \ldots, f_{p(v)}^v)$, $v \in V$ such that $\sum_{1 \le i \le p(v)} f_i^v = deg(v; G)$. A *p*-detachment G' of G is called an *f-detachment* if the degrees of pieces of each vertex $v \in V$ are given by $f(v)$.

A connected graph G such that the degree of each vertex is even admits an Eulerian trail, which is as well known as Euler's theorem in graph theory. Nash-Williams [264, 265] observed that this fact can be interpreted as the existence of a 2-vertex-connected *p*-detachment of G for the function p defined by $p(v) = deg(v; G)/2$, $v \in V$. He obtained the following results, where, for a subset $X \subseteq V$, $p(X)$ denotes $\sum_{v \in X} p(v)$ and $c(G)$ denotes the number of components in G.

Theorem 7.31 ([265]). *Let $G = (V, E)$ be a graph and $p : V \to \mathbf{Z}_+$. Then G has a connected p-detachment if and only if $d(X; G) + d(X, X; G) + 1 \geq c(G - X) + p(X)$ for every $X \in 2^V$. Furthermore, if G has a connected p-detachment, then G has a connected f-detachment for every r-degree specification f.* □

Theorem 7.32 ([265]). *Let $G = (V, E)$ be a graph, let $p : V \to \mathbf{Z}_+$ and let $k \geq 2$ be an integer. Then G has a k-edge-connected p-detachment if and only if*

(i) *G is k-edge-connected,*
(ii) *$deg(v; G) \geq kp(v)$ for each $v \in V$,*
(iii) *none of the followings holds:*
    (a) *k is odd, and G has a cut vertex v such that $deg(v; G) = 2k$ and $p(v) = 2$,*
    (b) *k is odd, $|V| = 2$, $|E| = 2k$, and $p(v) = 2$ and $d(v, v; G) = 0$ for all $v \in V$.*

Furthermore, if G has a k-edge-connected p-detachment, then G has a k-edge-connected f-detachment for every p-degree specification f such that $f_i^v \geq k$ for all $v \in V$ and $i = 1, 2, \ldots, p(v)$. □

Fleiner [69] proved that Theorem 7.32 can also be deduced from Theorem 7.29.

A graph is called *nonseparable* if it is connected and has no cut vertex, where a vertex v in a graph G which may have loops is called a *cut vertex* if $|E(G)| \geq 2$ and either v is incident to a loop or $G - v$ has more components than G.

Jackson and Jordán [154] gave a necessary and sufficient condition for a graph G to have a nonseparable detachment, answering an open question posed by Nash-Williams [264, 265].

Theorem 7.33 ([154]). *Let $G = (V, E)$ be a graph and $p : V \to \mathbf{Z}_+$, where V_1 (resp. V_2) denotes $\{v \in V \mid deg(v) \geq 4, \ p(v) = 1\}$ (resp. $\{v \in V \mid deg(v) \geq 4, p(v) \geq 2\}$). Then G has a nonseparable p-detachment if and only if*

(i) *G is 2-edge-connected,*
(ii) *$deg(v) \geq 2p(v)$ for all $v \in V$,*
(iii) *$d(v, v; G) = 0$ for all $v \in V_1$,*
(iv) *$d(X, V - X - y; G) + d(X, X; G) \geq p(X) + c(G - X \cup \{y\}) - 1$ for all $y \in V_1$ and $X \subseteq V_2$.* □

Jackson and Jordán [154] also gave a degree specification version of a nonseparable p-detachment.

Berg, Jackson, and Jordán [25] gave a counterpart of Theorems 7.31 and 7.32 for digraphs. For a digraph $G = (V, E)$, which may have loops and multiple edges, $E(X, X; G)$ for a subset $X \subseteq V$ denotes the set of edges from a vertex in X to a vertex in X (including loops incident to a vertex in X) and $d(X, X; G)$ denotes $|E(X, X; G)|$, and the *indegree* (resp. *outdegree*) of a vertex v is defined to be $deg^-(v; G) = d(V - v, v; G) + d(v, v; G)$ (resp. $deg^+(v; G) = d(v, V - v; G) + d(v, v; G)$). Given a function $p : V \to \mathbf{Z}_+$, a digraph G'

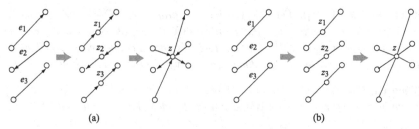

Figure 7.7. Pinching three edges e_1, e_2, e_3 in (a) a digraph G and (b) an undirected graph G.

with $E(G') = E$ is called a *p-detachment* of G if G' is obtained by splitting each vertex $v \in V$ into $p(v)$ vertices, that is, V' consists of $n = |V|$ subsets V_v, $v \in V$ such that contracting each subset V_v into a single vertex v results in the original G. For a function $p : V \to \mathbf{Z}_+$, a *p-degree specification* is a set f of sequence of pairs $f(v) = [(f_1^{-v}, f_1^{+v}), (f_2^{-v}, f_2^{+v}), \dots, (f_{p(v)}^{-v}, f_{p(v)}^{+v})]$, $v \in V$ such that $\sum_{1 \le i \le p(v)} f_i^{-v} = deg^-(v; G)$ and $\sum_{1 \le i \le p(v)} f_i^{+v} = deg^+(v; G)$. A *p*-detachment G' of G is called an *f-detachment* if the in- and outdegrees of pieces of each vertex $v \in V$ are given by the pairs in $f(v)$.

Theorem 7.34 ([25]). *Let $G = (V, E)$ be a digraph, let $p : V \to \mathbf{Z}_+$, and let $k \ge 1$ be an integer. Then G has a k-edge-connected p-detachment if and only if*

  (i) *G is k-edge-connected,*
  (ii) *$deg^-(v) \ge kp(v)$ and $deg^+(v) \ge kp(v)$ for all $v \in V$.*

Furthermore, if G has a k-edge-connected p-detachment then G has a k-edge-connected f-detachment for every p-degree specification f such that $f_i^{-v} \ge k$ and $f_i^{+v} \ge k$ for all $v \in V$ and $i = 1, 2, \dots, p(v)$. $\qquad\qquad\square$

7.6 Applications of Splittings

This section demonstrates the usefulness of edge splitting by showing some applications. The notion of edge splitting is used in the stated theorems, but again most of the proofs are omitted for simplicity.

7.6.1 Constructive Characterizations

Pinching a set of edges $e_1, e_2, \dots, e_r$ with a new vertex z in a digraph (or undirected graph) describes an operation that subdivides the edges by new vertices $z_1, z_2, \dots, z_r$ and then identifies $z_1, z_2, \dots, z_r$ as a new vertex z. Figures 7.7(a) and 7.7(b), respectively, illustrate pinching three edges e_1, e_2, e_3 in a digraph and in an undirected graph.

Mader [208] gave the following constructive characterization of *k*-edge-connected digraphs.

Theorem 7.35 ([208]). *A digraph $G = (V, E)$ which may have multiple edges and loops is k-edge-connected if and only if G can be constructed from a single vertex by repeating the following operations in an arbitrary order:*

   (i) *add a new edge (possibly a loop) joining existing vertices,*
   (ii) *pinch k existing edges.*   □

Theorem 7.36 ([208]). *A digraph $G = (V, E)$ with a vertex s, which may have multiple edges and loops, satisfies $\lambda(s, u; G) \geq k$ for all $u \in V - s$ if and only if G can be constructed from a single vertex s by repeating the following operation: pinch j existing edges with a new vertex z, where j is an integer $j \in [0, k]$, and add $k - j$ new edges entering z (outgoing from arbitrary existing vertices).*   □

For undirected graphs, Lovász [202] and Mader [206] gave the following characterizations, respectively.

Theorem 7.37 ([202]). *An undirected multigraph $G = (V, E)$ which may have loops is $2k$-edge-connected if and only if G can be constructed from a single vertex by repeating the following operations in an arbitrary order:*

   (i) *add a new edge (possibly a loop) joining existing vertices,*
   (ii) *pinch k existing edges.*   □

Theorem 7.38 ([206]). *An undirected multigraph $G = (V, E)$ which may have loops is $(2k + 1)$-edge-connected if and only if G can be constructed from a single vertex by repeating the following operations in an arbitrary order:*

   (i) *add a new edge (possibly a loop) joining existing vertices,*
   (ii) *pinch k existing edges with a new vertex z, and add a new edge joining z and an existing vertex u,*
   (iii) *pinch k existing edges with a new vertex z, pinch k existing edges (not all incident to z) with a new vertex z', and add a new edge joining z and z'.*   □

Theorem 7.39 ([83, 301]). *An undirected graph $G = (V, E)$ which may have loops is k-tree-connected if and only if G can be constructed from a single vertex by repeating the following operations in an arbitrary order:*

   (i) *add a new edge (possibly a loop) joining existing vertices,*
   (ii) *add a new vertex z and k new edges joining z with existing vertices,*
   (iii) *pinch i $(1 \leq i \leq k - 1)$ existing edges with a new vertex z and add $k - i$ new edges joining z with existing vertices.*   □

Frank and Szegö [86] gave constructive characterizations for many other connectivity notions by developing new edge-splitting methods.

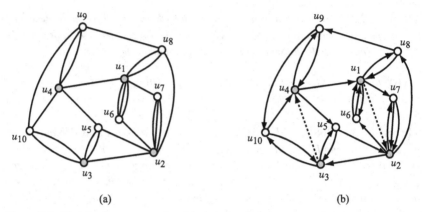

Figure 7.8. (a) A 4-edge-connected multigraph G, where u_1, u_2, u_3, and u_4 are the vertices of odd degrees; (b) a 2-edge-connected orientation of G, where, as explained later, dashed edges are introduced to obtain the orientation.

7.6.2 Orientation

For a given undirected graph G, an *orientation* of G is a digraph obtained from G by replacing each undirected edge $\{u, v\}$ with a directed edge (u, v) or (v, u).

Theorem 7.40 ([261]). *For any undirected multigraph $G = (V, E)$, there is an orientation G' of G such that $\lambda(u, v; G') \geq \lfloor \lambda(u, v; G)/2 \rfloor$ holds for all ordered pairs $u, v \in V$.*   □

In particular, from this theorem, we observe the following characterization of a $2k$-edge-connected graph.

Theorem 7.41. *Every $2k$-edge-connected graph admits a k-edge-connected orientation.*   □

Figures 7.8(a) and 7.8(b) show an example of a 4-edge-connected multigraph G and a 2-edge-connected orientation of G, respectively.

A characterization of $(2k + 1)$-edge-connected graphs is obtained by Frank et al. [90].

Theorem 7.42 ([90]). *Let $G = (V, E)$ be a $(2k + 1)$-edge-connected graph. For every pair $s, t \in V$, there is a k-edge-connected orientation G' of G such that $\lambda(s, t; G') \geq k + 1$.*   □

k-Edge-Connected Orientation of 2k-Edge-Connected Graphs

We consider the problem stated in Theorem 7.40 again more carefully, and we show that it can be done in polynomial time by using MA ordering and edge splitting.

Given a $2k$-edge-connected multigraph $G = (V, E)$, the k-edge-connected orientation problem asks to find an orientation of edges in G so that the resulting digraph $D = (V, A)$ is k-edge-connected. Gabow [97] gave an efficient algorithm for this problem. Following his idea partially, we show that the problem can be solved in $O(n^4 \log n)$ time if G is given as an edge-weight function or $O(|E| + kn^3 \log n)$ time if E is given as a set of unweighted edges.

Let $parity(v; G)$ for $v \in V$ denote the parity of $d(v; G)$ (i.e., $parity(v; G)$ is 0 if $d(v; G)$ is even, or 1 otherwise). A vertex v is called *odd* (resp. *even*) in G if $parity(v; G) = 1$ (resp. $parity(v; G) = 0$). A set F of new edges with $F \cap E = \emptyset$ is called a *pairing* of G if F forms a perfect matching on the set of odd vertices in G (i.e., a set of disjoint edges that spans all odd vertices). Let $H = (V, F)$. A pairing F is called an *h-pairing* of G for an integer h if

$$d(X; G) - d(X; H) \geq h \quad \text{for all cuts } X \subset V. \tag{7.23}$$

Nash-Williams showed the following result.

Theorem 7.43 ([261]). *G has an h-pairing if and only if G is h-edge-connected.*
□

Notice that a k-edge-connected orientation of a $2k$-edge-connected graph G can be easily obtained from a $2k$-pairing F of G: Find an orientation of $G + F = (V, E \cup F)$ such that the indegree is equal to the outdegree for each vertex in the resulting digraph D (such an orientation can be found in linear time since $G + F$ is an Eulerian undirected graph). Then this orientation gives a k-edge-connected orientation in G since (7.23) with $h = 2k$ implies that, for each nonempty set $X \subset V$, $d(X; G + F) \geq 2k + d(X; H) + d(X; H)$ holds and thereby $d(X; D) \geq k + d(X; H)$ holds; that is, at least k edges in G are directed from X to $V - X$ in the resulting digraph $\tilde{G} = D - F$.

For example, a 4-pairing F of the 4-edge-connected multigraph G in Fig. 7.8(a) is $\{e_1 = \{u_1, u_2\}, e_2 = \{u_3, u_4\}\}$, as shown in Fig. 7.8(b) as dashed edges. The obtained digraph (excluding dashed edges) is 2-edge-connected.

By using edge splitting, we give a constructive proof for Theorem 7.43 as follows.

Theorem 7.44. *Let $G = (V, E)$ be a 2k-edge-connected multigraph, where G is given by an edge-weight function. Then a 2k-pairing can be found in $O(n^4)$ time.*
□

Proof. We find a $2k$-pairing of $G = (V, E)$ by applying one of the following operations (a) or (b), until the resulting graph has no odd vertices.

(a) If there is an even vertex, say s in G (in addition to some odd vertices), then we remove s by a complete $2k$-feasible splitting. Clearly, any $2k$-pairing F in the resulting $2k$-edge-connected graph G' is also a $2k$-pairing of G, because the size of any cut $X \subset V - s$ does not decrease in the process of regaining G from G', and cut $X = \{s\}$ does not violate (7.23) with $h = 2k$ (since no edge in F is incident to the even vertex s). Let $G := G'$.

(b) If G consists only of odd vertices, then by Theorem 2.32 there is an edge $e = \{u, v\}$ with $\lambda(u, v; G) = d(v; G) \geq 2k + 1$, and such e can be found by computing an MA ordering in G in $O(m + n \log n)$ time. Note that $G - e$ remains $2k$-edge-connected from $\lambda(u, v; G) \geq 2k + 1$. It is easy to see that, for any $2k$-pairing F of $G - e$, $F \cup \{e\}$ is a $2k$-pairing of G. Let $G := G - e$.

After applying operation (a) or (b) until G contains no odd vertex (i.e., G has a trivial $2k$-pairing $F = \emptyset$), we recover a $2k$-pairing F by collecting all edges $e = \{u, v\}$ found in operation (b). As this computation contains the computation of $O(n)$ complete $2k$-feasible splittings, the running time becomes $O(n(nm' + n^2 \log n)) = O(n^4)$ time by Theorem 7.19, where $m' = O(n^2)$ denotes the maximum number of pairs of adjacent vertices in G during the algorithm.   □

Theorem 7.45. *Let $G = (V, E)$ be a $2k$-edge-connected multigraph, where set E is given as input. Then a $2k$-pairing can be found in $O(|E| + n^3(k + \log n))$ time.*   □

Proof. We first sparsify a given graph G into a $2k$-edge-connected spanning subgraph $G_{2k} = (V, E_{2k})$ in $O(n + |E|)$ time by Theorem 2.26. Let

$$V^* = \{v \in V \mid parity(v; G) \neq parity(v; G_{2k})\}$$

and let $r = |V^*|/2$ (note that $|V^*|$ is always even). To keep the parity of every vertex unchanged, we add a set E^* of r independent edges to G_{2k} as follows. Consider the spanning subgraph $\Delta G = (V, \Delta E = E - E_{2k})$ of G, where $parity(v; \Delta G) = 1$ if and only if $v \in V^*$. Then let us decompose ΔE into subsets, each of which induces a cycle C or a path $P(u, v)$ between two vertices u, v in V^*. Such a decomposition can be obtained in $O(n + |E|)$ time just by traversing each edge exactly once. Let $\mathcal{P} = \{P(u_1, v_1), \ldots, P(u_r, v_r)\}$ be the set of the resulting paths, where $r = |V^*|/2$ and $V^* = \{u_1, v_1, u_2, v_2, \ldots, u_r, v_r\}$. Then we add the set E^* of r new edges $\{u_1, v_1\}, \ldots, \{u_r, v_r\}$ to G_{2k}, which results in a graph $G_{2k}^* = (V, E_{2k} \cup E^*)$ such that

$$parity(v; G_{2k}^*) = parity(v; G), \quad v \in V. \tag{7.24}$$

Clearly, G_{2k}^* is $2k$-edge-connected (since so is G_{2k}) and has at most $2k(n - 1) + \frac{1}{2}n = O(kn)$ edges by Theorem 2.26. This preprocessing takes $O(n + |E|)$ time, as stated earlier. Then any $2k$-pairing F of G_{2k}^* is also a $2k$-pairing of G, since G_{2k}^* is a spanning subgraph of G and $d(X; G) \geq d(X; G_{2k}^*)$ for all cuts X. Let $m' = O(kn)$ be the number of edges in G_{2k}^*. Such a $2k$-pairing F can be found by repeatedly applying the same operation, (a) or (b), as in the proof of Theorem 7.44, until the resulting graph has no odd vertices. This is summarized as follows.

(a) If G_{2k}^* has an even vertex, say s, then we remove s by computing a complete $2k$-feasible splitting at s in $O(nm' + n^2 \log |\Gamma_G(s)|) = O(n^2(k + \log n))$ time by Theorem 7.19. We update the resulting graph as G_{2k}^*.

(b) If G_{2k}^* has no even vertex, then an edge $e = \{u, v\}$ with $\lambda(u, v; G_{2k}^*) = d(v; G_{2k}^*) \geq 2k + 1$ can be found in $O(m' + n) = O(kn)$ time by computing an

MA ordering in G. For any $2k$-pairing F of $2k$-edge-connected graph $G_{2k}^* - e$, $F \cup \{e\}$ is a $2k$-pairing of G_{2k}^*. Then let $G_{2k}^* := G_{2k}^* - e$.

Since operation (a) or (b) is repeated $O(n)$ times in the entire algorithm, the total running time of operations (a) and (b) becomes $O(n \cdot (n^2(k + \log n) + kn))$ time. Thus, the entire time complexity including the preprocessing is $O(n + |E|) + O(n^3(k + \log n)) = O(|E| + n^3(k + \log n))$. This proves the theorem. □

8

Connectivity Augmentation

The problem of increasing edge or vertex-connectivity of a given graph up to a specified target value k by adding the smallest number of new edges is called *connectivity augmentation*. These problems were first studied in 1976 by Eswaran and Tarjan [64] and Plesnik [275] and were shown to be polynomially solvable for $k = 2$. The problems have important applications such as the network construction problem [279], the rigidity problem in grid frameworks [13, 99], the data security problem [110, 172], and the rectangular dual graph problem in floor planning [303]. We refer to [81, 241] surveys for this study.

In this chapter, we mainly treat the edge-connectivity augmentation problem for a given target value k. For a general k, Watanabe and Nakamura [308] established in 1987 a min-max theorem, based on which they gave an $O(k^2(kn + m)n^4)$ time algorithm. Afterward, Frank [78] gave a unified approach to various edge-connectivity augmentation problems by making use of the edge-splitting theorems of Lovász [200, 202] and Mader [206, 208]. Then Nagamochi and Ibaraki [236] proposed an $O((nm + n^2 \log n) \log n)$ time algorithm by combining the minimum-cut algorithm in Section 3.2 and the approach of Frank. If the graph under consideration is weighted by real numbers, this algorithm can be further simplified and can be extended to solve the edge-connectivity augmentation problem for the entire range of target k in $O(nm + n^2 \log n)$ time [238], as will be explained in Section 8.4. By using extreme vertex sets in Section 1.5.3, Benczúr and Karger [20] gave an $O(n^2 \log^5 n)$ time randomized algorithm of Monte Carlo type to optimally increase a multigraph. Based on their augmentation method, an $O(nm + n^2 \log n)$ time edge-splitting algorithm was given in Sections 7.2 and 7.3, which is now used in Section 8.3 to solve the edge-connectivity augmentation in multigraphs in the same time complexity.

In this chapter, we first observe in Section 8.1 that the problem of increasing the edge-connectivity of a multigraph by 1 can be solved by using a cactus representation. In Section 8.2, we consider the problem of constructing a star augmentation of a given multigraph to satisfy k-edge-connectivity. In Section 8.3, we show that an optimal solution to the edge-connectivity augmentation problem in a multigraph G can be obtained from a star augmentation of G by applying an edge splitting algorithm. In Section 8.4, we consider the case of augmenting a weighted graph with the smallest sum of weights, and we give an algorithm that solves the problem for the entire range of target values. In Section 8.5, we discuss augmentation problems with additional constraints, some of which admit polynomial time algorithms, and we review some recent results for other augmentation problems.

8.1 Increasing Edge-Connectivity by One

Let $G = (V, E)$ be a multigraph which is stored as a simple graph with integer edge weights. In this subsection, we consider the problem of increasing the edge-connectivity of G by 1, which asks to find the smallest set F of new edges such that $\lambda(G + F) \geq \lambda(G) + 1$. In other words, the problem is to find the smallest set F of edges that destroy all minimum cuts in G. The system of minimum cuts in G is represented by a cactus, as studied in Chapter 5. It is a natural idea to find a desired set F that breaks all minimum cuts in the cactus representation. For a given multigraph $G = (V, E)$, let $(\mathcal{R} = (\mathcal{V}, \mathcal{E}), \varphi)$ be a cactus representation of G, where $\lambda(\mathcal{R}) = 2$ holds (see Chapter 5). For a set F of edges over V, let $\varphi(F)$ denote the set of edges mapped from F by the $\varphi : V \to \mathcal{V}$; that is, $\varphi(F) = \{\{\varphi(u), \varphi(v)\} \mid \{u, v\} \in F\}$. By the definition of cactus representations, we easily observe the next property.

Lemma 8.1 ([259]). *Given a set F of new edges to be added to G, $\lambda(G + F) \geq \lambda(G) + 1$ holds if and only if $\lambda(\mathcal{R} + \varphi(F)) \geq 3$ holds.* □

We call a cut of size 2 a *2-cut*. Then the problem involves finding a minimum edge set $\mathcal{F} = \varphi(F)$ to be added to a cactus $\mathcal{R}$ such that all 2-cuts in $\mathcal{R}$ are destroyed by $\mathcal{F}$, where every edge in $\mathcal{F}$ must join nonempty nodes in $\mathcal{R}$ (otherwise we cannot realize a set F of new edges in G such that $\varphi(F) = \mathcal{F}$).

A node with degree 2 in a cactus is called a *leaf node*. Each leaf node $x \in V(\mathcal{R})$ corresponds to a minimal minimum cut $\{\varphi^{-1}(x), V - \varphi^{-1}(x)\} \in \mathcal{C}(G)$ and vice versa, where a minimum cut $Z \subset V$ in G is *minimal* if no proper subset X of Z is a minimum cut. Let $\mathcal{M}(G)$ denote the set of all minimal minimum cuts in a graph G. Note that any two sets in $\mathcal{M}(G)$ are pairwise disjoint.

From this observation and Lemma 8.1, we have the following lemma describing the least number of edges to be added to increase the edge-connectivities of a graph G and a cactus $\mathcal{R}$.

Lemma 8.2. (i) *For a cactus $\mathcal{R}$ and a set $\mathcal{F}$ of new edges, if $\lambda(\mathcal{R} + \mathcal{F}) \geq 3$ holds then we have $|\mathcal{F}| \geq \lceil |L(\mathcal{R})|/2 \rceil$, where $L(\mathcal{R})$ denotes the set of leaf nodes.*

(ii) *For a multigraph $G = (V, E)$ and a set F of new edges, if $\lambda(G + F) \geq \lambda(G) + 1$ holds then we have $|F| \geq \lceil |\mathcal{M}(G)|/2 \rceil$.* □

Proof. We prove condition (ii) (condition (i) can be treated analogously). Consider any F such that $\lambda(G + F) \geq \lambda(G) + 1$. For each cut $X \in \mathcal{M}(G)$, F must contain an edge that is incident to a vertex in X, since otherwise $\lambda(G + F) \leq d(X; G + F) = d(X; G) = \lambda(G)$ would hold. Therefore, by the disjointness of cuts in $\mathcal{M}(G)$, the number of end vertices of edges in F is at least $|\mathcal{M}(G)|$, implying $|F| \geq \lceil |\mathcal{M}(G)|/2 \rceil$. $\qquad\square$

By definition, any leaf node x in a cactus representation is a nonempty node. We show that the edge-connectivity of $\mathcal{R}$ (resp. G) in Lemma 8.2 can be actually increased by 1 by adding $\lceil |L(\mathcal{R})|/2 \rceil$ (resp. $\lceil |\mathcal{M}(G)|/2 \rceil$) edges. For a cactus $\mathcal{R}$ with an even number of leaf nodes, a set σ of new $|L(\mathcal{R})|/2$ edges which pairwise join all leaf nodes is called a *leaf matching*. We show next that there is a leaf matching σ that realizes $\lambda(\mathcal{R} + \sigma) \geq 3$. If $|L(\mathcal{R})|$ is odd, then we choose an arbitrary node $z \in V(\mathcal{R})$ and create a new cycle $C = (z, z')$ by introducing a new leaf node z'; it suffices to show that the resulting cactus $\mathcal{R}'$ has a leaf matching σ such that $\lambda(\mathcal{R}' + \sigma) \geq 3$. Therefore, it suffices to consider only the case of even $|L(\mathcal{R})|$.

Lemma 8.3 ([259]). *Let $\mathcal{R}$ be a nontrivial cactus with even $|L(\mathcal{R})|$. Then*

(i) *The nodes in $L(\mathcal{R})$ have a cyclic ordering $(z_1, z_2, \ldots, z_\ell)$ (where the last z_ℓ is followed by the first z_1) such that, for any 2-cut $X \subset V(\mathcal{R})$ in $\mathcal{R}$, all nodes $z_i \in X$ have consecutive indices i. Moreover, such a cyclic ordering can be found in $O(|V(\mathcal{R})| + |E(\mathcal{R})|)$ time.*

(ii) *For the cyclic ordering $(z_1, z_2, \ldots, z_\ell)$ in condition (i), adding to $\mathcal{R}$ a set of new $\ell/2$ edges, $\mathcal{F} = \{\{z_i, z_{i+\ell/2}\} \mid i = 1, \ldots, \ell/2\}$, with unit weights increases the edge-connectivity up to 3.* $\qquad\square$

Proof. Take an Eulerian trail of $\mathcal{R}$ (see Section 1.1 for its definition), which can be found in linear time, say, by giving an orientation to the edges in $\mathcal{R}$ such that each undirected cycle becomes a directed cycle and by visiting all cycles in a depth-first search manner (i.e., whenever we encounter a new cycle we move to the edges in such a cycle; see Section 1.2.2). Then let $(z_1, z_2, \ldots, z_\ell)$ be a cyclic ordering of all nodes in $L(\mathcal{R})$ such that the first encounters of nodes in the Eulerian trail appear in the order $z_1, z_2, \ldots, z_\ell$. Then for any 2-cut $\{U, V(\mathcal{R}) - U\}$ in $\mathcal{R}$, all nodes $z \in L(\mathcal{R}) \cap U$ have consecutive numbers by the construction of the Euler trail.

(ii) Let X be an arbitrary 2-cut in $\mathcal{R}$. It suffices to show that $\mathcal{F} \cap E(X; \mathcal{R} + \mathcal{F}) \neq \emptyset$. Without loss of generality let $\{z_1, z_2, \ldots, z_\ell\} \cap X = \{z_1, z_2, \ldots, z_p\}$, where $p < \ell$. Consider edge $e = \{z_{\lfloor p/2 \rfloor}, z_{\lfloor p/2 \rfloor + \ell/2}\} \in \mathcal{F}$, where $p < \lfloor p/2 \rfloor + \ell/2 < \ell$ holds. Thus, $e \in \mathcal{F} \cap E(X; \mathcal{R} + \mathcal{F})$ holds, as required. $\qquad\square$

For example, we consider a multigraph G in Fig. 8.1(a) and its cactus representation $(\mathcal{R}, \varphi)$ in Fig. 8.1(b), where $\lambda(G) = 4$ and $\lambda(\mathcal{R}) = 2$. The cactus $\mathcal{R}$ has the set $L(\mathcal{R}) = \{z_1, z_2, \ldots, z_8\}$ of leaf nodes, which are labeled by a cyclic ordering

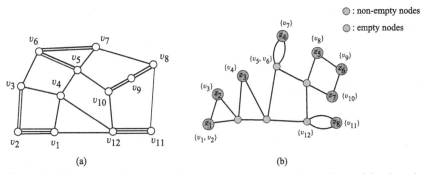

Figure 8.1. Illustration of a graph and its cactus representation: (a) an edge-weighted graph G (the number of lines between two vertices represents the weight of the edge between them), and (b) a cactus representation $\mathcal{R}$ for all minimum cuts in G (unshaded circles indicate empty nodes).

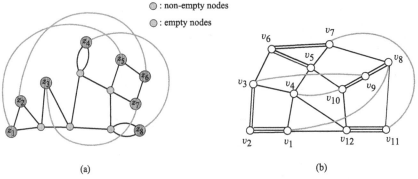

Figure 8.2. Illustration for increasing the edge-connectivity by 1: (a) a set $\mathcal{F}$ of edges to increase $\lambda(\mathcal{R})$ by 1, for the $\mathcal{R}$ in Fig. 8.1(b); (b) a set F of edges to increase $\lambda(G)$ by 1, for the G in Fig. 8.1(a).

in Lemma 8.3(i). By Lemma 8.3(ii), $\mathcal{F} = \{\{z_1, z_5\}, \{z_2, z_6\}, \{z_3, z_7\}, \{z_4, z_8\}\}$ satisfies $\lambda(\mathcal{R} + \mathcal{F}) \geq 3$ (see Fig. 8.2(a)). For this $\mathcal{F}$, we can choose a set F of new edges on V such that $\varphi(F) = \mathcal{F}$, for example, by $F = \{\{v_1, v_8\}, \{v_3, v_9\}, \{v_4, v_{10}\},$ $\{v_7, v_{11}\}\}$ (see Fig. 8.2(b)), where $|F| = |\mathcal{F}| = \lceil |L(\mathcal{R})|/2 \rceil = \lceil |\mathcal{M}(G)|/2 \rceil = 4$. By Lemma 8.1, $\lambda(G + F) \geq \lambda(G) + 1$ holds and, by Lemma 8.2, F is an optimal augmentation to G.

8.2 Star Augmentation

As a basis of the edge-connectivity augmentation problem discussed in the next section, this section considers the minimum star augmentation problem, which was discussed in Section 3.3. In this section, we consider the *minimum star augmentation problem with degree constraint* for a multigraph $G = (V, E)$, an integer $k \geq 1$, and a degree bound $\beta : V \to \mathbf{Z}_+$ such that $\beta(v) \geq d(v; G)$, $v \in V$, which asks to find an integer vertex weight $b : V \to \mathbf{Z}_+$ with the minimum total $b(V) = \sum_{v \in V} b(v)$ such that a star augmentation $G + b$ (defined in Section 1.1) satisfies $\lambda_s(G + b) \geq k$ under the degree bound β. Formally, the problem is to minimize $b(V)$ subject to

$$d(X; G + b) \, (= d(X; G) + b(X)) \geq k \text{ for all } X \in 2^V - \{\emptyset, V\} \qquad (8.1)$$

and

$$d(v; G + b) \, (= d(v; G) + b(v)) \leq \beta(v) \text{ for all } v \in V. \qquad (8.2)$$

A necessary condition for a multigraph G to have a star augmentation $G + b$ that satisfies (8.1) and (8.2) is

$$d(X; G) + \sum_{v \in X} (\beta(v) - d(v; G)) \geq k \text{ for all } X \in 2^V - \{\emptyset, V\}. \qquad (8.3)$$

We will see that (8.3) is also sufficient for the existence of a feasible star augmentation $G + b$. We easily observe the next property.

Lemma 8.4. *For a multigraph G and an integer $k \geq 1$, any feasible star augmentation $G + b$ must satisfy*

$$\sum_{Y \in \{Y_1, Y_2, \ldots, Y_t\}} b(Y) \geq \sum_{Y \in \{Y_1, Y_2, \ldots, Y_t\}} (k - d(Y; G))$$

for every family $\{Y_1, Y_2, \ldots, Y_t\}$ of disjoint subsets of V. □

In the following, we show an algorithm that constructs a minimum star augmentation $G + b$ satisfying (8.1) or that detects a subset X violating (8.3). For this, we first compute the family $\mathcal{X}(G)$ of extreme vertex sets of G, and we define

$$\mathcal{X}_k(G) = \{X \in \mathcal{X}(G) \mid d(X; G) < k\}. \qquad (8.4)$$

Then by Lemma 1.43, condition (8.1) is equivalent to

$$d(X; G + b) \geq k \text{ for all } X \in \mathcal{X}_k(G).$$

Let $\mathcal{T}$ be the tree representation for $\mathcal{X}_k(G)$. Starting with all nodes in $\mathcal{T}$ *unscanned* and $b(v) := 0$ for all $v \in V$, we repeatedly choose a lowest nodes X in the tree $\mathcal{T}$ among the unscanned nodes satisfying $d(X; G) + b(X) < k$ for the current b, and we increase $b(v)$ of arbitrarily chosen vertices, $v \in X$, so that $d(X; G) + b(X) = k$ holds. Note that if we failed to attain $d(X; G) + b(X) = k$ by increasing $b(v)$, $v \in X$, as much as possible under the degree constraint (8.2), then $d(X; G) + \sum_{v \in X} (\beta(v) - d(v; G)) < k$ holds for the X, indicating that (8.3) does not hold and the problem is infeasible.

Let b be the final weight function obtained by the aforementioned procedure. Consider all subsets $X \in \mathcal{X}_k(G)$ for which $d(X; G) + b(X) = k$ holds (note that some X may satisfy $d(X; G) + b(X) > k$) and let $\mathcal{M}$ be the family of inclusion-wise maximal subsets among such subsets. Note that all sets in $\mathcal{M}$ are pairwise

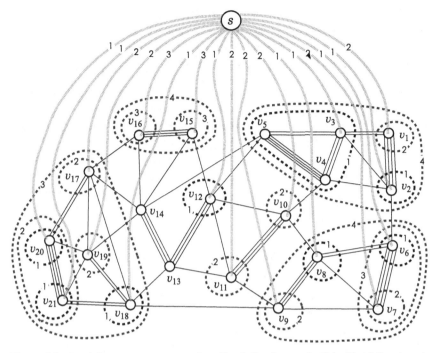

Figure 8.3. A minimum star augmentation $G + b$ for the graph G in Fig. 1.2, a target $k = 8$, and degree bounds $\beta(v) = 9$ for all $v \in V$, where an extreme vertex set $X \in \mathcal{X}_8(G)$ is enclosed by a black broken curve with the number indicating $k - d(X; G)$. Each edge $\{s, v\}$ between G and s is shown by a gray line with the number indicating the final $b(v)$.

disjoint since no two sets in $\mathcal{X}_k(G)$ are intersecting and $\mathcal{M}$ consists of inclusion-wise maximal subsets X such that $d(X; G) + b(X) = k$. Then we see that

$$b(V) \, (= d(s; G + b)) = \sum_{X \in \mathcal{M}} (k - d(X; G))$$

holds, which indicates that the obtained star augmentation is optimal by Lemma 8.4. Notice that, for a feasible instance, the final b will be obtained by checking (8.3) only for those $X \in \mathcal{X}_k(G)$.

For example, we consider a target $k = 8$ and a degree function $\beta(u) = 9$ for all $u \in V$, for the graph G in Fig. 1.3. Then $\mathcal{X}_8(G)$ is given in Fig. 8.3. A minimum star augmentation $G + b$, for example, is given by $b(v_1) = 2$, $b(v_2) = b(v_3) = b(v_6) = 1$, $b(v_7) = 2$, $b(v_8) = 1$, $b(v_9) = b(v_{10}) = b(v_{11}) = 2$, $b(v_{12}) = 1$, $b(v_{15}) = b(v_{16}) = 3, b(v_{17}) = 2, b(v_{18}) = 1, b(v_{19}) = 2$, and $b(v_{20}) = b(v_{21}) = 1$, where $b(V) = 28$ (see gray lines in Fig. 8.3). With these values of b, we obtain $\mathcal{M} = \{\{v_1, v_2, v_3, v_4, v_5\}, \{v_6, v_7\}, \{v_8\}, \{v_9\}, \{v_{10}\}, \{v_{11}\}, \{v_{12}\}, \{v_{15}\}, \{v_{16}\}, \{v_{17}\}, \{v_{18}\}, \{v_{19}\}, \{v_{20}, v_{21}\}\}$. For example, the set $X = \{v_6, v_7, v_8, v_9\} \in \mathcal{X}_8(G)$ does not belong to $\mathcal{M}$ since $d(X; G) + b(X) = (k - 4) + 1 + 2 + 1 + 2 = k + 2 > k$ holds.

Since the family $\mathcal{X}(G)$ of extreme vertex sets in G can be found in $O(mn + n^2 \log n)$ time and $O(n + m)$ space by Theorem 6.6, and other complexity is minor compared to this, the entire complexity is also $O(mn + n^2 \log n)$ time and $O(n + m)$ space. By summarizing the preceding argument, we have the next result.

Theorem 8.5. *Given a multigraph $G = (V, E)$ stored as an integer-weighted graph, a degree bound $\beta : V \rightarrow \mathbf{Z}_+$ with $\beta(v) \geq d(v; G)$, $v \in V$, and an integer $k \geq 1$, the minimum feasible star augmentation problem with degree constraint has a feasible star augmentation $G + b$ if and only if (8.3) holds for every $X \in \mathcal{X}_k(G)$. A subset $X \in \mathcal{X}_k(G)$ violating (8.3) or a minimum star augmentation $G + b$ together with a family $\{X_1, X_2, \ldots, X_t\}$ of disjoint subsets such that $b(V) = \sum_{1 \leq i \leq t}(k - d(X_i; G))$ can be found in $O(mn + n^2 \log n)$ time and $O(n + m)$ space.* $\qquad\square$

8.3 Augmenting Multigraphs

We are now ready to consider the *edge-connectivity augmentation problem under degree constraint*, which asks us to augment a given unweighted multigraph $G = (V, E)$ to a k-edge-connected multigraph $G + F$ (with $d(v; G + F) \leq \beta(u)$, $u \in V$) by adding the smallest set F of new edges, under a given degree bound $\beta : V \rightarrow \mathbf{Z}_+$ with $\beta(v) \geq d(v; G)$, $v \in V$. We represent multigraphs G and $G + F = (V, E \cup F)$ as simple graphs with integer edge weights. The problem is to find a minimum set F such that

$$d(X; G + F) (= d(X; G) + d(X; (V, F))) \geq k \text{ for all } X \in 2^V - \{\emptyset, V\} \qquad (8.5)$$

and

$$d(v; G + F) (= d(v; G) + d(v; (V, F))) \leq \beta(v) \text{ for all } v \in V. \qquad (8.6)$$

Given a family $\{Y_1, Y_2, \ldots, Y_t\}$ of disjoint subsets of V satisfying $d(Y_i; G) \leq k$, $i = 1, 2, \ldots, t$, at least $k - d(Y_i; G)$ edges need to be added to increase the cut size of Y_i up to k, and thereby at least $\lceil (1/2) \sum_{Y \in \{Y_1, Y_2, \ldots, Y_t\}} (k - d(Y; G)) \rceil$ edges are required to increase the cut size of all Y_i up to k. Hence, we obtain the next lemma.

Lemma 8.6. *For a multigraph G and an integer $k \geq 1$, any feasible augmentation $G + F$ must satisfy*

$$|F| \geq \left\lceil \frac{1}{2} \sum_{Y \in \{Y_1, Y_2, \ldots, Y_t\}} (k - d(Y; G)) \right\rceil$$

for every family $\{Y_1, Y_2, \ldots, Y_t\}$ of disjoint subsets of V. $\qquad\square$

This in particular says that if F has a family $\{Y_1, Y_2, \ldots, Y_t\}$ satisfying the inequality in the lemma, then $|F|$ is minimum.

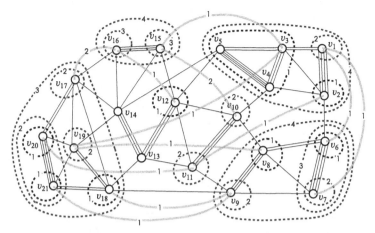

Figure 8.4. An optimal augmentation $G + F$ for the graph G in Fig. 1.2 and Fig. 1.3. a target $k = 8$, and degree bounds $\beta(v) = 9$ for all $v \in V$, where each edge $e \in F$ is denoted by a gray line, the number on which indicates its weight.

From this, a necessary condition for a multigraph G to have an augmentation $G + F$ that satisfies (8.5) and (8.6) is

$$d(X; G) + \sum_{v \in X}(\beta(v) - d(v; G)) \geq k \text{ for all } X \in 2^V - \{\emptyset, V\}, \qquad (8.7)$$

$$\frac{1}{2}\sum_{v \in V}(\beta(v) - d(v; G)) \geq \left\lceil \frac{1}{2}\sum_{Y \in \{Y_1, Y_2, \dots, Y_t\}}(k - d(Y; G))\right\rceil \qquad (8.8)$$

for every family $\{Y_1, Y_2, \dots, Y_t\}$ of disjoint subsets of V. Note that (8.7) is the same condition as (8.3).

We compute a minimum augmentation $G + F$ in the following two phases.

1. By applying Theorem 8.5, find a minimum star augmentation $H = G + b = (V \cup \{s\}, E \cup F_0)$ of G, which satisfies (8.1) and (8.2), where F_0 denotes the set of added edges incident to the introduced vertex s. If a subset $X \subset V$ violating (8.3) is detected then halt, concluding that the given instance is infeasible. Otherwise an added degree $b : V \to \mathbf{Z}_+$ and a family $\{X_1, X_2, \dots, X_t\}$ of disjoint subsets are obtained, for which $b(V) = \sum_{1 \leq i \leq t}(k - d(X_i; G))$ holds. Figure 8.3 gives an example of this phase.

   If $d(s; H)(= |F_0| = b(V))$ is odd, then we add to H one edge between s and an arbitrary vertex $u \in V$ with $\beta(u) - d(v; G) > b(u)$ to make $d(s; H)$ even; if no such u exists then halt, concluding that the given instance is infeasible (since $\sum_{v \in V}(\beta(v) - d(v; G)) < 1 + \sum_{1 \leq i \leq t}(k - d(X_i; G))$ holds, violating (8.8)).

2. By applying Theorem 7.19, compute a complete k-feasible splitting of H with the designated vertex s. Let F be the set of the split edges, and output graph $G + F$ as an optimally augmented graph. Figure 8.4 is obtained from the example of Fig. 8.3.

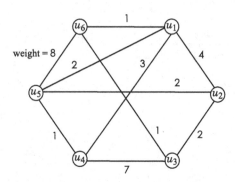

Figure 8.5. An edge-weighted undirected graph $G = (V, E)$.

Upon completing the first phase, we obtain $\lambda_s(G + b) \geq k$. Then the graph $G + F$ obtained from $H = G + b$ by a complete k-feasible splitting is k-edge-connected. By Theorems 8.5 and 7.19, the preceding algorithm can be implemented to run in $O(nm + n^2 \log n)$ time. We then prove the optimality of F. Since F is obtained from F_0 by a complete edge splitting, it holds that $|F| = \lceil |F_0|/2 \rceil = \lceil b(V)/2 \rceil$. Therefore, by Lemma 8.6, F is the smallest set to augment G into a k-edge-connected graph, establishing the next result.

Theorem 8.7. *Given a multigraph $G = (V, E)$ stored as an integer-weighted simple graph, a weight function $\beta : V \to \mathbf{Z}_+$ with $\beta(v) \geq d(v; G), v \in V$, and an integer $k \geq 2$, the edge-connectivity augmentation problem under degree constraint can be solved in $O(mn + n^2 \log n)$ time and $O(n + m)$ space. Moreover, the number of new weighted edges added to G is $O(n)$.* ◻

8.4 Augmenting Weighted Graphs

In this section, we treat a graph $G = (V, E)$ with edges weighted by nonnegative reals, and we consider the problem of increasing the edge-connectivity by increasing the weights of existing edges, creating new weighted edges, or both. This problem can be formulated as a linear programming problem since the local edge-connectivity between vertices u and v can be represented by the value of a maximum (u, v)-flow in G. Let $\Lambda_G(k)$ denote the smallest total amount of weights that needs to be added to make G k-edge-connected, where k is a nonnegative real. We call $\Lambda_G(k)$ for all $k \geq 0$ *the edge-connectivity augmentation function* of G, which is clearly nondecreasing. Note that $\Lambda_G(k)$ can be written as the objective function of a linear programming problem with a parameter $k \geq 0$. Hence, $\Lambda_G(k)$ is piecewise linear and convex. For example, for the graph G shown in Fig. 8.5, Fig. 8.6 illustrates function $\Lambda_G(k)$.

Let $G^*(k)$ denote an optimally augmented graph, that is, a k-edge-connected edge-weighted graph that is obtained from G by adding a total new weight of $\Lambda_G(k)$. In Section 8.4.1, we first see that the algorithm for augmenting multigraphs discussed in Section 8.3 can be used to solve the weighted version of this problem

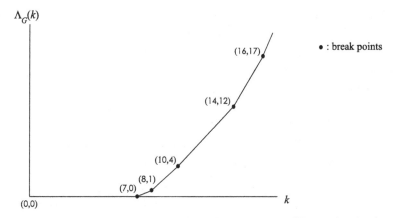

Figure 8.6. The edge connectivity augmentation function $\Lambda_G(k)$ of the graph G in Fig. 8.5.

for a single target k. In Section 8.4.2, we describe the main results about function Λ_G. For this, in Section 8.4.4 we give an algorithm for computing Λ_G from the family $\mathcal{X}(G)$ of extreme vertex sets in G after introducing the notions of ranged sets and ranged star augmentations in Section 8.4.3. Finally, in Section 8.4.5 we show that optimally augmented graphs $G^*(k)$ for all $k \in [\lambda(G), +\infty]$ can be compactly represented by a set of $O(n \log n)$ weighted cycles on V.

8.4.1 Algorithm for a Single Target k

In this section, we observe that the algorithm in Section 8.3 can be used to augment a given edge-weighted graph G to a k-edge-connected graph, where edge weights are not necessarily integers and there is no degree constraint. From this observation, we derive a characterization of $\Lambda_G(k)$.

We say that a family $\mathcal{X}$ of subsets of V *covers* a subset X (or is an X-*covering*) in a star augmentation G' of $G = (V, E)$ if every vertex $v \in X$ with $c_{G'}(s, v) > 0$ belongs to some subset $Y \in \mathcal{X}$. A subset $X \subset V$ is called k-*critical* in a star augmentation G' of $G = (V, E)$ if $d(X; G') = k$, and a family of k-critical subsets is called a k-*critical* family.

Let $c(F)$ denote the sum $\sum_{e \in F} c(e)$ of the weights of edges in F. Now the problem is to find a set F of new edges with minimum weight $c(F)$ such that

$$d(X; G + F) (= d(X; G) + d(X; (V, F))) \geq k \text{ for all } X \in 2^V - \{\emptyset, V\}. \quad (8.9)$$

Analogously with Lemma 8.6, we obtain the next lemma.

Lemma 8.8. *For an edge-weighted graph G and a real $k > 0$, any feasible augmentation $G + F$ must satisfy*

$$c(F) \geq \frac{1}{2} \sum_{Y \in \{Y_1, Y_2, \ldots, Y_t\}} (k - d(Y; G))$$

for every family $\{Y_1, Y_2, \ldots, Y_t\}$ of disjoint subsets of V. $\qquad\square$

We see that the argument used to derive Theorem 8.5 remains valid for the case where edges are weighted by nonnegative reals. Then, in the case of $\beta = +\infty$, we have the following result.

Theorem 8.9. *Given an edge-weighted graph $G = (V, E)$ and a real $k > 0$, a minimum feasible star augmentation $G + b$ with $b : V \to \mathfrak{R}_+$ and a family $\mathcal{X} = \{X_1, X_2, \ldots, X_t\}$ of disjoint subsets such that $b(V) = \sum_{1 \leq i \leq t}(k - d(X_i; G))$ can be found in $O(mn + n^2 \log n)$ time and $O(n + m)$ space.* $\qquad\square$

Note that the family $\mathcal{X}$ in Theorem 8.9 is a V-covering k-critical family. We compute a minimum augmentation $G + F$ in the following two phases.

1. By applying Theorem 8.9, find a minimum star augmentation $G' = G + b = (V \cup \{s\}, E \cup F_0)$ of G such that it satisfies (8.1), where F_0 denotes the set of weighted edges incident to the introduced vertex s. By Theorem 8.9, G' satisfies

$$\lambda_s(G') \geq k, \tag{8.10}$$

   there is a V-covering k-critical family $\mathcal{X}$ in G', $\tag{8.11}$

   and the sum of the weights $c(F_0) = d(s; G')$ of edges in F_0 is equal to $b(V) = \sum_{X \in \mathcal{X}}(k - d(X; G))$.
2. By applying Theorem 7.10, compute a complete k-feasible splitting of G' with the designated vertex s. Let F be the set of weighted edges obtained by the splitting, and output graph $G + F$ as an optimally augmented graph.

Note that, in the first phase, we do not have to increase $d(V)$ to an even number as in the case of multigraphs. Also, in the second phase, we use Theorem 7.10 to find a complete k-feasible splitting in a graph with edges weighted by reals instead of Theorem 7.19.

The graph $G + F$ obtained from $G' = G + b$ with $\lambda_s(G') \geq k$ by a complete k-feasible splitting in $G + F$ is k-edge-connected. By Theorems 8.9 and 7.10, the preceding algorithm can be implemented to run in $O(nm + n^2 \log n)$ time.

To prove the optimality of F, first note that $c(F) = c(F_0)/2 = d(s; G')/2 = b(V)/2$ holds since F is obtained from F_0 by a complete edge splitting. Therefore, by Lemma 8.8 and Theorem 8.9, F is a set with the minimum weight $c(F)$ needed to augment G into a k-edge-connected graph. From the preceding argument, we establish the next result.

Theorem 8.10. *Given an edge-weighted graph $G = (V, E)$ and a real $k > 0$, the edge-connectivity augmentation problem to the target connectivity k can be solved in $O(mn + n^2 \log n)$ time and $O(n + m)$ space. Moreover, the number of new weighted edges added to G is $O(n)$.* $\qquad\square$

It should be noted that the optimal value for $\Lambda_G(k)$ can be determined as $c(F_0) = b(V)$ after the first phase in the preceding algorithm. From any star augmentation G' satisfying (8.10) and (8.11), we can also construct an optimal augmentation

$G + F$ by Theorem 7.10. Therefore, we have the following optimality condition on $\Lambda_G(k)$.

Lemma 8.11. *For a star augmentation G' of an edge-weighted graph G with a target connectivity $k > 0$ of a real number, we have $\Lambda_G(k) = d(s; G')/2$ if (8.10) and (8.11) hold.* □

8.4.2 Function Λ_G

In this subsection, we present the main results on function Λ_G (see Fig. 8.6 in the beginning of Section 8.4), which will be proved in the subsequent subsections.

Theorem 8.12. *For an edge-weighted graph $G = (V, E)$, function Λ_G can be computed in $O(n(m + n \log n))$ time.* □

Theorem 8.13. *Let $G = (V, E)$ be an edge-weighted graph and let $(k_i^*, \Lambda_G(k_i^*))$, $i = 0, 1, 2, \ldots, r$, be all the break points of function $\Lambda_G(k)$, where $\lambda(G) = k_0^* < k_1^* < k_2^* < \cdots < k_r^*$. Then*

(i) *Function $\Lambda_G(k)$ $(k \geq 0)$ has at most $n - 1$ break points (i.e., $r \leq n - 2$), where n is the number of vertices in G.*

(ii) *Let $d\Lambda/dk$ denote the gradient of function $\Lambda_G(k)$ at $k \notin \{k_i^* \mid i = 0, 1, 2, \ldots, r\}$. Then $d\Lambda/dk \in \{0, \frac{2}{2}, \frac{3}{2}, \ldots, \frac{n}{2}\}$, and $d\Lambda/dk = \frac{n}{2}$ for $k > k_r^*$.*

(iii) *$\Lambda_G(k_r^*) = \frac{1}{2} \sum_{v \in V} \{k_r^* - d(v; G)\}$.*

(iv) *$\max_{v \in V} d(v; G) \leq k_r^* \leq \max \left[\max_{v \in V} d(v; G), \max_{X \subset V, |X| \geq 2} \frac{\sum_{v \in X} d(v; G) - d(X; G)}{|X| - 1} \right]$.*

□

8.4.3 Ranged Star Augmentations

This section introduces a *ranged star augmentation* of a graph to handle the entire range of target $k \in \Re_+$.

For two reals $a, b \in \Re_+$ with $a < b$, the interval $[a, b]$ is called a *range*, and its size $\pi([a, b])$ is defined as $b - a$. Let $R = \{[a_1, b_1], [a_2, b_2], \ldots, [a_t, b_t]\}$ be a set of ranges. The size of R, denoted by $\pi(R)$, is defined as the sum of all range sizes in R:

$$\pi(R) = (b_1 - a_1) + (b_2 - a_2) + \cdots + (b_t - a_t), \tag{8.12}$$

where $\pi(\emptyset)$ is defined to be 0. For a given real $k \in \Re_+$, we define the following operations on a set R of ranges. The *upper k-truncation* of a range $[a, b]$ is defined by

$$[a, b]|^k = \begin{cases} [a, \min\{b, k\}] & \text{if } a < k, \\ \emptyset & \text{otherwise.} \end{cases}$$

Based on this definition, the upper k-truncation of a set R of ranges is defined by

$$R|^k = \{[a_i, b_i]|^k \mid [a_i, b_i] \in R, \ a_i < k\}.$$

Similarly, the *lower k-truncation* of a range $[a, b]$ is defined by

$$[a, b]|_k = \begin{cases} [\max\{a, k\}, b] & \text{if } b > k \\ \emptyset & \text{otherwise,} \end{cases}$$

and the lower k-truncation of a set R of ranges is defined by

$$R|_k = \{[a_i, b_i]|_k \mid [a_i, b_i] \in R, \ b_i > k\}.$$

For example, $\{[1, 3], [2, 5], [4, 7]\}|^3 = \{[1, 3], [2, 3]\}$ and $\{[1, 3], [2, 5], [4, 7]\}|_3 = \{[3, 5], [4, 7]\}$ hold. For $k' \leq k$, we write $(R|^k)|_{k'} = (R|_{k'}|^k)$ as $R|_{k'}^k$.

Now we say that two range sets R and R' are *equivalent* if $\pi(R|^k) = \pi(R'|^k)$ holds for all $k \in \Re_+$. For example, $R = \{[5, 10], [8, 15]\}$ and $R' = \{[5, 15], [8, 10]\}$ are equivalent. A set R of ranges is called *gapless* from a to b if $\pi(R|^k) < \pi(R|^{k'})$ holds for any $a \leq k < k' \leq b$. A set R that is gapless from $a = \min\{a \mid [a, b] \in R\}$ to $b = \max\{b \mid [a, b] \in R\}$ is simply called *gapless*. For example, $R = \{[5, 10], [9, 15]\}$ is gapless, whereas $R = \{[5, 9], [10, 15]\}$ is not because $\pi(R|^9) = \pi(R|^{10}) = 4$.

For a real $\delta \in \Re_+$, we say that range $[a - \delta, b - \delta]$ is obtained by *lowering* $[a, b]$ by δ. Given a gapless set of ranges $R = \{[a_1, b_1], [a_2, b_2], \ldots, [a_t, b_t]\}$, in which $b_1 \leq b_2 \leq \cdots \leq b_t$ is assumed without loss of generality, we modify R into another gapless set of ranges

$$R' = \{[a_1 - \delta_1, b_1 - \delta_1], \ [a_2 - \delta_2, b_2 - \delta_2], \ldots, \ [a_t - \delta_t, b_t - \delta_t]\}$$

by lowering each range $[a_i, b_i] \in R$ by $\delta_i \geq 0$, such that R' satisfies $\delta_t = 0$ and

$$b_i - \delta_i = a_{i+1} - \delta_{i+1} \text{ for } i = 1, \ldots, t - 1$$

(i.e., R' is gapless and equivalent to a single range $[b_t - \pi(R), b_t]$). For example, for a set of ranges $R = \{[12, 14], [11, 14], [10, 16], [15, 18]\}$, such R' is given by $R' = \{[4, 6], [6, 9], [9, 15], [15, 18]\}$. We call such R' an *alignment* of R. By definition, an alignment R' is equivalent to a single range $[b_t - \pi(R), b_t]$. In the current example, $[b_t - \pi(R), b_t] = [4, 18]$.

Given a graph $G = (V, E)$, we consider a set $R(v)$ of ranges associated with each vertex $v \in V$. For notational convenience, we denote, for $X \subseteq V$,

$$R[X] = \{R(v) \mid v \in X\}, \quad R(X) = \cup_{v \in X} R(v), \tag{8.13}$$

and we define their sizes by $\pi(R[X]) = \sum_{v \in X} \pi(R(v)) (= \pi(R(X)))$. Given a set $R[V] = \{R(v) \mid v \in V\}$ of range sets, we define its *ranged star augmentation*

$$G' = G + R[V] \tag{8.14}$$

as follows. For each edge $\{s, v\}$, $v \in V$ incident to the designated vertex s, we assign the range set $R(v)$ instead of assigning a real weight and define its weight to be $\pi(R(v))$. For a real $k \geq 0$, we denote by

$$G'|^k = G + R[V]|^k$$

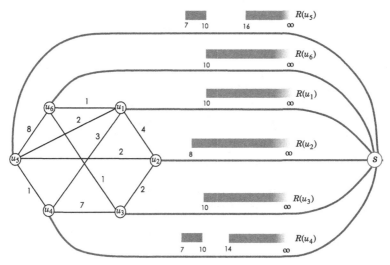

Figure 8.7. An example of a ranged star augmentation $G' = G + R[V]$ of the graph G in Fig. 8.5.

the ranged star augmentation obtained from $G' = G + R[V]$ by upper k-truncating $R(v)$ for all $v \in V$.

Based on these definitions, we can extend the optimality conditions in Lemma 8.11 to a ranged graph, where $G'|^k$ is identified with the star augmentation of G with weight $\pi(R(v)|^k)$ being attached to $\{s, v\}$, $v \in V$, when its connectivity or $d(X; G'|^k)$ is concerned.

Definition 8.14. *For a given graph $G = (V, E)$, a family $R[V]$ of sets of ranges is called* totally optimal *if the ranged star augmentation $G' = G + R[V]$ satisfies the following two conditions:*

$$\lambda_s(G'|^k) \geq k \text{ for all } k \in [0, +\infty], \tag{8.15}$$

$$G'|^k \text{ has a } V\text{-covering } k\text{-critical family } \mathcal{X}^k \text{ for every } k \in [0, +\infty]. \tag{8.16}$$

$\square$

If such a totally optimal family $R[V]$ of range sets is available, then, by Lemma 8.11, we can easily compute $\Lambda_G(k)$ for any $k \in \mathfrak{R}_+$ by

$$\Lambda_G(k) = d(s; G'|^k)/2 = \pi(R[V]|^k)/2. \tag{8.17}$$

Note that, by using $R(V) = \cup_{v \in V} R(v)$ instead of $R[V]$, $\pi(R[V]|^k)/2 = \pi(R(V)|^k)/2$ holds for all $k \geq 0$. Therefore, (8.17) is also stated as follows:

$$\Lambda_G(k) = \pi(R(V)|^k)/2, \tag{8.18}$$

where we call such $R(V)$ an *optimal set of range sets* of G. Taking the example of the family $R[V]$ of range sets in Fig. 8.7, which will be shown later to be totally

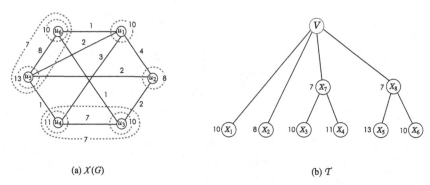

(a) $\mathcal{X}(G)$ (b) $\mathcal{T}$

Figure 8.8. (a) The family $\mathcal{X}(G) = \{X_1, X_2, \ldots, X_8\}$ of extreme vertex sets of the graph G in Fig. 8.5 and (b) the tree representation $\mathcal{T}$ for $\mathcal{X}(G)$.

optimal, its equivalent range set $R(V)$ is given by

$$R(V) = \{[7, +\infty], [7, +\infty], [8, +\infty], [10, +\infty], [14, +\infty], [16, +\infty]\}.$$
$$(8.19)$$

From this, we can obtain the edge-connectivity augmentation function Λ_G in Fig. 8.6 as follows. The maximum k with $\pi(R(V)|^k)/2 = 0$ is 7, which means $\lambda(G) = 7$ since we do not have to increase any edge weight to obtain a 7-edge-connected graph. Thus, the first break point of Λ_G is $(7, 0)$. Following (8.18), we then obtain

$$\Lambda_G(k) = \pi(R(V)|^k)/2 = \begin{cases} k - 7 & \text{for } 7 < k < 8 \\ 1 + 1.5(k - 8) & \text{for } 8 < k < 10 \\ 4 + 2(k - 10) & \text{for } 10 < k < 14 \\ 12 + 2.5(k - 14) & \text{for } 14 < k < 16 \\ 17 + 3(k - 16) & \text{for } 16 < k. \end{cases}$$

Observe that the gradient of Λ_G at any $k \geq 7$ with $k \notin \{7, 8, 10, 14, 16\}$ is given by one-half the number of ranges in $R(V)|^k$.

8.4.4 Simultaneous Augmentation

In this subsection, we show that a totally optimal family $R[V]$ of range sets can be constructed from the family $\mathcal{X}(G) = \{X_1, X_2, \ldots, X_p\}$ of extreme vertex sets of G. Let $\mathcal{T}$ be the tree representation for $\mathcal{X} \cup \{V\}$, where all X_i are indexed so that any node X_i in $\mathcal{T}$ has the largest index among all its descendants. For an extreme vertex set $X \in \mathcal{X}(G)$, we denote by $Ch(X)$ the family of extreme vertex sets Y that are the children of X in $\mathcal{T}$. For example, the family of extreme vertex sets of the graph G in Fig. 8.5 is $\mathcal{X}(G) = \{X_i = \{u_i\} \mid i = 1, 2, \ldots, 6\} \cup \{X_7 = \{u_3, u_4\}, X_8 = \{u_5, u_6\}\}$, as shown in Fig. 8.8(a). Its tree representation $\mathcal{T}$ is shown in Fig. 8.8(b).

Optimal Family of Range Sets

By Lemma 1.43, we see that condition (8.15) is equivalent to

$$d(X; G'|^k) \geq k \text{ for all } X \in \mathcal{X}(G) \text{ and } k \in [0, +\infty], \tag{8.20}$$

where it holds that

$$d(X; G'|^k) = d(X; G) + \sum_{v \in X} \pi(R(v)|^k) = d(X; G) + \pi(R(X)|^k).$$

To construct an optimal set $R[V]$ of range sets of G, we compute a family $R[X]$ of range sets for each extreme vertex set $X \in \mathcal{X}(G)$ such that

$$d(Y; G + R[X]|^k) \geq k \text{ for all } Y \in \mathcal{X}(G) \text{ with } Y \subset X \text{ and } k \in [0, +\infty] \tag{8.21}$$

and

$$G + R[X]|^k \text{ has an } X\text{-covering } k\text{-critical family } \mathcal{X}_X^k \text{ for every } k \in [0, +\infty]. \tag{8.22}$$

To represent such X-covering k-critical families $\mathcal{X}_X^k$ of $G'|^k$ for $k \in [0, +\infty]$, we use the following notion. A pair $(X, [a, b])$ of an extreme vertex set $X \in \mathcal{X}(G)$ and a range $[a, b]$ is called a *ranged extreme vertex set*. For a family $\mathcal{XR}$ of ranged extreme vertex sets and a real $k \geq 0$, we denote

$$\mathcal{XR}|^k = \{X \mid (X, [a, b]) \in \mathcal{XR}, \ a < k \leq b\}.$$

Construction of an Optimal Family $\mathcal{XR}_X$

We inductively construct for each extreme vertex set $X \in \mathcal{X}$ a range set $R[X]$ and a family $\mathcal{XR}_X$ of ranged extreme vertex sets for which (8.21) and (8.22) hold. Assuming that $R[Y]$ and $\mathcal{XR}_Y$ for all children $Y \in Ch(X)$ of an extreme vertex set X are available, we will show how $R[X]$ and $\mathcal{XR}_X$ can be obtained from $R[Y]$ and $\mathcal{XR}_Y$. For each extreme vertex set X with $Ch(X) = \emptyset$ (i.e., for each trivial extreme vertex set $X = \{v\}$, $v \in V$), we construct

$$R(v) = \{[d(v; G), +\infty]\}, \quad \mathcal{XR}_v = \{(\{v\}, [d(v; G), +\infty])\}.$$

Observe that, for any $k \geq 0$ and $v \in V$, $R[\{v\}]|^k = R(v)|^k$ and $\mathcal{X}_v^k = \mathcal{XR}_v^k$ satisfy (8.21) and (8.22), respectively. For example, in the graph G in Fig. 8.8(a), we have

$$R[X_1] = R(u_1) = \{[10, +\infty]\}, \quad \mathcal{XR}_{u_1} = \{(\{u_1\}, [10, +\infty])\},$$
$$R[X_2] = R(u_2) = \{[8, +\infty]\}, \quad \mathcal{XR}_{u_2} = \{(\{u_2\}, [8, +\infty])\},$$
$$R[X_3] = R(u_3) = \{[10, +\infty]\}, \quad \mathcal{XR}_{u_3} = \{(\{u_3\}, [10, +\infty])\},$$
$$R[X_4] = R(u_4) = \{[11, +\infty]\}, \quad \mathcal{XR}_{u_4} = \{(\{u_4\}, [11, +\infty])\},$$
$$R[X_5] = R(u_5) = \{[13, +\infty]\}, \quad \mathcal{XR}_{u_5} = \{(\{u_5\}, [13, +\infty])\},$$
$$R[X_6] = R(u_6) = \{[10, +\infty]\}, \quad \mathcal{XR}_{u_6} = \{(\{u_6\}, [10, +\infty])\}$$

(see the bottom layer of Fig. 8.9).

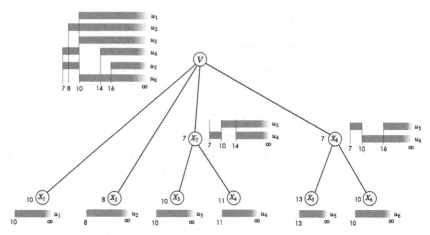

Figure 8.9. Illustration of a computation process of SIMULAUGMENT on the tree representation $\mathcal{T}$ for $\mathcal{X}(G)$ in Fig. 8.8(b).

Before describing a procedure for computing a range set $R(X)$ and a family $\mathcal{XR}_X$ of ranged extreme vertex sets from those for other $Y \in \mathcal{X}(G)$, we examine the example in Fig. 8.9. Consider the extreme vertex set $X_7 = \{u_3, u_4\}$. Suppose that we set $R[X_7] := \{R[X_3], R[X_4]\} = \{R(u_3) = \{[10, +\infty]\}, R(u_4) = \{[11, +\infty]\}\}$, and $\mathcal{XR}_{X_7} := \mathcal{XR}_{X_3} \cup \mathcal{XR}_{X_4} = \{(\{u_3\}, [10, +\infty)), (\{u_4\}, [11, +\infty))\}$, where $X_3 = \{u_3\}$ and $X_4 = \{u_4\}$. Then the current $R[X_7]$ does not satisfy (8.21) since $d(X_7; G + R[X_7]|^k) = d(X_7; G) = 7 < k$ holds for any $k \le 10$. However, just introducing a new range, say $[7, 10]$, to $R[X_7]$ does not remedy this because it violates condition (8.22); for any $k > 10$, each of $\{X_7\}$ and $\{X_3, X_4\}$ is no longer a k-critical family in $G + R(X_7)|^k$ since $d(X'; G + R[X_7]) > k$ holds for any $X' \in \{X_3, X_4, X_7\}$.

We show that there is a way of updating $R[X_3] \cup R[X_4]$ to obtain a set $R[X_7]$ that meets the criteria of both (8.21) and (8.22). We modify $R[X_3] \cup R[X_4]$ by splitting and lowering some ranges in the resulting set as follows. For $k^* = d(X_7; G) = 7$, compute k' such that $\pi(R[X_3]|^{k'} \cup R[X_4]|^{k'}) = k' - k^*$ holds. We see that $k' = 14$ satisfies the condition. We then split range $[11, +\infty] \in R(u_4)$ into two ranges, $[11, 14]$ and $[14, +\infty]$, and lower range $[11, 14]$ to $[7, 10]$ so that $\{[7, 10], [4, +\infty]\}$ and $[10, +\infty] \in R(u_3)$ become equivalent to $\{[7, +\infty], [14, \infty]\}$. As a result, we set

$$R[X_7] := \{R(u_3) := \{[10, +\infty]\}, R(u_4) := \{[7, 10], [14, +\infty]\}\}$$

and

$$\mathcal{XR}_{X_7} := \{(X_7, [7, 10]), (X_3, [10, +\infty]), (X_4, [14, +\infty])\},$$

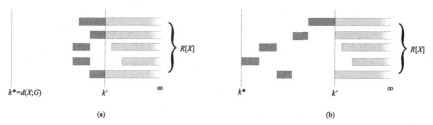

Figure 8.10. (a) A range set $R[X]$ before processing an extreme vertex set $X \in \mathcal{X}(G)$; (b) a range set $R[X]$ after processing X via the LOWER procedure.

as illustrated by the ranges beside node X_7 in Fig. 8.9. The new $R[X_7]$ satisfies the following:

$$d(X_7; G + R[X_7]|^k) = 7 + (k - 7) = k \text{ for } k \in [7, 14],$$
$$d(X_7; G + R[X_3]|^k) = 10 + (k - 10) = k \text{ for } k \in [14 + \infty],$$
$$d(X_7; G + R[X_4]|^k) = 11 + (k - 11) = k \text{ for } k \in [14 + \infty].$$

Thus, $\{X_7\}$ (resp. $\{X_3, X_4\}$) is a k-critical family in $G + R[X_7]|^k$ for $k \in [7, 14]$ (resp. $k \in [14, +\infty]$).

In general, we can obtain the desired $R[X]$ and $\mathcal{X}\mathcal{R}_X$ from those of $Y \in Ch(X)$ as follows. Let

$$k^* = d(X; G)$$

and determine k' such that

$$\pi(R[X]|^{k'}) = k' - k^*. \tag{8.23}$$

Then some (parts) of the ranges in $R[X]$ are lowered by the following procedure.

Procedure LOWER

Input: A family $R[X] = \{R(u) \mid u \in X\}$ of range sets for $X \subseteq V$, and k' satisfying (8.23) for $k^* = d(X; G)$.

Output: A family $R[X] = \{R(u) \mid u \in X\}$ of range sets such that $R[X]|^k$ is equivalent to range $[k^*, k']$ for $k \leq k'$ and $R[X]|_k$ remains unchanged for $k \geq k'$.

1 Define $A_u := R(u)|^{k'}$ for all $u \in X$, where $k^* + \pi(\cup_{u \in X} A_u) = k'$ holds by (8.23);

2 Align $\mathcal{A} = \cup_{u \in X} A_u$ to obtain $\mathcal{A}' = \cup_{u \in X} A'_u$ such that $\mathcal{A}'$ is equivalent to range $[k^*, k']$;

3 Finally, let $R(u) := A'_u \cup R(u)|_{k'}$ for each $u \in X$.

We remark that the result of aligning $\mathcal{A} = \cup_{u \in X} A_u$ in the LOWER procedure is not unique. A result of LOWER is illustrated in Fig. 8.10, where each range $[a, b]$ in $R(u) \in R[X]$ with $a < k' < b$ is split into two ranges $[a, k']$ and $[k', b]$ in Fig. 8.10(a), and then the split ranges $[a, k']$ colored darker gray are aligned from k^* to k' in Fig. 8.10(b) so that no two of them overlap each other. Note that, after updating $R(u)$, $u \in X$, by LOWER, $\pi(R[X]|^k)$ remains the same for all k with $k \in [0, k^*]$ or $k \in [k', +\infty]$ but increases for all $k \in (k^*, k')$. Therefore, any extreme vertex set $Y \subseteq X$ that was previously k-critical in $G + R[X]$ remains k-critical for all $k \in [k', +\infty]$. Furthermore, X is now a k-critical set for all $k \in [k^*, k']$. Based on these facts, we define $\mathcal{XR}_X$ by

$$\mathcal{XR}_X := \{(X, [k^*, k'])\} \cup \tag{8.24}$$
$$\{(Z, [\max\{a, k'\}, b]) \mid (Z, [a, b]) \in \mathcal{XR}_Y, \ Y \in Ch(X), \ k' < b\}.$$

Then it is not difficult to see that the resulting $R[X]$ and $\mathcal{XR}_X$ satisfy (8.21) and (8.22) for the current X.

Let us apply the preceding argument to the example of Fig. 8.9. For $X = X_8 = \{u_5, u_6\}$, we have $k^* = 7$, $k' = 16$, $A_{u_5} = \{[13, 16]\}$, and $A_{u_6} = \{[10, 16]\}$. Then $\mathcal{A} = A_{u_5} \cup A_{u_6}$ is aligned to $\mathcal{A}' = A'_{u_5} \cup A'_{u_6}$, where $A'_{u_5} = \{[7, 10]\}$ and $A'_{u_6} = \{[10, 16]\}$. Let $R(u_5) := A'_{u_5} \cup \{[16, +\infty]\}$ (which is not gapless) and let $R(u_6) := A'_{u_6} \cup \{[16, +\infty]\}$ (which will be replaced with the equivalent $\{[10, +\infty]\}$). Then

$$R[X_8] := \{R(u_5) := \{[7, 10], [16, +\infty]\}, R(u_6) := \{[10, +\infty]\}\},$$

as illustrated by the ranges beside node X_8 in Fig. 8.9, and

$$\mathcal{XR}_{X_8} := \{(X_8, [7, 16]), (X_5, [16, +\infty]), (X_6, [16, +\infty])\}.$$

Entire Augmentation Algorithm

By repeatedly applying the LOWER procedure to $X \in \mathcal{X}(G)$, which is located lowest in $\mathcal{T}$ among all unprocessed extreme vertex sets in $\mathcal{X}(G)$, we finally obtain a family $R[V]$ of range sets $R(v)$, $v \in V$, and the last family $\mathcal{XR}_V$ of ranged extreme vertex sets by taking the union of families $\mathcal{XR}_X$ over all inclusion-wise maximal extreme vertex sets $X \in \mathcal{X}(G)$. This $\mathcal{XR}_V$ satisfies (8.21) and (8.22), and the final range set $R[V]$ is totally optimal.

For our running example, we have already seen how $R[X_7]$, $\mathcal{XR}_{X_7}$, $R[X_8]$, and $\mathcal{XR}_{X_8}$ in Fig. 8.9 are computed from their children. Finally, $R[V]$ can be obtained by taking the union of $R[X_7]$ and $R[X_8]$. Thus, $R[V]$ consists of the following range sets:

$$R[V] = \Big\{ R(u_1) = \{[10, +\infty]\}, \ R(u_2) = \{[8, +\infty]\}, \ R(u_3) = \{[10, +\infty]\},$$
$$R(u_4) = \{[7, 10], [14, +\infty]\}, \ R(u_5) = \{[7, 10], [16, +\infty]\},$$
$$R(u_6) = \{[10, +\infty]\}\Big\} \tag{8.25}$$

(see Fig. 8.7).

The entire description of the preceding algorithm is given as follows.

Algorithm SIMULAUGMENT

Input: The family $\mathcal{X}(G)$ of extreme vertex sets of an edge-weighted graph
$G = (V, E)$.

Output: A totally optimal range set $R[V] = \{R(v) \mid v \in V\}$.

1 Let $R(v) := \{[d(v; G), +\infty]\}$, $\mathcal{X}\mathcal{R}_v := \{(\{v\}, [d(v; G), +\infty])\}$ for each $v \in V$;
2 Mark all nontrivial extreme vertex sets $X \in \mathcal{X}(G)$ unscanned;
3 **while** there is an unscanned extreme vertex set **do**
4   Let X be an inclusionwise minimal unscanned extreme vertex set;
5   Let $k^* := d(X; G)$, and let k' be the real determined by $\pi(R[X]|^{k'}) = k' - k^*$;
6   Update $R[X]$ by procedure LOWER;
7   Compute $\mathcal{X}\mathcal{R}_X$ according to (8.24)
8 **end**. /* while */

From the preceding discussion, SIMULAUGMENT correctly delivers a totally optimal range set $R[V]$.

Complexity of SIMULAUGMENT

In the following, we consider the complexity of SIMULAUGMENT. The number of ranges in a set $R[X]$ is denoted by $|R[X]|$. For a range $r = [a, b]$, a (resp. b) is called the *bottom* (resp. *top*) of r and is denoted by $bot(r)$ (resp. $top(r)$).

Lemma 8.15. *For an extreme vertex set $X \in \mathcal{X}(G)$, LOWER in SIMULAUGMENT can be implemented to run in $O(|R[V]| + |X| \log |R[V]|)$ time, where $R[V] = \{R(v) \mid v \in V\}$ denotes the family of range sets obtained after updating $R[X] = \{R(v) \mid v \in X\}$ by LOWER.* □

Proof. During the execution of SIMULAUGMENT, we maintain a list $List[R[V]]$ of all ranges in $R[V]$, where the ranges are sorted in nondecreasing order of their tops, and each range r in the list has two values, its bottom $bot(r)$ and the vertex u_r with $r \in R(u_r)$. Compute k' by (8.23). Using the preceding list, we then compute $\mathcal{A} := \cup_{u \in X} A_u := R(X)|^{k'}$ as follows.

(i) Let $R := List[R[V]]$ and remove all ranges $[a_u, b_u] \in R(u)$ satisfying $a_u < k' < b_u$ and $u \in X$ (if any) from R.
(ii) For each $u \in X$ detected in step (i), insert new ranges $[a_u, k']$ and $[k', b_u]$ into R.
(iii) Divide the resulting list R into two lists, $List[R[X]|^{k'}]$ and $List[R[X]|_{k'} \cup R[V - X]]$, where each of these lists is sorted with respect to the tops of the ranges.

The aforementioned step (i) can be carried out in $O(|R[V]|)$ time by traversing $List[R[V]]$, and step (ii) can be performed in $O(|X| \log |R[V]|)$ time by inserting one range into the list $List[R[V]]$ in $O(\log |R[V]|)$ time by using an appropriate data structure of priority queue. By picking up each $r \in List[R[V]]$ and attaching it to the end of $List[R[X]|^{k'}]$ if $r \in R[X]|^{k'}$ and $List[R[X]|_{k'} \cup R[V - X]]$ otherwise, step (iii) can be done in $O(|R[V]|)$ time.

For the list $List[R[X]|^{k'}]$, we can align $\mathcal{A} = \cup_{u \in X} A_u = R[X]|^{k'}$ and obtain a sorted list $List[\mathcal{A}']$ of the resulting set $\mathcal{A}'$ of ranges in $O(|\mathcal{A}|)$ time. Finally, a list for the entire set $R := List[\mathcal{A}'] \cup List[R[X]|_{k'} \cup R[V - X]]$ can be updated in $O(|R[V]|)$ time by merging all three sorted lists into a single list. Therefore, aligning $R[X]$ can be updated in $O(|R[V]| + |X| \log |R[V]|)$ time. □

Let r_{max} denote the maximum number of ranges in $R[V]$ attained during the execution of SIMULAUGMENT, for which $r_{max} \leq n^2$ obviously holds since at most $|X|$ $(\leq n)$ new ranges in $R[V]$ are created in each iteration of the while-loop. If we take this approach, the entire running time of the SIMULAUGMENT algorithm becomes $O(\sum_{X \in \mathcal{X}(G)}(|R[V]| + |X| \log |R[V]|)) = O(nr_{max} + n^2 \log n) = O(n^3)$ time. It has been shown [238] that a more sophisticated implementation of LOWER ensures $r_{max} \leq (2n - 1) + (2n - 3) \log_2(n - 1)$. This further improves the running time of SIMULAUGMENT as follows.

Theorem 8.16. *For an edge-weighted graph $G = (V, E)$, there are a family $\mathcal{X}\mathcal{R}_V$ of ranged extreme vertex sets satisfying (8.21) and (8.22), and a totally optimal range set $R[V]$ such that $|R[V]| \leq (2n - 1) + (2n - 3) \log_2(n - 1)$. Furthermore, such $R[V]$ can be obtained by SIMULAUGMENT in $O(n^2 \log n)$ time.* □

A totally optimal range set $R[V]$ in this theorem is used to construct all optimal solutions, that will be described in Section 8.4.5. However, to examine the structure of Λ_G, we only need to obtain a range set $R(V)$ that is equivalent to a totally optimal set $R[V]$ of range sets.

We are now able to prove Theorems 8.12 and 8.13.

Proof of Theorem 8.12. As already observed in (8.18), Λ_G can be computed from a range set $R(V)$. We show that $R(V)$ consists of gapless ranges, which is essential to prove Theorem 8.12. To prove this, we can modify the SIMULAUGMENT algorithm as follows, so that only a range set $R(X)$ equivalent to $R[X]$ is computed during the execution.

Algorithm SIMULAUGMENTEQUIV
Input: The family $\mathcal{X}(G)$ of extreme vertex sets of an edge-weighted graph
　　　$G = (V, E)$.
Output: A range set $R(V)$ equivalent to a totally optimal range set $R[V]$.
1　Let $R(v) := \{[d(v; G), +\infty]\}$ for each $v \in V$;
2　Mark all nontrivial extreme vertex sets $X \in \mathcal{X}(G)$ unscanned;
3　**while** there is an unscanned extreme vertex set **do**
4　　Let X be an inclusion-wise minimal unscanned extreme vertex set;
5　　Let $k^* := d(X; G)$;
6　　$R := \cup_{Y \in Ch(X)} R(Y)$;

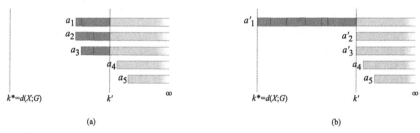

(a)   (b)

Figure 8.11. (a) A range set $R(X)$ that is equivalent to the $R[X]$ in Fig. 8.10(a), before processing an extreme vertex set $X \in \mathcal{X}(G)$; (b) a range set $R(X)$ that is equivalent to the $R[X]$ in Fig. 8.10(b) obtained by procedure LOWER.

7   /* We assume $R = \{[a_1, +\infty], [a_2, +\infty], \ldots, [a_r, +\infty]\}$, where
        $a_1 \leq a_2 \leq \cdots \leq a_r$ */
8   Find $k' \in \mathfrak{R}_+$ such that $\pi(R|^{k'}) = k' - k^*$;
9      $R(X) := (R - \{[a_1, +\infty]\})|_{k'} \cup \{[k^*, +\infty]\}$
10   **end**. /* while */

We easily see by induction that $R(X)$ consists of $|X|$ ranges with forms of $[a_i, +\infty]$ if so does $R(Y)$ for every child $Y \in Ch(X)$. See Fig. 8.11, where ranges in $R|^{k'} = \{[a_1, k'], [a_2, k'], [a_3, k']\}$ in Fig. 8.11(a) are replaced with a single range $[k^*, k']$ to construct $R(X)$ in Fig. 8.11(b). In this case, we can compute $R(X)$ in $O(|X|)$ time for each set $X \in \mathcal{X}(G)$. Hence, the final $R(V)$ can be obtained in $O(\sum_{X \in \mathcal{X}(G)} |X|) = O(n^2)$ time. Since $\mathcal{X}(G)$ can be computed in $O(mn + n^2 \log n)$ time by Theorem 6.6, the entire time bound is also $O(mn + n^2 \log n)$.

We finally prove Theorem 8.13.

Proof of Theorem 8.13. We assume that $R(V)$ for a given graph $G = (V, E)$ is given as $R(V) = \{[a_1, +\infty], [a_2, +\infty], \ldots, [a_n, +\infty]\}$, where $n = |V|$ and $a_1 \leq a_2 \leq \cdots \leq a_n$.

(i) From $\Lambda_G(k) = \pi(R(V)|^k)/2$, a real k becomes a break point of function $\Lambda_G(k)$ only at $k = a_i$. Therefore, the number of break points of function Λ_G is equal to the number of distinct values among these $a_1, a_2, \ldots, a_n$. We show $a_1 = a_2 = \lambda(G)$. Since a_1 is the smallest cut size among all extreme vertex sets, $a_1 = \lambda(G) = d(X'; G)$ holds for the extreme vertex set X', which is scanned last by SIMULAUGMENTEQUIV. By the definition of extreme vertex sets, $V - X'$ contains another extreme vertex set $X'' \in \mathcal{X}(G)$ with $d(X''; G) = \lambda(G)$. Thus, this range set $R(X'')$ contains a range $[a'', +\infty]$ with $a'' = \lambda(G)$. Therefore, the final $R(V)$ contains at least two ranges of the form $[\lambda(G), +\infty]$, and this shows that the number of break points in Λ_G is at most $n - 1$.

(ii) From (8.18), that is, $\Lambda_G(k) = \pi(R(V)|^k)/2$, the gradient $d\Lambda/dk$ of $\Lambda_G(k)$ at k is equal to $\frac{1}{2}|\{a_i \mid a_i < k\}|$. Then by considering $a_1 = a_2$, we see that $d\Lambda/dk \in \{\frac{2}{2}, \frac{3}{2}, \ldots, \frac{n}{2}\}$ for any k ($> a_1 = a_2$) with $k \notin \{a_1, a_2, \ldots, a_n\}$. In particular, $d\Lambda/dk = \frac{n}{2}$ for $k > a_n$.

(iii) Clearly $k_r^* = a_n$. By the construction of the final $R(V)$ by SIMULAUG-MENTEQUIV from initial range sets $R(v) = \{[d(v; G), +\infty]\}$, $v \in V$, we have $\max_{v \in V} d(v; G) \leq a_n$. From this, $\pi(R(V)|^k) = \sum_{v \in V} \pi(R(v)|^k)$ holds for any $k \in [0, a_n]$. Therefore, $\Lambda_G(k_r^*) = \frac{1}{2}\pi(R(V)|^{a_n}) = \frac{1}{2}\sum_{v \in V}\{k_r^* - d(v; G)\}$.

(iv) From condition (iii), $\max\{d(v; G)|v \in V\} \leq k_r^*$ hold. Recall that $k_r^* = a_n$ is equal to either $d(u; G)$ of some vertex u or some k' obtained in line 5 of SIMULAUGMENTEQUIV. If k_r^* is the former, then

$$k_r^* \leq \max\{d(v; G)|v \in V\}$$

clearly holds. To consider the latter case, assume that $k_r^* = k'$ is obtained when an extreme vertex set $X \in \mathcal{X}(G)$ is scanned in SIMULAUGMENTEQUIV. Let

$$\cup_{Y \in Ch(X)} R(Y) = \{[a_1', +\infty], [a_2', +\infty], \ldots, [a_{|X|}', +\infty]\}, \quad a_1' \leq a_2' \leq \cdots \leq a_{|X|}'$$

hold before scanning X. Furthermore, since k_r^* is the largest among all a_i', $R(X)$ after scanning X must be of the form

$$R(X) = \{[d(X; G), +\infty], [k_r^*, +\infty], \ldots, [k_r^*, +\infty]\}.$$

Therefore, by the assumption $k_r^* = k'$, it satisfies

$$k_r^* - d(X; G) = \sum_{1 \leq i \leq |X|} (k_r^* - a_i') = \sum_{u \in X}(k_r^* - d(u; G)),$$

from which

$$k_r^* = \frac{\sum_{u \in X} d(u; G) - d(X; G)}{|X| - 1}$$

follows. Combining the preceding results, we have

$$k_r^* \leq \max\left[\max\{d(v; G) \mid v \in V\}, \right.$$
$$\left. \max\left\{\frac{\sum_{u \in X} d(u; G) - d(X; G)}{|X| - 1} \mid X \subset V, |X| \geq 2\right\}\right]. \qquad \square$$

For our running example, $R(V)$ is given as in (8.19), and $k_r^* = 16$ is obtained after scanning $X = X_8 = \{u_5, u_6\}$, for which in fact $k_r^* = (\sum_{u \in X} d(u; G) - d(X; G))/(|X| - 1) = (d(u_5; G) + d(u_6; G) - d(X_8; G))/(2 - 1) = 16$ holds.

As a by-product of Theorems 8.12 and 8.13, we observe an interesting property of the graph $G^*(k)$, an optimally augmented k-edge-connected graph, when k is sufficiently large.

Corollary 8.17. *An optimally augmented k-edge-connected graph $G^*(k)$, obtained from $G = (V, E)$, is k-regular (i.e., $d(v; G^*(k)) = k$ for all $v \in V$) if $k \geq k_r^*$, where k_r^* is the largest break point of Λ_G.* $\qquad \square$

Proof. First consider the case of $k = k_r^*$. Clearly, $d(v; G^*(k_r^*)) \geq k_r^*$ for all $v \in V$ by $\lambda(G^*(k_r^*)) \geq k_r^*$. By Theorem 8.13(iii), we have

$$\sum_{v \in V} d(v; G) + 2\Lambda_G(k_r^*) = n \cdot k_r^*.$$

Since the total $\Lambda_G(k_r^*)$ amount of edge weights is added, G must have increased its total degree by $2\Lambda_G(k_r^*)$, and this equality implies that the inequality $d(v; G^*(k_r^*)) \geq k_r^*$ holds by equality for all $v \in V$. Thus, $G^*(k_r^*)$ is $k \ (= k_r^*)$ regular.

Now consider the case of $k > k_r^*$. By Theorem 8.13(iv), $d\Lambda/dk = n/2$ for $k > k_r^*$, which means that $\Lambda_G(k_r^*) + (k - k_r^*)n/2$ edge weights are added to make G k-edge-connected. Hence, the total degree of $G^*(k)$ is

$$\sum_{v \in V} d(v; G) + 2\Lambda_G(k_r^*) + (k - k_r^*)n = \sum_{v \in V} k_r^* + (k - k_r^*)n = kn.$$

Since $d(v; G^*(k)) \geq k$ must hold for all $v \in V$ by $\lambda(G^*(k)) \geq k$, this implies $d(v; G^*(k)) = k$ for all $v \in V$. □

8.4.5 Constructing All Optimal Solutions

In the previous subsections, we observed that the function $\Lambda_G(k)$, which gives the total amount of weights needed to make G k-edge-connected, can be computed in $O(mn + n^2 \log n)$ time for the entire range $k \in [0, +\infty]$. Now we show that all optimally augmented graphs $G^*(k)$ for the entire range $k \in [\lambda(G), +\infty]$ can be compactly represented by a set of $O(n \log n)$ cycles $\Pi = (C_1^*, C_2^*, \ldots, C_p^*)$ on V in the following sense. The cycles C_i^* have ranges $[\lambda_{i-1}, \lambda_i]$, $i = 1, 2, \ldots, p$, such that $\lambda(G) = \lambda_0 < \lambda_1 < \cdots < \lambda_{p-1} < \lambda_p = +\infty$. To compute $G^*(k)$ for a real $k \geq \lambda(G)$, first obtain the largest index $i = i_k$ such that $\lambda_i < k$ and then increase the weights of all edges in C_i^* by $(\lambda_i - \lambda_{i-1})/2$ for $i = 1, 2, \ldots, i_k$ and the weights of all edges in $C_{i_k+1}^*$ by $(k - \lambda_{i_k})/2$.

Such a hierarchical structure of optimal solutions over all k is also known for the integer version of the edge-connectivity augmentation problem in undirected graphs [259, 308] and directed graphs [37].

Our goal in this section is to establish the following theorem.

Theorem 8.18. *Given an edge-weighted graph $G = (V, E)$, there is a set*

$$\Pi = \{(C_i^*, [\lambda_{i-1}, \lambda_i]) \mid i = 1, 2, \ldots, p\}$$

of weighted cycles that provide all optimally augmented graphs $G^*(k)$ for the entire range $k \in [\lambda(G), +\infty]$, where p satisfies

$$p \leq 4n + 4n \log n.$$

Furthermore, such a set Π can be computed in $O(mn + n^2 \log n)$ time. □

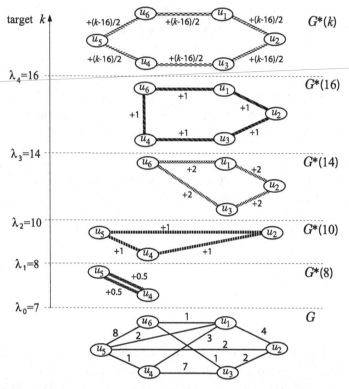

Figure 8.12. A scheme for generating optimally augmented graphs $G^*(k)$ of the initial graph G in Fig. 8.5, for all $k \geq \lambda(G)$, where $G^*(k)$ is obtained from G by increasing cycle weights up to the target k.

Illustration of Computing All Optimal Augmentations

As our running example, let us consider the graph G of Fig. 8.5, and the following set of weighted cycles:

$$\Pi = \{(C_1^* = \{u_4, u_5\}, [7, 8]), (C_2^* = \{u_2, u_4, u_5\}, [8, 10]),$$
$$(C_3^* = \{u_1, u_2, u_3, u_6\}, [10, 14]),$$
$$(C_4^* = \{u_1, u_2, u_3, u_4, u_6\}, [14, 16]),$$
$$(C_5^* = \{u_1, u_2, u_3, u_4, u_5, u_6\}, [16, +\infty])\}.$$

Figure 8.12 illustrates these cycles together with values of λ_i, where $G^*(k)$ is obtained from G by increasing the cycle weights up to the target k. Figure 8.13 shows the optimally augmented graph $G^*(k)$ for a target $k = 15$, constructed by adding G the first three cycles C_1^*, C_2^* and C_3^* with their weights 0.5, 1, and 2, and the fourth cycle C_4^* with weight $(k - \lambda_3)/2 = (15 - 14)/2 = 0.5$.

We show that the set Π of cycles in Theorem 8.18 can be constructed from a totally optimal range set $R[V]$ of G. Let $G' = G + R[V]$, for which we assume without loss of generality that $R[V]$ contains no range $[a, b]$ with $a = b$. Let

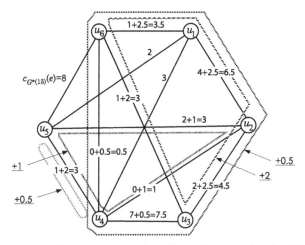

Figure 8.13. An optimally augmented graph $G^*(k)$ for the graph G in Fig. 8.5 and $k = 15$.

$\{\lambda_i \mid i = 0, 1, \ldots, p\} = \{top(r),\ bot(r) \mid r \in R[V]\}$, where we assume $\lambda_i < \lambda_{i+1}$, $i = 0, 1, \ldots, p - 1$ and $\lambda_p = +\infty$. In our running example, $R[V]$ is given in (8.25), and we have $\{top(r),\ bot(r) \mid r \in R[V]\} = \{7, 8, 10, 14, 16, +\infty\}$, $p = 5$ and $\lambda_0 = 7$, $\lambda_1 = 8$, $\lambda_2 = 10$, $\lambda_3 = 14$, $\lambda_4 = 16$, $\lambda_5 = +\infty$. In what follows, we treat λ_p as an arbitrary constant greater than λ_{p-1} in order to prove Theorem 8.18.

Graphs $G'|^{\lambda_i}$ and G_i^*

Now by Theorem 8.16 we can assume

$$p \leq 2|R[V]| < 4n + 4n \log_2 n.$$

Then we consider a sequence of $p + 1$ graphs $G'|^{\lambda_i} = (G + R[V])|^{\lambda_i}$, $i = 0, 1, \ldots, p$. Figure 8.14 illustrates these graphs $G'|^{\lambda_i}$ for our running example, where G' is the ranged star augmentation (8.14) defined in Section 8.4.3, and $\lambda_0 = 7$, $\lambda_1 = 8$, $\lambda_2 = 10$, $\lambda_3 = 14$, $\lambda_4 = 16$, and $\lambda_5 = +\infty$ as noted earlier. Note that the weights of edges $\{s, v\}$ are indicated by their thicknesses.

For each $i = 0, 1, \ldots, p - 1$, let $G_i^* = (V, E_i^*)$ denote a graph obtained from $G'|^{\lambda_i}$ by a complete λ_i-feasible splitting at s followed by the removal of the designated vertex s (see Figs. 8.15(a) and 8.15(b)). We can assume $\lambda(G_i^*) \geq \lambda_i$ by Theorem 7.10. In fact, $\lambda(G_i^*) = \lambda_i$ holds for all i, since Lemma 8.16 says that there exists a family $\mathcal{X}\mathcal{R}_V$ of ranged extreme vertex sets satisfying (8.21) and (8.22) for V and, hence, $G'|^{\lambda_i}$ has a V-covering λ_i-critical family $\mathcal{X}^{\lambda_i}$. Then G_i^*, $i = 0, 1, \ldots, p$, give optimally augmented graphs, $G^*(k)$, for $k = \lambda_i$.

We now show that such G_{i+1}^* can be easily obtained from G_i^* without really applying the splitting algorithm and that all G_i^* can be characterized by the cycles C_i^* as explained earlier. For this goal, we first show an important property of graphs

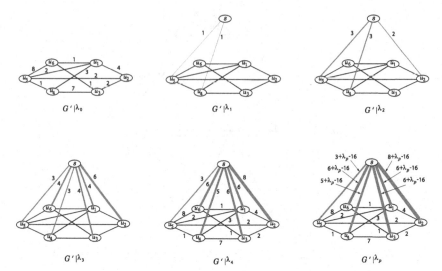

Figure 8.14. Graphs $G'|^{\lambda_0}, G'|^{\lambda_1}, \ldots, G'|^{\lambda_p}$ $(p = 5)$ for the initial graph G in Fig. 8.5.

G_i^*. Let $V_1, V_2, \ldots, V_h \subseteq V$ be the set of maximal sets such that

$$\lambda(u, v; G_i^*) > \lambda_i \text{ for all } u, v \in V_j,$$

where $\lambda(u, u; G_i^*) = +\infty$ by definition. We call such a subset V_j a λ_i-*component*.[1] By $\lambda(G_i^*) = \lambda_i$, we have $h \geq 2$. A λ_i-component V_j is called a λ_i-*leaf* if $d(V_j; G_i^*) = \lambda_i$ (i.e., $\{V_j, V - V_j\}$ itself is a minimum cut in G_i^*). From definitions, we easily see the following properties:

   (i) The set of λ_i-components is a partition of V.
   (ii) For any two λ_i-components V_ℓ and V_j, G_i^* has a minimum cut $X_{\ell,j}$ that separates V_ℓ and V_j.
   (iii) Every minimum cut X in G_i^* contains a λ_i-leaf $V_j \subseteq X$, since any minimum cut $X' \subseteq X$ with the minimal cardinality $|X'|$ is a λ_i-leaf of G_i^*.

Lemma 8.19. *Let V_j be a λ_i-component in $G_i^* = (V, E_i^*)$. Then $d(X; G_i^*) = d(X; G'|^{\lambda_i})$ holds for any subset $X \subseteq V_j$.* □

Proof. Let ΔE_i^* denote the set of edges e whose weights have been increased by the edge-splitting operation to obtain G_i^* from $G'|^{\lambda_i}$; that is,

$$\Delta E_i^* = \{e \in E \mid c_{G_i^*}(e) > c_G(e)\} \cup \{e \in E_i^* - E \mid c_{G_i^*}(e) > 0\}$$

(note that $c_G(e) = c_{G'|^{\lambda_i}}(e)$ holds for all $e \in E$). Then it is sufficient to show that ΔE_i^* contains no edge $\{u, v\}$ whose end vertices u and v both belong to some V_j. There exists a V-covering λ_i-critical family $\mathcal{X}^{\lambda_i}$ in $G'|^{\lambda_i}$, and the end vertices u and v of every edge $e = \{u, v\}$ in ΔE_i^* must belong to different critical

---

[1] A maximal subset $X \subseteq V(G)$ with $\lambda(u, v; G) \geq k$, $u, v \in X$ is defined as a k-edge-connected component in Section 1.5.2. The λ_i-component is a $(\lambda_i + \epsilon)$-edge-connected component for any $\epsilon > 0$.

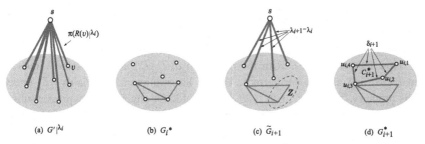

(a) $G'|^{\lambda_i}$ (b) G_i^* (c) $\tilde{G}_{i+1}$ (d) G_{i+1}^*

Figure 8.15. Illustration of graphs $G'|^{\lambda_i}$, G_i^*, $\tilde{G}_{i+1}$ and G_{i+1}^*.

subsets X', $X'' \in \mathcal{X}^{\lambda_i}$ in order to make G_i^* λ_i-edge-connected. This means that $\lambda(u, v; G_i^*) = \lambda_i$ holds for all $e = \{u, v\} \in \Delta E_i^*$. Therefore, no λ_i-component V_j contains both u and v since $\lambda(u', v'; G_i^*) > \lambda_i$ holds for any $u', v' \in V_j$. □

Computing G_{i+1}^* via $\tilde{G}_{i+1}$

We next introduce another sequence of graphs. Let $\tilde{G}_{i+1}$, $i = 0, 1, \ldots, p - 1$, denote the graph obtained from $G_i^* = (V, E_i^*)$ by putting back vertex s and edges $\{s, v\}$ with weights $\pi(R(v)|_{\lambda_i}^{\lambda_{i+1}}) = \lambda_{i+1} - \lambda_i$ for all $v \in V$; that is, $\tilde{G}_{i+1} = (V \cup \{s\}, E_i^* \cup E'(s))$, $E'(s) = \{\{s, v\} \mid v \in V\}$ and

$$c_{\tilde{G}_{i+1}}(e) = \begin{cases} \lambda_{i+1} - \lambda_i & \text{if } e = \{s, v\} \in E'(s) \text{ and } R|_{\lambda_i}^{\lambda_{i+1}}(v) \neq \emptyset \\ 0 & \text{if } e = \{s, v\} \in E'(s) \text{ and } R|_{\lambda_i}^{\lambda_{i+1}}(v) = \emptyset \\ c_{G_i^*}(e) & \text{if } e \in E_i^*. \end{cases}$$

In other words, $\tilde{G}_{i+1}$ is the graph obtained from $G'|^{\lambda_{i+1}}$ by splitting all edges $\{s, v\}$, $v \in V$ with weight $\pi(R(v)|^{\lambda_i})$ at s, leaving the weights $\pi(R(v)|_{\lambda_i}^{\lambda_{i+1}})$ in each edge $\{s, v\}$ (see Fig. 8.15(b) and 8.15(c)). The next lemma claims that an optimally augmented graph G_{i+1}^* can be obtained from this graph $\tilde{G}_{i+1}$.

Lemma 8.20. *For all* $i = 0, 1, \ldots, p - 1$, $\lambda(G_i^*) \geq \lambda_i$ *implies* $\lambda(\tilde{G}_{i+1}) \geq \lambda_{i+1}$. □

Proof. Consider the set $\Gamma_{\tilde{G}_{i+1}}(s)$ ($\neq \emptyset$) (i.e., vertices adjacent to s by positive weights in $\tilde{G}_{i+1}$). From the definitions of $\tilde{G}_{i+1}$ and G_i^*, any subset $X \subset V$ satisfies

$$d(X; \tilde{G}_{i+1}) = d(X; G_i^*) + |X \cap \Gamma_{\tilde{G}_{i+1}}(s)| \cdot (\lambda_{i+1} - \lambda_i).$$

Then, if $X \cap \Gamma_{\tilde{G}_{i+1}}(s) \neq \emptyset$, then $d(X; \tilde{G}_{i+1}) \geq \lambda_{i+1}$ follows from $\lambda(G_i^*) \geq \lambda_i$. To prove the theorem, therefore, we assume that $\tilde{G}_{i+1}$ has a subset Z such that

$$Z \cap \Gamma_{\tilde{G}_{i+1}}(s) = \emptyset \text{ and } d(Z; \tilde{G}_{i+1})(= d(Z; G_i^*)) < \lambda_{i+1}, \quad (8.26)$$

and we derive a contradiction.

We first show that such a subset Z is not contained in any λ_i-component V_j of G_i^*. If $Z \subseteq V_j$ for some λ_i-component V_j, then $d(Z; G_i^*) = d(Z; G'|^{\lambda_i})$

by Lemma 8.19 and, hence, $\lambda_{i+1} > d(Z; \tilde{G}_{i+1}) = d(Z; G_i^*) = d(Z; G'|^{\lambda_i}) = d(Z; G'|^{\lambda_{i+1}})$ by $Z \cap \Gamma_{\tilde{G}_{i+1}}(s) = \emptyset$, contradicting the fact that $G' = G + R(V)$ satisfies $\lambda_s(G'|^{\lambda_{i+1}}) \geq \lambda_{i+1}$. Hence, $Z \not\subseteq V_i$ holds for any λ_i-component V_j.

Now choose a cut Z with the minimum $d(Z; G_i^*)$ among all those cuts Z in (8.26) and assume furthermore that Z has minimum cardinality $|Z|$ under this property. Then $d(Z'; G_i^*) > d(Z; G_i^*)$ holds for any nonempty proper subset Z' of Z. Since Z is not contained in any λ_i-component, there are at least two λ_i-components, V_j and V_ℓ, such that $V_j \cap Z \neq \emptyset \neq V_\ell \cap Z$. By property (ii) of λ_i-components before Lemma 8.19, G_i^* has a cut $X \subset V$ with $d(X; G_i^*) = \lambda_i$ that separates V_j and V_ℓ. We now show that two cuts Z and X cross each other. From property (iii) before Lemma 8.19, X contains at least one λ_i-leaf V_a, for which

$$V_a \cap \Gamma_{\tilde{G}_{i+1}}(s) \neq \emptyset$$

must hold, because $V_a \cap \Gamma_{\tilde{G}_{i+1}}(s) = \emptyset$ (together with Lemma 8.19) would imply $\lambda_i = d(V_a; G_i^*) = d(V_a; G'|^{\lambda_i}) = d(V_a; G'|^{\lambda_{i+1}}) < \lambda_{i+1}$, a contradiction to $\lambda_s(G'|^{\lambda_{i+1}}) \geq \lambda_{i+1}$. Hence, $X - Z \supseteq V_a \cap \Gamma_{\tilde{G}_{i+1}}(s) \neq \emptyset$ by $Z \cap \Gamma_{\tilde{G}_{i+1}}(s) = \emptyset$. Similarly we have $(V - X) - Z \neq \emptyset$, since $\{X, V - X\}$ is also a minimum cut in G_i^*. Therefore, two cuts $\{Z, V - Z\}$ and $\{X, V - X\}$ cross each other, and we have the following inequality by (1.4):

$$d(Z; G_i^*) + d(X; G_i^*) \geq d(Z - X; G_i^*) + d(X - Z; G_i^*).$$

Note that $d(X; G_i^*) = \lambda_i$ $d(X - Z; G_i^*) \geq \lambda_i$ (by $\lambda(G_i^*) \geq \lambda_i$) and $d(Z - X; G_i^*) > d(Z; G_i^*)$ (from the choice of Z) hold. These, however, contradict the preceding inequality. Therefore, there is no cut Z satisfying (8.26), and the lemma is proved.   □

We now consider how to split the edges in $\tilde{G}_{i+1}$ at s to obtain G_{i+1}^*. Lemma 8.20 asserts that any cut X with $X \cap \Gamma_{\tilde{G}_{i+1}}(s) = \emptyset$ satisfies $d(X; \tilde{G}_{i+1}) \geq \lambda_{i+1}$. For a cut $X \supseteq \Gamma_{\tilde{G}_{i+1}}(s)$, we consider cut $X' = V - X$, which satisfies $X' \cap \Gamma_{\tilde{G}_{i+1}}(s) = \emptyset$ and $d(X; \tilde{G}_{i+1}) > d(X'; \tilde{G}_{i+1}) \geq \lambda_{i+1}$. That is, any cut X not dividing $\Gamma_{\tilde{G}_{i+1}}(s)$ satisfies $d(X; \tilde{G}_{i+1}) \geq \lambda_{i+1}$. Next we describe a way to increase the weight of every cut, dividing $\Gamma_{\tilde{G}_{i+1}}(s)$ at least by $\lambda_{i+1} - \lambda_i$. This means that the resulting graph after splitting can be considered G_{i+1}^*, because $\lambda_s(G_{i+1}^*) \geq \lambda_{i+1}$ follows from the assumption

$$\lambda(G_i^*) = \lambda_i$$

and from the preceding argument.

Now, arrange the vertices in $\Gamma_{\tilde{G}_{i+1}}(s)$ in an arbitrary order, say $u_{i,1}, u_{i,2}, \ldots, u_{i,q}$, to form a cycle

$$C_{i+1}^* = (u_{i,1}, u_{i,2}, \ldots, u_{i,q}), \tag{8.27}$$

where its edge set $E(C_{i+1}^*) = \{\{u_{i,j}, u_{i,j+1}\} \mid j = 1, \ldots, q\}$ (where $u_{i,q+1} = u_{i,1}$) may include new edges that were not in G_i^*. Then delete all edges $\{s, u\}$,

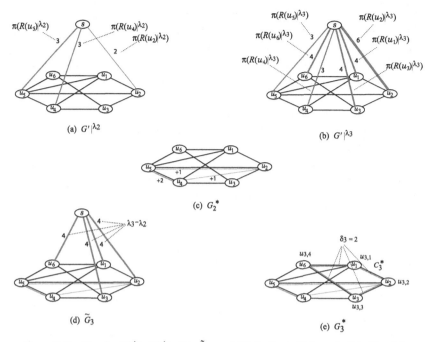

Figure 8.16. Graphs $G'|^{\lambda_2}$, $G'|^{\lambda_3}$, G_2^*, $\tilde{G}_3$, and G_3^* for the initial graph G in Fig. 8.5.

$u \in \Gamma_{\tilde{G}_{i+1}}(s)$ and increase the weights of edges e in E_i^* by $\delta_{i+1} = (\lambda_{i+1} - \lambda_i)/2$ as follows:

$$c_{G_{i+1}^*}(e) = \begin{cases} c_{G_i^*}(e) + \delta_{i+1} & \text{for } e \in E(C_{i+1}^*) \cap E_i^*, \\ \delta_{i+1} & \text{for } e \in E(C_{i+1}^*) - E_i^*, \\ c_{G_i^*}(e) & \text{for } e \in E_i^* - E(C_{i+1}^*). \end{cases}$$

In other words, G_{i+1}^* is obtained from G_i^* by adding the cycle C_{i+1}^* of (8.27) with weight δ_{i+1}, as illustrated in Fig. 8.15(d). (For $q = 2$, we distinguish $(u_{i,1}, u_{i,2})$ and $(u_{i,2}, u_{i,1})$ so that the total weight of edges between $u_{i,1}$ and $u_{i,2}$ is increased by $2\delta_{i+1}$.) Clearly, any cut X that divides $\Gamma_{\tilde{G}_{i+1}}(s)$ has the desired property; that is, $d(X; G_{i+1}^*) \geq d(X; G_i^*) + 2\delta_{i+1} \geq \lambda_{i+1}$.

Therefore, an optimally augmented λ_{i+1}-edge-connected graph G_{i+1}^* can be obtained from G_i^* via $\tilde{G}_{i+1}$ by adding the cycle C_{i+1}^* of weight δ_{i+1}.

For our running example, graph G_3^* is constructed from graphs $G'|^{\lambda_2}$, $G'|^{\lambda_3}$, and G_2^* as follows. Suppose that graphs $G'|^{\lambda_2}$, $G'|^{\lambda_3}$, and G_2^* are given as shown in Figs. 8.16(a), 8.16(b), and 8.16(c), respectively (see Fig. 8.14 for $G'|^{\lambda_2}$ and $G'|^{\lambda_3}$). Graph $\tilde{G}_3$ is constructed from G^* by adding s and putting back edges $\{s, v\}$ with weights $\pi(R(v)|_{\lambda_2}^{\lambda_3}) = \lambda_3 - \lambda_2 = 14 - 10 = 4$ for all $v \in V$, that is, the weight of each edge $\{s, v\}$ in $G'|^{\lambda_3}$ minus that of $\{s, v\}$ in $G'|^{\lambda_2}$ (see Fig 8.16(d)). Then G_3^* is obtained from $\tilde{G}_3$ as follows. The set of neighbors of s is $\Gamma_{\tilde{G}_3}(s) = \{u_1, u_2, u_3, u_6\}$, where each edge incident to s is weighted by $\lambda_3 - \lambda_2 = 4$, and we have a cycle $C_3^* = (u_{3,1}, u_{3,2}, u_{3,3}, u_{3,4}) = (u_1, u_2, u_3, u_6)$. After deleting all edges incident to

s, we increase the edge weight along the cycle C_3^* by $\delta_3 = (\lambda_3 - \lambda_2)/2 = 2$ to obtain graph G_3^* (see Fig 8.16(e)). Hence, G_3^* is obtained from G_2^* by adding the cycle C_3^* with weight 2, which is illustrated in Fig 8.12, where $G^*(14) = G_3^*$ is obtained from $G^*(10) = G_2^*$ by adding the cycle C_3^* with weight 2. Recall that G_i^* is an optimally augmented graph with $\lambda(G_i^*) = \lambda_i$, and $G^*(k)$ denotes an optimally augmented k-edge-connected graph.

The preceding construction also says that, for any intermediate k with $\lambda_i < k < \lambda_{i+1}$, we can obtain an optimally augmented graph $G^*(k)$ by adding the cycle C_{i+1}^* of weight $(k - \lambda_i)/2$.

Now we are ready to describe how to obtain $G^*(k)$ for the entire range of $k \in [\lambda(G), +\infty]$. For each λ_i, $i = 1, 2, \ldots, p$, choose a cycle C_i^* that visits all the neighbors of s in $G'|_{\lambda_{i-1}}^{\lambda_i}$. Then the set

$$\Pi = \{(C_i^*, [\lambda_{i-1}, \lambda_i]) \mid i = 1, 2, \ldots, p\}$$

of pairs $(C_i^*, [\lambda_{i-1}, \lambda_i])$ of cycles and ranges characterizes all optimal solutions for the entire range of k. Given $k \geq \lambda(G)$, $G^*(k)$ can be obtained by finding the maximum i_k, such that $\lambda_{i_k} < k$, and by increasing the weights of edges along all cycles C_i^* by $(\lambda_i - \lambda_{i-1})/2$, $i = 1, 2, \ldots, i_k$, and along the cycle $C_{i_k+1}^*$ by $(k - \lambda_{i_k})/2$. Since each cycle C_i^* can be obtained in $O(n)$ time, Π can be constructed in $O(np) = O(n^2 \log n)$ time. Together with Theorem 8.16, this finally establishes Theorem 8.18.

For our running example, the preceding construction was already made after Theorem 8.18.

8.5 More on Augmentation

8.5.1 Augmentation with Constraints

For the edge-connectivity augmentation problem in an undirected graph, several types of additional constraints have also been taken into consideration. We survey some of such results in this subsection.

Graph Simplicity

Let us assume that a given graph is simple and must be kept simple after adding new edges; that is, the edges must be added without creating multiple edges. For the general case where the target k is an input parameter, Jordán [159] proved the NP-hardness of this simplicity-preserving augmentation problem. However, for targets $k = 2$ and 3, the problem is solved polynomially as shown by Eswaran and Tarjan [64] and Watanabe and Yamakado [310], respectively. For the general target k, Bang-Jensen and Jordán [12] showed that if the optimal value is larger than a certain function that only depends on k then the smallest number of edges to be added to obtain a k-edge-connected graph is the same as the case without the simplicity-preserving constraint. Based on this, they gave an algorithm that solves the simplicity-preserving augmentation problem in polynomial time for any fixed target k.

(The article by Jordán [159] also contains the NP-hardness proof for the problem of increasing the edge connectivity of a given multigraph by adding a minimum number of edges without creating a new pair of adjacent vertices; i.e., only the existing edges are multiplied in G.)

Partition Constraint

For a multigraph $G = (V, E)$, a partition $\{V_1, \ldots, V_p\}$ of V is given as a constraint such that only edges between distinct subsets V_i and V_j are allowed to be added to G. (For example, if one needs to augment a p-partite graph while preserving the p-partiteness, then the problem can be formulated in this form.) This problem can be solved in polynomial time, as shown by Bang-Jensen et al. [13]. The result is based on edge splitting theorem, which preserves edge-connectivity without creating a split edge connecting vertices in the same subset V_i. If G is Eulerian or the target k is even, then such an edge splitting theorem has already been discovered in [153] and [236], respectively (see Theorems 7.23 and 7.24).

Planarity

Edges are requested to be added to a given planar graph while maintaining its planarity (this problem has an application in graph drawing [169]). The problem of augmenting a connected planar graph to a 2-vertex-connected planar graph is shown to be NP-hard [171], and a 5/3-approximation algorithm is obtained by Fialko and Mutzel [68]. However, it is still debatable whether the problem of augmenting a connected planar graph to a 2-edge-connected planar graph is NP-hard or not. If a given graph G is restricted to an outerplanar graph, then the following problems are polynomially solved: Augment an outerplanar G to a 2-edge-connected (resp. 2-vertex-connected) planar graph [170]. For an even k or $k = 3$, augmenting an outerplanar G to a k-edge-connected planar graph is solvable in polynomial time (see Theorems 7.27 and 7.28).

8.5.2 Other Augmentation Problems

In this subsection, we summarize the results on augmentation problems of other types, including problems of increasing vertex-connectivity.

Local-Edge-Connectivity Augmentation of Undirected Graphs

The local edge-connectivity augmentation problem asks to find a minimum set F of new edges to be added to a given undirected graph G such that, for each pair of vertices u and v, the resulting local edge-connectivity $\lambda_{G+F}(u, v)$ becomes larger than or equal to the target value $r(u, v)$ prescribed for each pair of $u, v \in V$.

Frank [78] proved that the problem can be solved in $O(n^3 m \log(n^2/m))$ time by applying Mader's edge splitting theorem (Theorem 7.20), a generalization of Lovász's theorem (Theorem 7.1), which preserves the local edge-connectivity in an undirected graph. Gabow [97] improved the running time of the local edge-connectivity augmentation algorithm of undirected graphs to $O(n^2 m \log(n^2/m))$.

Edge-Connectivity Augmentation of Digraphs

A digraph is k-edge-connected if it remains strongly connected after removal of any $(k-1)$ edges. The edge-connectivity augmentation problem in digraphs asks to find a minimum set of new directed edges to be added to a given digraph such that the augmented digraph becomes k-edge-connected for a prescribed target $k \geq 1$. Frank [78] pointed out that the edge-connectivity augmentation problem in a digraph can be solved in $O(n^3 m \log(n^2/m))$ time by using Mader's edge splitting theorem (Theorem 7.21) for digraphs, which preserves the edge-connectivity in a digraph. Gabow [97] improved the running time of this algorithm to $O(n^2 m \log(n^2/m))$. Frank [78] showed that the edge-connectivity augmentation problem in digraphs (and undirected graphs) is still polynomially solvable even if lower and upper bounds are imposed on the degree of each vertex.

One may consider the local edge-connectivity augmentation version for digraphs, whose undirected graph version is polynomially solved by an edge-splitting theorem. However, a corresponding edge splitting theorem does not exist that preserves the local edge-connectivity in a digraph. In fact, the problem of increasing the local edge-connectivity (or the local vertex-connectivity) in a directed graph is NP-hard even if the target values satisfy $r(u, v) \in \{0, 1\}$ for all pairs $u, v \in V$ [78].

Given a digraph $G = (V, E)$ with two specified subsets $S, T \subset V$ (which are not necessarily disjoint), Frank and Jordán [84] first studied the problem of finding a minimum number of new edges directed from S to T to make G k-edge-connected from S to T; that is, it has k-edge-disjoint directed paths from every vertex $s \in S$ to every vertex $t \in T$. They gave a min-max formula for the problem, based on which a polynomial time algorithm is obtained (where the algorithm is not combinatorial but relies on the ellipsoid method).

Vertex-Connectivity Augmentation of Undirected Graphs

The vertex-connectivity augmentation problem in undirected graphs asks to increase the vertex-connectivity of a given undirected graph G to a target k by adding a minimum number of new edges. The problem is polynomially solvable for $k = 2, 3$, and 4, due to [64, 133, 275], [132, 309], and [129, 130], respectively. For a general $k \geq 5$ (i.e., k is a parameter in the problem), it is not known whether the vertex-connectivity augmentation problem is NP-hard or not, even if a given graph G is assumed to be $(k-1)$-vertex-connected. As an approximate solution, Jordán [158] proved that a solution with its absolute error from the optimal value being at most $k - 3$ can be found in $O(n^5)$ time. Then Jordán reduced the absolute error of his algorithm to $\lceil (k - 1)/2 \rceil$ [160]. By investigating the structure of shredders (which are defined as vertex cuts, removal of which creates more than two components), Cheriyan and Thurimella [42] improved the time complexity of Jordán's algorithm [158] to $O(\min\{k, \sqrt{n}\}k^2 n^2 + kn^2 \log n)$ time. Afterwards Ishii and Nagamochi [138] obtained an approximation algorithm for the problem without assuming that a given graph G is $(k - 1)$-vertex-connected. Given an ℓ-vertex-connected graph G, they proved that a solution with absolute error $(k - \ell)(k - 1) + \max\{0, (k - \ell - 1)(\ell - 3) - 1\}(= O((k - \ell)k))$ can be found in $O((k - \ell)(k^2 n^2 + k^3 n^{3/2}))$ time (see also [155] for a slightly better error bound). For any *fixed* $k \in \mathbf{Z}_+$, Jackson and Jordán [156] proved that a minimum k-vertex-connectivity augmentation can be obtained in polynomial time, and they derived a min-max formula based on a complete solution of the augmentation problem for a new family of graphs called k-independence free graphs.

The problem of increasing the local vertex-connectivity to prescribed target values $r(u, v)$ by a minimum number of edges is NP-hard in general. Jordán [157] proved the NP-hardness in the case where a given graph $G = (V, E)$ is $(n/2)$-vertex-connected and there is a subset $S \subset V$ such that $r(u, v) = (n/2) + 1$ for all $u, v \in S$ and $r(u, v) = 0$ otherwise. Nagamochi and Ishii [242] proved that it is NP-hard even for the case of $r(u, v) \in \{0, 2\}$, $u, v \in V$, and Nagamochi [224] gave a $4/3$-approximation algorithm for this case.

Vertex-Connectivity Augmentation of Digraphs

A digraph is called k-*vertex-connected* if it has at least $(k + 1)$ vertices and remains strongly connected after removal of any $(k - 1)$ vertices. The vertex-connectivity augmentation problem in digraphs was shown to be polynomially solvable by Frank and Jordán [84]. This result is based on a min-max formula for the problem. They found that the minimum number of new directed edges to make a given digraph $G = (V, E)$ k-vertex-connected is given by the maximum of $\sum_i (k - |V - (A_i \cup B_i)|)$ over all families $\{(A_1, B_1), \ldots, (A_p, B_p)\}$ of pairs of disjoint subsets $A_i, B_i \subseteq V$ such that G has no directed edge from A_i to B_i for each i and $A_i \cap A_j = \emptyset$ or $B_i \cap B_j = \emptyset$ for each $i < j$. The algorithm obtained from this theorem again relies on the ellipsoid method. Afterward, they [85] observed that the vertex-connectivity augmentation problem can be directly reduced to the problem of increasing edge-connectivity from S to T in digraphs, where S and T are prescribed subsets. Recently Benczúr and Végh [21] gave a combinatorial algorithm to solve this problem.

Simultaneous Augmentation of Edge- and Vertex-Connectivities

The problem of increasing both edge- and vertex-connectivities a given graph has been studied [131, 140, 141, 142, 143, 144]. Hsu and Kao [131] first treated this problem, and presented a linear time algorithm for the case of augmenting an undirected graph $G = (V, E)$ with two specified vertex sets $X, Y \subseteq V$ by adding a minimum number of edges such that the local vertex-connectivity (resp. local edge-connectivity) between every two vertices in X (resp. in Y) becomes at least 2. Afterward, the problem of augmenting a multigraph $G = (V, E)$ by adding a minimum number of edges to make G ℓ-edge-connected and k-vertex-connected has been studied: polynomial time algorithms for $k = 2$ and a general ℓ [140, 145], for $k = 3$ and a fixed ℓ [141] when a given graph G is 2-vertex-connected and when G is an arbitrary graph [143]. For general ℓ and k, they also gave a polynomial time-approximation algorithm that produces a solution that contains at most $\max\{\ell + 1, 2k - 4\}$ extra edges from an optimum solution, assuming that a given graph is $(k - 1)$-vertex-connected [142, 144] (see [137] for a survey of these results).

Augmenting Hypergraphs and More General Objects

The problem of increasing the edge-connectivity of a hypergraph by adding hyperedges or graph edges has been studied [11, 36, 70, 294]. Cheng [36] gave a min-max formula for the problem of adding the minimum number of graph edges to a given $(k - 1)$-edge-connected hypergraph to obtain a k-edge-connected hypergraph. Fleiner and Jordán [70] extended the result to the problem of adding the minimum number of r hyperedges (i.e., each hyperedge contains r vertices) to a $(k - 1)$-edge-connected hypergraph to augment it to a k-edge-connected hypergraph. The problem of augmenting a hypergraph H by the smallest set F of hyperedges is polynomially solvable if each hyperedge in H and F has size at most 3 [163].

The edge-connectivity augmentation problem in hypergraphs can be generalized in terms of set functions as follows. For a given set function $f : 2^V \to \Re_+$ on a set V (where $\Re_+$ is the set of nonnegative reals), find a multigraph $H = (V, F)$ with a minimum number of edges such that $f(X) + d_H(X) \geq 0$ holds for all nonempty $X \subset V$. For example, the problem of increasing the edge-connectivity of a given graph $G = (V, E)$ to k can be formulated as this problem by setting f to be $f(X) = d(X; G) - k$ for the cut function $d : 2^V \to \Re_+$ of G. For a class of submodular functions f, the problem of augmenting f by a multigraph H is studied [18, 256]. Király [194] gave a min-max formula for the problem of covering a symmetric supermodular function by uniform hyperedges, which generalizes the results in the literature [18, 70]. However, Király et al. [195] proved that the problem of augmenting a hypergraph by the minimum number of graph edges to meet a local-edge-connectivity requirement is in general NP-hard.

Minimum-Cost Version

Let us finally mention the minimum-cost connectivity augmentation problem, where a cost function, $cost : V \times V \to \Re_+$, is given and the problem asks to find a minimum-cost set of new edges that makes a given graph k-edge-connected (or k-vertex-connected). There are surveys on this topic [188, 279].

The minimum cost augmentation problem is NP-hard even if the goal is to make an undirected graph 2-edge-connected (or 2-vertex-connected) [64]. Several approximation algorithms are proposed. Based on the fact that minimum-cost k pairwise edge-disjoint directed trees rooted at a vertex r can be computed in polynomial time, there is a 2-approximation algorithm for the minimum-cost edge-connectivity augmentation problem in an undirected graph G [191]. As to the problem of increasing the vertex-connectivity to k, currently the best approximation ratio is $6(1 + \frac{1}{2} + \frac{1}{3} + \cdots + \frac{1}{k})$ for any graph with at least $6k^2$ vertices, which is due to Cheriyan, Vempla and Vetta [44]. For small targets k, there are better approximation algorithms [55, 80, 254, 268, 272] which use the fact that a minimum-cost spanning subgraph $G' = (V, E')$ in a digraph $G = (V, E)$ with a root r can be obtained in polynomial time where G' has k vertex-disjoint paths from r to each vertex $v \in V - r$ (see [88]). However, it is still not certain whether a constant approximation ratio can be achieved for general k. If the cost function satisfies the triangle inequality, then a $(2 + \frac{2(k-1)}{n})$-approximation algorithm is known [189]. Given a simple graph G, the problem of finding a k-edge-connected (or k-vertex-connected) spanning subgraph with the minimum number of edges can be viewed as a minimum-cost connectivity augmentation problem. For this problem, which is NP-hard, Cheriyan and Thurimella [42] gave a good approximation algorithm with an approximation ratio that converges to 1 when k becomes large. The problem of finding a minimum spanning subgraph which preserves the reachability of a given graph (or digraph) is studied in the literature [128, 192, 193].

9

Source Location Problems

Problems that involve selection of the best location for facilities in a given network under certain requirements are called *location problems* [196]. Recently, the location problems with requirements measured by edge connectivity, vertex connectivity, or flow amount have been studied extensively [5, 125, 147, 149, 150, 295, 296]. In this chapter, we discuss the *source location problem* that finds an optimal set of sources in a graph under connectivity, flow-amount requirements, or both, which is defined as follows. Given an edge-weighted digraph $G = (V, E)$, a cost function $w : V \to \Re_+$, and two demand functions $r^+, r^- : V \to \Re_+$, we want to solve the following problem of choosing a subset of vertices $S \subseteq V$:

$$
\begin{aligned}
\text{Minimize} \quad & \sum_{v \in S} w(v) \\
\text{subject to} \quad & \emptyset \neq S \subseteq V, \\
& \psi^+(S, v) \geq r^+(v) \text{ for all } v \in V - S, \\
& \psi^-(S, v) \geq r^-(v) \text{ for all } v \in V - S,
\end{aligned} \tag{9.1}
$$

where $\psi^+(S, v)$ (resp. $\psi^-(S, v)$) is a measurement to be specified on the basis of edge-connectivity or vertex-connectivity from S to $v \in V$ (resp. from v to S) in G. A subset $S \subseteq V$ in G is called a *source set* if it satisfies the constraints in (9.1). A source set S with the minimum objective value $\sum_{v \in S} w(v)$ (resp. the minimum cardinality $|S|$) is called a *minimum cost source set* (resp. *minimum cardinality source set*).

On the other hand, if $G = (V, E)$ is an undirected graph, we consider the following source location problem:

$$
\begin{aligned}
\text{Minimize} \quad & \sum_{v \in S} w(v) \\
\text{subject to} \quad & \emptyset \neq S \subseteq V, \\
& \psi(S, v) \geq r(v) \text{ for all } v \in V - S,
\end{aligned} \tag{9.2}
$$

282

where $\psi(S, v)$ is a measurement to be specified on the basis of edge-connectivity or vertex-connectivity between S and $v \in V$ in G, and $r : V \to \Re_+$ is a demand function. A function $g : V \to \Re_+$ is called *uniform* if $g(v) = a$ for all $v \in V$, where $a \in \Re_+$ is a constant, and such a uniform function may be denoted as $g \equiv a$.

In Sections 9.1 and 9.2, we treat the source location problems with edge-connectivity and vertex-connectivity requirements, respectively.

9.1 Source Location Problem Under Edge-Connectivity Requirements

The source location problem with edge-connectivity requirement $\psi(S, v) = \lambda(S, v; G)$ in an undirected graph was first treated by Tamura et al. [295, 296], in which polynomial time algorithms were given for a uniform cost $w \equiv 1$. Sakashita et al. [285] proved that the problem is strongly NP-hard for a general cost $w : V \to \Re_+$. Honami et al. [125] then gave an $O(n^2 m)$ time algorithm for an unweighted digraph with $\psi(S, v) = \lambda(S, v; G)$, a uniform cost w, and a uniform demand $r \equiv k$ ($k \leq 3$).

Ito et al. [148] considered the problem of finding a minimum cardinality source set S in a digraph G for measurements $\psi^+(S, v) = \lambda(S, v; G)$ and $\psi^-(S, v) = \lambda(v, S; G)$, and for uniform demands $r^+ \equiv k$ and $r^- \equiv \ell$, where $\lambda(X, Y; G)$ denotes the minimum size of $d(Z, V - Z; G)$ with $X \subseteq Z \subseteq V - Y$. They derived a min-max formula for the problem and gave an algorithm that runs in polynomial time if k and ℓ are bounded by constants. Afterward, Bárász et al. [14] and van den Heuvel and Johnson [305] independently proved that this problem can be solved in polynomial time even if k and ℓ are not fixed.

9.1.1 Edge-Connectivity Requirement in Undirected Graphs

In this subsection, we treat an edge-weighted undirected graph $G = (V, E)$, and we consider the source location problem with $\psi(S, v) = \lambda(S, v; G)$, a general cost function $w : V \to \Re_+$, and a uniform demand $r \equiv k$ in G. The problem is to find a subset $S \subseteq V$ described as follows:

$$\begin{aligned} \text{Minimize} \quad & \sum_{v \in S} w(v) \\ \text{subject to} \quad & \emptyset \neq S \subseteq V, \\ & \lambda(S, v; G) \geq k \text{ for all } v \in V - S. \end{aligned} \quad (9.3)$$

If $\lambda(G) \geq k$ (i.e., $d(X; G) \geq k$ for all extreme vertex sets X in G) then $S = \{v\}$ is a minimum cost source set, where v is a vertex in V with the minimum weight $w(v)$. In the general case, we observe that $S \subseteq V$ is a source set (i.e., satisfying the constraints of (9.3)) if and only if $S \cap X \neq \emptyset$ holds for all nonempty subsets

$X \subset V$ with $d(X; G) < k$. Hence, if $k > \lambda(G)$ then we have the following min-max inequality:

$\min\{w(S) \mid$ source set $S \subseteq V\}$

$$\geq \max \left\{ \sum_{X \in \mathcal{X}} \min_{v \in X} w(v) \mid \mathcal{X} \text{ is a family of disjoint sets } X \text{ with } d(X; G) < k \right\}.$$
$$(9.4)$$

We show that the inequality can hold by equality.

Theorem 9.1. *Given an edge-weighted graph $G = (V, E)$, the source location problem (9.3) with a cost function $w : V \to \Re_+$, and a uniform demand $r \equiv k$ with $k > \lambda(G)$, there is an optimal source set S^* to (9.3), which is defined from a family $\mathcal{X}$ of $|S^*|$ disjoint subsets $X \subseteq V$ with $d(X; G) < k$ such that*

$$w(S^*) = \sum_{X \in \mathcal{X}} \min_{v \in X} w(v) \qquad (9.5)$$

(i.e., (9.4) holds by equality). Such a source set S^* and a family $\mathcal{X}$ can be found in $O(n)$ time from the family $\mathcal{X}(G)$ of extreme vertex sets in G. □

Proof. We construct such S^* and $\mathcal{X}$ from the family $\mathcal{X}(G)$ of extreme vertex sets in G (defined in Section 1.5.3). Let $\mathcal{X}_k(G) = \{X \in \mathcal{X}(G) \mid d(X; G) < k\}$. Given the tree representation $\mathcal{T}_k$ of $\mathcal{X}_k$ (see Section 1.1.7), consider the sets $X_1, X_2, \ldots, X_p$ in $\mathcal{X}_k(G)$ which correspond to the leaf nodes in $\mathcal{T}_k$. Let $\mathcal{X} = \{X_1, X_2, \ldots, X_p\}$, which consists of disjoint subsets, for which we define $S^* = \{v_1, v_2, \ldots, v_p\}$ by choosing a vertex v_i with the minimum weight $w(v_i)$ from each X_i. Since $|\mathcal{X}| = O(n)$, the previous construction can be executed in $O(n)$ time. We first show that S^* is a source set. For any subset $Y \subset V$ with $d(Y; G) < k$, by the definition of $\mathcal{T}_k$ and $\mathcal{X}_k$ there is at least one $X_i \subseteq Y$ satisfying $d(X_i; G) \leq d(Y; G)$, for which $S^* \cap Y \supseteq S \cap X_i \neq \emptyset$ holds. Therefore, S^* is a source set. This S^* attaining (9.5) is an optimal solution by inequality (9.4). □

For the source location problem (9.3) with a uniform cost, we show that, by using Theorem 6.11, source sets can be constructed under a more restricted condition. Assume that we start with a given set S_0 of sources in G, and then we add sources to S_0 in two phases (say, for some budget reason) as follows. Given a number q, we choose a set S_1 of q sources in the first phase so that $\min\{\lambda(S_0 \cup S_1, v; G) \mid v \in V - (S_0 \cup S_1)\}$ becomes as large as possible. Then in the second phase, for a given number k, we choose a set S_2 of sources such that $\lambda(S_0 \cup S_1 \cup S_2, v; G) \geq k$ holds for all $v \in V - (S_0 \cup S_1 \cup S_2)$. We wish to minimize the total number $|S_1 \cup S_2|$ of sources to be added in these phases. By Theorem 6.11, we see that S_1 can be chosen so as to maximize $\min\{\lambda(S_0 \cup S_1, v; G) \mid v \in V - S_1\}$ in the first phase without knowing the value of k for the second phase, while a subset $S_2 \subseteq V - (S_0 \cup S_1)$ can then be chosen so that $|S_1 \cup S_2| \leq |S|$ holds for any subset $S \subseteq V - S_0$ with $\lambda(S_0 \cup S, v; G) \geq k$, $v \in V - (S_0 \cup S)$.

Corollary 9.2. *Given an edge-weighted graph $G = (V, E)$ with $n \geq 2$ vertices and m edges, a subset $S_0 \subset V$, and an integer $q \in [2, n]$, there is a subset of S_1 of $V - S_0$ satisfying the following:*

(i) $|S_1| = q$ and $\min\{\lambda(S_0 \cup S_1, v; G) \mid v \in V - (S_0 \cup S_1)\} \geq \max_{S \subseteq V - S_0 : |S| = q}$ $[\min\{\lambda(S_0 \cup S, v; G) \mid v \in V - (S_0 \cup S)\}],$

(ii) *For any real $k \in \mathfrak{R}_+$ with $k \geq \max_{S \subseteq V : |S| = q}[\min\{\lambda(S_0 \cup S, v; G) \mid v \in V - (S_0 \cup S)\}],$ there is a subset S_2 of $V - S_0 - S_1$ such that $|S_1 \cup S_2| \leq |S|$ holds for any subset $S \subseteq V - S_0$ with $\lambda(S_0 \cup S, v; G) \geq k$ for all $v \in V - (S_0 \cup S).$*

For a given real k, such subsets S_1 and S_2 can be obtained in $O(n \log n)$ time if the family $\mathcal{X}(G)$ of extreme vertex sets of G is available. ☐

Proof. Observe that for a subset $S \subset V$, the minimum cut size over all cuts $\{X, V - X\}$ with $S \subseteq X \subset V$ is given by the edge-connectivity $\lambda(G/S)$ of the contracted graph G/S holds. Therefore, we see that

$$\lambda(G/S) = \min\{\lambda(S, v; G) \mid v \in V - S\}.$$

By applying Theorem 6.11 to $A = S_0$ and $B = V$, we compute an optimal ordering $v_1, v_2, \ldots, v_{|V - S_0|}$ of vertices in $V - S_0$ and $\lambda(G/S_0 \cup \{v_1, \ldots, v_i\}),$ $i = 1, 2, \ldots, |V - S_0|,$ in $O(n \log n)$ time.

(i) Let $S_1 = \{v_1, v_2, \ldots, v_q\}$. Then $S = S_1$ maximizes $\lambda(G/(S_0 \cup S_1))$ over all subsets $S \subseteq V - S_0$ with $|S| = q$.

(ii) Given a real $k \geq 0$, let $S_2 = \{v_{q+1}, v_{q+2}, \ldots, v_j\}$ for the smallest j such that $\lambda(G/S_0 \cup \{v_1, \ldots, v_j\}) \geq k$, where $j \geq q + 1$ or $S_2 = \emptyset$ holds by the assumption $k \geq \max_{S \subseteq V : |S| = q}[\min\{\lambda(S_0 \cup S, v; G) \mid v \in V - (S_0 \cup S)\}]$. Then $S_1 \cup S_2$ is a minimum subset $S \subseteq V - S_0$ such that $\lambda(G/(S_0 \cup S)) \geq k$, as required. ☐

9.1.2 Local-Edge-Connectivity Requirement in Undirected Graphs

In this section, we treat an edge-weighted undirected graph $G = (V, E)$, and we consider the source location problem with a cost function $w : V \rightarrow \mathfrak{R}_+$ and a local-edge-connectivity requirement $\psi(S, v) = \lambda(S, v; G) \geq r(v)$ for a demand function $r : V \rightarrow \mathfrak{R}_+$ in G. The problem is described as follows:

$$\text{Minimize} \quad \sum_{v \in S} w(v)$$
$$\text{subject to} \quad \emptyset \neq S \subseteq V, \tag{9.6}$$
$$\lambda(S, v; G) \geq r(v) \text{ for all } v \in V - S.$$

In this case, a subset $S \subseteq V$ is a source set if and only if, for every $v \in V - S$, there is no subset X such that $X \subseteq V - S$, $v \in X$, and $d(X; G) < r(v)$. For each vertex $v \in V$, we define

$$\mathcal{C}(v) = \{X \subset V \mid v \in X, \ d(X; G) < r(v)\}. \tag{9.7}$$

If $\bigcup_{v \in V} \mathcal{C}(v) = \emptyset$, then any vertex $v \in V$ with the minimum weight $w(v)$ gives a minimum cost source set $S = \{v\}$. Otherwise a source set is a subset $S \subseteq V$

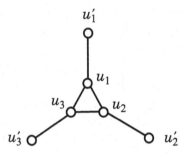

Figure 9.1. An instance (G, w, r) of problem (9.6), where the weight of every edge is 1 and $r(u_i) = 2, w(u_i) = 3, r(u_i') = 1, w(u_i') = 1, i = 1, 2, 3.$

satisfying

$$S \cap X \neq \emptyset \text{ for all } X \in \cup_{v \in V} C(v),$$

indicating

$$\min\{w(S) \mid \text{source set } S \subseteq V\}$$
$$\geq \max \left\{ \sum_{X \in \mathcal{X}} \min_{v \in X} w(v) \mid \mathcal{X} \text{ is a family of disjoint sets } X \in \cup_{v \in V} C(v) \right\}.$$
$$(9.8)$$

However, problem (9.6) is different from problem (9.3) in the sense that there is an instance that does not have a source set S^* and a family $\mathcal{X}$ of disjoint subsets in $\cup_{v \in V} C(v)$ that satisfy (9.5). For example, consider graph $G = (V = \{u_1, u_2, u_3, u_1', u_2', u_3'\}, E = \{\{u_i, u_i'\} \mid i = 1, 2, 3\} \cup \{\{u_i, u_j\} \mid 1 \leq i < j \leq 3\})$ with unit edge weights and $r(u_i) = 2, w(u_i) = 3, r(u_i') = 1, w(u_i') = 1, i = 1, 2, 3$ (see Fig. 9.1). For this instance, $C(u_i) = \{V - \{u_1'\}, V - \{u_2'\}, V - \{u_3'\}\}, i = 1, 2, 3,$ and $C(u_i') = \emptyset, i = 1, 2, 3$ hold, and $S = \{u_1', u_2'\}$ is a minimum cost source set with cost 2, for which no family of two disjoint sets $X_1, X_2 \in \cup_{v \in V} C(v)$ satisfies (9.5). In fact, problem (9.6) with a general cost $w : V \to \Re_+$ is shown to be weakly NP-hard [5].

We easily observe the following min-max inequality for the case of $w(v) = 1,$ $v \in V$:

$$\min\{|S| \mid \text{source set } S \subseteq V\}$$
$$\geq \max\{|\mathcal{X}| \mid \mathcal{X} \text{ is a family of disjoint sets } X \in \cup_{v \in V} C(v)\}. \quad (9.9)$$

We will show that the inequality can hold by equality, and Tamura et al. [295] proved that problem (9.6) is solvable in polynomial time. The problem is now described as follows:

$$\begin{aligned} \text{Minimize} \quad & |S| \\ \text{subject to} \quad & \emptyset \neq S \subseteq V, \\ & \lambda(S, v; G) \geq r(v) \text{ for all } v \in V - S. \end{aligned} \qquad (9.10)$$

In fact, Tamura et al. [295] proved that the following algorithm, DELSOURCE, correctly delivers a source set S with minimum $|S|$. Arata et al. [5] gave an $O(n \cdot F(n, m))$ time implementation of the algorithm, where $F(n, m)$ is the time bound for computing a maximum flow in an edge-weighted graph with n vertices and m edges.

Algorithm DELSOURCE

Input: An edge-weighted graph $G = (V, E)$ and a demand function $r : V \to \mathfrak{R}_+$.
Output: A source set $S^* \subseteq V$ with minimum $|S^*|$.
1   Let the vertices in V be numbered $v_1, v_2, \ldots, v_n$ so that
        $r(v_1) \le r(v_2) \le \cdots \le r(v_n)$ holds;
2    $S_0 := V$;
3   **for** $i = 1, 2, \ldots, n$ **do**
4   **if** $S_{i-1} - \{v_i\}$ remains a nonempty source set **then** $S_i := S_{i-1} - \{v_i\}$
5   **else** $S_i := S_{i-1}$;
     end; /* for */
6   Output $S^* := S_n$.

We prove here the correctness of DELSOURCE and its complexity via two claims.

Claim 9.3. *Let $S_{i-1} - \{v_i\}$ be a set in line 4 of* DELSOURCE. *Then*

(i) $S_{i-1} - \{v_i\} \ne \emptyset$ *is no longer a source set if and only if there is a set* $X \in \mathcal{C}(v_i)$ *(defined by (9.7)) with $S_{i-1} \cap X = \{v_i\}$.*
(ii) $S_{i-1} - \{v_i\}$ *becomes empty if and only if $i = n$ and $\cup_{v \in V - v_n} \mathcal{C}(v) = \emptyset$ hold.*   □

Proof. (i) The if part is trivial since $(S_{i-1} - \{v_i\}) \cap X = \emptyset$ holds for such a set X. To show the only-if part, assume that $S_{i-1} - \{v_i\}$ is not a source set in line 4. Recall that S_{i-1} is a source set and that it satisfies $S_{i-1} \cap X \ne \emptyset$ for all $X \in \cup_{v \in V} \mathcal{C}(v)$. If $(S_{i-1} \cap X) - v_i \ne \emptyset$ for all $X \in \cup_{v \in V} \mathcal{C}(v)$, then $S_{i-1} - v_i$ would be a source set. Therefore, we have a set $X \in \mathcal{C}(u)$ for some $u \in V$ such that

$$S_{i-1} \cap X = \{v_i\},$$

where $d(X; G) < r(u)$ holds. Note that $u = v_j$ holds for some $j \le i$, because $\{v_{i+1}, v_{i+2}, \ldots, v_n\} \subseteq S_{i-1}$ and $u \in X$. Moreover, by the numbering of vertices, $r(u) \le r(v_i)$ holds. This implies that $d(X; G) < r(u) \le r(v_i)$ holds; hence, X also belongs to $\mathcal{C}(v_i)$.

(ii) If $\cup_{v \in V} \mathcal{C}(v) = \emptyset$ holds, then $S_i = \{v_{i+1}, v_{i+1}, \ldots, v_n\}$ holds after the ith iteration of the for-loop and, hence, $S_{i-1} - \{v_i\}$ becomes empty only when $i = n$. If $S_{i-1} - \{v_i\} = \emptyset$ holds in line 4 of DELSOURCE, then $i = n$ since $S_i \subseteq \{v_{i+1}, v_{i+1}, \ldots, v_n\}$ holds after the ith iteration of the for-loop. If $S_{n-1} = \{v_n\}$ holds, then by condition (i) this implies that $\mathcal{C}(v) = \emptyset$ holds for all $v \in V - v_n$.   □

Claim 9.3 also tells that we can test whether $S_{i-1} - \{v_i\}$ $(1 \leq i < n)$ is a source set by checking whether $\lambda(S_{i-1} - \{v_i\}, v_i; G) \geq r(v_i)$ holds or not, where $\lambda(S_{i-1} - \{v_i\}, v_i; G)$ can be computed as the maximum-flow value between s and v_i in the graph $G/(S_{i-1} - \{v_i\})$ obtained from G by contracting $S_{i-1} - \{v_i\}$ into a vertex s. Hence, an iteration of the for-loop can be executed by using a maximum-flow algorithm, and DELSOURCE can be implemented to run in $O(nF(n, m))$ time.

Let S^* be a source set output by DELSOURCE. Now we prove the optimality of S^*. If $\cup_{v \in V} C(v) = \emptyset$, then by Claim 9.3(ii) we have $S^* = \{v_n\}$, which is a minimum source set.

Definition 9.4. *Assume $\cup_{v \in V} C(v) \neq \emptyset$. For each $v_i \in S^*$, there is a set $X_i \in C(v_i)$ with $S^* \cap X_i = \{v_i\}$ by Claim 9.3(i) and (ii). We define X_i to be inclusion-wise minimal among such sets X_i.* $\qquad\square$

A subset X_i in Definition 9.4 can be computed as a minimal minimum (s, v_i)-cut in $G/(S_{i-1} - \{v_i\})$ by using a maximum-flow algorithm (see Section 1.3.3). If $S_{n-1} = \{v_n\}(= S^*)$, then we can find such $X_n \in C(v_n)$, if any, by choosing each vertex in $V - v_n$ as s for computing a minimal minimum (s, v_n)-cut in G. Therefore, if $\cup_{v \in V} C(v) \neq \emptyset$, then a family $\mathcal{X}$ of minimal sets $X_i \in C(v_i)$, $v_i \in S^*$, can be obtained in $O(nF(n, m))$ time.

Claim 9.5. *Assume $\cup_{v \in V} C(v) \neq \emptyset$. Then, for any two vertices $v_i, v_j \in S^*$, the sets X_i, X_j in Definition 9.4 are disjoint.* $\qquad\square$

Proof. By the choice of X_i and X_j, we have $S^* \cap X_i = \{v_i\}$, $d(X_i; G) < r(v_i)$, $S^* \cap X_j = \{v_j\}$, and $d(X_j; G) < r(v_j)$. Assume $X_i \cap X_j \neq \emptyset$. Then we have $v_i \in X_i - X_j \subset X_i$, where by the minimality of $|X_i|$, $d(X_i - X_j; G) \geq r(v_i)$ must hold (otherwise $X_i' = X_i - X_j$ would satisfy $S^* \cap X_i' = \{v_i\}$ and $X_i' \in C(v_i)$). Analogously with X_j, we have $d(X_j - X_i; G) \geq r(v_j)$. Hence, we have

$$d(X_i; G) + d(X_j; G) < r(v_i) + r(v_j) \leq d(X_i - X_j; G) + d(X_j - X_i; G),$$

which contradicts that cut function d always satisfies $d(X_i; G) + d(X_j; G) \geq d(X_i - X_j; G) + d(X_j - X_i; G)$ (see (1.4)). $\qquad\square$

Let $\mathcal{X}$ be any family of disjoint subsets $X \in \cup_{v \in V} C(v)$. Then, since any source set S must contain at least one vertex from each set $X \in \cup_{v \in V} C(v)$, we have $|S| \geq |\mathcal{X}|$. Hence, a source set S is a minimum if there is a family $\mathcal{X}$ of disjoint subsets $X \in \cup_{v \in V} C(v)$ such that $|S| = |\mathcal{X}|$.

Theorem 9.6. *Assume $\cup_{v \in V} C(v) \neq \emptyset$. Let S^* be a subset obtained by DELSOURCE and let $\mathcal{X}$ be the family $\mathcal{X}$ of disjoint subsets $X \in \cup_{v \in V} C(v)$ constructed from S^* in Definition 9.4. Then $|S^*| = |\mathcal{X}|$ (i.e., (9.9) holds by equality).* $\qquad\square$

Proof. By Claim 9.5, $\mathcal{X} = \{X_i \mid v_i \in S^*\}(\subseteq \cup_{v \in V} C(v))$ is a family of disjoint sets such that $S^* \cap X_i = \{v_i\}$, indicating that $|\mathcal{X}| = |S^*|$. $\qquad\square$

This lemma proves the minimality of S^*.

The assumption that cost function w is uniform can be slightly weakened to the the following condition: Cost and demand functions w and r have a common ordering $v_1, v_2, \ldots, v_n$ of vertices in V such that

$$r(v_1) \le r(v_2) \le \cdots \le r(v_n) \quad \text{and} \quad w(v_1) \ge w(v_2) \ge \cdots \ge w(v_n). \quad (9.11)$$

Theorem 9.7. *Given an edge-weighted graph $G = (V, E)$, a cost function $w : V \to \Re_+$, and a requirement function $r : V \to \Re_+$, satisfying (9.11) and $\cup_{v \in V} C(v) \ne \emptyset$, there is an optimal source set S^* of (9.6) which can be obtained from a family $\mathcal{X}$ of $|S^*|$ disjoint subsets $X \in \cup_{v \in V} C(v)$ satisfying*

$$w(S^*) = \sum_{X \in \mathcal{X}} \min_{v \in X} w(v)$$

(i.e., (9.8) holds by equality). Such S^* and $\mathcal{X}$ can be obtained in $O(nF(n,m))$ time. □

Proof. Let S^* be the subset of V obtained by DELSOURCE applied to an ordering of (9.11). Let $\mathcal{X}$ be the family of disjoint subsets $X_i \in \cup_{v \in V} C(v)$ as defined in Definition 9.4. For each $v_i \in S^*$, $X_i \cap \{v_{i+1}, v_{i+2}, \ldots, v_n\} = \emptyset$ holds; thereby we have $i = \max\{h \mid v_h \in X_i\}$. From (9.11), such v_i has the minimum weight $w(v_i)$ among vertices in X_i; that is, $w(v_i) = \min_{v_h \in X_i} w(v_h)$. Therefore, S^* and $\mathcal{X}$ satisfy $w(S^*) = \sum_{X \in \mathcal{X}} \min_{v \in X} w(v)$. The time bound follows from the argument before Claim 9.5. □

9.1.3 Edge-Connectivity Requirement in Digraphs

We now let $G = (V, E)$ be an edge-weighted digraph, and we consider in (9.1) that $\psi^+(S, v) = \lambda(S, v; G)$ and $\psi^-(S, v) = \lambda(v, S; G)$ and that w, r^+ and r^- are uniform:

$$
\begin{aligned}
&\text{Minimize} \quad |S| \\
&\text{subject to} \quad \emptyset \ne S \subseteq V, \\
&\qquad\qquad \lambda(S, v; G) \ge k \text{ for all } v \in V - S, \\
&\qquad\qquad \lambda(v, S; G) \ge \ell \text{ for all } v \in V - S.
\end{aligned}
\qquad (9.12)
$$

A subset $S \subseteq V$ satisfying the conditions of (9.12) is called a (k, ℓ)-*source*.

For an edge-weighted digraph $G = (V, E)$, we denote $E^+(X; G) = E(X, V - X; G)$, $E^-(X; G) = E(V - X, X; G)$, $d^+(X; G) = d(X, V - X; G)$, and $d^-(X; G) = d(V - X, X; G)$ for each subset $X \subseteq V$. Given two reals $k, \ell \in \Re_+$, a nonempty and proper subset X of V is called k-*in-deficient* or simply *in-deficient* (resp. ℓ-*out-deficient* or simply *out-deficient*) if $d^-(X; G) < k$ (resp. $d^+(X; G) < \ell$). An in- or out-deficient set is called *deficient*. A deficient set X is called *minimal* if no proper subset of X is deficient. Let $\mathcal{E}_{k,\ell}$ be the family of all minimal deficient sets of an instance with G, k, and ℓ. Observe that a subset S is a (k, ℓ)-source if and only if

$$S \cap X \ne \emptyset \text{ for all } X \in \mathcal{E}_{k,\ell}. \qquad (9.13)$$

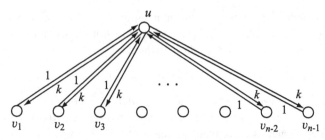

Figure 9.2. An instance (G, k, ℓ) of problem (9.12), where $\ell = 0$, $c_G(u, v_i) = k$, and $c_G(v_i, u) = 1, i = 1, 2, \ldots, n - 1$.

In general, $|\mathcal{E}_{k,\ell}|$ is exponential in n. For example, consider an instance with a real $k \in \Re_+$, $\ell = 0$ and a digraph $G = (V = \{u, v_1, v_2, \ldots, v_{n-1}\}$, $E = \{(u, v_i), (v_i, u) \mid i = 1, 2, \ldots, n - 1\})$ with edge weight $c_G(u, v_i) = k$ and $c_G(v_i, u) = 1, i = 1, 2, \ldots, n - 1$ (see Fig. 9.2), which has a minimal in-deficient set $V - X$ for any subset $X \subset \{v_1, v_2, \ldots, v_{n-1}\}$ of $k - 1$ vertices, implying $|\mathcal{E}_{k,\ell}| = \binom{n-1}{k-1}$.

By regarding $\mathcal{E}_{k,\ell}$ as a hypergraph, a subset S is a (k, ℓ)-source if and only if it is a transversal of the hypergraph. Hence problem (9.12) is now to find a minimum transversal of the hypergraph $\mathcal{E}_{k,\ell}$. Ito et al. [148] observed that the hypergraph $\mathcal{E}_{k,\ell}$ is a tree hypergraph, and by Theorem 1.50 we see that the transversal number $\tau(\mathcal{E})$ is equal to the matching number $\nu(\mathcal{E})$.

Theorem 9.8 ([148]). *The hypergraph $\mathcal{E}_{k,\ell}$ is a tree hypergraph and $\tau(\mathcal{E}) = \nu(\mathcal{E})$ holds. Hence, the minimum cardinality of a (k, ℓ)-source is equal to the maximum number of pairwise disjoint deficient sets.*   □

Based on the theorem, Ito et al. [148] gave an algorithm that runs in polynomial time if k and ℓ are bounded by constants. Afterward, Bárász et al. [14] and van den Heuvel and Johnson [305] independently proved that a minimum transversal of the hypergraph $\mathcal{E}_{k,\ell}$ can be computed in strongly polynomial time. In the following, we introduce the algorithm due to Bárász et al., from which a proof of Theorem 9.8 will be obtained. Their idea is as follows. If a basic tree T for the tree hypergraph $\mathcal{E}_{k,\ell}$ is available, then by Lemma 1.51 a minimum transversal for $\mathcal{E}_{k,\ell}$ can be obtained by performing $O(n)$ transversal tests. However $\mathcal{E}_{k,\ell}$ may consists of exponentially many hyperedges. To overcome this, Bárász et al. gave a characterization of a family $\mathcal{E}_G^*$ of an $O(n^2)$ number of subsets of V such that any basic tree T^* for $\mathcal{E}_G^*$ is a basic tree for $\mathcal{E}_{k,\ell}$. Hence, constructing a basic tree from such $\mathcal{E}_G^*$ by using Theorem 1.53 requires polynomial time.

Tree Hypergraph $\mathcal{E}_{k,\ell}$

For a given digraph $G = (V, E)$, a nonempty subset $X \subseteq V$ is called *in-solid* (resp. *out-solid*) if $d^-(Y) > d^-(X)$ (resp. $d^+(Y) > d^-(X)$) for every nonempty proper subset Y of X. An in- or out-solid set is called *solid*. Note that every singleton set

$\{v\}$ with $v \in V$ is in-solid and out-solid. Let $\mathcal{E}_G$ be the family of all solid sets of a digraph $G = (V, E)$.

Lemma 9.9. *For a digraph G and reals $k, \ell \in \Re_+$, it holds that $\mathcal{E}_{k,\ell} \subseteq \mathcal{E}_G$.* $\square$

Proof. A minimal k-in-deficient X satisfies $d^-(X) < k \leq d^-(Y)$ for all nonempty proper subsets Y of X, implying that it is in-solid. Similarly a minimal ℓ-out-deficient set is out-solid. $\square$

Lemma 9.10. *Let X be an in-solid set and let Y be an out-solid set. Then X and Y do not intersect each other.* $\square$

Proof. Assume that $X' = X - Y$, $Y' = Y - X$, and $Z = X \cap Y$ are all nonempty, and $\alpha = d(Z, X'; G)$, $\beta = d(Y', Z; G)$, $\gamma = d(V - (X \cup Y), Z; G)$, and $\gamma' = d(Z, V - (X \cup Y); G)$. Since $d^-(X') > d^-(X)$ and $d^+(Y') > d^+(Y)$, we have $\alpha > \beta + \gamma$ and $\beta > \alpha + \gamma'$. This leads to $0 > \gamma + \gamma'$, a contradiction. $\square$

Theorem 9.11. *The hypergraph $\mathcal{E}_G$ consisting of all solid sets of a digraph $G = (V, E)$ is a tree hypergraph.* $\square$

Proof. By Theorem 1.52, it suffices to show that (i) the line graph $L(\mathcal{E}_G)$ of $\mathcal{E}_G$ is chordal and (ii) $\mathcal{E}_G$ has the Helly property.

(i) Assume that $L(\mathcal{E}_G)$ is not chordal; that is, it has a chordless cycle of length at least 4. In other words, $\mathcal{E}_G$ contains solid sets $X_1, X_2, \ldots, X_h$ ($h \geq 4$) such that $X_i \cap X_j \neq \emptyset$ if and only if i and j are consecutive integers, where X_{h+1} is interpreted as X_1. By Lemma 9.10, either all X_i are in-solid or all X_i are out-solid. By symmetry, we assume that X_i are all in-solid. Let $Y_i = X_i \cap X_{i+1}$, $i = 1, 2, \ldots, h$, where $d^-(Y_i) > d^-(X_{i+1})$ holds for each i since Y_i is a proper subset of the in-solid set X_{i+1}. Hence, $\sum_{1 \leq i \leq h} d^-(Y_i) > \sum_{1 \leq i \leq h} d^-(X_i)$. On the other hand, Y_i and Y_j ($i \neq j$) are disjoint by assumption on X_i, and, since any edge entering some Y_i enters at least one of $X_1, X_2, \ldots, X_h$, we have $\sum_{1 \leq i \leq h} d^-(Y_i) \leq \sum_{1 \leq i \leq h} d^-(X_i)$, a contradiction.

(ii) Assume that $\mathcal{E}_G$ does not have the Helly property; that is, there are $h \geq 3$ solid sets $X_1, X_2, \ldots, X_h$ such that any two of these sets intersect each other but their intersection $Z = X_1 \cap X_2 \cap \cdots \cap X_h$ is empty. Let h be the minimum integer among such h. Again, by Lemma 9.10, either all X_i are in-solid or all X_i are out-solid. By symmetry, we assume that X_i are all in-solid. Let $Y_i = X_1 \cap X_2 \cap \cdots \cap X_{i-1} \cap X_{i+1} \cap \cdots \cap X_h$, $i = 1, 2, \ldots, h$. Each Y_i is nonempty by the minimality of h and satisfies $d^-(Y_i) > d^-(X_{i+1})$ since Y_i is a proper subset of in-solid set X_{i+1}. Hence, $\sum_{1 \leq i \leq h} d^-(Y_i) > \sum_{1 \leq i \leq h} d^-(X_i)$. On the other hand, $Z = \emptyset$ implies that Y_i and Y_j ($i \neq j$) are disjoint. Since any edge entering some Y_i enters at least one of the sets $X_1, \ldots, X_h$, we have $\sum_{1 \leq i \leq h} d^-(Y_i) \leq \sum_{1 \leq i \leq h} d^-(X_i)$, a contradiction. $\square$

Theorems 9.11 and 1.50 and Lemma 9.9 prove Theorem 9.8. Moreover, any basic tree T for $\mathcal{E}_G$ is a basic tree for $\mathcal{E}_{k,\ell}$. In the following, we choose a subfamily of $\mathcal{E}_G$ that gives rise to a basic tree for $\mathcal{E}_G$ (hence, for $\mathcal{E}_{k,\ell}$) after examining some structural properties of $\mathcal{E}_G$.

Lemma 9.12. *If the intersection of two in-solid (resp. out-solid) sets X and Y is nonempty, then $X \cup Y$ is in-solid (resp. out-solid).* ☐

Proof. We consider the case where X and Y are in-solid (the case of out-solid sets is analogous). Assume that $X \cup Y \neq \emptyset$ is not in-solid; that is, there is a proper subset Z of $X \cup Y$ with $d^-(Z) \leq d^-(X \cup Y)$. Assume without loss of generality that Z is inclusion-wise maximal subject to this property and satisfies $X \cap Z \neq \emptyset \neq X - Z$ (by exchanging the role of X and Y if necessary). Since $X \cup Z$ is a proper superset of Z, the maximality of Z implies $d^-(X \cup Z) > d^-(X \cup Y) \geq d^-(Z)$. Since $X \cap Z$ is a proper subset of in-solid set X, we have $d^-(X \cap Z) > d^-(X)$. Hence, by (1.2), we would have $d^-(X) + d^-(Z) \geq d^-(X \cap Z) + d^-(X \cup Z) > d^-(X) + d^-(Z)$, a contradiction. ☐

For a vertex $s \in V$, a set $X \in \mathcal{E}_G$ is called *s-avoiding* if $s \notin X$ and is called a *maximal s-avoiding* set if, in addition, X is inclusion-wise maximal among all s-avoiding sets in $\mathcal{E}_G$.

Lemma 9.13. *The family of maximal s-avoiding in-solid (resp. out-solid) sets is a partition of $V - s$.* ☐

Proof. Since every singleton set $\{v\}$, $v \in V - s$ is an s-avoiding in-solid set, $V - s$ is covered by the union of all maximal s-avoiding in-solid sets. On the other hand, by Lemma 9.12, maximal s-avoiding in-solid sets are pairwise disjoint. Therefore, they form a partition of $V - s$. The case of out-solid sets is treated analogously. ☐

A partition of $V - s$ into maximal s-avoiding in-solid (resp. out-solid) sets is called *in-solid partition* (resp. *out-solid partition*) of $V - s$. Therefore, Lemmas 9.10 and 9.13 imply the next lemma.

Lemma 9.14. *The family of maximal s-avoiding solid sets is a partition of $V - s$.* ☐

A partition in this lemma is called a *solid partition* of $V - s$. Let $\mathcal{E}_G^*$ denote the family of all maximal s-avoiding solid sets in $\mathcal{E}_G$ for all $s \in V$. An important consequence of the lemma is that, for each $s \in V$, the number of maximal s-avoiding solid sets is at most $n - 1$ and, hence, we have $|\mathcal{E}_G^*| = O(n^2)$. We remark that Bernáth [26] gave a sharp upper bound $2(n - 1)$ on $|\mathcal{E}_G^*|$.

Computing Solid Partitions

We show how to compute a solid partition of $V - s$. Lemma 9.14 tells that the union of in-solid and out-solid partitions of $V - s$ is a laminar family of $V - s$. Hence, it suffices to compute in-solid and out-solid partitions of $V - s$ separately and then to collect maximal members from the solid sets in the two partitions to form a solid partition of $V - s$.

Before describing a polynomial time algorithm for finding an in-solid partition of $V - s$, we observe a structural property of maximal s-avoiding in-solid sets. We consider a subset X such that $(V - X, X)$ is a minimum (t, s)-cut in the given graph G; that is, it satisfies $X \cap \{s, t\} = \{t\}$ and $d^-(X; G) = \lambda(s, t; G)$. Let N_t^s denote an inclusion-wise minimal set among all such subsets X. By Lemma 1.3, N_t^s is unique.

Lemma 9.15. *Given an $s \in V$, let N^s be a minimal member in the family $\{N_t^s \mid t \in V - s\}$. Then N^s is a maximal s-avoiding in-solid set.* □

Proof. We first claim that, for any $t, z \in V - s$, if $z \in N_t^s$ then $N_z^s \subseteq N_t^s$. If $N_z^s - N_t^s \neq \emptyset$, then $d^-(N_z^s \cap N_t^s) > d^-(N_z^s)$ (since N_z^s is in-solid) and $d^-(N_z^s \cup N_t^s) \geq \lambda(s, t; G) = d^-(N_t^s)$, which, however, contradicts inequality $d^-(N_z^s) + d^-(N_t^s) \geq d^-(N_z^s \cap N_t^s) + d^-(N_z^s \cup N_t^s)$ by (1.2). From this claim and the minimality of N^s, $N^s = N_z^s$ holds for all $z \in N^s$ and, hence, N^s is in-solid. This N^s is maximal, since any s-avoiding superset Z of N^s satisfies $d^-(Z) \geq \lambda(s, t; G) = d^-(N^s)$ and such a set Z cannot be in-solid. □

Let $\mathcal{N}$ be the in-solid partition of $V - s$ in G. A minimal member N^s of the family $\{N_t^s \mid t \in V - s\}$ can be computed by a maximum-flow algorithm in G. Let $N_1 := N^s$. By Lemma 9.15, we have $N_1 \in \mathcal{N}$. The remaining task is to find the other members in $\mathcal{N} - N_1$. Any member $N' \in \mathcal{N} - N_1$ satisfies $N' \cap (N_1 \cup \{s\}) = \emptyset$ and is an s-avoiding set in the graph $G/(N_1 \cup \{s\})$, where $N_1 \cup \{s\}$ is contracted into s. Hence, the remaining members in $\mathcal{N} - N_1$ form an in-solid partition of $V(G/(N_1 \cup \{s\})) - s$ in the contracted graph. By applying Lemma 9.15, we can find a second member N_2 from such an in-solid partition. Therefore, we can repeat this procedure until all members are found. That is, supposing that the first h members $N_1, \ldots, N_h$ are found, the next member, N_{h+1}, can be obtained as a minimal member of the family $\{N_t^s \mid t \in V(G/S) - s\}$ in the graph G/S with $S = N_1 \cup N_2 \cup \cdots \cup N_h \cup \{s\}$. The algorithm is formally described as follows.

Algorithm SOLIDPARTITION
Input: An edge-weighted digraph $G = (V, E)$ and a vertex $s \in V$.
Output: An in-solid partition $\mathcal{N}$ of $V - s$.
1 Initialize $\mathcal{N} := \emptyset$ and $S := \{s\}$;
2 **while** $V - S \neq \emptyset$ **do**
3   For each $t \in V - S$, let $N_t^s \subseteq V - S$ be the (unique) minimal set
        containing t such that $d^-(N_t^s) = \lambda(s, t; G/S)(= \lambda(S, t; G))$;
4   Let N be the smallest member of the family $\{N_t^s \mid t \in V(G/S) - s\}$;
5      $\mathcal{N} := \mathcal{N} \cup \{N\}$; $S := S \cup N$;
6 **end**; /* while */
7 Output $\mathcal{N}$.

SOLIDPARTITION can be implemented to run in $O(n^2 F(n,m))$ time, where $F(n,m)$ is the time bound for computing a maximum flow in an edge-weighted digraph with n vertices and m edges. Bárász et al. [14] improved the time bound of SOLIDPARTITION to $O(n^2 m \log(n^2/m))$ by using the Hao–Orlin algorithm [113] for computing a minimum cut in a digraph. Hence, we have the next lemma.

Lemma 9.16. *Given an edge-weighted graph $G = (V, E)$, the family $\mathcal{E}_G^*$ of maximal s-avoiding solid sets over all $s \in V$ can be obtained in $O(n^3 m \log(n^2/m))$ time.* □

Computing a Basic Tree

Knowing how to compute the family $\mathcal{E}_G^*$ of maximal s-avoiding solid sets, we are now ready to compute a basic tree for $\mathcal{E}_{k,\ell}$ from a given family $\mathcal{E}_G^*$. In fact, by Lemma 1.54, any basic tree T for $\mathcal{E}_G^*$ is a basic tree for $\mathcal{E}_G$ (hence, for $\mathcal{E}_{k,\ell}$). By Theorem 1.53, a basic tree for $\mathcal{E}_G$ can be obtained as a maximum-weight spanning tree T in an edge-weighted undirected graph G_w defined by (1.26) for an arbitrary hyperedge weight function $w : \mathcal{E}_G \to \Re_+ - \{0\}$. Since $|\mathcal{E}_G^*| = O(n^2)$, such a graph G_w and a maximum-weight spanning tree T in G_w can be computed in $O(n^3)$ time.

Computing a Minimum Transversal from a Basic Tree

We finally explain how to compute a minimum transversal of $\mathcal{E}_{k,\ell}$ from a given basic tree T of $\mathcal{E}_{k,\ell}$ in polynomial time. By Lemma 1.51, MINTRANSVERSAL in Section 1.7 computes a minimum transversal $R \subseteq V$ for $\mathcal{E}_{k,\ell}$ in $O(nC^*(\mathcal{E}_{k,\ell}))$ time, where $C^*(\mathcal{E}_{k,\ell})$ denote the time complexity for deciding whether a given set $R \subseteq V$ is a transversal of $\mathcal{E}_{k,\ell}$, when there is a vertex $v \in V - R$ that is contained in some hyperedge $X \in \mathcal{E}_{k,\ell}$ with $X \subseteq V - R$. Thus, we only have to show that $C^*(n)$ is polynomial in n and m.

Let $R \subseteq V$ and $v \in V - R$ be such that every hyperedge $X \in \mathcal{E}_{k,\ell}$ with $X \subseteq V - R$ (if any) contains v. In this situation, testing whether $R \subseteq V$ is a transversal of $\mathcal{E}_{k,\ell}$ or not can be conducted as follows. Compute $\lambda(v, R; G) = \lambda(v, r; G/R)$ and $\lambda(R, v; G) = \lambda(r, v; G/R)$ by using a maximum-flow algorithm, where G/R is the graph obtained from G by contracting R into a single vertex r. Observe that there is no out-deficient set X with $v \in X \subseteq V - R$ if and only if $\lambda(v, R; G) \geq k$. Analogously there is no in-deficient set Y with $v \in Y \subseteq V - R$ if and only if $\lambda(R, v; G) \geq \ell$. Therefore, we have $C^*(\mathcal{E}_{k,\ell}) = O(F(n,m)) = O(nm \log(n^2/m))$ for a hypergraph $\mathcal{E}_{k,\ell}$. A minimum transversal R for $\mathcal{E}_{k,\ell}$ can be computed from a basic tree T in $O(nC^*(\mathcal{E}_{k,\ell})) = O(n^2 m \log(n^2/m))$ time.

Summarizing the preceding argument, the next result is established.

Theorem 9.17 ([14]). *Given an edge-weighted digraph $G = (V, E)$ and two reals $k, \ell \in \Re_+$, a minimum (k, ℓ)-source can be computed in $O(n^3 m \log(n^2/m))$ time.* □

9.2 Source Location Problem Under Vertex-Connectivity Requirements

Now we turn to the case in which measurements $\psi^+(S, v)$, $\psi^-(S, v)$, and $\psi(S, v)$ are related to vertex connectivity in the source location problems (9.1) for digraphs and (9.2) for undirected graphs.

For the case of vertex-connectivity requirement $\psi(S, v) = \kappa(S, v; G)$, Ito et al. [150] proved that problem (9.2) is NP-hard for undirected graphs even with a uniform cost $w \equiv 1$. Here $\kappa(S, v; G)$ denotes the minimum size of a vertex cut $C \subseteq V - S - v$ that separates S and v (see Section 1.1).

Contrary to this, Nagamochi et al. [255] considered the measurements related to vertex-connectivity in a digraph G. Define $\hat{\kappa}^+(S, v; G)$ (resp. $\hat{\kappa}^-(S, v; G)$) to be the maximum number of internally vertex-disjoint directed paths from S to v (resp. from v to S) such that no two paths meet at the same vertex in S. Hence, $\hat{\kappa}^+(S, v; G) \leq |S|$ and $\hat{\kappa}^-(S, v; G) \leq |S|$. They proved that problem (9.1) with measurements $\psi^+(S, v) = \hat{\kappa}^+(S, v; G)$, $\psi^-(S, v) = 0$, with a general cost $w : V \to \Re_+$ and they uniform demands $r^+ \equiv k$ and $r^- \equiv 0$ $(k \in \mathbf{Z}_+)$ has a matroidal structure, and they gave an $O(\min\{k, \sqrt{n}\}nm)$ time algorithm. From this, they gave an $O(\min\{k, \sqrt{n}\}kn^2)$ time algorithm for problem (9.2) with $\psi(S, v) = \hat{\kappa}(S, v; G)$, a general cost $w : V \to \Re_+$, and a uniform demand $r \equiv k$ $(k \in \mathbf{Z}_+)$, where $\hat{\kappa}(S, v; G)$ denotes the maximum number of paths between S and v such that no two paths share any vertex other than v (see Section 1.1). They further gave an $O(n^4 m)$ time algorithm for problem (9.1) with measurements $\psi^+(S, v) = \hat{\kappa}^+(S, v; G)$, $\psi^-(S, v) = \hat{\kappa}^-(S, v; G)$ with a general cost $w : V \to \Re_+$, and uniform demands $r^+ \equiv k$ and $r^- \equiv \ell$ $(k, \ell \in \mathbf{Z}_+)$.

For the case of nonuniform demand with requirement $\psi(S, v) = \hat{\kappa}(S, v; G)$ in an unweighed graph $G = (V, E)$, Ishii et al. [139] gave a linear time algorithm that assumes a demand function $r : V \to \{0, 1, 2, 3\}$. They further showed that the problem is NP-hard if there exists a vertex $v \in V$ with $r(v) \geq 4$.

Ito et al. [150] considered the problem of finding a minimum cardinality source set in an unweighted graph $G = (V, E)$ with requirements $\kappa(S, v; G) \geq k$ and $\lambda(S, v; G) \geq \ell$ for all $v \in V - S$, and they presented an $O(\min\{\ell mn, \ell^2 n^2, mn^3\})$ time algorithm for $k \leq 2$.

9.2.1 Source Location Under Vertex-Connectivity Requirement and General Cost

In what follows, we describe a polynomial algorithm due to Nagamochi et al. [255] for solving the source location problem for directed graphs and the requirement $\psi(S, v) = \hat{\kappa}^+(S, v; G)$, with a general cost $w : V \to \Re_+$ and a uniform demand $r \equiv k$ $(k \in \mathbf{Z}_+)$.

Let $G = (V, E)$ be a digraph and let $w : V \to \Re_+$ be a cost function. For a subset $X \subseteq V$, let $w(X)$ denote $\sum\{w(v) \mid v \in X\}$. We consider the following source location problem:

$$\text{Minimize} \quad w(S)$$
$$\text{subject to} \quad \emptyset \neq S \subseteq V$$
$$\hat{\kappa}^+(S, v; G) \geq k \text{ for all } v \in V - S. \tag{9.14}$$

Notice that any source set S must satisfy $|S| \geq k$ and $\{v \in V \mid |\Gamma_G^-(v)| < k\} \subseteq S$. In the rest of this section, we shall prove the following three theorems related to source location problem (9.14).

Theorem 9.18. *Given a digraph $G = (V, E)$ and a cost function $w : V \to \Re_+$, source location problem (9.14) can be solved in $O(\min\{k, \sqrt{n}\}nm)$ time.* $\qquad \square$

If G is an undirected graph, the source location problem with measurement $\hat{\kappa}(S, v)$ can be solved in the same way, only by replacing each undirected edge with two oppositely oriented directed edges. As will be shown, the time complexity is slightly improved in this case.

Theorem 9.19. *Given an undirected graph $G = (V, E)$ and a cost function $w : V \to \Re_+$, a minimum cost subset $S \subseteq V$ such that $\hat{\kappa}(S, v; G) \geq k$ for all $v \in V - S$ can be computed in $O(\min\{k, \sqrt{n}\}kn^2)$ time.* $\qquad \square$

Furthermore, Theorem 9.18 can be extended to a more general problem in which, given two integers k and ℓ, we want to find a minimum cost subset $S \subseteq V$ under constraints $\hat{\kappa}^+(S, v; G) \geq k$ and $\hat{\kappa}^-(S, v; G) \geq \ell$ for all $v \in V - S$.

Theorem 9.20. *Given a digraph $G = (V, E)$ and a cost function $w : V \to \Re_+$, a minimum cost subset $S \subseteq V$ such that $\hat{\kappa}^+(S, v; G) \geq k$ and $\hat{\kappa}^-(S, v; G) \geq \ell$ for all $v \in V - S$ can be computed in $O(n^4m)$ time.* $\qquad \square$

Our first task for proving Theorem 9.18 is to characterize the set of sources S as s-basally k-connected digraphs, which will be introduced next, and then as a matroid based on such digraphs.

9.2.2 s-Basal k-Connectivity

Let H be a digraph with a designated vertex $s \in V(H)$, where multiple edges may be incident to s. We denote $G = H - s$. The graph H is called *s-basally k-connected* if

$$|\Gamma_G^-(X)| + d(s, X; H) \geq k \quad \text{for all nonempty, nondominating sets}$$
$$X \subset V(G) \text{ in } G, \tag{9.15}$$

where a subset $X \subseteq V$ is *dominating* in G if $V - X - \Gamma_G^-(X) = \emptyset$, and $d(s, X; H)$ denotes number of edges directed from s to X (see Section 1.1). A source set S to problem (9.14) is characterized as follows.

Lemma 9.21. (i) *Given a digraph G and a source set S in G (i.e., S satisfies the constraint in (9.14)), let H be the digraph obtained from G by adding a new* vertex s together with $\max\{1, k - |\Gamma_G^-(v)|\}$ edges from s to each vertex $v \in S$. Then H is s-basally k-connected.

(ii) *For an s-basally k-connected digraph H and $G = H - s$, let S be a subset of $V(G)$ such that $\Gamma_H^+(s) \subseteq S$ and $|S| \geq k$. Then S is a source in G.* ☐

The proof of this lemma will be given after introducing another characterization via matroids.

Given a digraph G, we define $V_0 = \{v \in V(G) \mid |\Gamma_G^-(v)| < k\}$, and we construct the digraph H_0 from G by adding a new vertex s and $\max\{1, k - |\Gamma_G^-(v)|\}$ edges from s to each vertex $v \in V(G)$. (Observe that V_0 is a set of vertices that must be included in any source set.) By Lemma 9.21(ii) with $S = V(G)$, H_0 is s-basally k-connected. For the ground set $U = V(G) - V_0$, we define a set system $\mathcal{M}^+ = (U, \mathcal{I}^+)$ by

$$\mathcal{I}^+ = \{X \subseteq U \mid |X| \leq |V(G)| - k \text{ and}$$
$$H_0 - E(s, X; H_0) \text{ remains } s\text{-basally } k\text{-connected}\}.$$

(Note that $|E(s, X; H_0)| = |X|$ since $X \subseteq U$.) A source set S is now characterized via system $\mathcal{M}^+ = (U, \mathcal{I}^+)$.

Lemma 9.22. *$S \subseteq V(G)$ is a source set in G if and only if $V(G) - S \in \mathcal{I}^+$.* ☐

Proof. For any $X \in \mathcal{I}^+$, $S = \Gamma_{H_0 - E(s,X;H_0)}^+(s)(= V(G) - X)$ is a source set in G by Lemma 9.21(i), since $|\Gamma_{H_0 - E(s,X;H_0)}^+(s)| \geq k$ holds and $H_0 - E(s, X; H_0)$ is s-basally k-connected. Conversely, for a given source set S in G, let $X = V(G) - S$. Then we have $X = V(G) - S \subseteq U$ (by $V_0 \subseteq S$) and $|X| \leq |V(G)| - k$ (by $|S| \geq k$). By Lemma 9.21(ii), $H_0 - E(s, X; H_0)$ is s-basally k-connected and, hence, $X \in \mathcal{I}^+$. ☐

After proving Lemma 9.21, we prove that $\mathcal{M}^+$ is a matroid; that is, it satisfies the following three axioms of a matroid:

(I1) $\emptyset \in \mathcal{I}^+$,

(I2) if $Y \subseteq X \subseteq U$ and $X \in \mathcal{I}^+$ then $Y \in \mathcal{I}^+$,

(I3) for $X, Y \in \mathcal{I}^+$ with $|X| < |Y|$, there exists a vertex $x \in Y - X$ such that $X \cup \{x\} \in \mathcal{I}^+$.

We now prove Lemma 9.21. For this, we first show that condition (9.15) can be rewritten as the following conditions:

$|\Gamma_G^-(X)| + |\Gamma_H^+(s) \cap X| \geq k$ for all nondominating sets $X \subset V(G)$ in G

$$\text{with } |\Gamma_G^-(X)| + |X| \geq k, \tag{9.16}$$

$|\Gamma_G^-(v)| + c_H(s, v) \geq k$ for all singleton sets $X = \{v\} \subset V(G)$. $\quad$ (9.17)

Lemma 9.23. *Condition* (9.15) *implies conditions* (9.16) *and* (9.17), *and vice versa.*   □

Proof. We first show that (9.15) implies (9.16) and (9.17). It is clear that (9.17) follows from (9.15) with $X = \{v\}$. Then consider a nondominating set X with $|\Gamma_G^-(X)| + |X| \geq k$. Assume that $|\Gamma_G^-(X)| + |\Gamma_H^+(s) \cap X| < k$. Then $Y = X - \Gamma_H^+(s)$ is not empty by $|\Gamma_G^-(X)| + |\Gamma_H^+(s) \cap X| < k \leq |\Gamma_G^-(X)| + |X|$. By $d(s, Y; H) = 0$ and (9.15), $|\Gamma_G^-(Y)| = |\Gamma_G^-(Y)| + d(s, Y; H) \geq k$. Since $\Gamma_G^-(Y) - (X - Y) \subseteq \Gamma_G^-(X)$ and $X - Y = \Gamma_H^+(s) \cap X$, we have $|\Gamma_G^-(X)| + |\Gamma_H^+(s) \cap X| \geq |\Gamma_G^-(Y)| \geq k$, contradicting $|\Gamma_G^-(X)| + |\Gamma_H^+(s) \cap X| < k$.

Next we show the converse. For a digraph H satisfying (9.16) and (9.17), let $X \subset V(G)$ be a nonempty, nondominating set in $G = H - s$. If $|\Gamma_G^-(X)| + |X| \geq k$, then $|\Gamma_G^-(X)| + d(s, X; H) \geq k$ follows from (9.16). Then assume $|\Gamma_G^-(X)| + |X| < k$ and let $h = k - |\Gamma_G^-(X)| - |X| (\geq 1)$. For each vertex $v \in X$, it holds that $|\Gamma_G^-(v)| \leq |\Gamma_G^-(X)| + |X - v| \leq k - h - 1$, and by (9.17) we have $c_H(s, v) \geq 1 + h$. Hence, we obtain $|\Gamma_G^-(X)| + d(s, X; H) \geq |\Gamma_G^-(X)| + (1 + h)|X| = k - h + h|X| \geq k$.   □

Proof of Lemma 9.21. (i) By construction of H from G, (9.17) holds. Assume that H is not s-basally k-connected. Thus, by Lemma 9.23, $G = H - s$ has a nonempty, nondominating set $X \subseteq V(G)$ that violates (9.16); that is, there is a subset $X \subseteq V(G)$ such that $|\Gamma_G^-(X)| + |X| \geq k$ and $k - 1 \geq |\Gamma_G^-(X)| + |\Gamma_H^+(s) \cap X| = |\Gamma_G^-(X)| + |S \cap X|$. This implies $X - S \neq \emptyset$. Take a vertex $v \in X - S$. Since S is a source set, G has a set P of k disjoint directed paths from S to v such that no two paths share a vertex in S. Since each of such paths starts from a vertex in $S \cap X$ or goes into X, the number of the paths satisfies $|P| \leq |S \cap X| + |\Gamma_G^-(X)| \leq k - 1$, a contradiction to $|P| = k$.

(ii) Assume that S is not a source set; that is, $\hat{\kappa}^+(S, v; G) < k$ holds for some $v \in V(G) - S$. That is, there is a set $C \subseteq V(G)$ of at most $k - 1$ vertices such that $G - C$ has no directed path from any vertex $u \in S - C$ to v, where $S - C \neq \emptyset$ by $|S| \geq k$. Let X be the set of vertices in $V(G) - C$ that have directed paths to v in $G - C$. Since $X \cap \Gamma_H^+(s) \subseteq X \cap S = \emptyset$, we have $d(s, X; H) = 0$. Note that X is not dominating in G by $V(G) - X - \Gamma_G^-(X) \supseteq S - C \neq \emptyset$. We see that $|\Gamma_G^-(X)| \leq k - 1$, since otherwise $|\Gamma_G^-(X)| \geq k > |C|$ would imply that all vertices in $\Gamma_G^-(X) - C$ are reachable to v, contradicting the choice of X. However, $d(s, X; H) = 0$ and $|\Gamma_G^-(X)| \leq k - 1$ contradict (9.15).   □

9.2.3 Matroidal Structure in the Source Location Problem

We are now ready to prove that $\mathcal{M}^+ = (U, \mathcal{I}^+)$ is a matroid.

Lemma 9.24. $\mathcal{M}^+ = (U, \mathcal{I}^+)$ *is a matroid.*   □

It is easy to see from the definition of $\mathcal{M}^+$ that axioms (I1) and (I2) hold. We will show axiom (I3) via three lemmas.

For an s-basally k-connected digraph H and an integer $i \in \{0, 1, \ldots, k-1\}$, we call a nondominating set $T \subseteq V(G)$ in $G = H - s$ i-critical in H, if T is an inclusion-wise minimal subset satisfying the following conditions:

$$|\Gamma_G^-(T)| = i, \quad |\Gamma_G^-(T)| + |\Gamma_H^+(s) \cap T| = k,$$

$$c_H(s, u) \le 1, \quad u \in T.$$

An i-critical set T satisfies $d(s, T; H) = |\Gamma_H^+(s) \cap T| = k - i$.

Lemma 9.25. *Let H be an s-basally k-connected digraph and let $G = H - s$. For a vertex $v \in \Gamma_H^+(s)$ with $|\Gamma_G^-(v)| \ge k$, if $H - (s, v)$ is not s-basally k-connected then v is contained in a $(k-1)$-critical set X_v.* $\square$

Proof. By $|\Gamma_G^-(v)| \ge k$, (9.17) holds in $H - (s, v)$. As $H - (s, v)$ is not s-basally k-z connected, vertex v is contained in a nondominating set X_v in G such that $|\Gamma_G^-(X_v)| + |\Gamma_H^+(s) \cap X_v| = k$ and $c_H(s, v) = 1$, where no proper subset $X' \subset X_v$ satisfies this property. Clearly, $|X_v| \ge 2$ by $|\Gamma_G^-(v)| \ge k$. To prove that this X_v is $(k-1)$-critical, it suffices to show that X_v satisfies $|\Gamma_G^-(X_v)| = k - 1$ and $d(s, X_v; H) = 1$. Assume $d(s, X_v; H) \ge 2$, which implies that $Z = \Gamma_H^+(s) \cap (X_v - v)$ is not empty by $c_H(s, v) = 1$. Then $|\Gamma_G^-(X_v - Z)| \le |\Gamma_G^-(X_v)| + |Z| = |\Gamma_G^-(X_v)| + |\Gamma_H^+(s) \cap (X_v - v)| = k - 1$. On the other hand, $|\Gamma_G^-(X_v - Z)| \ge k - d(s, X_v - Z; H) = k - c_H(s, v) = k - 1$ holds from (9.15). Hence, $|\Gamma_G^-(X_v - Z)| = k - 1$ and $d(s, X_v - Z; H) = 1$ follow, which contradicts the minimality of X_v. $\square$

Lemma 9.26. *Let H be an s-basally k-connected digraph and let $G = H - s$. Assume that H has an i-critical set T_i and a j-critical set T_j such that T_i and T_j intersect each other in G. If $|\Gamma_H^+(s)| \ge k + 1$, then it holds that $0 \le i + j - h \le k - 1$, where $h = |\Gamma_G^-(T_i \cap T_j)|$, and $T_i \cup T_j$ contains an $(i + j - h)$-critical set T satisfying $\Gamma_H^+(s) \cap (T_i \cup T_j) \subseteq T$.* $\square$

Proof. Since $V(G) - (T_i \cap T_j) - \Gamma_G^-(T_i \cap T_j) \ne \emptyset$ holds by $V(G) - T_i - \Gamma_G^-(T_i) \ne \emptyset$, the set $T_i \cap T_j$ satisfies

$$|\Gamma_G^-(T_i \cap T_j)| + d(s, T_i \cap T_j; H) \ge k \qquad (9.18)$$

by (9.15). By (1.6) for T_i and T_j, we obtain the following inequality:

$$\begin{aligned} |\Gamma_G^-(T_i)| + d(s, T_i; H) + |\Gamma_G^-(T_j)| + d(s, T_j; H) \\ \ge |\Gamma_G^-(T_i \cap T_j)| + d(s, T_i \cap T_j; H) + |\Gamma_G^-(T_i \cup T_j)| + d(s, T_i \cup T_j; H). \end{aligned} \qquad (9.19)$$

By the criticality of T_i and T_j, it holds that $|\Gamma_G^-(T_i)| + d(s, T_i; H) = |\Gamma_G^-(T_j)| + d(s, T_j; H) = k$, and (9.18) implies

$$|\Gamma_G^-(T_i \cup T_j)| + d(s, T_i \cup T_j; H) \le k. \qquad (9.20)$$

Therefore, $V(G) - (T_i \cup T_j) - \Gamma_G^-(T_i \cup T_j) \neq \emptyset$ since otherwise we would have $|\Gamma_H^+(s)| \leq |\Gamma_G^-(T_i \cup T_j)| + d(s, T_i \cup T_j; H) \leq k$, contradicting the assumption $|\Gamma_H^+(s)| \geq k + 1$. For this nondominating set $T_i \cup T_j$, we have $|\Gamma_G^-(T_i \cup T_j)| + d(s, T_i \cup T_j; H) \geq k$ by (9.15). Hence, $|\Gamma_G^-(T_i \cup T_j)| + d(s, T_i \cup T_j; H) = k$ holds by (9.20), and inequality (9.19) holds by equality, implying that $|\Gamma_G^-(T_i \cup T_j)| = |\Gamma_G^-(T_i)| + |\Gamma_G^-(T_j)| - |\Gamma_G^-(T_i \cap T_j)| = i + j - h$ for $|\Gamma_G^-(T_i)| = i$, $|\Gamma_G^-(T_j)| = j$ and $h = |\Gamma_G^-(T_i \cap T_j)|$. Clearly, $0 \leq |\Gamma_G^-(T_i \cup T_j)| \leq k - 1$ holds by $|\Gamma_G^-(T_i \cup T_j)| + d(s, T_i \cup T_j; H) = k$ and $d(s, T_i \cup T_j; H) \geq 1$. This means that there is an $(i + j - h)$-critical set $T \subseteq T_i \cup T_j$ with $\Gamma_H^+(s) \cap (T_i \cup T_j) \subseteq T$. $\qquad\square$

Lemma 9.27. *Let H be an s-basally k-connected digraph with $|\Gamma_H^+(s)| \geq k + 1$, let $G = H - s$, and let V be the family of i-critical sets for all $i = 0, 1, \ldots, k - 1$. Then for any nonempty subset $Z \subset \Gamma_H^+(s)$ such that $Z \subseteq \cup_{T \in V} T$, there is a family $\mathcal{T}_Z \subseteq V$ such that $Z \subseteq \cup_{T \in \mathcal{T}_Z} T$ holds and every two sets in $\mathcal{T}_Z$ are pairwise disjoint.* $\qquad\square$

Proof. Choose a family $\mathcal{T}_Z \subseteq V$ such that $Z \subseteq \cup_{T \in \mathcal{T}_Z} T$ so that $|\mathcal{T}_Z|$ is minimized. Assume that two sets T_i and T_j with $T_i \cap T_j \neq \emptyset$ exist in $\mathcal{T}_Z$. From the minimality of $|\mathcal{T}_Z|$, both $T_i - T_j$ and $T_j - T_i$ are nonempty. Hence, T_i and T_j intersect with each other in G (since $T_i \cap T_j \neq \emptyset$). By $|\Gamma_H^+(s)| \geq k + 1$, Lemma 9.26 says that $T_i \cup T_j$ contains a p-critical set T^* for some $p \in \{0, \ldots, k - 1\}$ with $T^* \supseteq \Gamma_H^+(s) \cap (T_i \cup T_j)$. Now $\mathcal{T}_Z' = (\mathcal{T}_Z - \{T_i, T_j\}) \cup \{T^*\}$ is a family of i-critical sets $(0 \leq i \leq k - 1)$ such that $Z \subseteq \cup_{T' \in \mathcal{T}_Z'} T'$, contradicting the minimality of $|\mathcal{T}_Z|$. $\qquad\square$

Now we are ready to prove axiom (I3). Let $X, Y \in \mathcal{I}^+$ such that $|X| < |Y|$, where $d(s, X; H_0) = |\Gamma_{H_0}^+(s) \cap X| = |X|$ and $d(s, Y; H_0) = |\Gamma_{H_0}^+(s) \cap Y| = |Y|$ hold. For the digraph $H^* = H_0 - E(s, X; H_0)$, we assume that, for each $v \in Y - X$, the digraph $H^* - d(s, v; H^*) = H^* - (s, v)$ is not s-basally k-connected (otherwise we have axiom (I3)). Then we derive a contradiction, which proves axiom (I3). Now $Y - X \subseteq \Gamma_H^+(s)$ holds. By Lemma 9.25, each vertex $v \in Y - X$ is contained in a $(k - 1)$-critical set X_v in H^* (since $|\Gamma_G^-(v)| \geq k$ holds for all $v \in Y - X \subseteq U = V(G) - V_0$). Thus, there exists a family $\mathcal{T}$ of i-critical sets $T \subset V(G)$, $0 \leq i \leq k - 1$, such that $Y - X \subseteq \cup_{T \in \mathcal{T}} T$ holds. By Lemma 9.27 with $H = H^*$ and $Z = Y - X$, we can choose $\mathcal{T}$ such that every two sets in $\mathcal{T}$ are disjoint. This implies that we need at least $|E(s, Y - X; H_0)|(= |Y - X|)$ edges that enter the sets in $\mathcal{T}$ to obtain an s-basally k-connected digraph. However, $H_0 - E(s, Y; H_0)$ is obtained from $H^* = H_0 - E(s, X; H_0)$ by removing edge set $E(s, Y - X; H_0)$ and adding edge set $E(s, X - Y; H_0)$. By $|X| < |Y|$, we have $|E(s, X - Y; H_0)| < |E(s, Y - X; H_0)|$, implying that $H_0 - E(s, Y; H_0)$ cannot be s-basally k-connected, a contradiction. This proves axiom (I3) and, hence, Lemma 9.24.

9.2.4 Algorithms

Since it turned out that $\mathcal{M}^+ = (U, \mathcal{I}^+)$ has the structure of a matroid, we can now obtain a subset $X \in \mathcal{I}^+$ with the maximum cost $w(X)$ via a greedy algorithm. An inclusion-wise maximal independent set in a matroid is called a *base*. Given a matroid $(N, \mathcal{I})$ and a cost function w, it is known [58] that a maximum cost base B is obtained by the following algorithm, GREEDY.

Algorithm GREEDY
Input: A matroid $(N, \mathcal{I})$ and a cost function $w : N \to \mathfrak{R}$.
Output: A maximum cost base $B \in \mathcal{I}$.
1    $N' := N; B := \emptyset;$
2   **while** B is not a maximal independent set **do**
3   Choose a maximum cost element u from N';
4        $N' := N' - u;$
5   **if** $B \cup \{u\} \in \mathcal{I}$ **then** $B := B \cup \{u\}$ **end** /* if */
6   **end**; /* while */
7   Output B.

By applying this algorithm to matroid $\mathcal{M}^+ = (U, \mathcal{I}^+)$ in Lemma 9.24, we obtain the following algorithm for solving the problem in Theorem 9.18. Let H_0 and V_0 be as defined before Lemma 9.22. Recall that H_0 is an s-basally k-connected digraph. Starting from $H := H_0$ and $X := \emptyset$, we scan edges $(s, v), v \in V(G) - V_0$ in the nonincreasing order of cost $w(v)$; that is, if $H - (s, v)$ remains s-basally k-connected then we remove edge (s, v) from the current digraph H and set $H := H - (s, v)$ and $X := X \cup \{v\}$. We repeat this operation until we obtain an s-basally k-connected digraph H' such that $E(s, V(G); H')$ becomes minimal subject to the s-basal k-connectivity or condition $|\Gamma_{H'}(s)| = k$. By Lemma 9.22, the maximum cost subset $X \in \mathcal{I}^+$ thus obtained gives a source set $S = V(G) - X$ satisfying $|S| \geq k$ with the minimum cost $w(S) = w(V(G)) - w(X)$. Hence, we obtain the next lemma.

Lemma 9.28. $S = \Gamma_{H'}^+(s)$ *in the resulting digraph H' is a minimum cost source set.* $\square$

Now we give an efficient implementation to obtain such a digraph H'. For this, we show that, given an s-basally k-connected digraph H and a vertex $v \in \Gamma_H^+(s)$, whether $H - (s, v)$ remains s-basally k-connected or not can be tested by computing local vertex-connectivities.

Lemma 9.29. *Let H be an s-basally k-connected digraph and let $G = H - s$. For each $(s, v) \in E(s, V(G); H)$ with $c_H(s, v) = 1$, the following conditions* (i) *and* (ii) *hold:*

(i) *If $\kappa(s, v; H - (s, v)) \geq k$ holds, then $H - (s, v)$ remains s-basally k-connected.*
(ii) *Assume that $|\Gamma_H^+(s)| \geq k + 1$. If $\kappa(s, v; H - (s, v)) < k$ holds, then $H - (s, v)$ is no longer s-basally k-connected.* $\square$

Proof. (i) Assume that $H - (s, v)$ is not s-basally k-connected. By Lemma 9.25, v is contained in a $(k - 1)$-critical set $X_v \subset V(G)$. Thus, $V(G) - X_v - \Gamma_G^-(X) \neq \emptyset$,

$v \in X_v$, $d(s, X_v; H) = 1$, and $|\Gamma_G^-(X_v)| = k - 1$ hold. Since $\Gamma_{H-(s,v)}^-(X_v) = \Gamma_G^-(X_v)$ separates v from s in $H - (s, v)$, we have $\kappa(s, v; H - (s, v)) < k$, a contradiction.

(ii) By $\kappa(s, v; H - (s, v)) < k$, there is a set $Y \subset V(G)$ with $v \in Y$ and $|\Gamma_{H-(s,v)}^-(Y)| < k$ such that $\Gamma_{H-(s,v)}^-(Y)$ separates v from s in $H - (s, v)$. We show that $V(G) - Y - \Gamma_G^-(Y) \neq \emptyset$. If $V(G) - Y \subseteq \Gamma_G^-(Y)$ then $\Gamma_{H-(s,v)}^+(s) \subseteq V(G) - Y \subseteq \Gamma_G^-(Y)$ implies $|\Gamma_H^+(s)| \leq |\Gamma_G^-(Y) \cup \{v\}| \leq k$, contradicting the assumption $|\Gamma_H^+(s)| \geq k + 1$. Hence, $V(G) - Y - \Gamma_G^-(Y) \neq \emptyset$. In this case, by $d(s, Y; H - (s, v)) = 0$ and $|\Gamma_{H-(s,v)}^-(Y)| < k$, Y violates (9.15) in $H - (s, v)$, showing that $H - (s, v)$ is not s-basally k-connected. $\square$

Recall that checking whether $\kappa(s, v; H - (s, v)) \geq k$ or not can be done in $O(\min\{k, \sqrt{n}\}m)$ time by using the network flow computation [66] (see Theorem 1.21 in Section 1.4). Hence, from Lemma 9.29 we have the next result.

Lemma 9.30. *Given an s-basally k-connected digraph H, the s-basal k-connectivity of $H - (s, v)$ can be tested in $O(\min\{k, \sqrt{n}\}m)$ time as long as $|\Gamma_H^+(s)| \geq k + 1$ holds.* $\square$

9.2.5 Proofs of Theorems 9.18, 9.19, and 9.20

Now we return to Theorems 9.18, 9.19, and 9.20 of this section, and we give their proofs. First, we consider Theorem 9.18. The GREEDY algorithm applied to matroid $\mathcal{M}^+ = (U, \mathcal{I}^+)$ for computing a minimum cost source set S needs $O(n)$ computations of $\kappa(s, v; H - (s, v))$, and the total time complexity is $O(\min\{k, \sqrt{n}\}nm)$. This proves Theorem 9.18.

For simple undirected graphs G, this complexity can be reduced to $O(m + \min\{k, \sqrt{n}\}kn^2)$ by using the following sparsification technique. Let G_k be a (k, α)-certificate of G for α with $\alpha(v) = 1$ for all $v \in V(G)$ (see Section 2.2). Such a subgraph G_k can be found in $O(m)$ time by Lemma 2.23 and has $O(kn)$ edges by Corollary 2.29. After replacing each undirected edge with two oppositely oriented directed edges, we apply GREEDY to this graph G_k, which now runs in $O(\min\{k, \sqrt{n}\}kn^2)$ time. Hence, it suffices to show that the set of all source sets S remains unchanged in G_k. For this, we assume that a source set S in G is not a source set in G_k. Then by $|S| \geq k$, there is a vertex cut C with $|C| < k$ that separates a vertex $u \in S$ from a vertex $v \in V(G) - S$. Since S is a source set in G, this C is not a vertex cut in G. This, however, contradicts that no new vertex cut C with $|C| < k$ appears in G_k by the sparsification, since $\mathcal{C}_j(u, v; G) = \mathcal{C}_j(u, v; G_k)$ holds for all pairs $u, v \in V(G)$ and integers $j < k$ by Corollary 2.29 and Lemma 2.27. This establishes Theorem 9.19.

Finally we consider the source location problem in Theorem 9.20, where a minimum cost set S is required to be chosen so that both $\hat{\kappa}^+(S, v; G) \geq k$ and $\hat{\kappa}^-(S, v; G) \geq \ell$ hold for all $v \in V(G) - S$. As observed in Lemma 9.24, all subsets S satisfying $\hat{\kappa}^+(S, v; G) \geq k$ for all $v \in V(G) - S$ can be represented by a matroid $\mathcal{M}^+ = (V(G), \mathcal{I}^+)$ (where we can extend the ground set from U to $V(G)$ without changing the set $\mathcal{I}^+$ of independent sets). Similarly, a matroid $\mathcal{M}^- = (V(G), \mathcal{I}^-)$ that represents all subsets S satisfying $\hat{\kappa}^-(S, v; G) \geq \ell$ for all $v \in V(G) - S$ can be defined by reversing the orientations of all directed edges in a given digraph. Thus, the problem is now to choose a maximum cost subset X that belongs to both $\mathcal{I}^+$ and $\mathcal{I}^-$ (where a minimum cost subset S in the source location problem is obtained by $S = V(G) - X$). This problem is known as the weighted matroid intersection problem, for which an $O(n^3)$ oracle time algorithm is known [58, 75, 197]. For matroids $\mathcal{M}^+$ and $\mathcal{M}^-$, an oracle of testing whether a given subset $X \subseteq V(G)$ is an independent set can be implemented to run in $O(nm)$ time [121]. Therefore, there exists an $O(n^4 m)$ time algorithm for solving the source location problem in Theorem 9.20.

10

Submodular and Posimodular Set Functions

In this chapter, we generalize the discussion on graphs given so far to submodular and posimodular set functions, and we present algorithms for some of the important problems.

Chapter 10 is organized as follows. Section 10.2 describes an efficient algorithm for minimizing submodular and posimodular set functions (see Section 10.1 for their definitions), which is an extension of the minimum-cut algorithm in undirected graphs studied in Chapter 3. Section 10.3 gives an analogous extension of the extreme vertex sets algorithm in Section 6.1 to the case of submodular and posimodular set functions. Based on the results in these sections, we then consider several optimization problems for submodular and posimodular set systems in Section 10.4, which include the aforementioned edge-connectivity augmentation problem with degree constraint. Section 10.5 discusses the extreme points of a base polyhedron of a submodular and posimodular set system. Finally, in Section 10.6 we study structure of the minimum transversal problem in posimodular set systems, which is an extension of source location problems with edge-connectivity requirement in Chapter 9.

10.1 Set Functions

Let V be a finite set, where we denote

$$n = |V|$$

in this chapter. For a set A and an element b, we may denote set $A \cup \{b\}$ by $A + b$. A *set function* f on V is a function $f : 2^V \to \Re$. A pair (V, f) of a finite set V and a set function f on V is called a *system*. For a vector $z \in \Re^n$ and a subset $X \subseteq V$, we denote

$$z(X) = \sum_{i \in X} z(i).$$

The function $z : 2^V \to \Re$ as just defined is called *modular*. A set function f is called *fully* (resp. *intersecting, crossing*) *submodular* if

$$f(X) + f(Y) \geq f(X \cap Y) + f(X \cup Y) \tag{10.1}$$

holds for every (resp. intersecting, crossing) pair of sets $X, Y \subseteq V$ [80, 92]. Recall that subsets X and Y are intersecting if $X \cup Y$, $X - Y$, and $Y - X$ are all nonempty, and they are crossing if in addition $V - (X \cup Y)$ is nonempty. For two fully (resp. intersecting, crossing) submodular set functions f and g, it is easy to show that set function $h = f + g$ (i.e., $h(X) = f(X) + g(X)$, $X \in 2^V$) is also fully (resp. intersecting, crossing) submodular. A set function f is called *fully* (resp. *intersecting, crossing*) *supermodular* if $-f$ is fully (resp. intersecting, crossing) submodular. A set function f is called *symmetric* if

$$f(X) = f(V - X) \text{ for all } X \subseteq V. \tag{10.2}$$

For example, the cut function $d : 2^V \to \Re^+$ is defined for an edge-weighted graph $G = (V, E)$ by $d(X; G) = \sum \{c_G(e) \mid e = \{u, v\} \in E, \ u \in X, \ v \in V - X\}$ (where $d(\emptyset; G) = d(V; G) = 0$), and it is a symmetric fully submodular set function (see property (1.3)). Analogously, given a hypergraph $H = (V, \mathcal{E})$ with a weight function $w : \mathcal{E} \to \Re_+$, we see that the set function $d : 2^V \to \Re_+$ defined by

$$d(X) = \sum \{w(E) \mid E \in \mathcal{E}, E \cap X \neq \emptyset, E - X \neq \emptyset\} \tag{10.3}$$

is symmetric fully submodular.

We call a set function f *fully* (resp. *intersecting, crossing*) *posimodular* if

$$f(X) + f(Y) \geq f(X - Y) + f(Y - X) \tag{10.4}$$

holds for every (resp. intersecting, crossing) pair of sets $X, Y \subseteq V$ [237]. For a non-negative vector $z \in \Re^n_+$, it is easily shown that the modular function $z : 2^V \to \Re_+$ is posimodular. For a fully (resp. intersecting, crossing) posimodular set function f and a nonnegative vector $z \in \Re^n_+$, the set function $h = f + z$ defined by $h(X) = f(X) + z(X)$, $X \in 2^V$, is also fully (resp. intersecting, crossing) posimodular. An f is called *fully* (resp. *intersecting, crossing*) *negamodular* if $-f$ is fully (resp. intersecting, crossing) posimodular.

A symmetric fully (crossing) submodular set function f is fully (crossing) posimodular, since (10.4) is obtained from $f(X) + f(Y) = f(V - X) + f(Y)$ by applying (10.1) to the pair of $X' = V - X$ and Y. However, the converse is not generally true.

Example 10.1. As an example of a fully submodular and posimodular set function f, which may not be symmetric, consider a multigraph $G = (V, E)$ and a weight function $w : V \to \mathbf{Z}_+$ and define

$$h_G(X) = d(X; G) + \sum \{w(v) \mid v \in X\} \text{ for } X \subseteq V,$$

where d is the cut function of G. Since d and w are both fully submodular and posimodular set functions, h_G is also a fully submodular and posimodular set function. However, this is not symmetric in general since the weight function w can be chosen so that h_G is not symmetric. For example, for a weight function $w : V \to \{1\}$, $f(X) \neq f(V - X)$ holds if $|X| \neq |V - X|$. As another example, let $\bar{d}(X)$ be the sum of the weights of edges incident to some vertex in a subset $X \subseteq V$; that is, $\bar{d}(X) = (d(X; G) + \sum_{v \in X} d(v; G))/2$. Then $\bar{d}$ is a fully submodular and posimodular set function, but it is not symmetric.   □

Given a multigraph $G = (V, E)$, a weight function $w: V \to \mathbf{Z}_+$ and an integer $k \geq 2$, the edge-connectivity augmentation problem with degree constraint [78] asks to find a set F of the smallest number of new edges such that the cut function d of the resulting multigraph $G' = (V, E \cup F)$ satisfies $d(X; G') \geq k$ for all $X \in 2^V - \{\emptyset, V\}$ (i.e., G' is k-edge-connected) while satisfying the given degree constraint $d(v; G') - d(v; G) \leq w(v)$ for all $v \in V$, where F can be chosen as an arbitrary multiset over $\{\{u, v\} \mid u, v \in V\}$. For each $X \in 2^V - \{\emptyset, V\}$, the value of $d(X; G)$ can be increased to at most $d(X; G) + \sum_{v \in X} w(v)$, since at most $\sum\{w(v) \mid v \in X\}$ edges are allowed between X and $V - X$. Thus, $\min\{h_G(X) \mid X \in 2^V - \{\emptyset, V\}\}$ of the set function h_G defined in Example 10.1 gives an upper bound on k such that G can be augmented to a k-edge-connected graph under the degree constraint of w.

10.2 Minimizing Submodular and Posimodular Functions

Since submodularity is observed in various combinatorial optimization problems, minimizing a submodular set function is posed as a fundamental problem in combinatorial optimization.

10.2.1 Submodular Minimization

The submodular minimization problem is as follows: Given a submodular system (V, f), find a subset X with $\emptyset \neq X \subset V$ that minimizes $f(X)$.

A subset X with $\emptyset \neq X \subset V$ that attains the minimum is called an *optimal solution*. An optimal solution X is called *minimal* (resp. *maximal*) if no proper and nonempty subset $X' \subset X$ (resp. no proper superset $X'' \supset X$ with $X'' \neq V$) is optimal.

The minimization problem can be solved in polynomial time by the algorithm of Grötschel, Lovász, and Schrijver [108] using the ellipsoid method. Recently, Iwata et al. [152] and Schrijver [288] independently discovered strongly polynomial combinatorial algorithms for minimizing submodular functions.

Queyranne [277] has found a simple combinatorial algorithm for a problem under the additional condition that f is symmetric, by extending the minimum-cut algorithm in Section 3.2 to the submodular minimization problem, which we shall describe in the following.

Theorem 10.2 ([277]). *For a given symmetric and fully submodular set function f on V with n $(= |V|) \geq 2$, an optimal solution can be found in $O(n^3 T_f)$*

time, where T_f denotes the time to evaluate the value $f(X)$ of a given subset $X \subset V$.   □

We slightly generalize this result of Queyranne by replacing symmetry condition (10.2) with posimodularity condition (10.4), and we present an algorithm that computes all minimal optimal solutions.

Algorithm to Obtain an Optimal Solution

Let us first review Queyranne's algorithm for a symmetric submodular function. We say that a subset $X \subset V$ *separates* u and v if $|\{u, v\} \cap X| = 1$. For a submodular system (V, f), an ordered pair (u, v) of elements of V is called a *pendent pair* if

$$f(v) \leq f(X) \text{ holds for all sets } X \subset V \text{ that separate } u \text{ and } v.$$

Note that a pendent pair of f is an extension of that of a cut function d, which is defined as a pair of vertices u and v in a graph G such that $\lambda(u, v; G) = d(v; G)$; that is, $\{v, V(G) - v\}$ gives the minimum cut among all cuts separating u and v (see Section 1.5.1).

We show that the PENDENTPAIR algorithm in Section 3.1 can be generalized to find a pendent pair in a symmetric and fully submodular set function.

Given a set function f on V and an element $x \in V$, the algorithm constructs an ordering $\sigma = (v_1, v_2, \ldots, v_n)$ of all the elements in V. After the ith iteration ($i = 1, \ldots, n - 1$), the algorithm has chosen the first i elements $v_1, v_2, \ldots, v_i$ in σ, where $v_1 = x$, and a data structure Q maintains the rest of the $n - i$ elements u according to the following key values:

$$\text{key}[u] := f(V_i + u) - f(u), \tag{10.5}$$

where

$$V_0 = \emptyset \text{ and } V_i = \{v_1, v_2, \ldots, v_i\} \text{ for } i = 1, \ldots, n. \tag{10.6}$$

The function UPDATE(key) updates these key values in Q after counter i and set V_i have been incremented. The EXTRACTMIN(Q) function then returns an element from Q with the least key value, deleting it from Q.

Algorithm PENDENTPAIR
Input: A set function f on V and an element $x \in V$.
Output: A pair (u, v) with $u, v \in V - x$.
    Let Q contain all $u \in V$ with $key[u] := 0$;
    $v_1 := x$;
    for $i = 2$ to n **do**
        UPDATE(key);
        $v_i := $ EXTRACTMIN(Q)
    end; /* for */
    Output $(u, v) := (v_{n-1}, v_n)$.

The ordering $\sigma = (v_1, v_2, \ldots, v_n)$ computed in PENDENTPAIR satisfies

$$f(V_{i-1} + v_i) - f(v_i) \le f(V_{i-1} + v_j) - f(v_j),$$
$$\text{for all } i, j \text{ with } 2 \le i \le j \le n. \tag{10.7}$$

This is an extension of a maximum adjacency (MA) ordering of a vertex set V of an edge-weighted graph $G = (V, E)$, which is defined as an ordering $(v_1, v_2, \ldots, v_n)$ of vertices in V such that $d(\{v_1, v_2, \ldots, v_{i-1}\}, v_i; G) \ge d(\{v_1, v_2, \ldots, v_{i-1}\}, v_j; G), 2 \le i \le j \le n$ in (3.1) in Section 3.1.

Lemma 10.3 ([277]). *Let f be a crossing submodular set function on a set V (not necessarily symmetric). Let an ordering $\sigma = (v_1, v_2, \ldots, v_n)$ of V satisfy (10.7) and define V_i by (10.6). Then for all $i = 1, \ldots, n - 1$, all $y \notin V_i$, and all $X \subseteq V_{i-1}$, it holds that*

$$f(V_i) + f(y) \le f(V_i - X) + f(X + y). \tag{10.8}$$

$\square$

Proof. For $i = 1$, (10.8) trivially follows from (10.7). By induction, assume that (10.8) holds for all $i = 1, \ldots, k - 1$. Consider an element $u \notin V_k$ and a subset $S \subseteq V_{k-1}$. By (10.7) for v_k, we have

$$f(V_{k-1} + v_k) - f(v_k) \le f(V_{k-1} + u) - f(u). \tag{10.9}$$

Let j be the smallest integer such that $S \subseteq V_{j-1}$.

Case 1: $j = k$. If $S = V_{k-1}$, then $f(V_k) + f(u) \le f(V_{k-1} + u) + f(v_k) = f(V_k - S) + f(S + u)$ follows from (10.9), indicating (10.8). Therefore, assume $S \subset V_{k-1}$. Then V_{k-1} and $S + u$ cross each other since $V_{k-1} - (S + u) \ne \emptyset$, $u \in (S + u) - V_{k-1} \ne \emptyset$, $v_{k-1} \in V_{k-1} \cap (S + u) \ne \emptyset$, and $v_k \in V - (V_{k-1} \cup (S + u)) \ne \emptyset$. Therefore,

$$\begin{aligned} f(V_k - S) + f(S + u) &= f((V_{k-1} - S) + v_k) + f(S + u) \\ &\ge f(V_{k-1}) + f(v_k) - f(S) + f(S + u) \\ &\ge f(V_{k-1} + u) + f(v_k) \\ &\ge f(V_k) + f(u), \end{aligned}$$

where the three inequalities follow respectively from the inductive assumption (10.8) with $i = k - 1$, $y = v_k$, and $X = V_{k-1} - S$; the submodular inequality (10.1) for crossing sets V_{k-1} and $S + u$ (i.e., $f(V_{k-1}) + f(S + u) \ge f(V_{k-1} + u) + f(S)$); and inequality (10.9).

Case 2: $j \le k - 1$. Then $v_{j-1} \in S$ and none of $v_j, \ldots, v_k$ is in S. Note that $V_k - S$ and V_j cross each other because $v_k \in (V_k - S) - V_j$, $v_{j-1} \in V_j - (V_k - S)$, $v_j \in (V_k - S) \cap V_j$, and $u \in V - (V_k - S) - V_j$. Therefore, we have

$$\begin{aligned} f(V_k - S) + f(S + u) &\ge f(V_k - S) + f(V_j) - f(V_j - S) + f(u) \\ &\ge f(V_k) + f(u), \end{aligned}$$

where the inequalities follow respectively from the inductive assumption (10.8) with $i = j$, $y = u$, and $X = S$, and the submodular inequality with crossing sets $V_k - S$ and V_j. Thus, (10.8) holds for $i = k$ and any $y = u \notin V_i$ and $X = S \subseteq V_{i-1}$. $\square$

Lemma 10.3 says that the pair (v_{n-1}, v_n) of the last two elements in the ordering σ of (10.7) satisfies

$$f(V - v_n) + f(v_n) \leq f(Y) + f(V - Y)$$

for all Y with $v_{n-1} \in Y \subseteq V - \{v_n\}$ since, by (10.8) with $i = n - 1$ and $y = v_n$, it holds that $f(V_{n-1}) + f(v_n) \leq f(V_{n-2} - X + v_{n-1}) + f(X + v_n)$ for all $X \subseteq V_{n-2}$ (then we let $Y = V_{n-2} - X + v_{n-1}$).

PENDENTPAIR runs in $O(n^2 T_f)$ time, since UPDATE(key) and EXTRACTMIN(Q) need $O(n)$ oracle calls and there are $O(n)$ iterations in the for-loops, where other computing time is minor compared to $O(n^2)$. Then we have the next.

Lemma 10.4 ([277]). *For a crossing submodular set function f on V with $|V| = n \geq 3$ and an arbitrarily chosen element $v_1 \in V$, an ordering σ with starting element v_1 in (10.7) can be obtained in $O(n^2 T_f)$ time, and the pair (v_n, v_{n-1}) of the last two elements satisfies that $f(v_n) + f(V - v_n) \leq f(Y) + f(V - Y)$ for all Y with $v_{n-1} \in Y \subseteq V - \{v_n\}$.* $\square$

Note that the pair (v_{n-1}, v_n) is a pendent pair with respect to function f' : $2^V \to \Re$ defined by $f'(X) = f(X) + f(V - X)$, $X \in 2^V$.

Now we prove the following statement, which is a slight extension of Theorem 10.2.

Corollary 10.5. *For a given symmetric and crossing submodular set function f on V with $n = |V| \geq 2$, an optimal solution $X \in 2^V - \{\emptyset, V\}$ that minimizes f can be found in $O(n^3 T_f)$ time.* $\square$

Proof. By symmetry of f, $f(v_n) + f(V - v_n) \leq f(Y) + f(V - Y)$ in Lemma 10.4 implies $f(v_n) \leq f(Y)$ for all Y with $v_{n-1} \in Y \subseteq V - \{v_n\}$; that is, (v_{n-1}, v_n) is a pendent pair. Then we can identify two elements v_{n-1} and v_n as a single element to find a nonempty subset X' with $X' \subseteq V - \{v_{n-1}, v_n\}$ and $f(X') < f(v_n)$ (if any). This can be done [92] while preserving the crossing submodularity in the new system (V', f') defined by $V' = V - v_n$ and

$$f'(X) = \begin{cases} f(X) & \text{if } v_{n-1} \notin X \subseteq V' \\ f(X + v_n) & \text{if } v_{n-1} \in X \subseteq V'. \end{cases} \tag{10.10}$$

Hence, for an optimal solution X of the system (V', f'), an optimal solution of the original system (V, f) is given by $\operatorname{argmin}\{f(S) \mid S \in \{\{v_n\}, X'\}\}$, where $X' = X$ if $v_{n-1} \notin X$ and $X' = X + v_n$ otherwise. By recursively applying this argument $n - 1$ times, we obtain a sequence of systems $(V^{(n)}, f^{(n)}), (V^{(n-1)}, f^{(n-1)}), \dots, (V^{(1)}, f^{(1)})$ such that $(V^{(n)}, f^{(n)}) = (V, f)$, and each $(V^{(i)}, f^{(i)})$ is obtained from $(V^{(i-1)}, f^{(i-1)})$ by contracting a pendent pair

(x_i, y_i) of $(V^{(i-1)}, f^{(i-1)})$. Hence, the optimal value in (V, f) is equal to $\min\{f^{(i)}(y_i) \mid i = n, n-1, \ldots, 2\}$ and an optimal solution to (V, f) is given by the set of elements that are contracted into the element $\arg\min\{f^{(i)}(y_i) \mid i = n, n-1, \ldots, 2\}$. For this, we need to find pendent pairs $O(n)$ times. Then by Lemma 10.4 an optimal solution to (V, f) can be found in $O(n^3 T_f)$ time. This completes the proof. □

Generalization to a Submodular and Posimodular Set Function

Now we relax the symmetry condition in the previous discussion to posimodularity.

Lemma 10.6. *Given a crossing submodular and posimodular set function f on a set V, let f' be the set function on V such that*

$$f'(X) = \min\{f(X), f(V-X)\} \text{ for all } X \in 2^V.$$

Then f' is a symmetric and crossing submodular set function on V. □

Proof. Clearly f' is symmetric. We show that $f'(X) + f'(Y) \geq f'(X \cap Y) + f'(X \cup Y)$ holds for any crossing $X, Y \subseteq V$. If $f'(X) = f(X)$ and $f'(Y) = f(Y)$, then

$$\begin{aligned} f'(X) + f'(Y) &= f(X) + f(Y) \\ &\geq f(X \cap Y) + f(X \cup Y) \\ &\geq f'(X \cap Y) + f'(X \cup Y) \end{aligned}$$

from the crossing submodularity of f and the definition of f'. If $f'(X) = f(V-X)$ and $f'(Y) = f(V-Y)$, then we have

$$\begin{aligned} f'(X) + f'(Y) &= f(V-X) + f(V-Y) \\ &\geq f((V-X) \cap (V-Y)) + f((V-X) \cup (V-Y)) \\ &= f(V-(X \cup Y)) + f(V-(X \cap Y)) \\ &\geq f'(X \cup Y) + f'(X \cap Y) \end{aligned}$$

from the crossing submodularity of f. Finally, assume $f'(X) = f(X)$ and $f'(Y) = f(V-Y)$ (and the case of $f'(X) = f(V-X)$ and $f'(Y) = f(Y)$ can be treated symmetrically). Then, by the crossing posimodularity of f, we have

$$\begin{aligned} f'(X) + f'(Y) &= f(X) + f(V-Y) \\ &\geq f(X - (V-Y)) + f((V-Y) - X) \\ &= f(X \cap Y) + f(V-(X \cup Y)) \\ &\geq f'(X \cap Y) + f'(X \cup Y). \end{aligned}$$

□

Theorem 10.7. *Given a crossing submodular and posimodular set function f on V with $|V| = n \geq 2$, an optimal solution $X \in 2^V - \{\emptyset, V\}$ that minimizes f can be found in $O(n^3 T_f)$ time.* ◻

Proof. For the given f, let f' be the set function defined in Lemma 10.6. Then we can apply Corollary 10.5 to the symmetric and crossing submodular set function f' to compute an optimal solution X of (V, f'). Then an optimal solution of the original system (V, f) is given by X or $V - X$, which can be directly determined by comparing $f(X)$ and $f(V - X)$. This proves the theorem. ◻

10.2.2 Minimal Optimal Solutions

Computing minimal and maximal optimal solutions of f plays a key role in many graph connectivity problems such as computing leaf-vertices in a cactus structure of all minimum cuts [259] and augmenting edge-connectivity by edge-splitting technique [78] (see Section 8.1). In what follows, we assume that f is an *intersecting* submodular and posimodular set function of V, and we consider how to compute minimal optimal solutions. Notice that two minimal solutions X and Y cannot intersect each other, since otherwise the posimodularity $f(X) + f(Y) \geq f(X - Y) + f(Y - X)$ would imply that $X - Y$ or $Y - X$ is also an optimal solution, contradicting the minimality of X and Y. However, two maximal optimal solutions X and Y may intersect each other (note that the submodularity $f(X) + f(Y) \geq f(X \cap Y) + f(X \cup Y)$ does not imply the optimality of $X \cap Y$ or $X \cup Y$ if $X \cup Y = V$).

In this subsection, we consider how to compute minimal optimal solutions in a system (V, f). For this, we remark that computing a minimal optimal solution X in (V, f') defined by Lemma 10.6 may not provide a minimal optimal solution in the original system (V, f) if $f(V - X) < f(X)$. Therefore, we now consider the following setting of the minimization problem: Given a symmetric and crossing submodular system $(V + s, g)$ with a designated element s ($\notin V$), find a subset X with $\emptyset \neq X \subset V$ (i.e., $s \notin X$ and $\emptyset \neq X \neq V$) that minimizes $g(X)$. If we apply Corollary 10.5 to $(V + s, g)$, its optimal solution X^* may satisfy $X^* = \{s\}$ or $X^* = V$, which is not allowed here. To avoid choosing a set $X = \{s\}$ or V as an optimal solution, we compute a pendent pair (x, y) such that $s \notin \{x, y\}$. This is possible by choosing s as the starting element v_1 in the ordering of (10.7). Then these x and y are contracted into a single element. We repeat this procedure so long as the system has at least *three* elements (i.e., at least two elements other than s). The entire algorithm is described as follows.

Algorithm MINIMIZE
Input: A symmetric and crossing submodular system $(V + s, g)$ with a
    designated element s, where $|V| \geq 2$ holds.
Output: $\lambda^* = \min\{g(X) \mid \emptyset \neq X \subset V\}$, and a nonempty set $X^* \subset V$ with
    $g(X^*) = \lambda^*$.
1   $V' := V + s$; $g' := g$;

2 **for** $i := 1$ to $|V| - 1$ **do**
3   Find a pendent pair (x, y) in (V', g') such that $s \notin \{x, y\}$;
4      $\lambda_i := g'(x)$; $x_i := x$;
5   Let (V', g') denote the system obtained from the current (V', g')
          by contracting x and y
6 **end**; /* for */
7 Choose $i^* \in \operatorname{argmin}\{\lambda_i \mid i = 1, 2, \ldots, |V| - 1\}$;
8 $\lambda^* := \lambda_{i^*}$; Let $X^* := V[x_{i^*}]$, where, for a set Z of elements, $V[Z]$ denotes
      the set of the elements in V that have been contracted into an element in Z
      in the preceding computation.

Since MINIMIZE computes pendent pairs $O(|V|)$ times, it runs in $O(|V|^3 T_g)$
time by Lemma 10.4.

The optimality of X^* is observed as follows. Assume indirectly that there is a
set Y such that $g(Y) < g(X^*)$ and $\emptyset \neq Y \subset V$. Then this Y must separate x and y
of some pendent pairs (x, y), which are computed during MINIMIZE (otherwise Y
would separate s and V). Let (x, y) be the earliest one among such pendent pairs.
Thus, $g'(x) \leq g(Y)$ must hold by the property of pendent pairs. This, however, con-
tradicts $g(Y) < g(X^*) = \lambda_{i^*} = \min\{\lambda_i \mid i = 1, \ldots, |V| - 1\} \leq g'(x)$. Therefore,
$\lambda^* = g(X^*)$.

Moreover, if we choose the smallest i^* among $\operatorname{argmin}\{\lambda_i \mid i = 1, \ldots, n - 1\}$
in line 7 of MINIMIZE, then the output X^* is a *minimal* optimal solution among
$X \subset V$ with $g(X) = \lambda^*$. To see this, assume indirectly that there is a set Y such that
$g(Y) = g(X^*)$ and $\emptyset \neq Y \subset X^*$. Let (x, y) be the first pendent pair constructed by
MINIMIZE and separated by Y, and let i_Y be the corresponding value of the for-loop
index i in lines 2–6 of MINIMIZE. Observe that $\{x, y\} \subseteq X^*$ and $i_Y < i^*$, because
otherwise X^* cannot be contracted into a single element during MINIMIZE. At
this iteration, $i_Y (< i^*)$, Y has been contracted into a subset Y' separating x and y
in the current system (V', g') and we have $\lambda_{i^*} < \lambda_{i_Y} = g'(x) \leq g'(Y') = g(Y) =
g(X^*) = \lambda_{i^*}$, a contradiction. Therefore, X^* is a minimal optimal solution.

We now show how to compute all minimal optimal solutions based on the
optimal value λ_{i^*}. We modify the preceding algorithm so that each time a minimal
optimal solution X is found we contract $X + s$ into s (in order to avoid finding an
optimal solution $X' \supset X$ in the subsequent computation).

Algorithm MINIMAL
Input: A symmetric and crossing submodular system $(V + s, g)$ with a
    designated element s, and the optimal value $\lambda^* = \min\{g(X) \mid \emptyset \neq X \subset V\}$,
    where $|V| \geq 2$ holds.
Output: The family $\mathcal{X}$ of minimal sets X with $\emptyset \neq X \subset V$, which
    satisfy $g(X) = \lambda^*$.
1      $V' := V + s$; $g' := g$; $\mathcal{X} := \emptyset$;
2   **for** each $v \in V$ with $g'(v) = \lambda^*$ **do**
3          $\mathcal{X} := \mathcal{X} \cup \{\{v\}\}$;

4 Let (V', g') denote the system obtained from the current (V', g')
    by contracting $\{v, s\}$ into s

5 **end**; /* for */

6 **while** $|V'| \geq 4$ **do**

7   Find a pendent pair (x, y) such that $s \notin \{x, y\}$ in (V', g');

8   Let (V', g') denote the system obtained from the current (V', g')
     by contracting x and y into a single element, say z;

9   **if** $g'(z) = \lambda^*$ **then**

10    $\mathcal{X} := \mathcal{X} \cup \{V[z]\}$, where $V[z] \subset V$ denotes the set of elements which
     have been contracted into z so far;

11   Let (V', g') denote the system obtained from the current (V', g')
     by contracting $\{z, s\}$ into s

12   **end** /* if */

13 **end**; /* while */

14 Denote the current set V' as $V' = \{s, a, b\}$; /* $g'(a) > \lambda^*$ and $g'(b) > \lambda^*$ */

15 **if** $g'(\{a, b\}) = \lambda^*$ and line 11 was executed at least once (i.e., at least
   one element in V has been contracted into s) **then**

16   $\mathcal{X} := \mathcal{X} \cup \{V[\{a, b\}]\}$, where $V[\{a, b\}] \subset V$ denotes the set of elements
   which have been contracted into a or b so far;

17 **end**. /* if */

Clearly, each subset $\{v\} \in \mathcal{X}$ with $g'(v) = \lambda^*$ after line 5 (if any) is a minimal optimal solution. We easily see by induction that the final family $\mathcal{X}$ contains only *minimal* optimal solutions among all $X \subset V$ with $g(X) = \lambda^*$. Next we show that there is no minimal optimal solution other than those in the final $\mathcal{X}$.

Assume that a nonempty subset $Z \subset V$ is a minimal optimal solution of (V, f) such that $Z \notin \mathcal{X}$. Let $(V' = \{s, a, b\}, g')$ be the final system obtained after the while-loop of MINIMAL. As observed at the beginning of this section, Z does not intersect any subset in $\mathcal{X}$; hence,

$$Z \subseteq V - \bigcup_{X \in \mathcal{X} - \{V[\{a,b\}]\}} X = V[\{a, b\}],$$

where the equality holds since all the vertices in $\bigcup_{X \in \mathcal{X} - \{V[\{a,b\}]\}} X$ have been contracted into s in the final (V', g'). Since we have checked whether $g'(\{a, b\})(= g(X_{a,b}))$ is equal to λ^* in line 15, Z must have been included in $\mathcal{X}$ if $Z = X_{a,b}$. Since $g'(a) > \lambda^*$ and $g'(b) > \lambda^*$ hold, we see that a pendent pair (x, y) that is separated by Z must have been chosen in line 7 during MINIMAL. Let (x, y) be the first pair among such pendent pairs. It must satisfy $g'(x) \leq g(Z) = \lambda^*$. This, however, contradicts that $g'(u) > \lambda^*$ holds for all $u \in V' - s$ during the while-loop.

Consequently, we obtain the next result, where the running time follows from Lemma 10.4 and from the fact that MINIMIZE computes pendent pairs $O(|V|)$ times.

Theorem 10.8. *Given a symmetric and crossing submodular system $(V + s, g)$ with $|V| = n \geq 2$, let $\lambda^* = \min\{g(X) \mid \emptyset \neq X \subset V\}$. Then the family X of all minimal solutions among those $X \subset V$ with $g(X) = \lambda^*$ can be obtained by MINIMIZE and MINIMAL in $O(n^3 T_g)$ time.*   □

Minimal Optimal Solutions in Intersecting Submodular and Posimodular Systems

We describe how to find minimal optimal solutions to an intersecting submodular and posimodular system (V, f). We work with the following set function g : $2^{V+s} \to \Re$ (where s is a new element), which is extended from $f : 2^V \to \Re$ as follows. For each $X \subseteq V + s$, let

$$g(X) = \begin{cases} f(X) & \text{if } s \notin X \\ f(V - (X - s)) & \text{if } s \in X. \end{cases} \tag{10.11}$$

Lemma 10.9. *Given an intersecting submodular and posimodular set function f on V, the preceding set function $g : 2^{V+s} \to \Re$ is symmetric and crossing submodular.*   □

Proof. The symmetry of g is immediate from definition (10.11). We show that $g(X) + g(Y) \geq g(X \cap Y) + g(X \cup Y)$ holds for any crossing $X, Y \subseteq V + s$. If $s \notin X \cup Y$, then it directly follows from the intersecting submodularity of f. If $s \in X \cap Y$, then for $X' = X - s$ and $Y' = Y - s$ we have the following:

$$\begin{aligned} g(X) + g(Y) &= f(V - X') + f(V - Y') \quad \text{(by (10.11))} \\ &\geq f((V - X') \cap (V - Y')) + f((V - X') \cup (V - Y')) \\ &\qquad\qquad \text{(by the intersecting submodularity of } f) \\ &= f(V - (X' \cup Y')) + f(V - (X' \cap Y')) \\ &= g((X' \cup Y') + s) + g((X' \cap Y') + s) \quad \text{(by (10.11))} \\ &= g(X \cup Y) + g(X \cap Y). \end{aligned}$$

For the remaining case, assume $s \in X - Y$ without loss of generality. Then for $X' = X - s$, it holds that

$$\begin{aligned} g(X) + g(Y) &= f(V - X') + f(Y) \quad \text{(by (10.11))} \\ &\geq f((V - X') - Y) + f(Y - (V - X')) \\ &\qquad\qquad \text{(by the intersecting posimodularity of } f) \\ &= f(V - (X' \cup Y)) + f(X' \cap Y) \\ &= g((X' \cup Y) + s) + f(X' \cap Y) \quad \text{(by (10.11))} \\ &= g(X \cup Y) + g(X \cap Y). \end{aligned}$$

□

Lemma 10.10. *For an intersecting submodular and posimodular set function f on V (where $n = |V| \geq 2$), there exists a pendent pair (x, y). Furthermore, such a pendent pair can be obtained in $O(n^2 T_f)$ time.* □

Proof. Given f, we add the new element s to V and define a set function g on $V + s$ by (10.11). By Lemma 10.9, g is symmetric and crossing submodular on $V + s$. We can apply Lemma 10.4 to the system $(V + s, g)$ and can find a pendent pair (x, y) in $(V + s, g)$ such that $s \notin \{x, y\}$ by choosing v_1 as s in the ordering of (10.7). For this pair (x, y), $g(x) \leq g(Y)$ holds for all $Y \subset V + s$ separating x and y. Hence, for any subset $X \subset V$ separating x and y, $f(x) = g(x) \leq g(X) = f(X)$. This implies that (x, y) is also a pendent pair in (V, f). □

Let g be defined from f by (10.11) and apply MINIMIZE to the system $(V + s, g)$. Then we observe that the subset X^* obtained by MINIMIZE is also optimal to the original system (V, f). Note that $g(X^*) = f(X^*)$ holds since $s \notin X^*$. If there is a solution Y such that $f(Y) < f(X^*)$ then Y satisfies $g(Y) = f(Y)$ and $\emptyset \neq Y \subset V$, contradicting the optimality of $g(X^*)$. Then, applying the argument before Theorem 10.8, we see that MINIMAL applied to $(V + s, g)$ gives all minimal optimal solutions to (V, f).

Theorem 10.11. *Given an intersecting submodular and posimodular system (V, f) with $|V| = n \geq 2$, the family $\mathcal{X}$ of all minimal solutions can be obtained by MINIMIZE and MINIMAL in $O(n^3 T_f)$ time.* □

10.3 Extreme Subsets in Submodular and Posimodular Systems

This section extends the results in Section 6.1 to the case of set functions.

Given a system (V, f), a nonempty proper subset X of V is called an *extreme subset* of f if

$$f(Y) > f(X) \text{ for all nonempty proper subsets } Y \text{ of } X.$$

We denote by $\mathcal{X}(f)$ the family of all extreme subsets of a set function f. Any trivial set $\{v\}$, $v \in V$ is an extreme subset. By definition, any nonempty subset X contains an extreme subset X' with $f(X') \leq f(X)$. In particular, $\mathcal{X}(f)$ contains a *minimizer* X (i.e., an optimal solution in the sense of Section 10.2) of f such that $f(X) = \min\{f(Y) \mid \emptyset \neq Y \subset V\}$.

Lemma 10.12. *Let f be set function on a finite set V. If f is intersecting posimodular or symmetric and crossing submodular, then the family $\mathcal{X}(f)$ of extreme subsets of f is laminar.* □

Proof. Recall that a symmetric and crossing submodular set function is crossing posimodular (see Section 10.1). Let $X, Y \in \mathcal{X}(f)$ be two intersecting extreme subsets. By definition of extreme subsets we would have $f(X) + f(Y) < f(X - Y) + f(Y - X)$, which is a contradiction. First consider the case where f is

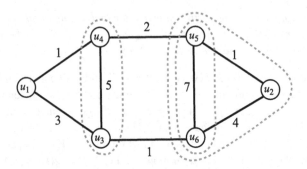

Figure 10.1. Extreme subsets in $\mathcal{X}(d)$ for the cut function d of an edge-weighted graph $G = (V, E)$, where the numbers beside edges indicate their weights and each nontrivial extreme subset $X \in \mathcal{X}(d)$ is depicted by a dotted closed curve.

intersecting posimodular. But the preceding inequality contradicts the posimodularity. Hence, we only have to consider the case where f is symmetric and crossing posimodular. If X and Y do not cross each other (i.e., $X \cup Y = V$), then we have $f(X-Y) = f(V-Y) = f(Y)$ and $f(Y-X) = f(V-X) = f(X)$, which again contradict the preceding inequality.   □

Extreme subsets are an extension of extreme vertex sets in graphs (see Section 6.1). Figure 10.1 illustrates all extreme subsets in $\mathcal{X}(d)$ for the cut function d of an edge-weighted graph $G = (V, E)$.

In this section, via subsections 10.3.1 and 10.3.2, we prove the next result, which also solves the problem of minimizing f since $\mathcal{X}(f)$ contains a minimizer of f.

Theorem 10.13. *Let f be a set function on V with $n = |V| \geq 2$. If f is symmetric and crossing submodular or intersecting submodular and posimodular, then the family $\mathcal{X}(f)$ of extreme subsets of f can be found in $O(n^3 T_f)$ time.*   □

10.3.1 Minimum Degree Orderings

We call a pair of elements $u, v \in V$ a *flat pair* of f if $f(X) \geq \min_{x \in X} f(x)$ holds for all subsets X that separate u and v (hence, no nontrivial extreme subset separates u and v).

Given a set function f on V with $n = |V| \geq 2$, we call an ordering $\pi = (v_1, v_2, \ldots, v_n)$ a *minimum degree (MD) ordering* of V if it satisfies

$$f(v_i) + f(V_{i-1} + v_i) \leq f(v_j) + f(V_{i-1} + v_j), \quad 1 \leq i \leq j \leq n, \quad (10.12)$$

where $V_0 = \emptyset$ and $V_i = \{v_1, v_2, \ldots, v_i\}$ $(1 \leq i \leq n - 1)$. It is not difficult to see that, after choosing V_{i-1}, the next element v_i can be chosen from $V - V_i$ by finding the smallest $f(v) + f(V_{i-1} + v)$ among all $v \in V - V_{i-1}$. Thus, an MD ordering can be found in $O(n^2 T_f)$ time.

Note that this is a generalization of the MD ordering in (6.1) defined for the cut function d of an edge-weighted graph $G = (V, E)$, since $d(x; G) + d(V_{i-1} + x; G) - d(V_{i-1}; G) = 2d(x; G - V_{i-1})$ holds for each $x \in V - V_{i-1}$. In Fig. 10.1, the vertices $u_1, u_2, \ldots, u_6$ in the graph are indexed by an MD ordering.

We show that a flat pair in a symmetric and crossing submodular function f can be found by an MD ordering of f.

Theorem 10.14 ([229]). *For a symmetric and crossing submodular set function f on V with $n = |V| \geq 2$, let $\pi = (v_1, v_2, \ldots, v_n)$ be an MD ordering of V. Then the last two vertices, v_{n-1} and v_n, give a flat pair.* □

We prove Theorem 10.14 after showing the next lemma.

Lemma 10.15. *Let f be a symmetric and crossing submodular set function on V. For a subset $Z \subset V$, let g be a set function on $V - Z$ such that $g(X) = f(X) + f(Z \cup X)$, $X \subseteq V - Z$. Then g is symmetric and crossing submodular.* □

Proof. Let X be an arbitrary subset of $V - Z$. We show $g(X) = g((V - Z) - X)$. By definition of g, we have $g((V-Z)-X)) = f((V-Z)-X)) + f(Z \cup ((V-Z)-X)) = f(V - (Z \cup X)) + f(V - X) = f(Z \cup X) + f(X) = g(X)$. Hence, g is symmetric. For two crossing subsets $X, Y \subseteq V - Z$, by the submodularity of f, we have

$$
\begin{aligned}
g(X) + g(Y) &= f(X) + f(Y) + f(Z \cup X) + f(Z \cup Y) \\
&\geq f(X \cap Y) + f(X \cup Y) + f(Z \cup (X \cap Y)) + f(Z \cup X \cup Y) \\
&\geq g(X \cap Y) + g(X \cup Y).
\end{aligned}
$$

Therefore, g is crossing submodular. □

Proof of Theorem 10.14. For each $i = 0, 1, \ldots, n - 2$, we define a set function f_i of $V - V_i$ by

$$f_i(X) = f(X) + f(V_i \cup X), \quad X \subseteq V - V_i,$$

which is symmetric and crossing submodular on $V - V_i$ by Lemma 10.15. By induction on $i = n - 2, n - 3, \ldots, 1, 0$, we prove that

$$f_i(X) \geq \min_{x \in X} f_i(x) \text{ for all } X \subseteq V - V_i \text{ that separate } v_{n-1} \text{ and } v_n. \quad (10.13)$$

Since $f_0(X) = 2f(X)$, property (10.13) for $i = 0$ proves the theorem. We easily see that (10.13) holds for $i = n - 2$ since $V - V_{n-2} = \{v_{n-1}, v_n\}$. Let $n \geq 3$ (otherwise we are done). Now we assume (10.13) for $i = j$, and we prove (10.13) for $i = j - 1$. Let X be an arbitrary subset of $V - V_{j-1}$ that separates v_{n-1} and v_n.

Case 1: $v_j \notin X$. Let $x^* = \mathrm{argmin}\{f_j(x) \mid x \in X\}$, where $f_j(X) \geq f_j(x^*)$ holds by induction hypothesis. We prove that

$$f_{j-1}(X) - f_{j-1}(x^*) \geq 0,$$

from which $f_{j-1}(X) \geq f_{j-1}(x^*) \geq \min_{x \in X} f_{j-1}(x)$ follows, indicating that (10.14) holds for $i = j - 1$. To show this, we can assume without loss of generality that $|X| \geq 2$ holds by symmetry of f_{j-1} and $n \geq 3$ (we let $X := (V - V_{j-1}) - X$ if $X = \{x^*\}$). Then subsets $V_{j-1} \cup X$ and $V_j + x^*$ are crossing, and we have, by submodularity of f,

$$f(V_{j-1} \cup X) + f(V_j + x^*) \geq f(V_j \cup X) + f(V_{j-1} + x^*).$$

From this and $f_j(X) \geq f_j(x^*)$, we have

$$\begin{aligned} f_{j-1}(X) - f_{j-1}(x^*) &= f(X) + f(V_{j-1} \cup X) - f(V_{j-1} + x^*) - f(x^*) \\ &\geq f(X) + f(V_j \cup X) - f(V_j + x^*) - f(x^*) \\ &= f_j(X) - f_j(x^*) \geq 0, \end{aligned}$$

as required.

Case 2: $v_j \in X$. By the choice of v_j, we have $f_{j-1}(v_j) = \min_{x \in V - V_{j-1}} f_{j-1}(x)$. Consider subset $Y = (V - V_j) - X$, which separates v_{n-1} and v_n; hence, $f_{j-1}(Y) \geq \min_{y \in Y} f_{j-1}(y)$ holds by the argument in Case 1. Since $f_{j-1}(Y) = f_{j-1}(X)$ holds by symmetry, we have $f_{j-1}(X) = f_{j-1}(Y) \geq \min_{y \in Y} f_{j-1}(y) \geq f_{j-1}(v_j) = \min_{x \in X} f_{j-1}(x)$, as required.

Therefore, (10.13) holds for $i = j$ and, hence, for $i = 0$ by induction, that is, Theorem 10.14. □

There is a symmetric and crossing submodular function f which has no flat pair that is at the same time pendent. For example, the cut function d in Fig. 10.1 has no such pairs, since $\{u_3, u_4\}$ and $\{u_5, u_6\}$ are the flat pairs of d, but neither of them is pendent.

Corollary 10.16. *Let f be a set function f on V with $n = |V| \geq 2$. If f is symmetric and crossing submodular or intersecting submodular and posimodular, then a flat pair of f can be found in $O(n^2 T_f)$ time.* □

Proof. If f is symmetric and crossing submodular, then we compute an MD ordering π of f in $O(n^2 T_f)$ time and choose the pair of the last two elements in π, which is flat by Theorem 10.14. Consider the case where f is intersecting submodular and posimodular, where we assume $f(\emptyset) = f(V) = -\infty$, as it does not lose the intersecting submodularity and posimodularity of f. In this case, we work with the set function $g : 2^{V+s} \to \Re \cup \{-\infty\}$ (where s is a new element) defined in (10.11). By Lemma 10.9, for an intersecting submodular and posi-modular set function f on V, this set function g is symmetric and crossing submodular on $V + s$. Let π_g be an MD ordering of g, where the first element in π_g must be s since $g(s) = f(V) = +\infty$. Then the last two elements $u, v \in V$ in π_g give a flat pair of g. We see that $\{u, v\}$ is also flat in f, since any subset $X \subseteq V$ with $f(X) < \min_{x \in X} f(x)$ would imply $g(X) < \min_{x \in X} g(x)$, contradicting that $\{u, v\}$ is flat in g. Therefore, we can find a flat pair in $O(n^2 T_f)$ time even if f is intersecting submodular and posimodular. □

10.3.2 Computing Extreme Subsets

This section presents an algorithm for computing all extreme subsets of a set function f by using flat pairs. For any nonempty subset $Y \subseteq V$, there is an extreme subset $Y^* \in \mathcal{X}(f)$ with $Y^* \subseteq Y$ and $f(Y^*) \le f(Y)$. Hence, we see that $f(Y) > f(X)$ for all nonempty $Y \subset X$ if and only if $f(Z) > f(X)$ for all $Z \subset X$ with $Z \in \mathcal{X}(f)$. From this observation and the fact that no nontrivial extreme subset $X \in \mathcal{X}(f)$ separates any flat pair, we obtain the following algorithm for computing all extreme subsets of a set function f.

After initializing by $\mathcal{X} := \{\{v\} \mid v \in V\} \ (\subseteq \mathcal{X}(f))$, we repeat a procedure of contracting a flat pair $n - 2$ times. Let V^i, $i = n, n - 1, \ldots, 2$, be the set of elements obtained after contracting the first $n - i$ flat pairs, where $|V^i| = i$ holds. For each element $x \in V^i$, let $V[x] \subseteq V$ denote the set of all elements that have been contracted into x. We maintain the property that

$$\mathcal{X} \text{ consists of all extreme subsets } X \in \mathcal{X}(f) \text{ with } X \subseteq V[x] \text{ and } x \in V^i.$$

$$(10.14)$$

After contracting a flat pair $u^i, v^i \in V^i$, into a single element z^i, we add $V[z^i]$ to $\mathcal{X}$ if $V[z^i]$ is an extreme subset of f so that (10.14) holds in the resulting set $V^{i-1} = (V^i - \{u^i, v^i\}) \cup \{z^i\}$. We note that $V[z^i]$ is an extreme subset of f if and only if $f(V[z^i]) < \min_{Y \in \mathcal{X}: Y \subset V[z^i]} f(Y)$ holds. To facilitate this test, we also maintain $\mu(x) = \min_{Y \in \mathcal{X}: Y \subset V[x]} f(Y)$ for all $x \in V^i$. The entire algorithm is described as follows.

Algorithm EXTREMESUBSETS
Input: A set function f on a finite set V, where $n = |V| \ge 2$.
Output: A laminar family $\mathcal{X} \subseteq 2^V - \{\emptyset, V\}$ of extreme subsets of f.
1   $\mathcal{X} := \{\{v\} \mid v \in V\}$;
2   Let $\mu(v) := f(v)$ for all $v \in V$;
3   $V^n := V$; $f^n := f$;
4   **for** $i := n$ **to** 3 **do**
5   Find a flat pair $\{u^i, v^i\}$ of f^i;
6       $V^{i-1} := (V^i - \{u^i, v^i\}) \cup \{z^i\}$;
7   Let f^{i-1} be the set function on V^{i-1} obtained from f^i by contracting
          elements u^i and v^i into a single element z^i (as defined in (10.10));
8   Let $V[z^i] \subseteq V$ be the set of all elements that have been contracted
          into z^i; /* $f(V[z^i]) = f^{i-1}(z^i)$ */
9   **if** $f^{i-1}(z^i) < \min\{\mu(u^i), \mu(v^i)\}$ **then**
10      $\mathcal{X} := \mathcal{X} \cup \{V[z^i]\}$; $\mu(z^i) := f^{i-1}(z^i)$
11   **else**
12       $\mu(z^i) := \min\{\mu(u^i), \mu(v^i)\}$
13   **end** /* if */
14 **end**. /* for */

From the preceding argument, we see that the EXTREMESUBSETS algorithm computes the set $\mathcal{X}(f)$ of all extreme sets of f correctly, assuming that we can always find a flat pair in line 5. If a given set function f is symmetric and crossing submodular or intersecting submodular and posimodular, then it is not difficult to see that each set function f^i obtained from f by contracting elements remains symmetric and crossing submodular or intersecting submodular and posimodular, respectively. Therefore, by Corollary 10.16, we can find a flat pair in $O(n^2 T_f)$ time. Then the run, time of EXTREMESUBSETS is $O(n^3 T_f)$. This establishes Theorem 10.13.

10.4 Optimization Problems over Submodular and Posimodular Systems

The optimization over a system (V, f) has been much studied. For example, the following problem asks to find a modular function z (i.e., a vector $z \in \Re^n$) under the constraint defined by (V, f).

Problem 1:   Minimize $\Phi(z)$
subject to $z(X) \le f(X)$ for all $X \in 2^V$
$0 \le z(v) \le b(v)$ for all $v \in V$

(where an additional constraint $z(V) = f(V)$ may also be imposed). Here $\Phi(z) :$ $R^V \to \Re$ is an objective function and $b \in \Re^n_+$ is a given constant vector. Problem 1 can be found in many applications [136, 186], where f is assumed to be fully submodular.

Given a system (V, g), a dual type of this problem is stated as follows.

Problem 2:   Minimize $\Phi(z)$
subject to $g(X) \le z(X)$ for all $X \in 2^V$
$0 \le z(v) \le b(v)$ for all $v \in V$

(where we may also impose an additional constraint, $z(V) = g(V)$). Problem 2 with a certain supermodular function g appears in the edge-connectivity augmentation problem [30, 78, 235] and the problem of computing the core of a convex game [290].

Problems 1 and 2 are generalized into the following common formulation. Given set functions f, f_1, f_2, g, g_1, g_2 on V, and vectors $b_1, b_2 \in \Re^n_+$, we consider the following problems.

Problem 3:   Minimize $\Phi(z)$
subject to $z(X) \le f(X)$ for all $X \in 2^V$
$g(X) \le z(X)$ for all $X \in 2^V$
$b_1(v) \le z(v) \le b_2(v)$ for all $v \in V$.

Problem 4:   Minimize $\Phi(z)$
subject to $g_1(X) \le z(X)$ for all $X \in 2^V$
$g_2(X) \le z(X)$ for all $X \in 2^V$
$b_1(v) \le z(v) \le b_2(v)$ for all $v \in V$.

Problem 5:   Minimize $\Phi(z)$

subject to $z(X) \leq f_1(X)$ for all $X \in 2^V$

$z(X) \leq f_2(X)$ for all $X \in 2^V$

$b_1(v) \leq z(v) \leq b_2(v)$ for all $v \in V$.

Concerning Problem 3, Frank [76] proves that for a fully supermodular function g and a fully submodular function f on V, where $g(X) \leq f(X)$ is assumed for all $X \in 2^V$, there exists a vector $z \in \Re^n$ such that $g(X) \leq z(X) \leq f(X)$ for all $X \in 2^V$. Problem 4 with fully supermodular set functions g_1 and g_2 has been studied as the g-polymatroid intersection problem [60, 87].

In this subsection, we consider Problems 1–5 with intersecting submodular and posimodular functions $f, f_1, f_2, -g, -g_1, -g_2$. We also consider integer versions of Problems 1–5, where we require an integer vector z as a solution, and all values of functions f, f_1, f_2, g, g_1, g_2 and vectors b, b_1, b_2 are integers.

Before proceeding further, we explain an application of Problem 2 with an intersecting submodular and posimodular function $-g$ to the edge-connectivity augmentation problem in some details.

Example 10.17. Let $G = (V, E)$ be an edge-weighted complete graph with a vertex set V, an edge set $E = \binom{V}{2}$, and an edge weight function $c_G : E \to \Re_+$. The *cut function* $d : 2^V \to \Re_+$ is defined by $d(X; G) = \sum \{c_G(e) \mid e = \{u, v\} \in E, \ u \in X, \ v \in V - X\}$ (where $d(\emptyset; G) = d(V; G) = 0$). For a vertex $v \in V$, $d(v; G)$ is called the *degree* of v. It is known (and easy to see) that the cut function d is symmetric and fully submodular. The *edge-connectivity augmentation problem* asks to increase edge weights c_G to obtain a k-edge-connected graph G' (i.e., $d(X; G') \geq k$ holds for all $X \in 2^V - \{\emptyset, V\}$ in the resulting graph G'). The integer version of this problem with integer edge weights c_G requires that output weights $c_{G'}$ are also integers. Frank [78] introduced an additional constraint, *the degree constraint*: Given a vector $b \in \Re_+^n$, the output k-edge-connected graph G' is required to satisfy $\sum_{e \in E(v)}(c_{G'}(e) - c_G(e)) \leq b(v)$ for all $v \in V$, where $E(v)$ denotes the set of edges incident to a vertex v.   □

The problem in the preceding example can be formulated as Problem 2 by the following result, which was already observed in Section 7.6.

Lemma 10.18. *Given an edge-weighted graph* $G = (V, E)$, $c_G : E \to \Re_+$, *a constant* $k \geq 0$, *and a vector* $t \in \Re_+^n$ *such that*

$$d(X; G) + t(X) \geq k \text{ for all } X \in 2^V - \{\emptyset, V\}, \tag{10.15}$$

there is a k-edge-connected graph $G' = (V, E)$ *with* $c_{G'} : E \to \Re_+$ *satisfying* $\sum_{e \in E(v)}(c_{G'}(e) - c_G(e)) = t(v)$ *for all* $v \in V$. *Also,* $c_{G'}$ *can be chosen as integers if* c_G, t, *and* $k \geq 2$ *are all integers and* $t(V) = \sum_{v \in V} t(v)$ *is an even integer.*   □

Notice that the total increase $\sum_{e \in E}(c_{G'}(e) - c_G(e))$ of weights in this lemma is $\frac{1}{2}t(V)$. As a result of the preceding lemma, we only need to find a vector $t \in \Re_+^n$ that minimizes $t(V) = \sum_{v \in V} t(v)$ under the constraint (10.15) (and $t(v) \leq b(v)$,

$v \in V$, if the degree constraint is imposed). Hence, by defining $\Phi(t) = \frac{1}{2}t(V)$ and a symmetric and fully supermodular set function g by $g(X) = k - d(X; G)$ for all $X \in 2^V$, we see that the smallest amount $\Lambda_G(k)$ of new weights to be added to obtain a k-edge-connected graph G' (as studied in Section 8.4.1) is given by the minimum value of $\Phi(t)$ over all $t \in \Re_+^n$ that satisfy $g(X) \le t(X)$, $X \in 2^V - \{\emptyset, V\}$ (and $t(v) \le b(v)$, $v \in V$ if the degree constraint is imposed). In the case of integer version, $\Lambda_G(k)$ is given by $\lceil \frac{1}{2}\Phi(t) \rceil$ (since if the minimum $t(V)$ is odd then $t(V) + 1$ is the smallest even integer satisfying (10.15)). In any case, the problem of finding such a vector t can be formulated as Problem 2 with these Φ, g, and b.

In this section, we first characterize the polyhedra defined by the constraints of Problems 1–5 with intersecting submodular and posimodular functions f, f_1, f_2, $-g$, $-g_1$, $-g_2$. Based on this, we then present a combinatorial algorithm for solving Problems 1–5, assuming a linear objective function $\Phi(t)$ (and assuming a further restriction on f, f_1, f_2).

These results, for example, provide us a polynomial time algorithm for the edge-connectivity augmentation problem with a more general degree constraint; for example, for each subset $X \subset V$, the total increase of degrees in X in the resulting graph G' is bounded by a given constant $f(X)$.

We also show that Problem 2 can be solved for another objective function $\Phi(t) = |\{v \in V \mid t(v) > 0\}|$ in $O(n^3)$ oracle calls of function values. This, for example, says that we can solve in polynomial time the problem of augmenting the edge-connectivity of a graph to minimize the number of vertices with edges whose weights are increased.

10.4.1 Laminar Polyhedral Structures of Problems 1–5

A *polyhedron* of a system (V, f) is defined by

$$P(f) = \{z \in \Re^n \mid z(X) \le f(X), \forall X \in 2^V - \{\emptyset, V\}\}, \qquad (10.16)$$

where $X = \emptyset$ and V are not considered in the definition, and a *base polyhedron* of (V, f) by

$$B(f) = \{z \in P(f) \mid z(V) = f(V)\}, \qquad (10.17)$$

where possibly $B(f) = \emptyset$. Note that, in these definitions, constraint $z \ge 0$ is not imposed as in Problems 1 and 2. Let

$$\begin{aligned} P_-(f) &= P(f) \cap \Re_-^n, \quad B_-(f) = B(f) \cap \Re_-^n, \\ P_+(f) &= P(f) \cap \Re_+^n, \quad B_+(f) = B(f) \cap \Re_+^n. \end{aligned} \qquad (10.18)$$

For two set functions f_1 and f_2 on V, we denote by $(f_1 - f_2)$ the set function f' such that $f'(X) = f_1(X) - f_2(X)$ holds for all $X \in 2^V$.

Polyhedral Structure of $P_-(f)$

We consider the set of all feasible vectors to Problem 2, where we assume that g is an intersecting supermodular and negamodular set function and that a vector

$b \in \mathfrak{R}_+^n$ is given by $b(v) = +\infty$ $(v \in V)$. In this case, $f = -g$ is intersecting submodular and posimodular. Then a vector z is feasible to Problem 2 if and only if $-z \in P_-(f)$ holds for a system (V, f).

We shall now prove Theorem 10.19, which tells that, given a system (V, f) with an intersecting submodular and posimodular set function f, there is a laminar family $\mathcal{X} \subseteq 2^V - \{\emptyset, V\}$ that characterizes $P_-(f)$ as follows:

$$P_-(f) = \{t \in \mathfrak{R}_-^n \mid t(X) \le f(X) \text{ for all } X \in \mathcal{X}\}. \tag{10.19}$$

Because $|\mathcal{X}| \le 2n$ always holds for a laminar family $\mathcal{X}$, this says that $P_-(f)$ essentially requires at most $2n$ inequalities among all $2^n - 2$ inequalities of the form $t(X) \le f(X)$; furthermore, those essential inequalities are independent of the objective function $\Phi(z)$ in Problem 2.

Given an intersecting submodular and posimodular set function f on V, we first compute the laminar family $\mathcal{X}(f)$ of extreme subsets of f, which in fact satisfies property (10.19), as will be shown later. We then compute a vector $-z \in P_-(f)$ based on the family $\mathcal{X}(f)$, and we discard some sets from $\mathcal{X}(f)$ to obtain a minimal family $\mathcal{X} \subseteq \mathcal{X}(f)$ that satisfies property (10.19). More precisely, we compute a vector $z \in \mathfrak{R}_+^n$ such that

$$f(X) + z(X) \ge 0 \text{ for all } X \in \mathcal{X}(f).$$

Initially we set $\mathcal{X} := \emptyset$ and $z(v) := 0$ for all $v \in V$. For each set $X \in \mathcal{X}(f)$, we check whether $f(X) + z(X) \ge 0$ holds or not, where we choose sets $X \in \mathcal{X}(f)$ with a smaller cardinality first. If $f(X) + z(X) < 0$, then we add to $\mathcal{X}$ the set X, and we increase $z(v)$ of some $v \in X$ so that $f(X) + z(X) = 0$ holds (where more than one $z(v)$ may be increased as long as $f(X) + z(X) = 0$ is satisfied). On the other hand, if $f(Z) + z(Z) \ge 0$ holds, then no $z(v)$ is changed. After checking all sets in $\mathcal{X}(f)$, we output the final z and $\mathcal{X}$. The entire algorithm is described as follows.

Algorithm LAMINAR
Input: A system (V, f) with an intersecting submodular and posimodular set
  function f on V, where $n = |V| \ge 2$.
Output: A vector $-z \in P_-(f)$, and a laminar family $\mathcal{X}$ of V satisfying (10.19).
1 Compute the family $\mathcal{X}(f)$ of extreme subsets of f;
2 $\mathcal{X}^* := \mathcal{X}(f)$;
3 $\mathcal{X} := \emptyset$; $V' := V$; $z(v) := 0$ for all $v \in V$;
4 **while** $\mathcal{X}^* \ne \emptyset$ **do**
5   Choose a minimal set $X \in \mathcal{X}^*$; $\mathcal{X}^* := \mathcal{X}^* - X$;
6   **if** $f(X) + z(X) < 0$ **then**
7   Increase $z(v)$, $v \in X$ arbitrarily so that the resulting $f + z$ satisfies
        $f(X) + z(X) = 0$;
8      $\mathcal{X} := \mathcal{X} \cup \{X\}$
9   **end** /* if */
10 **end**; /* while */
11 Output $-z$ and $\mathcal{X}$.

By Theorem 10.13, the family $\mathcal{X}(f)$ of extreme subsets of f in line 1 can be obtained in $O(n^3)$ calls to the function value oracle of f, and algorithm LAMINAR runs in the same time complexity. Note that the vector $-z$ output by LAMINAR may not be unique because there are many ways of increasing $z(v)$, $v \in X$, in line 7.

Given a laminar family $\mathcal{X} \subseteq 2^V$ on V, a subset $Y \in \mathcal{X}$ is called a *child* of a subset $X \in \mathcal{X}$ (and X is called the *parent* of Y) if $Y \subset X$ and there is no other subset $Y' \in \mathcal{X}$ with $Y \subset Y' \subset X$. For a subset $X \in \mathcal{X}$, let $Ch(X)$ denote the set of children of X and let $pa(X)$ denote the parent of X (possibly $pa(X) = \emptyset$).

Let $\mathcal{X}$ be the family of subsets of V output by LAMINAR, which is clearly laminar. For the laminar family

$$\mathcal{V} = \mathcal{X} \cup \{V\} \cup \{\{v\} \mid v \in V\},$$

let $\mathcal{T} = (\mathcal{V}, \mathcal{E})$ be its tree representation (as defined in Section 1.1), where the parent–child relation in the tree is given by $pa(X)$ and $Ch(X)$, and V is the root of $\mathcal{T}$. Define $f' : \mathcal{V} \to \Re$ by

$$f'(X) = \begin{cases} 0 & \text{if } X = \{v\} \text{ and } f(v) \geq 0 \\ f(X) & \text{otherwise.} \end{cases} \qquad (10.20)$$

We use the following notations:

$$P(f; \mathcal{X}) = \{t \in \Re^n \mid t(X) \leq f(X) \text{ for all } X \in \mathcal{X}\},$$

$$P_-(f; \mathcal{X}) = P(f; \mathcal{X}) \cap \Re^n_-.$$

Clearly, $P_-(f) \subseteq P_-(f; \mathcal{X})$ holds, where $P_-(f)$ is defined by (10.18).

Theorem 10.19. *For a system (V, f) with an intersecting submodular and posimodular set function f on V, where $|V| \geq 2$, let $-z$ and $\mathcal{X}$ $(\subseteq \mathcal{X}(f))$ be the vector and the laminar family output by algorithm LAMINAR. Let f' be defined by (10.20) and let $\mathcal{T}$ be the tree as defined earlier. Then*

   (i) *$-z \in P_-(f)$.*
   (ii) *For each nonroot node X in $\mathcal{T}$, $f'(X) < \sum_{Y \in Ch(X)} f'(Y)$ holds, and $f(v) < 0$ holds when $X = \{v\}$ is a minimal subset in $\mathcal{X}$*
   (iii) *$P_-(f) = P_-(f; \mathcal{X}(f)) = P_-(f; \mathcal{X})$.*
   (iv) *$B_-(f) \neq \emptyset$ if and only if $f(V) \leq \sum_{Y \in Ch(V)} f'(Y)$ holds.*   □

Proof. (i) We first show $P_-(f) = P_-(f; \mathcal{X}(f))$. For each nonempty set $X \subset V$, there is an extreme subset $X^* \in \mathcal{X}(f)$ such that $X^* \subseteq X$ and $f(X^*) \leq f(X)$. Hence, $f(X^*) + z(X^*) \geq 0$ implies $f(X) + z(X) \geq 0$ since $z(X) \geq z(X^*) \geq 0$. This proves $P_-(f) = P_-(f; \mathcal{X}(f))$. We next show that $f(X) + z(X) \geq 0$ holds for all $X \in \mathcal{X}(f)$. During the execution of LAMINAR, we check $f(X) + z(X)$ of each set $X \in \mathcal{X}(f)$, and we increase $z(v)$, $v \in X$, so that $f(X) + z(X) = 0$ holds if $f(X) + z(X) < 0$. Since z never decreases during the computation, $f(X) + z(X)$ for every processed set X remains nonnegative. Therefore, the final z satisfies $f(X) + z(X) \geq 0$ for all $X \in \mathcal{X}(f)$. Hence, $-z \in P_-(f; \mathcal{X}(f)) = P_-(f)$, as required.

(ii) LAMINAR adds a set $X \in \mathcal{X}(f)$ to $\mathcal{X}$ only when $f(X) + z(X) < 0$ holds in line 6. Since $z \geq 0$, we have $f(X) < 0$ for all $X \in \mathcal{X}$. First consider a minimal set $X \in \mathcal{X}$. Clearly $f(v) < 0$ holds when $X = \{v\}$ is a minimal subset in $\mathcal{X}$. If $|X| \geq 2$, then $f(v) \geq 0$ holds for all $v \in X$ (otherwise $\{v\}$ must have been chosen in $\mathcal{X}$) and, hence, $f'(X) < 0 = \sum_{v \in X} f'(v) = \sum_{Y \in Ch(X)} f'(Y)$ holds (where $Ch(X) = \{\{v\} \mid v \in X\}$ by the definition of $\mathcal{T}$). Next consider a set $X \in \mathcal{X}$ such that $Ch(X)$ contains some sets in $\mathcal{X}$. When LAMINAR detects $f(X) + z(X) < 0$ in line 6, we see by induction that $f(Y) + z(Y) = 0$ holds for all $Y \in Ch(X) \cap \mathcal{X}$, and $\sum_{\{v\} \in Ch(X) - \mathcal{X}} z(v) = 0$ holds. Hence, $f(X) + z(X) < 0 = \sum_{Y \in Ch(X) \cap \mathcal{X}} (f(Y) + z(Y)) + \sum_{\{v\} \in Ch(X) - \mathcal{X}} z(v)$ holds, from which we have $f(X) < \sum_{Y \in Ch(X) \cap \mathcal{X}} f(Y) = \sum_{Y \in Ch(X)} f'(Y)$ (note that $f'(v) = 0$ for all $\{v\} \in Ch(X) - \mathcal{X}$), as required.

(iii) Since we have proved $P_-(f) = P_-(f; \mathcal{X}(f))$ in condition (i) and $P_-(f; \mathcal{X}(f)) \subseteq P_-(f; \mathcal{X})$ is trivial, we show $P_-(f; \mathcal{X}(f)) \supseteq P_-(f; \mathcal{X})$. Consider a set $W \in \mathcal{X}(f) - \mathcal{X}$ and assume $f(W) < 0$ (since $f(W) \geq 0$ implies $P_-(f; \mathcal{X}(f)) \supseteq P_-(f; \mathcal{X}(f) - W)$). Let $Ch'(W)$ denote the set of maximal sets $Y \in \mathcal{X}$ with $Y \subset W$. When set W was discarded in line 6 of LAMINAR, $f(W) + z(W) \geq 0$ and $z(W) = \sum_{Y \in Ch'(W)} z(Y)$ hold. As observed in condition (ii), we see by induction that $f(Y) + z(Y) = 0$ for all $Y \in Ch'(W)$ and $z(v) = 0$ for all $v \in W - \cup_{Y \in Ch'(W)} Y$. Hence, $f(W) + z(W) \geq 0 = \sum_{Y \in Ch'(W)} (f(Y) + z(Y)) + \sum_{v \in W : v \notin Y \in Ch'(W)} z(v)$, from which we have $f(W) \geq \sum_{Y \in Ch'(W)} f(Y)$. This implies that $f(W) + z'(W) \geq 0$ holds for any $z' \geq 0$ such that $f(Y) + z'(Y) \geq 0$ holds for all $Y \in Ch'(W)$. Therefore, for any $-z' \in P_-(f; \mathcal{X})$, it holds that $-z' \in P_-(f; \mathcal{X}(f))$.

(iv) From condition (iii), we have $B_-(f) = \{t \in \mathfrak{R}^n_- \mid t(V) = f(V)\} \cap P_-(f; \mathcal{X})$. If $f(V) > \sum_{Y \in Ch(V)} f'(Y)$, then for any vector $t \in P_-(f; \mathcal{X})$, we have $f(V) > \sum_{Y \in Ch(V)} f'(Y) \geq \sum_{Y \in Ch(V)} t(Y) \geq t(V)$, indicating that $f(V) > t(V)$ and $B_-(f) = \emptyset$ hold.

Now assume $f(V) \leq \sum_{Y \in Ch(V)} f'(Y)$. By condition (ii), we can obtain a vector $t \in P_-(f; \mathcal{X})$ such that $t(Y) = f'(Y)$ for all $Y \in Ch(V)$ and $t(v) = 0$ for all $V - \cup_{Y \in Ch(V)} Y$, as $t = -z$ constructed by LAMINAR. Hence, such t satisfies $t(V) = \sum_{Y \in Ch(V)} f'(Y)$ and can be modified by reducing any entries of t so that $t(V) = f(V)$ holds since $f(V) \leq \sum_{Y \in Ch(V)} f'(Y)$. Therefore, $B_-(f) \neq \emptyset$. $\square$

Fujishige [94] proved that a laminar family $\mathcal{X} \subseteq 2^V - \{\emptyset\}$ with $P_-(f) = P_-(f; \mathcal{X})$ exists for more general set functions. A set function $f : 2^V \to \mathfrak{R}$ is called *weakly posimodular* if, for each intersecting pair of $X, Y \subseteq V$, there exist nonempty subsets $X_0 \subseteq X$ and $Y_0 \subseteq Y$, satisfying either $X_0 \subset X$ or $Y_0 \subset Y$, such that $f(X) + f(Y) \geq f(X_0) + f(Y_0)$.

Theorem 10.20 ([94]). *For a system (V, f) with a weakly posimodular set function f on V, there exists a laminar family $\mathcal{X} \subseteq 2^V - \{\emptyset\}$ with $P_-(f) = P_-(f; \mathcal{X})$.* $\square$

We omit the proof of this theorem. Unlike the case of intersecting submodular and posimodular set functions, no efficient algorithm for identifying such a laminar family $\mathcal{X}$ is currently known for a weakly posimodular set function.

Based on Theorem 10.19, we can solve Problem 2 if its objective function is linear; that is, $\Phi(z) = \sum_{v \in V} w(v)z(v)$ for some cost vector $w \in \Re^n$. The proof for this case will be given in Section 10.4.4 under a more general setting of Problem 3. In the following, we consider another special case of Problem 2.

10.4.2 An Efficient Algorithm for a Special Case of Problem 2

We consider Problem 2 with the following objective function:

$$\Phi(z) = |\{v \in V \mid z(v) > 0\}| \text{ (i.e., the number of nonzero entries in vector } z).$$

For simplicity, we first consider the case in which the constraint $z \leq b$ is not imposed on Problem 2. For an intersecting supermodular and negamodular set function g in Problem 2, let $f = -g$ and $\mathcal{X} \subseteq 2^V$ be the laminar family obtained from system (V, f) by applying Theorem 10.19. A subset $X \in \mathcal{X}$ is called *minimal* (resp. *maximal*) if $\mathcal{X}$ contains no set X' such that $X' \subset X$ (resp. $X' \supset X$). Let $\mathcal{M}(\mathcal{X})$ denote the set of all minimal subsets $X \in \mathcal{X}$. Since all subsets in $\mathcal{M}(\mathcal{X})$ are pairwise disjoint (by their minimality) and $f(X) < 0$ holds for each $X \in \mathcal{M}(\mathcal{X})$, a vector $-z \in P_-(f)$ must contain an element v with $z(v) > 0$ in each minimal subset X. This implies that the number of nonzero entries of a vector $-z \in P_-(f)$ is at least $|\mathcal{M}(\mathcal{X})|$. That is,

$$\min_{-z \in P_-(f)} \Phi(z) = \min_{-z \in P_-(f)} |\{v \in V \mid z(v) > 0\}| \geq |\mathcal{M}(\mathcal{X})|.$$

Furthermore, we show in what follows that we can choose a vector $-z \in P_-(f)$ such that $|\{v \in V \mid z(v) > 0\}| = |\mathcal{M}(\mathcal{X})|$ (this tells us that $\Phi(z) = |\mathcal{M}(\mathcal{X})|$ is the optimum value). For each $X \in \mathcal{M}(\mathcal{X})$, choose one element $u_X \in X$ and let $I = \{u_X \mid X \in \mathcal{M}(\mathcal{X})\}$. Based on this I, we construct z as follows. After setting $z(v) := 0$ for all $v \in V$ and $\mathcal{X}' := \mathcal{X}$, repeat the following until $\mathcal{X}'$ becomes empty: (i) Choose an inclusion-wise minimal subset X among subsets in the current family $\mathcal{X}'$ such that $X \cap I \neq \emptyset$, (ii) choose an element $v \in I \cap X$ and increase $z(v)$ by $-(f(X) + z(X))$ (so that the new $z(X)$ satisfies $f(X) + z(X) = 0$), and (iii) remove the X from $\mathcal{X}'$. Note that any subset $X \in \mathcal{X}$ contains a minimal subset $Y \in \mathcal{M}(\mathcal{X})$ and, hence, an element $u_Y \in I \cap Y$, implying that $\mathcal{X}'$ will become empty only by increasing values $z(v)$ with $v \in I$. By induction, we see that a subset X is removed from $\mathcal{X}'$ only when either $X \in \mathcal{M}(\mathcal{X})$ holds or all subsets $Y \in \mathcal{X}$ with $Y \subset X$ have been eliminated, and that, in the latter case, $f(Y) + z(Y) = 0$ holds for all $Y \in Ch(X)$, and $f(X) < \sum_{Y \in Ch(X)} f(Y) = \sum_{Y \in Ch(X)} -z(Y)$ holds by Theorem 10.19(ii). Here we only need to increase $z(v)$ for some $v \in I \subset X$ to attain $f(X) = -z(X)$ without increasing $z(v') \in X - v$. Upon termination, therefore, $f(Y) + z(Y) \geq 0$ holds for all Y in the original $\mathcal{X}$. Thus, the resulting $-z$ belongs to $P_-(f; \mathcal{X})$ (and, hence, $-z \in P_-(f)$ by Theorem 10.19). Clearly, the z minimizes $\Phi(z)$ since $|\{v \in V \mid z(v) > 0\}| = |I| = |\mathcal{M}(\mathcal{X})|$ holds.

Notice that the output vector $-z$ satisfies $f(Y) + z(Y) = 0$ for all inclusion-wise maximal subsets $Y \in \mathcal{X}$, since each of such Y is eliminated from $\mathcal{X}'$ after satisfying $f(Y) + z(Y) = 0$ and no proper superset of Y will be later processed in the algorithm. We see that z also minimizes $\Phi'(z) = \sum_{v \in V} z(v)$ among all feasible vectors in Problem 2. This is because maximal subsets $Y \in \mathcal{X}$ are disjoint and thereby $\sum \{-f(Y) \mid Y$ is a maximal subset in $\mathcal{X}\}$ is a lower bound on $\sum_{v \in V} z(v)$ and $-z$ attains the lower bound.

Now we proceed to the general case in which bounds on z, $0 \le z \le b$, are also considered.

Theorem 10.21. *For an intersecting supermodular and negamodular set function g on V, and a vector $b \in \mathfrak{R}^n_+$, let $\mathcal{X} \subseteq 2^V$ be a laminar family that satisfies $P_-(-g) = P_-(-g; \mathcal{X})$. Then an instance of Problem 2 is feasible if and only if $b(X) \ge g(X)$ for all subsets $X \in \mathcal{X}$. If Problem 2 is feasible, then there is a feasible vector z which minimizes two objective functions $\Phi(z) = |\{v \in V \mid z(v) > 0\}|$ and $\Phi'(z) = \sum_{v \in V} z(v)$ at the same time. Such a solution z can be computed from $\mathcal{X}$ in $O(n^2)$ time.* $\qquad\square$

Proof. Note that if $b(X) < g(X)$ for some $X \in 2^V$, then there is no vector z satisfying $b(X) \ge z(X) \ge g(X)$. Let $f = -g$, where f is intersecting submodular and posimodular. In the following, we either construct a vector $-z \in P_-(f; \mathcal{X}) \cap \{t \in \mathfrak{R}^n_- \mid -t \le b\}$, which minimizes the number of nonzero entries, or we conclude the infeasibility $P_-(f; \mathcal{X}) \cap \{t \in \mathfrak{R}^n_- \mid -t \le b\} = \emptyset$ by detecting an $X \in \mathcal{X}$ with $b(X) < -f(X)$. We consider the parent–child relation on $\mathcal{X} \cup \{V\}$, where, for each $X \in \mathcal{X} \cup \{V\} - \mathcal{M}(\mathcal{X})$, $Ch(X)$ denotes the set of children of X, and $f(X) < \sum_{Y \in Ch(X)} f(Y)$ is assumed without loss of generality (otherwise such an X satisfies $P_-(f; \mathcal{X} - X) = P_-(f; \mathcal{X})$ and can be discarded in order to find a vector in $P_-(f; \mathcal{X})$). For each subset $X \in \mathcal{X} \cup \{V\}$, an $|X|$-dimensional vector z_X on X is called X-*feasible* if it satisfies the following:

$$f(X') + z_X(X') \ge 0 \text{ for all } X' \in \mathcal{X} \text{ with } X' \subseteq X, \ z_X(v) \le b(v) \text{ for all } v \in X.$$

We now define an X-*optimal* vector z_X as an X-feasible vector that can be obtained by either condition (i) or (ii):

(i) X is a minimal subset in $\mathcal{X}$; that is, $X \in \mathcal{M}(\mathcal{X})$. Let $X = \{v_1, v_2, \ldots, v_{|X|}\}$, where we assume $b(v_1) \ge b(v_2) \ge \cdots \ge b(v_{|X|})$ without loss of generality. An X-optimal vector z_X is defined by

$$z_X(v_j) := \begin{cases} b(v_j) & \text{for } 1 \le j < p, \\ -\sum_{1 \le h \le p-1} b(v_h) - f(X) & \text{for } j = p, \\ 0 & \text{for } p+1 \le j \le |X|, \end{cases}$$

where p is the smallest index such that $-f(X) \le \sum_{1 \le j \le p} b(v_j)$.

(ii) X is a set in $\mathcal{X} \cup \{V\} - \mathcal{M}(\mathcal{X})$, where we assume (by induction) that, for each set $Y \in Ch(X)$, a Y-optimal vector z_Y with $z_Y(Y) = -f(Y)$ has already been defined. For each $v \in X$, let $z_X(v) := z_Y(v)$ for a set $Y \in Ch(X)$ with $v \in Y$ and let $z_X(v) := 0$ for all $v \in X - \bigcup_{Y \in Ch(X)} Y$. Then $z_X(X) = -\sum_{Y \in Ch(X)} f(Y) < -f(X)$ holds by assumption. Let $X' = \{v_1, \ldots, v_h\}$

be the set of all $v \in X$ with $z_X(v) = b(v)$, let $X'' = \{v_{h+1}, \ldots, v_q\}$ be the set of all $v \in X$ with $0 < z_X(v) < b(v)$, and let $X - X' - X'' = \{v_{q+1}, \ldots, v_{|X|}\}$ be the set of all $v \in X$ with $0 = z_X(v) < b(v)$, where we assume $b(v_{q+1}) \geq \cdots \geq b(v_{|X|})$ while we order $v_{h+1}, \ldots, v_q$ arbitrarily. Then an X-optimal vector z_X is defined by performing

$$z_X(v_j) := z_X(v_j) + \min\{b(v_j) - z_X(v_j), -z_X(X) - f(X)\},$$
$$j = h + 1, \ldots, q,$$

(updating $z_X(X)$ after each j) and by setting (if $f(X) + z_X(X) < 0$ still holds)

$$z_X(v_j) := \begin{cases} b(v_j) & \text{for } q + 1 \leq j < p, \\ -\sum_{q+1 \leq h \leq p-1} b(v_h) - f(X) - z_X(X) & \text{for } j = p, \\ 0 & \text{for } p + 1 \leq j \leq |X|, \end{cases}$$

where p is the smallest index such that $\sum_{q+1 \leq j \leq p} b(v_j) + z_X(X) \geq -f(X)$. (If such p cannot be chosen, then $b(X) < -f(X)$ holds for this X, indicating the infeasibility of the problem instance.)

Obviously the vector z_X defined in condition (i) is X-feasible. In condition (ii), the vector z_X is constructed from vectors z_Y with $Y \in Ch(X)$ to satisfy $z_X(X) = f(X)$, where each $z_X(v)$ with $v \in X$ is not decreased and takes a value equal to or less than $b(v)$. (This is possible because the initial z_X satisfies $z_X(X) < -f(X)$ and we assume $-f(X) \leq b(X)$.) Hence, the resulting vector z_X in condition (ii) is also X-feasible.

Consequently, a V-optimal vector z_V can be constructed via the following procedure.

Procedure MinNonzero
1 $\mathcal{X}' := \mathcal{X}$; $z(v) := 0$ for all $v \in V$;
2 **while** $\mathcal{X}' \neq \emptyset$ **do**
3   Choose a minimal subset X in the current $\mathcal{X}'$;
4   **while** $f(X) + z(X) < 0$ and there is an element $v \in X$ with $0 < z(v)$
          $< b(v)$ **do**
5   Update $z(v) := z(v) + \min\{b(v) - z(v), -z(X) - f(X)\}$
6   **end**; /* while */
7   **while** $f(X) + z(X) < 0$ **do**
8   **if** there is no $v \in X$ with $z(v) = 0$ **then** halt by concluding that
             there is no feasible vector
9   **end**; /* if */
10   Choose $v \in X$ such that $z(v) = 0$ and $b(v)$ is maximum;
11   Set $z(v) := \min\{-z(X) - f(X), b(v)\}$
12   **end**; /* while */
       /* now $f(X) + z(X) = 0$ holds */
13    $\mathcal{X}' := \mathcal{X}' - X$
14 **end**. /* while */

We have already observed that the V-feasible vector $z \in \mathfrak{R}_+^n$ output by MIN-NONZERO is then feasible by the assumption on $\mathcal{X}$. MINNONZERO can be implemented to run in $O(n^2)$ time as follows. We first find a sorted list $L : b(v_1) \geq b(v_2) \geq \cdots \geq b(v_n)$ for $V = \{v_1, v_2, \ldots, v_n\}$. Then, after the first while-loop, we can obtain a sorted list of $b(v)$, $v \in X$, with $z(v) = 0$ in $O(n)$ time by choosing those $b(v)$ from list L. Hence, for each $X \in \mathcal{X}$, we can compute z_X in $O(n)$ time, proving that the entire time complexity is $O(n|\mathcal{X}|) = O(n^2)$.

Assuming that a given instance is feasible, we now show that the preceding V-optimal vector z minimizes both $\Phi(z)$ and $\Phi'(z)$. By construction,

$$\Phi'(z) = \sum_{v \in V} z(v) = \sum \{-f(Y) \mid Y \text{ is a maximal subset in } \mathcal{X}\}$$

holds; that is, z minimizes $\Phi'(z)$. To show that z also minimizes $\Phi(z)$, we prove that $|\{v \in V \mid z(v) > 0\}| \leq |\{v \in V \mid \tilde{z}(v) > 0\}|$ holds for any V-feasible vector $\tilde{z}$.

For this, we show that any V-feasible vector $\tilde{z}$ can be modified so that $\tilde{z}(v) \geq z(v)$ holds for all $v \in V$ without changing $\Phi'(\tilde{z})$ or introducing nonzero entries. We modify $\tilde{z}$ by following the process of MINNONZERO in which z is constructed by computing z_X, $X \in \mathcal{X} \cup \{V\}$ recursively.

For a minimal set $X \in \mathcal{M}(\mathcal{X})$, assume that there is an element $v \in X$ such that $z_X(v) > \tilde{z}(v)$ for an X-optimal vector z_X on X. Then there is an entry $u \in X - \{v\}$ such that $\tilde{z}(u) > 0$ (such an entry u exists since $f(X) + \tilde{z}(X) \geq 0 = f(X) + z_X(X)$). If $\tilde{z}(v) > 0$, then we can increase $\tilde{z}(v)$ by $z_X(v) - \tilde{z}(v)$ by decreasing other elements $\tilde{z}(u) > 0$ with $u \in X - \{v\}$ while keeping the V-feasibility of $\tilde{z}$. If $\tilde{z}(v) = 0$, then there is an entry $u \in X - \{v\}$ such that $0 < \tilde{z}(u) \leq b(u) \leq b(v) = z_X(v)$ (since z_X is constructed by increasing $z_X(v)$ in a nonincreasing order of $b(v)$, $v \in X$), for which we can increase $\tilde{z}(v)$ by $\tilde{z}(u)$ by decreasing $\tilde{z}(u) > 0$ to $\tilde{z}(u) = 0$. In this modification, the number of nonzero entries is not increased.

By repeating this, the resulting vector $\tilde{z}$ satisfies

$$\tilde{z}(v) \geq z_X(v) \text{ for all } v \in X,$$

and the number of nonzero entries is not increased. We can apply a similar argument to all sets $X \in \mathcal{X} - \mathcal{M}(\mathcal{X})$ to modify $\tilde{z}$ into a V-optimal vector without increasing the number of nonzero entries. For all maximal subsets $X \in \mathcal{X}$, it holds that $\tilde{z}(v) \geq z_X(v)$ for all $v \in X$, and $z(v) = 0$ for all $v \in V - \cup_{X \in \mathcal{X}} X$; we have $|\{v \in V \mid z(v) > 0\}| \leq |\{v \in V \mid \tilde{z}(v) > 0\}|$, as required. $\qquad \square$

This result can be applied to the degree-constrained edge-connectivity augmentation problem of a graph, under the additional constraint that we minimize the number of vertices incident to the edges whose weights are increased. That is, given a complete graph $G = (V, E = \binom{V}{2})$ with an edge weight function c_G, and a vector $b \in \mathfrak{R}_+^n$, we need to find a k-edge-connected graph $G' = (V, E)$ with edge weight function $c_{G'}$ that minimizes $|\{v \in V \mid \sum_{e \in E(v;G)} (c_{G'}(e) - c_G(e)) > 0\}|$ under constraint $d(v; G') \leq d(v; G) + b(v)$, $v \in V$. To apply Theorem 10.21 to this problem, we define an intersecting submodular and posimodular function f by

$d(X; G) - k$ for all $X \in 2^V$. Then by Theorem 10.21, we can find a vector z that minimizes $|\{v \in V \mid z(v) = \sum_{e \in E(v;G)}(c_{G'}(e) - c_G(e)) > 0\}|$ and $\sum_{v \in V} z(v)$ at the same time. If weights are restricted to integers, together with Lemma 10.18 we obtain an algorithm for solving the edge-connectivity augmentation problem to minimize the number of vertices whose degrees are increased.

Theorem 10.22. *For an edge-weighted complete graph $G = (V, E = \binom{V}{2})$, $k \geq 2$ and $b \in \mathfrak{R}^n_+$, where all $c_G(e)$, k, and $b(v)$ are integers, let $c_{G'}$ ($\geq c_G$) be a new integer-valued edge weight function such that $G' = (V, E)$ is k-edge-connected under the degree constraint that the new degree of each vertex $i \in V$ is at most $b(v) + d(v; G)$. If there exists a feasible $c_{G'}$ (i.e., $d(X; G) + b(X) \geq k$ for all $X \in 2^V - \{\emptyset, V\}$), then there is a $c_{G'}$ that simultaneously minimizes* (i) *the number of vertices to which an edge with increased weight is incident and* (ii) *the total amount of increment $\sum_{e \in E}(c_{G'}(e) - c_G(e))$. Testing the feasibility and finding such a $c_{G'}$ can be done in $O(nm + n^2 \log n)$ time, where $n = |V|$ and m is the number of edges with positive weights in G.* $\square$

Proof. To find $z \in \mathfrak{R}^n_+$ such that

$$d(X; G) + z(X) \geq k \; for \, all \, X \in 2^V - \{\emptyset, V\}, \tag{10.21}$$

we compute a laminar family $\mathcal{X} \subset 2^V$ of Theorem 10.19(iii) for $f = d - k$ by using LAMINAR. For the cut function d of G, we can compute the family $\mathcal{X}(d) = \mathcal{X}(G)$ in $O(n(m + n \log n))$ time by Theorem 6.6. Therefore, LAMINAR can be implemented to run in $O(n(m + n \log n))$ time, similarly to the h-MINIMALEDGESET algorithm in Section 3.3. Given such a laminar family $\mathcal{X}$, we can find z that minimizes $|z(V)|$ and $|\{v \in V \mid z(v) \neq 0\}|$ simultaneously under condition (10.21) by procedure MINNONZERO in $O(n^2)$ time. If $|z(V)|$ is odd, we increase an arbitrary $z(v)$ by 1. We see from Lemma 10.18 that, given z such that $|z(V)|$ is even and satisfies (10.21), there is a k-edge-connected graph $G' = (V, E)$ satisfying $c_{G'} \geq c_G$ and $d(v; G') = d(v; G) + z(v)$ for all $v \in V$. Given $d(v; G')$ for all $v \in V$, such G' (i.e., $c_{G'}$) can be computed in $O(nm + n^2 \log n)$ time by applying the splitting algorithm as stated in Theorem 8.7 in Section 8.3. $\square$

10.4.3 A Polynomial Time Algorithm for the Polyhedra of Problem 1

In this subsection, we consider polyhedra $P(f)$ and $P_+(f)$ for an intersecting submodular and posimodular function f on V, which appear in Problem 1. Meanwhile, we do not consider the constraint $z \leq b$, because this more general case will be considered in the next subsection as Problem 3.

To generalize Theorem 10.19 to this case, we further assume that the set function $\hat{f}$ defined by

$$\hat{f}(X) = f(X) - m_f(X), \quad X \in 2^V$$

is intersecting submodular and posimodular, where m_f denotes the modular function on V defined from f by

$$m_f(v) = f(v), \quad v \in V. \tag{10.22}$$

Note that if $\hat{f}$ is intersecting submodular and posimodular, then so is $f = \hat{f} + m_f$. However, the converse is not true in general (for example, consider function f with $f(X) = k$ for all $X \in 2^V$).

We now give an example of a nonmodular function f such that $\hat{f} = f - m_f$ is also intersecting submodular and posimodular.

Example 10.23. Consider an unweighted multigraph $G = (V, E)$ and assume that $d(v; G) = k$ for all vertices $v \in V$ (i.e., G is k-regular). Let

$$\bar{d}(X) = (d(X; G) + \sum_{v \in X} d(v; G))/2,$$

where $\bar{d}$ is a fully submodular and posimodular set function, as observed in Example 10.1. Let $p \le k/2$. Then function f defined by $f(X) = \bar{d}(X) - k + p$, $X \in 2^V$ is fully submodular and posimodular. This f satisfies $f(v) = \bar{d}(v) - k + p = d(v; G) - k + p = p$ for all $v \in V$ and, hence, we have

$$\hat{f}(X) = f(X) - m_f(X) = \bar{d}(X) - p|X| - k + p \text{ for all } X \in 2^V.$$

We see that $\hat{f}$ is fully submodular because, for two subsets $X, Y \subseteq V$,

$$\begin{aligned}
\hat{f}(X) + \hat{f}(Y) &= \bar{d}(X) + \bar{d}(Y) - (p|X| + p|Y|) - 2k + 2p \\
&\ge \bar{d}(X \cap Y) + \bar{d}(X \cup Y) - (p|X| + p|Y|) - 2k + 2p \\
&= \hat{f}(X \cap Y) + \hat{f}(X \cup Y).
\end{aligned}$$

Function $\hat{f}$ is fully posimodular since, for two subsets $X, Y \subseteq V$,

$$\begin{aligned}
\hat{f}(X) + \hat{f}(Y) &- (\hat{f}(X - Y) + \hat{f}(Y - X)) \\
&\ge k|X \cap Y| - 2p|X \cap Y| \ge 0 \quad \text{(by } p \le k/2\text{)},
\end{aligned}$$

where the first inequality holds since an edge incident to a vertex in $X \cap Y$ is counted at most once in $\bar{d}(X - Y) + \bar{d}(Y - X)$ and twice in $\bar{d}(X) + \bar{d}(Y)$. $\quad \square$

Now we discuss how to compute a vector $z \in P_+(f)$. Let us consider $y = z - m_f$. Then $0 \le z(X) \le f(X)$ holds if and only if $0 \le y(X) + m_f(X) \le f(X) = \hat{f}(X) + m_f(X)$. Thus, the problem is equivalent to finding a vector $y \in P(\hat{f}) \cap \{y \in \Re^n \mid y + m_f \ge 0\}$.

We first consider $P(f)$. Note that $P(\hat{f}) = P_-(\hat{f})$ since $\hat{f}(i) = 0$ holds for all $i \in V$. Therefore,

$$P(f) = \{z = y + m_f \mid y \in P_-(\hat{f})\}.$$

By applying Theorem 10.19 to system $(V, \hat{f})$, we obtain a laminar family $\mathcal{X}$, such that $P_-(\hat{f}) = P_-(\hat{f}; \mathcal{X})$, by using $O(n^3)$ calls to the function value oracle of

$\hat{f}$. Clearly, for any $z \in P(f; \mathcal{X})$, we have $y = z - m_f \in P_-(\hat{f}; \mathcal{X}) = P_-(\hat{f})$ and, hence, $z \in P(f)$. The converse is also clear. Thus, $P(f) = P(f; \mathcal{X})$ holds.

Now, we see that $P_+(f) \neq \emptyset$ holds if and only if $f(X) \geq 0$ holds for all $X \in \mathcal{X}$. If $P_+(f) \neq \emptyset$, then the vector $z \in \mathfrak{R}^n$ with $z(v) = 0$ for all $v \in V$ belongs to $P_+(f)$, establishing the next theorem.

Theorem 10.24. *For a system (V, f) with a set function f on V with $n = |V| \geq 2$ such that $f - m_f$ is intersecting submodular and posimodular, there is a laminar family $\mathcal{X}$ such that $P(f) = P(f; \mathcal{X})$. Such a family $\mathcal{X}$ can be found by $O(n^3)$ function value oracle calls. Furthermore, $P_+(f) \neq \emptyset$ holds if and only if $f(X) \geq 0$ holds for all $X \in \mathcal{X}$ and $0 \in P_+(f)$.* $\square$

10.4.4 A Polynomial Time Algorithm for Problem 3

In this subsection, we solve Problem 3 with a linear objective function

$$\Phi(z) = \sum_{v \in V} w(v)z(v)$$

for a given weight vector $w \in \mathfrak{R}^n$. Recall that Problem 3 includes Problems 1 and 2 as its special cases.

Theorem 10.25. *Let g and f be set functions on V, and $b_1, b_2 \in \mathfrak{R}^n_+$ and $w \in \mathfrak{R}^n$. If $-g$ and $f - m_f$ are both intersecting submodular and posimodular (where m_f is defined in (10.22)), then an optimal solution z to Problem 3 that minimizes the objective function $\Phi(z) = \sum_{v \in V} w(v)z(v)$ can be found by using $O(n^3)$ calls to the function value oracle of f and by solving a minimum cost flow problem with $O(n)$ vertices and edges. If g, f, w, b_1, b_2 are all integer-valued, then an integer optimal solution z can be found in the same time complexity.* $\square$

Proof. By Theorem 10.19, there is a laminar family $\mathcal{X}_1$ such that

$$\{z \in \mathfrak{R}^n_+ \mid g(X) \leq z(X) \text{ for all } X \in 2^V - \{\emptyset, V\}\}$$
$$= \{z \in \mathfrak{R}^n_+ \mid g(X) \leq z(X) \text{ for all } X \in \mathcal{X}_1\}.$$

Analogously, by Theorem 10.24, there is a laminar family $\mathcal{X}_2$ such that

$$\{z \in \mathfrak{R}^n \mid z(X) \leq f(X) \text{ for all } X \in 2^V - \{\emptyset, V\}\}$$
$$= \{z \in \mathfrak{R}^n \mid z(X) \leq f(X) \text{ for all } X \in \mathcal{X}_2\}.$$

Thus, the problem is restated as follows:

$$
\begin{array}{lll}
\text{minimize} & \Phi(z) = \sum_{v \in V} w(v)z(v) & \\
\text{subject to} & g(X) \leq z(X) & \text{for all } X \in \mathcal{X}'_1 \\
& z(X) \leq f(X) & \text{for all } X \in \mathcal{X}'_2 \\
& b_1(v) \leq z(v) \leq b_2(v) & \text{for all } v \in V,
\end{array}
\qquad (10.23)
$$

where $\mathcal{X}'_i = \mathcal{X}_i \cup \{\emptyset, V\}$ for $i = 1, 2$.

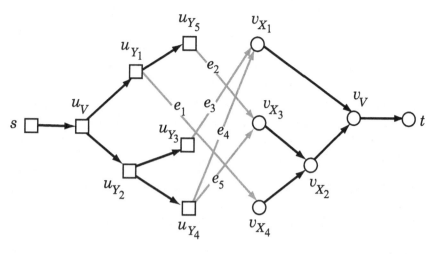

Figure 10.2. An example of digraph $D = (W = W_1 \cup W_2, A = A_1 \cup A_2 \cup A_3)$.

To show that this problem can be solved efficiently, it is formulated as the minimum cost flow problem in a digraph. Let $N = (D = (W, A), \underline{c}, \overline{c}, w')$ be the edge-weighted digraph defined as follows, where D is the digraph with a vertex set W, an edge set A, $\underline{c}, \overline{c} : A \to \Re^+$ are lower and upper capacity functions, and $w' : A \to \Re$ is a cost function. The vertex set W in the digraph D consists of W_1 and W_2. W_1 contains a sink t and vertices v_X, associated with subsets $X \in \mathcal{X}'_1$. Similarly, W_2 contains a source s and vertices u_Y, associated with subsets $Y \in \mathcal{X}'_2$. The edge sets A consists of the following edge sets: A_1, A_2, and A_3. For two vertices $v, v' \in W_1$, A_1 contains an edge (v, v') if and only if $v = v_X$ and $v' = v_{X'}$ hold for $X, X' \in \mathcal{X}'_1$ such that $pa(X) = X'$ (or $X = V$ and $v' = t$). Similarly, for two vertices $u, u' \in W_2$, A_2 contains an edge (u, u') if and only if $u = u_Y$, $u' = u_{Y'}$ for $Y, Y' \in \mathcal{X}'_1$ such that $pa(Y') = Y$ (or $u = s$ and $Y' = V$). Finally, A_3 consists of edges $e_i = (u, v)$, associated with the elements $i \in V$, in such a way that $e_i = (u, v)$ joins vertices $v = v_X \in W_1$ and $u = u_Y \in W_2$ for sets $X \in \mathcal{X}'_1$ and $Y \in \mathcal{X}'_2$, which are minimal subject to $i \in X$ and $i \in Y$, respectively.

For example, given two laminar families $\mathcal{X}'_1 = \{V = \{1, 2, 3, 4, 5\}, X_1 = \{3, 4\}, X_2 = \{1, 2, 5\}, X_3 = \{2, 5\}, X_4 = \{1\}\}$ and $\mathcal{X}'_2 = \{V = \{1, 2, 3, 4, 5\}, Y_1 = \{1, 2\}, Y_2 = \{3, 4, 5\}, Y_3 = \{3\}, Y_4 = \{4, 5\}, Y_5 = \{2\}\}$, Fig. 10.2 shows the corresponding digraph $D = (W = W_1 \cup W_2, A = A_1 \cup A_2 \cup A_3)$.

The lower and upper capacity functions $\underline{c}, \overline{c} : A \to \Re^n_+$ and cost function $w' : A \to \Re^n$ are then defined by

$$\underline{c}(e) = g(X), \overline{c}(e) = +\infty \text{ for } e = (v, v') \in A_1 \text{ with } v = v_X \text{ and } X \in \mathcal{X}'_1,$$
$$\underline{c}(e) = 0, \overline{c}(e) = f(Y) \text{ for } e = (u, u') \in A_2 \text{ with } u' = u_Y \text{ and } Y \in \mathcal{X}'_2,$$
$$w'(e) = 0 \text{ for } e \in A_1 \cup A_2,$$
$$\underline{c}(e_i) = b_1(i), \overline{c}(e_i) = b_2(i), w'(e_i) = w(i) \text{ for } e_i \in A_3.$$

$$(10.24)$$

Let $\hat{n} = |A|$. For a vector $z \in \mathfrak{R}_+^n$, the vector $x \in \mathfrak{R}_+^{\hat{n}}$ defined by

$$x(e) = \begin{cases} \sum_{i \in X} z(i) & \text{if } e = (v_X, v_{X'}) \in A_1, \\ \sum_{i \in Y'} z(i) & \text{if } e = (v_Y, v_{Y'}) \in A_2, \\ z(i) & \text{if } e = e_i \in A_3 \end{cases}$$

satisfies the flow conservation and is a feasible flow in N if z is feasible to problem (10.23), since $\underline{c}(e) = g(X) \le z(X) = x(e)$ holds for $e \in A_1$, $x(e) = z(Y) \le f(Y) = \overline{c}(e)$ holds for $e \in A_2$, and $\underline{c}(e_i) = b_1(i) \le x(e_i) = z(i) \le b_2(i) = \overline{c}(e_i)$ holds for $e_i \in A_3$. Conversely, we see that any feasible flow $x \in \mathfrak{R}_+^{\hat{n}}$ in N gives a vector $z_x \in \mathfrak{R}_+^n$ with $z_x(i) = x(e_i)$, $i \in V$, which is feasible to problem (10.23). Also, if x is a minimum cost flow $x \in \mathfrak{R}_+^{\hat{n}}$ in N, then the corresponding vector z_x is optimal to the problem since x minimizes the cost function $\sum_{e_i \in A_3} w(e_i) x(e_i)$, which is equal to $\sum_{i \in V} w(i) z_x(i)$. Note that $|W| = O(n)$ and $\hat{n} = |A| = O(n)$ hold. Thus, the feasibility of the flow problem can be tested in $O(n^2 \log n)$ time by using the $O(|A||W| \log(|A|/|W|^2)$ time maximum-flow algorithm of Goldberg and Tarjan [103], and an optimal solution (if the problem is feasible) can be obtained in $O(n^2 (\log n)^2)$ time by using the minimum cost flow algorithm of Orlin [270]. It is also known that, when g, f, w, b_1, b_2 are all integers, there always exits an integer minimum cost flow (hence, an integer optimal solution z) and such a minimum cost flow can also be obtained by the aforementioned procedure. This proves the theorem. □

10.4.5 Polynomial Time Algorithms for Problems 4 and 5

Analogously to Problem 3, we solve Problems 4 and 5 with a linear objective function $\Phi(z) = \sum_{i \in V} w(i) z(i)$ by transforming them to minimum cost flow problems.

By Theorem 10.19, for two intersecting submodular and posimodular set functions $-g_1$ and $-g_2$ on V, there are laminar families $\mathcal{X}_1$ and $\mathcal{X}_2$ such that

$$\{z \in \mathfrak{R}_+^n \mid g_j(X) \le z(X) \text{ for all } X \in 2^V - \{\emptyset, V\}\}$$
$$= \{z \in \mathfrak{R}_+^n \mid g_j(X) \le z(X) \text{ for all } X \in \mathcal{X}_j\}, \quad j = 1, 2.$$

Thus, it is not difficult to see that Problem 4 can be formulated as the minimum cost flow problem for the digraph $N = (D = (W, A), \underline{c}, \overline{c}, w')$, which was introduced in the proof of Theorem 10.25, just by changing lower and upper capacities in (10.24) as follows:

$$\underline{c}(e) = g_1(X), \overline{c}(e) = +\infty \text{ for } e = (v, v') \in A_1 \text{ with } v = v_X \text{ and } X \in \mathcal{X}_1',$$

$$\underline{c}(e) = g_2(X), \overline{c}(e) = +\infty \text{ for } e = (u, u') \in A_2 \text{ with } u' = u_X \text{ and } X \in \mathcal{X}_2'.$$

Theorem 10.26. *Let $-g_1$ and $-g_2$ be intersecting submodular and posimodular set functions on V, and $b_1, b_2 \in \mathfrak{R}_+^n$ and $w \in \mathfrak{R}^n$. Then an optimal solution z to Problem 4 with objective function $\Phi(z) = \sum_{i \in V} w(i) z(i)$ can be found by using $O(n^3)$ calls to the function value oracles of g_1 and g_2 and by solving a minimum* *cost flow problem with $O(n)$ vertices and edges. If g_1, g_2, w, b_1, b_2 are all integer-valued, then an integer optimal solution z to Problem 4 can be found in the same time complexity.* ☐

We now consider Problem 5. Given two set functions f_1 and f_2 such that both $f_1 - m_{f_1}$ and $f_2 - m_{f_2}$ are intersecting submodular and posimodular, we apply Theorem 10.24 to obtain laminar families $\mathcal{X}_1$ and $\mathcal{X}_2$ such that

$$\{z \in \mathfrak{R}^n \mid z(X) \leq f_j(X) \text{ for all } X \in 2^V - \{\emptyset, V\}\}$$
$$= \{z \in \mathfrak{R}^n \mid z(X) \leq f_j(X) \text{ for all } X \in \mathcal{X}_j\}, \quad j = 1, 2.$$

Similarly to Problem 4, Problem 5 can be formulated as the minimum cost flow problem in the digraph N, which was introduced in the proof of Theorem 10.25, by changing lower and upper capacities in (10.24) as follows:

$$\underline{c}(e) = 0, \overline{c}(e) = f_1(X) \text{ for } e = (v, v') \in A_1 \text{ with } v = v_X \text{ and } X \in \mathcal{X}'_1,$$

$$\underline{c}(e) = 0, \overline{c}(e) = f_2(X) \text{ for } e = (u, u') \in A_2 \text{ with } u' = u_X \text{ and } X \in \mathcal{X}'_2.$$

Theorem 10.27. *Let f_1 and f_2 be set functions on V, and $b_1, b_2 \in \mathfrak{R}^n_+$ and $w \in \mathfrak{R}^n$. If $f_1 - m_{f_1}$ and $f_2 - m_{f_2}$ are both intersecting submodular and posimodular, then an optimal solution z to Problem 5 with objective function $\Phi(z) = \sum_{i \in V} w(i)z(i)$ can be found by using $O(n^3)$ calls to the function value oracles of f_1 and f_2, and by solving a minimum cost flow problem with $O(n)$ vertices and edges. If f_1, f_2, w, b_1, b_2 are all integer-valued, then an integer optimal solution z to Problem 5 can be found in the same time complexity.* ☐

To conclude this subsection, we present two applications of Theorem 10.26.

Given two multigraphs $G_1 = (V, E_1)$ and $G_2 = (V, E_2)$ on the same vertex set V and two integers k_1 and k_2, Jordán [161] solved the problem of finding the smallest set F of new edges such that each graph $G_j + F = (V, E_j \cup F)$ augmented by F is k_j-edge-connected. His algorithm needs to compute a vector $z \in \mathfrak{R}^n_+$ of the minimum size $\sum_{v \in V} z(v)$ such that $k_j - d(X; G_j) \leq z(X)$ holds for all $X \in 2^V - \{\emptyset, V\}$ and $j = 1, 2$. The problem of computing such a minimum z can be viewed as a submodular flow problem [60, 87] (and, hence, polynomially solvable [50]). We point out here that a fast algorithm can be obtained by formulating it as Problem 4 with intersecting supermodular and negamodular set functions $g_j(X) = k_j - d(X; G_j)$ for $X \subseteq V$ and $j = 1, 2$, $b_1(v) = 0$, $b_2(v) = +\infty$ for $v \in V$ and the objective function $\Phi(z) = \sum_{v \in V} z(v)$. To compute a laminar family $\mathcal{X}$ in Theorem 10.19, LAMINAR can be implemented to run in $O(n(m + n \log n))$ time as observed in the proof of Theorem 10.22. Thus, by Theorem 10.26, we have a fast algorithm for computing such a minimum vector z.

Corollary 10.28. *Given two multigraphs $G_1 = (V, E_1)$ and $G_2 = (V, E_2)$ on the same vertex set V, and two integers k_1 and k_2, a vector $z \in \mathfrak{R}^n_+$ of the minimum size $\sum_{v \in V} z(v)$, such that $k_j - d(X; G_j) \leq z(X)$ holds for all $X \in 2^V - \{\emptyset, V\}$ and $j = 1, 2$, can be computed in $O(nm + n^2(\log n)^2)$ time.* ☐

A graph G is ℓ-vertex-connected if $|\Gamma_G(X)| \geq \ell$ for all $X \in 2^V - \{\emptyset, V\}$ with $V - \Gamma_G(X) \neq \emptyset$, where $\Gamma_G(X)$ denotes the set of vertices in $V - X$ that are adjacent to some vertex in X. Ishii et al. [143] showed an efficient algorithm for augmenting a 2-vertex-connected multigraph $G = (V, E)$ to a k-edge-connected and 3-vertex-connected graph by adding a smallest edge set F. For this, it is required to compute a vector $z \in \mathfrak{R}_+^n$ with the minimum size $\sum_{v \in V} z(v)$ such that $k - d(X; G) \leq z(X)$ holds for all $X \in 2^V - \{\emptyset, V\}$ and $1 \leq z(X)$ holds for all $X \in \mathcal{M}$, where $\mathcal{M}$ is the family of minimal subsets $T \subseteq V$ with $|\Gamma_G(X)| = 2$ and $V - \Gamma_G(X) \neq \emptyset$. Since $\mathcal{M}$ is easily shown to be a family of disjoint subsets (and, hence, a laminar family), we see that a desired vector z can be computed efficiently as in the proof of Corollary 10.28.

Corollary 10.29. *Given a 2-vertex-connected multigraph $G = (V, E)$, let $\mathcal{M}$ be the family of minimal subsets $T \subseteq V$ with $|\Gamma_G(X)| = 2$ and $V - \Gamma_G(X) \neq \emptyset$. Then a vector $z \in \mathfrak{R}_+^n$ of the minimum size $\sum_{v \in V} z(v)$, such that $k - d(X; G) \leq z(X)$ holds for all $X \in 2^V - \{\emptyset, V\}$ and $1 \leq z(X)$ for all $X \in \mathcal{M}$, can be computed in $O(nm + n^2 (\log n)^2)$ time.* $\square$

10.5 Extreme Points of Base Polyhedron

In this section, we characterize all extreme points of a base polyhedron $B_-(f)$ defined in (10.17) and (10.18) for an intersecting submodular and posimodular set function f. Given a set function f, we denote by $EP_-(f)$ the set of all extreme points in $B_-(f)$, where a vector $z \in B_-(f)$ is called an *extreme point* if there is no pair of vectors $z', z'' \in B_-(f)$ such that $z = a \cdot z' + (1 - a) \cdot z''$ holds for some real $a \in (0, 1)$.

Let Π_n be the set of all permutations of $(1, 2, \ldots, n)$. For a subset $P \subseteq \mathfrak{R}_-^n$ and a permutation $\pi \in \Pi_n$, a vector $z \in \mathfrak{R}_-^n$ is called *lexicographically π-minimal* (π-minimal, for short) in P if there is no other vector $z' \in P$ which is lexicographically smaller than z with respect to π; i.e., no j satisfies $z'(\pi(i)) = z(\pi(i))$ for $i = 1, 2, \ldots, j - 1$ and $z'(\pi(j)) < z(\pi(j))$. Note that, for each $z \in \mathfrak{R}_-^n$, a π-minimal vector in P is unique.

For a set function f, we consider the π-minimal vector in $B_-(f)$ for each $\pi \in \Pi_n$, and we denote by $L(f)$ the set of all these π-minimal vectors. The following characterization for the set of extreme points in $B_-(f)$ is known.

Theorem 10.30 ([58, 290]). *For a fully submodular set function f with $f(\emptyset) = 0$ and $f(X) \leq 0$ for all $X \in 2^V$, $B_-(f)$ is nonempty and $L(f) = EP_-(f)$ holds.* $\square$

More generally, it is known [92, Theorems 2.5(ii) and 2.6(ii)] that $L(f) = EP_-(f)$ holds for a crossing submodular function f if $B_-(f)$ is nonempty. Hence, Theorem 10.30 follows from this fact only by showing that $B_-(f)$ is always nonempty for any fully submodular set function f with $f(\emptyset) = 0$ and $f(X) \leq 0$ for all $X \in 2^V$ (since a fully submodular function is crossing submodular).

Based on Theorem 10.20, we will show in the following that $L(f) = EP_-(f)$ holds (if $B_-(f) \neq \emptyset$) for a weakly posimodular set function f. This does not directly follow from Fujishige's result [92], since a crossing submodular function may not be weakly posimodular. We first prove the next property.

Lemma 10.31. *For a finite set V, let $\mathcal{X} \subseteq 2^V - \{\emptyset\}$ be a laminar family and $h : \mathcal{X} \to \mathfrak{R}_+$ be a function such that $h(X) \geq \sum_{Y \in Ch(X)} h(Y)$ holds for all $X \in \mathcal{X}$, where $Ch(X)$ denotes the set of children of X in the tree $\mathcal{T}$ representing $\mathcal{X}$. Then there is a fully supermodular set function $h^* : 2^V \to \mathfrak{R}_+$ such that $h^*(\emptyset) = 0$ and*

$$\{t \in \mathfrak{R}_+^n \mid h(X) \leq t(X), \ \forall X \in \mathcal{X}\} = \{t \in \mathfrak{R}_+^n \mid h^*(X) \leq t(X), \ \forall X \in 2^V\}.$$

Moreover, if $V \in \mathcal{X}$, then $h^*(V) = h(V)$ holds. $\qquad\square$

Proof. For a subset $X \subseteq V$, we denote by $\mathcal{M}(\mathcal{X}; X)$ the set of all maximal subsets $Z \in \mathcal{X}$ with $Z \subseteq X$ (note that sets in $\mathcal{M}(\mathcal{X}; X)$ are disjoint since $\mathcal{X}$ is a laminar family). Define a set function $h^* : 2^V \to \mathfrak{R}_+$ by

$$h^*(X) = \sum_{Z \in \mathcal{M}(\mathcal{X};X)} h(Z) \text{ for all } X \in 2^V,$$

where $h^*(X) = 0$ if $\mathcal{M}(\mathcal{X}; X) = \emptyset$. Clearly, $h^*(\emptyset) = 0$, and if $V \in \mathcal{X}$, then $V = \mathcal{M}(\mathcal{X}; V)$ and $h^*(V) = \sum_{Z \in \mathcal{M}(\mathcal{X};V)} h(Z) = h(V)$ hold. We prove that, for any $X, Y \subseteq V$, it holds that $h^*(X) + h^*(Y) \leq h^*(X \cap Y) + h^*(X \cup Y)$. Let $\mathcal{M}(\mathcal{X}; X) \cup \mathcal{M}(\mathcal{X}; Y) = \{Z_1, \ldots, Z_d\}$ and assume, without loss of generality, that

$$\{Z_1, \ldots, Z_c\} = \{Z \subseteq X \cap Y \mid Z \in \mathcal{M}(\mathcal{X}; X) \cup \mathcal{M}(\mathcal{X}; Y)\},$$

$$\{Z_1, \ldots, Z_a\} = \mathcal{M}(\mathcal{X}; X) \cap \mathcal{M}(\mathcal{X}; Y),$$

$$\{Z_{a+1}, \ldots, Z_b\} = \{Z \subseteq X \cap Y \mid Z \in \mathcal{M}(\mathcal{X}; X) - \mathcal{M}(\mathcal{X}; Y)\}$$

(i.e., those $Z \in \mathcal{M}(\mathcal{X}; X)$ such that $Z \subset Z'$ for some $Z' \in \mathcal{M}(\mathcal{X}; Y)$) and

$$\{Z_{b+1}, \ldots, Z_c\} = \{Z \subseteq X \cap Y \mid Z \in \mathcal{M}(\mathcal{X}; Y) - \mathcal{M}(\mathcal{X}; X)\},$$

where $a \leq b \leq c \leq d$ holds. See Fig. 10.3, which illustrates the sets Z_i in $\mathcal{M}(\mathcal{X}; X) \cup \mathcal{M}(\mathcal{X}; Y)$.

Clearly, $\{Z_1, \ldots, Z_c\} \subseteq \mathcal{M}(\mathcal{X}; X \cap Y)$, which implies $\sum_{1 \leq i \leq c} h(Z_i) \leq h^*(X \cap Y)$. We claim that sets in $\{Z_i \mid 1 \leq i \leq a \text{ or } c + 1 \leq i \leq d\}$ are all disjoint. By definition, set Z_i with $i \in \{1, 2, \ldots, a\}$ is disjoint with any other Z_j with $j \in \{1, 2, \ldots, d\} - i$. Then assume that there are two sets Z_i and Z_j with $c + 1 \leq i < j \leq d$, which are not disjoint; that is, one of them contains the other, say $Z_i \subset Z_j$ (since they belong to a laminar family $\mathcal{X}$). Moreover, if $Z_i \subseteq X$ (resp. $Z_i \subseteq Y$) then $Z_j \subseteq Y$ (resp. $Z_j \subseteq Y$), since both $\mathcal{M}(\mathcal{X}; X)$ and $\mathcal{M}(\mathcal{X}; Y)$ are families of maximal sets. However, neither $X \supseteq Z_i \subset Z_j \subseteq Y$ nor $Y \supseteq Z_i \subset Z_j \subseteq Z$ holds, since none of Z_i and Z_j is contained in $X \cap Y$. This proves the claim.

Since $\mathcal{X}$ is a laminar family, we see that $\mathcal{M}(\mathcal{X}; X \cup Y)$ contains a family of disjoint subsets $\{Z'_1, \ldots, Z'_p\} \subseteq \mathcal{X}$ such that each Z_i ($1 \leq i \leq a$ or $c + 1 \leq i \leq d$)

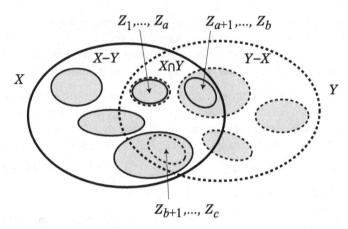

Figure 10.3. Sets Z_i in $\mathcal{M}(\mathcal{X}; X) \cup \mathcal{M}(\mathcal{X}; Y)$, which are represented by shaded circles, where dotted (resp. solid) circles stand for sets in $\mathcal{M}(\mathcal{X}; Y)$ (resp. $\mathcal{M}(\mathcal{X}; X)$).

is contained in some Z'_j. For each Z'_j, $h(Z'_j) \geq \sum_{Z_i \subseteq Z'_j} h(Z_i)$ holds by the assumption on h. This implies that $\sum_{1 \leq i \leq a, \, c+1 \leq i \leq d} h(Z_i) \leq h^*(X \cup Y)$. Thus, we obtain $h^*(X) + h^*(Y) = \sum_{1 \leq i \leq c} h(Z_i) + \sum_{1 \leq i \leq a, \, c+1 \leq i \leq d} h(Z_i) \leq h^*(X \cap Y) + h^*(X \cup Y)$. $\qquad \square$

Corollary 10.32. *For a system (V, f) with a weakly posimodular set function f, $L(f) = EP_-(f)$ holds if $B_-(f) \neq \emptyset$.* $\qquad \square$

Proof. Assume $B_-(f) \neq \emptyset$. By Theorem 10.20, there exists a laminar family $\mathcal{X}$ such that $P_-(f) = P_-(f; \mathcal{X})$, where $f(X) \leq 0$ for all $X \in \mathcal{X}$. Let $h = -f$. We can assume without loss of generality that $h(X) \geq \sum_{Y \in Ch(X)} h(Y)$ for all $X \in \mathcal{X}$ (discarding constrains those X with $h(X) < \sum_{Y \in Ch(X)} h(Y)$ as they are redundant in constraint $h(X) \leq t(X)$). Let $\mathcal{X}' = \mathcal{X} \cup \{V\}$. Then $P_-(f; \mathcal{X}') = \{-t \in \mathfrak{R}^n_- \mid h(X) \leq t(X), \, \forall X \in \mathcal{X}'\}$, which is not empty since $B_-(f) \neq \emptyset$. By Lemma 10.31, there is a fully supermodular set function $h^* : 2^V \to \mathfrak{R}_+$ such that $h^*(\emptyset) = 0$, $h^*(V) = h(V) = -f(V)$ and $\{-t \in \mathfrak{R}^n_- \mid h^*(X) \leq t(X), \, \forall X \in 2^V\} = P_-(f; \mathcal{X})$. Then recall that $B_-(f)$ is given by $B_-(f) = \{-t \in \mathfrak{R}^n_- \mid t(V) = h^*(V)$ and $h^*(X) \leq t(X), \, \forall X \in 2^V\} = B_-(-h^*)$, and we have $L(-h^*) = EP_-(-h^*)$ (hence, $L(f) = EP_-(f)$) by Theorem 10.30. $\qquad \square$

10.5.1 Mean Vectors of All π-Minimal Vectors

For a set function f on $V = \{1, 2, \ldots, n\}$ such that $B_-(f)$ and $L(f) = EP_-(f)$, we define the *mean vector* ψ_f of all π-minimal vectors z_π, $\pi \in \Pi_n$, in $B_-(f)$ by

$$\psi_f = \frac{1}{n!} \sum_{\pi \in \Pi_n} z_\pi, \qquad (10.25)$$

where possibly $z_\pi = z_{\pi'}$ holds for two permutations $\pi, \pi' \in \Pi_n$. This mean vector ψ_f of $B_-(f)$ for a fully submodular function f plays a key concept in convex games [290], but computing the mean vector ψ_f for a fully submodular function f is shown to be intractable [240]. We now show, however, that, for an intersecting submodular and posimodular set function f, the mean vector ψ_f can be efficiently computed from its laminar family $\mathcal{X}$.

Lemma 10.33. *For a system (V, f), where f is an intersecting submodular and posimodular set function, let $\mathcal{X}$ be a laminar family that satisfies (10.19). Then, given a permutation $\pi \in \Pi_n$, the π-minimal vector $z_\pi \in B_-(f)$ can be obtained from $\mathcal{X}$ in $O(n)$ time.* $\square$

Proof. Let $\mathcal{V} = \mathcal{X} \cup \{V\} \cup \{\{v\} \mid v \in V\}$ and $\mathcal{T} = (\mathcal{V}, \mathcal{E})$, respectively, be the laminar family and its tree representation defined before Theorem 10.19. Observe that $X = \cup_{Y \in Ch(X)} Y$ always holds for each set $X \in \mathcal{V}$ with $Ch(X) \neq \emptyset$.

For each $X \in \mathcal{X}$, we call an $|X|$-dimensional vector z_X on X *X-feasible* if it satisfies $z_X(X') \leq f(X')$ for all $X' \in \mathcal{X}$ with $X' \subseteq X$. By Theorem 10.19(ii)–(iv), $f'(X) < \sum_{Y \in Ch(X)} f'(Y)$ holds for all $X \in \mathcal{X} \cup \{V\}$, where f' is the set function defined from f by (10.20). Thus, we can see by induction that the following property holds.

Lemma 10.34. *Let $\mathcal{X}$ and f' be as defined earlier. For each $X \in \mathcal{X} \cup \{V\}$ and an $a \in \Re_-$, there is an X-feasible vector z_X on X with $z_X(X) = a$ if and only if $a \leq f'(X)$ holds.* $\square$

Now we construct the π-minimal vector $z_\pi \in B_-(f)$. We first determine a value $a(X)$ for each $X \in \mathcal{V}$, based on which we finally determine $z_\pi(i)$, $i \in V$, such that $z_\pi(X) = a(X)$ holds for all $X \in \mathcal{V}$. Since $z_\pi \in B_-(f)$, $z_\pi(V) = f'(V)$ must hold, hence we let $a(V) = f'(V)$. Assuming that $a(X)$ for a set $X \in \mathcal{V}$ has been determined, we show how to determine values $a(Y)$ for its children $Y \in Ch(X)$ in $\mathcal{T}$. Let $Ch(X) = \{Y_1, Y_2, \ldots, Y_p\}$. Clearly, $z_\pi(Y_i)$ needs to satisfy $z_\pi(Y_i) \leq f'(Y_i)$ for all Y_i. So values $a(Y_i)$ must satisfy

$$a(Y_i) \leq f'(Y_i), i = 1, 2, \ldots, p \text{ and } \sum_{1 \leq i \leq p} a(Y_i) = a(X) \qquad (10.26)$$

(since $V = Y_1 \cup Y_2 \cup \cdots \cup Y_p$ holds and z_π is a modular function). Conversely, given an arbitrary set of reals $a(Y_1), a(Y_2), \ldots, a(Y_p) \in \Re_-$ satisfying (10.26), there exists a Y_i-feasible vector z_{Y_i} with $z_{Y_i}(Y_i) = a(Y_i)$ for each Y_i by Lemma 10.34, implying that there also exists an X-feasible vector z_X with $z_X(X) = a(X)$ and $z_X(Y_i) = a(Y_i)$ for all $Y_i \in Ch(X)$. By repeating this procedure, a V-feasible vector $z \in \Re_-^n$ will be constructed. To obtain a π-minimal vector z from this procedure, we choose a special set of reals $a(Y_1), a(Y_2), \ldots, a(Y_p) \in \Re_-$ for the children of each set $X \in \mathcal{V}$. As observed earlier, we can construct an X-feasible vector as long as a satisfies (10.26). Since we want to construct a π-minimal vector z_π, the value of $z_\pi(\pi(i))$ with the minimum i such that $\pi(i) \in X$ should be as small as possible subject to (10.26). Thus, for the $i^* = \min\{i \mid \pi(i) \in X\}$ and the child $Y^* \in Ch(X)$ with $\pi(i^*) \in Y^*$, the value $a(Y^*)$ to be as small as possible.

Note that this can be attained by setting values $a(Y)$ for $Y \in Ch(X) - Y^*$ to be as large as possible. Thus, we set

$$
\begin{aligned}
a(Y) &= f'(Y) \text{ for } Y \in Ch(X) - \{Y^*\} \\
a(Y^*) &= a(X) - \sum_{Y \in Ch(X) - Y^*} f'(Y).
\end{aligned}
\tag{10.27}
$$

The entire algorithm for computing the π-minimal vector z_π is described as follows.

Algorithm LEXICOMIN
Input: A laminar family $\mathcal{X}$ that satisfies (10.19), and a permutation $\pi \in \Pi_n$.
Output: The π-minimal vector $z_\pi \in B_-(f)$.
1   $\mathcal{V} := \mathcal{X} \cup \{V\} \cup \{\{v\} \mid v \in V\}$; Let f' be the set function defined from f
      by (10.20);
2   $a(V) := f'(V)$;
3   **while** $\mathcal{V} \neq \emptyset$ **do**
4   Choose a maximal subset X in the current $\mathcal{V}$, and $\mathcal{V} := \mathcal{V} - X$;
5   **if** $Ch(X) \neq \emptyset$ **then** /* $|Ch(X)| \geq 2$ */
6         $i^* := \min\{i \mid \pi(i) \in X\}$; Let $Y^* \in Ch(X)$ be the subset containing $\pi(i^*)$;
7         $a(Y) := f'(Y)$ for all $Y \in Ch(X) - Y^*$;
8         $a(Y^*) := a(X) - \sum_{Y \in Ch(X) - Y^*} f'(Y)$
9   **else** /* $|X| = 1$ */
10        $z_\pi(v) := a(X)$ for the $v \in V$ with $X = \{v\}$
11   **end** /* if */
12 **end**; /* while */
13 Output vector z_π given by $z_\pi(v) = a(v)$, $v \in V$.

For each set X, $|Ch(X)|$ values $a(Y)$, $Y \in Ch(X)$ can be computed in $O(|Ch(X)|)$ time. Hence, the entire run time of LEXICOMIN is $O(\sum_{X \in \mathcal{V}} | Ch(X)|) = O(|\mathcal{V}|) = O(n)$.

We now show that the vector z_π output by LEXICOMIN is in fact π-minimal. For this, we show by induction that, for each $i \in V$, $z_\pi(\pi(i))$ is minimized over all V-feasible vectors that minimize entries $z_\pi(\pi(j))$, $j = 1, 2, \ldots, i - 1$, in this order. For $i = 1$, let $X_1 = V, X_2, \ldots, X_q = \{\pi(1)\}$ be the sets in $\mathcal{V}$ containing $\pi(1)$, where $X_k = pa(X_{k+1})$ for $k = 1, 2, \ldots, q - 1$. By the choice of values $a(X_k)$, $z_\pi(X_k) = a(X_k)$ holds for $k = 1, 2, \ldots, q$. Since $a(X_1) = a(V)$ is chosen so that $z_\pi(X_1)$ can take the minimum possible value among all V-feasible vectors, there is no V-feasible vector z with $z(X_1) < a(X_1) = z_\pi(X_1)$. Under the constraint $a(X_1) = z_\pi(X_1)$, we see that $a(X_2)$ is the minimum possible value that $z_\pi(X_2)$ can take, similarly for $X_2, \ldots, X_q = \{\pi(1)\}$. Hence, there is no V-feasible vector z with $z(\pi(1)) < a(\pi(1)) = z_\pi(\pi(1))$. For these sets $X_1, X_2, \ldots, X_q$, $z_\pi(X_k) = a(X_k)$ must hold to obtain a vector z_π such that $z_\pi(\pi(1)) \leq z(\pi(1))$ holds for all V-feasible vectors z. Under this constraint, we see that, for each set $X \in \mathcal{V}$ with $\pi(1) \notin X$ and $\pi(2) \in X$, $a(X)$ is set to be the minimum possible value so that $z_\pi(\pi(2)) \leq z(\pi(2))$ holds for all V-feasible vectors z with $z(\pi(1)) = z_\pi(\pi(1))$.

By repeating this argument, we conclude that the resulting z_π is a π-minimal vector, and the proof of Lemma 10.33 is complete. $\qquad\square$

Let us now consider how to compute the mean vector ψ_f of all π-minimal vectors defined by (10.25). For each $X \in \mathcal{V}$, let $A(X)$ denote the set of reals $a \in \mathfrak{R}_-$ such that $a = z_\pi(X)$ holds for some permutation $\pi \in \Pi_n$ and let $\mu(X)$ denote the mean value of $z_\pi(X)$ over all $\pi \in \Pi_n$. Since we have seen that $a(V) = f'(V)$ holds for any π, we see that $\mu(V) = f'(V)$. We then execute the LEXICOMIN algorithm under the assumption that a permutation π has been chosen randomly from Π_n. Suppose that a set $X \in \mathcal{V}$ is chosen in the while-loop of LEXICOMIN and assume that $z_\pi(X) = a \ (\in A(X))$ has already been determined. Then the values $a(Y)$ for $Y \in Ch(X)$ will be determined as follows. Note that the probability that a set $Y \in Ch(X)$ contains the element i^* defined in line 6 of LEXICOMIN is $|Y|/|X|$. By (10.27), the mean value of $z_\pi(Y)$ assuming $z_\pi(X) = a$ is given by

$$\frac{|Y|}{|X|}\left(a - \sum_{Z \in Ch(X) - \{Y\}} f'(Z)\right) + \left(1 - \frac{|Y|}{|X|}\right)f'(Y)$$

$$= f'(Y) + \frac{|Y|}{|X|}\left(a - \sum_{Z \in Ch(X)} f'(Z)\right).$$

Therefore, by letting $p(X; a)$ denote the probability that $z_\pi(X)$ takes $a \in A(X)$, we have

$$\mu(Y) = \sum_{a \in A(X)} p(X; a)\left[f'(Y) + \frac{|Y|}{|X|}\left(a - \sum_{Z \in Ch(X)} f'(Z)\right)\right]$$

$$= \left[f'(Y) + \frac{|Y|}{|X|}\left(\sum_{a \in A(X)} p(X; a)a - \sum_{Z \in Ch(X)} f'(Z)\right)\right]$$

$$= f'(Y) + \frac{|Y|}{|X|}\left(\mu(X) - \sum_{Z \in Ch(X)} f'(Z)\right). \qquad (10.28)$$

Hence, $\mu(Y)$, $Y \in Ch(X)$, can be computed from $\mu(X)$. Given a laminar family $\mathcal{X}$ with a set function f satisfying (10.19), we first execute line 1of LEXICOMIN to obtain f'. Then starting with $\mu(V) := f'(V)$, we compute $\mu(Y)$ from its parent X recursively by (10.28) to determine the mean value $\mu(\{u\})$ of each singleton set $\{u\} \in V$. Then mean vector ψ_f is given by setting $\psi_f(i) := \mu(i)$ for each $i \in V$.

For each set X, values $\mu(Y)$ for all children $Y \in Ch(X)$ can be computed in $O(|Ch(X)|)$ time by (10.28). The total time for computing the vector μ is $O(\sum_{X \in \mathcal{V}} |Ch(X)|) = O(n)$. Then the time complexity for computing ψ_f from a laminar family $\mathcal{X}$ is $O(n)$. Thus, we have the next result.

Theorem 10.35. *For a system (V, f) with an intersecting submodular and posimodular set function f on V, where $n = |V| \geq 2$, let $\mathcal{X}$ be the laminar family* *that satisfies* (10.19). *Then the mean vector* ψ_f *of all lexicographically minimal vectors in* $B_-(f)$ *can be computed from* $\mathcal{X}$ *in* $O(n)$ *time.*   □

10.6 Minimum Transversal in Set Systems

In this section, we consider a system (V, f, g) on a finite set V consisting two set functions $f : 2^V \rightarrow \Re$ and $g : 2^V \rightarrow \Re$, and we introduce the following problem:

$$\begin{array}{ll} \text{Minimize} & |R| \\ \text{subject to} & R \subseteq V \\ & f(X) \geq g(X) \text{ for all } X \subseteq V - R. \end{array} \qquad (10.29)$$

We call the function g a *demand function*. Throughout this section, submodular (resp. posimodular) set functions mean fully submodular (resp. fully posimodular) set functions unless stated otherwise.

Problem (10.29) can be regarded as a problem of finding a minimum transversal in a hypergraph associated with given set functions f and g. A vertex subset $X \subseteq V$ is called *deficient* if $f(X) < g(X)$. A deficient set X is called *minimal* if no proper subset X is deficient. Let $\mathcal{W}(f, g)$ denote the family of all minimal deficient sets of (V, f, g). Then the constraint in problem (10.29) is equivalent to

$$R \cap X \neq \emptyset \text{ for all } X \in \mathcal{W}(f, g). \qquad (10.30)$$

In other words, problem (10.29) finds a minimum transversal R of $\mathcal{W}(f, g)$.

We observe here that the source location problems in Sections 9.1.2 and 9.1.3 can be formulated as (10.29) and (10.30).

Example 10.36. In Section 9.1.2, a subset $R \subseteq V$ in an edge-weighted undirected graph $G = (V, E)$ in problem (9.6) is defined as a source if $\lambda(R, v; G) \geq r(v)$ for all $v \in V - R$ for a demand function $r : V \rightarrow \Re_+$ in G. The condition $\lambda(R, v; G) \geq r(v)$ is equivalent to $d(X; G) \geq r(v)$ for all $X \subseteq V - R$ with $v \in X$. Hence, the constraint in (9.6) can be restated as

$$d(X; G) \geq \max_{v \in X} r(v) \text{ for all nonempty } X \subseteq V - R,$$

and the problem of finding a minimum cardinality source R in (9.6) is problem (10.29) with $f(X) = d(X; G)$, $X \in 2^X$ and

$$g(X) = \begin{cases} \max_{v \in X} r(v) & \text{if } X \in 2^V - \{\emptyset\}, \\ 0 & \text{if } X = \emptyset. \end{cases} \qquad (10.31)$$

Moreover, after defining $\mathcal{C}(v) = \{X \subset V \mid v \in X, \ d(X; G) < r(v)\}$ in (9.7), we have observed that a source set is a subset $R \subseteq V$ satisfying

$$R \cap X \neq \emptyset \text{ for all } X \in \mathcal{W}$$

for $\mathcal{W} = \cup_{v \in V} \mathcal{C}(v)$, which has the same form as (10.30).   □

Note that the condition $\lambda(R, v; G) \geq r(v)$ for all $v \in V - R$ in problem (9.6) is also equivalent to $\lambda(x^*, v; G/R) \geq r(v)$ for all $v \in V(G) - \{x^*\}$, where G/R is the graph obtained from G by contracting R into a single vertex x^*.

Example 10.37. As an extension of problem (9.6), van den Heuvel and Johnson [306] introduced the external network problem, which, given edge-weighted undirected graph $G = (V, E)$ and a function $r : \binom{V}{2} \to \Re_+$, asks to find a minimum cardinality subset $R \subseteq V$ such that the graph G/R obtained by contracting R into a single vertex x^* satisfies

$$\lambda(u, v; G/R) \geq r(u, v) \text{ for all } u, v \in V - R,$$
$$\lambda(x^*, v; G/R) \geq r(u, v) \text{ for all } u \in R \text{ and } v \in V - R.$$

Then the problem of finding a minimum such subset R is problem (10.29) with $f(X) = d(X; G)$, $X \in 2^V$ and

$$g(X) = \begin{cases} \max_{u \in X, v \in V - X} r(u, v) & \text{if } X \in 2^V - \{\emptyset, V\}, \\ 0 & \text{if } X \in \{\emptyset, V\}. \end{cases} \tag{10.32}$$

$\square$

Example 10.38. In Section 9.1.3, a subset $R \subseteq V$ in an edge-weighted digraph $G = (V, E)$ is defined as a (k, ℓ)-source if $\lambda(R, v; G) \geq k$ for all $v \in V - R$, and $\lambda(v, R; G) \geq \ell$ for all $v \in V - R$ in (9.12). As observed in (9.13), a subset S is a (k, ℓ)-source if and only if

$$R \cap X \neq \emptyset \text{ for all } X \in \mathcal{E}_{k,\ell},$$

where $\mathcal{E}_{k,\ell}$ is the family of all subsets $X \subset V$ such that $d^-(X; G) < k$ or $d^+(X; G) < \ell$, and this constraint has the same form as (10.30). (For problem (9.12), finding functions f and g that represent the constraint in the form of (10.29) is not straightforward.) $\square$

As observed in Section 1.7, the transversal number $\tau(\mathcal{E})$ of a tree hypergraph $\mathcal{E}$ is equal to the matching number $\nu(\mathcal{E})$ of $\mathcal{E}$ by Theorem 1.50. Note that the number of minimal deficient sets may be exponential in $n = |V|$. Our main interest in this section is to know whether the hypergraph $\mathcal{W}(f, g)$ with a submodular or posimodular function f is a tree hypergraph. In Example 10.38, representing problem (9.12) in the form of (10.29) was not straightforward. However, we will see that there exists a representation by (10.29) with some pair of set functions f and g in Theorem 10.50 of this section.

The rest of this section is organized as follows. Section 10.6.1 shows that problem (10.29) for a fully submodular function f is intractable in general and that the hypergraph $\mathcal{W}(f, g)$ may not be a tree hypergraph. Section 10.6.2 reveals some structural properties of a posimodular function f, and Section 10.6.3 introduces a new class of set functions called *modulotone*. Based on this, Section 10.6.4 shows the hypergraph $\mathcal{W}(f, g)$ becomes a tree hypergraph if and only if f is posimodular and g is modulotone. Section 10.6.5 then describes an efficient algorithm for problem (10.29) with a submodular and posimodular function f and a modulotone function g with some special structure.

10.6.1 Deficient Sets in Submodular Systems

This section shows the hardness of problem (10.29) with a submodular function f and that $\mathcal{W}(f, g)$ may not be a tree hypergraph in general. We first prove that every graph $G = (V, E)$ can be realized as $\mathcal{W}(f, g)$ of a submodular function f and a uniform demand function g (i.e., $g(X) = g(Y)$ holds for all nonempty $X, Y \in 2^V$).

Lemma 10.39 ([286]). *Given an undirected graph $G = (V, E)$, there exist a submodular function $f : 2^V \to \Re$ and a uniform demand function $g : 2^V \to \Re$ such that*

$$E = \mathcal{W}(f, g). \qquad \square$$

Proof. Given an undirected graph $G = (V, E)$ and a real k, we define f and g as follows. Let g be a demand function given by $g(\emptyset) = 0$ and

$$g(X) = k \ \text{ for all nonempty } X \subseteq V. \tag{10.33}$$

For a subset $X \subseteq V$, let $E(X) = \{\{u, v\} \in E \mid \{u, v\} \subseteq X\}$. We define a set function $f : 2^V \to \Re$ on V by

$$f(X) = k - |E(X)|. \tag{10.34}$$

Then a subset X of V is deficient if and only if X contains at least one edge in E. It follows that the family $\mathcal{W}(f, g)$ of all minimal deficient sets is given by

$$\mathcal{W}(f, g) = \{\{u, v\} \mid \{u, v\} \in E\}. \tag{10.35}$$

We next show that f is submodular, which completes the proof. It is easy to see that $|E(X)| + |E(Y)| = |E(X) \cap E(Y)| + |E(X) \cup E(Y)| \leq |E(X \cap Y)| + |E(X \cup Y)|$ for arbitrary $X, Y \subseteq V$, since $E(X) \cap E(Y) = E(X \cap Y)$ and $E(X) \cup E(Y) \subseteq E(X \cup Y)$ hold. Hence, we have

$$
\begin{aligned}
f(X) + f(Y) &= (k - |E(X)|) + (k - |E(X)|) \\
&\geq (k - |E(X \cap Y)|) + (k - |E(X \cup Y)|) \\
&= f(X \cap Y) + f(X \cup Y),
\end{aligned}
$$

that is, f is submodular. $\qquad \square$

Lemma 10.40 ([286]). *There are a submodular function f and a uniform demand function g such that $\mathcal{W}(f, g)$ is not a tree hypergraph.* $\qquad \square$

Proof. We give an instance such that $\mathcal{W}(f, g)$ is not a tree hypergraph. Let $G = (V, E)$ be an undirected graph given by

$$V = \{v_1, v_2, v_3, v_4\} \quad \text{and} \quad E = \{\{v_1, v_2\}, \{v_2, v_3\}, \{v_3, v_4\}, \{v_4, v_1\}\},$$

that is, E forms a cycle of length 4. The family $\mathcal{W}(f, g)$ constructed in Lemma 10.39 is equal to E. Then the line graph L of $\mathcal{W}(f, g)$ has a cycle of length 4, which corresponds to E and this cycle has no chord. That is, L is not chordal and, hence, $\mathcal{W}(f, g)$ is not a tree hypergraph. $\qquad\square$

From Lemma 10.39, we have the following results.

Theorem 10.41 ([286]). *For a submodular function f, there is no oracle polynomial time algorithm for finding a minimum transversal of $\mathcal{W}(f, g)$ unless $P = NP$, even if the demand function g is uniform.* $\qquad\square$

Proof. We give a reduction from the minimum vertex cover problem to the problem of finding a minimum transversal of $\mathcal{W}(f, g)$. Given an undirected graph $G = (V, E)$, the minimum vertex cover problem is described as follows:

$$\begin{aligned}
\text{Minimize} \quad & |R| \\
\text{subject to} \quad & R \cap \{u, v\} \neq \emptyset \text{ for all } \{u, v\} \in E \qquad (10.36) \\
& R \subseteq V.
\end{aligned}$$

Lemma 10.39 says that there are a submodular function f and a uniform demand function g such that the family $\mathcal{W}(f, g)$ of all minimal deficient sets is E. Hence, a subset $R \subseteq V$ satisfies the constraint (10.36) if and only if R is a transversal of $\mathcal{W}(f, g)$. Since function value oracles to f and g in this case can be executed in polynomial time in $|V|$, we would have a polynomial time algorithm for the minimum vertex cover problem if there is an oracle polynomial time algorithm for finding a minimum transversal of $\mathcal{W}(f, g)$. This means that there exists no oracle polynomial time algorithm for finding a minimum transversal of $\mathcal{W}(f, g)$ unless $P = NP$, since the minimum vertex cover problem is known to be NP-hard (see [101]). $\qquad\square$

10.6.2 Structure of Posimodular Functions

For an element $v \in V$, we call a nonempty subsets X of V v-*solid* (with respect to f) if

$$v \in X \text{ and } f(X) < f(Y) \text{ for every proper subset } Y \subset X \text{ with } v \in Y.$$

For each $v \in V$ the family of all v-solid sets is denoted by $\mathcal{S}_v$. Define

$$\mathcal{S}(f) = \cup_{v \in V} \mathcal{S}_v.$$

This subsection proves the next theorem via a number of lemmas.

Theorem 10.42 ([286]). *If f is a posimodular set function, then $S(f)$ is a tree hypergraph.*   □

By Theorem 1.52 it suffices to show that the line graph of $S(f)$ is chordal and $S(f)$ has the Helly property.

Lemma 10.43 ([286]). *Let f be a posimodular set function on V. Let $X_0, X_1, \ldots, X_{h-1}, X_h \; (= X_0) \; (h \geq 3)$ be subsets of V such that $X_i \cap X_j \neq \emptyset$ if and only if i and j are consecutive integers. For each $i = 0, \ldots, h-1$, let $Y_i = X_i \cap X_{i+1}$. Then*

$$\sum_{i=0}^{h-1} f(X_i) \geq \sum_{i=0}^{h-1} f(Y_i)$$

holds.   □

Proof. By the posimodularity of f, we have

$$2\sum_{i=0}^{h-1} f(X_i) = \sum_{i=0}^{h-1}\{f(X_i) + f(X_{i+1})\}$$

$$\geq \sum_{i=0}^{h-1}\{f(X_i - X_{i+1}) + f(X_{i+1} - X_i)\}$$

$$= \sum_{i=0}^{h-1}\{f(X_{i+1} - X_i) + f(X_{i+1} - X_{i+2})\}$$

$$\geq \sum_{i=0}^{h-1}\{f(X_i \cap X_{i+1}) + f(X_{i+1} \cap X_{i+2})\}$$

$$= \sum_{i=0}^{h-1}\{f(Y_i) + f(Y_{i+1})\} \;\; = \;\; 2\sum_{i=0}^{h-1} f(Y_i),$$

where the second inequality follows from $(X_{i+1} - X_i) - (X_{i+1} - X_{i+2}) = X_{i+1} \cap X_{i+2}$ and $(X_{i+1} - X_{i+2}) - (X_{i+1} - X_i) = X_i \cap X_{i+1}$.   □

Lemma 10.44 ([286]). *Let f be a posimodular set function on V. Let $\mathcal{F} = \{X_1, \ldots, X_h\} \subseteq 2^V$ and $I = \{1, \ldots, h\}$. For each subset J of I, we define $Z_J = \bigcap\{X_j \mid j \in J\}$. If $\mathcal{F}$ is pairwise intersecting (i.e., $X_i \cap X_j \neq \emptyset$ for all $i, j \in I$) then*

$$\sum_{i \in I} f(X_i) \geq \sum_{i \in I} f(Z_{I\setminus\{i\}} - Z_I) \tag{10.37}$$

holds.   □

Proof. We proceed by induction on the size h of $\mathcal{F}$. First, in the case of $h = 2$, (10.37) is obtained directly from the posimodularity of f since $Z_{I\setminus\{1\}} - Z_I =$

$X_2 - X_1$ and $Z_{I\setminus\{2\}} - Z_I = X_1 - X_2$. Next, assuming the lemma for $h \leq \ell$, we consider the case for $h = \ell + 1$. Then we have

$$
\begin{aligned}
(h - 1) \sum_{i \in I} f(X_i) &= \sum_{i \in I} \sum_{j \in I \setminus \{i\}} f(X_j) \\
&\geq \sum_{i \in I} \sum_{j \in I \setminus \{i\}} f(Z_{I \setminus \{i,j\}} - Z_{I \setminus \{i\}}) \quad \text{(by induction)} \\
&= \sum_{i,j \in I : i < j} \{ f(Z_{I \setminus \{i,j\}} - Z_{I \setminus \{i\}}) + f(Z_{I \setminus \{i,j\}} - Z_{I \setminus \{j\}}) \} \\
&\geq \sum_{i,j \in I : i < j} \{ f(Z_{I \setminus \{i\}} - Z_I) + f(Z_{I \setminus \{j\}} - Z_I) \} \\
&= (h - 1) \sum_{i \in I} f(Z_{I \setminus \{i\}} - Z_I),
\end{aligned}
$$

where the second inequality follows from the posimodularity of f and the relation $(Z_{I \setminus \{i,j\}} - Z_{I \setminus \{i\}}) - (Z_{I \setminus \{i,j\}} - Z_{I \setminus \{j\}}) = (Z_{I \setminus \{i,j\}} - Z_{I \setminus \{i\}}) \cap Z_{I \setminus \{j\}} = Z_{I \setminus \{j\}} - Z_I$. □

Lemma 10.45 ([286]). *Let f be a posimodular set function on V, and for each subset $X \subseteq V$ define*

$$
A_X = \{ v \in X \mid X \in \mathcal{S}_v \}.
$$

If the intersection of two members X, Y of $\mathcal{S}(f)$ is nonempty, then A_X or A_Y is included in $X \cap Y$. □

Proof. We suppose that $X - Y$ and $Y - X$ are nonempty, since the lemma clearly holds if $X \subseteq Y$ or $Y \subseteq X$ holds. By the posimodularity, we have

$$
f(X) \geq f(X - Y) \quad \text{or} \quad f(Y) \geq f(Y - X),
$$

and by symmetry we may assume that $f(X) \geq f(X - Y)$. Then X cannot be v-solid for any $v \in X - Y$ since $X - Y$ is a nonempty proper subset of X. Therefore, all elements $v \in X$ such that $X \in \mathcal{S}_v$ belong to $X \cap Y$, i.e., $A_X \subseteq X \cap Y$. □

Lemma 10.46 ([286]). *Let f be a posimodular set function. Then the line graph L of $\mathcal{S}(f)$ is chordal.* □

Proof. Assuming that L is not chordal, we derive a contradiction. Let X_0, $X_1, \ldots, X_{h-1}, X_h (= X_0)$ be a chordless cycle in $\mathcal{S}(f)$ of length at least 4. For each $i = 0, \ldots, h - 1$, let $Y_i = X_i \cap X_{i+1}$. Then the assumption means that $Y_i \neq \emptyset$ for all $i = 0, \ldots, h - 1$ and $Y_i \cap Y_j = \emptyset$ if $|i - j| \geq 2$. It follows from Lemma 10.45 that

$$
A_{X_0} \subseteq Y_0 \quad \text{or} \quad A_{X_1} \subseteq Y_0
$$

holds. By symmetry, we may assume $A_{X_1} \subseteq Y_0$. Then Lemma 10.45 implies that $A_{X_2} \subseteq Y_1$ since $Y_0 \cap Y_1 = \emptyset$. By repeating this, we have

$$A_{X_{i+1}} \subseteq Y_i \quad \text{for} \quad i = 0, 1, \dots, h - 1.$$

From this,

$$f(Y_i) > f(X_{i+1}) \quad \text{for} \quad i = 0, 1, \dots, h - 1$$

since Y_i is a nonempty proper subset of X_{i+1} and $X_{i+1} \in \mathcal{S}_v$ holds for some $v \in Y_i$. Therefore, we have

$$\sum_{i=0}^{h-1} f(Y_i) > \sum_{i=0}^{h-1} f(X_i),$$

contradicting Lemma 10.43.   □

Lemma 10.47 ([286]). *Let f be a posimodular set function and consider a family $\mathcal{F} = \{X_1, \dots, X_h\} \subseteq \mathcal{S}(f)$ such that $X_i \cap X_j \neq \emptyset$ for all $i, j \in I = (\{1, \dots, h\})$. Then $\mathcal{F}$ has a member X_i such that $A_{X_i} \subseteq Z_I = (\cap_{i \in I} X_i)$.*   □

Proof. We prove by induction on the size h of $\mathcal{F}$. First, the lemma clearly holds from Lemma 10.45 when $h = 2$. Next, assuming the lemma statement for $h \leq \ell$, we consider the case of $h = \ell + 1$. We assume $A_{X_i} \not\subseteq Z_I$ for all $i \in I$, and we derive a contradiction. By the induction hypothesis and the assumption, for each $j \in I$, there exists $i(j) \in I \setminus \{j\}$ such that

$$A_{X_{i(j)}} \subseteq Z_{I \setminus \{j\}} \quad \text{and} \quad A_{X_{i(j)}} \cap (Z_{I \setminus \{j\}} - Z_I) \neq \emptyset.$$

Then

$$f(X_{i(j)}) < f(Z_{I \setminus \{j\}} - Z_I)$$

holds, since $Z_{I \setminus \{j\}} - Z_I$ is a nonempty proper subset of $X_{i(j)}$ and $X_{i(j)} \in \mathcal{S}_v$ holds for some $v \in Z_{I \setminus \{j\}} - Z_I$. Note that $i(j) \neq i(j')$ for $j \neq j'$, since otherwise we would have

$$A_{X_{i(j)}} = A_{X_{i(j')}} \subseteq Z_{I \setminus \{j\}} \cap Z_{I \setminus \{j'\}} = Z_I,$$

contradicting the assumption. Therefore, we have

$$\sum_{i \in I} f(X_i) < \sum_{i \in I} f(Z_{I \setminus \{i\}} - Z_I),$$

which contradicts Lemma 10.44.   □

Lemma 10.47 directly implies the following corollay.

Corollary 10.48 ([286]). *Let f be a posimodular set function. Then $\mathcal{S}(f)$ has the Helly property.*   □

Finally Lemma 10.46 and Corollary 10.48 establish Theorem 10.42.

10.6.3 Modulotone Set Functions

Let V be a finite set. We call a set function $g : 2^V \to \mathfrak{R}_+$ *modulotone* if every nonempty $X \subseteq V$ has an element $v_X \in X$ such that

$$g(Y) \geq g(X) \text{ for all } Y \subseteq X \text{ with } v_X \in Y.$$

Clearly a uniform set function g is modulotone. The next lemma says that set functions g introduced in Examples 10.36 and 10.37 are modulotone.

Lemma 10.49. *Let V be a finite set.*

(i) *Given a function $r : V \to \mathfrak{R}_+$, the set function $g : 2^V \to \mathfrak{R}_+$ defined from r by (10.31) is modulotone.*

(ii) *Given a function $r : V^2 \to \mathfrak{R}_+$, the set function $g : 2^V \to \mathfrak{R}_+$ defined from r by (10.32) is modulotone.* □

Proof. (i) Let $X \in 2^V - \{\emptyset\}$. Choose an element $v^* \in X$ with $r(v^*) = \max_{v \in X} r(v)$. Then, for any subset $Y \subseteq X$ with $v^* \in Y$, it holds that $g(X) = \max_{v \in X} r(v) = r(v^*) = \max_{v \in Y} r(v) = g(Y)$, as required.

(ii) Let $X \in 2^V - \{\emptyset, V\}$. Choose an ordered pair (u^*, v^*) such that $u^* \in X$, $v^* \in V - X$ and $r(u^*, v^*) = \max_{u \in X, \, v \in V - X} r(u, v)$. Then, for any subset $Y \subseteq X$ with $u^* \in Y$, it holds that $g(X) = r(u^*, v^*) \leq \max_{u \in Y, v \in V - Y} r(u, v) = g(Y)$, as required. □

10.6.4 Deficient Sets in Posimodular Systems

This section proves that any tree hypergraph $\mathcal{E} \subseteq 2^V$ is realized as $\mathcal{W}(f, g)$ for a posimodular function f and a modulotone demand function g. This provides a new characterization of tree hypergraphs.

A family $\mathcal{E} \subseteq 2^V$ of subsets of a finite set V is called a *Sperner family* if neither $E \subseteq E'$ nor $E' \subseteq E$ holds for any two distinct sets $E, E' \in \mathcal{E}$.

Theorem 10.50 ([286]). *A Sperner family $\mathcal{E} \subseteq 2^V$ is a tree hypergraph if and only if $\mathcal{E} = \mathcal{W}(f, g)$ for a posimodular function $f : 2^V \to \mathfrak{R}_+$ and a modulotone demand function $g : 2^V \to \mathfrak{R}_+$.* □

To prove the sufficiency, we first show

$$\mathcal{W}(f, g) \subseteq \mathcal{S}(f). \tag{10.38}$$

Let $X \in \mathcal{W}(f, g)$. Then $f(X) < g(X)$ and $f(Y) \geq g(Y)$ for all nonempty proper subsets Y of X. Since g is modulotone, there is an element $v \in X$ such that $g(Y) \geq g(X)$ for all $Y \subseteq X$ containing v. Therefore, we have $f(Y) \geq g(Y) \geq g(X) > f(X)$ for all proper subsets Y of X containing v; that is, X is v-solid and, hence, $X \in \mathcal{S}(f)$. This together with Theorem 10.42 proves the sufficiency.

To prove the necessity, we show that the next theorem tells how f and g satisfying $\mathcal{E} = \mathcal{W}(f, g)$ can be constructed.

Theorem 10.51 ([286]). *Given a Sperner family $\mathcal{E} \subseteq 2^V$, which is also a tree hypergraph, there is a weight function $w : \mathcal{E} \to \Re_+$ such that $\mathcal{E} = \mathcal{W}(f, g)$ holds for the two set functions $f, g : 2^V \to \Re_+$ constructed from $\mathcal{E}$ and w by*

$$f(X) = \sum \{w(E) \mid E \in \mathcal{E}, E \cap X \neq \emptyset, E - X \neq \emptyset\}, \qquad (10.39)$$

$$g(X) = \max_{v \in X} r(v), \qquad (10.40)$$

where $g(\emptyset) = 0$ and

$$r(v) = \sum \{w(E) \mid v \in E \in \mathcal{E}\}, \quad v \in V. \qquad (10.41)$$

$\square$

As observe in (10.3), the f of (10.39) is a cut function of hypergraph $\mathcal{E}$, which is symmetric and submodular and, hence, it is posimodular. By Lemma 10.49, $g : 2^V \to \Re_+$ is modulotone. We prove Theorem 10.51 by showing several claims in the following.

Claim 10.52. *For any weight function $w : \mathcal{E} \to \Re_+$, the f and g constructed by (10.39) and (10.40) have a property that each set $X \in \mathcal{W}(f, g)$ contains a set $E \in \mathcal{E}$.* $\square$

Proof. Let $X \in \mathcal{W}(f, g)$ and let $v \in X$ be an element such that $r(v) = g(X)$ (i.e., $r(v) = \max_{u \in X} r(u)$). Then we have $g(X) = r(v) \leq \sum \{w(E) \mid E \in \mathcal{E}, E \cap X \neq \emptyset\}$ by (10.41). Assume that no $E \in \mathcal{E}$ satisfies $E \subseteq X$. Then we have

$$f(X) = \sum \{w(E) \mid E \in \mathcal{E}, E \cap X \neq \emptyset\} \geq g(X),$$

implying that X is not a deficient set. Therefore, if $X \in \mathcal{W}(f, g)$ then it contains a set $E \in \mathcal{E}$. $\square$

Claim 10.52 tells that, if $E \in \mathcal{E}$ is deficient, then E is *minimal* deficient.

Let us assume that a Sperner family $\mathcal{E}$ is a tree hypergraph, and we let $|\mathcal{E}| = m$. Note that the line graph $L(\mathcal{E})$ of $\mathcal{E}$ is chordal by definition. Hence, $L(\mathcal{E})$ has a perfect elimination ordering $\sigma = (v_1, v_2, \ldots, v_m)$ (see Section 2.6 for the definition of perfect elimination orderings). Let E_i be the hyperedge of $\mathcal{E}$ corresponding to v_i. For each $i = 1, 2, \ldots, m$, the set of adjacent vertices v_j ($j > i$) of v_i induces a complete subgraph from $L(\mathcal{E})$ by the definition of perfect elimination orderings, and thereby the intersection of all E_j with $E_j \cap E_i \neq \emptyset$ and $j > i$ (as subsets of V) is nonempty, since $\mathcal{E}$ has the Helly property by Theorem 1.52. That is,

$$\bigcap \{E_j \cap E_i \mid E_j \cap E_i \neq \emptyset, \ j > i\} \neq \emptyset \qquad (10.42)$$

if there is an E_j satisfying $E_j \cap E_i \neq \emptyset$ and $j > i$. Let

$$\mathcal{E}_i^{\downarrow} = \{E_j \in \mathcal{E} \mid E_j \cap E_i \neq \emptyset, \ j < i\},$$
$$\mathcal{E}_i^{\uparrow} = \{E_j \in \mathcal{E} \mid E_j \cap E_i \neq \emptyset, \ j > i\}, \text{ and}$$
$$\mathcal{E}_i = \mathcal{E}_i^{\downarrow} \cup \mathcal{E}_i^{\uparrow}.$$

The following claim clearly follows from (10.42).

Claim 10.53. $\mathcal{E}_i^{\uparrow} \neq \emptyset$ implies that the intersection of all $E \in \mathcal{E}_i^{\uparrow}$ (as subsets of V) is nonempty; that is, $\bigcap \{E \cap E_i \mid E \in \mathcal{E}_i^{\uparrow}\} \neq \emptyset$. □

We define inductively the weight $w(E_i)$ from $i = 1$ to m by $w(E_1) := 1$, and

$$w(E_i) := \sum \{w(E) \mid E \in \mathcal{E}_i^{\downarrow}\} + 1. \tag{10.43}$$

For the functions f in (10.39) and g in (10.40) defined from this weight function w, we have the following claim.

Claim 10.54. Each $E_i \in \mathcal{E}$ is deficient. □

Proof. For a hyperedge $E_i \in \mathcal{E}$, we distinguish two cases: (i) $\mathcal{E}_i^{\uparrow} = \emptyset$ and (ii) $\mathcal{E}_i^{\uparrow} \neq \emptyset$.

(i) $\mathcal{E}_i^{\uparrow} = \emptyset$: From the definition of w, we have

$$f(E_i) = \sum \{w(E) \mid E \in \mathcal{E}_i^{\downarrow}\} < \sum \{w(E) \mid E \in \mathcal{E}_i^{\downarrow}\} + 1 = w(E_i) \leq g(E_i).$$

(ii) $\mathcal{E}_i^{\uparrow} \neq \emptyset$: From Claim 10.53, there is an element $v^* \in V$ with $v^* \in E_j \cap E_i$ for all $E_j \cap E_i \neq \emptyset$ $(j > i)$. Then we have

$$\begin{aligned}
g(E_i) &= \max_{v \in E_i} r(v) \\
&\geq r(v^*) \\
&= \sum \{w(E) \mid v^* \in E \in \mathcal{E}\} \\
&\geq w(E_i) + \sum \{w(E) \mid E \in \mathcal{E}_i^{\uparrow}\} \\
&= 1 + \sum \{w(E) \mid E \in \mathcal{E}_i^{\downarrow}\} + \sum \{w(E) \mid E \in \mathcal{E}_i^{\uparrow}\} \\
&> \sum \{w(E) \mid E \in \mathcal{E}_i\} \\
&= f(E_i).
\end{aligned}$$

For each of conditions (i) and (ii), we have $f(E_i) < g(E_i)$; that is, E_i is deficient. □

Claims 10.52 and 10.54 imply Theorem 10.51. This theorem tells that problem (10.29) with a posimodular function f and a modulotone function d is characterized by a problem of finding a minimum transversal R in a tree hypergraph. For the latter problem, we know that there is a min-max formula, and a minimum transversal R can be obtained in polynomial time in $n = |V|$ if a basic tree of the tree hypergraph is available, as observed in Section 1.7. However, finding a basic tree of the tree hypergraph corresponding to a given instance of problem (10.29) is another important task, and no efficient algorithm has been found for a posimodular function f and a modulotone function g. The next section shows that there exists an efficient algorithm for computing a basic tree if f is additionally assumed to be submodular and g has a special structure.

10.6.5 Deficient Sets in Submodular and Posimodular Systems

In this section, we assume that f is a posimodular and submodular function and g is a modulotone demand function, and we describe polynomial time algorithms for some cases of problem (10.29). We see by Theorem 10.50 that the family $\mathcal{W}(f, g)$ of all minimal deficient sets is a tree hypergraph. Theorem 1.53 tells that, given a tree hypergraph with an explicit list of hyperedges, we can compute a basic tree in polynomial time in the number of hyperedges. However, $|\mathcal{W}(f, g)|$ can be exponential in $|V|$. In this case, we use Lemma 1.54 to choose a small subset of $\mathcal{W}(f, g)$ that still provides a basic tree for $\mathcal{W}(f, g)$.

s-Avoiding Solid Sets

Given $s, t \in V$ with $s \neq t$, an s-avoiding t-solid set X is defined as a t-solid subset of $V - \{s\}$. An s-avoiding t-solid set X is called maximal if X is not included in any other s-avoiding t-solid set. For each $s \in V$, let $S_t^{(s)}$ be the family of maximal s-avoiding t-solid sets for $t \in V - \{s\}$ and let $S^{(s)} = \cup_{t \in V - s} S_t^{(s)}$ and $S'(f) = \cup_{s \in V} S^{(s)}$.

To compute $S'(f)$, we minimize the submodular function f to find a subset X of $V - s$ containing t such that

$$f(X) = \min\{f(Y) \mid t \in Y \subseteq V - \{s\}\}. \qquad (10.44)$$

From the submodularity of f, the minimizer sets X are closed under taking union and intersection (as observed in Lemma 1.3 for the case where f is a cut function). Let N_t^s denote the unique minimal member in the family of X satisfying (10.44).

Lemma 10.55 ([286]). *Given a submodular set function f on V, let N_t^s be defined as before.*

  (i) *For two distinct $s, t \in V$, a maximal s-avoiding t-solid set is unique and is given by N_t^s.*
  (ii) *$|S'(f)| \leq n(n - 1)$.*   □

Proof. (i) Let N be a maximal s-avoiding t-solid set. We first prove its uniqueness. By the submodularity of f, any $X \subseteq V - \{s\}$ with $t \in X \not\subseteq N$ satisfies

$$f(X) + f(N) \geq f(X \cap N) + f(X \cup N) \geq f(X \cap N) + f(N),$$

implying that $f(X) \geq f(X \cap N)$ holds for a nonempty proper subset $X \cap N$ of X containing t and, therefore, X is not t-solid. This proves that N is unique. Next we show that $N = N_t^s$ is a maximal s-avoiding t-solid set. Since N_t^s is the unique minimal minimizer of (10.44), any proper subset Y of N_t^s with $t \in Y$ satisfies $f(Y) > f(N_t^s)$, implying that N_t^s is an s-avoiding t-solid set. Since N_t^s is a minimizer of (10.44), any proper superset $Z \subseteq V - s$ of N_t^s satisfies $f(N_t^s) \leq f(Z)$ and cannot be an s-avoiding t-solid set, indicating the maximality of N_t^s.

(ii) Immediate from condition (i) by considering all combinations of s and t.   □

Based on this, the family $\mathcal{S}^{(s)}$ can be obtained by computing sets N_t^s for all $t \in V - \{s\}$.

We can compute the unique minimal minimizer set for a submodular function by using strongly polynomial algorithms for submodular function minimization [152, 288]. For example, the algorithm by Schrijver [288] outputs the minimal minimizer set and that by Iwata, Fleischer, and Fujishige [152] outputs the maximal minimizer set. In the case of the latter algorithm, we can obtain the minimal minimizer set by executing for the submodular function f' defined by $f'(X) = f(V - X)$ for all $X \subseteq V$.

It is easy to see that, to find the minimal minimizer set N_t^s for (10.44), the preceding algorithms can be applied to the function $f' : 2^{V-\{s,t\}} \to \Re$ defined by $f'(X) = f(X \cup \{t\})$ for all $X \subseteq V - \{s, t\}$. Note that this f' is submodular as well.

Computing a Basic Tree for $\mathcal{S}(f)$

By Lemma 10.55(ii), $|\mathcal{S}'(f)| = O(n^2)$ holds. Therefore, one can compute a basic tree T for $\mathcal{S}'(f)$ in polynomial time by using Theorem 1.53. Moreover, this T is also a basic tree for $\mathcal{S}(f)$ by Lemma 1.54.

Lemma 10.56 ([286]). *If T is a basic tree for $\mathcal{S}'(f)$, then T is basic for $\mathcal{S}(f)$.* □

Computing a Minimum Transversal

Now we consider how to solve problem (10.29), which is equivalent to the problem of computing a minimum transversal R of $\mathcal{W}(f, g)$ (i.e., a minimum size set $R \subseteq V$ such that $R \cap X \neq \emptyset$ for all $X \in \mathcal{W}(f, g)$).

Property (10.38) tells that $\mathcal{W}(f, g)$ is a tree hypergraph and a basic tree T for $\mathcal{S}(f)$ is basic for $\mathcal{W}(f, g)$. It also follows from Lemma 10.56 that a basic tree T for $\mathcal{W}(f, g)$ can be computed in polynomial time. By Lemma 1.51, the MINTRANSVERSAL algorithm in Section 1.7 outputs a minimum transversal of $\mathcal{W}(f, g)$.

Transversal Check

Here we consider how to check whether a given set $R \subseteq V$ is a transversal when the problem has a submodular and posimodular function f and a modulotone demand function g.

Given a function $r : V^2 \to \mathfrak{R}_+$, we consider a demand function $g : 2^V \to \mathfrak{R}_+$ defined by (10.32). By Lemma 10.49, g is modulotone. Then a subset $R \subseteq V$ is a transversal; that is, $f(X) \geq g(X)$ for all $X \subseteq V - R$, if and only if

$$\min\{f(X) \mid u \in X \subseteq V - (R \cup \{v\})\} \geq r(u, v) \qquad (10.45)$$

holds for each ordered pair (u, v) of elements such that $u \in V - R$ and $v \in V - \{u\}$.

The left-hand side of (10.45) gives the minimum value of the set function $f' : 2^{V-(R \cup \{u,v\})} \to \mathfrak{R}_+$ defined by

$$f'(X) = f(X \cup \{u\}) \qquad (10.46)$$

for all $X \subseteq V - (R \cup \{u, v\})$. The resulting function f' is submodular [92]. Therefore, we can check whether R is a transversal by (10.45) by minimizing the submodular function f' for every ordered pair (u, v) such that $u \in V - R$ and $v \in V - \{u\}$. As we mentioned in Section 10.2.1, strongly polynomial algorithms for submodular function minimization are known [152, 288].

Given a function $r : V \to \mathfrak{R}_+$ on a finite set V, the demand function $g : 2^V \to \mathfrak{R}_+$ given by (10.31) is also modulotone by Lemma 10.49. Analogously, a subset $R \subseteq V$ is a transversal; that is, $f(X) \geq g(X)$ for all $X \subseteq V - R$ if and only if

$$\min\{f(X) \mid u \in X \subseteq V - R\} \geq r(u) \qquad (10.47)$$

holds for each element $u \in V - R$, and we can test whether a given R is a transversal or not by minimizing a submodular function.

The algorithm just outlined for finding a minimum set $R \subseteq V$ to problem (10.29) is summarized as follows.

Algorithm TRANSVERSAL
Input: A posimodular and submodular function $f : 2^V \to \mathfrak{R}_+$ and
    a modulotone demand function $g : 2^V \to \mathfrak{R}_+$ with $g(\emptyset) = 0$.
Output: A minimum set $R \subseteq V$ such that $f(X) \geq g(X)$ for each $X \subseteq V - R$.
Step 1. Compute the family $\mathcal{S}'(f) = \cup_{s \in V} \mathcal{S}^{(s)}$ by Lemma 10.55;
Step 2. Compute a basic tree T for the tree hypergraph $\mathcal{S}'(f)$ by Lemma 1.53;
       /* T is also basic tree for the family $\mathcal{W}(f, g)$ of all minimal deficient
       sets */
Step 3. Compute a minimum transversal R of tree hypergraph $\mathcal{W}(f, g)$ from T
       by using the MINTRANSVERSAL algorithm in Section 1.7.

Let $SFM(n)$ denote the time complexity for minimizing a submodular function on 2^V, where $n = |V|$, and let $C^*(n)$ denote the time complexity for deciding whether a set $R \subseteq V$ is a transversal of $\mathcal{W}(f, g)$.

Theorem 10.57. *Given a posimodular and submodular function $f : 2^V \to \mathfrak{R}_+$ and a modulotone demand function $g : 2^V \to \mathfrak{R}_+$ with $g(\emptyset) = 0$, the* TRANSVER-SAL *algorithm correctly finds a minimum set $R \subseteq V$ such that $f(X) \geq g(X)$*

for all $X \subseteq V - R$, *in time complexity of* $O(n^2 SFM(n) + nC^*(n))$, *which is* $O(n^3 SFM(n))$ *if g is given as* (10.32) *or* (10.31). $\qquad\qquad\square$

Proof. As mentioned after Lemma 10.55, the unique maximal s-avoiding t-solid set for $s \in V$ and $t \in V - \{s\}$ can be obtained by executing an algorithm for the submodular function minimization once. For each $s \in V$, the family $\mathcal{S}^{(s)}$ of maximal s-avoiding t-solid sets for all $t \in V - \{s\}$ can be computed in $O(nSFM(n))$ time. Hence, the total time of Step 1 to compute $\mathcal{S}'(f) = \cup_{s \in V}\mathcal{S}^{(s)}$ is $O(n^2 SFM(n))$. To compute a basic tree for $\mathcal{S}'(f)$, we first set a weight function c in Section 10.6.5, and then we construct a maximum weight spanning tree T, which will be a basic tree for $\mathcal{S}'(f)$ by Theorem 1.53. The first and second part can be executed in $O(n^2|\mathcal{S}'(f)|)$ and $O(n^2)$ time, respectively (see [91] for an $O(m + n \log n) = O(n^2)$ time algorithm for computing an optimal spanning tree). Then the total time of Step 2 is $O(n^4)$ time, since $|\mathcal{S}'(f)| = O(n^2)$. A minimum transversal R of a tree hypergraph $\mathcal{W}(f, g)$ with its basic tree T can be found by applying the MINTRANSVERSAL algorithm in Section 1.7. Then Step 3 can be done in $O(nC^*(n))$ time by Theorem 1.51. Hence, the total time of the entire algorithm is $O(n^2 SFM(n) + nC^*(n))$.

As mentioned in Section 10.6.5, $C^*(n)$ is $O(n^2 SFM(n))$ if g is given as (10.32) or (10.31). Then, in this case, the total time is $O(n^3 SFM(n))$. $\qquad\qquad\square$

Bibliography

[1] A. V. Aho, J. E. Hopcroft, and J. D. Ullman, *Data Structures and Algorithms*, Addison-Wesley, 1983.

[2] R. K. Ahuja, T. L. Magnanti, and J. B. Orlin, Network flows, in *Optimization, Handbooks in Management Science and Operations Research*, edited by G. L. Nemhauser, A. H. G. Rinnooy Kan, and M. J. Todd, Vol. 1, Chap. IV, pp. 211–369. North-Holland, 1989.

[3] R. K. Ahuja, T. L. Magnanti, and J. B. Orlin, *Network Flows: Theory, Algorithms, and Applications*, Prentice-Hall, Englewood Cliffs, NJ, 1993.

[4] S. Alstrup, J. Holm, K. Lichtenberg, and M. Thorup, *Maintaining information in fully-dynamic trees with top trees*, CoRR cs.DS/0310065, 2003.

[5] K. Arata, S. Iwata, K. Makino, and S. Fujishige, Locating sources to meet flow demands in undirected networks, *J. Algorithms*, **42** (2002), 54–68.

[6] S. R. Arikati and K. Mehlhorn, A correctness certificate for the Stoer-Wagner min-cut algorithm, *Inform. Process. Lett.*, **70** (1999), 251–254.

[7] G. Ausiello, P. Crescenzi, G. Gambosi, V. Kann, A. Marchetti-Spaccamela, and M. Protasi, *Complexity and Approximation: Combinatorial Optimization Problems and Their Approximability Properties*, Springer, Berlin, 1999.

[8] M. Baïou, F. Barahona, and A. R. Mahjoub, Separation of partition inequalities, *Math. Oper. Res.* **25**:2 (1999), 243–254.

[9] M. O. Ball and J. S. Provan, Calculating bounds on reachability in computer networks, *Networks* **18** (1988), 1–12.

[10] J. Bang-Jensen and G. Gutin, *Digraphs: Theory, Algorithms and Applications*, Springer-Verlag, 2002.

[11] J. Bang-Jensen and B. Jackson, Augmenting hypergraphs by edges of size two, *Math. Progr.* **B-84** (1999), 467–482.

[12] J. Bang-Jensen and T. Jordán, Edge-connectivity augmentation preserving simplicity, *SIAM J. Disc. Math.*, **11** (1998), 603–623.

[13] J. Bang-Jensen, H. N. Gabow, T. Jordán, and Z. Szigeti, Edge-connectivity augmentation with partition constraints, *SIAM J. Disc. Math.*, **12** (1999), 160–207.

[14] M. Bárász, J. Becker, and A. Frank, An algorithm for source location in directed graphs, *Oper. Res. Lett.* **33** (2005), 221–230.

[15] J. F. Bard, G. Kontoravdis, and G. Yu, A branch-and-cut procedure for the vehicle routing problem with time windows, *Transportation Science* **36**:2 (2002), 250–269.

[16] A. A. Benczúr, Counterexamples for directed and node capacitated cut-trees, *SIAM J. Comput.* **24** (1995), 505–510.

[17] A. A. Benczúr, A representation of cuts within 6/5 times the edge connectivity with applications, *Proc. 36th IEEE Symp. Found. Comp. Sci.*, 1995, pp. 92–102.

357

[18]   A. Benczúr and A. Frank, Covering symmetric supermodular functions by graphs, *Math. Progr.* **B-84** (1999), 483–504.

[19]   A. A. Benczúr and D. R. Karger, Approximate *s-t* min-cuts in $\tilde{O}(n^2)$ time, *Proc. 28th ACM Symp. Theory Computing*, 1996, pp. 47–55.

[20]   A. A. Benczúr and D. R. Karger, Augmenting undirected edge connectivity in $\tilde{O}(n^2)$ time, *J. Algorithms* **37** (2000), 2–36.

[21]   A. A. Benczúr and L. Végh, Primal-dual approach for directed vertex connectivity augmentation and generalizations, Proc. *16th ACM-SIAM Symp. on Discrete Algorithms*, 2005, pp. 186–194 (see EGRES TR-2005-06 the Egerváry Research Group, Budapest, Hungary, for the full version).

[22]   S. W. Bent, D. D. Sleator, and R. E. Tarjan, Biased search tree, *SIAM J. Comput.* **14** (1985), 545–568.

[23]   A. R. Berg and T. Jordán, Sparse certificates and removable cycles in ℓ-mixed p-connected graphs, *Oper. Res. Lett.* **33** (2005), 111–114.

[24]   A. R. Berg and T. Jordán, Two-connected orientations of Eulerian graphs, *J. Graph Theory* **52** (2006), 230–242.

[25]   A. R. Berg, B. Jackson, and T. Jordán, Highly edge-connected detachments of graphs and digraphs, *J. Graph Theory* **43** (2003), 67–77.

[26]   A. Bernáth, A note on the directed source location algorithm, Egerváry Research Report 2004–12, 2004.

[27]   R. E. Bixby, The minimum number of edges and vertices in a graph with edge connectivity n and m n-bonds, *Networks* **5** (1975), 253–298.

[28]   R. A. Botafogo, Cluster analysis for hypertext systems, *Proceedings of the 16th Annual International ACM SIGIR Conference on Research and Development in Information Retrieval*, Pittsburgh, PA, 1993, pp. 116–125.

[29]   A. Brandstädt, V. B. Le, and J. P. Spinrad, *Graph Classes: A Survey*, SIAM Monographs on Discrete Mathematics and Applications, SIAM, Philadelphia, 1999.

[30]   G.-R. Cai and Y.-G. Sun, The minimum augmentation of any graph to k-edge-connected graph, *Networks* **19** (1989), 151–172.

[31]   T. F. Chan, J. Cong, T. Kong, and J. R. Shinnerl, Multilevel optimization for large-scale circuit placement, *Proceedings of the 2000 IEEE International Conference on Computer-Aided Design, 2000*, San Jose, CA, 2000, pp. 171–176.

[32]   L. S. Chandran and L. S. Ram, On the number of minimum cuts in a graph, *Lect. Notes Comp. Sci.*, **2387**, Springer-Verlag, *Proc. 8th International Computing and Combinatorics Conference*, 2002, pp. 220–229.

[33]   G. Chartrand and L. Lesniak, *Graphs and Digraphs*, 4th edition, Chapman & Hall, 2004.

[34]   S. Chatterjee, J. R. Gilbert, R. Schreiber, and T. Sheffler, Array distribution in data-parallel programs, *Languages and Compliers for Parallel Computing, Lect. Notes Comp. Sci.* **896**, Springer-Verlag, 1994.

[35]   C. S. Chekuri, A. V. Goldberg, D. R. Karger, M. S. Levine, and C. Stein, Experimental study of minimum cut algorithms, *Proc. 8th Annual ACM-SIAM Symposium on Discrete Algorithms*, 1997, pp. 324–333.

[36]   E. Cheng, Edge-augmentation of hypergraphs, *Math. Progr.* **B-84** (1999), 443–466.

[37]   E. Cheng and T. Jordán, Successive edge-connectivity augmentation problems, *Math. Progr.* **B-84** (1999), 577–594.

[38]   J. Cheriyan and S. N. Maheshwari, Finding nonseparating induced cycles and independent spanning trees in 3-connected graphs, *J. Algorithms*, **9** (1988), 507–537.

[39]   J. Cheriyan and S. N. Maheshwari, Analysis of preflow push algorithms for maximum network flow, *SIAM J. Comput.* **18** (1989), 1057–1086.

[40]   J. Cheriyan and J. H. Reif, Directed $s - t$ numberings, rubber bands, and testing digraph k-vertex connectivity, *Proc. 3rd ACM-SIAM Symp. on Discrete Algorithms*, Orlando, FL, 1992, pp. 335–344.

[41]   J. Cheriyan and R. Thurimella, Algorithms for parallel k-vertex connectivity and sparse certificates, *Proc. 23rd ACM Symp. Theory of Computing*, New Orleans, LA, 1991, pp. 391–401.

[42] J. Cheriyan and R. Thurimella, Fast algorithms for k-shredders and k-node connectivity augmentation, *J. Algorithms* **33** (1999), 15–50.

[43] J. Cheriyan, M.-Y. Kao, and R. Thurimella, Scan-first search and sparse certificates: An improved parallel algorithm for k-vertex connectivity, *SIAM J. Comput.* **22** (1993), 157–174.

[44] J. Cheriyan, S. Vempla, and A. Vetta, An approximation algorithm for the minimum-cost k-vertex connected subgraph, *SIAM J. Comput.*, **32**:4 (2003), 1050–1055.

[45] C. J. Colbourn, *The Combinatorics of Network Reliability*, Oxford University Press, New York, Oxford, 1987.

[46] J. Cong and S. K. Lim, Edge separability based circuit clustering with application to circuit partitioning, *Proceedings of Asia and South Pacific Design Automation Conference 2000*, Yokohama, Japan, 2000, pp. 429–434.

[47] A. Corberan, A. N. Letchford, and J. M. Sanchis, A cutting plane algorithm for the general routing problem, *Math. Progr.* **A-90**:2 (2001), 291–316.

[48] T. H. Cormen, C. E. Leiserson, R. L. Rivest, and C. Stein, *Introduction to Algorithms*, 2nd edition, MIT Press and McGraw-Hill Book Company, 2001.

[49] W. H. Cunningham, Optimal attack and reinforcement of a network, *J. Assoc. Comput. Mach.* **32** (1985), 549–561.

[50] W. H. Cunningham and A. Frank, A primal-dual algorithm for submodular flows, *Math. Oper. Res.* **10** (1985), 251–262.

[51] S. Curran, O. Lee, and X. Yu, Chain decompositions and independent trees in 4-connected graphs, *Proc. 14th ACM-SIAM Symp. on Discrete Algorithms*, 2003, pp. 186–191.

[52] R. Diestel, *Graph Theory*, Springer-Verlag, New York, 1997.

[53] E. A. Dinic, Algorithm for solution of a problem of maximum flow in a network with power estimation, *Soviet Math. Dokl.* **11** (1970), 1277–1280.

[54] E. A. Dinits, A. V. Karzanov, and M. V. Lomonosov, On the structure of a family of minimal weighted cuts in a graph, in *Studies in Discrete Optimization* (in Russian) edited by A. A. Fridman, Nauka, Moscow, 1976, pp. 290–306.

[55] E. A. Dinits and Z. Nutov, Finding minimum weight k-vertex connected spanning subgraphs: Approximation algorithms with factor 2 for $k = 3$ and factor 3 for $k = 4, 5$, *Lect. Notes Comp. Sci.* **1203**, Springer-Verlag, *Proc. 3rd Italian Conf. on Algorithms and Complexity*, 1997, pp. 13–24.

[56] P. Duchet, Hypergraphs, in *Handbook of Combinatorics*, edited by R. Graham, M. Grötschel, and L. Lovász, Elsevier, Amsterdam, 1995, pp. 381–432.

[57] J. Edmonds, Submodular functions, matroids and certain polyhedra, *Calgary International Conf. on Combinatorial Structures and their Applications*, Gordon and Breach, New York, 1969, pp. 69–87.

[58] J. Edmonds, Matroids, submodular functions, and certain polyhedra, in *Combinatorial Structures and Their Applications*, edited by R. K. Guy, H. Hanani, N. Sauer, and J. Schönheim, Gordon and Breach, New York, 1970, pp. 69–87.

[59] J. Edmonds, Edge-disjoint branchings, in *Combinatorial Algorithms*, edited by R. Rustin, Algorithmics Press, New York, 1972, pp. 91–96.

[60] J. Edmonds and R. Giles, A min-max relation for submodular functions on graphs, *Ann. Discrete Math.* **1** (1977), 185–204.

[61] J. Edmonds and R. M. Karp, Theoretical improvements in algorithmic efficiency for network flow problems, *J. Assoc. Comput. Mach.* **19** (1972), 248–264.

[62] Y. Egawa, A. Kaneko, and M. Matsumoto, A mixed version of Menger's theorem, *Combinatorica*, **11**:1 (1991), 71–74.

[63] P. Elias, A. Feinstein, and C. F. Shannon, A note on the maximum flow through a network, *IRE Trans. Inform. Theory* **2** (1956), 117–119.

[64] K. P. Eswaran and R. E. Tarjan, Augmentation problems, *SIAM J. Comput.* **5** (1976), 653–665.

[65] S. Even, An algorithm for determining whether the connectivity of a graph is at least k, *SIAM J. Comput.* **4** (1975), 393–396.

[66] S. Even and R. E. Tarjan, Network flow and testing graph connectivity, *SIAM J. Comput.* **4** (1975), 507–518.

[67] S. Even, G. Itkis, and S. Rajsbaum, On mixed connectivity certificates, *Theoret. Comp. Sci.* **203** (1998), 253–269.

[68] S. Fialko and P. Mutzel, A new approximation algorithm for the planar augmentation problem, *Proc. of 9th Annual ACM-SIAM Symposium on Discrete Algorithms*, 1998, pp. 260–269.

[69] B. Fleiner, Detachments of vertices of graphs preserving edge-connectivity, *SIAM J. Discr. Math.* **18**:3 (2005), 581–591.

[70] T. Fleiner and T. Jordán, Coverings and structure of crossing families, *Math. Progr.* **B-84** (1999), 505–518.

[71] L. L. Fleischer, Building chain and cactus representations of all minimum cuts from Hao-Orlin in the same asymptotic run time, *J. Algorithms* **33** (1999), 51–72.

[72] L. R. Ford and D. R. Fulkerson, Maximal flow through a network, *Can. J. Math.* **8** (1956), 399–404.

[73] L. R. Ford and D. R. Fulkerson, *Flows in Networks*, Princeton Univ. Press, Princeton, NJ, 1962.

[74] A. Frank, Some polynomial algorithms for certain graphs and hypergraphs, in *Proceedings of the Fifth British Combinatorial Conference*, edited by C. Nash-Williams, and J. Sheehan, Congressus Numerantium XV, pp. 211–226.

[75] A. Frank, A weighted matroid intersection algorithm, *J. Algorithms*, **2** (1981), 328–336.

[76] A. Frank, Finding feasible vectors of Edmonds-Giles polyhedra, *J. Combinatorial Theory*, **B-36** (1984), 221–239.

[77] A. Frank, On connectivity properties of Eulerian digraphs, in *Graph Theory in Memory of G. A. Dirac, Ann. Discrete Math.* **41**, North-Holland, Amsterdam, 1989, pp. 179–194.

[78] A. Frank, Augmenting graphs to meet edge-connectivity requirements, *SIAM J. Discrete Math.* **5** (1992), 25–53.

[79] A. Frank, On a theorem of Mader, *Discrete Math.* **101** (1992), 49–57.

[80] A. Frank, Applications of submodular functions, in *Surveys in Combinatorics*, edited by K. Walker, *London Math. Soc. Lect. Notes*, **187** 1993, pp. 85–136.

[81] A. Frank, Connectivity augmentation problems in network design, in *Mathematical Programming: State of the Art*, edited by J. R. Birge and K. G. Murty, The University of Michigan, Ann Arbor, MI, 1994, pp. 34–63.

[82] A. Frank, On the edge-connectivity algorithm of Nagamochi and Ibaraki, Laboratoire Artemis, IMAG, Université J. Fourier, Grenoble, March, 1994.

[83] A. Frank, Connectivity and network flows, in *Handbook of Combinatorics*, edited by R. Graham, M. Grötschel, and L. Lovász, Elsevier, Amsterdam, 1995, pp. 111–177.

[84] A. Frank and T. Jordán, Minimal edge-coverings of pairs of sets, *J. Combinatorial Theory* **B-65** (1995), 73–110.

[85] A. Frank and T. Jordán, Directed vertex-connectivity augmentation, *Math. Progr.* **B-84** (1999), 537–554.

[86] A. Frank and L. Szegö, Constructive characterizations for packing and covering with trees, *Discrete Appl. Math.* **131** (2003), 347–371.

[87] A. Frank and É. Tardos, Generalized polymatroids and submodular flows, *Math. Progr.* **42** (1988), 489–563.

[88] A. Frank and É. Tardos, An application of submodular flows, *Linear Algebra Appl.* **114/115** (1989), 320–348.

[89] A. Frank, T. Ibaraki, and H. Nagamochi, On sparse subgraphs preserving connectivity properties, *J. Graph Theory* **17** (1993), 275–281.

[90] A. Frank, T. Király, and Z. Király, On the orientation of graphs and hypergraphs, *Discrete Appl. Math.* **131** (2003), 489–563.

[91] M. L. Fredman and R. E. Tarjan, Fibonacci heaps and their uses in improved network optimization algorithms, *J. Assoc. Comp. Mach.* **34** (1987), 596–615.

[92] S. Fujishige, *Submodular Functions and Optimization*, North-Holland, Amsterdam, 1991.

[93]   S. Fujishige, Another simple proof of the validity of Nagamochi and Ibaraki's mincut algorithm and Queyranne's extension to symmetric submodular function minimization, *J. Oper. Res. Soc. Jpn.* **41** (1998), 626–628.

[94]   S. Fujishige, A laminarity property of the polyhedron described by a weakly posimodular set function, *Discrete Appl. Math.* **100**:1-2 (2000), 123–126.

[95]   S. Fujishige, A maximum flow algorithm using MA ordering, *Oper. Res. Lett.* **31** (2003), 176–178.

[96]   H. N. Gabow, A matroid approach to finding edge connectivity and packing arborescences, *Proc. 23rd ACM Symp. Theory of Computing*, New Orleans, LA, 1991, pp. 112–122.

[97]   H. N. Gabow, Efficient splitting off algorithms for graphs, *Proc. 26th ACM Symposium on Theory of Computing*, 1994, pp. 696–705.

[98]   H. N. Gabow, Using expander graphs to find vertex connectivity, *Proc. 41st IEEE Symp. Found. Comp. Sci.*, 2000, pp. 410–420.

[99]   H. N. Gabow and T. Jordán, How to make a square grid framework with cables rigid, *SIAM J. Comput.* **30**:2 (2000), 649–680.

[100] Z. Galil and G. F. Italiano, Reducing edge connectivity to vertex connectivity, *SIGACT News*, **22** (1991), 57–61.

[101] M. R. Gary and D. S. Johnson, *Computers and Intractability: A Guide to the Theory of NP-completeness*, Freeman, San Francisco, 1978.

[102] Y. Gdalyahu, D. Weinshall, and M. Werman, Self-organization in vision: Stochastic clustering for image segmentation, perceptual grouping, and image database organization, *IEEE Trans. Pattern Anal. Mach. Intell.* **23**:10 (2001), 1053–1074.

[103] A. Goldberg and R. E. Tarjan, A new approach to the maximum flow problem, *J. ACM*, **35** (1988), 921–940.

[104] A. Goldberg and K. Tsioutsiouliklis, Cut tree algorithms: An experimental study, *J. Algorithms*, **38** (2001), 51–83.

[105] A. V. Goldberg and S. Rao, Flows in undirected unit capacity networks, *SIAM J. Discrete Math.*, **12** (1999), 1–5.

[106] O. Goldschmidt and D. S. Hochbaum, Polynomial algorithm for the *k*-cut problem for fixed *k*, *Math. Oper. Res.* **19** (1994), 24–37.

[107] R. E. Gomory and T. C. Hu, Multi-terminal network flows, *SIAM J. Appl. Math.*, **9** (1961), 551–570.

[108] M. Grötschel, L. Lovász, and A. Schrijver, *Geometric Algorithms and Combinatorial Optimization*, Springer, Berlin, 1988.

[109] D. Gusfield, Connectivity and edge-disjoint spanning trees. *Inf. Process. Lett.* **16** (1983), 87–89.

[110] D. Gusfield, Optimal mixed graph augmentation, *SIAM J. Comput.* **16** (1987), 599–612.

[111] H. W. Hamacher, J.-C. Picard, and M. Queyranne, Ranking the cuts and cut-sets of a network, *Ann. Discrete Appl. Math.* **19** (1984), 183–200.

[112] H. W. Hamacher, J.-C. Picard, and M. Queyranne, On finding the *K* best cuts in a network, *Oper. Res. Lett.* **2** (1984), 303–305.

[113] J. Hao and J. B. Orlin, A faster algorithm for finding the minimum cut in a directed graph, *J. Algorithms*, **17** (1994), 424–446.

[114] E. Hartuv and R. Shamir, A clustering algorithm based on graph connectivity, *Inform. Process. Lett.* **76** (2000), 175–181.

[115] E. Hartuv, A. Schmitt, J. Lange, S. Meier-Ewert, H. Lehrach, and R. Shamir, An algorithm for clustering cDNAs for gene expression analysis, *Proc. Third Annual ACM International Conference on Research in Computational Molecular Biology*, Lyon, France, 1999, pp. 188–197.

[116] E. Hartuv, A. Schmitt, J. Lange, S. Meier-Ewert, H. Lehrach, and R. Shamir, An algorithm for clustering cDNA fingerprints, *Genomics* (2000), 249–259.

[117] T. Hasunuma, Completely independent spanning trees in the underlying graph of a line digraph, *Discrete Math.* **234** (2001), 149–157.

[118] T. Hasunuma, Completely independent spanning trees in maximal planar graphs, *Lect. Notes Comp. Sci.* **2573**, Springer-Verlag, *Proceedings of the 28th International Workshop*

on Graph-Theoretic Concepts in Computer Science (WG2002), Cesky Krumlov, Czech Republic, 2002, pp. 235–245.

[119] T. Hasunuma and H. Nagamochi, Independent spanning trees with small depths in iterated line digraphs, *Discrete Appl. Math.* **110** (2001), 189–211.

[120] M. R. Henzinger, A static 2-approximation algorithm for vertex connectivity and incremental approximation algorithms for edge and vertex connectivity, *J. Algorithms*, **24** (1997), 194–220.

[121] M. R. Henzinger, S. Rao, and H. N. Gabow, Computing vertex connectivity: New bounds from old techniques, *J. Algorithms* **34** (2000), 222–250.

[122] M. R. Henzinger, P. Klein, S. Rao, and D. Williamson, Faster shortest-path algorithms for planar graphs, *J. Comp. Syst. Sc.* **53** (1997), 2–23.

[123] M. R. Henzinger and D. Williamson, On the number of small cuts, *Inform. Process. Lett.* **59** (1996), 21–30.

[124] D. S. Hochbaum and A. Pathria, Path costs in evolutionary tree reconstruction, *J. Comput. Biol.* **4** (1997), 163–176.

[125] S. Honami, H. Ito, H. Uehara, and M. Yokoyama, An algorithm for finding a node-subset having high connectivity from other nodes, *IPSJ SIG Notes*, AL-66, 1999, pp. 9–16 (in Japanese).

[126] J. Hopcroft and R. E. Tarjan, An $O(V^2)$ algorithm for determining isomorphism of planar graphs, *Inform. Process. Lett.* **1** (1971), 32–34.

[127] J. Hopcroft and R. E. Tarjan: Dividing a graph into triconnected components, *SIAM J. Comput.* **2** (1973), 135–158.

[128] H. Hsu, An algorithm for finding a minimal equivalent graph of digraph, *J. ACM*, **22** (1975), 11–16.

[129] T. Hsu, On four-connecting a triconnected graph, *J. Algorithms* **35** (2000), 202–234.

[130] T. Hsu, Undirected vertex-connectivity structure and smallest four-vertex-connectivity augmentation, *Lect. Notes Comput. Sci.* **1004**, Springer-Verlag, *6th International Symp. on Algorithms and Computation*, 1995, pp. 274–283.

[131] T. Hsu and M. Kao, A unifying augmentation algorithm for two-edge-connectivity and biconnectivity, *J. Comb. Optimiz.* **2** (1998), 237–256.

[132] T. Hsu and V. Ramachandran, A linear time algorithm for triconnectivity augmentation, *Proc. 32nd IEEE Symp. Found. Comp. Sci.* 1991, pp. 548–559.

[133] T. Hsu and V. Ramachandran, Finding a smallest augmentation to biconnect a graph, *SIAM J. Comput.* **22** (1993), 889–912.

[134] A. Huck, Independent trees in graphs. *Graphs Combin.* **10** (1994), 29–45.

[135] A. Huck, Disproof of a conjecture about independent spanning trees in k-connected directed graphs, *J. Graph Theory* **20** (1995), 235–239.

[136] T. Ibaraki and N. Katoh, *Resource Allocation Problems – Algorithmic Approaches*, MIT Press, Cambridge, MA, 1988.

[137] T. Ishii, *Studies on multigraph connectivity augmentation problems*, Ph.D. Thesis, Dept. of Applied Mathematics and Physics, Kyoto University, Kyoto, Japan, 2000.

[138] T. Ishii and H. Nagamochi, On the minimum augmentation of an ℓ-connected graph to a k-connected graph, *Lect. Notes Comput. Sci.* **1851**, Springer-Verlag, *7th Biennial Scandinavian Workshop on Algorithm Theory*, Bergen, Norway, 2000, pp. 286–299.

[139] T. Ishii, H. Fujita, and H. Nagamochi, Source location problem with local 3-vertex-connectivity requirements, *Proc. of the 3rd Hungarian-Japanese Symposium on Discrete Mathematics and Its Applications*, Tokyo, 2003, pp. 368–377.

[140] T. Ishii, H. Nagamochi, and T. Ibaraki, Augmenting edge and vertex connectivities simultaneously, *Lect. Notes Comput. Sci.* **1350**, Springer-Verlag, *8th International Symp. on Algorithms and Computation*, 1997, pp. 102–111.

[141] T. Ishii, H. Nagamochi, and T. Ibaraki, k-edge and 3-vertex connectivity augmentation in an arbitrary multigraph, *Lect. Notes Comput. Sci.* **1533**, Springer-Verlag, *9th International Symp. on Algorithms and Computation*, 1998, pp. 159–168.

[142] T. Ishii, H. Nagamochi, and T. Ibaraki, Augmenting a $(k - 1)$-vertex-connected multigraph to an l-edge-connected and k-vertex-connected multigraph, *Lect. Notes Comput.*

Sci. **1643**, Springer-Verlag, *7th Annual European Symposium on Algorithms*, 1999, pp. 414–425.

[143] T. Ishii, H. Nagamochi, and T. Ibaraki, Optimal augmentation of a 2-vertex-connected multigraph to a k-edge-connected and 3-vertex-connected multigraph, *J. Comb. Optimiz.* **4** (2000), 35–78.

[144] T. Ishii, H. Nagamochi, and T. Ibaraki, Augmenting a $(k-1)$-vertex-connected multigraph to an l-edge-connected and k-vertex-connected multigraph, *Algorithmica* **44** (2006), 257–280.

[145] T. Ishii, H. Nagamochi, and T. Ibaraki, Multigraph augmentation under biconnectivity and general edge-connectivity requirements, *Networks* **37**:3 (2001), 144–155.

[146] A. Itai and M. Rodeh, The multi-tree approach to reliability in distributed networks, *Inform. Comput.* **79** (1988), 43–59.

[147] H. Ito and M. Yokoyama, Edge connectivity between nodes and node-subsets, *Networks* **31** (1998), 157–163.

[148] H. Ito, K. Makino, K. Arata, S. Honami, Y. Itatsu, and S. Fujishige, Source location problem with flow requirements in directed networks, *Optimiz. Method Software* **18** (2003), 427–435.

[149] H. Ito, H. Uehara, and M. Yokoyama, A faster and flexible algorithm for a location problem on undirected flow networks, *Inst. Electron. Inform. Comm. Eng. Trans. Fundament.* **E83-A** (2000), 704–712.

[150] H. Ito, M. Ito, Y. Itatsu, K. Nakai, H. Uehara, and M. Yokoyama, Source Location problems consdering vertex-connectivity and edge-connectivity simultaneously, *Networks* **40** (2000), 63–70.

[151] Y. Iwasaki, Y. Kajiwara, K. Obokata, and Y. Igarashi, Independent spanning trees of chordal rings, *Inform. Process. Lett.* **69** (1999), 155–160.

[152] S. Iwata, L. Fleischer, and S. Fujishige, A combinatorial strongly polynomial algorithm for minimizing submodular functions, *J. ACM* **48**:4 (2001), 761–777.

[153] B. Jackson, Some remarks on arc-connectivity, vertex splitting, and orientation in graphs and digraphs, *J. Graph Theory* **12** (1988), 429–436.

[154] B. Jackson and T. Jordán, A near optimal algorithm for vertex connectivity augmentation, *Lect. Notes in Comp. Sci.* **1969**, Springer, *International Symp. on Algorithms and Computation*, 2000, pp. 313–325.

[155] B. Jackson and T. Jordán, Non-separable detachments of graphs, *J. Comb. Theory* **B-87** (2003), 17–37.

[156] B. Jackson and T. Jordán, Independence free graphs and vertex connectivity augmentation, *J. Comb. Theory* **B-94**:1 (2005), 31–77.

[157] T. Jordán, *Connectivity augmentation problem in graphs*, Ph.D. thesis, Dept. of Computer Science, Eötvös University, Budapest, Hungary, 1994.

[158] T. Jordán, On the optimal vertex-connectivity augmentation, *J. Combinatorial Theory, Ser.* **B-63** (1995), 8–20.

[159] T. Jordán, A note on the vertex-connectivity augmentation problem, *J. Comb. Theory* **B-71** (1997a), 294–301.

[160] T. Jordán, Two NP-complete augmentation problems, Odense University Preprints #8 (1997b).

[161] T. Jordán, Edge-splitting problems with demands, *Lect. Notes Comp. Sci.* **1610**, Springer-Verlag, *7th Conference on Integer Programming and Combinatorial Optimization*, 1999, pp. 273–288.

[162] T. Jordán, Constrained edge-splitting problems. *SIAM J. Discrete Math.* **17**:1 (2003), 88–102.

[163] T. Jordán and Z. Szigeti, Detachments preserving local edge-connectivity of graphs, *SIAM J. Discrete Math.* **17**:1 (2003), 72–87.

[164] M. Jünger, G. Reinelt, and G. Rinaldi, The traveling salesman problem, in *Handbook on Operations Research and Management Sciences*, edited by M. Ball, T. Magnanti, C. L. Monma, and G. L. Nemhauser, North-Holland, Amsterdam, 1995, pp. 225–330.

[165] M. Jünger, G. Rinaldi, and S. Thienel, Practical performance of efficient minimum cut algorithms, *Algorithmica*, **26**:1 (2000), 172–195.

[166] Y. Kamidoi, N. Yoshida, and H. Nagamochi, A deterministic algorithm for finding all minimum k-way cuts, *SIAM J. Comput.* **36**:5 (2006), 943–955.

[167] A. Kaneko and K. Ota, On minimally (n, λ)-connected graphs, *J. Comb. Theory* **B-80** (2000), 156–171.

[168] A. Kanevsky, R. Tamassia, G. D. Battsia, and J. Chen, On-line maintenance of the four-connected components of a graph, *Proc. 32nd IEEE Symp. Found. Comp. Sci.*, San Juan, Puerto Rico, 1991, pp. 793–801.

[169] G. Kant, *Algorithms for Drawing Planar Graphs*, Ph.D. thesis, Dept. of Computer Science, Utrecht University, 1993.

[170] G. Kant, Augmenting outerplanar graphs, *J. Algorithms* **21** (1996), 1–25.

[171] G. Kant and H. L. Bodlaender, Planar graph augmentation problems, *Lect. Notes Comp. Sci.* **621**, Springer, 1992, pp. 258–271.

[172] M. Kao, Data security equals graph connectivity, *SIAM J. Discrete Math.* **9** (1996), 87–100.

[173] S. Kapoor, On minimum 3-cuts and approximating k-cuts using cut trees, *Lect. Notes Comp. Sci.*, **1084**, Springer, 1996, pp. 132–146.

[174] D. R. Karger, Global min-cuts in RNC, and other ramifications of a simple min-cut algorithm, *Proc. the 4th ACM-SIAM Symposium on Discrete Algorithms*, 1993, pp. 21–30.

[175] D. R. Karger, Random sampling in cuts, flow and network design problems, *Proc. 26th ACM Symposium on Theory of Computing*, 1994, pp. 648–659.

[176] D. R. Karger, A randomized fully polynomial approximation scheme for the all terminal network reliability problem, *Proce. 27th ACM Symposium on Theory of Computing*, 1995, pp. 11–17.

[177] D. R. Karger, Minimum cuts in near-linear time, *Proc. 28th ACM Symposium on Theory of Computing*, 1996, pp. 56–63.

[178] D. R. Karger, Using random sampling to find maximum flows in uncapacitated undirected graphs, *Proc. 29th ACM Symposium on Theory of Computing*, 1997, pp. 240–249.

[179] D. R. Karger and M. S. Levine, Finding maximum flows in undirected graphs seems easier than bipartite matching, *Proc. 30th ACM Symp. Theory of Computing*, 1998, pp. 69–78.

[180] D. R. Karger and R. Motwani, An NC algorithm for minimum cuts, *SIAM J. Comput.* **26** (1997), 255–272.

[181] D. R. Karger and C. Stein, An $\tilde{O}(n^2)$ algorithm for minimum cuts, *Proceedings 25th ACM Symposium on Theory of Computing*, 1993, pp. 757–765.

[182] D. R. Karger and C. Stein, A new approach to the minimum cut problems, *J. ACM*, **43** (1996), 601–640.

[183] A. V. Karzanov, O nakhozhdenii maksimal'nogo potoka v setyakh spetsial'nogo vida i nekotorykh prilozheniyakh [On finding maximum flows in networks with special structure and some applications], in *Mathematicheskie Voprosy Upravleniya Proizvodstvom* 5, Moscow State University Press, Moscow, 1973 (in Russian).

[184] A. V. Karzanov, Determining the maximum flow in a network by the method of preflow, *Soviet Math. Dokl.* **15** (1974), 434–437.

[185] A. V. Karzanov and E. A. Timofeev, Efficient algorithm for finding all minimal edge cuts of a nonoriented graph, *Kibernetika* **2** (1984), 8–12; translated in *Cybernetics* (1986), 156–162.

[186] N. Katoh and T. Ibaraki, Resource allocation problems, in *Handbook of Combinatorial Optimization*, edited by D.-Z. Du and P.M. Pardalos, Kluwer Academic Publishers, 1998.

[187] N. Katoh, T. Ibaraki, and H. Mine, An efficient algorithm for K shortest simple paths, *Networks* **12** (1982), 441–427.

[188] S. Khuller, Approximation algorithms for finding highly connected subgraphs, in *Approximation Algorithms*, edited by D. Hochbaum, PWS Publishing, 1997.

[189] S. Khuller and B. Raghavachari, Improved approximation algorithms for uniform connectivity problems, *J. Algorithms* **21** (1996), 434–450.

[190] S. Khuller and B. Schieber, On independent spanning trees, *Inform. Process. Lett.* **42** (1992), 321–323.

[191] S. Khuller and U. Vishkin, Biconnectivity approximations and graph carvings, *J. ACM*, **41** (1994), 214–235.

[192] S. Khuller, B. Raghavachari, and N. Young, Approximating the minimum equivalent digraph, *SIAM J. Comput.* **24** (1995), 859–872.

[193] S. Khuller, B. Raghavachari, and N. Young, On strongly connected digraphs with bounded cycle length, *Discrete Appl. Math.* **69** (1996), 281–289.

[194] T. Király, Covering symmetric supermodular functions by uniform hypergraphs, *J. Combin. Theory* **B-91** (2004), 185–200.

[195] Z. Király, B. Cosh, and B. Jackson, *Local connectivity augmentation in hypergraphs is NP-complete*, Ph.D. Thesis, Goldsmiths College, University of London, 2000.

[196] M. Labbe, D. Peeters, and J.-F. Thisse, Location on networks, in *Handbooks in OR & MS*, **8**, edited by M. O. Ball et al., North-Holland, 1995, pp. 551–624.

[197] E. L. Lawler, Matroid intersection algorithms, *Math. Progr.* **9** (1975), 31–56.

[198] J. Lehel, F. Maffary, and M. Preissmann, Graphs with largest number of minimum cuts, *Discrete Appl. Math.* **65** (1996), 387–407.

[199] A. N. Letchford and A. Lodi, Primal separation algorithms, *4OR: Quart. J. Belgian, French Italian Oper. Res. Soc.* Springer-Verlag, **1**:3 (2003), 209–224.

[200] L. Lovász, A talk delivered at a conference on graph theory, Prague, 1974.

[201] L. Lovász, On two min-max theorems in graph theory, *J. Combin. Theory* **B-21** (1976), 26–30.

[202] L. Lovász, *Combinatorial Problems and Exercises*, North-Holland, Amsterdam, 1979.

[203] W. Mader: Über minimal n-fach zusammenhängende, unendliche Graphen und ein Extremalproblem, *Arch. Mat.* **23** (1972), 553–560.

[204] W. Mader, Grad und lokaler Zusammenhang in unendliche Graphen, *Math. Ann.* **205** (1973), 9–11.

[205] W. Mader, Kreuzungsfreie a, b-Wedge in endlichen Graphen, *Abh. Math. Sem. Univ. Hamburg*, Univ. Hamburg, **42** (1974), 187–204.

[206] W. Mader, A reduction method for edge-connectivity in graphs, *Ann. Discrete Math.* **3** (1978), 145–164.

[207] W. Mader, Connectivity and edge-connectivity in finite graphs, in *Surveys on Combinatorics*, edited by B. Bollobas, London Math. Soc. Lecture Note, **38**, 1979, pp. 293–309.

[208] W. Mader, Konstruktion aller n-fach kantenzusammenhängenden Digraphen, *Eur. J. Combinatorics* **3** (1982), 63–67.

[209] W. Mader, Minimal n-fach zusammenhängende Digraphen, *J. Comb. Theory* **B-38** (1985), 102–117.

[210] W. K. Mak and D. F. Wong, A fast hypergraph min-cut algorithm for circuit partitioning, *Integration* **30**:1 (2000), 1–11.

[211] V. Malhotra, P. Kumar, and S. Maheshwari, An $O(|V|^3)$ algorithm for finding maximum flows in networks, *Inform. Process. Lett.* **7** (1978), 277–278.

[212] Y. Mansour and B. Schieber, Finding the edge connectivity of directed graphs, *J. Algorithms* **10** (1989), 76–85.

[213] D. W. Matula, k-Components, clusters, and slicings in graphs, *SIAM J. Appl. Math.* **22** (1972), 459–480.

[214] D. W. Matula, A linear time $2 + \varepsilon$ approximation algorithm for edge connectivity, *Proc. 4th Annual ACM-SIAM Symposium on Discrete Algorithms*, 1993, pp. 500–504.

[215] D. W. Matula and L. L. Beck, Smallest-last ordering and clustering and graph coloring algorithms, *J. ACM* **30** (1983), 417–427.

[216] T. A. Mckee and F. R. Mcmorris, *Topics in Intersection Graph Theory, SIAM Monographs on Discrete Mathematics and Applications*, SIAM, Philadelphia, 1999.

[217] K. Menger, Zur allgemeinen Kurventheorie, *Fund. Math.* **10** (1927), 96–115.

[218] P. Mutzel, A polyhedral approach to planar augmentation and related problems, *Lect. Notes Comp. Sci.* **979**, Springer-Verlag, *Annual European Symposium on Algorithms*, 1995, pp. 494–507.

[219] D. Naddef and S. Thienel, Efficient separation routines for the symmetric traveling salesman problem I: General tools and comb separation, *Math. Progr.* **92**:2 (2002), 237–255.

[220] H. Nagamochi, Computing extreme sets in graphs and its applications, *Proc. 3rd Hungarian-Japanese Symposium on Discrete Mathematics and Its Applications*, Tokyo, 2003, pp. 349–357.

[221] H. Nagamochi, Graph algorithms for network connectivity problems, *Oper. Res. Soc. Jpn* **47**:4 (2004), 199–223.

[222] H. Nagamochi, On 2-approximation to the vertex-connectivity in graphs, *Inst. Electron. Inform. Comm. Eng. Trans. Information and Systems*, **E88-D**:1 (2005), 12–16.

[223] H. Nagamochi, On computing minimum (s, t)-cuts in digraphs, *Inform. Process. Lett.* **93**:5 (2005), 231–237.

[224] H. Nagamochi, A $\frac{4}{3}$-approximation for the minimum 2-local-vertex-connectivity augmentation in a connected graph, *J. Algorithms* **56**:2 (2005), 77–95.

[225] H. Nagamochi, Increasing the edge-connectivity by contracting a vertex subset, *IEICE Trans. Inform. Systems* **E89-D**:2 (2006), 744–750.

[226] H. Nagamochi, A fast edge-splitting algorithm in edge-weighted graphs, *Inst. Electron. Inform. Comm. Eng. Trans. Fundam.* **E89-A**:5 (2006), 1263–1268.

[227] H. Nagamochi, Sparse connectivity certificates via MA orderings in graphs, *Discrete Appl. Math.* **154**:16 (2006), 2411–2417.

[228] H. Nagamochi, Computing a minimum cut in a graph with dynamic edges incident to a designated vertex, *Inst. Electron. Inform. Comm. Eng. Trans. Fundam.* **E90-D**:2 (2007), 428–431.

[229] H. Nagamochi, Minimum degree orderings, *Lect. Notes Comp. Sci.* **4835**, Springer, 2007, pp. 17–28. *The 18th International Symposium on Algorithms and Computation (ISAAC 2007)*.

[230] H. Nagamochi and P. Eades, An edge-splitting algorithm in planar graphs, *J. Comb. Optimiz.* **7** (2003), 137–159.

[231] H. Nagamochi and T. Ibaraki, A linear-time algorithm for finding a sparse k-connected spanning subgraph of a k-connected graph, *Algorithmica* **7** (1992), 583–596.

[232] H. Nagamochi and T. Ibaraki, Computing edge-connectivity of multigraphs and capacitated graphs, *SIAM J. Discrete Math.* **5** (1992), 54–66.

[233] H. Nagamochi and T. Ibaraki, A linear time algorithm for computing 3-edge-connected components of a multigraph, *Jpn. J. Ind. Appl. Math.* **9** (1992), 163–180.

[234] H. Nagamochi and T. Ibaraki, A faster edge splitting algorithm in multigraphs and its application to the edge-connectivity augmentation problem, *Lect. Notes Comp. Sci.* **920**, Springer-Verlag, edited by E. Balas and J. Clausen, *4th Integer Programming and Combinatorial Optimization*, Copenhagen, 1995, pp. 403–413.

[235] H. Nagamochi and T. Ibaraki, Deterministic $\tilde{O}(nm)$ time edge-splitting in undirected graphs, *Proceedings 28th ACM Symposium on Theory of Computing*, 1996, pp. 64–73.

[236] H. Nagamochi and T. Ibaraki, Deterministic $\tilde{O}(nm)$ time edge-splitting in undirected graphs, *J. Comb. Optimiz.* **1** (1997), 5–46.

[237] H. Nagamochi and T. Ibaraki, A note on minimizing submodular functions, *Inform. Process. Lett.* **67** (1998), 239–244.

[238] H. Nagamochi and T. Ibaraki, Augmenting edge-connectivity over the entire range in $\tilde{O}(nm)$ time, *J. Algorithms* **30** (1999), 253–301.

[239] H. Nagamochi and T. Ibaraki, A fast algorithm for computing minimum 3-way and 4-way cuts, *Math. Progr.* **88** (2000), 507–520.

[240] H. Nagamochi and T. Ibaraki, Polyhedral structure of submodular and posimodulara systems, *Discrete Appl. Math.* **107** (2000), 165–189.

[241] H. Nagamochi and T. Ibaraki, Graph connectivity and its augmentation: Applications of MA orderings, *Discrete Applied Mathematics* **123** (2002), 447–472.

[242] H. Nagamochi and T. Ishii, On the minimum local-vertex-connectivity augmentation in graphs, *Discrete Appl. Math.* **129**:2 (2003), 475–486.

[243] H. Nagamochi and T. Kameda, Canonical cactus representation for minimum cuts, *Jpn J. Ind. Appl. Math.* **11** (1994), 343–361.

[244] H. Nagamochi and T. Kameda, Constructing cactus representation for all minimum cuts in an undirected network, *Oper. Res. Soc. Jpn* **39** (1996), 135–158.

[245] H. Nagamochi and Y. Kamidoi, Minimum cost subpartitions in graphs, *Inform. Process. Lett.* **102** (2007), 79–84.

[246] H. Nagamochi and T. Watanabe, Computing *k*-edge-connected components in multi-graphs, *Inst. Electron. Inform. Comm. Eng. Trans. Fundam.* **E76-A**:4 (1993), 513–517.

[247] H. Nagamochi, Z. Sun, and T. Ibaraki, Counting the number of minimum cuts in undirected multigraphs, *IEEE Trans. Reliability* **40** (1991), 610–614.

[248] H. Nagamochi, T. Ono, and T. Ibaraki, Implementing an efficient minimum capacity cut algorithm, *Math. Progr.* **67** (1994), 325–341.

[249] H. Nagamochi, K. Nishimura, and T. Ibaraki, Computing all small cuts in undirected networks, *SIAM J. Discrete Math.* **10** (1997), 469–481.

[250] H. Nagamochi, T. Ishii, and T. Ibaraki, A simple and constructive proof of a minimum cut algorithm, *Inst. Electron. Inform. Comm. Eng. Trans. Fundam.* **E82-A** (1999), 2231–2236.

[251] H. Nagamochi, S. Katayama, and T. Ibaraki, A faster algorithm for computing minimum 5-way and 6-way cuts in graphs, *J. Comb. Optimiz.* **4** (2000), 151–169.

[252] H. Nagamochi, S. Nakamura, and T. Ibaraki, A simplified $\tilde{O}(nm)$ time edge-splitting algorithm in undirected graphs, *Algorithmica* **26** (2000), 56–67.

[253] H. Nagamochi, Y. Nakao, and T. Ibaraki, A fast algorithm for cactus representations of minimum cuts, *J. Jpn Soc. Ind. Appl. Math.* **17** (2000), 245–264.

[254] H. Nagamochi, K. Seki, and T. Ibaraki, A 7/3-approximation for the minimum weight 3-connected spanning subgraph problem, *Inst. Electron. Inform. Comm. Eng. Trans. Fundam.* **E83-A**:4 (2000), 687–691.

[255] H. Nagamochi, T. Ishii, and H. Ito, Minimum cost source location problem with vertex-connectivity requirements in digraphs, *Inform. Process. Lett.* **80** (2001), 287–294.

[256] H. Nagamochi, T. Shiraki, and T. Ibaraki, Augmenting a submodular and posimodular set function by a multigraph, *J. Comb. Optimiz.* **5**:2 (2001), 175–212.

[257] H. Nagamochi, S. Nakamura, and T. Ishii, Constructing a cactus for minimum cuts of a graph in $O(mn + n^2 \log n)$ time and $O(m)$ space, *Inst. Electron. Inform. Comm. Eng. Trans. Inform. Systems*, **E86-D** (2003), 179–185.

[258] D. Naor and V. V. Vazirani, Representing and enumerating edge connectivity cuts in RNC, *Lect. Notes Comp. Sci.* **519**, *WADS'91*, edited by F. Dehne, J.-R. Sack, and N. Santoro, Springer Verlag, 1991, pp. 273–285.

[259] D. Naor, D. Gusfield, and C. Martel, A fast algorithm for optimally increasing the edge connectivity, *SIAM J. Comput.* **26** (1997), 1139–1165.

[260] J. Naor and Y. Rabani, Tree packing and approximating *k*-cuts, *Proc. 12th Annual ACM-SIAM Symposium on Discrete Algorithms*, 2001, pp. 26–27.

[261] C. St. J. A. Nash-Williams, On orientations, connectivity and odd vertex pairings in finite graphs, *Can. J. Math.* **12** (1960), 555–567.

[262] C. St. J. A. Nash-Williams, Edge-disjoint spanning trees in finite graphs, *J. London Math. Soc.* **36** (1961), 445–450.

[263] C. St. J. A. Nash-Williams, Decomposition of finite graphs into forest, *J. London Math. Soc.* **39** (1964), 12.

[264] C. St. J. A. Nash-Williams, Detachments of graphs and generalised Euler trails, in *Surveys in Combinatorics 1985*, edited by I. Anderson, *Lond. Math. Soc. Lect. Note* **103**, Cambridge University Press, Cambrige, 1985, pp. 137–151.

[265] C. St. J. A. Nash-Williams, Connected detachments of graphs and generalised Euler trails, *J. Lond. Math. Soc.* **31** (1985), 17–29.

[266] T. Nishizeki and S. Poljak, *k*-connectivity and decomposition of graphs into forests, *Discrete Appl. Math.* **55** (1994), 295–301.

[267] T. Nishizeki and Md. S. Rahman, *Planar Graph Drawing*, Word Scientific, Singapore, 2004.

[268] Z. Nutov and M. Penn, Faster approximation algorithms for weighted triconnectivity augmentation problems, *Oper. Res. Lett.* **21** (1997), 219–223.

[269] K. Obokata, Y. Iwasaki, F. Bao, and Y. Igarashi, Independent spanning trees in product graphs and their construction, *IEICE Trans.* **E79-A** (1996), 1894–1903.

[270] J. B. Orlin, A faster strongly polynomial minimum cost flow algorithm, *Proc. 20th ACM Symp. Theory of Computing*, 1988, pp. 377–387.

[271] M. Padberg and G. Rinaldi, An efficient algorithm for the minimum capacity cut problem, *Math. Progr.* **47** (1990), 19–36.

[272] M. Penn and H. Shasha-Krupnik, Improved approximation algorithms for weighted 2- and 3-vertex connectivity augmentation problems, *J. Algorithms* **22**:1 (1997), 187–196.

[273] J.-C. Picard and M. Queyranne, On the structure of all minimum cuts in a network and applications, *Math. Progr. Study* **13** (1980), 8–16.

[274] J.-C. Picard and H. D. Ratliff, Minimum cuts and related problems, *Networks* **5** (1975), 357–370.

[275] J. Plesnik, Minimum block containing a given graph, *Archiv der Mathematik*, XXVII (1976), 668–672.

[276] J. S. Provan and D. R. Shier, A paradigm for listing (s, t)-cuts in graphs, *Algorithmica* **15** (1996), 351–372.

[277] M. Queyranne, Minimizing symmetric submodular functions, *Math. Progr.* **82** (1998), 3–12.

[278] T. Radzik, Implementation of dynamic trees with in-subtree operations, *ACM J. Exp. Algorithms* **3** (1998).

[279] S. Raghavan and T. L. Magnanti, Network connectivity, in *Annotated Bibliographies in Combinatorial Optimization*, edited by M. Dell'Amico, F. Maffioli, and S. Martello, John Wiley & Sons, 1997.

[280] T. K. Ralphs, L. Kopman, W. R. Pulleyblank, and L. E. Trotter, On the capacitated vehicle routing problem, *Math. Progr.* **B-94** (2003), 343–359.

[281] A. Ramanathan and C. J. Colbourn, Counting almost minimum cutsets with reliability applications, *Math. Progr.* **39** (1987), 253–261.

[282] R. Ravi and A. Sinha, Approximating k-cuts via network strength, *Proc. 13th Annual ACM-SIAM Symposium on Discrete Algorithms*, 2002, pp. 621–622.

[283] R. Rizzi, On minimizing symmetric set functions, *Combinatorica* **20** (2000), 445–450.

[284] R. Rizzi, Excluding a simple good pair approach to directed cuts, *Graphs and Combinatorics* **17** (2001), 741–744.

[285] M. Sakashita, K. Makino, and S. Fujishige, Minimum cost source location problems with flow requirements, *Lect. Notes Comp. Sci.* **3887**, Springer, *7th Latin American Symposium on Theoretical Informatics (LATIN 2006)*, Valdivia, Chile, 2006, pp. 769–780.

[286] M. Sakashita, K. Makino, H. Nagamochi, and S. Fujishige, Minimum transversal in a posi-modular system, *Lect. Notes Comp. Sci.* **4168**, Springer, *14th Annual European Symposium on Algorithms*, ETH Zurich, Switzerland, 2006, pp. 576–587.

[287] H. Saran and V. V. Vazirani, Finding k cuts within twice the optimal, *SIAM J. Comput.* **24** (1995), 101–108.

[288] A. Schrijver, A combinatorial algorithm minimizing submodular function in strongly polynomial time, *J. Comb. Theory* **B-80** (2000), 346–355.

[289] A. Schrijver, *Combinatorial Optimization, Polyhedra and Efficiency*, Springer-Verlag, Berlin, 2003.

[290] L. S. Shapley, Cores of convex games, *Int. J. Game Theory* **1** (1971), 11–26.

[291] D. D. Sleator and R. E. Tarjan, A data structure for dynamic trees, *J. Comp. System Sci.* **26**:3 (1983), 362–391.

[292] M. Stoer, *Design of Survivable Networks*, *Lect. Notes Math.* **1531**, Springer-Verlag, Heidelberg, 1992.

[293] M. Stoer and F. Wagner, A simple min cut algorithm, *J. ACM* **44** (1997), 585–591.

[294] Z. Szigeti, Hypergraph connectivity augmentation, *Math. Progr.* **B-84** (1999), 519–528.

[295] H. Tamura, M. Sengoku, S. Shinoda, and T. Abe, Location problems on undirected flow networks, *Inst. Electron. Inform. Comm. Eng. Trans.* **E73** (1990), 1989–1993.

[296] H. Tamura, H. Sugawara, M. Sengoku, and S. Shinoda, Plural cover problem on undirected flow networks, *Inst. Electron. Inform. Comm. Eng. Trans. Fundam.* **J81-A** (1998), 863–869 (in Japanese).

[297] R. E. Tarjan, Depth-first search and linear graph algorithms, *SIAM J. Comput.* **1** (1972), 146–160.

[298] R. E. Tarjan, *Data Structures and Network Algorithms*, Society for Industrial and Applied Mathematics, 1983.

[299] R. E. Tarjan, Simple version of Karzanov's blocking flow algorithm, *Oper. Res. Lett.* **2** (1984), 265–268.

[300] R. E. Tarjan and M. Yannakakis, Simple linear-time algorithms to test chordality of graphs, test acyclicity of hypergraphs, and selectively reduce acyclic hypergraphs, *SIAM J. Comput.* **13** (1984), 566–579.

[301] T.-S. Tay, Henneberg's method for bar and body frameworks, *Struct. Topol.* **17** (1991), 53–58.

[302] M. Thorup, Fully-dynamic min-cut, *Proc. ACM Symp. on Theory of Computing*, 2001, pp. 224–230.

[303] S. Tsukiyama, K. Koike, and I. Shirakawa, An algorithm to eliminate all complex triangles in a maximal planar graph for use in VLSI floor-plan, *Proc. ISCAS'86*, 1986, pp. 321–324.

[304] W. T. Tutte, On the problem of decomposing a graph into n connected factors, *J. Lond. Math. Soc.* **36** (1961), 221–230.

[305] J. van den Heuvel and M. Johnson, Transversals of subtree hypergraphs and the source location problem in digraphs, *CDAM Research Report*, LSE-CDAM-2004-10, London School of Economics, 2004.

[306] J. van den Heuvel and M. Johnson, The external network problem with edge- or arc-connectivity requirements, *Workshop on Combinatorial and Algorithmic Aspects of Networking, CAAN 2004, Lect. Notes Comp. Sci.* **3405**, Springer, 2004, pp. 114–126.

[307] V. V. Vazirani and M. Yannakakis, Suboptimal cuts: Their enumeration, weight, and number, *Lect. Notes Comp. Sci.* **623**, Springer-Verlag, 1992, pp. 366–377.

[308] T. Watanabe and A. Nakamura, Edge-connectivity augmentation problems, *J. Comp. System Sci.* **35** (1987), 96–144.

[309] T. Watanabe and A. Nakamura, A minimum 3-connectivity augmentation of a graph, *J. Comp. System Sci.* **46** (1993), 91–128.

[310] T. Watanabe and M. Yamakado, A linear time algorithm for smallest augmentation to 3-edge-connect a graph, *Inst. Electron. Inform. Comm. Eng. Trans. Fundam.* **E76-A** (1993), 518–530.

[311] K. M. Wenger, *Generic cut generation methods for routing problems*, Ph.D. Thesis, University of Heidelberg, Institute of Computer Science, Heidelberg, Germany, Shaker Verlag, 2003.

[312] R. W. Whitty, Vertex-disjoint paths and edge-disjoint branchings in directed graphs, *J. Graph Theory* **11** (1987), 349–358.

[313] M. J. Zaki, V. Nadimpally, D. Bardhan, and C. Bystroff, Predicting protein folding pathways, *Bioinformatics* **20** (2004), 386–393.

[314] A. Zehavi and A. Itai, Three tree-paths, *J. Graph Theory* **13** (1989), 175–188.

[315] L. Zhao, H. Nagamochi, and T. Ibaraki, Approximating the minimum k-way cut in a graph via minimum 3-way cuts, *J. Comb. Optimiz.* **5** (2001), 397–410.

Index

Printed in the United States
By Bookmasters